Demographics
OF THE U.S.

Demographics OF THE U.S.

TRENDS AND PROJECTIONS

BY CHERYL RUSSELL

2nd EDITION

New Strategist Publications, Inc.
Ithaca, New York

New Strategist Publications, Inc.
P.O. Box 242, Ithaca, New York 14851
800-848-0842
<www.newstrategist.com>

ISBN 1-885070-48-9

Printed in the United States of America

Table of Contents

Chapter 8. Population

Chapter 9. Spending

Chapter 10. Wealth

List of Tables

Chapter 2. Education

Chapter 3. Health

Chapter 4. Housing

Chapter 5. Income

Chapter 6. Labor Force

Chapter 7. Living Arrangements

Chapter 8. Population

Chapter 9. Spending

Chapter 10. Wealth

List of Charts

Chapter 9. Spending

Chapter 10. Wealth

Introduction

It may be hard to believe in this day and age that certain statistics are getting harder to find, but it's true. As online publishing abounds, invaluable older books are disappearing. As the volume of statistics produced by our number-driven society grows, historical figures are becoming more elusive. Although many government agencies have put their historical statistics on the Internet, the figures available online rarely are comprehensive, leaving researchers dependent on the whims of busy statisticians who have better things to do than upload old data. As the quantity of new books climbs, librarians are throwing away earlier editions of important reference works in a desperate hunt for shelf space as budgets tighten. One example is the *Statistical Abstract of the U.S.*, published annually by the Census Bureau. New editions replace old editions on many library shelves, although new editions of the *Abstract* do not include the same historical data.

Into this chaos we introduce the second edition of *Demographics of the U.S.: Trends and Projections*, a reference book of historical statistics covering the years 1950 to 2000 and an archive of the socioeconomic trends of the last half of the twentieth century. *Demographics of the U.S.* is a reference book for those who want perspective on the many changes in American life—a perspective critical for understanding what the twenty-first century is likely to hold and as difficult to come by as historical statistics themselves.

Demographics of the U.S. collects in one volume much of the demographic data that can be found only hit or miss elsewhere. New Strategist's editors scoured volume after volume of government references to locate trendline data on adult education, births, deaths, union membership, employee benefits, working mothers, computer ownership, food consumption, and so on. The result is a compilation of statistics that cannot be found in one single volume anywhere else, documenting the past half-century of trends and culminating in a look at American lifestyles in the iconic year 2000.

New to this edition of *Demographics of the U.S.* is more comprehensive coverage of historical statistics, including single-year data on many topics, such as school enrollment, SAT scores, hospital admissions, AIDS victims, employment status of men and women, living arrangements of children, marital status, and geographical mobility. Also new to this edition are exclusive New Strategist projections of the population by age, sex, race, and Hispanic origin to the year 2010 based on 2000 census counts—projections that are not yet available from the Census Bureau.

The presentation of data in *Demographics of the U.S.* is not a dry regurgitation of numbers, but an analytical look at the trends that have reshaped the norms of our society and created opportunity for millions. The book examines not only the past, but also the ongoing changes that will transform us in the future. The most important trends of the next fifty years are not difficult to spot because many are demographically driven and already set in motion.

Since 1950, our society has been reshaped by five big trends. They are:

1. Women's expanded roles Women's labor force participation rate has soared over the past few decades and today nearly matches that of men. Women's lifestyles have become much more similar to men's, and dual-income couples are now the norm. While some have resisted these changes, most of the population—especially young and middle-aged adults—now readily accept women's (and men's) new roles. One happy consequence is our record level of affluence as dual-income couples boost household income.

2. A more diverse population Blacks, Hispanics, and Asians represent growing shares of the U.S. population. The non-Hispanic white share is shrinking, especially among the young. Not only is the face of America changing, but so are the attitudes of the public toward diversity. In the past quarter-century, racial tolerance has grown enormously as blacks and other minorities made gains in education and income, joining the middle and upper classes of American society.

3. Alternative living arrangements To be married and have children once was the norm in the U.S. Today, such nuclear families represent a relatively small share of house-holds (25 percent) and married couples are barely hanging on to their majority status. People who live alone now outnumber couples with children. Nonfamilies (people living alone or with nonrelatives) have grown rapidly as a share of households as people postponed marriage, divorced readily, and chose to live with partners outside of marriage. The consequence is a fracturing of the mass market into ever-smaller segments, each with its own wants and needs.

4. Gains in educational attainment As recently as 1966, the majority of adults in the U.S. had not graduated from high school. Today, nearly 90 percent of young adults are high school graduates, and more than half continue on to college. The enormous rise in educational attainment has boosted the sophistication of the American public, led to improvements in health and life expectancy, and created the affluent, high-tech society we now enjoy.

5. Rising standard of living Thanks to the expanded roles of women and the rise in educational attainment, America's standard of living has risen to new heights. And thanks to our embrace of diversity, the record-high standard of living has been available to more people than ever before. American affluence hit a new high in 2000, when one in seven households had an income of $100,000 or more. Homeownership also is at a record level, as is life expectancy. There can be little doubt we are better off today than ever before.

The most important trends of the next fifty years will be substantially different from the trends of the past. Three of the major trends described above will come to an end, not because of a shift in lifestyles or opinions, but because they will have become the norm rather than the new. Women's expanded roles, for example, have been adopted by middle-aged and younger Americans. As they age and replace older, more traditional generations, the trend—meaning the ongoing change—will end. Similarly with educational attainment, in a few years well-educated younger generations will have entirely replaced less-educated older Americans. Living arrangements have already diversified, and they are unlikely to fracture much more.

One of the big trends of the past half-century will become even more important during the next fifty years—the increasing diversity of Americans. Non-Hispanic whites will become a minority in many states and metropolitan areas over the next few decades. They will soon become a minority among the nation's children as well. The non-Hispanic white share of children under age 15 will drop from 60 to 56 percent between 2000 and 2010.

The aging of the population is the second major trend reshaping our society. Boomers entering their sixties, seventies, and eighties will afford a new perspective on aging as highly educated, active, and sophisticated older Americans banish old-age stereotypes.

The high-tech revolution is the third overarching trend. Not only do computers and the Internet transform communication, but the communications revolution is transforming every other field such as medicine, banking, and entertainment.

The fourth important trend is the rise of individualism. While the trend of growing individualism began in earnest with the baby-boom generation, it will see its culmination among boomers' children and grandchildren. Policy makers as well as businesses will have to learn how to make our economy and democracy work by engaging individuals rather than markets, political parties, or special interest groups.

Finally, thanks to the foregoing trends, the fifth major trend of the next fifty years is one also important in the past—the rise in our standard of living, including higher incomes, improving health, and greater material, if not mental, well-being.

The American Well-Being Index

To measure the ongoing rise in our standard of living, New Strategist has created the American Well-Being Index. The index is comprised of fourteen items that include most of the important aspects of life in our society, from racial tolerance to having fun. The fourteen measures are: personal happiness, health status, job satisfaction, financial satisfaction, homeownership, percentage of children living in two-parent households, percentage of college-educated (a measure of opportunity), health insurance coverage, percentage voting in presidential elections (a measure of citizenship), percentage disagreeing with the statement, "blacks shouldn't push where they are not wanted" (a measure of racial tolerance), percentage saying crime is down in their area (a measure of personal security), percentage owning a computer (a measure of how connected households are to the new economy), percentage of households with no outstanding credit card debt, and household spending on entertainment as a share of food spending (a measure of how much households devote to having fun).

If our society were ideal, our score on the American Well-Being Index would be 1400. In our imperfect society, we are destined to achieve a far lower score. But we are doing better than we did a quarter-century ago, which is as far as we can peer into the past using the indicators shown on the facing page.

In 2000, we were more than halfway to achieving perfection, scoring a 738 out of the possible 1400, or 53 percent of the highest possible score. The 2000 score is substantially better than the 621 we scored in 1974 (44 percent of the highest possible score). It is also an improvement over the 1998 score of 725 published in the first edition of *Demographics of the U.S.*

Many indicators improved over the past few decades, including the percentage of people with a college degree, the percentage of Americans who say their health is excellent or very good, homeownership, racial tolerance, and personal security. Computer ownership, as measured by the percentage of households with a computer, experienced the biggest rise. While some may claim this is an unfair indicator since home computers were virtually nonexistent in the early 1970s, the measure reveals the percentage of households wired into the high-tech future, one of the five major trends of the next fifty years. Even excluding computer ownership, the American Well-Being Index improved substantially since 1974.

Since our last compilation of the index, several indicators have continued to improve, most notably computer ownership. The percentage of households owning a computer rose from 42 to 51 percent between 1998 and 2000 and accounted for 9 points of the 13-point gain in the index during those years, or 70 percent of the improvement. But other important indicators also rose, albeit by much less. Personal happiness increased some, as did the percentage of people reporting their health as excellent or very good. College education was up, as was health insurance coverage. The percentage of people voting in the 2000 presidential election was slightly greater than in 1996.

American Well-Being Index

(percent of people or households by selected indicators of well-being, 1974, 1998, and 2000; total score is sum of percentages; highest possible score is 1400)

	2000	1998	1974	change 1998–00	change 1974–00
Total score	**738**	**725**	**621**	**13**	**117**
1. People who are very happy	34%	32%	38%	2%	0%
2. People who are in excellent/very good health	80	79	73	1	7
3. People who are very satisfied with their work	45	48	48	0	0
4. People who are very satisfied with their finances	31	30	31	1	0
5. Households owning their home	67	67	63	0	4
6. Children living with two parents	69	68	85	1	0
7. People who are college educated	26	24	13	2	13
8. People with health insurance coverage	86	84	86	2	0
9. People voting in the last presidential election	55	54	63	1	0
10. People who disagree with the statement, "blacks shouldn't push where they're not wanted"	56	56	25	0	31
11. People who say there is less crime in their area than one year ago	46	48	10	0	36
12. Households owning a computer	51	42	0	9	51
13. Households without outstanding credit card debt	56	56	63	0	0
14. Entertainment spending as a percent of food spending	36	37	23	0	13

Note: Some 1974 data are for other years: indicators 5, 6, and 8 are for 1970; indicators 9, 11, and 14 are for 1972; indicator 10 is for 1975; and indicator 13 is for 1983. 2000 data for indicator 13 is for 1998. For indicator 14, to enable comparisons, entertainment spending includes reading, and food spending includes alcohol for all years shown.

Sources: Indicators 1, 2, 3, 4, and 10: General Social Surveys, National Opinion Research Center, University of Chicago; Indicator 5: Bureau of the Census, Internet site http://www.census.gov/hhes/www/housing/hvs/historic/histt12.html, and Historical Statistics of the United States, Colonial Times to 1970, Part 1, 1975; Indicator 6: Bureau of the Census, Internet site http://www.census.gov/population/socdemo/hh-fam/tabCH-1.txt; Indicator 7: Bureau of the Census, Internet site http://www.census.gov/population/socdemo/education/tableA-2.txt; Indicator 8: Bureau of the Census, Internet site http://www.census.gov/hhes/hlthins/historic/hihistt1.html, and Statistical Abstract of the United States: 1990; Indicator 9: Bureau of the Census, Voting and Registration in the Election of November 1998, Current Population Report P20-523RV, 2000, and Voting and Registration in the Election of November 2000, Current Population Report P20-542, 2002; Indicator 11: The Gallup Organization, Internet site http://www.gallup.com; Indicator 12: Bureau of the Census, Access Denied: Changes in Computer Ownership and Use: 1984–1997, Robert Kominski and Eric Newburger, 1999, and National Telecommunications and Information Administration, Falling through the Net: Defining the Digital Divide, 1999, and Bureau of the Census, Home Computers and Internet Use in the United States: August 2000, Current Population Reports, P23-207, 2001; Indicator 13: Federal Reserve Bulletin, Changes in Family Finances from 1983 to 1989: Evidence from the Survey of Consumer Finances, January 1992; and Recent Changes in U.S. Family Finances: Results from the 1998 Survey of Consumer Finances, January 2000; Indicator 14: Bureau of Labor Statistics, How Family Spending Has Changed in the U.S., Monthly Labor Review, March 1990, and data from the 1998 and 2000 Consumer Expenditure Surveys, Internet site http://www.bls.gov/cex/; calculations by New Strategist

Five indicators declined between 1974 and 2000. These were satisfaction with work, the percentage of people voting in the last presidential election (although this measure rose slightly between 1998 and 2000), the percentage of children living with two parents, the percentage of households with no outstanding credit card debt, and personal happiness.

Only three indicators declined between 1998 and 2000, most of them reflecting the end of the dot-com and stock market boom of the late 1990s. The percentage of people who are very satisfied with their work fell 3 percentage points, accounting for the entire decline in this indicator since 1974. Entertainment spending as a share of food spending fell 1 percentage point as paying for necessities captured a larger share of the household budget. And the public felt a bit less secure in 2000 than in 1998, with the crime indicator moving up 1 percentage point.

Among the indicators that declined between 1974 and 2000, one of the most intriguing is the drop in personal happiness. Although the figure rose slightly between 1998 and 2000, that still left it 4 percentage points below its 1974 level. Why would personal happiness decline despite the overall rise in well-being? One explanation may be the communication revolution itself. People today are keenly aware of how their own life compares with that of others. The more the media glorify the rich and famous, the more dissatisfied becomes the average and unknown American. The antidote may be greater resistance to the media's influence, something that may be occurring since the public's confidence in the media has plummeted during the past few decades.

Whether Americans will continue to resist the siren call of bigger and better and find greater personal happiness will be shown in forthcoming updates of *Demographics of the U.S.: Trends and Projections*. New Strategist will continue to track America's well-being with these indicators in later editions of this book.

How to Use This Book

Demographics of the U.S.: Trends and Projections is designed for easy use. It is divided into ten chapters, organized alphabetically: Attitudes and Behavior, Education, Health, Housing, Income, Labor Force, Living Arrangements, Population, Spending, and Wealth.

Most of the tables in the book are based on data published online or in a variety of printed volumes by the federal government, in particular the Bureau of the Census, the Bureau of Labor Statistics, the National Center for Education Statistics, the National Center for Health Statistics, and the Federal Reserve Board. The federal government continues to be the best source of up-to-date, reliable information on the changing characteristics of Americans.

To explore changes in attitudes, New Strategist extracted data from the nationally representative General Social Survey of the University of Chicago's National Opinion Research Center. NORC conducts the biennial survey through face-to-face interviews with an independently drawn, representative sample of 1,500 to 3,000 noninstitutionalized English-speaking people aged 18 or older who live in the United States. The GSS is one of the best sources of attitudinal data on Americans available today, and because the same, or similar, questions have been asked every year or two since the early 1970s, it is also one of the best longitudinal sources of attitudinal data.

During the past few years, dramatic technological change has reshaped the demographic reference industry. The government's detailed demographic data, once widely available to all in printed reports, is now accessible only to Internet users or in unpublished tables obtained by contacting the appropriate government agency with a specific request. In the rush to put the latest data online, historical statistics have been left behind—either they are missing altogether or they are available only for selected years or data sets. Consequently, many historical data are now out of reach unless researchers are willing to travel to libraries that have not yet discarded older references. In many ways, the shift from printed reports to web sites has made demographic analysis a bigger chore. It can be more time-consuming than ever to get no-nonsense answers to questions about the changing demographics of Americans.

Demographics of the U.S.: Trends and Projections has the answers. It shows where we came from and where we're going. Thumbing through its pages, you can gain more insight into American society than you could by spending all afternoon surfing databases on the Internet.

Whenever possible, *Demographics of the U.S.: Trends and Projections* presents data from 1950 to the latest available year, including projections if they are available. Because the 2000 census counted 6 million more Americans than demographers had predicted, the Census Bureau's population projections, produced several years earlier, instantly became obsolete. The bureau has not yet released new projections. To make up for the loss, New Strategist produced its own, exclusive population projections for *Demographics of the U.S.* These projections, based on 2000 census counts and shown in the Population chapter, reveal the size and shape of the U.S. population in 2010 by age, sex, race, and Hispanic origin.

For most demographic and socioeconomic topics, it is impossible to uncover data for the entire fifty-year span from 1950 to 2000 because many demographic concepts and classifications have emerged only in the past few decades or have changed so much that comparable historical data are nonexistent.

Modern racial and ethnic classifications, for example, did not exist before the late 1970s or 1980s (and they changed again with the 2000 census, which allowed people to choose more than one racial category for the first time). Some household types now considered important received little attention until the 1960s and 1970s. The obsessive focus on generations and age groups occurred after the birth of the baby-boom generation. Analysts revised educational attainment categories in 1991, so that data collected before and after that year are not strictly comparable. Important health indicators were unknown fifty years ago, and therefore were untracked. No one collected comparable spending and wealth data until the 1980s. Despite the limitations of the data, however, *Demographics of the U.S.: Trends and Projections* reveals much about our past and clarifies where we are headed in the future. It informs without overwhelming through a combination of tables, text, and charts.

While most of the data published here are produced by the government, the tables in *Demographics of the U.S.: Trends and Projections* are not simply reprints of government spreadsheets, as is the case in many other reference books. Instead, New Strategist's statisticians individually compiled and created each of the book's tables, with calculations designed to reveal the stories behind the numbers.

Each chapter of *Demographics of the U.S.: Trends and Projections* includes the demographic and lifestyle data most important to researchers. A page of text accompanies many of the tables, analyzing the data and highlighting the trends. Readers who want more statistical detail than the tables provide can plumb the original source, listed at the bottom of each table.

The book contains a lengthy table list to help researchers locate the information they need. For a more detailed search, use the index at the back of the book. Also at the back of the book is the glossary, which defines the terms commonly used in tables and text. A list of telephone and Internet contacts also appears at the end of the book, allowing researchers to access government specialists and web sites.

Demographics of the U.S.: Trends and Projections explains our complex, confusing, and ever-changing society, making sense of our past and shedding light on our future.

—CHERYL RUSSELL

1

Attitudes and Behavior

■ Americans are not as happy as they used to be, but they find life more exciting. In 2000, 34 percent of people aged 18 or older said they were "very happy," down from 38 percent in 1974. Forty-six percent of Americans find life exciting, up from 42 percent in 1974.

■ Most people—particularly baby boomers and younger adults—approve of the sweeping changes in men's and women's roles over the past half-century. The proportion of Americans who believe it is better if men are the achievers and women the homemakers fell sharply over the past quarter-century, from the 65 percent majority in 1977 to a 39 percent minority in 2000.

■ Racial tolerance increased enormously during the past half-century. The proportion of Americans who agree with the statement that "blacks shouldn't push themselves where they're not wanted" fell to 15 percent in 2000.

■ Americans are more likely to be political independents than either Democrats or Republicans. In 2000, 41 percent of people aged 18 or older identified themselves as independents, up from 31 percent in 1974. The share of people identifying themselves as Democrats fell from 42 to 32 percent during those years, while the Republican share grew from 22 to 26 percent.

■ Note: The exact wording of the General Social Survey questions is shown in the tables.

More Excitement, Less Happiness

Americans are not as happy as they used to be, but they find life more exciting. In 2000, 34 percent of people aged 18 or older said they were "very happy," down from 38 percent who felt that way a quarter-century earlier in 1974. Happiness has declined for every demographic segment except among those with bachelor's or higher degrees. More than 40 percent of Americans with a college degree are very happy—perhaps because the well-educated are the ones benefiting from ongoing economic change.

Forty-six percent of Americans find life exciting, up from 42 percent in 1974. The only people who do not find life more exciting are the youngest and the oldest age groups and those without a bachelor's degree. Among people aged 50 to 59, the percentage who find life exciting grew from 36 to fully 58 percent.

One factor contributing to the decline in happiness is the growing lack of trust in others. Nearly half (45 percent) of people aged 18 or older say most people are just looking out for themselves, up from 37 percent in 1975. The lack of faith in others has grown in most demographic segments, rising the most among young adults (up 19 percentage points).

Happiness has increased for the well-educated

(percent of people who say they are "very happy," by education, 1974 and 2000)

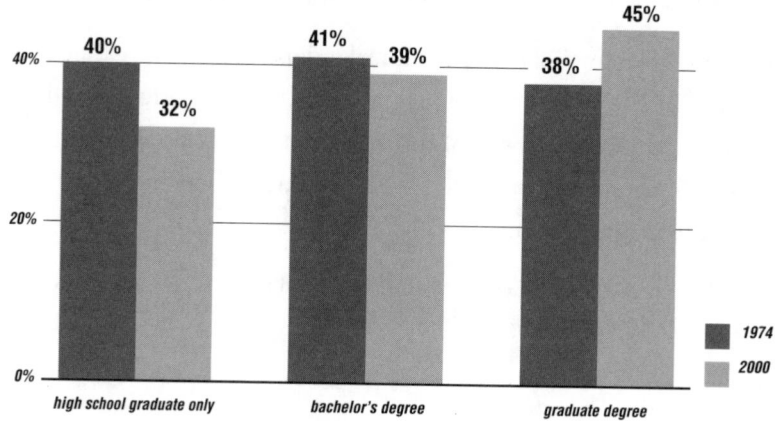

Table 1.1 Personal Happiness, 1974 to 2000

"Taken all together, how would you say things are these days—would you say that you are very happy, pretty happy, or not too happy?"

(percent of people aged 18 or older saying they are very happy, and percentage point change, 1974 to 2000)

	2000	1990	1980	1974	percentage point change 1974–00
Total	34%	33%	34%	38%	−4
Men	33	34	31	34	−1
Women	34	33	36	41	−7
Black	26	22	20	27	−1
White	36	35	36	39	−3
Aged 18 to 29	28	35	29	29	−1
Aged 30 to 39	35	34	32	38	−3
Aged 40 to 49	32	30	32	38	−6
Aged 50 to 59	39	33	34	41	−2
Aged 60 to 69	37	34	41	45	−8
Aged 70 or older	37	34	44	43	−6
Not a high school graduate	28	30	32	34	−6
High school graduate	32	32	33	40	−8
Bachelor's degree	41	45	38	39	2
Graduate degree	45	37	46	38	7

Source: General Social Surveys, National Opinion Research Center, University of Chicago; calculations by New Strategist

Table 1.2 Is Life Exciting? 1974 to 2000

"In general, do you find life exciting, pretty routine, or dull?"

(percent of people aged 18 or older who find life exciting, and percentage point change, 1974 to 2000)

	2000	1990	1980	1974	percentage point change 1974–00
Total	46%	45%	46%	42%	4
Men	52	50	50	47	5
Women	42	42	43	38	4
Black	46	33	40	35	11
White	47	47	47	43	4
Aged 18 to 29	46	48	47	50	−4
Aged 30 to 39	49	46	51	42	7
Aged 40 to 49	45	47	46	42	3
Aged 50 to 59	58	45	48	36	23
Aged 60 to 69	40	40	41	39	1
Aged 70 or older	34	40	37	40	−6
Not a high school graduate	29	21	34	32	−3
High school graduate	43	47	47	44	−1
Bachelor's degree	62	61	63	59	3
Graduate degree	67	67	65	63	4

Source: General Social Surveys, National Opinion Research Center, University of Chicago; calculations by New Strategist

Table 1.3 Helpfulness of Others, 1975 to 2000

"Would you say that most of the time people try to be helpful,
or that they are mostly just looking out for themselves?"

(percent of people aged 18 or older who say people are just looking out for themselves, and percentage point change, 1975 to 2000)

	2000	1990	1980	1975	percentage point change 1975–00
Total	45%	52%	47%	37%	8
Men	47	49	49	42	5
Women	44	55	45	33	11
Black	55	57	65	47	8
White	44	49	45	35	9
Aged 18 to 29	60	48	59	41	19
Aged 30 to 39	44	47	50	38	6
Aged 40 to 49	42	43	40	29	13
Aged 50 to 59	42	42	37	36	6
Aged 60 to 69	41	29	43	37	4
Aged 70 or older	35	33	38	36	−1
Not a high school graduate	55	50	52	45	10
High school graduate	48	45	47	35	13
Bachelor's degree	32	29	35	22	10
Graduate degree	30	18	28	24	6

Source: General Social Surveys, National Opinion Research Center, University of Chicago; calculations by New Strategist

Most Would Work If Rich

For most Americans, work is an important part of their identity. Even if they had enough money to live comfortably for the rest of their lives, 66 percent of workers would continue going to the office every day. This figure grew slightly from the 63 percent of 1974. People in nearly every demographic segment are more likely to say they would continue to work even if they didn't need the money. But people with bachelor's and graduate-level degrees are much less likely to say they would continue to work if rich.

Despite the ups and downs of the economy over the past few decades, people's feelings about their jobs and finances have changed surprisingly little in most demographic groups. Thirty-one percent say they are "pretty well satisfied" with their finances, the same as in 1974. Forty-five percent are "very satisfied" with the work they do (including housework for those without jobs), only slightly lower than in 1974. People with graduate degrees experienced the greatest increase in satisfaction with their finances between 1974 and 2000 (up 6 percentage points to 49 percent). Interestingly, this group also experienced the greatest decline in job satisfaction between 1974 and 2000, a 16 percentage point drop to 51 percent.

Fiftysomethings less likely to continue working if rich

(percent of workers who say they would continue to work even if they had enough money to live comfortably for the rest of their lives, by age, 1974 and 2000)

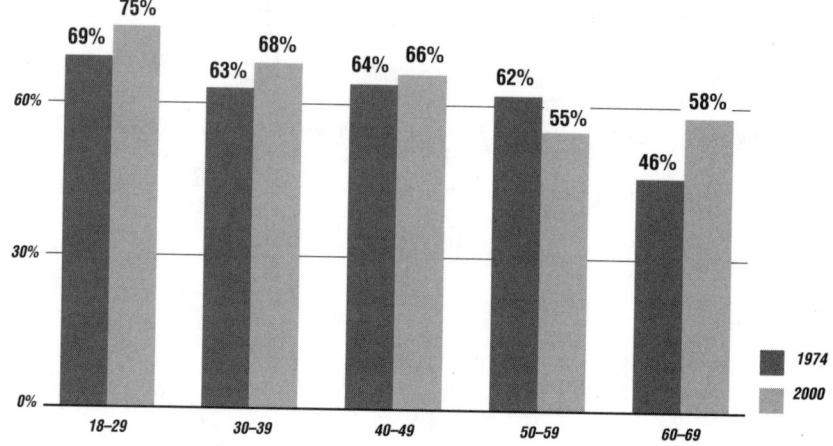

Table 1.4 Would You Work If You Were Rich? 1974 to 2000

"If you were to get enough money to live as comfortably as you would like for the rest of your life, would you continue to work or would you stop working?"

(percent of people aged 18 or older saying they would continue to work, and percentage point change, 1974 to 2000)

	2000	*1990*	*1980*	*1974*	*percentage point change 1974–00*
Total	**66%**	**73%**	**77%**	**63%**	**3**
Men	69	78	80	68	1
Women	64	68	73	55	9
Black	68	67	81	55	13
White	66	73	76	64	2
Aged 18 to 29	75	78	78	69	6
Aged 30 to 39	68	77	82	63	5
Aged 40 to 49	66	75	77	64	2
Aged 50 to 59	55	56	74	62	–7
Aged 60 to 69	58	53	58	46	12
Not a high school graduate	62	74	71	56	6
High school graduate	66	69	76	61	5
Bachelor's degree	67	77	85	79	–12
Graduate degree	66	86	82	82	–16

Note: Asked of people currently working or temporarily not at work. Aged 70 or older not shown because of small sample size.
Source: General Social Surveys, National Opinion Research Center, University of Chicago; calculations by New Strategist

Table 1.5 Satisfaction with Finances, 1974 to 2000

"So far as you and your family are concerned, would you say that you are pretty well satisfied with your present financial situation, more or less satisfied, or not satisfied at all?"

(percent of people aged 18 or older who are pretty well satisfied, and percentage point change, 1974 to 2000)

	2000	1990	1980	1974	percentage point change 1974–00
Total	31%	30%	29%	31%	0
Men	33	31	30	32	1
Women	29	29	28	31	–2
Black	16	18	18	22	–6
White	34	31	30	32	2
Aged 18 to 29	25	28	22	22	3
Aged 30 to 39	22	24	23	26	–4
Aged 40 to 49	29	23	26	30	–1
Aged 50 to 59	38	31	29	36	2
Aged 60 to 69	40	39	40	41	–1
Aged 70 or older	43	43	43	47	–4
Not a high school graduate	26	25	29	33	–7
High school graduate	28	29	27	27	1
Bachelor's degree	39	36	32	36	3
Graduate degree	49	51	39	43	6

Source: General Social Surveys, National Opinion Research Center, University of Chicago; calculations by New Strategist

Table 1.6 Satisfaction with Job, 1974 to 2000

"On the whole, how satisfied are you with the work you do?"

(percent of people aged 18 or older who are very satisfied, and percentage point change, 1974 to 2000)

	2000	1990	1980	1974	percentage point change 1974–00
Total	45%	46%	47%	48%	–3
Men	45	45	46	49	–4
Women	46	47	48	47	–1
Black	37	38	38	33	4
White	48	48	48	50	–2
Aged 18 to 29	40	39	35	39	1
Aged 30 to 39	43	45	43	44	–1
Aged 40 to 49	46	48	50	49	–3
Aged 50 to 59	50	48	52	53	–3
Aged 60 to 69	54	59	59	59	–5
Aged 70 or older	64	55	66	63	1
Not a high school graduate	40	41	50	42	–2
High school graduate	43	44	46	49	–6
Bachelor's degree	51	54	39	46	5
Graduate degree	51	60	59	67	–16

Note: Question asked regardless of labor force status.
Source: General Social Surveys, National Opinion Research Center, University of Chicago; calculations by New Strategist

Americans Are Strongly Religious

Sixty-two percent of people aged 18 or older believe in God without any doubt, a proportion that has barely budged since 1988, the year the question was first asked. Blacks are especially likely to believe in God without a doubt, 80 percent saying so.

The 53 percent majority of Americans are Protestants, but the figure has declined from 64 percent in 1974. The Catholic share has remained stable at 25 percent, while the Jewish proportion has fallen from 3 to 2 percent. People of "other" religion have grown from 1 to 6 percent as immigrants from Asia and the Middle East enter the United States. The share of Americans who say they have no religious preference has doubled from 7 to 14 percent during the past quarter century. One in five young adults claims to have no religious preference.

Thirty percent of people aged 18 or older attend religious services at least weekly, down from 36 percent in 1974. The biggest decline occurred among young adults, a 12 percentage point drop.

Protestant religion declining in importance

(percent of people who say their religious preference is Protestant, by age, 1974 and 2000)

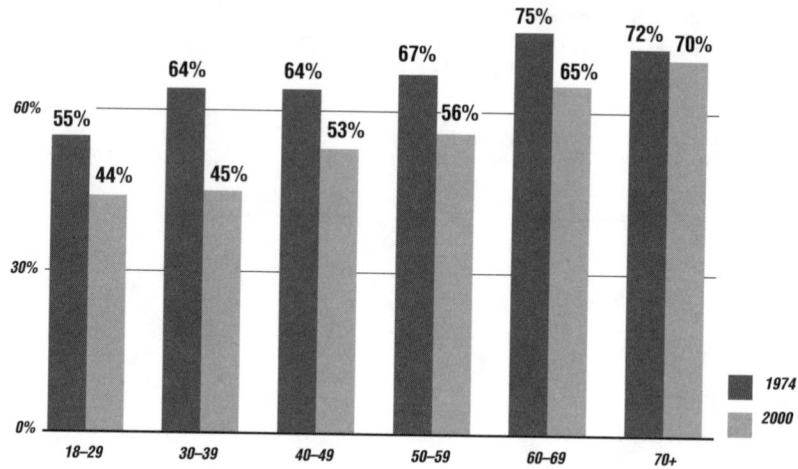

Table 1.7 Belief about God, 1988 and 2000

"I know God really exists and I have no doubts about it."

(percent of people aged 18 or older who agree, and percentage point change, 1988 to 2000)

	2000	1988	percentage point change 1988–00
Total	**62%**	**64%**	**−2**
Men	53	55	−2
Women	70	70	0
Black	80	75	5
White	59	62	−3
Aged 18 to 29	51	56	−5
Aged 30 to 39	62	62	0
Aged 40 to 49	60	63	−3
Aged 50 to 59	68	65	3
Aged 60 to 69	62	69	−7
Aged 70 or older	81	73	8
Not a high school graduate	63	72	−9
High school graduate	65	66	−1
Bachelor's degree	54	50	4
Graduate degree	53	47	6

Source: General Social Surveys, National Opinion Research Center, University of Chicago; calculations by New Strategist

Table 1.8 Religious Preference, 1974 and 2000

"What is your religious preference? Is it Protestant, Catholic,
Jewish, some other religion, or no religion?"

(percent of people aged 18 or older responding, 1974 and 2000)

	Protestant		Catholic		Jewish		Other		None	
	2000	1974	2000	1974	2000	1974	2000	1974	2000	1974
Total	53%	64%	25%	25%	2%	3%	6%	1%	14%	7%
Men	49	64	25	24	3	2	6	1	18	10
Women	56	65	26	27	2	4	5	1	11	4
Black	76	86	7	8	1	1	5	1	12	5
White	51	62	27	28	3	3	4	0	14	7
Aged 18 to 29	44	55	28	30	1	3	7	1	20	11
Aged 30 to 39	45	64	26	24	2	4	9	0	18	8
Aged 40 to 49	53	64	25	29	3	1	5	0	14	6
Aged 50 to 59	56	67	25	25	3	3	4	0	12	5
Aged 60 to 69	65	75	26	19	1	3	2	0	5	4
Aged 70 or older	70	72	21	19	2	5	1	0	6	4
Not a high school graduate	56	71	25	22	1	2	5	0	13	6
High school graduate	54	62	27	29	1	2	5	1	13	7
Bachelor's degree	47	60	24	22	6	7	7	1	16	10
Graduate degree	49	59	18	16	6	11	10	1	16	12

Note: Numbers may not add to 100 because "don't know" is not shown.
Source: General Social Surveys, National Opinion Research Center, University of Chicago; calculations by New Strategist

Table 1.9 Attendance at Religious Services, 1974 to 2000

"How often do you attend religious services?"

(percent of people aged 18 or older who attend religious services at least weekly, 1974 to 2000; percentage point change, 1974–00)

	2000	1990	1980	1974	percentage point change 1974–00
Total people	30%	35%	35%	36%	–6
Men	27	28	27	32	–5
Women	33	41	42	40	–7
Black	37	36	38	34	3
White	29	35	35	36	–7
Aged 18 to 29	21	24	24	26	–5
Aged 30 to 39	24	28	33	36	–12
Aged 40 to 49	28	34	37	35	–7
Aged 50 to 59	36	37	38	41	–5
Aged 60 to 69	42	51	40	42	0
Aged 70 or older	47	52	54	49	–2
Not a high school graduate	25	36	38	33	–8
High school graduate	29	33	34	37	–8
Bachelor's degree	34	40	35	38	–4
Graduate degree	40	41	34	45	–5

Source: General Social Surveys, National Opinion Research Center, University of Chicago; calculations by New Strategist

Marital Happiness Declines as Roles Change

The marriages of Americans are less happy than they once were—perhaps because of the confusion generated by the changing roles of men and women. Sixty-two percent of the married described their relationship as "very happy" in 2000, down from the 69 percent who felt that way in 1974. The biggest declines in marital happiness occurred among people in their fifties. The percentage of fiftysomethings with very happy marriages fell by 13 percentage points between 1974 and 2000.

Behind the decline in marital happiness may be the confusion generated by sweeping changes in the roles of men and women. Most people—particularly baby boomers and younger adults—approve of those changes, however. The proportion of Americans who believe it is better if men are the achievers outside the home fell sharply over the past quarter century, from 65 percent in 1977 to just 39 percent in 2000. The share of those who think a working mother can have just as good a relationship with her children as a mother who does not work rose from a 48 percent minority in 1977 to the 61 percent majority in 2000.

Fewer married couples are very happy

(percent of married people aged 18 or older who describe their marriage as "very happy," 1974 and 2000)

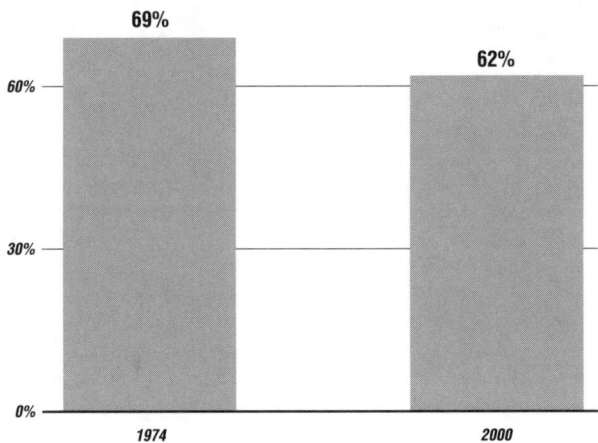

Table 1.10   Marital Happiness, 1974 to 2000

"Taking all things together, how would you describe your marriage? Would you say that your marriage is very happy, pretty happy, or not too happy?"

(percent of people aged 18 or older who say their marriage is very happy, and percentage point change, 1974 to 2000)

	2000	1990	1980	1974	percentage point change 1974–00
Total	62%	65%	68%	69%	–7
Men	64	69	70	69	–5
Women	61	61	66	68	–7
Black	55	50	57	60	–5
White	64	66	69	70	–6
Aged 18 to 29	61	79	68	69	–8
Aged 30 to 39	60	63	66	67	–7
Aged 40 to 49	61	57	61	65	–4
Aged 50 to 59	64	61	67	77	–13
Aged 60 to 69	64	68	75	64	0
Aged 70 or older	66	66	75	74	–8
Not a high school graduate	57	61	67	66	–9
High school graduate	60	64	67	69	–9
Bachelor's degree	70	71	71	74	–4
Graduate degree	76	67	79	77	–1

Note: Asked of people who were married at the time of the survey.
Source: General Social Surveys, National Opinion Research Center, University of Chicago; calculations by New Strategist

Table 1.11 Female Homemakers and Male Breadwinners, 1977 to 2000

"It is much better for everyone involved if the man is the achiever
outside the home and the woman takes care of the home
and family—do you agree or disagree?"

(percent of people aged 18 or older who agree/strongly agree, and percentage point change, 1977 to 2000)

	2000	1990	1977	percentage point change 1977–00
Total	39%	41%	65%	–26
Men	41	39	68	–27
Women	38	48	62	–24
Black	34	44	61	–27
White	40	40	65	–25
Aged 18 to 29	25	24	45	–20
Aged 30 to 39	30	27	51	–21
Aged 40 to 49	37	31	67	–30
Aged 50 to 59	41	51	79	–38
Aged 60 to 69	57	71	84	–27
Aged 70 or older	75	70	88	–13
Not a high school graduate	52	62	79	–27
High school graduate	42	39	61	–19
Bachelor's degree	29	34	45	–16
Graduate degree	25	25	45	–20

Source: General Social Surveys, National Opinion Research Center, University of Chicago; calculations by New Strategist

Table 1.12 Is a Working Mother as Good? 1977 to 2000

"A working mother can establish just as warm and secure a relationship with her children as a mother who does not work—do you agree or disagree?"

(percent of people aged 18 or older who agree/strongly agree, and percentage point change, 1977 to 2000)

	2000	1990	1977	percentage point change 1977–00
Total	61%	63%	48%	13
Men	55	57	41	14
Women	66	68	54	12
Black	66	70	56	10
White	59	62	47	12
Aged 18 to 29	68	71	60	8
Aged 30 to 39	63	71	61	2
Aged 40 to 49	62	70	45	17
Aged 50 to 59	61	62	43	18
Aged 60 to 69	49	46	32	17
Aged 70 or older	47	44	30	17
Not a high school graduate	56	50	37	19
High school graduate	59	65	52	7
Bachelor's degree	67	65	61	6
Graduate degree	72	74	64	8

Source: General Social Surveys, National Opinion Research Center, University of Chicago; calculations by New Strategist

More Tolerance for Sex Outside of Marriage

Americans are far more tolerant of premarital and homosexual sex today than they were in 1974. The proportion of people who say it is "not wrong at all" for a man and woman to have sex before marriage rose from 30 to 41 percent between 1974 and 2000.

The proportion of people who say it is "not wrong at all" for adults of the same sex to have sexual relations more than doubled between 1974 and 2000, rising from 12 to 27 percent. Young adults are most likely to see nothing wrong with homosexual relations. Forty percent feel this way, up from 22 percent in 1974.

Premarital and homosexual sex gain approval

(percent of people aged 18 or older who say it is "not wrong at all" for a man and woman to have sex before marriage, or for adults of the same sex to have sexual relations, 1974 and 2000)

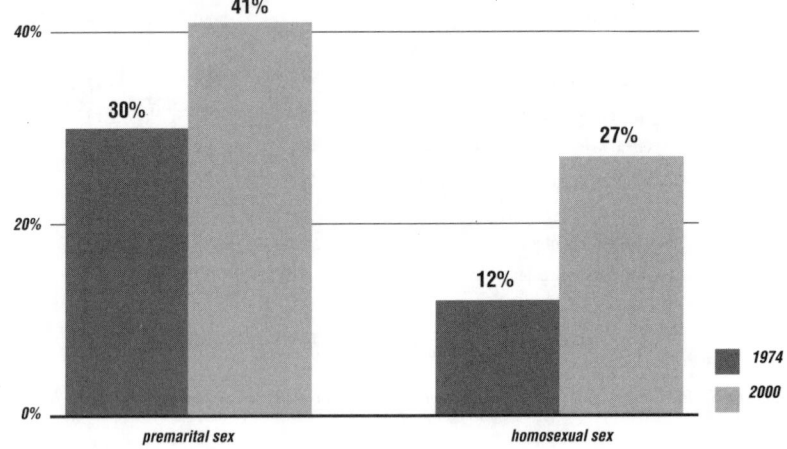

Table 1.13 Premarital Sex, 1974 to 2000

"If a man and woman have sex relations before marriage, do you think it is always wrong, almost always wrong, wrong only sometimes, or not wrong at all?"

(percent of people aged 18 or older saying it is not wrong at all, and percentage point change, 1974 to 2000)

	2000	1990	1974	percentage point change 1974–00
Total	41%	40%	30%	11
Men	45	45	35	10
Women	38	36	25	13
Black	38	46	46	–8
White	41	40	28	13
Aged 18 to 29	51	43	50	1
Aged 30 to 39	46	48	35	11
Aged 40 to 49	44	45	25	19
Aged 50 to 59	36	46	18	18
Aged 60 to 69	27	28	17	10
Aged 70 or older	18	18	11	7
Not a high school graduate	38	35	23	15
High school graduate	40	40	32	8
Bachelor's degree	42	37	41	1
Graduate degree	44	56	30	14

Source: General Social Surveys, National Opinion Research Center, University of Chicago; calculations by New Strategist

Table 1.14 Homosexual Sex, 1974 to 2000

"What about sexual relations between two adults of the same sex—do you think it is always wrong, almost always wrong, wrong only sometimes, or not wrong at all?"

(percent of people aged 18 or older who say it is not wrong at all, and percentage point change, 1974 to 2000)

	2000	1990	1980	1974	percentage point change 1974–00
Total	27%	13%	15%	12%	15
Men	25	11	16	12	13
Women	28	15	14	13	15
Black	18	14	14	15	3
White	28	13	15	12	16
Aged 18 to 29	40	16	18	22	18
Aged 30 to 39	27	18	23	12	15
Aged 40 to 49	27	14	13	15	12
Aged 50 to 59	29	5	10	7	22
Aged 60 to 69	12	12	9	6	6
Aged 70 or older	8	6	4	3	5
Not a high school graduate	16	4	8	8	8
High school graduate	27	12	14	12	15
Bachelor's degree	32	19	31	25	7
Graduate degree	41	30	29	19	22

Source: General Social Surveys, National Opinion Research Center, University of Chicago; calculations by New Strategist

Big Gains in Racial Tolerance

Racial tolerance has grown enormously during the past several decades. The proportion of Americans who agree with the statement that "blacks shouldn't push themselves where they're not wanted" has fallen from 35 to 15 percent between 1980 (the first year this question was asked of both blacks and whites) and 2000. Among adults under age 40, only 11 percent agree with the statement, as do 8 percent of college graduates.

The percentage of people aged 18 or older who think there should be laws against interracial marriage fell from 30 percent in 1980 to just 9 percent in 2000. The attitudes of older Americans are lagging behind, however. In 2000, 26 percent of people aged 70 or older still believed interracial marriage should be illegal—but this share declined from the 51 percent majority who felt that way in 1980.

Few Americans believe interracial marriage should be illegal

(percent of people aged 18 or older who think there should be laws against marriages between blacks and whites, 1974 and 2000)

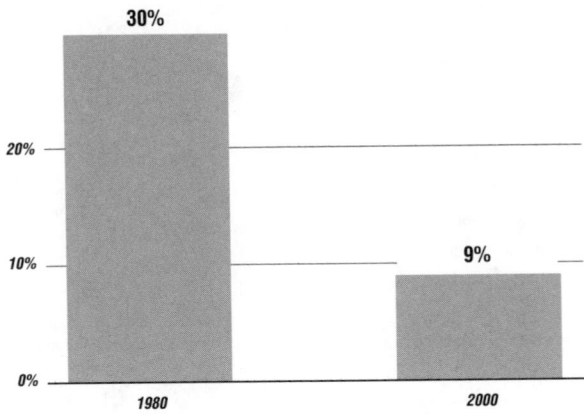

Table 1.15 Should Blacks Push Where They're Not Wanted? 1980 and 2000

"Here is an opinion other people have expressed in connection with black-white relations: 'Blacks shouldn't push themselves where they're not wanted.' How do you feel about that statement?"

(percent of people aged 18 or older who agree, and percentage point change, 1980 to 2000)

	2000	1980	percentage point change 1980–00
Total	15%	35%	–20
Men	17	36	–19
Women	14	33	–19
Black	20	24	–4
White	15	36	–21
Aged 18 to 29	11	25	–14
Aged 30 to 39	11	25	–14
Aged 40 to 49	13	37	–24
Aged 50 to 59	18	42	–24
Aged 60 to 69	22	50	–28
Aged 70 or older	26	43	–17
Not a high school graduate	25	51	–26
High school graduate	16	31	–15
Bachelor's degree	8	13	–5
Graduate degree	8	18	–10

Source: General Social Surveys, National Opinion Research Center, University of Chicago; calculations by New Strategist

Table 1.16 Interracial Marriage, 1980 to 2000

"Do you think there should be laws against marriages between
(Negroes/Blacks/African-Americans) and whites?"

(percent of people aged 18 or older answering yes, and percentage point change, 1980 to 2000)

	2000	1990	1980	percentage point change 1980–00
Total	**9%**	**19%**	**30%**	**−21**
Men	10	17	28	−18
Women	9	21	31	−22
Black	4	7	18	−14
White	11	21	31	−20
Aged 18 to 29	5	10	16	−11
Aged 30 to 39	6	12	19	−13
Aged 40 to 49	7	14	30	−23
Aged 50 to 59	10	26	36	−26
Aged 60 to 69	12	28	49	−37
Aged 70 or older	26	41	51	−25
Not a high school graduate	17	45	53	−36
High school graduate	10	16	25	−15
Bachelor's degree	3	6	7	−4
Graduate degree	2	2	3	−1

Source: General Social Surveys, National Opinion Research Center, University of Chicago; calculations by New Strategist

Most Agree Gun Control Is Needed

If Americans can agree on one issue, it's gun control. This consensus makes it all the more surprising that gun control is such a political hot potato. Fully 79 percent of Americans favor a law that would require a person to obtain a police permit before he or she can buy a gun. The figure is up slightly from 75 percent in 1974.

Almost every demographic segment favored gun control more highly in 2000 than in 1974. The biggest gains occurred among blacks (up 12 percentage points to 87 percent), people with graduate degrees (up 12 percentage points to 88 percent), and people in their fifties (up 12 percentage points to 83 percent).

Most people favor gun control

(percent of people who favor a law requiring a person to obtain a police permit before he or she can buy a gun, 1974 and 2000)

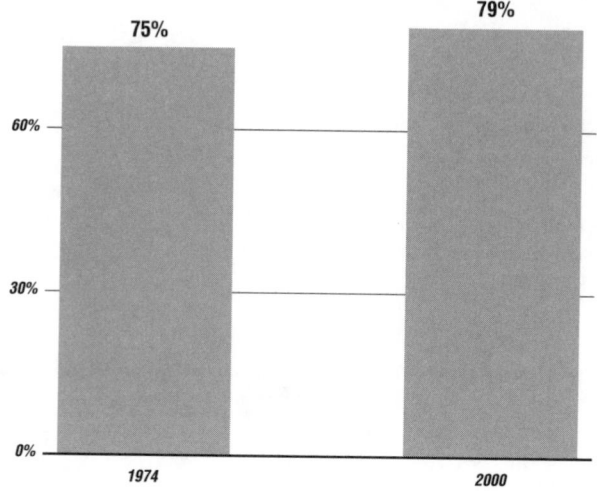

Table 1.17 Gun Control, 1974 to 2000

"Would you favor or oppose a law which would require a person to obtain a police permit before he or she could buy a gun?"

(percent of people aged 18 or older in favor, and percentage point change, 1974 to 2000)

	2000	1990	1980	1974	percentage point change 1974–00
Total	79%	80%	71%	75%	4
Men	70	73	64	66	4
Women	86	86	76	83	3
Black	87	87	83	75	12
White	77	79	69	75	2
Aged 18 to 29	80	86	73	76	4
Aged 30 to 39	80	76	74	77	3
Aged 40 to 49	79	77	66	74	5
Aged 50 to 59	80	81	65	70	10
Aged 60 to 69	71	80	68	74	-3
Aged 70 or older	81	81	79	81	0
Not a high school graduate	83	81	72	73	10
High school graduate	78	79	70	76	2
Bachelor's degree	79	75	70	77	2
Graduate degree	83	88	81	71	12

Source: General Social Surveys, National Opinion Research Center, University of Chicago; calculations by New Strategist

Confidence in America's Institutions Plummets

The confidence of the American public in the nation's institutions has spiraled downward over the past quarter-century. In some institutions—such as the executive branch of the federal government and Congress—people have had little faith for decades. For other institutions, the loss of confidence has occurred more recently.

Only 14 percent of people aged 18 or older say they have a "great deal of confidence" in the executive branch of the federal government, a figure that hasn't changed since 1974. Even fewer people have a great deal of confidence in Congress, with only 13 percent feeling that way in 2000, down from 17 percent in 1974. The Supreme Court fares better, as 32 percent have a great deal of confidence in it, down slightly from 33 percent in 1974.

Confidence in the press, education, and medicine experienced double-digit declines between 1974 and 2000. But confidence in the people running major companies fell only 3 percentage points during those years. (The latest data—from the 2000 General Social Survey—were collected well before the business and accounting scandals of 2001 and 2002.

Confidence in the press, education, and medicine have fallen sharply

(percent of people having a "great deal of confidence" in the people running selected institutions, 1974 and 2000)

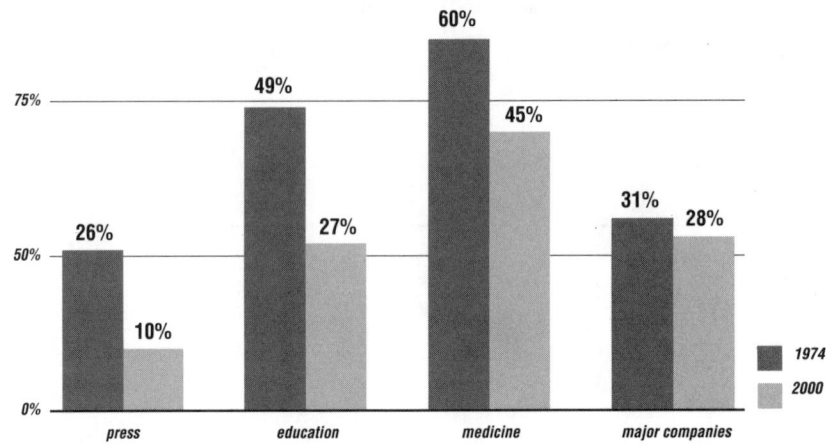

Table 1.18 Confidence in the Executive Branch of Government, 1974 to 2000

"As far as the people running the executive branch of the federal government
are concerned, would you say you have a great deal of confidence,
only some confidence, or hardly any confidence at all in them?"

(percent of people aged 18 or older who have a great deal of confidence, and percentage point change, 1974 to 2000)

	2000	1990	1980	1974	percentage point change 1974–00
Total	14%	24%	13%	14%	0
Men	13	24	12	15	–2
Women	14	25	13	12	2
Black	20	14	15	12	8
White	12	26	12	14	–2
Aged 18 to 29	20	31	13	9	11
Aged 30 to 39	12	20	9	8	4
Aged 40 to 49	10	17	12	15	–5
Aged 50 to 59	12	28	12	18	–6
Aged 60 to 69	11	22	15	19	–8
Aged 70 or older	14	30	18	20	–6
Not a high school graduate	18	19	17	16	2
High school graduate	12	25	11	13	–1
Bachelor's degree	17	27	8	10	7
Graduate degree	11	31	12	14	–3

Source: General Social Surveys, National Opinion Research Center, University of Chicago; calculations by New Strategist

Table 1.19 Confidence in Congress, 1974 to 2000

"As far as the people running Congress are concerned, would you say
you have a great deal of confidence, only some confidence,
or hardly any confidence at all in them?"

(percent of people aged 18 or older who have a great deal of confidence, and percentage point change, 1974 to 2000)

	2000	1990	1980	1974	percentage point change 1974–00
Total	**13%**	**16%**	**10%**	**17%**	**–4**
Men	12	15	9	19	–7
Women	13	17	10	15	–2
Black	16	14	12	12	4
White	12	16	10	18	–6
Aged 18 to 29	18	21	9	15	3
Aged 30 to 39	11	15	8	17	–6
Aged 40 to 49	11	10	8	20	–9
Aged 50 to 59	11	20	9	17	–6
Aged 60 to 69	13	17	10	17	–4
Aged 70 or older	9	13	18	18	–9
Not a high school graduate	16	13	15	16	0
High school graduate	12	17	8	17	–5
Bachelor's degree	14	14	5	17	–3
Graduate degree	13	18	7	25	–12

Source: General Social Surveys, National Opinion Research Center, University of Chicago; calculations by New Strategist

Table 1.20   Confidence in the Supreme Court, 1974 to 2000

"As far as the people running the Supreme Court are concerned, would you say you have a great deal of confidence, only some confidence, or hardly any confidence at all in them?"

(percent of people aged 18 or older who have a great deal of confidence, and percentage point change, 1974 to 2000)

	2000	1990	1980	1974	percentage point change 1974–00
Total	**32%**	**37%**	**26%**	**33%**	**–1**
Men	36	37	28	38	–2
Women	29	37	25	29	0
Black	30	24	30	26	4
White	33	38	26	34	–1
Aged 18 to 29	44	41	31	36	8
Aged 30 to 39	29	37	27	32	–3
Aged 40 to 49	31	36	22	36	–5
Aged 50 to 59	28	35	25	32	–4
Aged 60 to 69	33	28	19	30	3
Aged 70 or older	26	40	30	29	–3
Not a high school graduate	28	28	26	30	–2
High school graduate	28	35	25	32	–4
Bachelor's degree	42	46	28	42	0
Graduate degree	53	49	31	48	5

Source: General Social Surveys, National Opinion Research Center, University of Chicago; calculations by New Strategist

Table 1.21 Confidence in the Press, 1974 to 2000

"As far as the people running the press are concerned, would you say you have a great deal of confidence, only some confidence, or hardly any confidence at all in them?"

(percent of people aged 18 or older who have a great deal of confidence, and percentage point change, 1974 to 2000)

	2000	1990	1980	1974	percentage point change 1974–00
Total	**10%**	**15%**	**23%**	**26%**	**–16**
Men	9	18	25	28	–19
Women	11	13	21	24	–13
Black	10	11	30	30	–20
White	10	16	22	25	–15
Aged 18 to 29	14	22	23	31	–17
Aged 30 to 39	11	12	23	24	–13
Aged 40 to 49	8	14	22	22	–14
Aged 50 to 59	8	14	23	23	–15
Aged 60 to 69	10	10	23	24	–14
Aged 70 or older	7	19	20	30	–23
Not a high school graduate	13	18	25	30	–17
High school graduate	10	15	23	24	–14
Bachelor's degree	11	14	20	23	–12
Graduate degree	9	16	21	25	–16

Source: General Social Surveys, National Opinion Research Center, University of Chicago; calculations by New Strategist

Table 1.22 Confidence in Education, 1974 to 2000

"As far as the people running education are concerned, would you say you have a great deal of confidence, only some confidence, or hardly any confidence at all in them?"

(percent of people aged 18 or older who have a great deal of confidence, and percentage point change, 1974 to 2000)

	2000	1990	1980	1974	percentage point change 1974–00
Total	27%	27%	31%	49%	−22
Men	28	23	28	49	−21
Women	27	31	33	49	−22
Black	40	26	53	65	−25
White	25	27	28	47	−22
Aged 18 to 29	36	27	30	48	−12
Aged 30 to 39	20	26	28	49	−29
Aged 40 to 49	22	22	28	45	−23
Aged 50 to 59	28	30	36	46	−18
Aged 60 to 69	31	26	26	54	−23
Aged 70 or older	32	37	41	58	−26
Not a high school graduate	33	32	37	55	−22
High school graduate	27	29	27	48	−21
Bachelor's degree	26	19	29	38	−12
Graduate degree	28	26	38	43	−15

Source: General Social Surveys, National Opinion Research Center, University of Chicago; calculations by New Strategist

Table 1.23 Confidence in Medicine, 1974 to 2000

"As far as the people running medicine are concerned, would you
say you have a great deal of confidence, only some confidence,
or hardly any confidence at all in them?"

(percent of people aged 18 or older who have a great deal of confidence, and percentage point change, 1974 to 2000)

	2000	1990	1980	1974	percentage point change 1974–00
Total	**45%**	**46%**	**53%**	**60%**	**–15**
Men	48	47	55	59	–11
Women	42	46	52	61	–19
Black	46	38	54	58	–12
White	45	47	53	61	–16
Aged 18 to 29	57	58	58	71	–14
Aged 30 to 39	48	43	49	62	–14
Aged 40 to 49	39	37	52	59	–20
Aged 50 to 59	37	43	52	55	–18
Aged 60 to 69	36	38	54	52	–16
Aged 70 or older	42	57	52	52	–10
Not a high school graduate	44	47	52	57	–13
High school graduate	42	46	54	63	–21
Bachelor's degree	49	46	54	58	–9
Graduate degree	51	47	54	60	–9

Source: General Social Surveys, National Opinion Research Center, University of Chicago; calculations by New Strategist

Table 1.24   Confidence in Major Companies, 1974 to 2000

"As far as the people running major companies are concerned, would you say you have a great deal of confidence, only some confidence, or hardly any confidence at all in them?"

(percent of people aged 18 or older who have a great deal of confidence, and percentage point change, 1974 to 2000)

	2000	1990	1980	1974	percentage point change 1974–00
Total	28%	26%	29%	31%	–3
Men	31	29	31	36	–5
Women	27	23	27	28	–1
Black	22	13	19	15	7
White	30	28	30	33	–3
Aged 18 to 29	30	30	18	26	4
Aged 30 to 39	30	19	29	26	4
Aged 40 to 49	26	24	31	35	–9
Aged 50 to 59	30	34	36	39	–9
Aged 60 to 69	29	27	35	36	–7
Aged 70 or older	27	28	34	34	–7
Not a high school graduate	18	24	27	30	–12
High school graduate	26	25	27	30	–4
Bachelor's degree	41	34	37	35	6
Graduate degree	41	23	44	44	–3

Source: General Social Surveys, National Opinion Research Center, University of Chicago; calculations by New Strategist

Independents Outnumber Party Loyalists

Americans are more likely to be political independents than either Democrats or Republicans. In 2000, 41 percent of people aged 18 or older identified themselves as independents, up from 31 percent in 1974. The percentage of Americans who identify themselves as Democrats fell from 42 to 32 percent during those years, while Republicans grew slightly from 22 to 26 percent.

Political identification is irrelevant if people don't vote, and increasingly that's the case. The percentage of people voting in presidential elections has fallen from 69 to 55 percent between 1964 and 2000. The percentage voting in Congressional elections is also down sharply, falling from 55 percent in 1966 to just 42 percent in 1998.

By age, the biggest declines in voting rates have been entirely among people under age 65—which gives more political clout to the older population. Both men and women are less likely to vote than they once were, but women are now more likely to vote than men—a reversal of the past pattern. The voting rate has also fallen in every racial and ethnic group, declining more sharply for whites than blacks—which increases the power of the black vote. A small minority of Hispanics and Asians go to the polls.

Voting rate declines

(percent of people voting in presidential elections, 1964 to 2000)

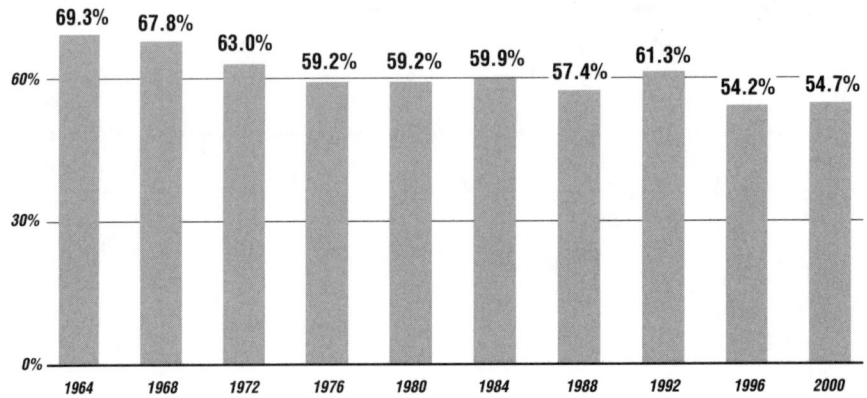

Table 1.25 Political Party Identification, 1974 and 2000

"Generally speaking, do you usually think of yourself as
a Republican, Democrat, independent, or what?"

(percent of people aged 18 or older responding, and percentage point change, 1974 and 2000)

	Democrat		independent		Republican		percentage point change, 1974–00		
	2000	*1974*	*2000*	*1974*	*2000*	*1974*	*Democrat*	*Independent*	*Republican*
Total	32%	42%	41%	31%	26%	22%	–10	10	4
Men	27	41	42	33	29	21	–14	9	8
Women	36	43	41	29	22	23	–7	12	–1
Black	59	62	34	20	6	10	–3	14	–4
White	26	39	42	32	30	24	–13	10	6
Aged 18 to 29	23	35	55	44	21	15	–12	11	6
Aged 30 to 39	28	41	43	34	27	19	–13	9	8
Aged 40 to 49	35	46	38	30	26	19	–11	8	7
Aged 50 to 59	35	45	37	26	25	27	–10	11	–2
Aged 60 to 69	34	45	36	22	31	27	–11	14	4
Aged 70 or older	44	45	30	13	26	36	–1	17	–10
Not a high school graduate	36	51	46	23	16	19	–15	23	–3
High school grad.	31	40	43	33	25	22	–9	10	3
Bachelor's degree	28	25	37	46	34	27	3	–9	7
Graduate degree	32	36	33	40	32	22	–4	–7	10

Note: Numbers may not add to 100 because "other party" and "don't know" are not shown.
Source: General Social Surveys, National Opinion Research Center, University of Chicago; calculations by New Strategist

Table 1.26 Voting Rates by Age, 1964 to 2000

(percent of people who reported voting in elections by age, and percentage point change, 1964 to 2000)

	total	18–24	25–44	45–64	65+
Presidential election years					
2000	54.7%	32.3%	49.8%	64.1%	67.6%
1996	54.2	32.4	49.2	64.4	67.0
1992	61.3	42.8	58.3	70.0	70.1
1988	57.4	36.2	54.0	67.9	68.8
1984	59.9	40.8	58.4	69.8	67.7
1980	59.2	39.9	58.7	69.3	65.1
1976	59.2	42.2	58.7	68.7	62.2
1972	63.0	49.6	62.7	70.8	63.5
1968	67.8	50.4	66.6	74.9	65.8
1964	69.3	50.9	69.0	75.9	66.3
Percentage point change					
1964 to 2000	−14.6	−18.6	−19.2	−11.8	1.3
Congressional election years					
1998	41.9%	16.7%	34.8%	53.6%	59.5%
1994	45.0	20.1	39.4	56.7	61.3
1990	45.0	20.4	40.7	55.8	60.3
1986	46.0	21.9	41.4	58.7	60.9
1982	48.5	24.8	45.4	62.2	59.9
1978	45.9	23.5	43.1	58.5	55.9
1974	44.7	23.8	42.2	56.9	51.4
1970	54.6	30.4	51.9	64.2	57.0
1966	55.4	31.2	53.1	64.5	56.1
Percentage point change					
1966 to 1998	−13.5	−14.5	−18.3	−10.9	3.4

Note: Before 1972, data for 18-to-24-year-olds include only 21-to-24-year-olds.
Source: Bureau of the Census, Voting and Registration in the Election of November 1998, *Current Population Report P20-523RV, 2000; and* Voting and Registration in the Election of November 2000, *Current Population Report P20-542, 2002; calculations by New Strategist*

Table 1.27   Voting Rate by Sex, 1964 to 2000

(percent of people who reported voting in elections by sex, and percentage point change, 1964 to 2000)

	total	men	women
Presidential election years			
2000	54.7%	53.1%	56.2%
1996	54.2	52.8	55.5
1992	61.3	60.2	62.3
1988	57.4	56.4	58.3
1984	59.9	59.0	60.8
1980	59.2	59.1	59.4
1976	59.2	59.6	58.8
1972	63.0	64.1	62.0
1968	67.8	69.8	66.0
1964	69.3	71.9	67.0
Percentage point change			
1964 to 2000	−14.6	−18.8	−10.8
Congressional election years			
1998	41.9%	41.4%	42.4%
1994	45.0	44.7	45.3
1990	45.0	44.6	45.4
1986	46.0	45.8	46.1
1982	48.5	48.7	48.4
1978	45.9	46.6	45.3
1974	44.7	46.2	43.4
1970	54.6	56.8	52.7
1966	55.4	58.2	50.3
Percentage point change			
1966 to 1998	−13.5	−16.8	−7.9

Source: Bureau of the Census, Voting and Registration in the Election of November 1998, *Current Population Report P20-523RV, 2000; and* Voting and Registration in the Election of November 2000, *Current Population Report P20-542, 2002; calculations by New Strategist*

Table 1.28 Voting Rate by Race and Hispanic Origin, 1964 to 2000

(percent of people who reported voting in elections by race and Hispanic origin, and percentage point change, 1964 to 2000)

	total	Asian	black	Hispanic	white total	white non-Hispanic
Presidential election years						
2000	54.7%	25.4%	53.5%	27.5%	56.4%	60.4%
1996	54.2	25.7	50.6	26.7	56.0	59.6
1992	61.3	27.3	54.0	28.9	63.6	66.9
1988	57.4	–	51.5	28.8	59.1	61.8
1984	59.9	–	55.8	32.6	61.4	63.3
1980	59.2	–	50.5	29.9	60.9	62.8
1976	59.2	–	48.7	31.8	60.9	–
1972	63.0	–	52.1	37.5	64.5	–
1968	67.8	–	57.6	–	69.1	–
1964	69.3	–	58.5	–	70.7	–
Percentage point change						
1964 to 2000	–14.6	–	–5.0	–	–14.3	–
Congressional election years						
1998	41.9%	19.2%	39.6%	20.0%	43.3%	46.5%
1994	45.0	21.8	37.1	20.2	47.3	50.1
1990	45.0	–	39.2	21.0	46.7	–
1986	46.0	–	43.2	24.2	47.0	–
1982	48.5	–	43.0	25.3	49.9	–
1978	45.9	–	37.2	23.5	47.3	–
1974	44.7	–	33.8	22.9	46.3	–
1970	54.6	–	43.5	–	56.0	–
1966	55.4	–	41.7	–	57.0	–
Percentage point change						
1966 to 1998	–13.5	–	–2.1	–	–13.7	–

Note: (–) means data not available.
Source: Bureau of the Census, Voting and Registration in the Election of November 1998, *Current Population Report P20-523RV, 2000; and* Voting and Registration in the Election of November 2000, *Current Population Report P20-542, 2002;* calculations by New Strategist

Crime Is Down

The drop in crime rates is being felt in homes across the country. Forty-six percent of people aged 18 or older believe there's less crime in their area now than there was a year ago, a proportion that has grown from a low of just 10 percent in 1972.

Police records confirm the perception that crime is down. After rising rapidly from 1960 to 1990, the number of crimes and the crime rate fell during the 1990s. The number of crimes fell 20 percent between 1990 and 2000, while the crime rate fell 29 percent. Crime would have to drop a lot more before it matched the levels of 1960, however. Between 1960 and 1990, the crime rate more than doubled.

People feel safer

(percent of people aged 18 or older who say there is less crime in their area than there was a year ago, 1972 to 2000)

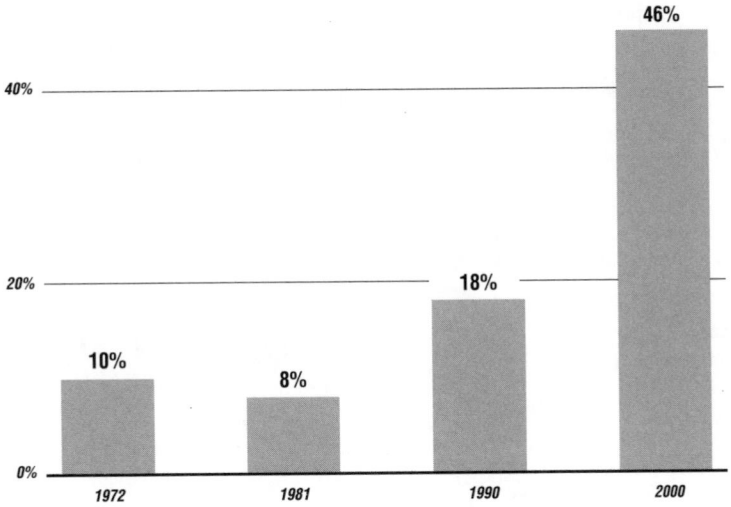

Table 1.29 More Crime in Area? 1972 to 2000

"Is there more crime in your area than there was a year ago, or less?"

(percent of people aged 18 or older by attitude toward crime in area, and percentage point change, 1972 to 2000)

	more	*less*	*same*	*no opinion*
2000	34%	46%	15%	5%
1998	31	48	16	5
1997	46	32	20	2
1996	46	24	25	5
1992	54	19	23	4
1990	51	18	24	8
1989	47	21	27	5
1983	37	17	36	10
1981	54	8	29	9
1977	43	17	21	8
1975	50	12	29	9
1972	51	10	27	12
Percentage point change				
1972 to 2000	−17	36	−12	−7

Source: Reprinted with permission from The Gallup Organization, Internet site http://www.gallup.com

Table 1.30   Crimes Reported to Police, 1960 to 2000: Number of Crimes

(number of criminal offenses reported to police by type of crime, 1960 to 2000; percent change for selected years)

	total	murder	forcible rape	robbery	aggravated assault	burglary	larceny-theft	motor vehicle theft
2000	11,605,751	15,517	90,186	407,842	910,744	2,049,946	6,965,957	1,165,559
1999	11,634,378	15,522	89,411	409,371	911,740	2,100,739	6,955,520	1,152,075
1998	12,485,714	16,974	93,144	447,186	976,583	2,332,735	7,376,311	1,242,781
1997	13,194,571	18,208	96,153	498,534	1,023,201	2,460,526	7,743,760	1,354,189
1996	13,493,863	19,645	96,252	535,594	1,037,049	2,506,400	7,904,685	1,394,238
1995	13,862,727	21,606	97,470	580,509	1,099,207	2,593,784	7,997,710	1,472,441
1994	13,989,543	23,326	102,216	618,949	1,113,179	2,712,774	7,879,812	1,539,287
1993	14,144,794	24,526	106,014	659,870	1,135,607	2,834,808	7,820,909	1,563,060
1992	14,438,191	23,760	109,062	672,478	1,126,974	2,979,884	7,915,199	1,610,834
1991	14,872,883	24,703	106,593	687,732	1,092,739	3,157,150	8,142,228	1,661,738
1990	14,475,613	23,438	102,555	639,271	1,054,863	3,073,909	7,945,670	1,635,907
1989	14,251,449	21,500	94,504	578,326	951,707	3,168,170	7,872,442	1,564,800
1988	13,923,086	20,675	92,486	542,968	910,092	3,218,077	7,705,872	1,432,916
1987	13,508,708	20,096	91,111	517,704	855,088	3,236,184	7,499,851	1,288,674
1986	13,211,869	20,613	91,459	542,775	834,322	3,241,410	7,257,153	1,224,137
1985	12,430,357	18,976	87,671	497,874	723,246	3,073,348	6,926,380	1,102,862
1984	11,881,755	18,692	84,233	485,008	685,349	2,984,434	6,591,874	1,032,165
1983	12,108,630	19,308	78,918	506,567	653,294	3,129,851	6,712,759	1,007,933
1982	12,974,400	21,010	78,770	553,130	669,480	3,447,100	7,142,500	1,062,400
1981	13,423,800	22,520	82,500	592,910	663,900	3,779,700	7,194,400	1,087,800
1980	13,408,300	23,040	82,990	565,840	672,650	3,795,200	7,136,900	1,131,700
1979	12,249,500	21,460	76,390	480,700	629,480	3,327,700	6,601,000	1,112,800
1978	11,209,000	19,560	67,610	426,930	571,460	3,128,300	5,991,000	1,004,100
1977	10,984,500	19,120	63,500	412,610	534,350	3,071,500	5,905,700	977,700
1976	11,349,700	18,780	57,080	427,810	500,530	3,108,700	6,270,800	966,000
1975	11,292,400	20,510	56,090	470,500	492,620	3,265,300	5,977,700	1,009,600
1974	10,253,400	20,710	55,400	442,400	456,210	3,039,200	5,262,500	977,100
1973	8,718,100	19,640	51,400	384,220	420,650	2,565,500	4,347,900	928,800
1972	8,248,800	18,670	46,850	376,290	393,090	2,375,500	4,151,200	887,200
1971	8,588,200	17,780	42,260	387,700	368,760	2,399,300	4,424,200	948,200
1970	8,098,000	16,000	37,990	349,860	334,970	2,205,000	4,225,800	928,400
1969	7,410,900	14,760	37,170	298,850	311,090	1,981,900	3,888,600	878,500
1968	6,720,200	13,800	31,670	262,840	286,700	1,858,900	3,482,700	783,600
1967	5,903,400	12,240	27,620	202,910	257,160	1,632,100	3,111,600	659,800
1966	5,223,500	11,040	25,820	157,990	235,330	1,410,100	2,822,000	561,200
1965	4,739,400	9,960	23,410	138,690	215,330	1,282,500	2,572,600	496,900
1964	4,564,600	9,360	21,420	130,390	203,050	1,213,200	2,514,400	472,800
1963	3,109,500	8,640	17,650	116,470	174,210	1,086,400	2,297,800	408,300
1962	3,752,200	8,530	17,550	110,860	164,570	994,300	2,089,600	366,800
1961	3,488,000	8,740	17,220	106,670	156,760	949,600	1,913,000	336,000
1960	3,384,200	9,110	17,190	107,840	154,320	912,100	1,855,400	328,200
Percent change								
1990 to 2000	–19.8%	–33.8%	–12.1%	–36.2%	–13.7%	–33.3%	–12.3%	–28.8%
1960 to 2000	242.9	70.3	424.6	278.2	490.2	124.8	275.4	255.1

Source: Bureau of Justice Statistics, Sourcebook of Criminal Justice Statistics; *Internet site http://www.albany.edu/sourcebook; calculations by New Strategist*

Table 1.31 Crimes Reported to Police, 1960 to 2000: Rate of Crime

(number of criminal offenses reported to police per 100,000 people by type of crime, 1960 to 2000; percent change for selected years)

	total	murder	forcible rape	robbery	aggravated assault	burglary	larceny-theft	motor vehicle theft
2000	4,124.0	5.5	32.0	144.9	323.6	728.4	2,475.3	414.2
1999	4,266.5	5.7	32.8	150.1	334.3	770.4	2,550.7	422.5
1998	4,620.1	6.3	34.5	165.5	361.4	863.2	2,729.5	459.9
1997	4,927.3	6.8	35.9	186.2	382.1	918.8	2,891.8	505.7
1996	5,087.6	7.4	36.3	201.9	391.0	945.0	2,980.3	525.7
1995	5,274.9	8.2	37.1	220.9	418.3	987.0	3,043.2	560.3
1994	5,373.8	9.0	39.3	237.8	427.6	1,042.1	3,026.9	591.3
1993	5,487.1	9.5	41.1	256.0	440.5	1,099.7	3,033.9	606.3
1992	5,661.4	9.3	42.8	263.7	441.9	1,168.4	3,103.6	631.6
1991	5,898.4	9.8	42.3	272.7	433.4	1,252.1	3,229.1	659.0
1990	5,802.7	9.4	41.1	256.3	422.9	1,232.2	3,185.1	655.8
1989	5,774.0	8.7	38.3	234.3	385.6	1,283.6	3,189.6	634.0
1988	5,694.5	8.5	37.8	222.1	372.2	1,316.2	3,151.7	586.1
1987	5,575.5	8.3	37.6	213.7	352.9	1,335.7	3,095.4	531.9
1986	5,501.9	8.6	38.1	226.0	347.4	1,349.8	3,022.1	509.8
1985	5,224.5	8.0	36.8	209.3	304.0	1,291.7	2,911.2	463.5
1984	5,038.4	7.9	35.7	205.7	290.6	1,265.5	2,795.2	437.7
1983	5,179.2	8.3	33.8	216.7	279.4	1,338.7	2,871.3	431.1
1982	5,600.5	9.1	34.0	238.8	289.0	1,488.0	3,083.1	458.6
1981	5,850.0	9.8	36.0	258.4	289.3	1,647.2	3,135.3	474.1
1980	5,950.0	10.2	36.8	251.1	298.5	1,684.1	3,167.0	502.2
1979	5,565.5	9.7	34.7	218.4	286.0	1,511.9	2,999.1	505.6
1978	5,140.3	9.0	31.0	195.8	262.1	1,434.6	2,747.4	460.5
1977	5,077.6	8.8	29.4	190.7	240.0	1,419.8	2,729.9	451.9
1976	5,287.3	8.8	26.6	199.3	233.2	1,448.2	2,921.3	450.0
1975	5,298.5	9.6	26.3	220.8	231.1	1,532.1	2,804.8	473.7
1974	4,850.4	9.8	26.2	209.3	215.8	1,437.7	2,489.5	462.2
1973	4,154.4	9.4	24.5	183.1	200.5	1,222.5	2,071.9	442.6
1972	3,961.4	9.0	22.5	180.7	188.8	1,140.8	1,993.6	426.1
1971	4,164.7	8.6	20.5	188.0	178.8	1,163.5	2,145.5	459.8
1970	3,984.5	7.9	18.7	172.1	164.8	1,084.9	2,079.3	456.8
1969	3,680.0	7.3	18.5	148.4	154.5	984.1	1,930.9	436.2
1968	3,370.2	6.9	15.9	131.8	143.8	932.3	1,746.6	393.0
1967	2,989.7	6.2	14.0	102.8	130.2	826.6	1,575.8	334.1
1966	2,670.8	5.6	13.2	80.8	120.3	721.0	1,442.9	286.9
1965	2,449.0	5.1	12.1	71.7	111.3	662.7	1,329.3	256.8
1964	2,388.1	4.9	11.2	68.2	106.2	634.7	1,315.5	247.4
1963	2,180.3	4.6	9.4	61.8	92.4	576.4	1,219.1	216.6
1962	2,019.8	4.6	9.4	59.7	88.6	535.2	1,124.8	197.4
1961	1,906.1	4.8	9.4	58.3	85.7	518.9	1,045.4	183.6
1960	1,887.2	5.1	9.6	60.1	86.1	508.6	1,034.7	183.0
Percent change								
1990 to 2000	−28.9%	−41.5%	−22.1%	−43.5%	−23.5%	−40.9%	−22.3%	−36.8%
1960 to 2000	118.5	7.8	233.3	141.1	275.8	43.2	139.2	126.3

Source: Bureau of Justice Statistics, Sourcebook of Criminal Justice Statistics; *Internet site http://www.albany.edu/sourcebook; calculations by New Strategist*

Food Preferences Are Changing

The American diet is different than it used to be. People are eating less red meat and more poultry. They're eating more fresh fruits and vegetables and fewer eggs. The changes in food consumption between 1970 and 1999 have been striking.

Per capita consumption of red meat fell 11 percent between 1970 and 1999, while consumption of poultry rose more than 100 percent. Americans ate 17 percent fewer eggs in 1999 than they did in 1970, but 161 percent more cheese. While people are drinking 67 percent less whole milk, they're drinking 167 percent more reduced-fat milk. Interestingly, between 1990 and 1999, consumption of red meat and eggs climbed somewhat, although they remain well below levels of 1970.

Despite concerns over too much fat in the diet, consumption of fats and oils rose 30 percent between 1970 and 1999. Fresh fruit consumption is up 31 percent, while fresh vegetable consumption rose 26 percent.

Americans drank more than twice as many gallons of soft drinks per capita in 1999 than they did in 1970. They also drink more beer and wine, but less distilled spirits. Bottled water consumption has grown from just 2.4 gallons per person in 1980 to more than 18 gallons in 1999.

People are eating more of both the good and the bad

(percent change in per capita consumption of selected foods, 1970–99)

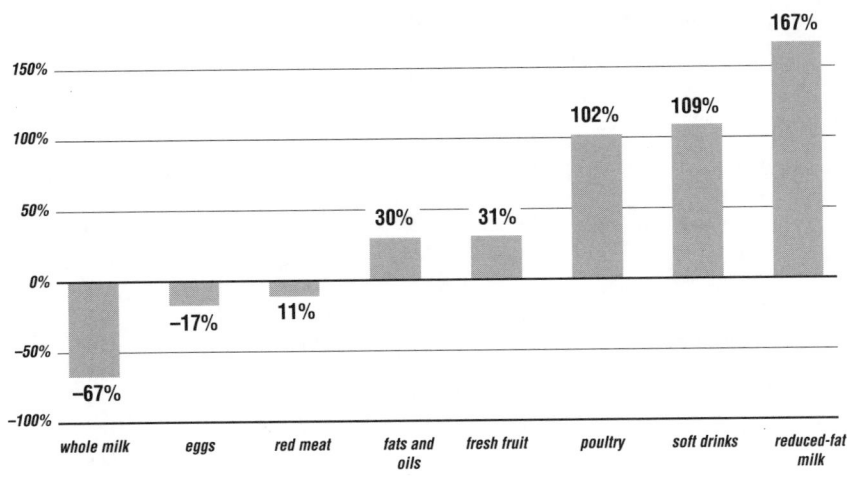

Table 1.32 Food and Beverage Consumption, 1970 to 1999

(number of pounds of selected foods and gallons of selected beverages consumed per person, and percent change, 1970 to 1999)

	1999	1990	1980	1970	percent change 1970–99
Red meat	**117.7**	**112.3**	**126.4**	**131.7**	**–10.6%**
Beef	65.8	63.9	72.1	79.6	–17.3
Pork	50.5	46.4	52.1	48.0	5.2
Poultry	**68.3**	**56.3**	**40.8**	**33.8**	**102.1**
Chicken	54.2	42.4	32.7	27.4	97.8
Turkey	14.1	13.8	8.1	6.4	120.3
Fish and shellfish	**15.2**	**15.0**	**12.4**	**11.7**	**29.9**
Eggs (number)	**255**	**234**	**271**	**309**	**–17.4**
Processed	74	48	35	33	124.2
Shell	181	186	236	276	–34.4
Cheese	**29.8**	**24.6**	**17.5**	**11.4**	**161.4**
Cheddar	10.1	9.0	6.9	5.8	74.1
Mozzarella	9.2	6.9	3.0	1.2	666.7
Swiss	1.1	1.4	1.3	0.9	22.2
Beverage milk	**23.6**	**25.7**	**27.6**	**31.2**	**–24.4**
Whole	8.4	10.5	17.0	25.5	–67.1
Reduced fat	15.2	15.2	10.5	5.7	166.7
Yogurt	**9.1**	**7.4**	**4.6**	**0.8**	**1,037.5**
Frozen dairy products	**29.3**	**28.4**	**26.4**	**28.5**	**2.8**
Ice cream	16.8	15.8	17.5	17.8	–5.6
Fats and oils	**68.5**	**63.0**	**56.9**	**52.6**	**30.2**
Butter	4.8	4.4	4.5	5.4	–11.1
Margarine	8.1	10.9	11.3	10.8	–25.0
Salad and cooking oils	29.4	25.2	21.2	15.4	90.9
Fresh fruits	**132.5**	**116.3**	**104.7**	**101.2**	**30.9**
Apples	18.8	19.6	19.2	17.0	10.6
Bananas	31.4	24.4	20.8	17.4	80.5
Cantaloupe	11.9	9.2	5.8	7.2	65.3
Grapefruit	5.9	4.4	7.3	8.2	–28.0
Grapes	8.2	7.9	3.9	2.9	182.8
Oranges	8.6	12.4	14.3	16.2	–46.9
Peaches and nectarines	5.3	5.5	7.1	5.8	–8.6
Pears	3.4	3.2	2.6	1.9	78.9
Strawberries	4.5	3.2	2.0	1.7	164.7
Watermelon	15.8	13.3	10.7	13.5	17.0
Canned fruits	**19.6**	**21.0**	**24.6**	**23.3**	**–15.9**
Frozen fruits	**3.7**	**3.8**	**3.1**	**3.3**	**12.1**
Fruit juices	**9.6**	**7.9**	**9.5**	**5.7**	**68.4**
Fresh vegetables	**192.1**	**167.1**	**149.1**	**152.9**	**25.6**
Bell peppers	6.7	4.5	2.9	2.2	204.5
Broccoli	6.0	3.4	1.4	0.5	1,100.0
Cabbage	8.1	8.8	8.1	8.8	–8.0
Carrots	13.6	8.3	6.2	6.0	126.7
Celery	6.2	7.2	7.4	7.3	–15.1

(continued)

(continued from previous page)

	1999	1990	1980	1970	percent change 1970–99
Corn	9.9	6.7	6.5	7.8	26.9%
Cucumbers	6.9	4.7	3.9	2.8	146.4
Head lettuce	25.3	27.8	25.6	22.4	12.9
Onions	18.6	15.1	11.4	10.1	84.2
Potatoes	49.2	46.8	51.1	61.8	−20.4
Tomatoes	17.8	15.5	12.8	12.1	47.1
Flour, cereal products	**201.9**	**181.0**	**144.7**	**135.6**	**48.9**
Ready-to-eat cereals	13.1	12.6	9.7	8.6	52.3
Ready-to-cook cereals	2.4	2.9	2.3	1.7	41.2
Caloric sweeteners	**158.4**	**136.9**	**123.0**	**122.3**	**29.5**
Sugar	67.9	64.4	83.6	101.8	−33.3
Corn sweeteners	89.1	71.1	38.2	19.1	366.5
Bottled water	**18.1**	**8.0**	**2.4**	**–**	**–**
Coffee	**25.7**	**26.9**	**26.7**	**33.4**	**−23.1**
Tea	**8.4**	**6.9**	**7.3**	**6.8**	**23.5**
Soft drinks	**50.8**	**46.2**	**35.1**	**24.3**	**109.1**
Diet	11.7	10.7	5.1	2.1	457.1
Regular	39.1	35.6	29.9	22.2	76.1
Alcoholic beverages*	**36.3**	**39.5**	**42.8**	**35.7**	**1.7**
Beer	31.9	34.4	36.6	30.6	4.2
Wine	2.7	2.9	3.2	2.2	22.7
Distilled spirits	1.8	2.2	3.0	3.0	−40.0

* Per person aged 21 or older.
Note: (–) means data not available.
Source: USDA, Economic Research Service, Food Consumption, Prices, and Expenditures, 1970–1997; and Bureau of the Census, Statistical Abstracts of the United States for 1995 and 2001; calculations by New Strategist

Most Households Own a Computer

Computers have been eagerly adopted by American households. In 1984, only 8 percent of households were computer owners. By 2000, the 51 percent majority owned a computer. The proportion of households with computers is much greater in some demographic segments than others.

Asians and non-Hispanic whites are more likely to own computers than blacks or Hispanics. The well-educated are more likely to be have computers at home than those with less education. Households with children are much more likely to own a computer than those without. Overall, 67 percent of households with children aged 6 to 17 owned a computer in 2000 versus 45 percent of those without school-aged children at home.

Internet access was available in 42 percent of homes in 2000. Again, those most likely to have Internet access are Asians, non-Hispanic whites, householders aged 25 to 44, and those with school-aged children at home. Internet access peaks at 66 percent for householders with a college degree.

Computer ownership has grown rapidly

(percent of households with a computer, 1984 to 2000)

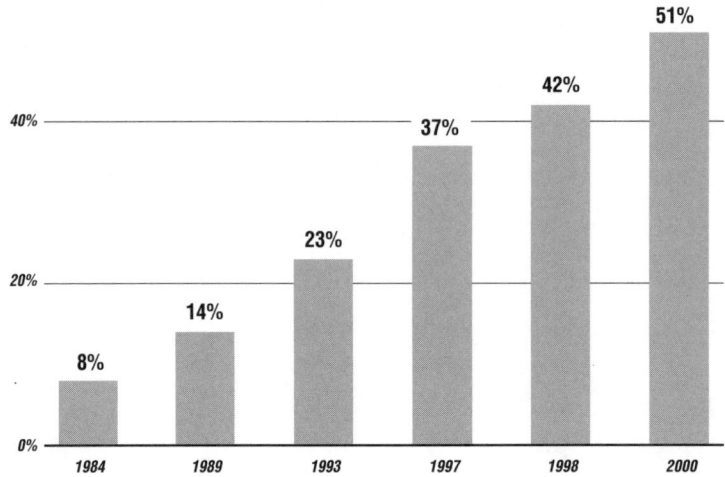

Table 1.33 Households with Computers, 1984 to 1998

(percent of households with a computer by selected characteristics, 1984 to 1998)

	1998	*1997*	*1993*	*1989*	*1984*
Total households	**42.1%**	**36.6%**	**22.8%**	**14.4%**	**7.9%**
Age of householder					
Under age 25	32.3	28.0	18.2	8.5	5.1
Aged 25 to 34	46.0	40.0	23.4	14.5	9.4
Aged 35 to 44	54.9	49.0	31.9	23.5	15.5
Aged 45 to 54	54.7	48.0	33.5	22.0	10.2
Aged 55 or older	25.8	21.0	11.6	6.4	2.5
Race and Hispanic origin of householder					
Black, not Hispanic	23.2	19.3	11.3	6.6	3.8
Hispanic	25.5	19.4	12.1	7.1	4.3
White, not Hispanic	46.6	40.8	25.1	16.0	8.8
Type of household					
Married couples with children < 18	61.8	57.2	35.6	23.7	15.4
Male householder with children < 18	35.0	30.5	18.0	16.1	6.9
Female householder with children < 18	31.7	25.0	12.1	9.1	6.7
Family households without children <18	43.2	36.4	24.2	14.8	5.1
Nonfamily households	27.5	23.5	14.3	7.6	3.7
Household income					
Under $5,000	15.9	16.5	6.8	5.8	1.6
$5,000 to $9,999	12.3	9.9	5.1	3.7	1.7
$10,000 to $14,999	15.9	12.9	8.0	4.5	3.3
$15,000 to $19,999	21.2	17.4	11.7	8.0	5.3
$20,000 to $24,999	25.7	23.0	15.0	9.7	8.1
$25,000 to $34,999	35.8	31.7	20.8	14.6	11.7
$35,000 to $49,999	50.2	45.6	30.8	22.5	17.0
$50,000 to $74,999	66.3	60.6	45.2	31.6	22.4
$75,000 or more	79.9	75.9	60.2	43.8	22.1
Education of householder					
Elementary, 0 to 8 years	7.9	6.8	3.0	1.9	0.9
Some high school, no diploma	15.7	10.9	5.4	4.5	2.3
High school diploma/GED	31.2	25.7	13.5	9.1	5.9
Some college	49.3	43.4	27.7	18.1	11.3
Bachelor's degree or more	68.7	63.2	46.9	30.6	16.4

Source: Bureau of the Census, Access Denied: Changes in Computer Ownership and Use: 1984–1997, *Robert Kominski and Eric Newburger, 1999; and National Telecommunications and Information Administration,* Falling Through the Net: Defining the Digital Divide, *1999*

Table 1.34 Households with Computers and Internet Access, 2000

(percent of households with computers and Internet access, by selected characteristics, 2000)

	computer	Internet access
Total households	**51.0%**	**41.5%**
Age of householder		
Under age 25	43.8	35.7
Aged 25 to 44	61.0	50.2
Aged 45 to 64	56.9	46.7
Aged 65 or older	24.3	17.7
Race and Hispanic origin of householder		
Asian	65.1	56.2
Black	32.8	23.6
Hispanic	33.7	23.6
White, not Hispanic	55.7	46.1
Type of household		
Married couples	63.6	52.7
Female-headed family	42.1	30.6
Male-headed family	45.0	34.8
Nonfamily household	34.6	28.1
Presence of children		
Without children aged 6 to 17	45.1	37.0
With children aged 6 to 17	66.8	53.3
Education of householder		
Less than high school diploma	18.2	11.7
High school diploma/GED	39.6	29.9
Some college	60.3	49.0
Bachelor's degree or more	75.7	66.0

Source: Bureau of the Census, Home Computers and Internet Use in the United States: August 2000, *Current Population Reports, P23-207, 2001*

2

Education

■ The educational attainment of the American population has soared over the past half-century. In 1950, only 34 percent of people aged 25 or older were high school graduates. By 2000, the figure had climbed to 84 percent.

■ Going to college is no longer an elite privilege, but the norm. Most high school graduates now continue their education on a college campus. In 2000, 66 percent of girls and 60 percent of boys had enrolled in college within 12 months of graduating from high school.

■ On college campuses, women rule. In 1950, only 32 percent of college students were women. Today, they account for the 56 percent majority.

■ Men once dominated all degree levels earned at the nation's college campuses. Today, women earn the majority of associate's, bachelor's, and master's degrees.

Education Levels Climb

The educational attainment of the American population has soared over the past half-century. In 1950, only 34 percent of people aged 25 or older were high school graduates. By 2000, the figure had climbed to 84 percent. The proportion of Americans with a college degree rose from 6 to 26 percent during those years.

Some demographic segments are better educated than others, but the gaps have closed substantially over the past 50 years. Men and women are equally likely to have a high school diploma, and women are almost as likely as men to have a college degree. Blacks have nearly closed the gap with whites in high school graduation rate, although whites are still considerably more likely to have a college degree. Hispanics have made the least progress. Nearly half lack a high school diploma, in part because many are immigrants with little education.

More high school and college graduates

(percent of people aged 25 or older who are high school or college graduates, 1950 and 2000)

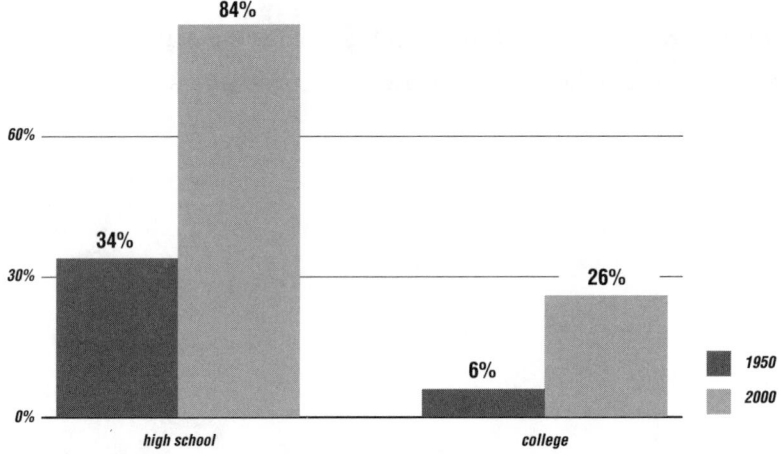

Table 2.1 High School Graduates by Sex, 1950 to 2000

(percent of people who have completed four or more years of high school, by sex, 1950 to 2000; percentage point change for selected years)

	total	men	women
2000	84.1%	84.2%	84.0%
1999	83.4	83.4	83.4
1998	82.8	82.8	82.9
1997	82.1	82.0	82.2
1996	81.7	81.9	81.6
1995	81.7	81.7	81.6
1994	80.9	81.0	80.7
1993	80.2	80.5	80.0
1992	79.4	79.7	79.2
1991	78.4	78.5	78.3
1990	77.6	77.7	77.5
1989	76.9	77.2	76.6
1988	76.2	76.4	76.0
1987	75.6	76.0	75.3
1986	74.7	75.1	74.4
1985	73.9	74.4	73.5
1984	73.3	73.7	73.0
1983	72.1	72.7	71.5
1982	71.0	71.7	70.3
1981	69.7	70.3	69.1
1980	68.6	69.2	68.1
1979	67.7	68.4	67.1
1978	65.9	66.8	65.2
1977	64.9	65.6	64.4
1976	64.1	64.7	63.5
1975	62.5	63.1	62.1
1974	61.2	61.6	60.9
1973	59.8	60.0	59.6
1972	58.2	58.2	58.2
1971	56.4	56.3	56.6
1970	55.2	55.0	55.4
1969	54.0	53.6	54.4
1968	52.6	52.0	53.2
1967	51.1	50.5	51.7
1966	49.9	49.0	50.8
1965	49.0	48.0	49.9
1964	48.0	47.0	48.9
1962	46.3	45.0	47.5
1959	43.7	42.2	45.2
1957	41.6	39.7	43.3
1952	38.8	36.9	40.5
1950	34.3	32.6	36.0
Percentage point change			
1990 to 2000	6.5	6.5	6.5
1950 to 2000	49.8	51.6	48.0

Source: Bureau of the Census, Current Population Surveys, Internet site http://www.census.gov/population/socdemo/education/ tableA-2.txt; calculations by New Strategist

Table 2.2 High School Graduates by Age, 1950 to 2000

(percent of people who have completed four or more years of high school, by age, 1950 to 2000; percentage point change for selected years)

	total	25–34	35–54	55+
2000	84.1%	88.2%	88.8%	74.6%
1999	83.4	87.7	88.2	73.4
1998	82.8	87.9	87.7	72.1
1997	82.1	87.3	87.5	70.4
1996	81.7	86.9	87.3	69.9
1995	81.7	87.1	87.5	69.2
1994	80.9	86.4	87.2	67.7
1993	80.2	86.9	87.0	66.0
1992	79.4	86.5	86.0	65.2
1991	78.4	86.1	85.1	63.7
1990	77.6	86.2	84.6	61.6
1989	76.9	86.6	83.3	60.9
1988	76.2	86.4	82.7	59.8
1987	75.6	86.5	82.5	58.4
1986	74.7	86.8	81.4	57.0
1985	73.9	86.8	80.4	56.0
1984	73.3	86.5	79.3	55.8
1983	72.1	86.4	77.8	54.3
1982	71.0	86.3	76.0	53.1
1981	69.7	85.6	74.6	51.5
1980	68.6	85.4	73.5	50.1
1979	67.7	84.7	72.5	49.4
1978	65.9	84.0	70.3	47.2
1977	64.9	83.4	68.9	46.4
1976	64.1	82.7	68.3	45.2
1975	62.5	81.1	67.5	43.2
1974	61.2	80.1	66.6	41.3
1973	59.8	78.1	65.4	40.3
1972	58.2	77.2	63.2	39.1
1971	56.4	75.3	62.4	36.9
1970	55.2	73.8	61.2	35.8
1969	54.0	72.6	59.9	34.8
1968	52.6	71.1	58.6	33.3
1967	51.1	70.4	56.9	31.8
1966	49.9	69.2	55.4	30.9
1965	49.0	68.0	54.8	29.3
1964	48.0	67.0	53.5	28.5
1962	46.3	64.3	51.6	27.2
1960	41.0	58.0	45.3	22.8
1959	42.9	60.5	47.0	23.9
1957	40.8	57.8	43.7	23.0
1952	38.4	55.7	39.3	21.7
1950	33.3	47.0	32.9	19.2
Percentage point change				
1990 to 2000	6.5	2.0	4.2	13.0
1950 to 2000	50.8	41.2	55.9	55.4

Source: Bureau of the Census, Current Population Surveys, Internet site http://www.census.gov/population/socdemo/education/ tableA-1.txt; calculations by New Strategist

Table 2.3 High School Graduates by Race and Hispanic Origin, 1950 to 2000

(percent of people who have completed four or more years of high school by race and Hispanic origin, 1950 to 2000; percentage point change for selected years)

	black	Hispanic	white
2000	78.5%	57.0%	84.9%
1999	77.0	56.1	84.3
1998	76.0	55.5	83.7
1997	74.9	54.7	83.0
1996	74.3	53.1	82.8
1995	73.8	53.4	83.0
1994	72.9	53.3	82.0
1993	70.4	53.1	81.5
1992	67.7	52.6	80.9
1991	66.7	51.3	79.9
1990	66.2	50.8	79.1
1989	64.6	50.9	78.4
1988	63.5	51.0	77.7
1987	63.4	50.9	77.0
1986	62.3	48.5	76.2
1985	59.8	47.9	75.5
1984	58.5	47.1	75.0
1983	56.8	46.2	73.8
1982	54.9	45.9	72.8
1981	52.9	44.5	71.6
1980	51.2	45.3	70.5
1979	49.4	42.0	69.7
1978	47.6	40.8	67.9
1977	45.5	39.6	67.0
1976	43.8	39.3	66.1
1975	42.5	37.9	64.5
1974	40.8	36.5	63.3
1973	39.2	–	61.9
1972	36.6	–	60.4
1971	34.7	–	58.6
1970	33.7	–	57.4
1969	32.3	–	56.3
1968	30.1	–	54.9
1967	29.5	–	53.4
1966	27.8	–	52.2
1965	27.2	–	51.3
1964	25.7	–	50.3
1962	24.8	–	48.7
1959	20.7	–	46.1
1957	18.4	–	43.2
1952	15.0	–	–
1950	13.7	–	–
Percentage point change			
1990 to 2000	12.3	6.2	5.8
1950 to 2000	64.8	–	–

Note: (–) means data are not available. Source: Bureau of the Census, Current Population Surveys, Internet site http://www.census.gov/population/socdemo/education/tableA-2.txt; calculations by New Strategist

Table 2.4 College Graduates by Sex, 1950 to 2000

(percent of people who have completed four or more years of college, by sex, 1950 to 2000; percentage point change for selected years)

	total	men	women
2000	25.6%	27.8%	23.6%
1999	25.2	27.5	23.1
1998	24.4	26.5	22.4
1997	23.9	26.2	21.7
1996	23.6	26.0	21.4
1995	23.0	26.0	20.2
1994	22.2	25.1	19.6
1993	21.9	24.8	19.2
1992	21.4	24.3	18.6
1991	21.4	24.3	18.8
1990	21.3	24.4	18.4
1989	21.1	24.5	18.1
1988	20.3	24.0	17.0
1987	19.9	23.6	16.5
1986	19.4	23.2	16.1
1985	19.4	23.1	16.0
1984	19.1	22.9	15.7
1983	18.8	23.0	15.1
1982	17.7	21.9	14.0
1981	17.1	21.1	13.4
1980	17.0	20.9	13.6
1979	16.4	20.4	12.9
1978	15.7	19.7	12.2
1977	15.4	19.2	12.0
1976	14.7	18.6	11.3
1975	13.9	17.6	10.6
1974	13.3	16.9	10.1
1973	12.6	16.0	9.6
1972	12.0	15.4	9.0
1971	11.4	14.6	8.5
1970	11.0	14.1	8.2
1969	10.7	13.6	8.1
1968	10.5	13.3	8.0
1967	10.1	12.8	7.6
1966	9.8	12.5	7.4
1965	9.4	12.0	7.1
1964	9.1	11.7	6.8
1962	8.9	11.4	6.7
1959	7.9	10.3	6.0
1957	7.5	9.6	5.8
1952	6.9	8.3	5.8
1950	6.0	7.3	5.2
Percentage point change			
1990 to 2000	4.3	3.4	5.2
1950 to 2000	19.6	20.5	18.4

Source: Bureau of the Census, Current Population Surveys, Internet site http://www.census.gov/population/socdemo/education/tableA-2.txt; calculations by New Strategist

Table 2.5 College Graduates by Age, 1950 to 2000

(percent of people who have completed four or more years of college, by age, 1950 to 2000; percentage point change for selected years)

	total	25–34	35–54	55+
2000	25.6%	29.3%	28.5%	18.9%
1999	25.2	28.7	28.2	18.4
1998	24.4	27.5	27.4	17.8
1997	23.9	27.1	26.8	17.2
1996	23.6	26.5	27.0	16.5
1995	23.0	25.0	27.2	15.4
1994	22.2	23.4	26.7	15.1
1993	21.9	23.8	26.1	14.7
1992	21.4	23.2	25.7	14.2
1991	21.4	23.7	25.8	14.1
1990	21.3	23.9	25.4	13.9
1989	21.1	24.2	25.5	13.3
1988	20.3	23.6	24.5	12.5
1987	19.9	23.9	23.7	12.1
1986	19.4	24.0	22.9	11.7
1985	19.4	23.8	23.0	11.7
1984	19.1	24.3	22.0	11.6
1983	18.8	24.4	21.2	11.6
1982	17.7	23.8	19.6	10.8
1981	17.1	23.2	18.9	10.2
1980	17.0	24.1	18.3	9.9
1979	16.4	23.8	17.4	9.7
1978	15.7	23.6	16.3	8.9
1977	15.4	23.8	15.5	8.9
1976	14.7	22.6	14.6	8.9
1975	13.9	21.4	14.1	8.1
1974	13.3	20.0	13.8	7.9
1973	12.6	18.2	13.2	7.9
1972	12.0	17.9	12.2	7.9
1971	11.4	16.3	11.8	7.7
1970	11.0	15.8	11.4	7.5
1969	10.7	15.3	11.2	7.1
1968	10.5	14.7	11.2	7.0
1967	10.1	14.2	10.7	6.7
1966	9.8	13.8	10.4	6.7
1965	9.4	13.1	10.0	6.3
1964	9.1	12.9	9.7	5.9
1962	8.9	12.9	9.4	5.7
1960	7.7	11.0	8.1	4.6
1959	7.9	10.8	8.4	5.1
1957	7.5	10.0	7.9	4.9
1952	6.9	8.9	7.2	4.8
1950	6.0	5.3	6.5	4.0
Percentage point change				
1990 to 2000	4.3	5.4	3.0	5.0
1950 to 2000	19.6	24.0	21.9	15.0

Source: Bureau of the Census, Current Population Surveys, Internet site http://www.census.gov/population/socdemo/education/ tableA-1.txt; calculations by New Strategist

Table 2.6 College Graduates by Race and Hispanic Origin, 1950 to 2000

(percent of people who have completed four or more years of college by race and Hispanic origin, 1950 to 2000; percentage point change for selected years)

	black	Hispanic	white
2000	16.6%	10.6%	28.1%
1999	15.5	10.9	27.7
1998	14.7	11.0	25.0
1997	13.3	10.3	24.6
1996	13.6	9.3	24.3
1995	13.2	9.3	24.0
1994	12.9	9.1	22.9
1993	12.2	9.0	22.6
1992	11.9	9.3	22.1
1991	11.5	9.7	22.2
1990	11.3	9.2	22.0
1989	11.8	9.9	21.8
1988	11.2	10.1	20.9
1987	10.7	8.6	20.5
1986	10.9	8.4	20.1
1985	11.1	8.5	20.0
1984	10.4	8.2	19.8
1983	9.5	7.9	19.5
1982	8.8	7.8	18.5
1981	8.2	7.7	17.8
1980	7.9	7.9	17.8
1979	7.9	6.7	17.2
1978	7.2	7.0	16.4
1977	7.2	6.2	16.1
1976	6.6	6.1	15.4
1975	6.4	6.3	14.5
1974	5.5	5.5	14.0
1973	6.0	–	13.1
1972	5.1	–	12.6
1971	4.5	–	12.0
1970	4.5	–	11.6
1969	4.6	–	11.2
1968	4.3	–	11.0
1967	4.0	–	10.6
1966	3.8	–	10.4
1965	4.7	–	9.9
1964	3.9	–	9.6
1962	4.0	–	9.5
1959	3.3	–	8.6
1957	2.9	–	8.0
1952	2.4	–	–
1950	2.3	–	–
Percentage point change			
1990 to 2000	5.3	1.4	6.1
1950 to 2000	14.3	–	–

Note: (–) means data are not available.
Source: Bureau of the Census, Current Populations Surveys, Internet site http://www.census.gov/population/socdemo/education/tableA-2.txt; calculations by New Strategist

Most Preschoolers Are in School

As mothers have gone to work, young children have gone to school. Sixty-four percent of the nation's 3-to-5-year-olds were enrolled in nursery school or kindergarten in 2000, up from just 27 percent in 1965. Slightly more than half attend school all day, up from only 17 percent who did in 1970. As the nursery school experience has become common, a growing proportion of children are attending public nursery schools. The proportion stood at about 50 percent in 2000. More than 80 percent of kindergarteners attend public programs.

The nation's elementary and secondary schools have experienced boom and bust over the past 50 years. Behind the cycles of growth and decline are the baby boom, baby bust (or Generation X), and Millennial generations. In 2000, the number of students in elementary school (grades 1 through 8) stood at just under 33 million, close to the all-time high of 34 million reached in 1970. The number of students in secondary school (grades 9 through 12) reached a record high of 15.8 million in 1999.

The percentage of students attending private school has fallen slightly

(percent of students enrolled in private school by attendance level, 1955 and 2000)

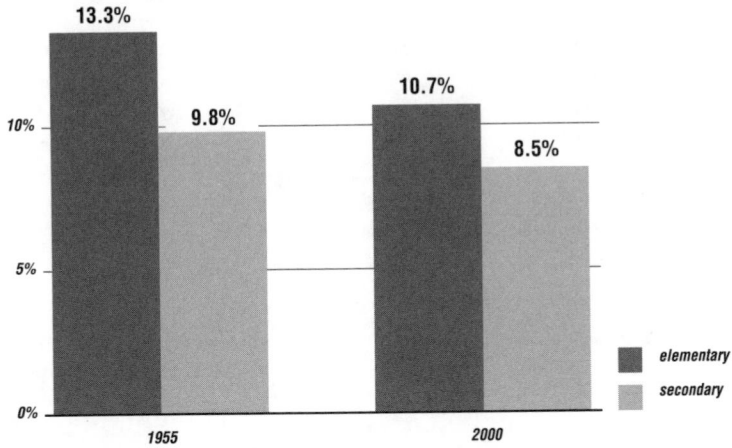

Table 2.7 Enrollment of 3-to-5-Year-Olds in Preprimary Programs, 1965 to 2000

(total number of people aged 3 to 5, and number and percent enrolled in nursery school or kindergarten, 1965 to 2000; percent and percentage point change for selected years; numbers in thousands)

	total population aged 3 to 5	enrolled in nursery school or kindergarten		
		number	share of total	percent attending full-day
2000	11,858	7,592	64.0%	52.8%
1999	11,920	7,844	65.8	53.0
1998	12,078	7,788	64.5	50.8
1997	12,121	7,860	64.9	49.9
1996	12,378	7,580	61.2	47.0
1995	12,518	7,739	61.8	47.7
1994	12,328	7,514	61.0	46.2
1993	11,954	6,581	55.1	40.1
1992	11,545	6,402	55.5	37.6
1991	11,370	6,334	55.7	38.0
1990	11,207	6,659	59.4	38.7
1989	11,039	6,026	54.6	37.1
1988	10,993	5,978	54.4	34.2
1987	10,872	5,931	54.6	35.2
1986	10,866	5,971	55.0	37.5
1985	10,733	5,865	54.6	36.6
1984	10,612	5,480	51.6	35.2
1980	9,284	4,878	52.5	31.8
1975	10,185	4,955	48.7	26.1
1970	10,949	4,104	37.5	17.0
1965	12,549	3,407	27.1	–

	percent change		percentage point change	
1990 to 2000	5.8%	14.0%	4.6	14.1
1965 to 2000	–5.5	122.8	36.9	–

Note: (–) means data are not available.
Source: National Center for Education Statistics, Digest of Education Statistics 2001; *calculations by New Strategist*

Table 2.8 Enrollment in Nursery School and Kindergarten, 1955 to 2000

(number of people enrolled in nursery school and kindergarten by control of institution, 19505 to 2000; percent and percentage point change for selected years; numbers in thousands)

	nursery school				kindergarten			
			private				private	
	total	*public*	*number*	*share of total*	*total*	*public*	*number*	*share of total*
2000	4,401	2,217	2,184	49.6%	3,832	3,173	659	17.2%
1999	4,578	2,270	2,309	50.4	3,825	3,167	658	17.2
1998	4,577	2,265	2,313	50.5	3,828	3,128	700	18.3
1997	4,500	2,254	2,246	49.9	3,933	3,271	663	16.9
1996	4,212	1,868	2,344	55.7	4,034	3,353	681	16.9
1995	4,399	2,012	2,387	54.3	3,877	3,174	704	18.2
1994	4,259	1,940	2,319	54.4	3,863	3,278	585	15.1
1993	3,032	1,258	1,774	58.5	4,275	3,589	686	16.0
1992	2,899	1,098	1,801	62.1	4,130	3,507	623	15.1
1991	2,933	1,094	1,839	62.7	4,152	3,531	621	15.0
1990	3,401	1,212	2,188	64.3	3,899	3,332	567	14.5
1989	2,877	971	1,906	66.2	3,868	3,293	575	14.9
1988	2,639	838	1,770	67.1	3,958	3,420	538	13.6
1987	2,587	848	1,739	67.2	4,018	3,423	595	14.8
1986	2,554	835	1,719	67.3	3,961	3,328	633	16.0
1985	2,491	854	1,637	65.7	3,815	3,221	594	15.6
1984	2,354	761	1,593	67.7	3,484	2,953	531	15.2
1983	2,350	809	1,541	65.6	3,361	2,706	656	19.5
1982	2,153	729	1,423	66.1	3,299	2,746	553	16.8
1981	2,058	663	1,396	67.8	3,161	2,616	545	17.2
1980	1,987	633	1,354	68.1	3,176	2,690	486	15.3
1979	1,869	636	1,233	66.0	3,025	2,593	432	14.3
1978	1,824	587	1,237	67.8	2,989	2,493	496	16.6
1977	1,618	562	1,056	65.3	3,191	2,665	526	16.5
1976	1,526	476	1,050	68.8	3,490	2,962	528	15.1
1975	1,748	574	1,174	67.2	3,393	2,851	542	16.0
1974	1,607	423	1,184	73.7	3,252	2,726	526	16.2
1973	1,324	400	924	69.8	3,074	2,582	493	16.0
1972	1,283	402	881	68.7	3,135	2,636	499	15.9
1971	1,066	317	749	70.3	3,263	2,689	574	17.6
1970	1,096	333	763	69.6	3,183	2,647	536	16.8
1969	860	245	615	71.5	3,276	2,682	594	18.1
1968	816	262	554	67.9	3,268	2,709	559	17.1
1967	713	230	484	67.9	3,312	2,678	635	19.2
1966	688	215	473	68.8	3,115	2,527	588	18.9
1965	520	127	393	75.6	3,057	2,439	618	20.2
1964	471	91	380	80.7	2,830	2,349	481	17.0
1963	–	–	–	–	2,340	1,936	404	17.3
1962	–	–	–	–	2,319	1,914	405	17.5
1961	–	–	–	–	2,299	1,926	373	16.2
1960	–	–	–	–	2,092	1,691	401	19.2
1959	–	–	–	–	2,032	1,678	354	17.4
1958	–	–	–	–	1,991	1,569	422	21.2
1957	–	–	–	–	1,824	1,471	353	19.4
1956	–	–	–	–	1,758	1,566	192	10.9
1955	–	–	–	–	1,628	1,365	263	16.2

	percent change		percentage point change		percent change		percentage point change	
1990 to 2000	29.4%	82.9%	–0.2	–14.7	–1.7%	–4.8%	16.2	2.7
1955 to 2000	–	–	–	–	135.4	132.5	150.6	1.0

Note: (–) means data not available or not applicable.
Source: Bureau of the Census, Current Population Surveys, Internet site http://www.census.gov/population/socdemo/school/ tabA-1.txt; calculations by New Strategist

Table 2.9 Enrollment in Elementary and Secondary School, 1955 to 2000

(number of people enrolled in 1st through 12th grades, by control of institution, 1955 to 2000; percent and percentage point change for selected years; numbers in thousands)

| | elementary | | | | secondary | | | |
| | | | private | | | | private | |
	total	public	number	share of total	total	public	number	share of total
2000	32,874	29,355	3,520	10.7%	15,647	14,323	1,324	8.5%
1999	32,863	29,253	3,609	11.0	15,830	14,559	1,271	8.0
1998	32,543	29,096	3,447	10.6	15,470	14,198	1,272	8.2
1997	32,333	29,281	3,054	9.4	15,631	14,481	1,148	7.3
1996	31,476	28,112	3,364	10.7	15,140	13,956	1,184	7.8
1995	31,788	28,357	3,431	10.8	14,828	13,620	1,208	8.1
1994	31,487	28,109	3,378	10.7	14,521	13,453	1,068	7.4
1993	31,219	28,278	2,941	9.4	13,989	12,985	1,004	7.2
1992	30,165	27,066	3,102	10.3	13,219	12,268	952	7.2
1991	29,591	26,632	2,958	10.0	13,010	12,069	945	7.3
1990	29,265	26,591	2,674	9.1	12,719	11,818	903	7.1
1989	28,637	25,897	2,740	9.6	12,786	11,980	806	6.3
1988	28,223	25,443	2,778	9.8	13,093	12,095	998	7.6
1987	27,524	24,760	2,765	10.0	13,647	12,577	1,070	7.8
1986	27,121	24,163	2,958	10.9	13,912	12,746	1,166	8.4
1985	26,866	23,803	3,063	11.4	13,979	12,764	1,215	8.7
1984	26,838	24,120	2,718	10.1	13,777	12,721	1,057	7.7
1983	27,198	24,203	2,994	11.0	14,010	12,792	1,218	8.7
1982	27,412	24,381	3,031	11.1	14,123	13,004	1,118	7.9
1981	27,795	24,758	3,037	10.9	14,642	13,523	1,119	7.6
1980	27,449	24,398	3,051	11.1	14,556	–	–	–
1979	27,865	24,756	3,109	11.2	15,116	13,994	1,122	7.4
1978	28,490	25,252	3,238	11.4	15,475	14,231	1,244	8.0
1977	29,234	25,983	3,251	11.1	15,753	14,505	1,248	7.9
1976	29,774	26,698	3,075	10.3	15,742	14,541	1,201	7.6
1975	30,446	27,166	3,279	10.8	15,683	14,503	1,180	7.5
1974	31,126	27,956	3,169	10.2	15,447	14,275	1,172	7.6
1973	31,469	28,201	3,268	10.4	15,347	14,162	1,184	7.7
1972	32,242	28,693	3,549	11.0	15,169	14,015	1,155	7.6
1971	33,507	29,829	3,678	11.0	15,183	14,057	1,126	7.4
1970	33,950	30,001	3,949	11.6	14,715	13,545	1,170	8.0
1969	33,788	29,825	3,964	11.7	14,553	13,400	1,153	7.9
1968	33,761	29,527	4,234	12.5	14,145	12,793	1,352	9.6
1967	33,440	28,877	4,562	13.6	13,790	12,498	1,292	9.4
1966	32,916	28,208	4,706	14.3	13,364	11,985	1,377	10.3
1965	32,474	27,596	4,878	15.0	12,975	11,517	1,457	11.2
1964	31,734	26,811	4,923	15.5	12,812	11,403	1,410	11.0
1963	31,245	26,502	4,742	15.2	12,438	11,186	1,251	10.1
1962	30,661	26,148	4,513	14.7	11,516	10,431	1,085	9.4
1961	30,718	26,221	4,497	14.6	10,959	9,817	1,141	10.4
1960	30,349	25,814	4,535	14.9	10,249	9,215	1,033	10.1
1959	29,382	24,680	4,702	16.0	9,616	8,571	1,045	10.9
1958	28,184	23,800	4,385	15.6	9,482	8,485	998	10.5
1957	27,248	23,076	4,172	15.3	8,956	8,059	897	10.0
1956	26,169	22,474	3,695	14.1	8,543	7,668	875	10.2
1955	25,458	22,078	3,379	13.3	7,961	7,181	780	9.8
	percent change		percentage point change		percent change		percentage point change	
1990 to 2000	12.3%	10.4%	31.6	1.6	23.0%	21.2%	46.6	1.4
1955 to 2000	29.1	33.0	4.2	–2.6	96.5	99.5	69.7	–1.3

Note: Secondary school is 9th through 12th grade; (–) means data not available.
Source: Bureau of the Census, Current Population Surveys, Internet site http://www.census.gov/population/socdemo/school/tabA-1.txt; calculations by New Strategist

Table 2.10 High School Graduates, 1949–50 to 1999–00

(number of high school graduates, 1949–50 to 1999–00; percent change for selected years; numbers in thousands)

	high school graduates
1999–00	2,824
1998–99	2,762
1997–98	2,704
1996–97	2,612
1995–96	2,518
1994–95	2,520
1993–94	2,464
1992–93	2,480
1991–92	2,478
1990–91	2,493
1989–90	2,589
1988–89	2,744
1987–88	2,773
1986–87	2,694
1985–86	2,643
1984–85	2,677
1983–84	2,767
1982–83	2,888
1981–82	2,995
1980–81	3,020
1979–80	3,043
1978–79	3,101
1977–78	3,127
1976–77	3,152
1975–76	3,148
1974–75	3,133
1973–74	3,073
1972–73	3,035
1971–72	3,002
1970–71	2,938
1969–70	2,889
1968–69	2,822
1967–68	2,695
1966–67	2,672
1965–66	2,665
1964–65	2,658
1963–64	2,283
1962–63	1,943
1961–62	1,918
1960–61	1,964
1959–60	1,858
1958–59	1,627
1957–58	1,506
1956–57	1,434
1955–56	1,415
1953–54	1,276
1951–52	1,197
1949–50	1,200
Percent change	
1989–90 to 1999–00	8.5%
1949–50 to 1999–00	134.1

Source: National Center for Education Statistics, Digest of Education Statistics 2001*; calculations by New Strategist*

Table 2.11 High School Graduates, 2000–01 to 2011–12

(number of high school graduates, 2000–01 to 2011–12; percent change 2001–2012; numbers in thousands)

	high school graduates
2011–12	3,074
2010–11	3,127
2009–10	3,153
2008–09	3,181
2007–08	3,168
2006–07	3,092
2005–06	3,021
2004–05	2,965
2003–04	2,942
2002–03	2,920
2001–02	2,869
2000–01	2,839
Percent change	
2000–01 to 2011–12	8.3%

Source: National Center for Education Statistics, Projections of Education Statistics to 2012*; calculations by New Strategist*

SAT Scores Are Down, But . . .

The number of high school students who take the Scholastic Assessment Test expanded enormously over the past few decades. Once limited to the elite, the SAT has been embraced by the masses. As larger numbers of "average" students took the test, SAT scores fell. Verbal scores, in particular, declined between 1966–67 and 2000–01.

Most racial and ethnic groups have boosted their SAT scores since the late 1980s, however. While the average verbal score fell 1 point overall between 1986–87 and 2000–01, verbal scores rose during those years for every racial and ethnic group except Mexican Americans. Math scores rose 13 points overall between 1986–87 and 2000–01, including a 25 point gain for Asians.

Verbal down, math up

(average verbal and math SAT scores, 1966–67 and 2000–01)

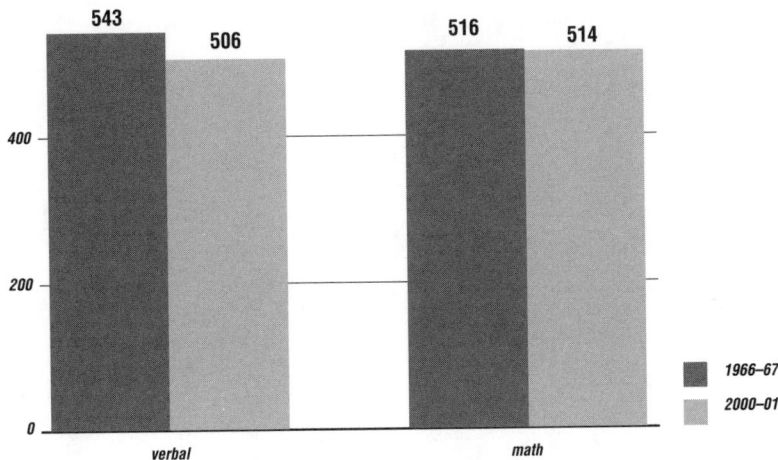

Table 2.12 Scholastic Assessment Test Scores by Sex, 1966–67 to 2000–01

(average SAT scores and change in scores, by sex, 1966–67 to 2000–01)

	math			verbal		
	total	*female*	*male*	*total*	*female*	*male*
2000–01	514	498	533	506	502	509
1999–00	514	498	533	505	504	507
1998–99	511	495	531	505	502	509
1997–98	512	496	531	505	502	509
1996–97	511	494	530	505	503	507
1995–96	508	492	527	505	503	507
1994–95	506	490	525	504	502	505
1993–94	504	487	523	499	497	501
1992–93	503	484	524	500	497	504
1991–92	501	484	521	500	496	504
1990–91	500	482	520	499	495	503
1989–90	501	483	521	500	496	505
1988–89	502	482	523	504	498	510
1987–88	501	483	521	505	499	512
1986–87	501	481	523	507	502	512
1985–86	500	479	523	509	504	515
1984–85	500	480	522	509	503	514
1983–84	497	478	518	504	498	511
1982–83	494	474	516	503	498	508
1981–82	493	473	516	504	499	509
1980–81	492	473	516	502	496	508
1979–80	492	473	515	502	498	506
1978–79	493	473	516	505	501	509
1977–78	494	474	517	507	503	511
1976–77	496	474	520	507	505	509
1975–76	497	475	520	509	508	511
1974–75	498	479	518	512	509	515
1973–74	505	488	524	521	520	524
1972–73	506	489	525	523	521	523
1971–72	509	489	527	530	529	531
1970–71	513	494	529	532	534	531
1969–70	512	493	531	537	538	536
1968–69	517	498	534	540	543	536
1967–68	516	497	533	543	543	541
1966–67	516	495	535	543	545	540
Change in score						
1990–91 to 2000–01	14	16	13	7	7	6
1966–67 to 2000–01	–2	3	–2	–37	–43	–31

Source: National Center for Education Statistics, Digest of Education Statistics 2001*; calculations by New Strategist*

Table 2.13 Scholastic Assessment Test Scores by Race and Hispanic Origin, 1986–87 to 2000–01

(average SAT scores and change in scores by race and Hispanic origin, 1986–87 to 2000–01)

	total students	American Indian	Asian	black	Mexican American	Puerto Rican	white	other
Math								
2000–01	514	479	566	426	458	451	531	512
1999–00	514	481	565	426	460	451	530	515
1998–99	511	481	560	422	456	448	526	511
1997–98	512	483	562	426	460	447	528	514
1996–97	511	475	560	423	458	447	526	514
1995–96	508	477	558	422	459	445	523	512
1990–91	500	468	548	419	459	439	513	492
1986–87	501	463	541	411	455	432	514	482
Change in score								
1986–87 to 2000–01	13	16	25	15	3	19	17	30
Verbal								
2000–01	506	481	501	433	451	457	529	503
1999–00	505	482	499	434	453	456	528	508
1998–99	505	484	498	434	453	455	527	511
1997–98	505	480	498	434	453	452	526	511
1996–97	505	475	496	434	451	454	526	512
1995–96	505	483	496	434	455	452	526	511
1990–91	499	470	485	427	454	436	518	486
1986–87	507	471	479	428	457	436	524	480
Change in score								
1986–87 to 2000–01	–1	10	22	5	–6	21	5	23

Source: National Center for Education Statistics, Digest of Education Statistics 2001; calculations by New Strategist

Most Go to College

Going to college is no longer an elite privilege, but the norm. Most high school graduates now continue their education on a college campus. Forty years ago, boys who graduated from high school were much more likely than girls to go to college-54 versus 38 percent. Today, the opposite is the case, with 66 percent of girls continuing their education versus 60 percent of boys.

Whites are more likely than blacks to enroll in college. Sixty-four percent of whites and a smaller 56 percent of blacks go to college within 12 months of graduating from high school. The black enrollment rate has grown since 1977, when only 50 percent of blacks went on to college. Hispanics are less likely than blacks to enroll in college after high school, with an enrollment rate of only 48 percent in 1999-slightly lower than their 1977 enrollment rate.

Black and white enrollment rates are rising

(percent of people aged 16 to 24 who graduated from high school in the previous 12 months and had enrolled in college as of October of each year, by race, 1977 to 2000)

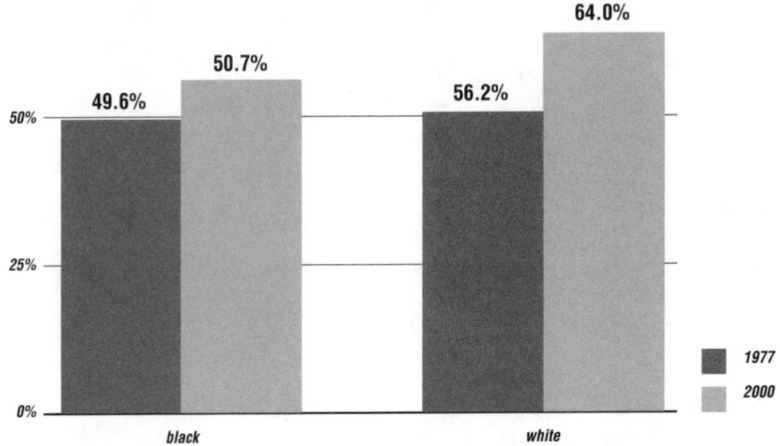

Table 2.14   College Enrollment Rate by Sex, 1960 to 2000

(percent of people aged 16 to 24 who graduated from high school in the previous 12 months and had enrolled in college as of October of each year, by sex, and difference between men and women, 1960 to 2000; percentage point change in enrollment rates for selected years)

	men	women	difference between men and women
2000	59.9%	66.2%	−6.3
1999	61.4	64.4	−3.0
1998	62.4	69.1	−6.7
1997	63.5	70.3	−6.8
1996	60.1	69.7	−9.6
1995	62.6	61.4	1.2
1994	60.6	63.2	−2.6
1993	59.7	65.4	−5.7
1992	59.6	63.8	−4.2
1991	57.6	67.1	−9.5
1990	57.8	62.0	−4.2
1989	57.6	61.6	−4.0
1988	57.0	60.8	−3.8
1987	58.4	55.3	3.1
1986	55.9	51.9	4.0
1985	58.6	56.9	1.7
1984	56.0	54.5	1.5
1983	51.9	53.4	−1.5
1982	49.0	52.1	−3.1
1981	54.8	53.1	1.7
1980	46.7	51.8	−5.1
1979	50.4	48.4	2.0
1978	51.0	49.3	1.7
1977	52.2	49.3	2.9
1976	47.2	50.3	−3.1
1975	52.6	49.0	3.6
1974	49.4	45.8	3.6
1973	50.1	43.4	6.7
1972	52.7	45.9	6.8
1971	57.6	49.7	7.9
1970	55.2	48.5	6.7
1969	60.1	47.2	12.9
1968	63.2	48.9	14.3
1966	58.7	42.7	16.0
1965	57.3	45.3	12.0
1964	57.2	40.7	16.5
1962	55.0	43.5	11.5
1960	54.0	37.9	16.1
Percentage point change			
1990 to 2000	2.1	4.2	−
1960 to 2000	5.9	28.3	−

Note: (−) means not applicable.
Source: National Center for Education Statistics, Digest of Education Statistics 2001; *calculations by New Strategist*

Table 2.15 College Enrollment Rates by Race and Hispanic Origin, 1977 to 2000

(percent of people aged 16 to 24 who graduated from high school in the previous 12 months and had enrolled in college as of October of each year, by race and Hispanic origin, 1977 to 2000; percentage point change in enrollment rates for selected years)

	blacks	Hispanics	whites
2000	56.2%	–	64.0%
1999	59.2	47.6%	62.8
1998	62.1	51.7	65.8
1997	59.6	54.5	67.5
1996	55.3	56.7	65.8
1995	51.4	51.1	62.6
1994	50.9	55.1	63.6
1993	55.6	55.4	62.8
1992	47.9	58.1	63.4
1991	45.6	53.1	64.6
1990	46.3	53.3	61.5
1989	52.8	53.2	60.4
1988	45.0	48.6	60.7
1987	51.9	45.0	56.6
1986	36.5	43.0	56.0
1985	42.3	46.5	59.4
1984	40.2	49.9	57.9
1983	38.5	47.3	55.0
1982	36.5	49.8	52.0
1981	42.9	49.3	54.6
1980	41.8	49.9	49.9
1979	45.4	46.8	49.6
1978	45.7	46.3	50.1
1977	49.6	48.9	50.7
Percentage point change			
1990 to 2000	9.9	–5.7	2.5
1977 to 2000	6.6	–1.3	13.3

Note: Hispanic enrollment rates are three-year moving averages. 1990–2000 percentage point change for Hispanics is the difference between 1990 and 1999 moving averages.
Source: National Center for Education Statistics, Digest of Education Statistics 2001; *calculations by New Strategist*

In College, Women Outnumber Men

In 1950, only 32 percent of college students were women. Today, women account for the 56 percent majority of college students.

The demographics of college students have changed in other ways as well. Not only are students older, but they are more racially and ethnically diverse. The number of students aged 25 or older has grown enormously over the past half-century, with 37 percent of students aged 25 or older in 2000. The figure is projected to rise slightly during the next decade.

The minority share of students has grown from 15 percent in 1976 to 27 percent in 1999. Blacks are the largest minority group on college campuses, accounting for 11 percent of students. Nine percent of college students are Hispanic and 6 percent are Asian.

More than one-third of college students are aged 25 or older

(college students aged 25 or older as a share of total students, 1950 to 2012)

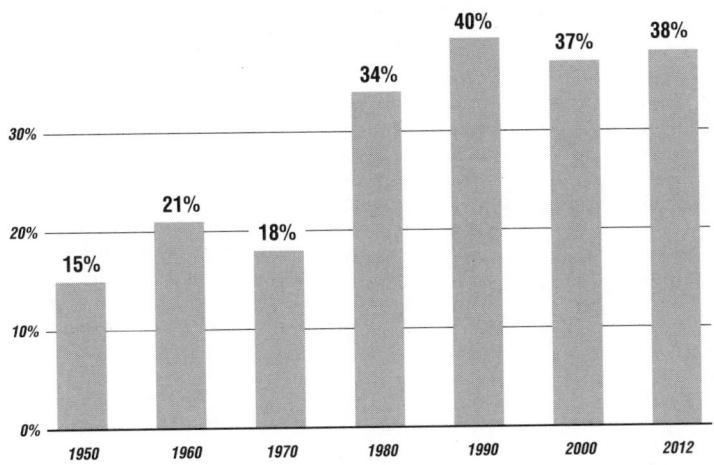

Table 2.16   College Enrollment by Sex, 1950 to 2000

(number of people aged 14 or older enrolled in college by sex, and women's share of total, 1950 to 2000; percent and percentage point change for selected years; numbers in thousands)

			women	
	total	*men*	*number*	*share of total*
2000	15,314	6,682	8,631	56.4%
1999	15,203	6,956	8,247	54.2
1998	15,546	6,905	8,641	55.6
1997	15,436	6,843	8,593	55.7
1996	15,226	6,820	8,406	55.2
1995	14,715	6,703	8,013	54.5
1994	15,022	6,764	8,258	55.0
1993	14,394	6,599	7,795	54.2
1992	14,035	6,192	7,844	55.9
1991	14,057	6,439	7,618	54.2
1990	13,621	6,192	7,429	54.5
1989	13,180	5,950	7,231	54.9
1988	13,116	5,950	7,166	54.6
1987	12,719	6,030	6,689	52.6
1986	12,651	5,957	6,694	52.9
1985	12,524	5,906	6,618	52.8
1984	12,304	5,989	6,315	51.3
1983	12,320	6,010	6,310	51.2
1982	12,308	5,899	6,410	52.1
1981	12,127	5,825	6,303	52.0
1980	11,387	5,430	5,957	52.3
1979	11,380	5,480	5,900	51.8
1978	11,141	5,580	5,559	49.9
1977	11,546	5,889	5,657	49.0
1976	11,139	5,785	5,354	48.1
1975	10,880	5,911	4,969	45.7
1974	9,852	5,402	4,449	45.2
1973	8,966	5,048	3,918	43.7
1972	9,096	5,218	3,877	42.6
1971	8,087	4,850	3,236	40.0
1970	7,413	4,401	3,013	40.6
1969	7,435	4,448	2,987	40.2
1968	6,801	4,124	2,677	39.4
1967	6,401	3,841	2,560	40.0
1966	6,085	3,749	2,337	38.4
1965	5,675	3,503	2,172	38.3
1964	4,643	2,888	1,755	37.8
1963	4,336	2,742	1,594	36.8
1962	4,208	2,742	1,466	34.8
1961	3,731	2,356	1,375	36.9
1960	3,570	2,339	1,231	34.5
1959	3,340	2,187	1,153	34.5
1958	3,242	2,129	1,113	34.3
1957	3,138	2,028	1,110	35.4
1956	2,883	1,932	951	33.0
1955	2,379	1,579	800	33.6
1950	2,175	1,474	701	32.2

	percent change			*percentage point change*
1990 to 2000	12.4%	7.9%	16.2%	3.1
1950 to 2000	604.1	353.3	1,131.2	25.4

Source: Bureau of the Census, Current Population Surveys, Internet site http://www.census.gov/population/socdemo/school/tabA-6.txt; calculations by New Strategist

Table 2.17 College Enrollment by Sex, 2001 to 2012

(number of people aged 14 or older enrolled in college by sex, and women's share of total, 2001 to 2012; percent and percentage point change, 2001–12; numbers in thousands)

			women	
	total	*men*	*number*	*share of total*
2012	17,673	7,542	10,131	57.3%
2011	17,418	7,460	9,958	57.2
2010	17,185	7,380	9,805	57.1
2009	16,978	7,309	9,669	57.0
2008	16,738	7,216	9,522	56.9
2007	16,503	7,124	9,380	56.8
2006	16,321	7,052	9,269	56.8
2005	16,135	6,985	9,150	56.7
2004	15,947	6,919	9,027	56.6
2003	15,756	6,860	8,896	56.5
2002	15,608	6,817	8,791	56.3
2001	15,442	6,772	8,670	56.1
	percent change			*percentage point change*
2001 to 2012	14.4%	11.4%	16.9%	1.2

Source: National Center for Education Statistics, Projections of Education Statistics to 2012; *calculations by New Strategist*

Table 2.18 College Enrollment by Age, 1950 to 2000

(number of people aged 14 or older enrolled in college by age; 1950 to 2000; percent change for selected years; numbers in thousands)

	total	under 20	20 to 21	22 to 24	25 to 29	30 to 34	35 or older
2000	15,314	3,748	3,169	2,683	1,962	1,244	2,507
1999	15,203	3,671	3,120	2,620	1,940	1,155	2,697
1998	15,546	3,793	3,092	2,561	2,148	1,266	2,685
1997	15,436	3,533	3,143	2,699	2,154	1,116	2,791
1996	15,226	3,546	2,907	2,551	2,215	1,228	2,778
1995	14,715	3,259	2,940	2,498	2,143	1,206	2,669
1994	15,022	3,201	3,028	2,650	2,026	1,393	2,725
1993	14,394	3,200	2,892	2,668	1,914	1,226	2,493
1992	14,035	3,097	2,938	2,512	1,829	1,296	2,364
1991	14,057	3,061	2,939	2,304	1,983	1,302	2,468
1990	13,621	3,197	2,767	2,178	1,927	1,235	2,319
1989	13,180	3,249	2,570	2,168	1,889	1,192	2,112
1988	13,116	3,228	2,681	2,064	1,735	1,228	2,179
1987	12,719	3,284	2,642	2,006	1,826	1,159	1,802
1986	12,651	3,168	2,374	2,136	1,860	1,245	1,867
1985	12,524	3,169	2,616	2,014	1,884	1,180	1,661
1984	12,304	3,120	2,597	2,127	1,857	1,158	1,445
1983	12,320	3,200	2,495	2,042	1,921	1,167	1,495
1982	12,308	3,183	2,689	2,060	1,859	1,129	1,389
1981	12,127	3,276	2,545	1,986	1,717	1,211	1,393
1980	11,387	3,182	2,423	1,870	1,641	1,062	1,207
1979	11,380	3,155	2,353	1,794	1,679	996	1,402
1978	11,141	3,173	2,298	1,798	1,619	950	1,303
1977	11,546	3,187	2,430	1,799	1,809	992	1,329
1976	11,139	3,218	2,398	1,846	1,686	803	1,189
1975	10,880	3,236	2,313	1,679	1,616	853	1,183
1974	9,852	2,906	2,192	1,527	1,482	720	1,025
1973	8,966	2,812	2,073	1,465	1,278	551	787
1972	9,096	2,975	2,116	1,461	1,229	531	783
1971	8,087	3,010	1,997	1,487	1,067	527	–
1970	7,413	2,854	1,857	1,354	939	410	–
1969	7,435	2,843	1,945	1,294	918	435	–
1968	6,801	2,782	1,826	1,029	790	373	–
1967	6,401	2,525	1,816	998	707	356	–
1966	6,085	2,694	1,472	987	679	254	–
1965	5,675	2,479	1,326	940	614	316	–
1964	4,643	1,907	1,287	670	523	256	–
1963	4,336	1,684	1,212	717	482	241	–
1962	4,208	1,845	996	630	486	251	–
1961	3,731	1,683	892	507	437	212	–
1960	3,570	1,521	790	509	491	259	–
1959	3,340	1,385	739	489	503	224	–
1958	3,242	1,281	1,221*		534	206	–
1957	3,138	1,165	1,236		553	184	–
1956	2,883	1,101	1,105		494	183	–
1955	2,379	892	931		406	150	–
1950	2,175	913	939		324	–	–
Percent change							
1990 to 2000	12.4%	17.2%	14.5%	23.2%	1.8%	0.7%	8.1%
1950 to 2000	604.1	310.5	–	–	–	–	–

* Prior to 1959, data are for 20 to 24 age group
Note: (–) means data not available.
Source: Bureau of the Census, Current Population Surveys, Internet site http://www.census.gov/population/socdemo/school/ tabA-6.txt; calculations by New Strategist

Table 2.19   College Enrollment by Age, 2001 to 2012

(number of people aged 14 or older enrolled in college by age, 2001 to 2012; percent change in number, 2001–12; numbers in thousands)

	total	under 20	20 to 21	22 to 24	25 to 29	30 to 34	35 or older
2012	17,673	4,268	3,702	2,999	2,368	1,460	2,877
2011	17,418	4,289	3,661	2,884	2,326	1,409	2,849
2010	17,185	4,310	3,561	2,819	2,288	1,361	2,846
2009	16,978	4,299	3,445	2,786	2,264	1,320	2,864
2008	16,738	4,197	3,372	2,751	2,232	1,287	2,899
2007	16,503	4,067	3,330	2,727	2,183	1,265	2,931
2006	16,321	3,974	3,304	2,704	2,128	1,258	2,953
2005	16,135	3,912	3,234	2,703	2,062	1,275	2,948
2004	15,947	3,864	3,189	2,679	1,998	1,283	2,934
2003	15,756	3,762	3,203	2,634	1,948	1,289	2,920
2002	15,608	3,730	3,161	2,605	1,923	1,287	2,902
2001	15,442	3,673	3,118	2,578	1,925	1,280	2,868
Percent change							
2001 to 2012	14.4%	16.2%	18.7%	16.3%	23.0%	14.1%	0.3%

Source: National Center for Education Statistics, Projections of Education Statistics to 2012*; calculations by New Strategist*

Table 2.20 College Enrollment by Race and Hispanic Origin, 1955 to 2000

(number of people aged 15 or older enrolled in institutions of higher education by race and Hispanic origin, 1955 to 2000; percent change for selected years; numbers in thousands)

					white	
	total	*Asian*	*black*	*Hispanic*	*total*	*non-Hispanic*
2000	15,314	1,049	2,164	1,426	11,999	10,636
1999	15,203	1,041	1,998	1,307	12,053	10,818
1998	15,546	–	2,016	1,363	12,401	11,004
1997	15,436	–	1,903	1,260	12,442	11,185
1996	15,226	–	1,901	1,223	12,189	10,969
1995	14,715	–	1,772	1,207	12,021	10,982
1994	15,022	–	1,800	1,187	12,222	11,075
1993	14,394	–	1,599	1,169	11,735	10,554
1992	14,035	–	1,424	918	11,710	–
1991	14,057	–	1,477	830	11,686	–
1990	13,621	–	1,393	748	11,488	–
1989	13,180	–	1,287	754	11,243	–
1988	13,116	–	1,321	747	11,140	–
1987	12,719	–	1,351	739	10,731	–
1986	12,651	–	1,359	794	10,707	–
1985	12,524	–	1,263	580	10,781	–
1984	12,304	–	1,332	524	10,520	–
1983	12,320	–	1,273	521	10,565	–
1982	12,308	–	1,294	494	10,551	–
1981	12,127	–	1,335	510	10,353	–
1980	11,387	–	1,163	443	9,925	–
1979	11,380	–	1,156	439	9,956	–
1978	11,141	–	1,175	377	9,661	–
1977	11,546	–	1,284	417	9,962	–
1976	11,139	–	1,217	426	9,679	–
1975	10,880	–	1,099	411	9,546	–
1974	9,852	–	930	354	8,689	–
1973	8,966	–	781	289	8,014	–
1972	9,096	–	727	242	7,458	–
1971	8,087	–	680	–	7,273	–
1970	7,413	–	522	–	6,759	–
1969	7,435	–	492	–	6,827	–
1968	6,801	–	434	–	6,255	–
1967	6,401	–	370	–	5,905	–
1966	6,085	–	282	–	5,708	–
1965	5,675	–	274	–	5,317	–
1964	4,643	–	234	–	4,337	–
1963	4,336	–	286	–	4,050	–
1962	4,208	–	274	–	3,934	–
1961	3,731	–	233	–	3,498	–
1960	3,570	–	227	–	3,342	–
1959	3,340	–	222	–	3,118	–
1958	3,242	–	212	–	3,030	–
1957	3,138	–	206	–	2,932	–
1956	2,883	–	196	–	2,687	–
1955	2,379	–	155	–	2,224	–
Percent change						
1990 to 2000	12.4%	–	55.3%	90.6%	4.4%	–
1955 to 2000	543.7	–	1,296.1	–	439.5	–

Note: Enrollment figures by race and Hispanic origin are based on reports by householders. They differ from race and Hispanic origin enrollment figures in the following table, which are based on reports by institutions of higher education. Numbers will not add to total because Hispanics may be of any race and not all races are shown.
Source: Bureau of the Census, Current Population Surveys, Internet site http://www.census.gov/population/socdemo/school/ tabA-6.txt; calculations by New Strategist

Table 2.21 College Enrollment by Race and Hispanic Origin, 1976 to 1999

(number and percent distribution of people aged 15 or older enrolled in institutions of higher education by race and Hispanic origin, 1976 to 1999; percent and percentage point change for selected years; numbers in thousands)

	total	minority total	American Indian	Asian	black, non-Hispanic	Hispanic	white, non-Hispanic	nonresident alien
1999	14,791	4,012	145	910	1,641	1,317	10,263	516
1998	14,507	3,885	144	901	1,583	1,257	10,179	444
1997	14,502	3,771	143	859	1,551	1,219	10,266	465
1996	14,368	3,637	138	828	1,506	1,166	10,264	466
1995	14,262	3,496	131	797	1,474	1,094	10,311	454
1990	13,819	2,705	103	572	1,247	782	10,723	392
1980	12,087	1,949	84	286	1,107	472	9,833	305
1976	10,986	1,691	76	198	1,033	384	9,076	219
Percent change								
1990 to 1999	7.0%	48.3%	41.1%	58.9%	31.6%	68.3%	−4.3%	31.9%
1976 to 1999	34.6	137.3	91.2	359.4	58.8	242.9	13.1	135.8
Percent distribution by race and Hispanic origin								
1999	100.0%	27.1%	1.0%	6.2%	11.1%	8.9%	69.4%	3.5%
1998	100.0	26.8	1.0	6.2	10.9	8.7	70.2	3.1
1997	100.0	26.0	1.0	5.9	10.7	8.4	70.8	3.2
1996	100.0	25.3	1.0	5.8	10.5	8.1	71.4	3.2
1995	100.0	24.5	0.9	5.6	10.3	7.7	72.3	3.2
1990	100.0	19.6	0.7	4.1	9.0	5.7	77.6	2.8
1980	100.0	16.1	0.7	2.4	9.2	3.9	81.4	2.5
1976	100.0	15.4	0.7	1.8	9.4	3.5	82.6	2.0
Percentage point change								
1990 to 1999	–	7.6	0.2	2.0	2.1	3.2	−8.2	0.7
1976 to 1999	–	11.7	0.3	4.3	1.7	5.4	−13.2	1.5

Note: Enrollment figures by race and Hispanic origin are based on reports by institutions of higher education. They differ from race/Hispanic origin enrollment figures in the preceding table, which are based on reports by householders.
Source: National Center for Education Statistics, Digest of Education Statistics 2001; *calculations by New Strategist*

Women Earn Most Degrees

Before 1977, men dominated all degree levels on the nation's college campuses. Today, women earn more than 60 percent of associate's degrees, 57 percent of bachelor's degrees, and the 58 percent majority of master's degrees. Women earn slightly more than 40 percent of doctoral and first-professional degrees—figures that are projected to rise slightly during the next decade.

Over the past quarter-century, minorities have accounted for an ever-larger share of degrees awarded by institutions of higher education. Nevertheless, as the level of degree rises, the proportion earned by minorities falls. Blacks earned 11 percent of associate's degrees in 1999–00, 9 percent of bachelor's degrees, 8 percent of master's degrees, and just 5 percent of doctorates. One in four doctorates is earned by a nonresident alien, meaning a foreign student.

Most bachelor's degrees go to women

(percent of bachelor's degrees awarded to women, 1949–50 to 2011–12)

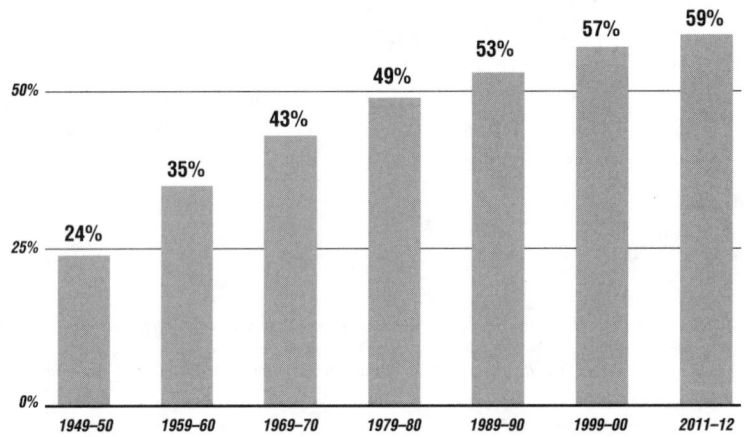

Table 2.22 Degrees Conferred by Level of Degree, 1949–50 to 1999–00

(number of degrees conferred by institutions of higher education by level of degree, 1949–50 to 1999–00; percent change for selected years)

	associate's	bachelor's	master's	doctoral	first professional
1999–00	564,933	1,237,875	457,056	44,808	80,057
1998–99	559,954	1,200,303	439,986	44,077	78,439
1997–98	558,555	1,184,406	430,164	46,010	78,598
1996–97	571,226	1,172,879	419,401	45,876	78,730
1995–96	555,216	1,164,792	406,301	44,652	76,734
1994–95	539,691	1,160,134	397,629	44,446	75,800
1993–94	530,632	1,169,275	387,070	43,185	75,418
1992–93	514,756	1,165,178	369,585	42,132	75,387
1991–92	504,231	1,136,553	352,838	40,659	74,146
1990–91	481,720	1,094,538	337,168	39,294	71,948
1989–90	455,102	1,051,344	324,301	38,371	70,988
1988–89	436,764	1,018,755	310,621	35,720	70,856
1987–88	435,085	994,829	299,317	34,870	70,735
1986–87	436,304	991,264	289,349	34,041	71,617
1985–86	446,047	987,823	288,567	33,653	73,910
1984–85	454,712	979,477	286,251	32,943	75,063
1983–84	452,240	974,309	284,263	33,209	74,468
1982–83	449,620	969,510	289,921	32,775	73,054
1981–82	434,526	952,998	295,546	32,707	72,032
1980–81	416,377	935,140	295,739	32,958	71,956
1979–80	400,910	929,417	298,081	32,615	70,131
1978–79	402,702	921,390	301,079	32,730	68,848
1977–78	412,246	921,204	311,620	32,131	66,581
1976–77	406,377	919,549	317,164	33,232	64,359
1975–76	391,454	925,746	311,771	34,064	62,649
1974–75	360,171	922,933	292,450	34,083	55,916
1973–74	343,924	945,776	277,033	33,816	53,816
1972–73	316,174	922,362	263,371	34,777	50,018
1971–72	292,014	887,273	251,633	33,363	43,411
1970–71	252,311	839,730	230,509	32,107	37,946
1969–70	206,023	792,316	208,291	29,866	34,918
1968–69	183,279	728,845	193,756	26,158	35,114
1967–68	159,441	632,289	176,749	23,089	33,939
1966–67	139,183	558,534	157,726	20,617	31,695
1965–66	111,607	520,115	140,602	18,237	30,124
1964–65	–	493,757	121,167	16,467	28,290
1963–64	–	461,266	109,183	14,490	27,209
1962–63	–	1,051,344	324,301	38,371	70,988
1961–62	–	929,417	298,081	32,615	70,131
1960–61	–	792,316	208,291	29,866	34,918
1959–60	–	392,440	74,435	9,829	–
1949–50	–	432,058	58,183	6,420	–
Percent change					
'89–90 to '99–00	24.1%	17.7%	40.9%	16.8%	12.8%
'49–50 to '99–00	–	186.5	685.5	597.9	–

Note: Bachelor's degrees granted in 1950 and 1960 include first-professional degrees; (–) means data not available.
Source: National Center for Education Statistics, Digest of Education Statistics 2001; calculations by New Strategist

Table 2.23 Degrees Conferred by Level of Degree, 2000–01 to 2011–12

(number of degrees conferred by institutions of higher education by level of degree, 2000–01 to 2011–12; percent change 2000–01 to 2011–12)

	associate's	bachelor's	master's	doctoral	first-professional
2011–12	669,000	1,437,000	501,000	46,800	86,400
2010–11	662,000	1,414,000	491,000	46,300	85,700
2009–10	656,000	1,397,000	488,000	46,100	84,900
2008–09	652,000	1,382,000	484,000	45,900	84,100
2007–08	647,000	1,368,000	480,000	45,800	83,500
2006–07	643,000	1,353,000	477,000	45,600	82,900
2005–06	638,000	1,343,000	473,000	45,400	82,300
2004–05	637,000	1,327,000	470,000	45,100	82,200
2003–04	632,000	1,322,000	467,000	45,000	82,200
2002–03	633,000	1,301,000	468,000	45,000	80,200
2001–02	619,000	1,282,000	468,000	44,900	80,800
2000–01	615,000	1,268,000	475,000	44,900	80,100
Percent change					
2000–01 to 2011–12	8.8%	13.3%	5.5%	4.2%	7.9%

Source: National Center for Education Statistics, Projections of Education Statistics to 2012*; calculations by New Strategist*

Table 2.24 Associate's Degrees Conferred by Sex, 1965–66 to 1999–00

(number of associate's degrees conferred by institutions of higher education by sex and women's share of total, 1965–66 to 1999–00; percent and percentage point change for selected years)

	total associate's degrees	men	women number	women share of total
1999–00	564,933	224,721	340,212	60.2%
1998–99	559,954	218,417	341,537	61.0
1997–98	558,555	217,613	340,942	61.0
1996–97	571,226	223,948	347,278	60.8
1995–96	555,216	219,514	335,702	60.5
1994–95	539,691	218,352	321,339	59.5
1993–94	530,632	215,261	315,371	59.4
1992–93	514,756	211,964	302,792	58.8
1991–92	504,231	207,481	296,750	58.9
1990–91	481,720	198,634	283,086	58.8
1989–90	455,102	191,195	263,907	58.0
1988–89	436,764	186,316	250,448	57.3
1987–88	435,085	190,047	245,038	56.3
1986–87	436,304	190,839	245,465	56.3
1985–86	446,047	196,166	249,881	56.0
1984–85	454,712	202,932	251,780	55.4
1983–84	452,240	202,704	249,536	55.2
1982–83	449,620	203,991	245,629	54.6
1981–82	434,526	196,944	237,582	54.7
1980–81	416,377	188,638	227,739	54.7
1979–80	400,910	183,737	217,173	54.2
1978–79	402,702	192,091	210,611	52.3
1977–78	412,246	204,718	207,528	50.3
1976–77	406,377	210,842	195,535	48.1
1975–76	391,454	209,996	181,458	46.4
1974–75	360,171	191,017	169,154	47.0
1973–74	343,924	188,591	155,333	45.2
1972–73	316,174	175,413	140,761	44.5
1971–72	292,014	166,227	125,787	43.1
1970–71	252,311	144,144	108,167	42.9
1969–70	206,023	117,432	88,591	43.0
1968–69	183,279	105,661	77,618	42.3
1967–68	159,441	90,317	69,124	43.4
1966–67	139,183	78,356	60,827	43.7
1965–66	111,607	63,779	47,828	42.9
	percent change			percentage point change
1989–90 to 1999–00	24.1%	17.5%	28.9%	2.2
1965–66 to 1999–00	406.2	252.3	611.3	17.4

Source: National Center for Education Statistics, Digest of Education Statistics 2001; *calculations by New Strategist*

Table 2.25 Associate's Degrees Conferred by Sex, 2000–01 to 2011–12

(number of associate's degrees conferred by institutions of higher education by sex, and women's share of total, 2000–01 to 2011–12; percent and percentage point change 2000–01 to 2011–12)

	total associate's degrees	men	women number	women share of total
2011–12	669,000	238,000	431,000	64.4%
2010–11	662,000	236,000	426,000	64.4
2009–10	656,000	235,000	421,000	64.2
2008–09	652,000	234,000	418,000	64.1
2007–08	647,000	233,000	414,000	64.0
2006–07	643,000	232,000	411,000	63.9
2005–06	638,000	231,000	407,000	63.8
2004–05	637,000	231,000	406,000	63.7
2003–04	632,000	231,000	401,000	63.4
2002–03	633,000	233,000	400,000	63.2
2001–02	619,000	227,000	392,000	63.3
2000–01	615,000	227,000	388,000	63.1

	percent change			percentage point change
2000–01 to 2011–12	8.8%	4.8%	11.1%	1.3

Source: National Center for Education Statistics, Projections of Education Statistics to 2012; *calculations by New Strategist*

Table 2.26 Associate's Degrees Conferred by Race and Hispanic Origin, 1976–77 to 1999–00

(number and percent distribution of associate's degrees conferred by insitutions of higher education, by race and Hispanic origin, 1976–77 to 1999–00; percent and percentage point change for selected years)

	total associate's degrees	American Indian	Asian	black, non-Hispanic	Hispanic	white, non-Hispanic	nonresident alien
1999–00	564,933	6,494	27,764	60,181	51,541	408,508	10,445
1998–99	559,954	6,417	27,566	57,405	48,643	408,844	11,079
1997–98	555,538	6,220	25,047	55,008	45,627	411,336	12,300
1996–97	563,620	5,927	24,829	55,260	42,645	424,364	10,595
1995–96	553,625	5,556	23,091	51,672	38,163	425,028	10,115
1994–95	538,545	5,492	20,717	47,142	36,013	419,323	9,858
1993–94	529,106	4,871	18,433	45,461	32,074	418,301	9,966
1992–93	508,154	4,379	16,632	42,340	29,991	405,883	8,929
1991–92	494,387	4,008	15,596	39,411	26,905	400,530	7,937
1990–91	462,030	3,672	13,725	37,657	24,251	376,081	6,644
1989–90	450,263	3,530	13,482	35,327	22,195	369,580	6,149
1988–89	432,144	3,331	12,519	34,664	20,384	354,865	6,381
1986–87	436,304	3,195	11,779	35,447	19,334	361,861	4,688
1984–85	429,815	2,953	9,914	35,791	19,407	355,343	6,407
1980–81	410,174	2,584	8,650	35,330	17,800	339,167	6,643
1978–79	396,745	2,336	7,518	34,979	16,269	331,092	4,551
1976–77	404,956	2,498	7,044	33,159	16,636	342,290	3,329

Percent change

'89–90 to '99–00	25.5%	84.0%	105.9%	70.4%	132.2%	10.5%	69.9%
'76–77 to '99–00	39.5	160.0	294.2	81.5	209.8	19.3	213.8

Percent distribution by race and Hispanic origin

1999–00	100.0%	1.1%	4.9%	10.7%	9.1%	72.3%	1.8%
1998–99	100.0	1.1	4.9	10.3	8.7	73.0	2.0
1997–98	100.0	1.1	4.5	9.9	8.2	74.0	2.2
1996–97	100.0	1.1	4.4	9.8	7.6	75.3	1.9
1995–96	100.0	1.0	4.2	9.3	6.9	76.8	1.8
1994–95	100.0	1.0	3.8	8.8	6.7	77.9	1.8
1993–94	100.0	0.9	3.5	8.6	6.1	79.1	1.9
1992–93	100.0	0.9	3.3	8.3	5.9	79.9	1.8
1991–92	100.0	0.8	3.2	8.0	5.4	81.0	1.6
1990–91	100.0	0.8	3.0	8.2	5.2	81.4	1.4
1989–90	100.0	0.8	3.0	7.8	4.9	82.1	1.4
1988–89	100.0	0.8	2.9	8.0	4.7	82.1	1.5
1986–87	100.0	0.7	2.7	8.1	4.4	82.9	1.1
1984–85	100.0	0.7	2.3	8.3	4.5	82.7	1.5
1980–81	100.0	0.6	2.1	8.6	4.3	82.7	1.6
1978–79	100.0	0.6	1.9	8.8	4.1	83.5	1.1
1976–77	100.0	0.6	1.7	8.2	4.1	84.5	0.8

Percentage point change

'89–90 to '99–00	–	0.4	1.9	2.8	4.2	–9.8	0.5
'76–77 to '99–00	–	0.5	3.2	2.5	5.0	–12.2	1.0

Source: National Center for Education Statistics, Digest of Education Statistics 2001; *calculations by New Strategist*

Table 2.27 Bachelor's Degrees Conferred by Sex, 1949–50 to 1999–00

(number of bachelor's degrees conferred by institutions of higher education by sex, and women's share of total, 1949–50 to 1999–00; percent and percentage point change for selected years)

	total bachelor's degrees	men	women number	women share of total
1999–00	1,237,875	530,367	707,508	57.2%
1998–99	1,200,303	518,746	681,557	56.8
1997–98	1,184,406	519,956	664,450	56.1
1996–97	1,172,879	520,515	652,364	55.6
1995–96	1,164,792	522,454	642,338	55.1
1994–95	1,169,275	532,422	636,853	54.5
1993–94	1,160,134	526,131	634,003	54.6
1992–93	1,165,178	532,881	632,297	54.3
1991–92	1,136,553	520,811	615,742	54.2
1990–91	1,094,538	504,045	590,493	53.9
1989–90	1,051,344	491,696	559,648	53.2
1988–89	1,018,755	483,346	535,409	52.6
1987–88	994,829	477,203	517,626	52.0
1986–87	991,264	480,782	510,482	51.5
1985–86	987,823	485,923	501,900	50.8
1984–85	979,477	482,528	496,949	50.7
1983–84	974,309	482,319	491,990	50.5
1982–83	969,510	479,140	490,370	50.6
1981–82	952,998	473,364	479,634	50.3
1980–81	935,140	469,883	465,257	49.8
1979–80	929,417	473,611	455,806	49.0
1978–79	921,390	477,344	444,046	48.2
1977–78	921,204	487,347	433,857	47.1
1976–77	919,549	495,545	424,004	46.1
1975–76	925,746	504,925	420,821	45.5
1974–75	945,776	527,313	418,463	44.2
1973–74	922,933	504,841	418,092	45.3
1972–73	922,362	518,191	404,171	43.8
1971–72	887,273	500,590	386,683	43.6
1970–71	839,730	475,594	364,136	43.4
1969–70	792,316	451,097	341,219	43.1
1968–69	728,845	410,595	318,250	43.7
1967–68	632,289	357,682	274,607	43.4
1966–67	558,534	322,711	235,823	42.2
1965–66	520,115	299,287	220,828	42.5
1964–65	493,757	282,173	211,584	42.9
1963–64	461,266	265,349	195,917	42.5
1962–63	411,420	241,309	170,111	41.3
1961–62	383,961	230,456	153,505	40.0
1960–61	365,174	224,538	140,636	38.5
1959–60	392,440	254,063	138,377	35.3
1949–50	432,058	328,841	103,217	23.9
	percent change			*percentage point change*
1989–90 to 1999–00	17.8%	7.9%	26.4%	4.0
1949–50 to 1999–00	186.5	61.3	585.5	34.0

Note: Bachelor's degrees granted in 1949–50 and 1959–60 include first-professional degrees.
Source: National Center for Education Statistics, Digest of Education Statistics 2001; *calculations by New Strategist*

Table 2.28 Bachelor's Degrees Conferred by Sex, 2000–01 to 2011–12

(number of bachelor's degrees conferred by institutions of higher education by sex, and women's share of total, 2000–01 to 2011–12; percent and percentage point change 2000–01 to 2011–12)

	total bachelor's degrees	men	women number	women share of total
2011–12	1,437,000	587,000	850,000	59.2%
2010–11	1,414,000	580,000	834,000	59.0
2009–10	1,397,000	574,000	823,000	58.9
2008–09	1,382,000	570,000	812,000	58.8
2007–08	1,368,000	566,000	802,000	58.6
2006–07	1,353,000	562,000	791,000	58.5
2005–06	1,343,000	559,000	784,000	58.4
2004–05	1,327,000	557,000	770,000	58.0
2003–04	1,322,000	553,000	769,000	58.2
2002–03	1,301,000	543,000	758,000	58.3
2001–02	1,282,000	538,000	744,000	58.0
2000–01	1,268,000	535,000	733,000	57.8
		percent change		percentage point change
2000–01 to 2011–12	13.3%	9.7%	16.0%	1.3

Source: National Center for Education Statistics, Projections of Education Statistics to 2012; *calculations by New Strategist*

Table 2.29 Bachelor's Degrees Conferred by Race and Hispanic Origin, 1976–77 to 1999–00

(number and percent distribution of bachelor's degrees conferred by institutions of higher education, by race and Hispanic origin, 1976–77 to 1999–00; percent and percentage point change for selected years)

	total bachelor's degrees	American Indian	Asian	black, non-Hispanic	Hispanic	white, non-Hispanic	nonresident alien
1999–00	1,237,875	8,711	77,793	107,891	74,963	928,013	40,504
1998–99	1,200,303	8,418	74,102	102,106	70,008	906,305	39,364
1997–98	1,183,033	7,894	71,592	98,132	65,937	900,317	39,161
1996–97	1,168,023	7,409	67,969	94,053	61,941	898,224	38,427
1995–96	1,163,036	6,970	64,359	91,166	58,288	904,709	37,544
1994–95	1,158,788	6,606	60,478	87,203	54,201	913,377	36,923
1993–94	1,165,973	6,189	55,660	83,576	50,241	936,227	34,080
1992–93	1,159,931	5,671	51,463	77,872	45,376	947,309	32,240
1991–92	1,129,833	5,176	46,720	72,326	40,761	936,771	28,079
1990–91	1,081,280	4,513	41,618	65,341	36,612	904,062	29,134
1989–90	1,048,631	4,392	39,248	61,063	32,844	884,376	26,708
1988–89	1,016,350	3,951	37,674	58,078	29,918	859,703	27,026
1986–87	991,264	3,968	32,624	56,560	26,988	841,818	29,306
1984–85	968,311	4,246	25,395	57,473	25,874	826,106	29,217
1980–81	934,800	3,593	18,794	60,673	21,832	807,319	22,589
1978–79	919,540	3,410	15,407	60,246	20,096	802,542	17,839
1976–77	917,900	3,326	13,793	58,636	18,743	807,688	15,714

Percent change

'89–90 to '99–00	18.0%	98.3%	98.2%	76.7%	128.2%	4.9%	51.7%
'76–77 to '99–00	34.9	161.9	464.0	84.0	300.0	14.9	157.8

Percent distribution by race and Hispanic origin

1999–00	100.0%	0.7%	6.5%	9.0%	6.3%	77.5%	0.7%
1998–99	100.0	0.7	6.4	8.8	6.0	78.1	0.7
1997–98	100.0	0.7	6.3	8.6	5.8	78.7	0.7
1996–97	100.0	0.7	6.0	8.3	5.5	79.5	0.7
1995–96	100.0	0.6	5.7	8.1	5.2	80.4	0.6
1994–95	100.0	0.6	5.4	7.8	4.8	81.4	0.6
1993–94	100.0	0.5	4.9	7.4	4.4	82.7	0.5
1992–93	100.0	0.5	4.6	6.9	4.0	84.0	0.5
1991–92	100.0	0.5	4.2	6.6	3.7	85.0	0.5
1990–91	100.0	0.4	4.0	6.2	3.5	85.9	0.4
1989–90	100.0	0.4	3.8	6.0	3.2	86.5	0.4
1988–89	100.0	0.4	3.8	5.9	3.0	86.9	0.4
1986–87	100.0	0.4	3.4	5.9	2.8	87.5	0.4
1984–85	100.0	0.5	2.7	6.1	2.8	88.0	0.5
1980–81	100.0	0.4	2.1	6.7	2.4	88.5	0.4
1978–79	100.0	0.4	1.7	6.7	2.2	89.0	0.4
1976–77	100.0	0.4	1.5	6.5	2.1	89.5	0.4

Percentage point change

'89–90 to '99–00	–	0.3	2.7	3.0	3.0	–9.0	0.3
'76–77 to '99–00	–	0.4	5.0	2.5	4.2	–12.0	0.4

Source: National Center for Education Statistics, Digest of Education Statistics 2001; *calculations by New Strategist*

Table 2.30 Master's Degrees Conferred by Sex, 1949–50 to 1999–00

(number of master's degrees conferred by insitutions of higher education by sex, and women's share of total, 1949–50 to 1999–00; percent and percentage point change for selected years)

	total master's degrees	men	women number	women share of total
1999–00	457,056	191,792	265,264	58.0%
1998–99	439,986	186,148	253,838	57.7
1997–98	430,164	184,375	245,789	57.1
1996–97	419,401	180,947	238,454	56.9
1995–96	406,301	179,081	227,220	55.9
1994–95	397,629	178,598	219,031	55.1
1993–94	387,070	176,085	210,985	54.5
1992–93	369,585	169,258	200,327	54.2
1991–92	352,838	161,842	190,996	54.1
1990–91	337,168	156,482	180,686	53.6
1989–90	324,301	153,653	170,648	52.6
1988–89	310,621	149,354	161,267	51.9
1987–88	299,317	145,163	154,154	51.5
1986–87	289,349	141,269	148,080	51.2
1985–86	288,567	143,508	145,059	50.3
1984–85	286,251	143,390	142,861	49.9
1983–84	284,263	143,595	140,668	49.5
1982–83	289,921	144,697	145,224	50.1
1981–82	295,546	145,532	150,014	50.8
1980–81	295,739	147,043	148,696	50.3
1979–80	298,081	150,749	147,332	49.4
1978–79	301,079	153,370	147,709	49.1
1977–78	311,620	161,212	150,408	48.3
1976–77	317,164	167,783	149,381	47.1
1975–76	311,771	167,248	144,523	46.4
1974–75	292,450	161,570	130,880	44.8
1973–74	277,033	157,842	119,191	43.0
1972–73	263,371	154,468	108,903	41.3
1971–72	251,633	149,550	102,083	40.6
1970–71	230,509	138,146	92,363	40.1
1969–70	208,291	125,624	82,667	39.7
1968–69	193,756	121,531	72,225	37.3
1967–68	176,749	113,552	63,197	35.8
1966–67	157,726	103,109	54,617	34.6
1965–66	140,602	93,081	47,521	33.8
1964–65	121,167	81,319	39,848	32.9
1963–64	109,183	73,850	35,333	32.4
1962–63	98,684	67,302	31,382	31.8
1961–62	91,418	62,603	28,815	31.5
1960–61	84,609	57,830	26,779	31.7
1959–60	74,435	50,898	23,537	31.6
1949–50	58,183	41,220	16,963	29.2
	percent change			percentage point change
'89–90 to '99–00	40.9%	24.8%	55.4%	5.4
'49–50 to '99–00	685.5	365.3	1,463.8	28.9

Source: National Center for Education Statistics, Digest of Education Statistics 2001*; calculations by New Strategist*

Table 2.31 Master's Degrees Conferred by Sex, 2000–01 to 2011–12

(number of master's degrees conferred by institutions of higher education by sex, and women's share of total, 2000–01 to 2011–12; percent and percentage point change 2000–01 to 2011–12)

	total master's degrees	men	women number	women share of total
2011–12	501,000	204,000	297,000	59.3%
2010–11	491,000	201,000	290,000	59.1
2009–10	488,000	201,000	287,000	58.8
2008–09	484,000	200,000	284,000	58.7
2007–08	480,000	199,000	281,000	58.5
2006–07	477,000	198,000	279,000	58.5
2005–06	473,000	197,000	276,000	58.4
2004–05	470,000	197,000	273,000	58.1
2003–04	467,000	197,000	270,000	57.8
2002–03	468,000	199,000	269,000	57.5
2001–02	468,000	201,000	267,000	57.1
2000–01	475,000	202,000	273,000	57.5
	percent change			percentage point change
2000–01 to 2011–12	5.5%	1.0%	8.8%	1.8

Source: National Center for Education Statistics, Projections of Education Statistics to 2012; *calculations by New Strategist*

Table 2.32 Master's Degrees Conferred by Race and Hispanic Origin, 1976–77 to 1999–00

(number and percent distribution of master's degrees conferred by institutions of higher education, by race and Hispanic origin, 1976–77 to 1999–00; percent and percentage point change for selected years)

	total master's degrees	American Indian	Asian	black, non-Hispanic	Hispanic	white, non-Hispanic	nonresident alien
1999–00	457,056	2,232	22,899	35,625	19,093	317,999	59,208
1998–99	439,986	2,004	21,803	32,344	17,708	311,299	54,828
1997–98	429,296	2,049	21,088	30,097	16,215	307,587	52,260
1996–97	414,882	1,924	18,477	28,224	15,187	302,541	48,529
1995–96	405,521	1,778	18,161	25,801	14,412	297,558	47,811
1994–95	397,052	1,621	16,842	24,171	12,907	292,784	48,727
1993–94	385,419	1,697	15,267	21,937	11,913	288,288	46,317
1992–93	368,701	1,407	13,866	19,780	10,665	278,829	44,154
1991–92	348,682	1,273	12,658	18,116	9,358	268,371	38,906
1990–91	328,645	1,136	11,180	16,139	8,386	255,281	36,523
1989–90	322,465	1,101	10,577	15,446	7,950	251,690	35,701
1988–89	309,770	1,086	10,335	14,095	7,277	242,764	34,213
1986–87	289,349	1,103	8,559	13,873	7,044	228,874	29,896
1984–85	280,421	1,256	7,782	13,939	6,864	223,628	26,952
1980–81	294,183	1,034	6,282	17,133	6,461	241,216	22,057
1978–79	300,255	999	5,496	19,418	5,555	249,360	19,427
1976–77	316,602	967	5,122	21,037	6,071	266,061	17,344

Percent change

'89–90 to '99–00	41.7%	102.7%	116.5%	130.6%	140.2%	26.3%	65.8%
'76–77 to '99–00	44.4	130.8	347.1	69.3	214.5	19.5	241.4

Percent distribution by race and Hispanic origin

1999–00	100.0%	0.5%	5.0%	7.8%	4.2%	69.6%	13.0%
1998–99	100.0	0.5	5.0	7.4	4.0	70.8	12.5
1997–98	100.0	0.5	4.9	7.0	3.8	71.6	12.2
1996–97	100.0	0.5	4.5	6.8	3.7	72.9	11.7
1995–96	100.0	0.4	4.5	6.4	3.6	73.4	11.8
1994–95	100.0	0.4	4.2	6.1	3.3	73.7	12.3
1993–94	100.0	0.4	4.0	5.7	3.1	74.8	12.0
1992–93	100.0	0.4	3.8	5.4	2.9	75.6	12.0
1991–92	100.0	0.4	3.6	5.2	2.7	77.0	11.2
1990–91	100.0	0.3	3.4	4.9	2.6	77.7	11.1
1989–90	100.0	0.3	3.3	4.8	2.5	78.1	11.1
1988–89	100.0	0.4	3.3	4.6	2.3	78.4	11.0
1986–87	100.0	0.4	3.0	4.8	2.4	79.1	10.3
1984–85	100.0	0.4	2.8	5.0	2.4	79.7	9.6
1980–81	100.0	0.4	2.1	5.8	2.2	82.0	7.5
1978–79	100.0	0.3	1.8	6.5	1.9	83.0	6.5
1976–77	100.0	0.3	1.6	6.6	1.9	84.0	5.5

Percentage point change

'89–90 to '99–00	–	0.1	1.7	3.0	1.7	–8.5	1.9
'76–77 to '99–00	–	0.2	3.4	1.1	2.3	–14.5	7.5

Source: National Center for Education Statistics, Digest of Education Statistics 2001; *calculations by New Strategist*

Table 2.33 Doctoral Degrees Conferred by Sex, 1949–50 to 1999–00

(number of doctoral degrees conferred by institutions of higher education by sex and women's share of total, 1949–50 to 1999–00; percent and percentage point change for selected years)

	total doctoral degrees	men	women number	women share of total
1999–00	44,808	25,028	19,780	44.1%
1998–99	44,077	25,146	18,931	42.9
1997–98	46,010	26,664	19,346	42.0
1996–97	45,876	27,146	18,730	40.8
1995–96	44,652	26,841	17,811	39.9
1994–95	44,446	26,916	17,530	39.4
1993–94	43,185	26,552	16,633	38.5
1992–93	42,132	26,073	16,059	38.1
1991–92	40,659	25,557	15,102	37.1
1990–91	39,294	24,756	14,538	37.0
1989–90	38,371	24,401	13,970	36.4
1988–89	35,720	22,648	13,072	36.6
1987–88	34,870	22,615	12,255	35.1
1986–87	34,041	22,061	11,980	35.2
1985–86	33,653	21,819	11,834	35.2
1984–85	32,943	21,700	11,243	34.1
1983–84	33,209	22,064	11,145	33.6
1982–83	32,775	21,902	10,873	33.2
1981–82	32,707	22,224	10,483	32.1
1980–81	32,958	22,711	10,247	31.1
1979–80	32,615	22,943	9,672	29.7
1978–79	32,730	23,541	9,189	28.1
1977–78	32,131	23,658	8,473	26.4
1976–77	33,232	25,142	8,090	24.3
1975–76	34,064	26,267	7,797	22.9
1974–75	34,083	26,817	7,266	21.3
1973–74	33,816	27,365	6,451	19.1
1972–73	34,777	28,571	6,206	17.8
1971–72	33,363	28,090	5,273	15.8
1970–71	32,107	27,530	4,577	14.3
1969–70	29,866	25,890	3,976	13.3
1968–69	26,158	22,722	3,436	13.1
1967–68	23,089	20,183	2,906	12.6
1966–67	20,617	18,163	2,454	11.9
1965–66	18,237	16,121	2,116	11.6
1964–65	16,467	14,692	1,775	10.8
1963–64	14,490	12,955	1,535	10.6
1962–63	12,822	11,448	1,374	10.7
1961–62	11,622	10,377	1,245	10.7
1960–61	10,575	9,463	1,112	10.5
1959–60	9,829	8,801	1,028	10.5
1949–50	6,420	5,804	616	9.6

	percent change			percentage point change
1989–90 to 1999–00	16.8%	2.6%	41.6%	7.7
1949–50 to 1999–00	597.9	331.2	3,111.0	34.5

Source: National Center for Education Statistics, Digest of Education Statistics 2001; *calculations by New Strategist*

Table 2.34 Doctoral Degrees Conferred by Sex, 2000–01 to 2011–12

(number of doctoral degrees conferred by institutions of higher education by sex, and women's share of total, 2000–01 to 2010–12; percent and percentage point change 2000–01 to 2011–12)

	total doctoral degrees	men	women	
			number	share of total
2011–12	46,800	26,000	20,800	44.4%
2010–11	46,300	25,800	20,500	44.3
2009–10	46,100	25,700	20,400	44.3
2008–09	45,900	25,600	20,300	44.2
2007–08	45,800	25,500	20,300	44.3
2006–07	45,600	25,400	20,200	44.3
2005–06	45,400	25,300	20,100	44.3
2004–05	45,100	25,200	19,900	44.1
2003–04	45,000	25,200	19,800	44.0
2002–03	45,000	25,200	19,800	44.0
2001–02	44,900	25,200	19,700	43.9
2000–01	44,900	24,800	20,100	44.8
		percent change		percentage point change
2000–01 to 2011–12	4.2%	4.8%	3.5%	–0.3

Source: National Center for Education Statistics, Projections of Education Statistics to 2012; *calculations by New Strategist*

Table 2.35 Doctoral Degrees Conferred by Race and Hispanic Origin, 1976–77 to 1999–00

(number and percent distribution of doctoral degrees conferred by institutions of higher education, by race and Hispanic origin, 1976–77 to 1999–00; percent and percentage point change for selected years)

	total doctoral degrees	American Indian	Asian	black, non-Hispanic	Hispanic	white, non-Hispanic	nonresident alien
1999–00	44,808	159	2,380	2,220	1,291	27,520	11,238
1998–99	44,077	192	2,262	2,116	1,284	27,492	10,731
1997–98	45,925	187	2,334	2,066	1,270	28,747	11,321
1996–97	45,394	173	2,607	1,847	1,098	28,344	11,325
1995–96	44,645	158	2,646	1,636	999	27,756	11,450
1994–95	44,427	130	2,690	1,667	984	27,826	11,130
1993–94	43,149	134	2,025	1,393	903	27,156	11,538
1992–93	42,021	106	1,582	1,352	827	26,700	11,454
1991–92	40,090	118	1,559	1,223	811	25,813	10,566
1990–91	38,547	102	1,459	1,211	732	25,328	9,715
1989–90	38,113	99	1,235	1,153	788	25,880	8,958
1988–89	35,659	85	1,323	1,066	629	24,884	7,672
1986–87	34,041	105	1,098	1,057	751	24,434	6,596
1984–85	32,307	119	1,106	1,154	677	23,934	5,317
1980–81	32,839	130	877	1,265	456	25,908	4,203
1978–79	32,675	104	811	1,268	439	26,138	3,915
1976–77	33,126	95	658	1,253	522	26,851	3,747

Percent change

'89–90 to '99–00	17.6%	60.6%	92.7%	92.5%	63.8%	6.3%	25.5%
'76–77 to '99–00	35.3	67.4	261.7	77.2	147.3	2.5	199.9

Percent distribution by race and Hispanic origin

1999–00	100.0%	0.4%	5.3%	5.0%	2.9%	61.4%	25.1%
1998–99	100.0	0.4	5.1	4.8	2.9	62.4	24.3
1997–98	100.0	0.4	5.1	4.5	2.8	62.6	24.7
1996–97	100.0	0.4	5.7	4.1	2.4	62.4	24.9
1995–96	100.0	0.4	5.9	3.7	2.2	62.2	25.6
1994–95	100.0	0.3	6.1	3.8	2.2	62.6	25.1
1993–94	100.0	0.3	4.7	3.2	2.1	62.9	26.7
1992–93	100.0	0.3	3.8	3.2	2.0	63.5	27.3
1991–92	100.0	0.3	3.9	3.1	2.0	64.4	26.4
1990–91	100.0	0.3	3.8	3.1	1.9	65.7	25.2
1989–90	100.0	0.3	3.2	3.0	2.1	67.9	23.5
1988–89	100.0	0.2	3.7	3.0	1.8	69.8	21.5
1986–87	100.0	0.3	3.2	3.1	2.2	71.8	19.4
1984–85	100.0	0.4	3.4	3.6	2.1	74.1	16.5
1980–81	100.0	0.4	2.7	3.9	1.4	78.9	12.8
1978–79	100.0	0.3	2.5	3.9	1.3	80.0	12.0
1976–77	100.0	0.3	2.0	3.8	1.6	81.1	11.3

Percentage point change

'89–90 to '99–00	–	0.2	1.9	1.8	0.8	–5.5	0.8
'76–77 to '99–00	–	0.4	5.1	4.8	2.9	62.4	24.3

Source: National Center for Education Statistics, Digest of Education Statistics 2001; *calculations by New Strategist*

Table 2.36   First Professional Degrees Conferred by Sex, 1960–61 to 1999–00

(number of first professional degrees conferred by institutions of higher education by sex, and women's share of total, 1960–61 to 1999–00; percent and percentage point change for selected years)

	total first professional degrees	men	women	
			number	share of total
1999–00	80,057	44,239	35,818	44.7%
1998–99	78,439	44,339	34,100	43.5
1997–98	78,598	44,911	33,687	42.9
1996–97	78,730	45,564	33,166	42.1
1995–96	76,734	44,748	31,986	41.7
1994–95	75,800	44,853	30,947	40.8
1993–94	75,418	44,707	30,711	40.7
1992–93	75,387	45,153	30,234	40.1
1991–92	74,146	45,071	29,075	39.2
1990–91	71,948	43,846	28,102	39.1
1989–90	70,988	43,961	27,027	38.1
1988–89	70,856	45,046	25,810	36.4
1987–88	70,735	45,484	25,251	35.7
1986–87	71,617	46,523	25,094	35.0
1985–86	73,910	49,261	24,649	33.4
1984–85	75,063	50,455	24,608	32.8
1983–84	74,468	51,378	23,090	31.0
1982–83	73,054	51,250	21,804	29.8
1981–82	72,032	52,223	19,809	27.5
1980–81	71,956	52,792	19,164	26.6
1979–80	70,131	52,716	17,415	24.8
1978–79	68,848	52,652	16,196	23.5
1977–78	66,581	52,270	14,311	21.5
1976–77	64,359	52,374	11,985	18.6
1975–76	62,649	52,892	9,757	15.6
1974–75	55,916	48,956	6,960	12.4
1973–74	53,816	48,530	5,286	9.8
1972–73	50,018	46,489	3,529	7.1
1971–72	43,411	40,723	2,688	6.2
1970–71	37,946	35,544	2,402	6.3
1969–70	34,918	33,077	1,841	5.3
1968–69	35,114	33,595	1,519	4.3
1967–68	33,939	32,402	1,537	4.5
1966–67	31,695	30,401	1,294	4.1
1965–66	30,124	28,982	1,142	3.8
1964–65	28,290	27,283	1,007	3.6
1963–64	27,209	26,357	852	3.1
1962–63	26,590	25,753	837	3.1
1961–62	25,607	24,836	771	3.0
1960–61	25,253	24,577	676	2.7
		percent change		percentage point change
1989–90 to 1999–00	12.8%	0.6%	32.5%	6.7
1949–50 to 1999–00	217.0	80.0	5,198.5	42.1

Source: National Center for Education Statistics, Digest of Education Statistics 2001; *calculations by New Strategist*

Table 2.37 First Professional Degrees Conferred by Sex, 2000–01 to 2011–12

(number of first professional degrees conferred by institutions of higher education by sex, and women's share of total, 2000–01 to 2011–12; percent and percentage point change 2000–01 to 2011–12)

	total first professional degrees	men	women	
			number	share of total
2011–12	86,400	44,800	41,600	48.1%
2010–11	85,700	44,600	41,100	48.0
2009–10	84,900	44,300	40,600	47.8
2008–09	84,100	44,000	40,100	47.7
2007–08	83,500	43,800	39,700	47.5
2006–07	82,900	43,600	39,300	47.4
2005–06	82,300	43,600	38,700	47.0
2004–05	82,200	44,000	38,200	46.5
2003–04	82,200	44,300	37,900	46.1
2002–03	80,200	42,500	37,700	4.7
2001–02	80,800	42,700	38,100	47.2
2000–01	80,100	43,400	36,700	45.8
		percent change		percentage point change
2000–01 to 2011–12	7.9%	3.2%	13.4%	2.3

Source: National Center for Education Statistics, Projections of Education Statistics to 2012; *calculations by New Strategist*

Table 2.38　First-Professional Degrees Conferred by Race and Hispanic Origin, 1976–77 to 1999–00

(number and percent distribution of first-professional degrees conferred by institutions of higher education, by race and Hispanic origin, 1976–77 to 1999–00; percent and percentage point change for selected years)

	total first-professional degrees	American Indian	Asian	black, non-Hispanic	Hispanic	white, non-Hispanic	nonresident alien
1999–00	80,057	564	8,576	5,552	3,865	59,601	1,899
1998–99	78,439	612	8,147	5,332	3,863	58,688	1,797
1997–98	78,353	561	7,712	5,483	3,547	59,273	1,777
1996–97	77,815	511	7,037	5,251	3,553	59,852	1,611
1995–96	76,641	463	6,617	5,016	3,476	59,456	1,613
1994–95	75,800	412	6,397	4,747	3,231	59,402	1,611
1993–94	75,418	371	5,892	4,444	3,134	60,140	1,437
1992–93	74,960	368	5,160	4,100	2,984	60,830	1,518
1991–92	72,129	296	4,455	3,560	2,766	59,800	1,252
1990–91	71,515	261	3,755	3,575	2,527	60,327	1,070
1989–90	70,744	257	3,362	3,410	2,427	60,240	1,048
1988–89	70,856	264	2,976	3,148	2,269	61,214	985
1986–87	71,617	304	2,270	3,420	2,051	62,688	884
1984–85	71,057	248	1,816	3,029	1,884	63,219	861
1980–81	71,340	192	1,456	2,931	1,541	64,551	669
1978–79	68,611	216	1,205	2,836	1,283	62,430	641
1976–77	63,953	196	1,021	2,537	1,076	58,422	701

Percent change

'89–90 to '99–00	13.2%	119.5%	155.1%	62.8%	59.3%	−1.1%	81.2%
'76–77 to '99–00	10.6	31.1	229.3	34.4	125.6	3.1	49.5

Percent distribution by race and Hispanic origin

1999–00	100.0%	0.7%	10.7%	6.9%	4.8%	74.4%	2.4%
1998–99	100.0	0.8	10.4	6.8	4.9	74.8	2.3
1997–98	100.0	0.7	9.8	7.0	4.5	75.6	2.3
1996–97	100.0	0.7	9.0	6.7	4.6	76.9	2.1
1995–96	100.0	0.6	8.6	6.5	4.5	77.6	2.1
1994–95	100.0	0.5	8.4	6.3	4.3	78.4	2.1
1993–94	100.0	0.5	7.8	5.9	4.2	79.7	1.9
1992–93	100.0	0.5	6.9	5.5	4.0	81.1	2.0
1991–92	100.0	0.4	6.2	4.9	3.8	82.9	1.7
1990–91	100.0	0.4	5.3	5.0	3.5	84.4	1.5
1989–90	100.0	0.4	4.8	4.8	3.4	85.2	1.5
1988–89	100.0	0.4	4.2	4.4	3.2	86.4	1.4
1986–87	100.0	0.4	3.2	4.8	2.9	87.5	1.2
1984–85	100.0	0.3	2.6	4.3	2.7	89.0	1.2
1980–81	100.0	0.3	2.0	4.1	2.2	90.5	0.9
1978–79	100.0	0.3	1.8	4.1	1.9	91.0	0.9
1976–77	100.0	0.3	1.6	4.0	1.7	91.4	1.1

Percentage point change

'89–90 to '99–00	–	0.3	6.0	2.1	1.4	−10.7	0.9
'76–77 to '99–00	–	0.4	9.1	3.0	3.1	−16.9	1.3

Source: National Center for Education Statistics, Digest of Education Statistics 2001; *calculations by New Strategist*

3

Health

■ Americans feel better than ever. The proportion of people aged 18 or older who say their health is "excellent" or "good" rose from 73 to 80 percent between 1974 and 2000.

■ Most babies are born to women in their twenties, but the proportion is much lower than it once was. In 1950, fully 59 percent of births were to women aged 20 to 29. By 2000, the figure had fallen to 52 percent. At the same time, the share of births to women aged 30 or older grew from 27 to 36 percent.

■ The percentage of the population covered by health insurance has changed little since 1980. In 2000, 86 percent of Americans had health insurance, up slightly from 85 percent in 1980. Because the population has grown, however, the number of uninsured has increased.

■ As health care costs have soared, in-patient hospital care increasingly has become restricted to the most dire cases. Although the U.S. population grew 38 percent between 1970 and 2000, the number of people admitted to hospitals as in-patients climbed only 10 percent. Outpatient visits rose 227 percent during those years, however.

■ The death rate from heart disease, the leading cause of death, fell by 56 percent between 1950 and 2000. As the death rate has dropped, life expectancy has grown. Between 1950 and 2000, life expectancy at birth grew from 68.2 to 76.9 years.

Americans Feel Better than Ever

Americans feel better than they did a quarter century ago. The proportion of people aged 18 or older who say their health is "excellent" or "good" rose from 73 to 80 percent between 1974 and 2000.

Nearly everyone feels better today than their counterparts did in 1974. Young adults are the only demographic segment reporting a decline in health status, a two percentage point drop to 86 percent.

Blacks, people in their fifties, and those with graduate degrees have shown the greatest improvement in health status. The percentage of people aged 50 to 59 who say their health is excellent or very good climbed from 63 to 80 percent between 1974 and 2000. Among Americans aged 70 or older, the proportion saying their health is excellent or good rose from a 48 percent minority in 1974 to the 58 percent majority in 2000. Behind the improvement in health status is the rising educational level of the population. Because the educated are more health conscious, they take better care of themselves.

Older Americans made the biggest gains

(percent of people aged 50 or older who say their health is "excellent" or "very good," by age, 1974 and 2000)

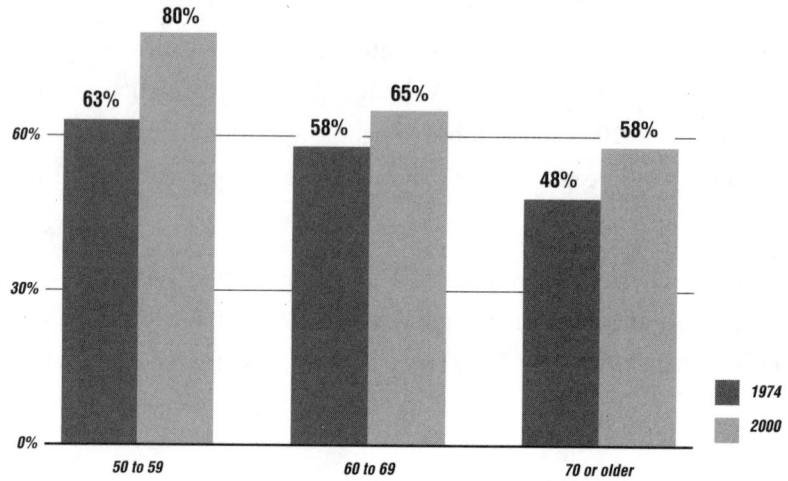

Table 3.1 Health Status, 1974 to 2000

"Would you say your own health, in general, is excellent, good, fair, or poor?"

(percent of people aged 18 or older responding "excellent" or "good" by selected characteristics, and percentage point change, 1974 to 2000)

	2000	1990	1980	1974	percentage point change 1974–00
Total	80%	77%	74%	73%	7
Men	82	80	78	77	5
Women	78	75	71	69	9
Black	71	68	59	57	14
White	81	78	75	74	7
Aged 18 to 29	86	87	87	88	-2
Aged 30 to 39	87	87	84	82	5
Aged 40 to 49	83	81	75	74	9
Aged 50 to 59	80	70	63	63	17
Aged 60 to 69	65	72	56	58	7
Aged 70 or older	58	52	60	48	10
Not a high school graduate	58	52	55	56	2
High school graduate	80	82	81	80	0
Bachelor's degree	91	88	84	90	1
Graduate degree	91	88	90	81	10

Source: General Social Surveys, National Opinion Research Center, University of Chicago; calculations by New Strategist

Most Babies Are Born to Women Aged 20 to 29

During the past half-century, the annual number of births has fluctuated through cycles of baby boom and baby bust. Births peaked at 4.3 million in 1957, fell below 4 million in 1965, surpassed 4 million again in 1989, fell below 4 million in 1994, and topped 4 million yet again in 2000.

Behind the fluctuating number of births are the changing roles of women. As women went to work, they postponed childbearing. In 1950, fully 59 percent of births were to women aged 20 to 29. By 2000, the figure had fallen to 52 percent. The share of births to women aged 30 or older grew from 27 to 36 percent during those years. The proportion of births to women under age 20 has barely changed in the past 50 years.

Only 58 percent of babies were born to non-Hispanic white women in 2000, a proportion that is falling steadily. Twenty percent of births were to Hispanics in 2000, up from just 10 percent in 1985. Fifteen percent of births are to blacks, a figure that has remained fairly stable over the past half century. One in three babies is born to an unmarried woman, up from just 4 percent in 1950.

One-third of babies are born out-of-wedlock

(percent of births to unmarried women, 1950 to 2000)

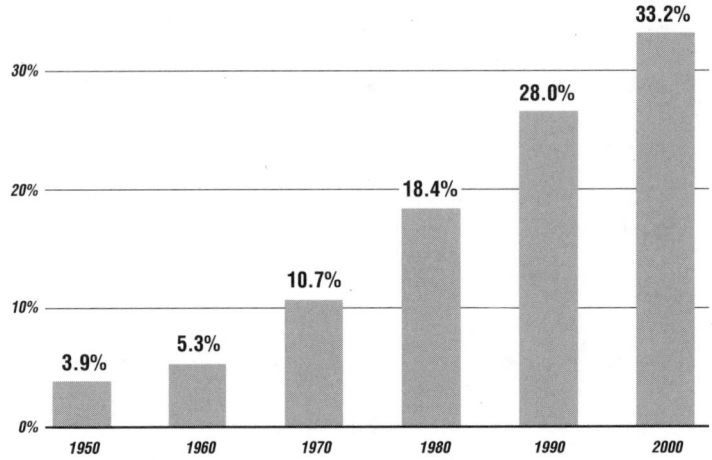

Table 3.2 Contraceptive Use by Age, 1982 to 1995

(percent of women aged 15 to 44 who use contraception, by method and age, 1982 to 1995; percentage point change, 1982–95)

	1995	1988	1982	percentage point change 1982–95
Any method				
Total, aged 15 to 44	**64.2%**	**60.3%**	**55.7%**	**8.5%**
Aged 15 to 19	29.8	32.1	24.2	5.6
Aged 20 to 24	63.5	59.0	55.8	7.7
Aged 25 to 34	71.1	66.3	66.7	4.4
Aged 35 to 44	72.3	68.3	61.6	10.7
Birth control pill				
Total, aged 15 to 44	**26.9**	**30.7**	**28.0**	**–1.1**
Aged 15 to 19	43.8	58.8	63.9	–20.1
Aged 20 to 24	52.1	68.2	55.1	–3.0
Aged 25 to 34	33.3	32.6	25.7	7.6
Aged 35 to 44	8.7	4.3	3.7	5.0
Condom				
Total, aged 15 to 44	**20.4**	**14.6**	**12.0**	**8.4**
Aged 15 to 19	36.7	32.8	20.8	15.9
Aged 20 to 24	26.4	14.5	10.7	15.7
Aged 25 to 34	21.1	13.7	11.4	9.7
Aged 35 to 44	14.7	11.2	11.3	3.4
Diaphragm				
Total, aged 15 to 44	**1.9**	**5.7**	**8.1**	**–6.2**
Aged 15 to 19	0.1	–	6.0	–5.9
Aged 20 to 24	0.6	3.7	10.2	–9.6
Aged 25 to 34	1.7	7.3	10.3	–8.6
Aged 35 to 44	2.8	6.0	4.0	–1.2
Intrauterine device				
Total, aged 15 to 44	**0.8**	**2.0**	**7.1**	**–6.3**
Aged 15 to 19	0.0	–	1.3	–1.3
Aged 20 to 24	0.3	4.2	4.2	–3.9
Aged 25 to 34	0.8	9.7	9.7	–8.9
Aged 35 to 44	1.1	6.9	6.9	–5.8
Sterilization, female				
Total, aged 15 to 44	**27.7**	**27.5**	**23.2**	**4.5**
Aged 15 to 19	0.3	–	0.0	0.3
Aged 20 to 24	4.0	4.6	4.5	–0.5
Aged 25 to 34	23.8	25.0	22.1	1.7
Aged 35 to 44	45.0	47.6	43.5	1.5
Sterilization, male				
Total, aged 15 to 44	**10.9**	**11.7**	**10.9**	**0.0**
Aged 15 to 19	0.0	–	0.4	–0.4
Aged 20 to 24	1.1	–	3.6	–2.5
Aged 25 to 34	7.8	7.8	10.1	–2.3
Aged 35 to 44	19.4	19.4	19.9	–0.5

Note: Method of contraception used in the month of interview. (–) Means sample too small to make a reliable estimate.
Source: National Center for Health Statistics, Health, United States, 2001; *calculations by New Strategist*

Table 3.3 Number of Births, 1950 to 2000

(number of births by year and decade, 1950 to 2000; percent change from preceding year and decade, 1950–2000; numbers in thousands)

	number	percent change from preceding year or decade
1991–2000	**39,760**	**4.5%**
2000	4,058	2.5
1999	3,959	0.4
1998	3,942	1.6
1997	3,881	–0.3
1996	3,891	–0.2
1995	3,900	–1.3
1994	3,953	–1.2
1993	4,000	–1.6
1992	4,065	–1.1
1991	4,111	–1.1
1981–1990	**38,054**	**14.7**
1990	4,158	2.9
1989	4,041	3.4
1988	3,910	2.7
1987	3,809	1.4
1986	3,757	–0.1
1985	3,761	2.5
1984	3,669	0.8
1983	3,639	–1.1
1982	3,681	1.4
1981	3,629	0.5
1971–1980	**33,189**	**–13.3**
1980	3,612	3.4
1979	3,494	4.8
1978	3,333	0.2
1977	3,327	5.0
1976	3,168	0.8
1975	3,144	–0.5
1974	3,160	0.7
1973	3,137	–3.7
1972	3,258	–8.4
1971	3,556	–4.7
1961–1970	**38,280**	**–7.0**
1970	3,731	3.6
1969	3,600	2.8
1968	3,502	–0.5
1967	3,521	–2.4
1966	3,606	–4.1
1965	3,760	–6.6
1964	4,027	–1.7
1963	4,098	–1.7
1962	4,167	–2.4
1961	4,268	0.2
1951–1960	**41,160**	**–**
1960	4,258	0.3
1959	4,245	–0.2
1958	4,255	–1.2
1957	4,308	2.1
1956	4,218	3.0
1955	4,097	0.5
1954	4,078	2.8
1953	3,965	1.3
1952	3,913	2.4
1951	3,823	5.3
1950	3,632	–

Note: (–) means not applicable.
Source: National Center for Health Statistics, Births: Final Data for 2000, National Vital Statistics Report, Vol. 50, No. 5, 2002; and Bureau of the Census, Historical Statistics of the United States: Colonial Times to 1970, Part 1, 1975; calculations by New Strategist

Table 3.4 Births by Age, 1950 to 2000

(number of births by age of mother, 1950 to 2000; percent change for selected years; numbers in thousands)

	total	under 20	20 to 24	25 to 29	30 to 34	35 to 39	40 or older
2000	4,059	478	1,018	1,088	929	452	95
1999	3,959	485	982	1,078	892	434	87
1998	3,942	494	965	1,083	889	425	85
1997	3,881	493	942	1,069	887	410	80
1996	3,891	503	945	1,071	898	400	75
1995	3,900	512	966	1,064	905	384	70
1994	3,953	518	1,001	1,089	906	372	66
1993	4,000	514	1,038	1,129	901	357	61
1992	4,065	517	1,070	1,179	895	345	58
1991	4,111	532	1,090	1,220	885	331	54
1990	4,158	534	1,094	1,277	886	318	50
1989	4,041	518	1,078	1,263	842	294	46
1988	3,910	489	1,067	1,239	804	270	41
1987	3,809	473	1,076	1,216	761	248	36
1986	3,757	472	1,102	1,200	721	230	31
1985	3,761	478	1,141	1,201	696	214	29
1984	3,669	480	1,142	1,166	658	196	28
1983	3,639	499	1,160	1,148	625	180	27
1982	3,681	524	1,206	1,152	605	168	26
1981	3,629	537	1,212	1,128	581	146	25
1980	3,612	562	1,226	1,108	550	141	24
1975	3,144	595	1,094	937	376	115	28
1970	3,731	656	1,419	995	428	180	53
1965	3,760	599	1,337	926	529	283	86
1960	4,258	594	1,427	1,093	688	360	97
1955	4,097	490	1,274	1,119	722	345	93
1950	3,632	425	1,131	1,022	598	293	80
Percent change							
1990 to 2000	−2.4%	−10.5%	−6.9%	−14.8%	4.9%	42.1%	90.0%
1950 to 2000	11.8	12.5	−10.0	6.5	55.4	54.3	18.8

Note: Numbers may not add to total because "age not stated" is not shown.
Source: National Center for Health Statistics, Births: Final Data for 2000, *National Vital Statistics Report, Vol. 50, No. 5, 2002;*
and Births: Final Data for 1999, *National Vital Statistics Report, Vol. 49, No. 1, 2001; and Bureau of the Census,* Statistical
Abstract of the United States 1980, 1990, *and 1992; calculations by New Strategist*

Table 3.5 Distribution of Births by Age, 1950 to 2000

(percent distribution of births by age of mother, 1950 to 2000; percentage point change for selected years)

	total	under age 20	20 to 24	25 to 29	30 to 34	35 to 39	40 or older
2000	100.0%	11.8%	25.1%	26.8%	22.9%	11.1%	2.3%
1999	100.0	12.3	24.8	27.2	22.5	11.0	2.2
1998	100.0	12.5	24.5	27.5	22.6	10.8	2.2
1997	100.0	12.7	24.3	27.5	22.9	10.6	2.1
1996	100.0	12.9	24.3	27.5	23.1	10.3	1.9
1995	100.0	13.1	24.8	27.3	23.2	9.8	1.8
1994	100.0	13.1	25.3	27.5	22.9	9.4	1.7
1993	100.0	12.8	25.9	28.2	22.5	8.9	1.5
1992	100.0	12.7	26.3	2.9	22.0	8.5	1.4
1991	100.0	12.9	26.5	29.7	21.5	8.1	1.3
1990	100.0	12.8	26.3	30.7	21.3	7.6	1.2
1989	100.0	12.8	26.7	31.3	20.8	7.3	1.1
1988	100.0	12.5	27.3	31.7	20.6	6.9	1.1
1987	100.0	12.4	28.2	31.9	20.0	6.5	0.9
1986	100.0	12.6	29.3	31.9	19.2	6.1	0.8
1985	100.0	12.7	30.3	31.9	18.5	5.7	0.8
1984	100.0	13.1	31.1	31.8	17.9	5.3	0.8
1983	100.0	13.7	31.9	31.5	17.2	4.9	0.7
1982	100.0	14.2	32.8	31.3	16.4	4.6	0.7
1981	100.0	14.8	33.4	31.1	16.0	4.0	0.7
1980	100.0	15.6	33.9	30.7	15.2	3.9	0.7
1975	100.0	18.9	34.8	29.8	12.0	3.7	0.9
1970	100.0	17.6	38.0	26.7	11.5	4.8	1.4
1965	100.0	15.9	35.6	24.6	14.1	7.5	2.3
1960	100.0	14.0	33.5	25.7	16.2	8.5	2.3
1955	100.0	12.0	31.1	27.3	17.6	8.4	2.3
1950	100.0	11.7	31.1	28.1	16.5	8.1	2.2
Percentage point change							
1990 to 2000	–	−1.1	−1.2	−3.9	1.6	3.5	1.1
1950 to 2000	–	0.1	−6.1	−1.3	6.4	3.1	0.1

Note: Numbers may not add to 100 because "age not stated" is not shown; (–) means not applicable.
Source: National Center for Health Statistics, Births: Final Data for 2000, National Vital Statistics Report, Vol. 50, No. 5, 2002;
and Births: Final Data for 1999, National Vital Statistics Report, Vol. 49, No. 1, 2001; and Bureau of the Census, Statistical
Abstract of the United States 1980, 1990, and 1992; calculations by New Strategist

Table 3.6 Birth Rates by Age, 1950 to 2000

(number of births per 1,000 women aged 15 to 44, and per 1,000 women in specified age group, 1950 to 2000; percent change for selected years)

	total	15 to 19	20 to 24	25 to 29	30 to 34	35 to 39	40 to 44	45 to 49
2000	67.5	48.5	112.3	121.4	94.1	40.4	7.9	0.5
1999	65.9	49.6	111.0	117.8	89.6	38.3	7.4	0.4
1998	65.6	51.1	111.2	115.9	87.4	37.4	7.3	0.4
1997	65.0	52.3	110.4	113.8	85.3	36.1	7.1	0.4
1996	65.3	54.4	110.4	113.1	83.9	35.3	6.8	0.3
1995	65.6	56.8	109.8	112.2	82.5	34.3	6.6	0.3
1994	66.7	58.9	111.1	113.9	81.5	33.7	6.4	0.3
1993	67.6	59.6	112.6	115.5	80.8	32.9	6.1	0.3
1992	68.9	60.7	114.6	117.4	80.2	32.5	5.9	0.3
1991	69.6	62.1	115.7	118.2	79.5	32.0	5.5	0.2
1990	70.9	59.9	116.5	120.2	80.8	31.7	5.5	0.2
1989	69.2	58.1	115.4	116.6	76.2	29.7	5.2	0.2
1988	67.2	53.6	111.5	113.4	73.7	27.9	4.8	0.2
1987	65.7	51.1	108.9	110.8	71.3	26.2	4.4	0.2
1986	65.4	50.6	108.2	109.2	69.3	24.3	4.1	0.2
1985	66.2	51.3	108.9	110.5	68.5	23.9	4.0	0.2
1984	65.4	50.9	107.3	108.3	66.5	22.8	3.9	0.2
1983	65.8	51.7	108.3	108.7	64.6	22.1	3.8	0.2
1982	67.3	52.9	111.3	111.0	64.2	21.1	3.9	0.2
1981	67.4	52.7	111.8	112.0	61.4	20.0	3.8	0.2
1980	68.4	53.0	115.1	112.9	61.9	19.8	3.9	0.2
1975	66.0	55.6	113.0	108.2	52.3	19.5	4.6	0.3
1970	87.9	68.3	167.8	145.1	73.3	31.7	8.1	0.5
1965	96.6	70.5	195.3	161.6	94.4	46.2	12.8	0.8
1960	118.0	89.1	258.1	197.4	112.7	56.2	15.5	0.9
1955	118.3	90.5	242.0	190.5	116.2	58.7	16.1	1.0
1950	106.2	81.6	196.6	166.1	103.7	52.9	15.1	1.2
Percent change								
1990 to 2000	−4.8%	−19.0%	−3.6%	1.0%	16.5%	27.4%	43.6%	150.0%
1950 to 2000	−36.4	−40.6	−42.9	−26.9	−9.3	−23.6	−47.7	−58.3

Source: National Center for Health Statistics, Health, United States, 2001; *and* Births: Final Data for 2000, *National Vital Statistics Report, Vol. 50, No. 5, 2002; and* Births: Final Data for 1999, *National Vital Statistics Report, Vol. 49, No. 1, 2001; and Bureau of the Census,* Historical Statistics of the United States: Colonial Times to 1970, Part 1, *1975; and* Statistical Abstracts of the United States 1980, 1990, *and* 1992; *calculations by New Strategist*

Table 3.7 Births by Race and Hispanic Origin, 1950 to 2000

(number of births by race and Hispanic origin, 1950 to 2000; percent change for selected years; numbers in thousands)

	total	American Indian	Asian	black	Hispanic	white total	white non-Hispanic
2000	4,059	42	201	623	816	3,194	2,363
1999	3,959	40	181	606	764	3,133	2,346
1998	3,942	40	173	610	735	3,119	2,361
1997	3,881	39	170	600	710	3,073	2,333
1996	3,892	38	166	595	701	3,093	2,359
1995	3,900	37	160	603	680	3,099	2,383
1994	3,953	38	158	636	665	3,121	2,439
1993	4,000	39	153	659	654	3,150	2,472
1992	4,065	40	150	674	643	3,202	2,527
1991	4,111	39	145	683	623	3,241	2,590
1990	4,158	39	142	684	595	3,290	2,627
1989	4,041	39	133	673	532	3,192	2,526
1988	3,910	37	129	639	450	3,102	–
1987	3,809	35	117	611	406	3,044	–
1986	3,757	34	108	593	–	3,019	–
1985	3,761	34	105	581	373	3,038	–
1984	3,669	33	99	568	–	2,967	–
1983	3,639	33	96	563	–	2,946	–
1982	3,681	32	93	569	–	2,985	–
1981	3,629	30	85	565	–	2,948	–
1980	3,612	29	74	568	–	2,936	–
1975	3,168	28	–	512	–	2,552	–
1970	3,731	26	–	572	–	3,091	–
1965	3,760	24	–	581	–	3,124	–
1960	4,258	21	–	602	–	3,601	–
1955	4,097	–	–	613	–	3,485	–
1950	3,632	–	–	524	–	3,108	–
Percent change							
1990 to 2000	–2.4%	7.6%	41.9%	–9.0%	37.1%	–2.9%	–10.0%
1950 to 2000	11.8	–	–	18.9	–	2.8	–

Note: Race of child before 1980, race of mother 1980 and after; blacks in 1955 and 1950 include black and "other" races; numbers will not add to total because Hispanics may be of any race; (–) means data not available or not applicable.
Source: National Center for Health Statistics, Births: Final Data for 2000, *National Vital Statistics Report, Vol. 50, No. 5, 2002; and Bureau of the Census,* Statistical Abstract of the United States 1990 *and* 1991; *calculations by New Strategist*

Table 3.8   Distribution of Births by Race and Hispanic Origin, 1950 to 2000

(percent distribution of births by race and Hispanic origin, 1950 to 2000; percentage point change for selected years)

	total	American Indian	Asian	black	Hispanic	white total	white non-Hispanic
2000	100.0%	1.0%	5.0%	15.3%	20.1%	78.7%	58.2%
1999	100.0	1.0	4.6	15.3	19.3	79.1	59.3
1998	100.0	1.0	4.4	15.5	18.6	79.1	59.9
1997	100.0	1.0	4.4	15.5	18.3	79.2	60.1
1996	100.0	1.0	4.3	15.3	18.0	79.5	60.6
1995	100.0	1.0	4.1	15.5	17.4	79.5	61.1
1994	100.0	1.0	4.0	16.1	16.8	79.0	61.7
1993	100.0	1.0	3.8	16.5	16.4	78.7	61.8
1992	100.0	1.0	3.7	16.6	15.8	78.8	62.2
1991	100.0	0.9	3.5	16.6	15.2	78.8	63.0
1990	100.0	0.9	3.4	16.5	14.3	79.1	63.2
1989	100.0	1.0	3.3	16.7	13.2	79.0	62.5
1988	100.0	0.9	3.3	16.3	11.5	79.3	–
1987	100.0	0.9	3.1	16.0	10.7	79.9	–
1986	100.0	0.9	2.9	15.8	–	80.4	–
1985	100.0	0.9	2.8	15.4	9.9	80.8	–
1984	100.0	0.9	2.7	15.5	–	80.9	–
1983	100.0	0.9	2.6	15.5	–	81.0	–
1982	100.0	0.9	2.5	15.5	–	81.1	–
1981	100.0	0.8	2.3	15.6	–	81.2	–
1980	100.0	0.8	2.1	15.7	–	81.3	–
1975	100.0	0.9	–	16.2	–	80.6	–
1970	100.0	0.7	–	15.3	–	82.8	–
1965	100.0	0.6	–	15.5	–	83.1	–
1960	100.0	0.5	–	14.1	–	84.6	–
1955	100.0	–	–	15.0	–	85.1	–
1950	100.0	–	–	14.4	–	85.6	–
Percentage point change							
1990 to 2000	–	0.1	1.5	–1.1	5.8	–0.4	–4.9
1950 to 2000	–	–	–	0.9	–	–6.9	–

Note: Race of child before 1980, race of mother 1980 and after; blacks in 1955 and 1950 include black and "other" races; numbers will not add to 100 because Hispanics may be of any race; (–) means data not available or not applicable.
Source: National Center for Health Statistics, Births: Final Data for 2000, *National Vital Statistics Report, Vol. 50, No. 5, 2002; and Bureau of the Census,* Statistical Abstract of the United States 1990 *and* 1991; *calculations by New Strategist*

Table 3.9 Birth Rates by Race and Hispanic Origin, 1950 to 2000

(number of live births per 1,000 women aged 15 to 44 by race and Hispanic origin, 1950 to 2000; percent change for selected years)

	total	American Indian	Asian	black	Hispanic	white total	white non-Hispanic
2000	67.5	71.4	70.7	71.7	105.9	66.5	58.5
1999	65.9	69.7	65.6	70.1	102.0	65.1	57.8
1998	65.6	70.7	64.0	71.0	101.1	64.6	57.7
1997	65.0	69.1	66.3	70.7	102.8	63.9	57.0
1996	65.3	68.7	65.9	70.7	104.9	64.3	57.3
1995	65.6	69.1	66.4	72.3	105.0	64.4	57.6
1994	66.7	70.9	66.8	76.9	105.6	64.9	58.3
1993	67.6	73.4	66.7	80.5	106.9	65.4	59.0
1992	68.9	75.4	67.2	83.2	108.6	66.5	60.2
1991	69.6	75.1	67.6	85.2	108.1	67.0	61.0
1990	70.9	76.2	69.6	86.8	107.7	68.3	62.8
1989	69.2	79.0	68.2	86.2	104.9	66.4	60.5
1988	67.3	76.8	70.2	82.6	–	64.5	–
1987	65.8	75.6	67.1	80.1	–	63.3	–
1986	65.4	75.9	66.0	78.9	–	63.1	–
1985	66.3	78.6	68.4	78.8	–	64.1	–
1984	65.5	79.8	69.2	78.2	–	63.2	–
1983	65.7	81.8	71.7	78.7	–	63.4	–
1982	67.3	83.6	74.8	80.9	–	64.8	–
1981	67.3	79.6	73.7	82.0	–	64.8	–
1980	68.4	82.7	73.2	84.7	–	65.6	–
1975	66.0	–	–	87.9	–	62.5	–
1970	87.9	–	–	115.4	–	84.1	–
1965	96.3	–	–	133.2	–	91.3	–
1960	118.0	–	–	153.5	–	113.2	–
1955	118.3	–	–	155.3	–	113.7	–
1950	106.2	–	–	137.3	–	102.3	–
Percent change							
1990 to 2000	–4.8%	–6.3%	1.6%	–17.4%	–1.7%	–2.6%	–6.8%
1950 to 2000	–36.4	–	–	–47.8	–	–35.0	–

Note: Race of child before 1980, race of mother 1980 and after; blacks in 1955 and 1950 include black and "other" races; (–) means data not available or not applicable.
Source: Bureau of the Census, Historical Statistics of the United States: Colonial Times to 1970, Part 1, *1975; National Center for Health Statistics,* Births: Final Data for 2000, *National Vital Statistics Report, Vol. 50, No. 5, 2002; calculations by New Strategist*

Table 3.10 Births to Unmarried Women, 1950 to 2000

(total number of births, number to unmarried women, and unmarried share of total, 1950 to 2000; percent and percentage point change for selected years; numbers in thousands)

	total births	births to unmarried women	
		number	share of total
2000	4,059	1,347	33.2%
1999	3,959	1,305	33.0
1998	3,942	1,294	32.8
1997	3,881	1,257	32.4
1996	3,891	1,260	32.4
1995	3,900	1,254	32.2
1994	3,953	1,290	32.6
1993	4,000	1,240	31.0
1992	4,065	1,225	30.1
1991	4,111	1,214	29.5
1990	4,158	1,165	28.0
1989	4,041	1,094	27.1
1988	3,910	1,005	25.7
1987	3,809	933	24.5
1986	3,757	878	23.4
1985	3,761	828	22.0
1984	3,669	770	21.0
1983	3,639	738	20.3
1982	3,681	715	19.4
1981	3,629	687	18.9
1980	3,612	666	18.4
1979	3,494	598	17.1
1978	3,333	544	16.3
1977	3,327	516	15.5
1976	3,168	468	14.8
1975	3,144	448	14.3
1974	3,160	418	13.2
1973	3,137	407	13.0
1972	3,258	403	12.4
1971	3,556	401	11.3
1970	3,731	399	10.7
1969	3,600	361	10.0
1968	3,502	339	9.7
1967	3,521	318	9.0
1966	3,606	302	8.4
1965	3,760	291	7.7
1964	4,027	276	6.9
1963	4,098	259	6.3
1962	4,167	245	5.9
1961	4,268	240	5.6
1960	4,258	224	5.3
1959	4,245	221	5.2
1958	4,255	209	5.0
1957	4,308	202	4.7
1956	4,218	194	4.7
1955	4,097	183	4.5
1954	4,078	177	4.4
1953	3,965	161	4.1
1952	3,913	150	3.9
1951	3,823	147	3.9
1950	3,632	142	3.9

	percent change		percentage point change
1990 to 2000	−2.4%	15.6%	5.2
1950 to 2000	11.8	848.6	29.3

Source: National Center for Health Statistics, Births: Final Data for 2000, *National Vital Statistics Report, Vol. 50, No. 5, 2002; and* Nonmarital Childbearing in the United States, 1940–99, *National Vital Statistics Report, Vol. 48, No. 16, 2000; calculations by New Strategist*

Table 3.11 Births to Unmarried Women by Race and Hispanic Origin, 1950 to 2000

(births to unmarried women as a percent of total births by race and Hispanic origin, 1950 to 2000)

	total	American Indian	Asian	black	Hispanic	white total	white non-Hispanic
2000	33.2%	58.4%	14.8%	68.5%	42.7%	27.1%	22.1%
1999	33.0	58.9	15.4	68.9	42.2	26.8	22.1
1998	32.8	59.3	15.6	69.1	41.6	26.3	21.9
1997	32.4	58.7	15.6	69.2	40.9	25.8	21.5
1996	32.4	58.0	16.7	69.8	40.7	25.7	21.5
1995	32.2	57.2	16.3	69.9	40.8	25.3	21.2
1994	32.6	57.0	16.2	70.4	43.1	25.4	20.8
1993	31.0	55.8	15.7	68.7	40.0	23.6	19.5
1992	30.1	55.3	14.7	68.1	39.1	22.6	18.5
1991	29.5	55.0	13.9	67.9	38.5	21.8	18.0
1990	28.0	53.6	13.2	66.5	36.7	20.4	16.9
1989	27.1	–	–	65.7	35.5	19.2	–
1988	25.7	45.6	12.0	64.7	34.0	18.0	–
1987	24.5	–	–	63.4	32.7	16.9	–
1986	23.4	–	–	62.4	–	15.9	–
1985	22.0	40.7	9.5	61.2	29.5	14.7	12.4
1984	21.0	–	–	60.3	–	13.6	–
1983	20.3	–	–	59.2	–	12.9	–
1982	19.4	–	–	57.7	–	12.3	–
1981	18.9	–	–	56.9	–	11.8	–
1980	18.4	39.2	7.3	56.1	23.6	11.2	9.6
1975	14.3	32.7	–	49.5	–	7.3	–
1970	10.7	22.4	–	37.6	–	5.7	–
1965	7.7	–	–	26.3	–	4.0	–
1960	5.3	–	–	21.6	–	2.3	–
1955	4.5	–	–	19.4	–	1.8	–
1950	4.0	–	–	16.8	–	1.7	–
Percentage point change							
1990 to 2000	5.2	5.7	2.4	2.6	4.9	5.9	5.0
1950 to 2000	29.2	–	–	51.7	–	25.4	–

Note: Births to unmarried blacks before 1970 are to black and "other" races; (–) means data not available.
Source: National Center for Health Statistics, Health, United States, 2001; and Births: Final Data for 2000, National Vital Statistics Report, Vol. 50, No. 5, 2002; and Nonmarital Childbearing in the United States, 1940–99, National Vital Statistics Report, Vol. 48, No. 16, 2000; and Bureau of the Census, Statistical Abstract of the United States 1980, 1990, 1991, and 1992; calculations by New Strategist

People Are Fatter but Fitter

Americans may feel better than they once did, but they're fatter than ever. The proportion of people aged 20 to 74 who can be classified as obese (meaning they have a body mass index of 30 or higher) rose from 14 percent in 1960–62 to 26 percent in 1999.

Despite the weight gain, people were less likely to have high cholesterol or hypertension in the early 1990s than in the 1960s. The percentage of people aged 20 to 74 with high cholesterol fell from 34 percent in 1960–62 to 19 percent in 1988–94. Similarly, the percentage of Americans with hypertension fell from 39 to 23 percent during those years. Every age group experienced a decline in these indicators as people learned of the dangers of high cholesterol and hypertension.

One lifestyle change that contributed significantly to Americans' improved health is the decline in cigarette smoking. The percentage of people aged 18 or older who smoke fell from 42 to 23 percent between 1965 and 2000. Cigarette smoking also fell among high school seniors between 1975 and 2000, but marijuana use increased.

More Americans are obese

(percent of people aged 20 to 74 who are obese, 1960–62 to 1999)

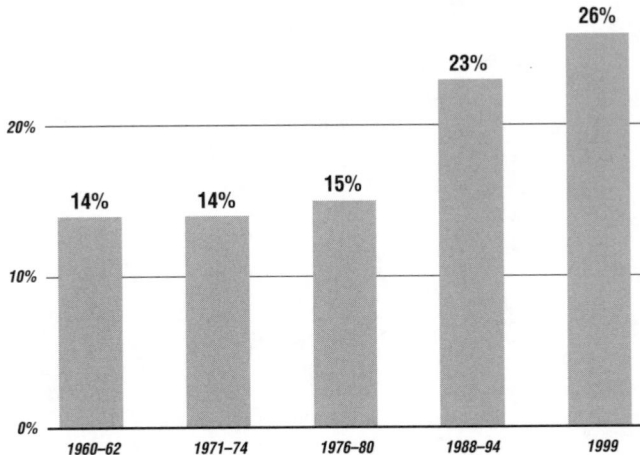

Table 3.12 Obesity by Sex and Age, 1960–62 to 1999

(percent of people aged 20 to 74 who are obese by sex and age, 1960–62 to 1999)

	1999	*1988–94*	*1976–80*	*1971–74*	*1960–62*
Total people	26%	23%	15%	14%	14%
Total men	–	20	12	12	11
Aged 20 to 34	–	14	9	10	9
Aged 35 to 44	–	22	14	14	12
Aged 45 to 54	–	23	17	14	13
Aged 55 to 64	–	27	14	14	9
Aged 65 to 74	–	24	13	11	10
Total women	–	26	17	17	16
Aged 20 to 34	–	19	11	10	7
Aged 35 to 44	–	26	18	18	15
Aged 45 to 54	–	32	20	19	20
Aged 55 to 64	–	34	23	24	24
Aged 65 to 74	–	27	22	22	23

Note: People with a body mass index of 30 or higher are considered obese. BMI is defined as weight in kilograms divided by height in meters squared. (–) means data are not available.
Source: National Center for Health Statistics, Health, United States, 2001; *and Health E-Stats, Internet site http://www.cdc.gov/ nchs/products/pubs/pubd/hestats/obese/obse99.htm; calculations by New Strategist*

Table 3.13 Hypertension by Sex and Age, 1960–62 to 1988–94

(percent of people aged 20 to 74 with hypertension by sex and age, 1960–62 to 1988–94; and percentage point change, 1960–62 to 1988–94)

	1988–94	*1976–80*	*1971–74*	*1960–62*	*percentage point change 1960–62 to 1988–94*
Total people	**23%**	**40%**	**40%**	**39%**	**–16**
Total men	**25**	**44**	**43**	**42**	**–17**
Aged 20 to 34	9	29	25	23	–14
Aged 35 to 44	21	41	39	38	–17
Aged 45 to 54	34	54	55	48	–14
Aged 55 to 64	43	62	63	60	–17
Aged 65 to 74	57	67	67	69	–12
Total women	**22**	**36**	**37**	**37**	**–15**
Aged 20 to 34	3	11	11	9	–6
Aged 35 to 44	13	29	28	24	–11
Aged 45 to 54	25	47	44	43	–18
Aged 55 to 64	44	61	63	66	–22
Aged 65 to 74	61	72	78	82	–21

Note: A person who has systolic pressure of at least 140 mmHg or diastolic pressure of at least 90 mmHg, or who takes antiphypertensive medication, is considered to have hypertension.
Source: National Center for Health Statistics, Health, United States, 2001; *calculations by New Strategist*

Table 3.14 High Cholesterol by Sex and Age, 1960–62 to 1988–94

(percent of people aged 20 to 74 with high serum cholesterol by sex and age, 1960–62 to 1988–94; and percentage point change, 1960–62 to 1988–94)

	1988–94	1976–80	1971–74	1960–62	percentage point change 1960–62 to 1988–94
Total people	19%	27%	28%	34%	–15
Total men	18	25	27	31	–13
Aged 20 to 34	8	12	12	15	–7
Aged 35 to 44	19	28	32	34	–15
Aged 45 to 54	27	37	38	39	–13
Aged 55 to 64	28	37	36	42	–14
Aged 65 to 74	22	32	35	38	–16
Total women	20	29	30	36	–16
Aged 20 to 34	7	10	11	12	–5
Aged 35 to 44	12	21	19	23	–11
Aged 45 to 54	27	41	39	47	–20
Aged 55 to 64	41	53	53	70	–29
Aged 65 to 74	41	52	58	69	–27

Note: High cholesterol is defined as 240 mg/dL or more.
Source: National Center for Health Statistics, Health, United States, 2001; *calculations by New Strategist*

Table 3.15 Cigarette Smoking by Sex and Age, 1965 to 2000

(percent of people aged 18 or older who smoke cigarettes by sex and age, 1965 to 2000; percentage point change for selected years)

	total, both sexes	men						women					
		total	18–24	25–34	35–44	45–64	65+	total	18–24	25–34	35–44	45–64	65+
2000	23.3%	25.7%	28.5%	29.0%	30.2%	26.4%	10.2%	21.0%	25.1%	22.5%	26.2%	21.6%	9.3%
1999	23.5	25.7	29.5	29.1	30.0	25.8	10.5	21.5	26.3	23.5	26.5	21.0	10.7
1998	24.1	26.4	31.3	28.5	30.2	27.7	10.4	22.0	24.5	24.6	26.4	22.5	11.2
1997	24.7	27.6	31.7	30.3	32.1	27.6	12.8	22.1	25.7	24.8	27.2	21.5	11.5
1995	24.7	27.0	27.8	29.5	31.5	27.1	14.9	22.6	21.8	26.4	27.1	24.0	11.5
1994	25.5	28.2	29.8	31.4	33.2	28.3	13.2	23.1	25.2	28.8	26.8	22.8	11.1
1993	25.0	27.7	28.8	30.2	32.0	29.2	13.5	22.5	22.9	27.3	27.4	23.0	10.5
1992	26.5	28.6	28.0	32.8	32.9	28.6	16.1	24.6	24.9	30.1	27.3	26.1	12.4
1991	25.6	28.1	23.5	32.8	33.1	29.3	15.1	23.5	22.4	28.4	27.6	24.6	12.0
1990	25.5	28.4	26.6	31.6	34.5	29.3	14.6	22.8	22.5	28.2	24.8	24.8	11.5
1988	28.1	30.8	25.5	36.2	36.5	31.3	18.0	25.7	26.3	31.3	27.8	27.7	12.8
1987	28.8	31.2	28.2	34.8	36.8	33.5	17.2	26.5	26.1	31.8	29.6	28.6	13.7
1985	30.1	32.6	28.0	38.2	37.6	33.4	19.6	27.9	30.4	32.0	31.5	29.9	13.5
1983	32.1	35.1	32.9	38.8	41.0	35.9	22.0	29.5	35.5	32.6	33.8	31.0	13.1
1979	33.5	37.5	35.0	43.9	41.8	39.3	20.9	29.9	33.8	33.7	37.0	30.7	13.2
1974	37.1	43.1	42.1	50.5	51.0	42.6	24.8	32.1	34.1	38.8	39.8	33.4	12.0
1965	42.4	51.9	54.1	60.7	58.2	51.9	28.5	33.9	38.1	43.7	43.7	32.0	9.6
Percentage point change													
1990 to 2000	–2.2	–2.7	1.9	–2.6	–4.3	–2.9	–4.4	–1.8	2.6	–5.7	1.4	–3.2	–2.2
1965 to 2000	–19.1	–26.2	–25.6	–31.7	–28.0	–25.5	–18.3	–12.9	–13.0	–21.2	–17.5	–10.4	–0.3

Source: National Center for Health Statistics, Health, United States, 2002; and Bureau of the Census, calculations by New Strategist

Table 3.16 Lifetime Drug Use by 12th Graders, 1975 to 2000

(percent of 12th graders who have ever used drugs, drunk alcohol, or smoked cigarettes, by type of substance, 1975 to 2000; percentage point change for selected years)

Class of:	any illicit drug	any illicit drug except marijuana	marijuana/ hashish	inhalants	hallucinogens any	LSD	PCP	Ecstasy	cocaine	heroin	amphet- amines	sedatives	tranquilizers	alcohol	cigarettes
2000	54.0%	29.0%	48.8%	14.6%	13.6%	11.1%	3.4%	11.0%	8.6%	2.4%	15.6%	9.3%	8.9%	80.3%	62.5%
1999	54.7	29.4	49.7	16.0	14.2	12.2	3.4	8.0	9.8	2.0	16.3	9.5	9.3	80.0	64.6
1998	54.1	29.4	49.1	16.5	14.4	12.6	3.9	5.8	9.3	2.0	16.4	9.2	8.5	81.4	65.3
1997	54.3	30.0	49.6	16.9	15.4	13.6	3.9	6.9	8.7	2.1	16.5	8.7	7.8	81.7	65.4
1996	50.8	28.5	44.9	17.5	14.5	12.6	4.0	6.1	7.1	1.8	15.3	8.2	7.2	79.2	63.5
1995	48.4	28.1	41.7	17.8	13.1	11.7	2.7	–	6.0	1.6	15.3	7.6	7.1	80.7	64.2
1994	45.6	27.6	38.2	18.3	11.7	10.5	2.8	–	5.9	1.2	15.7	7.3	6.6	80.4	62.0
1993	42.9	26.7	35.3	17.7	11.3	10.3	2.9	–	6.1	1.1	15.1	6.4	6.4	80.0	61.9
1992	40.7	25.1	32.6	17.0	9.4	8.6	2.4	–	6.1	1.2	13.9	6.1	6.0	87.5	61.8
1991	44.1	26.9	36.7	18.0	10.0	8.8	2.9	–	7.8	0.9	15.4	6.7	7.2	88.0	63.1
1990	47.9	29.4	40.7	18.5	9.7	8.7	2.8	–	9.4	1.3	17.5	7.5	7.2	89.5	64.4
1989	50.9	31.4	43.7	18.6	9.9	8.3	3.9	–	10.3	1.3	19.1	7.4	7.6	90.7	65.7
1988	53.9	32.5	47.2	17.5	9.2	7.7	2.9	–	12.1	1.1	19.8	7.8	9.4	92.0	66.4
1987	56.6	35.8	50.2	18.6	10.6	8.4	3.0	–	15.2	1.2	21.6	8.7	10.9	92.2	67.2
1986	57.6	37.7	50.9	20.1	11.9	7.2	4.8	–	16.9	1.1	23.4	10.4	10.9	91.3	67.6
1985	60.6	39.7	54.2	18.1	12.1	7.5	4.9	–	17.3	1.2	26.2	11.8	11.9	92.2	68.8
1984	61.6	40.3	54.9	18.0	12.3	8.0	5.0	–	16.1	1.3	27.9	13.3	12.4	92.6	69.7
1983	62.9	40.4	57.0	18.2	13.6	8.9	5.6	–	16.2	1.2	26.9	14.4	13.3	92.6	70.6
1982	64.4	41.1	58.7	17.7	14.3	9.6	6.0	–	16.0	1.2	27.9	15.2	14.0	92.8	70.1
1981	65.6	42.8	59.5	17.2	15.3	9.8	7.8	–	16.5	1.1	32.2	16.0	14.7	92.6	71.0
1980	65.4	38.7	60.3	17.3	15.6	9.3	9.6	–	15.7	1.1	26.4	14.9	15.2	93.2	71.0

(continued)

(continued from previous page)

Class of:	any illicit drug	any illicit drug except marijuana	marijuana/hashish	inhalants	hallucinogens any	LSD	PCP	Ecstasy	cocaine	heroin	amphet-amines	sedatives	tranquilizers	alcohol	cigarettes
1979	65.1%	37.4%	60.4%	18.2%	17.7%	9.5%	12.8%	–	15.4%	1.1%	24.2%	14.6%	16.3%	93.0%	74.0%
1978	64.1	36.5	59.2	12.0	14.3	9.7	–	–	12.9	1.6	22.9	16.0	17.0	93.1	75.3
1977	61.6	35.8	56.4	11.1	13.9	9.8	–	–	10.8	1.8	23.0	17.4	18.0	92.5	75.7
1976	58.3	35.4	52.8	10.3	15.1	11.0	–	–	9.7	1.8	22.6	17.7	16.8	91.9	75.4
1975	55.2	36.2	47.3	–	16.3	11.3	–	–	9.0	2.2	22.3	18.2	17.0	90.4	73.6
Percentage point change															
1990 to 2000	6.1	–0.4	8.1	–3.9	3.9	2.4	0.6	–	–0.8	1.1	–1.9	1.8	1.7	–9.2	–1.9
1975 to 2000	–1.2	–7.2	1.5	–	–2.7	–0.2	–	–	–0.4	0.2	–6.7	–8.9	–8.1	–10.1	–11.1

Note: Beginning in 1979, percentages of inhalant and hallucinogen users were adjusted for underreporting; beginning in 1993, the question regarding alcohol use was changed to indicate that having a drink meant drinking more than a few sips. (–) means data not available.
Source: University of Michigan, Monitoring the Future Study, Internet site http://monitoringthefuture.org/; calculations by New Strategist

Outpatient Care at Hospitals Has Soared

The percentage of the population covered by health insurance has remained stable since 1980. In 2000, 86 percent of Americans had health insurance, up slightly from 85 percent in 1985. Because the population has grown, however, the number of people without health insurance has increased.

As health care costs mounted and health insurers limited medical care reimbursements, hospitals have shifted their services toward less expensive outpatient care. The number of people admitted to hospitals grew only 10 percent between 1970 and 2000, much slower than the 38 percent population growth during those years. Outpatients visits soared, however, rising 227 percent. Hospitals cared for 593,000 outpatients in 2000, up from 181,000 in 1970.

Even surgery has become an outpatient service. Outpatient surgery accounted for 63 percent of all surgeries in 2000, up from just 16 percent in 1980.

Hospitals see many more outpatients

(percent change in number of hospital admissions and outpatient visits, 1970 to 2000)

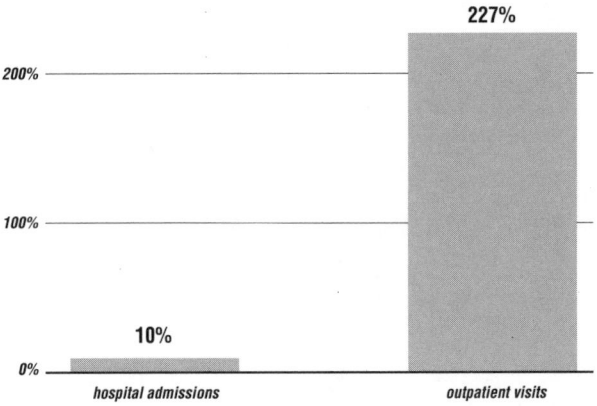

Table 3.17   Heath Insurance Coverage, 1985 to 2000

(total number of people, and number and percent covered by health insurance, 1985 to 2000; numbers in thousands)

	total	with private or government health insurance	
		number	percent
2000	276,540	237,857	86.0%
1999	274,087	234,807	85.7
1998	271,743	227,462	83.7
1997	269,094	225,646	83.9
1996	266,792	225,077	84.4
1995	264,314	223,733	84.6
1994	262,105	222,387	84.8
1993	259,753	220,040	84.7
1992	256,830	218,189	85.0
1991	251,447	216,003	85.9
1990	248,886	214,167	86.1
1989	246,191	212,807	86.4
1988	243,685	211,005	86.6
1987	241,187	210,161	87.1
1986	236,700	202,600	85.6
1985	234,000	199,400	85.2

Source: Bureau of the Census, Statistical Abstract of the United States 1990*; and Internet site http://www.census.gov/hhes/ hlthins/historic/hihistt1.html*

Table 3.18   Hospital Admissions, Outpatient Visits, and Outpatient Surgery, 1970 to 2000

(number of admissions to hospitals, number of outpatient visits to hospitals, and outpatient surgery as a percent of total surgery in community hospitals, 1970 to 2000; percent change in admissions and outpatient visits, and percentage point change in outpatient surgery for selected years; numbers in thousands)

	hospital admissions	outpatient visits	outpatient surgery (community hospitals only)
2000	34,891	592,673	62.7%
1999	34,181	573,461	62.4
1998	33,766	545,481	61.6
1997	33,624	520,600	60.7
1996	33,307	505,455	59.5
1995	33,282	483,195	58.1
1994	33,125	453,584	57.2
1993	33,201	435,619	55.4
1992	33,536	417,874	53.8
1991	33,567	387,675	52.3
1990	33,774	368,184	50.6
1989	33,742	352,200	48.7
1988	34,107	336,200	46.8
1987	34,439	310,700	43.4
1986	35,219	294,600	40.3
1985	36,304	282,140	34.6
1984	37,938	276,566	27.8
1983	38,887	273,168	23.8
1982	39,095	313,667	20.8
1981	39,169	265,332	18.5
1980	38,892	262,951	16.3
1979	37,802	262,009	–
1978	37,243	263,606	–
1977	37,060	263,775	–
1976	36,776	270,951	–
1975	36,157	254,844	–
1974	35,506	250,481	–
1973	34,352	233,555	–
1972	33,265	219,182	–
1971	32,664	199,725	–
1970	31,759	181,370	–

	percent change		percentage point change
1990 to 2000	3.3%	61.0%	12.1
1970 to 2000	9.9	226.8	–

Note: Community hospitals include all short-term care, nonfederal hospitals; (–) means data not available.
Source: Hospital Statistics™ 2000 *edition, Health Forum LLC, An American Hospital Association Company,* © 2002

Increasingly, Cancer Is a Treatable Condition

The incidence of many types of cancers in the U.S. is declining. The overall cancer incidence rate remained stable for women between 1990 and 1997, while it fell 6 percent for men. Women experienced double-digit declines in the incidence of cervical and stomach cancer. Men experienced double-digit declines for many more types of cancer including colon, leukemia, lung, oral cavity, and stomach. The incidence of breast cancer and non-Hodgkin's lymphoma increased among women, while the incidence of prostate cancer and non-Hodgkin's lymphoma rose among men.

Cancer survival rates are increasing for most types of cancer thanks to early detection and better medical care. Cancer is becoming a treatable condition rather than a death sentence. Among whites, 60 percent of men and 63 percent of women with cancer survive at least five years. The five-year survival rate for breast cancer grew from 75 to 86 percent between 1974–79 and 1989–96. Among blacks, cancer survival rates rose as well, but they remain below 50 percent.

More survive cancer

(percent of people with cancer surviving five years relative to the survival rate of their cohort, 1974–75 and 1989–96)

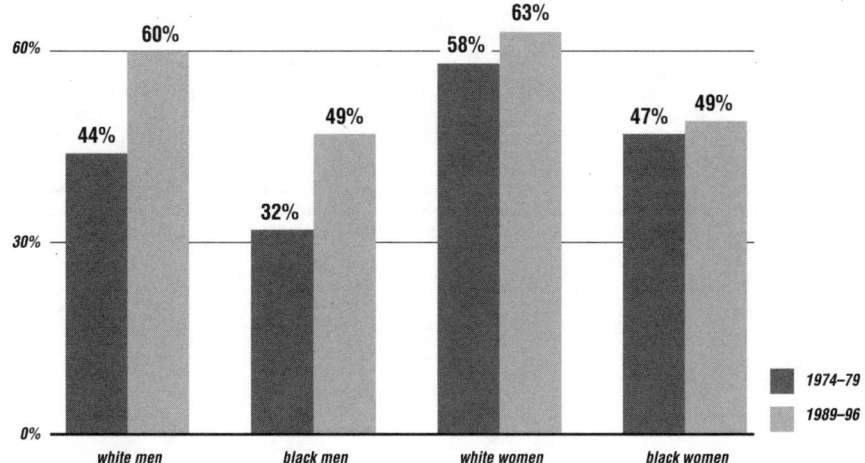

Table 3.19 Cancer Incidence Rate by Sex, 1990 to 1997

(number of new cases of cancer per 100,000 age-adjusted population by sex and selected cancer site, 1990 to 1997; percent change in rate, 1990–97)

	1997	1996	1995	1994	1993	1992	1991	1990	percent change 1990–97
Female, total	**343.4**	**343.5**	**342.7**	**341.3**	**340.0**	**344.3**	**347.2**	**345.7**	**–0.7%**
Breast	113.1	110.9	110.1	108.6	107.1	109.4	109.8	108.6	4.1
Cervix uteri	8.0	8.8	8.3	9.0	9.0	9.2	9.1	9.9	–19.2
Colon and rectum	36.0	35.6	35.8	36.2	37.3	37.8	38.6	39.5	–8.9
Corpus uteri	21.5	21.0	21.5	21.1	20.5	21.2	21.1	21.5	0.0
Lung and bronchus	40.7	41.9	41.7	41.8	41.8	42.0	41.9	41.0	–0.7
Non-Hodgkin's lymphoma	12.5	12.3	12.3	12.6	12.0	12.0	11.9	12.1	3.3
Oral cavity and pharynx	5.7	5.8	5.8	5.7	6.1	5.8	6.3	6.3	–9.5
Ovary	13.9	14.2	14.6	14.4	15.1	15.0	15.1	15.3	–9.2
Pancreas	7.5	7.6	7.8	7.8	7.7	7.9	8.1	7.9	–5.1
Stomach	4.6	4.7	4.8	4.8	5.0	5.1	5.4	5.2	–11.5
Urinary bladder	7.2	7.0	7.4	7.3	7.5	7.6	7.4	7.5	–4.0
Male, total	**443.4**	**454.1**	**458.2**	**472.5**	**498.6**	**527.2**	**507.1**	**472.8**	**–6.2**
Colon and rectum	51.0	50.4	49.6	51.7	52.8	54.8	56.8	57.2	–10.8
Leukemia	12.2	12.8	13.8	13.1	13.3	14.2	13.8	14.0	–12.9
Lung and bronchus	63.7	66.7	69.7	71.2	73.1	75.8	77.2	79.0	–19.4
Non-Hodgkin's lymphoma	18.7	19.9	20.5	20.0	19.1	19.0	19.2	18.6	0.5
Oral cavity and pharynx	13.9	14.7	14.3	15.1	15.5	15.8	15.8	16.3	–14.7
Pancreas	9.7	9.9	9.9	10.3	10.0	10.3	10.2	10.5	–7.6
Prostate gland	136.0	135.7	136.4	145.3	167.8	187.4	165.6	129.7	4.9
Stomach	10.2	10.7	10.7	11.3	11.3	11.4	11.6	11.6	–12.1
Urinary bladder	27.2	27.4	27.6	28.4	28.9	29.1	29.4	29.5	–7.8

Note: Age-adjusted incidence rates are calculated by applying age specific incidence rates in each year to a standard population with a fixed age distribution. They should be viewed as an index rather than an actual measure of cancer risk.
Source: National Center for Health Statistics, Health United States, 2001; *calculations by New Strategist*

Table 3.20 Cancer Survival Rates by Sex and Race, 1974–79 to 1989–96

(ratio of the five-year survival rate for the patient group to the expected five-year survival rate for people of that age, sex, and race, 1974–79 to 1989–96; percentage point change in rate, 1974–79 to 1989–96)

	1989–96	1986–88	1983–85	1980–82	1974–79	percentage point change 1974–79 to 1989–96
White male, total	**60.1**	**51.8**	**48.5**	**46.7**	**43.5**	**16.6**
Oral cavity and pharynx	53.7	52.2	54.5	54.4	54.3	-0.6
Esophagus	13.1	11.4	7.8	6.6	5.0	8.1
Stomach	17.1	16.1	14.5	15.4	13.9	3.2
Colon	63.2	62.4	59.0	56.0	50.9	12.3
Rectum	60.2	58.8	55.3	51.4	49.0	11.2
Pancreas	3.8	2.9	2.6	2.6	2.7	1.1
Lung and bronchus	12.9	12.1	12.1	12.2	11.6	1.3
Prostate gland	94.1	82.7	76.3	74.5	70.4	23.7
Urinary bladder	84.0	82.2	79.6	80.0	76.0	8.0
Non-Hodgkin's lymphoma	48.7	50.2	53.5	50.9	47.1	1.6
Leukemia	46.5	45.2	41.3	39.6	35.8	10.7
Black male, total	**48.5**	**37.7**	**34.6**	**34.4**	**32.1**	**16.4**
Oral cavity and pharynx	29.0	29.3	30.0	26.3	31.2	-2.2
Esophagus	8.6	7.1	5.2	4.6	2.3	6.3
Stomach	20.5	14.8	18.5	18.5	15.4	5.1
Colon	52.8	52.1	48.4	46.7	45.4	7.4
Rectum	52.4	46.7	42.3	35.9	36.9	15.5
Pancreas	4.0	6.5	4.8	3.6	2.4	1.6
Lung and bronchus	10.1	12.0	10.2	11.0	10.0	0.1
Prostate gland	86.7	69.3	63.9	64.7	60.8	25.9
Urinary bladder	67.3	67.5	64.8	63.5	59.1	8.2
Non-Hodgkin's lymphoma	37.4	46.7	43.6	47.0	45.0	-7.6
Leukemia	31.9	35.9	32.3	30.4	31.0	0.9
White female, total	**63.0**	**61.5**	**58.8**	**57.1**	**57.5**	**5.5**
Colon	62.1	60.7	57.9	55.4	52.6	9.5
Rectum	61.5	59.6	56.6	54.6	50.9	10.6
Pancreas	4.5	3.4	3.2	3.0	2.2	2.3
Lung and bronchus	16.6	15.9	17.1	16.3	16.7	-0.1
Melanoma of skin	91.7	91.2	89.3	88.3	86.0	5.7
Breast	86.3	83.9	79.3	77.1	75.4	10.9
Cervix uteri	71.6	71.7	70.3	68.0	69.7	1.9
Corpus uteri	85.6	84.4	84.6	82.8	87.8	-2.2
Ovary	50.1	42.0	40.2	38.8	37.2	12.9
Non-Hodgkin's lymphoma	57.5	56.1	55.4	52.9	49.3	8.2
Black female, total	**49.3**	**47.8**	**45.4**	**45.9**	**46.8**	**2.5**
Colon	51.8	53.1	50.0	50.9	48.7	3.1
Rectum	52.2	55.5	44.5	40.7	43.3	8.9
Pancreas	3.6	5.6	5.9	5.8	4.1	-0.5
Lung and bronchus	13.5	11.8	14.2	15.5	15.5	-2.0
Melanoma of skin	78.5	–	70.1	–	69.9	8.6
Breast	71.4	69.4	63.5	65.8	63.1	8.3
Cervix uteri	58.6	55.3	50.2	61.2	62.9	-4.3
Corpus uteri	56.9	56.7	53.9	54.5	59.3	-2.4
Ovary	47.5	38.5	41.7	38.3	40.1	7.4
Non-Hodgkin's lymphoma	49.4	54.1	46.5	53.6	57.6	-8.2

Note: (–) means data not available.

Source: National Center for Health Statistics, Health, United States, 2001; *calculations by New Strategist*

AIDS Threat Diminishes

Nearly 775,000 Americans were diagnosed with AIDS from the time the disease was identified in the early 1980s through 2000. While still a significant cause of death, human immunodeficiency virus infection—like cancer—is becoming a more treatable condition. New drug concoctions have extended the life expectancy of AIDS patients and reduced deaths. In 1996, AIDS was the eighth leading cause of death. By 2000, it did not rank among the top 15, although it was the fifth ranking cause of death among 25-to-44-year-olds.

Among those diagnosed with AIDS through 2000, 83 percent were males and 17 percent females. The female share has been rising, reaching 25 percent among those diagnosed in 2000. Forty-three percent of people diagnosed with AIDS through 2000 were non-Hispanic white and 38 percent non-Hispanic black. But among those diagnosed in 2000, the black share stood at 47 percent, larger than the 32 percent white share. Hispanics account for 18 percent of those diagnosed with AIDS through 2000.

AIDS strikes blacks hard

(percent of people diagnosed with AIDS who are non-Hispanic black, 1981–82 to 2000)

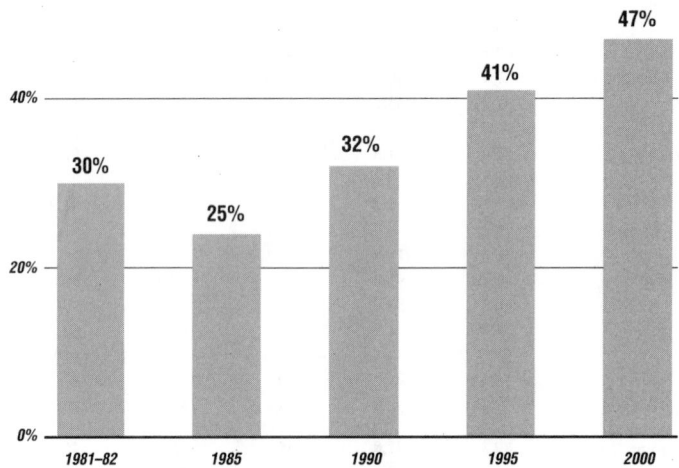

Table 3.21 AIDS Cases by Sex, 1981–82 to 2000

(number and percent distribution of diagnosed AIDS cases diagnosed by sex, by year of diagnosis, 1981–82 to 2000)

	total	*male*	*female*
Total cases	**774,467**	**640,022**	**134,441**
2000	42,156	31,588	10,588
1999	46,400	35,482	10,918
1998	48,269	37,076	11,190
1997	58,443	45,696	12,747
1996	66,497	52,969	13,528
1995	70,864	57,451	13,413
1994	77,103	63,301	13,802
1993	102,166	85,781	16,385
1992	45,789	39,457	6,332
1991	43,653	37,997	5,656
1990	41,529	36,667	4,862
1989	33,559	29,921	3,638
1988	30,657	27,375	3,282
1987	21,478	19,643	1,835
1986	13,083	12,028	1,055
1985	8,210	7,622	588
1984	4,442	4,146	296
1983	2,059	1,902	157
1981–82	838	780	58
Total cases	**100.0%**	**82.6%**	**17.4%**
2000	100.0	74.9	25.1
1999	100.0	76.5	23.5
1998	100.0	76.8	23.2
1997	100.0	78.2	21.8
1996	100.0	79.7	20.3
1995	100.0	81.1	18.9
1994	100.0	82.1	17.9
1993	100.0	84.0	16.0
1992	100.0	86.2	13.8
1991	100.0	87.0	13.0
1990	100.0	88.3	11.7
1989	100.0	89.2	10.8
1988	100.0	89.3	10.7
1987	100.0	91.5	8.5
1986	100.0	91.9	8.1
1985	100.0	92.8	7.2
1984	100.0	93.3	6.7
1983	100.0	92.4	7.6
198–82	100.0	93.1	6.9

Note: Numbers will not add to total because total includes cases of unknown sex.
Source: Bureau of the Census, Statistical Abstracts of the United States, 1990 to 2001; calculations by New Strategist

Table 3.22 AIDS Cases by Race and Hispanic Origin, 1981–82 to 2000

(number and percent distribution of diagnosed AIDS cases by race and Hispanic origin, by year of diagnosis, 1981–82 to 2000)

	total	black, non-Hispanic	Hispanic	white, non-Hispanic
Total cases	774,467	292,522	141,694	331,160
2000	42,156	19,890	8,173	13,392
1999	46,400	21,900	9,021	14,813
1998	48,269	21,752	9,650	16,118
1997	58,443	26,995	10,387	20,170
1996	66,497	28,639	10,796	26,172
1995	70,864	29,060	11,544	29,386
1994	77,103	30,923	12,556	32,729
1993	102,166	38,014	15,438	47,507
1992	45,789	16,052	6,766	22,446
1991	43,653	14,638	6,417	22,125
1990	41,529	13,199	5,657	22,258
1989	33,559	10,254	4,364	18,571
1988	30,657	9,123	4,232	17,029
1987	21,478	5,429	2,601	13,239
1986	13,083	3,392	1,810	7,769
1985	8,210	2,081	1,039	4,968
1984	4,442	1,123	609	2,689
1983	2,059	565	311	1,174
1981–82	838	251	117	467
Total cases	100.0%	37.8%	18.3%	42.8%
2000	100.0	47.2	19.4	31.8
1999	100.0	47.2	19.4	31.9
1998	100.0	45.1	20.0	33.4
1997	100.0	46.2	17.8	34.5
1996	100.0	43.1	16.2	39.4
1995	100.0	41.0	16.3	41.5
1994	100.0	40.1	16.3	42.4
1993	100.0	37.2	15.1	46.5
1992	100.0	35.1	14.8	49.0
1991	100.0	33.5	14.7	50.7
1990	100.0	31.8	13.6	53.6
1989	100.0	30.6	13.0	55.3
1988	100.0	29.8	13.8	55.5
1987	100.0	25.3	12.1	61.6
1986	100.0	25.9	13.8	59.4
1985	100.0	25.4	12.6	60.5
1984	100.0	25.3	13.7	60.5
1983	100.0	27.4	15.1	57.0
1981–82	100.0	30.0	14.0	55.7

Note: Numbers will not add to total because not all races are shown.
Source: Bureau of the Census, Statistical Abstracts of the United States, 1990 to 2001; calculations by New Strategist

Longer Lives, More Deaths

As the U.S. population has grown, so has the number of deaths. From 16 million deaths during the 1950s, the figure climbed to 23 million in the 1990s as the population grew by more than 100 million.

Dying is different today than it was at mid-century. Many Americans would prefer to have more control over their death. The percentage of people aged 18 or older who think doctors should be allowed to end the lives of terminally ill patients at their request rose from 59 to 65 percent between 1977 and 2000. Those most in favor are young adults, but even among older Americans the majority favor physician-assisted suicide.

Death rates have dropped dramatically for many causes of death as cigarette smoking declined and seat belt use increased. The death rate from heart disease, the leading cause of death, fell 56 percent between 1950 and 2000. The rate for cerebrovascular disease (the third ranking cause of death) fell 67 percent during those years. The death rate from motor vehicle accidents declined 38 percent between 1950 and 2000. The death rate rose for cancer (up 3 percent) and diabetes (up 8 percent), however.

As the death rate dropped, life expectancy grew. Between 1950 and 2000, life expectancy at birth grew from 68.2 to 76.9 years. Life expectancy at age 65 now stands at 17.9 years, up from 13.9 years in 1950.

Life expectancy rises

(number of years of life remaining at birth, by sex, 1950 and 2000)

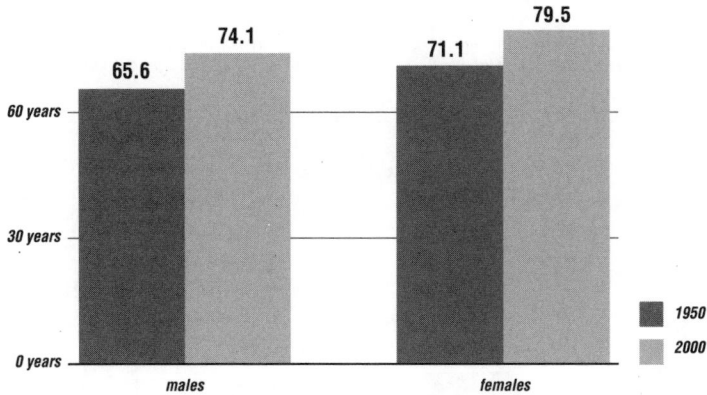

Table 3.23 Physician-Assisted Suicide, 1977 to 2000

"When a person has a disease that cannot be cured, do you think doctors should be allowed by law to end the patient's life by some painless means if the patient and his family request it?"

(percent of people aged 18 or older responding "yes," by selected characteristcs, 1977 to 2000; percentage point change, 1977–00)

	2000	1990	1977	percentage point change 1977–00
Total	65%	72%	59%	6%
Men	69	76	65	4
Women	62	69	55	7
Black	47	62	36	11
White	68	74	62	6
Aged 18 to 29	69	74	70	–1
Aged 30 to 39	67	77	60	7
Aged 40 to 49	66	76	57	9
Aged 50 to 59	64	71	58	6
Aged 60 to 69	58	72	55	3
Aged 70 or older	54	56	45	9
Not a high school graduate	58	60	52	6
High school graduate	65	75	62	3
Bachelor's degree	67	70	61	6
Graduate degree	67	79	74	–7

Note: Numbers may not add to 100 because "don't know" and no answer are not shown.
Source: General Social Surveys, National Opinion Research Center, University of Chicago; calculations by New Strategist

Table 3.24 Number of Deaths, 1950 to 2000

(number of deaths by year and decade, 1950 to 2000; percent change from preceding year and decade, 1950–2000; numbers in thousands)

	number	percent change from preceding year or decade
1991–2000	**22,969**	**10.5%**
2000	2,405	0.6
1999	2,391	2.3
1998	2,338	1.0
1997	2,314	–0.0
1996	2,315	0.1
1995	2,312	1.4
1994	2,279	0.4
1993	2,269	4.3
1992	2,176	0.3
1991	2,170	1.0
1981–1990	**20,791**	**7.5**
1990	2,148	–0.1
1989	2,150	–0.8
1988	2,168	2.1
1987	2,123	0.9
1986	2,105	0.9
1985	2,086	2.3
1984	2,039	1.0
1983	2,019	2.2
1982	1,975	–0.2
1981	1,978	–0.6
1971–1980	**19,347**	**5.2**
1980	1,990	4.0
1979	1,914	–0.7
1978	1,928	1.5
1977	1,900	–0.5
1976	1,909	0.8
1975	1,893	–2.1
1974	1,934	–2.0
1973	1,973	0.5
1972	1,964	1.1
1971	1,942	1.1
1961–1970	**18,386**	**17.0%**
1970	1,921	–0.1
1969	1,922	–0.4
1968	1,930	4.3
1967	1,851	–0.6
1966	1,863	1.9
1965	1,828	1.7
1964	1,798	–0.9
1963	1,814	3.2
1962	1,757	3.2
1961	1,702	–0.6
1951–1960	**15,721**	–
1960	1,712	3.3
1959	1,657	0.5
1958	1,648	0.9
1957	1,633	4.4
1956	1,564	2.3
1955	1,529	3.2
1954	1,481	–2.4
1953	1,518	1.4
1952	1,497	1.0
1951	1,482	2.1
1950	1,452	–

Source: Bureau of the Census, Statistical Abstract of the United States: 1980; *and* Historical Statistics of the United States: Colonial Times to 1970, Part 1, *1975; and National Center for Health Statistics*, Deaths: Preliminary Data for 2000, *National*

Table 3.25 Death Rate by Cause of Death, 1950 to 2000

(number of age-adjusted deaths per 100,000 population by selected cause of death, and percent change, 1950 to 2000)

	2000	1990	1980	1970	1960	1950	percent change 1950–00
All causes	**872.4**	**938.7**	**1,039.1**	**1,222.6**	**1,339.2**	**1,446.0**	**–39.7%**
Diseases of heart	257.5	321.8	412.1	492.7	559.0	586.8	–56.1
Malignant neoplasms	200.5	216.0	207.9	198.6	193.9	193.9	3.4
Cerebrovascular disease	60.2	65.3	96.2	147.7	177.9	180.7	–66.7
Chronic lower respiratory diseases	44.9	37.2	28.3	–	–	–	–
Accidents and adverse effects	33.9	36.3	46.4	62.2	63.1	78.4	–56.8
Motor vehicle injuries	15.2	18.5	22.3	27.6	23.1	24.6	–38.2
Diabetes mellitus	24.9	20.7	18.1	24.3	22.5	23.1	7.8
Influenza and pneumonia	24.3	36.8	31.4	41.7	53.7	48.1	–49.5
Alzheimer's disease	17.8	–	–	–	–	–	–
Suicide	10.3	12.5	12.2	13.1	12.5	13.2	–22.0
Chronic liver disease and cirrhosis	9.5	11.1	15.1	17.8	13.3	11.3	–15.9
Homicide	5.8	9.4	10.4	8.8	5.0	5.1	13.7
Human immunodeficiency virus (HIV)	5.2	10.2	–	–	–	–	–

Note: Age-adjusted death rates are calculated by applying age-specific death rates in each year to the 2000 standard population. They should be viewed as an index rather than an actual measure of mortality risk. (–) means data not available.
Source: National Center for Health Statistics, Health, United States, 2001 (updated tables); and Deaths: Preliminary Data for 2000, National Vital Statistics Report, Vol. 49, No. 12, 2001; calculations by New Strategist

Table 3.26 Life Expectancy by Age, 1950 to 2000

(years of life remaining at birth and age 65, 1950 to 2000; change in years of life remaining for selected years)

	at birth	at age 65
2000	76.9	17.9
1999	76.7	17.7
1998	76.7	17.8
1997	76.5	17.7
1996	76.1	17.5
1995	75.8	17.4
1994	75.7	17.4
1993	75.5	17.3
1992	75.8	17.5
1991	75.5	17.4
1990	75.4	17.2
1980	73.7	16.4
1970	70.8	15.2
1960	69.7	14.3
1950	68.2	13.9
Change in years		
1990 to 2000	1.5	0.7
1950 to 2000	8.7	4.0

Source: National Center for Health Statistics, Health, United States, 2001 *(updated tables); and* Deaths: Preliminary Data for 2000, *National Vital Statistics Report, Vol. 49, No. 12, 2001; calculations by New Strategist*

Table 3.27 Life Expectancy by Race, 1950 to 2000

(years of life remaining at birth by race, 1950 to 2000; change in years of life remaining for selected years)

	at birth		at age 65	
	black	*white*	*black*	*white*
2000	71.8	77.4	16.2	17.9
1999	71.4	77.3	16.0	17.8
1998	71.3	77.3	16.1	17.8
1997	71.1	77.1	16.1	17.8
1996	70.2	76.8	15.8	17.6
1995	69.6	76.5	15.6	17.6
1994	69.5	76.5	15.7	17.5
1993	69.2	76.3	15.5	17.4
1992	69.6	76.5	15.7	17.6
1991	69.3	76.3	15.5	17.5
1990	69.1	76.1	15.4	17.3
1980	68.1	74.4	15.1	16.5
1970	64.1	71.7	14.2	15.2
1960	63.6	70.6	13.9	14.4
1950	60.8	69.1	13.9	–
Change in years				
1990 to 2000	2.7	1.3	0.8	0.6
1950 to 2000	11.0	8.3	2.3	–

Note: (–) means data not available.
Source: National Center for Health Statistics, Health, United States, 2001 *(updated tables); and* Deaths: Preliminary Data for 2000, *National Vital Statistics Report, Vol. 49, No. 12, 2001; calculations by New Strategist*

Table 3.28 Life Expectancy by Sex, 1950 to 2000

(years of life remaining at birth and age 65 by sex, 1950 to 2000; change in years of life remaining for selected years)

	at birth		at age 65	
	female	*male*	*female*	*male*
2000	79.5	74.1	19.2	16.3
1999	79.4	73.9	19.1	16.1
1998	79.5	73.8	19.2	16.0
1997	79.4	73.6	19.2	15.9
1996	79.1	73.1	19.0	15.7
1995	78.9	72.5	18.9	15.6
1994	79.0	72.4	19.0	15.5
1993	78.8	72.2	18.9	15.3
1992	79.1	72.3	19.2	15.4
1991	78.9	72.0	19.1	15.3
1990	78.8	71.8	18.9	15.1
1980	77.4	70.0	18.3	14.1
1970	74.7	67.1	17.0	13.1
1960	73.1	66.6	15.8	12.8
1950	71.1	65.6	15.0	12.8
Change in years				
1990 to 2000	0.7	2.3	0.3	1.2
1950 to 2000	8.4	8.5	4.2	3.5

Source: National Center for Health Statistics, Health, United States, 2001 *(updated tables); and* Deaths: Preliminary Data for 2000, *National Vital Statistics Report, Vol. 49, No. 12, 2001; calculations by New Strategist*

4

Housing

■ The proportion of American households owning a home hit an all-time high in 2000, at 67.4 percent. In 1950, just 55.0 percent of households owned their home.

■ The homeownership rate has increased the most for householders aged 65 or older—up 6 percentage points between 1982 and 2000. The rate also rose for householders aged 55 to 64, but it fell among householders under age 45.

■ The homeownership rate is highest in the Midwest, where 73 percent of households owned their home in 2000. It is lowest in the West, where only 62 percent of households own a home. Since 1960, the homeownership rate has fallen in the West, the only region to lose ground.

■ During the past half-century, the nation's housing improved dramatically. In 1950, one-third of housing units did not have complete plumbing facilities. By 2000, fewer than 1 percent lacked complete plumbing.

Homeownership Is at Record High

The proportion of American households owning a home hit an all-time high in 2000, at 66.2 percent. In 1950, just 55.0 percent of households owned their home. The homeownership rate rose between 1950 and 1980, then stabilized until rising again in the mid-1990s thanks to the booming economy and the aging of the baby-boom generation.

Since 1982, the homeownership rate has increased the most for householders aged 65 or older—up 6 percentage points. The rate also rose for householders aged 55 to 64, but it was lower in 2000 than in 1982 for householders under age 45. For younger householders, however, the homeownership rate increased in the late 1990s.

By household type, the homeownership rate rose for all but male-headed families between 1982 and 2000. By race and Hispanic origin, homeownership rose for blacks, Hispanics, and whites between 1976 and 2000. The 71 percent majority of white households owned a home in 2000 versus 47 percent of blacks and 45 percent of Hispanics.

Homeownership rate rose during the 1990s

(percent of households owning a home, 1950 to 2000)

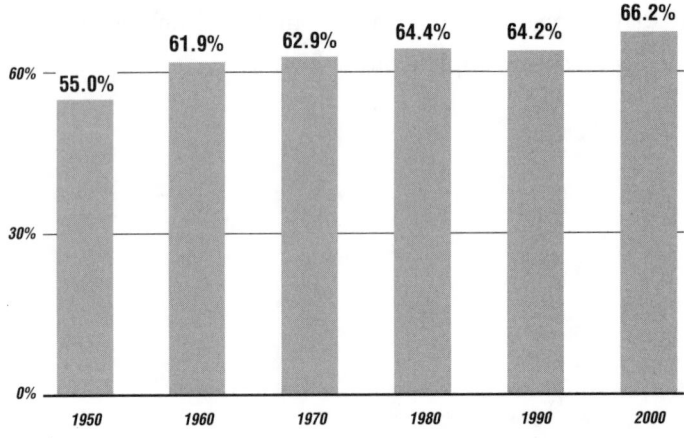

Table 4.1 Homeownership, 1950 to 2000 Censuses

(total number of households, and number and percent of households owning their home, 1950 to 2000; percent and percentage point change for selected years; numbers in thousands)

	total households	homeowners	
		number	share of total
2000	105,480	69,816	66.2%
1990	91,947	59,025	64.2
1980	80,390	51,795	64.4
1970	63,445	39,886	62.9
1960	53,024	32,797	61.9
1950	42,826	23,560	55.0
	percent change		percentage point change
1990 to 2000	14.7%	18.3%	2.0
1950 to 2000	146.3	196.3	11.2

Source: Bureau of the Census, Census 2000, Table DP-1. Profile of General Demographic Characteristics; *and* Statistical Abstract of the United States 1995; *calculations by New Strategist*

Table 4.2 Homeowners by Age, 1982 to 2000

(number of households owning a home by age of householder, 1982 to 2000; percent change for selected years; numbers in thousands)

	total homeowners	under 35	35 to 44	45 to 54	55 to 64	65 or older
2000	71,249	10,161	16,429	16,058	11,100	17,501
1999	70,098	9,949	16,228	15,499	10,989	17,433
1998	68,638	9,802	16,159	14,969	10,601	17,106
1997	67,142	9,630	15,880	14,536	10,150	16,946
1996	66,042	9,793	15,534	13,996	9,850	16,869
1995	64,738	9,803	15,093	13,501	9,712	16,629
1994	63,136	9,453	14,733	12,962	9,714	16,273
1993	62,535	9,559	14,611	12,516	9,746	16,103
1992	61,823	9,480	14,223	11,977	10,031	16,106
1991	61,010	9,664	14,137	11,249	9,999	15,962
1990	60,248	9,955	13,789	10,957	10,011	15,536
1989	59,755	10,348	13,429	10,774	10,096	15,106
1988	58,700	10,038	12,905	10,440	10,146	14,888
1987	57,915	10,057	12,631	10,075	10,344	14,549
1986	56,844	10,090	12,178	9,827	10,390	14,118
1985	56,152	10,089	11,943	9,615	10,437	13,841
1984	55,671	10,150	11,516	9,580	10,487	13,676
1983	54,671	9,997	11,008	9,610	10,442	13,341
1982	54,237	10,241	10,711	9,709	10,370	12,978
Percent change						
1990 to 2000	18.3%	2.1%	19.1%	46.6%	10.9%	12.6%
1982 to 2000	31.4	–0.8	53.4	65.4	7.0	34.9

Note: Numbers may not add to total because "age not stated" is not shown.
Source: Bureau of the Census, Housing Vacancy Surveys, Internet site http://www.census.gov/hhes/www/housing/hvs/historic/histt12.html; calculations by New Strategist

Table 4.3   Homeownership Rate by Age, 1982 to 2000

(percent of households owning their home by age of householder, 1982 to 2000; percentage point change for selected years)

	total households	under 35	35 to 44	45 to 54	55 to 64	65 or older
2000	67.4%	40.5%	68.0%	78.8%	81.8%	80.4%
1999	66.8	39.7	67.2	76.0	81.0	80.1
1998	66.3	39.3	66.9	75.7	80.9	79.3
1997	65.7	38.7	66.1	75.8	80.1	79.1
1996	65.4	39.1	65.5	75.6	80.0	78.9
1995	64.7	38.6	65.2	75.2	79.5	78.1
1994	64.0	37.3	64.5	75.2	79.3	77.4
1993	64.0	37.3	65.1	75.3	79.9	77.3
1992	64.1	37.6	65.1	75.1	80.2	77.1
1991	64.1	37.8	65.8	74.8	80.0	77.2
1990	63.9	38.5	66.3	75.2	79.3	76.3
1989	63.9	39.1	66.6	75.5	79.6	75.8
1988	63.8	39.3	66.9	75.6	79.5	75.6
1987	64.0	39.5	67.2	76.1	80.2	75.5
1986	63.8	39.6	67.3	76.0	79.9	75.0
1985	63.9	39.9	68.1	75.9	79.5	74.8
1984	64.5	40.5	68.9	76.5	80.0	75.1
1983	64.6	40.7	69.3	77.0	79.9	75.0
1982	64.8	41.2	70.0	77.4	80.0	74.4
Percentage point change						
1990 to 2000	3.5	2.0	1.7	3.6	2.5	4.1
1982 to 2000	2.6	-0.7	–2.0	1.4	1.8	6.0

Source: Bureau of the Census, Housing Vacancy Surveys, Internet site http://www.census.gov/hhes/www/housing/hvs/annual01/ ann01t15.html; calculations by New Strategist

Table 4.4   Homeowners by Household Type, 1982 to 2000

(number of households owning a home by type of household, 1982 to 2000; percent change for selected years; numbers in thousands)

	total homeowners	family households			nonfamily households			
		married couples	female hh no spouse present	male hh no spouse present	female householder		male householder	
					living alone	other	living alone	other
2000	71,249	45,535	6,283	2,427	9,135	1,011	5,480	1377
1999	70,098	45,053	6,097	2,341	8,965	941	5,375	1,324
1998	68,637	44,280	5,865	2,289	8,761	922	5,248	1,270
1997	67,142	43,582	5,784	2,139	8,548	867	4,968	1,255
1996	66,042	43,222	5,661	2,075	8,313	743	4,810	1,217
1995	64,738	42,733	5,489	1,925	8,184	638	4,638	1,131
1994	63,136	41,846	5,404	1,777	7,898	676	4,432	1,102
1993	62,535	41,591	5,286	1,801	7,847	650	4,355	1,005
1992	61,823	41,417	5,105	1,743	7,701	600	4,293	958
1991	61,010	41,088	5,057	1,640	7,536	583	4,176	931
1990	60,248	40,793	4,902	1,646	7,449	546	4,016	895
1989	59,755	40,814	4,838	1,608	7,178	512	3,919	886
1988	58,700	39,927	4,929	1,830	6,849	469	3,619	798
1987	57,915	39,685	4,921	1,751	6,635	440	3,451	769
1986	56,844	39,198	4,770	1,640	6,497	427	3,365	709
1985	56,152	38,907	4,697	1,604	6,470	401	3,150	693
1984	55,671	38,722	4,702	1,555	6,413	366	3,014	631
1983	54,671	38,405	4,567	1,470	6,107	356	2,860	611
1982	54,237	38,382	4,498	1,437	5,971	346	2,804	569
Percent change								
1990 to 2000	18.3%	11.6%	28.2%	47.4%	22.6%	85.2%	36.5%	53.9%
1982 to 2000	31.4	18.6	39.7	68.9	53.0	192.2	95.4	142.0

Source: Bureau of the Census, Housing Vacancy Surveys, Internet site http://www.census.gov/hhes/www/housing/hvs/historic/ histt15.html; calculations by New Strategist

Table 4.5 Homeownership Rate by Household Type, 1982 to 2000

(percent of households owning a home by type of household, 1982 to 2000; percentage point change for selected years)

| | total homeowners | family households | | | nonfamily households | | | |
| | | married couples | female hh no spouse present | male hh no spouse present | female householder | | male householder | |
					living alone	other	living alone	other
2000	67.4%	82.4%	49.1%	57.5%	58.1%	40.6%	47.4%	38.0%
1999	66.8	81.8	48.2	56.1	57.6	41.5	46.3	37.2
1998	66.3	81.5	47.0	55.7	56.9	40.3	45.7	36.7
1997	65.7	80.8	46.1	54.0	56.7	39.5	45.2	35.9
1996	65.4	80.2	46.1	55.5	56.0	35.9	44.9	35.5
1995	64.7	79.6	45.1	55.3	55.4	33.0	43.8	34.2
1994	64.0	78.8	44.2	52.8	54.5	34.3	43.1	33.6
1993	64.0	78.7	43.9	53.7	54.6	35.0	42.8	32.6
1992	64.1	78.7	43.6	53.6	54.1	34.0	43.5	32.4
1991	64.1	78.5	43.9	54.3	53.8	33.8	43.1	31.8
1990	63.9	78.1	44.0	55.2	53.6	32.5	42.4	31.7
1989	63.9	78.3	44.1	55.7	52.6	30.8	41.8	31.5
1988	63.8	78.9	45.3	56.1	51.8	30.5	39.9	31.3
1987	64.0	78.7	45.8	56.5	51.6	30.7	39.9	31.1
1986	63.8	78.4	45.3	56.8	50.9	31.4	40.0	29.8
1985	63.9	78.2	45.8	57.8	51.3	30.6	38.8	30.1
1984	64.5	78.2	46.9	59.2	52.2	30.0	38.9	28.8
1983	64.6	78.3	47.0	59.2	52.0	29.7	38.3	29.5
1982	64.8	78.5	47.1	59.3	51.2	30.1	38.0	28.3
Percentage point change								
1990 to 2000	3.5	4.3	5.1	2.3	4.5	8.1	5.0	6.3
1982 to 2000	2.6	3.9	2.0	−1.8	6.9	10.5	9.4	9.7

Source: Bureau of the Census, Housing Vacancy Surveys, Internet site http://www.census.gov/hhes/www/housing/hvs/annual01/ann01t15.html; calculations by New Strategist

Table 4.6 Homeowners by Race and Hispanic Origin, 1976 to 2000

(number of households owning a home by race and Hispanic origin of householder, 1976 to 2000; percent change for selected years; numbers in thousands)

	total homeowners	black	Hispanic	white
2000	70,370	6,055	4,243	62,077
1999	69,241	5,723	4,096	61,350
1998	67,873	5,735	3,857	60,050
1997	66,356	5,510	3,543	58,826
1996	65,143	5,085	3,274	58,282
1995	64,045	4,888	3,278	57,449
1994	62,374	4,791	3,060	55,879
1993	62,220	4,726	2,654	55,915
1992	61,310	4,683	2,547	55,117
1991	60,395	4,526	2,423	54,527
1990	59,846	4,445	2,443	54,094
1989	59,419	4,417	2,457	53,737
1988	58,214	4,323	2,292	52,697
1987	57,258	4,505	2,198	51,657
1986	56,408	4,361	2,115	51,017
1985	55,845	4,185	2,007	50,661
1984	55,157	4,204	1,749	50,055
1983	54,494	4,043	1,684	49,484
1982	56,317	4,230	1,852	51,110
1981	55,881	4,230	1,822	50,737
1980	54,891	4,173	1,753	49,913
1979	52,283	3,887	1,514	47,751
1978	49,398	3,553	1,408	45,291
1977	48,083	3,431	1,302	44,148
1976	47,408	3,313	1,259	43,628
Percent change				
1990 to 2000	17.6%	36.2%	73.7%	14.8%
1976 to 2000	46.1	72.7	225.3	40.6

Note: Numbers will not add to total because Hispanics may be of any race and not all races are shown. Estimated total homeowners in this table differ slightly from those in other tables because they are based on different sources of data. Source: Bureau of the Census, Current Population Surveys, Internet site http://www.census.gov/population/socdemo/hh-fam/ tabHH-5.txt; calculations by New Strategist

Table 4.7 Homeownership Rate by Race and Hispanic Origin, 1976 to 2000

(percent of households owning a home by race and Hispanic origin of householder, 1976 to 2000; percentage point change in rate for selected years)

	total households	black	Hispanic	white
2000	67.2%	47.1%	45.5%	70.8%
1999	66.7	45.5	45.2	70.3
1998	66.2	46.0	44.9	69.7
1997	65.7	45.5	43.1	69.2
1996	65.4	45.5	41.2	69.0
1995	64.7	43.9	42.4	68.6
1994	64.2	41.9	41.6	67.8
1993	64.5	42.5	40.1	68.1
1992	64.1	42.2	39.9	67.5
1991	64.0	42.3	39.0	67.3
1990	64.1	42.4	41.2	67.5
1989	64.0	42.4	41.6	67.4
1988	63.9	41.8	40.2	67.2
1987	64.0	42.4	40.6	66.8
1986	63.8	45.4	40.6	66.6
1985	64.3	44.5	41.1	67.3
1984	64.6	44.1	40.4	67.3
1983	64.9	45.5	41.2	67.6
1982	67.4	45.3	46.5	70.2
1981	67.8	47.2	46.6	70.6
1980	68.0	47.8	47.6	70.5
1979	67.6	48.6	46.0	70.2
1978	65.0	48.2	42.6	67.7
1977	64.9	44.5	42.3	67.6
1976	65.1	44.1	42.7	67.8
Percentage point change				
1990 to 2000	3.1	4.7	4.4	3.3
1976 to 2000	2.1	3.0	2.8	3.1

Note: Estimated total homeownership rates in this table differ slightly from those in other tables because they are based on different sources of data.
Source: Bureau of the Census, Current Population Surveys, Internet site http://www.census.gov/population/socdemo/hh-fam/ tabHH-5.txt; calculations by New Strategist

Homeownership Is Highest in the Midwest

The homeownership rate is highest in the Midwest, where 73 percent of households owned their home in 2000. It is lowest in the West, where only 62 percent of households own a home. Between 1960 and 2000, the homeownership rate fell in the West, the only region to lose ground. Behind the decline is the rapidly growing immigrant population of the West, since immigrants are less likely to own a home than native-born Americans. In addition, home prices are higher in the West than in other regions of the country, making it difficult for people to afford a home of their own.

By state, homeownership increased the most in Alaska (up 8.8 percentage points) and South Carolina (up 7.4 percentage points) between 1984 and 2000. The rate fell in five states, the biggest decline occurring in Kansas.

Seventy-five percent of households in nonmetropolitan areas own their home, as do 74 percent of suburban households. Only 51 percent of central city householders are homeowners.

Homeownership rate fell in the West

(percent of households that own their home, by region, 1960 and 2000)

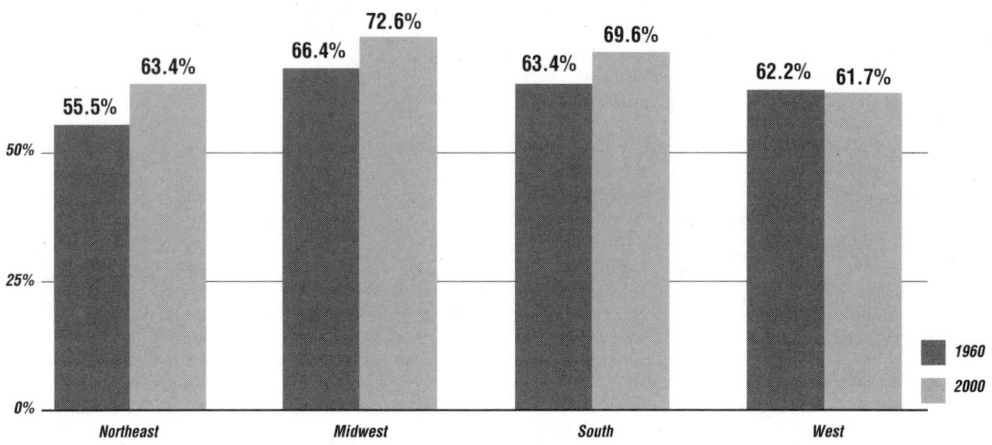

Table 4.8 Homeownership Rate by Region, 1960 to 2000

(percent of households owning a home by region, 1960 to 2000; percentage point change for selected years)

	total households	Northeast	Midwest	South	West
2000	67.4%	63.4%	72.6%	69.6%	61.7%
1999	66.8	63.1	71.7	69.1	60.9
1998	66.3	62.6	71.1	68.6	60.5
1997	65.7	62.4	70.5	68.0	59.6
1996	65.4	62.2	70.6	67.5	59.2
1995	64.7	62.0	69.2	66.7	59.2
1994	64.0	61.5	67.7	65.6	59.4
1993	64.0	61.8	67.1	65.7	59.9
1992	64.1	62.5	67.2	65.8	59.3
1991	64.1	62.3	67.2	66.1	58.6
1990	63.9	62.6	67.5	65.7	58.0
1989	63.9	62.0	67.7	65.9	57.8
1988	63.8	61.3	67.5	65.8	58.5
1987	64.0	61.7	67.3	66.3	58.4
1986	63.8	61.4	66.9	66.1	58.3
1985	63.9	60.8	66.9	66.4	59.0
1984	64.5	61.2	68.4	67.0	58.5
1983	64.6	61.5	69.3	67.0	58.2
1982	64.8	61.1	69.4	66.7	59.4
1981	65.4	60.8	69.7	68.2	60.2
1980	65.6	60.8	68.9	68.7	60.0
1970	64.2	58.1	69.5	66.0	60.0
1960	62.1	55.5	66.4	63.4	62.2
Percentage point change					
1990 to 2000	3.5	0.8	5.1	3.9	3.7
1960 to 2000	5.3	7.9	6.2	6.2	–0.5

Source: Bureau of the Census, Housing Vacancy Surveys, Internet site http://www.census.gov/hhes/www/housing/hvs/annual01/ann01t12.html; calculations by New Strategist

Table 4.9 Homeownership Rate by State, 1984 to 2000

(percent of households owning a home by state, 1984 to 2000; percentage point change for selected years)

	2000	1990	1984	percentage point change 1990–00	percentage point change 1984–00
Total households	**67.4%**	**63.9%**	**64.5%**	**3.5%**	**2.9%**
Alabama	73.2	68.4	73.7	4.8	–0.5
Alaska	66.4	58.4	57.6	8.0	8.8
Arizona	68.0	64.5	65.2	3.5	2.8
Arkansas	68.9	67.8	65.9	1.1	3.0
California	57.1	53.8	53.7	3.3	3.4
Colorado	68.3	59.0	64.7	9.3	3.6
Connecticut	70.0	67.9	67.8	2.1	2.2
Delaware	72.0	67.7	70.4	4.3	1.6
District of Columbia	41.9	36.4	37.3	5.5	4.6
Florida	68.4	65.1	66.5	3.3	1.9
Georgia	69.8	64.3	63.6	5.5	6.2
Hawaii	55.2	55.5	50.7	–0.3	4.5
Idaho	70.5	69.4	69.7	1.1	0.8
Illinois	67.9	63.0	62.4	4.9	5.5
Indiana	74.9	67.0	69.9	7.9	5.0
Iowa	75.2	70.7	71.3	4.5	3.9
Kansas	69.3	69.0	72.7	0.3	–3.4
Kentucky	73.4	65.8	70.2	7.6	3.2
Louisiana	68.1	67.8	70.1	0.3	–2.0
Maine	76.5	74.3	74.1	2.3	2.4
Maryland	69.9	64.9	67.8	5.0	2.1
Massachusetts	59.9	58.6	61.7	1.3	–1.8
Michigan	77.2	72.3	72.7	4.9	4.5
Minnesota	76.1	68.0	72.6	8.1	3.5
Mississippi	75.2	69.4	72.3	5.8	2.9
Missouri	74.2	64.0	69.5	10.2	4.7
Montana	70.2	69.1	66.4	1.1	3.8
Nebraska	70.2	67.3	69.3	2.9	0.9
Nevada	64.0	55.8	58.9	8.2	5.1
New Hampshire	69.2	65.0	67.1	4.2	2.1
New Jersey	66.2	65.0	63.4	1.2	2.8
New Mexico	73.7	68.6	68.0	5.1	5.7
New York	53.4	53.3	51.1	0.1	2.3
North Carolina	71.1	69.0	68.8	2.1	2.3
North Dakota	70.7	67.2	70.1	3.5	0.6
Ohio	71.3	68.7	67.7	2.6	3.6
Oklahoma	72.7	70.3	71.0	2.4	1.7
Oregon	65.3	64.4	61.9	0.9	3.4
Pennsylvania	74.7	73.8	71.1	0.9	3.6
Rhode Island	61.5	58.5	60.9	3.0	0.6
South Carolina	76.5	71.4	69.1	5.1	7.4
South Dakota	71.2	66.2	69.6	5.0	1.6
Tennessee	70.9	68.3	67.6	2.6	3.3
Texas	63.8	59.7	62.5	4.1	1.3
Utah	72.7	70.1	69.9	2.6	2.8
Vermont	68.7	72.6	66.9	–3.9	1.8
Virginia	73.9	69.8	68.3	4.1	5.6
Washington	63.6	61.8	65.7	1.8	–2.1
West Virginia	75.9	72.0	72.0	3.9	3.9
Wisconsin	71.8	68.3	65.2	3.5	6.6
Wyoming	71.0	68.9	68.8	2.1	2.2

Source: Bureau of the Census, Housing Vacancy Surveys, Internet site http://www.census.gov/hhes/www/housing/hvs/annual01/ann01t13.html; calculations by New Strategist

Table 4.10 Homeownership Rate by Metropolitan Status, 1965 to 2000

(percent of households owning a home by metropolitan status, 1965 to 2000; percentage point change for selected years)

| | total households | metropolitan area | | | nonmetro area |
		total	central city	suburb	
2000	67.4%	65.5%	51.4%	74.0%	75.2%
1999	66.8	64.7	50.4	73.6	75.4
1998	66.3	64.2	50.0	73.2	74.7
1997	65.7	63.7	49.9	72.5	73.7
1996	65.4	63.4	49.7	72.2	73.5
1995	64.7	62.7	49.5	71.2	72.7
1994	64.0	61.7	48.5	70.3	72.0
1993	64.0	61.5	48.6	70.3	72.6
1992	64.1	61.6	49.3	70.1	72.8
1991	64.1	61.4	48.7	70.2	73.2
1990	63.9	61.3	48.7	70.1	73.2
1989	63.9	61.3	48.7	70.2	72.8
1988	63.8	61.3	48.3	70.6	72.6
1987	64.0	61.4	48.7	70.8	72.8
1986	63.8	61.2	48.5	70.8	72.3
1985	63.9	60.2	47.7	69.1	71.9
1984	64.5	60.8	49.0	69.7	72.3
1983	64.6	60.9	49.2	69.8	72.9
1982	64.8	61.0	49.1	70.0	73.0
1981	65.4	61.5	49.4	70.8	73.8
1980	65.6	61.6	49.6	70.8	74.1
1970	64.2	60.3	48.9	70.6	71.6
1965	63.3	59.7	48.0	72.0	69.1
Percentage point change					
1990 to 2000	3.5	4.2	2.7	3.9	2.0
1965 to 2000	4.1	5.8	3.4	2.0	6.1

Source: Bureau of the Census, Housing Vacancy Surveys, Internet site http://www.census.gov/hhes/www/housing/hvs/annual01/ ann01t12.html; calculations by New Strategist

Table 4.11 Homeownership Rate by Metropolitan Area, 1986 to 2000

(percent of households owning a home in the 75 largest metropolitan areas, 1986 to 2000; percentage point change for selected years)

	2000	1990	1986	percentage point change 1990–00	percentage point change 1986–00
Total metropolitan areas	65.5%	61.3%	61.2%	4.2	4.3
Akron, OH	63.6	–	–	–	–
Albany–Schenectady–Troy, NY	71.1	69.9	62.4	1.2	8.7
Atlanta, GA	67.7	61.0	57.5	6.7	10.2
Austin–San Marcos, TX	54.7	–	–	–	–
Baltimore, MD	68.2	63.0	58.8	5.2	9.4
Bergen–Passaic, NJ	63.2	61.4	58.6	1.8	4.6
Birmingham, AL	69.9	65.7	68.6	4.2	1.3
Boston, MA–NH	58.7	55.0	55.9	3.7	2.8
Buffalo, NY	72.5	61.4	64.1	11.1	8.4
Charlotte–Gastonia–Rock Hill, NC–SC	75.8	64.8	63.0	11.0	12.8
Chicago, IL	66.4	56.9	54.7	9.5	11.7
Cincinnati, OH–KY–IN	72.5	57.9	63.8	14.6	8.7
Cleveland–Lorain–Elyria, OH	72.0	64.5	64.7	7.5	7.3
Columbus, OH	61.6	61.8	59.2	–0.2	2.4
Dallas, TX	62.4	54.0	51.2	8.4	11.2
Dayton–Springfield, OH	62.8	67.6	62.8	–4.8	0.0
Denver, CO	68.2	55.7	60.7	12.5	7.5
Detroit, MI	75.3	71.4	70.5	3.9	4.8
Fresno, CA	56.2	–	–	–	–
Ft. Lauderdale, FL	76.3	68.2	74.3	8.1	2.0
Ft. Worth–Arlington, TX	62.4	61.4	64.8	1.0	–2.4
Grand Rapids–Muskegon–Holland, MI	80.1	–	–	–	–
Greensboro–Winston-Salem–High Point, NC	68.9	68.2	68.2	0.7	0.7
Greenville–Spartanburg–Anderson, SC	76.5	–	–	–	–
Hartford, CT	69.7	65.5	68.3	4.2	1.4
Honolulu, HI	56.8	52.9	50.0	3.9	6.8
Houston, TX	53.6	53.9	56.3	–0.3	–2.7
Indianapolis, IN	67.5	55.3	61.4	12.2	6.1
Jacksonville, FL	70.4	61.0	61.0	9.4	9.4
Kansas City, MO–KS	73.6	61.7	63.8	11.9	9.8
Las Vegas, NV–AZ	61.9	–	–	–	–
Los Angeles–Long Beach, CA	49.0	47.9	48.3	1.1	0.7
Louisville, KY–IN	70.2	69.3	66.4	0.9	3.8
Memphis, TN–AR–MS	61.1	60.8	60.2	0.3	0.9
Miami, FL	56.2	47.9	47.9	8.3	8.3
Middlesex–Somerset–Hunterton, NJ	69.7	72.4	67.5	–2.7	2.2
Milwaukee–Waukesha, WI	67.5	72.2	65.9	–4.7	1.6
Minneapolis–St. Paul, MN–WI	73.1	62.5	64.2	10.6	8.9
Monmouth–Ocean, NJ	83.5	76.1	76.6	7.4	6.9
Nashville, TN	67.9	57.3	60.6	10.6	7.3
Nassau–Suffolk, NY	79.7	81.8	81.8	–2.1	–2.1
New Orleans, LA	64.6	59.9	59.9	4.7	4.7
New York, NY	34.1	34.0	32.1	0.1	2.0
Newark, NJ	60.3	60.7	62.0	–0.4	–1.7
Norfolk–Virginia Beach–Newport News, VA	70.1	62.6	57.2	7.5	12.9
Oakland, CA	60.3	54.2	57.0	6.1	3.3
Oklahoma City, OK	70.5	65.1	67.8	5.4	2.7

(continued)

(continued from previous page)

| | 2000 | 1990 | 1986 | percentage point change | |
				1990–00	1986–00
Omaha, NE–IA	69.6%	–	–	–	–
Orange County, CA	62.3	55.1%	57.3%	7.2	5.0
Orlando, FL	60.5	66.8	71.2	–6.3	–10.7
Philadelphia, PA–NJ	74.7	73.6	69.8	1.1	4.9
Phoenix–Mesa, AZ	70.7	64.3	61.8	6.4	8.9
Pittsburgh, PA	71.8	71.9	70.5	–0.1	1.3
Portland–Vancouver, OR–WA	62.1	66.5	65.2	–4.4	–3.1
Providence–Fall River–Pawtucket, RI	61.2	59.5	63.0	1.7	–1.8
Raleigh–Durham–Chapel Hill, NC	65.6	–	–	–	–
Richmond–Petersburg, VA	74.1	69.4	71.5	4.7	2.6
Rochester, NY	65.2	65.9	61.7	–0.7	3.5
Sacramento, CA	61.6	53.5	54.3	8.1	7.3
Salt Lake City–Ogden, UT	72.1	73.6	71.2	–1.5	0.9
San Antonio, TX	66.6	57.9	60.1	8.7	6.5
San Bernardino–Riverside, CA	62.6	60.0	65.9	2.6	–3.3
San Diego, CA	59.1	51.2	53.6	7.9	5.5
San Francisco, CA	48.9	48.8	48.7	0.1	0.2
San Jose, CA	60.9	63.2	50.9	–2.3	10.0
Scranton–Wilkes-Barre-Hazelton, PA	71.8	–	–	–	–
Seattle–Bellevue–Everett, WA	63.4	64.8	63.0	–1.4	0.4
St. Louis, MO–IL	70.6	59.4	64.8	11.2	5.8
Syracuse, NY	59.2	–	–	–	–
Tampa–St. Petersburg–Clearwater, FL	70.0	67.0	67.6	3.0	2.4
Tucson, AZ	60.5	–	–	–	–
Tulsa, OK	65.2	–	–	–	–
Ventura, CA	66.2	–	–	–	–
Washington, DC–MD–VA–WV	67.1	63.2	60.2	3.9	6.9
West Palm Beach–Boca Raton, FL	71.3	–	–	–	–

Note: Data for 1986 and 1990 are based on 1980 metropolitan definitions. Data for 2000 are based on 1990 metropolitan definitions; (–) means data are not available.
Source: Bureau of the Census, Housing Vacancy Surveys, Internet site http://www.census.gov/hhes/www/housing/hvs/annual01/ann01t14.html; calculations by New Strategist

Housing Stock Has Improved

During the past half-century, the nation's housing has improved dramatically. In 1950, one-third of housing units did not have complete plumbing facilities, meaning they lacked either hot and cold piped water, a bathtub or shower, or a flush toilet. By 2000, fewer than 1 percent of housing units lacked complete plumbing.

The primary fuel used to heat homes also has changed during the past 50 years. In 1950, one-third of housing units depended on coal for their primary heating fuel, while another 10 percent used wood. By 2000, fewer than 2 percent of households used coal or wood. The 51 percent majority depended on utility gas in 2000, up from 27 percent in 1950. Another 30 percent used electricity, up from fewer than 1 percent in 1950.

While dramatic changes have occurred in the use of heating fuels and the prevalence of plumbing facilities, there has been surprisingly little change in the proportion of households owning a second home. The share rose from 2.3 percent in 1950 to just 3.1 percent in 2000. As the baby-boom generation enters the prime ages of second-home ownership, the figure may rise.

Big changes in heating fuels used

(percent distribution of households by primary heating fuel, 1950 and 2000)

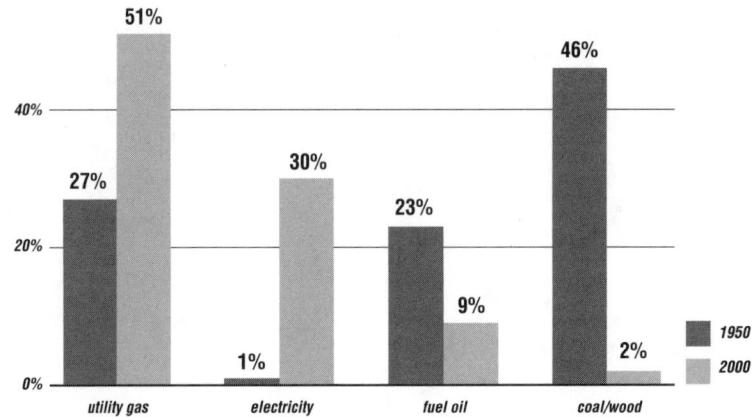

Table 4.12 House Heating Fuel, 1950 to 2000 Censuses

(total number of occupied housing units reporting heating fuel use and percent distribution by primary house heating fuel, 1950–00; numbers in thousands)

	total occupied housing units		utility gas	electricity	fuel oil	bottled, tank or LP gas	coal or coke	wood	other/none
	number	percent							
2000	105,480	100.0%	51.2%	30.3%	9.0%	6.5%	0.1%	1.7%	1.1%
1990	91,947	100.0	51.0	25.8	12.2	5.7	0.4	3.9	1.0
1980	80,390	100.0	53.1	18.4	18.2	5.6	0.6	3.2	0.9
1970	63,447	100.0	55.2	7.7	26.0	6.0	2.9	1.3	1.0
1960	53,022	100.0	43.1	1.8	32.4	5.1	12.2	4.2	1.3
1950	41,829	100.0	26.6	0.7	22.6	2.3	34.6	10.0	3.2

Source: Bureau of the Census, 1950 to 2000 censuses, Internet sites http://www.census.gov/hhes/www/housing/census/historic/fuels.html and http://censtats.census.gov/data/US/01000.pdf; calculations by New Strategist

Table 4.13 Plumbing Facilities in Housing Units, 1950 to 2000 Censuses

(total number of housing units reporting plumbing facilities, and number and percent without complete plumbing, 1950–00; numbers in thousands)

		lacking complete plumbing	
	total	number	percent
2000	115,905	671	0.6%
1990	102,264	1,102	1.1
1980	86,693	2,334	2.7
1970	67,657	4,672	6.9
1960	58,315	9,778	16.8
1950	44,502	15,773	35.4

Note: Complete plumbing facilities are defined as hot and cold piped water, a bathtub or shower, and a flush toilet.
Source: Bureau of the Census, 1950 to 2000 censuses, Internet sites http://www.census.gov/hhes/www/housing/census/historic/plumbing.html and http://censtats.census.gov/data/US/01000.pdf

Table 4.14 Ownership of Vacation Homes, 1950 to 2000 Censuses

(total number of housing units, and number and percent that are seasonal, recreational, or occasional use, 1950–00; percent and percentage point change for selected years; numbers in thousands)

		vacation housing units	
	total	*number*	*percent*
2000	115,905	3,579	3.1%
1990	102,264	3,082	3.0
1980	88,411	2,794	3.2
1970	68,679	2,020	2.9
1960	58,326	2,024	3.5
1950	45,983	1,050	2.3

Source: Bureau of the Census, 1950 to 2000 censuses, Housing Characteristics 2000, *2000 Census Brief, C2KBR/01–13, 2001; and Internet site http://www.census.gov/hhes/www/housing/census/historic/vacation.html; calculations by New Strategist*

5

Income

■ Never before have so many Americans been so well off. In 2000, 13 percent of households had incomes of $100,000 or more, up from just 3 percent in 1967, after adjusting for inflation.

■ Household income has been growing as our standard of living has improved. Median household income grew 34 percent between 1967 and 2000, after adjusting for inflation.

■ As women have gone to work over the past few decades, the share of two-earner households has grown, boosting affluence. For couples in which both husband and wife work full-time, median household income was a lofty $78,604 in 2000.

■ Women are closing the earnings gap with men. Among full-time workers in 1960, women earned only 61 percent as much as men. By 2000, the figure had grown to 73 percent.

■ The number of Americans living in poverty has fallen since 1959, despite the expanding population. Behind the decline in the number of poor is the plummeting poverty rate, which fell from 22 to 11 percent between 1959 and 2000.

Nation Enjoys Record Affluence

Never before have so many Americans been so well off. In 2000, 13.4 percent of households had incomes of $100,000 or more, up from just 2.8 percent in 1967, after adjusting for inflation. Forty-three percent of households had incomes of $50,000 or more in 2000, up from 22 percent in 1967. The proportion of households with incomes below $15,000 fell from 23 to 16 percent of the total during those years.

While affluence has grown for all Americans, the most affluent are gaining control of an expanding share of household income. Households with incomes in the top fifth of the income distribution control half of all household income. Those in the top 5 percent control 22 percent of household income. Meanwhile, the bottom three income quintiles have lost share, now controlling only 27 percent of household income, down from 32 percent in 1967.

Behind the growing affluence of American households is the rise of working women. Many of the most affluent households are dual-income couples, while the less affluent are single-parent and single-earner households.

Nearly one in seven households has an income of $100,000 or more

(percent of households with incomes of $100,000 or more, 1967 to 2000; in 2000 dollars)

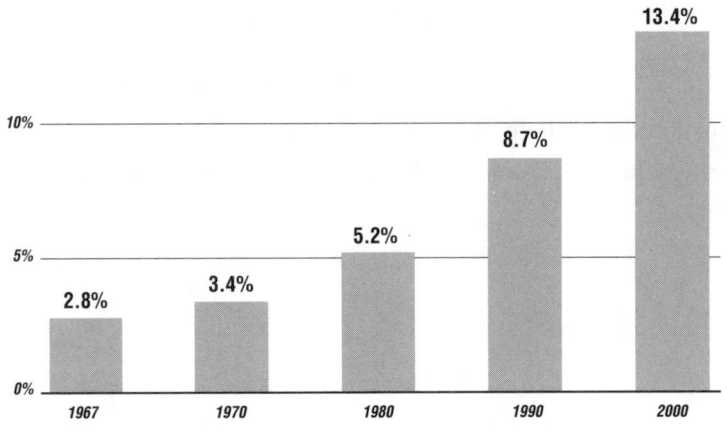

Table 5.1 Distribution of Households by Income, 1967 to 2000

(total number of households and percent distribution by income, 1967 to 2000; percentage point change for selected years; in 2000 dollars; households in thousands as of the following year)

| | total households | | under $15,000 | $15,000–$24,999 | $25,000–$34,999 | $35,000–$49,999 | $50,000–$74,999 | $75,000–$99,999 | $100,000 or more |
	number	percent							
2000	106,418	100.0%	16.0%	13.4%	12.5%	15.5%	18.9%	10.4%	13.4%
1999	104,705	100.0	16.0	13.8	12.4	15.8	18.5	10.5	13.2
1998	103,874	100.0	17.1	13.4	13.1	15.5	18.8	10.2	12.0
1997	102,528	100.0	17.8	14.2	12.7	16.0	18.5	9.7	11.1
1996	101,018	100.0	18.3	14.3	13.5	15.7	18.6	9.5	10.2
1995	99,627	100.0	18.3	14.9	13.1	16.4	18.3	9.4	9.6
1994	98,990	100.0	19.4	14.9	13.3	16.2	17.7	9.1	9.5
1993	97,107	100.0	19.7	14.9	13.1	16.6	17.7	8.8	9.1
1992	96,426	100.0	19.7	14.9	13.2	16.7	18.4	8.7	8.4
1991	95,669	100.0	19.0	14.7	13.7	16.8	18.4	9.0	8.4
1990	94,312	100.0	18.4	14.1	13.7	17.2	18.8	9.1	8.7
1989	93,347	100.0	18.0	14.1	13.1	17.1	19.2	9.2	9.3
1988	92,830	100.0	18.5	14.3	12.8	17.3	19.2	9.3	8.5
1987	91,124	100.0	18.9	14.5	12.9	17.1	19.1	9.3	8.2
1986	89,479	100.0	19.1	14.8	13.3	17.2	18.7	9.1	7.8
1985	88,458	100.0	19.6	15.1	13.7	17.7	18.3	8.7	6.8
1984	86,789	100.0	19.8	15.5	14.0	17.6	18.3	8.2	6.4
1983	85,290	100.0	20.4	16.0	14.4	17.8	17.9	7.6	5.8
1982	83,918	100.0	20.8	15.7	14.5	18.2	17.9	7.4	5.5
1981	83,527	100.0	20.6	16.0	14.1	18.2	18.6	7.5	5.1
1980	82,368	100.0	20.2	15.5	14.0	18.9	18.7	7.5	5.2
1979	80,776	100.0	19.3	15.2	13.8	18.5	19.7	7.8	5.6
1978	77,330	100.0	19.6	15.1	13.7	18.8	19.7	7.7	5.3
1977	76,030	100.0	20.6	15.8	14.3	19.1	18.9	6.7	4.4
1976	74,142	100.0	20.8	16.0	14.8	19.4	18.6	6.4	4.0
1975	72,867	100.0	21.4	16.0	15.4	19.4	18.2	6.0	3.7
1974	71,163	100.0	20.1	15.8	15.3	20.0	18.4	6.5	4.0
1973	69,859	100.0	20.1	15.0	14.8	19.7	19.3	6.6	4.4
1972	68,251	100.0	20.8	14.7	15.1	20.1	18.8	6.3	4.3
1971	66,676	100.0	21.5	15.5	15.7	21.1	17.4	5.4	3.4
1970	64,778	100.0	21.1	15.2	16.3	21.0	17.6	5.4	3.4
1969	63,874	100.0	20.8	15.0	16.4	21.6	17.6	5.2	3.3
1968	62,214	100.0	21.5	15.4	17.8	21.2	16.8	4.5	2.7
1967	60,813	100.0	22.9	16.1	17.4	21.8	14.9	4.1	2.8
Percentage point change									
1990 to 2000	–	–	–2.4	–0.7	–1.2	–1.7	0.1	1.3	4.7
1967 to 2000	–	–	–25.0	–27.6	–28.5	–25.5	–22.1	–30.6	–27.6

Note: (–) means not applicable.
Source: Bureau of the Census, Current Population Surveys, Internet site http://www.census.gov/hhes/income/histinc/h17.html; calculations by New Strategist

Table 5.2 Share of Aggregate Income Received by Each Fifth and Top 5 Percent of Households, 1967 to 2000

(total number of households and percent distribution of aggregate income by household income quintile, 1967 to 2000; percentage point change for selected years; households in thousands as of the following year)

	total households	total	bottom fifth	second fifth	third fifth	fourth fifth	top fifth	top 5 percent
2000	106,418	100.0%	3.6%	8.9%	14.9%	23.0%	49.6%	21.9%
1999	104,705	100.0	3.6	8.9	14.9	23.2	49.4	21.5
1998	103,874	100.0	3.6	9.0	15.0	23.2	49.2	21.4
1997	102,528	100.0	3.6	8.9	15.0	23.2	49.4	21.7
1996	101,018	100.0	3.7	9.0	15.1	23.3	49.0	21.4
1995	99,627	100.0	3.7	9.1	15.2	23.3	48.7	21.0
1994	98,990	100.0	3.6	8.9	15.0	23.4	49.1	21.2
1993	97,107	100.0	3.6	9.0	15.1	23.5	48.9	21.0
1992	96,426	100.0	3.8	9.4	15.8	24.2	46.9	18.6
1991	95,669	100.0	3.8	9.6	15.9	24.2	46.5	18.1
1990	94,312	100.0	3.9	9.6	15.9	24.0	46.6	18.6
1989	93,347	100.0	3.8	9.5	15.8	24.0	46.8	18.9
1988	92,830	100.0	3.8	9.6	16.0	24.3	46.3	18.3
1987	91,124	100.0	3.8	9.6	16.1	24.3	46.2	18.2
1986	89,479	100.0	3.9	9.7	16.2	24.5	45.7	17.5
1985	88,458	100.0	4.0	9.7	16.3	24.6	45.3	17.0
1984	86,789	100.0	4.1	9.9	16.4	24.7	44.9	16.5
1983	85,290	100.0	4.1	10.0	16.5	24.7	44.7	16.4
1982	83,918	100.0	4.1	10.1	16.6	24.7	44.5	16.2
1981	83,527	100.0	4.2	10.2	16.8	25.0	43.8	15.6
1980	82,368	100.0	4.3	10.3	16.9	24.9	43.7	15.8
1979	80,776	100.0	4.2	10.3	16.9	24.7	44.0	16.4
1978	77,330	100.0	4.3	10.3	16.9	24.8	43.7	16.2
1977	76,030	100.0	4.4	10.3	17.0	24.8	43.6	16.1
1976	74,142	100.0	4.4	10.4	17.1	24.8	43.3	16.0
1975	72,867	100.0	4.4	10.5	17.1	24.8	43.2	15.9
1974	71,163	100.0	4.4	10.6	17.1	24.7	43.1	15.9
1973	69,859	100.0	4.2	10.5	17.1	24.6	43.6	16.6
1972	68,251	100.0	4.1	10.5	17.1	24.5	43.9	17.0
1971	66,676	100.0	4.1	10.6	17.3	24.5	43.5	16.7
1970	64,374	100.0	4.1	10.8	17.4	24.5	43.3	16.6
1969	62,874	100.0	4.1	10.9	17.5	24.5	43.0	16.6
1968	62,214	100.0	4.2	11.1	17.5	24.4	42.8	16.6
1967	60,813	100.0	4.0	10.8	17.3	24.2	43.8	17.5
Percentage point change								
1990 to 2000	–	–	–0.3	–0.7	–1.0	–1.0	3.0	3.3
1967 to 2000	–	–	–0.4	–1.9	–2.4	–1.2	5.8	4.4

Note: (–) means not applicable.
Source: Bureau of the Census, Current Population Surveys, Internet site http://www.census.gov/hhes/income/histinc/h02.html; calculations by New Strategist

Most Households Have Enjoyed Rising Incomes

Household income has been growing for decades, although not steadily, as our standard of living has improved. In 2000, median household income stood at $42,151, up from $31,397 in 1967, after adjusting for inflation. Median household income grew 22 percent between 1967 and 1990, then gained another 10 percent during the 1990s. These gains occurred even though today's households are less likely to include married couples, the most affluent household type.

Not all households have experienced rising incomes. Householders under age 25 saw their median household income fall 6 percent between 1967 and 1990 before making gains in the 1990s. Married couples and female-headed families have seen their incomes grow faster than average. Black householders have made bigger gains than any other racial or ethnic group.

Households in the Midwest posted the strongest gains during the 1990s with a 16 percent rise in median income, after adjusting for inflation. The South posted the second-largest gain during the 1990s, an increase of 11 percent, but still has the lowest median household income among the four regions.

Households make income gains

(median household income, 1967 to 2000; in 2000 dollars)

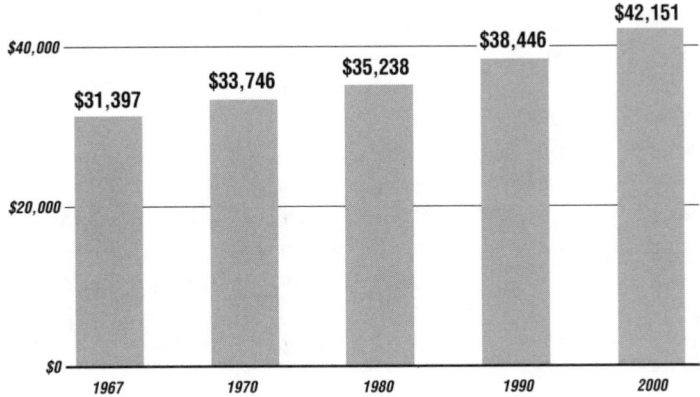

Table 5.3 Median Income of Households by Age of Householder, 1967 to 2000

(median income of households by age of householder, 1967 to 2000; percent change in income for selected years; in 2000 dollars)

	total households	under age 25	aged 25 to 34	aged 35 to 44	aged 45 to 54	aged 55 to 64	aged 65 or older
2000	$42,151	$27,711	$44,477	$53,243	$58,217	$44,993	$23,047
1999	42,187	26,017	43,591	52,582	58,829	46,095	23,578
1998	41,032	24,865	42,281	51,126	57,137	45,550	22,929
1997	39,594	24,163	40,845	49,603	55,505	44,250	22,214
1996	38,798	23,435	39,231	48,558	55,174	43,524	21,260
1995	38,262	23,556	38,963	48,804	53,961	42,754	21,442
1994	37,136	22,260	38,157	47,959	54,398	40,552	20,827
1993	36,746	22,740	36,793	48,063	54,350	39,373	20,879
1992	36,965	21,312	37,693	48,087	53,616	41,016	20,675
1991	37,314	22,682	38,200	48,737	54,189	41,250	21,025
1990	38,446	23,114	38,980	49,511	53,827	41,556	21,641
1989	38,979	25,167	40,216	50,750	55,993	41,559	21,267
1988	38,309	23,978	39,974	51,437	53,771	40,671	20,999
1987	38,007	23,986	39,327	51,313	54,259	40,193	21,063
1986	37,546	23,089	39,056	49,445	53,778	40,380	20,879
1985	36,246	23,095	38,497	47,676	50,986	39,222	20,341
1984	35,568	22,260	37,663	47,261	50,009	38,232	20,309
1983	34,462	22,115	35,883	45,673	50,084	37,586	19,336
1982	34,667	23,745	36,575	45,321	48,097	37,940	18,976
1981	34,696	24,088	37,314	46,174	49,194	38,274	18,014
1980	35,238	25,292	38,476	47,012	49,984	38,894	17,472
1979	36,399	26,342	40,251	48,859	50,964	39,660	17,422
1978	36,440	26,643	39,918	48,206	51,236	38,771	17,129
1977	34,242	24,148	38,034	45,606	48,888	36,107	16,013
1976	34,050	23,786	37,563	44,880	47,411	35,998	16,002
1975	33,489	23,096	37,255	44,109	46,322	35,433	15,850
1974	34,409	24,929	38,174	45,746	47,242	35,248	16,263
1973	35,504	25,318	39,969	47,160	47,559	36,737	15,479
1972	34,802	25,341	39,037	45,536	47,104	36,011	14,962
1971	33,398	24,346	37,279	42,972	44,452	34,567	14,106
1970	33,746	25,767	37,439	43,007	44,096	34,410	13,515
1969	33,973	25,756	37,768	43,462	44,292	33,479	13,482
1968	32,723	25,475	36,311	41,526	41,298	32,241	13,439
1967	31,397	24,681	35,217	39,542	39,990	30,579	12,131

Percent change

1990 to 2000	9.6%	19.9%	14.1%	7.5%	8.2%	8.3%	6.5%
1967 to 2000	34.3	12.3	26.3	34.6	45.6	47.1	90.0

Source: Bureau of the Census, Current Population Surveys, Internet site http://www.census.gov/hhes/income/histinc/h10.html; calculations by New Strategist

Table 5.4 Median Income of Households by Type of Household, 1980 to 2000

(median income of households by household type, 1980 to 2000; percent change in income for selected years; in 2000 dollars)

| | | family households | | | nonfamily households | | | |
	total households	married couples	female householder no spouse present	male householder no spouse present	female householder total	female householder living alone	male householder total	male householder living alone
2000	$42,151	$59,343	$28,126	$42,143	$20,929	$18,163	$31,269	$26,723
1999	42,187	58,736	27,043	43,243	20,586	17,930	31,786	27,754
1998	41,032	57,272	25,740	41,590	19,643	17,312	32,093	27,458
1997	39,594	55,297	24,652	39,197	18,845	16,617	29,523	25,541
1996	38,798	54,502	23,573	38,980	17,926	15,988	29,806	26,290
1995	38,262	52,918	23,970	37,653	17,844	16,091	29,219	25,360
1994	37,136	51,842	22,873	35,073	17,205	15,459	28,307	24,420
1993	36,746	50,729	21,813	35,109	17,506	15,285	29,086	25,138
1992	36,965	50,636	22,160	36,572	17,421	15,605	27,886	24,107
1991	37,314	50,875	22,251	38,409	17,745	15,896	28,515	25,093
1990	38,446	51,354	23,200	40,512	18,103	16,111	28,875	25,633
1989	38,979	52,138	23,441	40,907	18,548	16,438	30,237	26,453
1988	38,309	51,271	22,586	40,303	18,120	16,354	29,549	25,728
1987	38,007	50,975	22,576	38,946	17,171	15,631	29,057	24,784
1986	37,546	49,579	21,621	39,665	–	15,044	–	24,835
1985	36,246	47,822	21,970	37,375	–	15,000	–	25,034
1984	35,568	47,106	21,379	38,957	–	15,295	–	24,122
1983	34,462	45,096	20,196	37,758	–	15,084	–	23,299
1982	34,667	44,800	20,423	36,463	–	14,019	–	23,747
1981	34,696	45,669	20,812	37,367	–	13,470	–	23,351
1980	35,238	46,122	21,549	37,358	–	13,311	–	22,936
Percent change								
1990 to 2000	9.6%	15.6%	21.2%	4.0%	15.6%	12.7%	8.3%	4.3%
1980 to 2000	19.6	28.7	30.5	12.8	–	36.5	–	16.5

Note: (–) means data are not available.
Source: Bureau of the Census, Internet site http://www.census.gov/hhes/income/histinc/h09.html; calculations by New Strategist

Table 5.5 Median Income of Households by Race and Hispanic Origin of Householder, 1967 to 2000

(median income of households by race and Hispanic origin of householder, 1967 to 2000; percent change for selected years; in 2000 dollars)

	total households	Asian	black	Hispanic	white total	white non-Hispanic
2000	$42,151	$55,525	$30,436	$33,455	$44,232	$45,910
1999	42,187	52,925	28,848	31,767	43,932	45,856
1998	41,032	49,212	26,751	29,894	43,171	44,782
1997	39,594	48,415	26,803	28,491	41,699	43,416
1996	38,798	47,307	25,669	27,226	40,623	42,400
1995	38,262	45,603	25,144	25,668	40,159	41,745
1994	37,136	46,595	24,202	26,958	39,166	40,430
1993	36,746	45,105	22,975	26,919	38,768	40,195
1992	36,965	45,611	22,630	27,266	38,863	40,168
1991	37,314	45,145	23,294	28,105	39,101	40,035
1990	38,446	49,369	23,979	28,671	40,100	41,016
1989	38,979	48,683	24,385	29,560	41,002	41,884
1988	38,309	45,404	23,087	28,648	40,499	41,615
1987	38,007	46,998	22,856	28,199	40,044	41,145
1986	37,546	45,404	22,742	27,676	39,474	40,371
1985	36,246	46,998	22,742	26,803	38,226	39,085
1984	35,568	–	21,376	26,963	37,523	38,302
1983	34,462	–	20,509	26,246	36,140	(NA)
1982	34,667	–	20,569	26,086	36,293	36,901
1981	34,696	–	20,571	27,831	36,659	37,188
1980	35,238	–	21,418	27,162	37,176	37,835
1979	36,399	–	22,406	28,839	38,163	38,701
1978	36,440	–	22,765	28,551	37,881	38,595
1977	34,242	–	21,249	26,862	36,008	36,722
1976	34,050	–	21,209	25,684	35,668	36,396
1975	33,489	–	21,024	25,159	35,021	35,285
1974	34,409	–	21,401	27,369	35,986	36,293
1973	35,504	–	21,903	27,506	37,210	37,538
1972	34,802	–	21,311	27,552	36,510	37,030
1971	33,398	–	20,635	27,506	34,934	37,538
1970	33,746	–	21,393	27,552	35,148	37,030
1969	33,973	–	21,431	–	35,456	–
1968	32,723	–	20,091	–	34,071	–
1967	31,397	–	19,010	–	32,742	–
Percent change						
1990 to 2000	9.6%	12.5%	26.9%	16.7%	10.3%	11.9%
1967 to 2000	34.3	–	60.1	–	35.1	–

Note: (–) means data not available.
Source: Bureau of the Census, Current Population Surveys, Internet site http://www.census.gov/hhes/income/histinc/h05.html; calculations by New Strategist

Table 5.6 Median Income of Households by Educational Attainment of Householder, 1991 to 2000

(median income of households by educational attainment of householder, and percent change, 1991 to 2000; in 2000 dollars)

	total households	less than 9th grade	9th to 12th grade (no diploma)	high school graduate	some college, no degree	associate's degree	bachelor's degree or more				
							total	bachelor's degree	master's degree	professional degree	doctoral degree
2000	$43,556	$17,557	$22,753	$36,722	$44,449	$50,356	$71,437	$65,922	$77,935	$100,000	$93,361
1999	43,450	17,841	22,467	36,945	45,632	50,934	72,149	66,570	76,978	103,359	100,594
1998	42,521	17,046	21,868	36,271	43,958	51,287	70,144	65,621	75,010	100,571	88,743
1997	40,862	16,628	21,240	36,143	42,815	48,425	67,721	63,180	72,881	98,682	93,336
1996	39,918	16,808	21,483	35,303	41,975	48,655	65,565	60,273	69,838	98,760	88,719
1995	39,563	16,891	20,546	35,230	41,720	47,291	65,183	59,349	72,939	92,083	89,832
1994	38,543	16,431	20,192	34,612	41,297	46,337	66,114	60,278	70,263	89,781	89,959
1993	37,834	16,373	21,132	33,758	41,427	46,558	66,005	60,552	70,975	103,115	87,926
1992	38,127	16,193	20,901	34,896	42,516	46,184	65,061	59,583	69,678	102,218	84,484
1991	38,436	16,375	21,719	35,284	43,536	49,172	64,741	60,325	68,337	96,547	87,092
Percent change											
1991 to 2000	13.3%	7.2%	4.8%	4.1%	2.1%	2.4%	10.3%	9.3%	14.0%	3.6%	7.2%

Note: Because educational attainment categories changed in 1991, earlier data are not strictly comparable.
Source: Bureau of the Census, Current Population Surveys, Internet site http://www.census.gov/hhes/income/histinc/h13.html; calculations by New Strategist

Table 5.7 Median Income of Households by Educational Attainment of Householder, 1967 to 1990

(median income of households by educational attainment of householder, and percent change, 1967 to 1990; in 2000 dollars)

	total households	fewer than 9 years	high school 1–3 years	high school 4 years	college, 1–3 years	college, 4 years or more total	college, 4 years or more 4 years	college, 4 years or more 5+ years
1990	$39,491	$17,363	$23,357	$36,906	$45,869	$64,903	$60,453	$4,450
1989	40,271	17,120	23,958	37,838	47,309	66,318	61,779	$4,539
1988	39,577	17,396	23,357	38,005	46,060	65,128	59,207	$5,921
1987	39,147	17,398	24,661	37,811	46,746	64,126	59,754	$4,372
1986	38,768	17,563	24,331	37,951	45,320	63,993	59,996	$3,997
1985	37,641	17,414	24,292	37,021	44,024	62,064	57,842	$4,222
1984	36,896	17,355	24,681	37,021	42,724	60,206	56,834	$3,372
1983	35,603	17,158	23,679	35,604	42,441	58,504	54,721	$3,783
1982	35,679	17,482	24,111	36,211	42,214	57,596	53,916	$3,680
1981	36,024	17,601	24,801	37,385	42,935	56,694	52,767	$3,927
1980	36,578	17,659	26,291	39,075	43,257	57,464	54,398	$3,066
1979	37,677	18,296	27,176	40,302	44,901	58,613	55,110	$3,503
1978	37,535	18,479	28,065	40,087	44,275	58,215	54,834	$3,381
1977	35,650	17,739	26,996	38,625	42,424	56,056	53,127	$2,929
1976	35,413	18,080	28,032	38,393	42,647	56,067	52,953	$3,114
1975	34,896	17,962	27,194	37,621	42,925	55,969	52,813	$3,156
1974	35,768	18,939	29,695	39,047	43,389	57,264	54,553	$2,711
1973	36,896	–	31,255	40,645	45,188	60,039	–	–
1972	36,094	–	31,249	40,052	44,642	59,418	–	–
1971	34,567	–	30,920	38,503	42,858	55,994	–	–
1970	34,607	–	31,346	38,880	43,583	55,792	–	–
1969	34,885	–	32,070	39,040	43,883	55,708	–	–
1968	33,463	–	31,447	37,469	42,096	53,617	–	–
1967	32,236	–	30,588	36,324	40,895	52,152	–	–
Percent change								
1967 to 1990	22.5%	–	–23.6%	1.6%	12.2%	24.4%	–	–

Note: Because educational attainment categories changed in 1991, earlier data are not strictly comparable. (–) means data not available.

Source: Bureau of the Census, Current Population Surveys, Internet site http://www.census.gov/hhes/income/histinc/h14.html; calculations by New Strategist

Table 5.8   Median Income of Households by Region, 1975 to 2000

(median income of households by region, 1975 to 2000; percent change in income for selected years; in 2000 dollars)

	total households	Northeast	Midwest	South	West
2000	$42,151	$45,118	$44,647	$38,402	$44,759
1999	42,187	43,394	44,113	38,700	44,155
1998	41,032	42,877	42,851	37,773	43,246
1997	39,594	41,653	40,997	36,748	41,902
1996	38,798	40,891	39,986	35,442	40,583
1995	38,262	40,547	40,241	34,743	40,398
1994	37,136	40,200	37,413	34,554	39,654
1993	36,746	39,694	36,933	33,453	39,685
1992	36,965	39,817	37,168	33,313	40,209
1991	37,314	41,452	37,067	33,662	39,948
1990	38,446	41,955	38,387	34,593	40,780
1989	38,979	44,018	38,769	34,885	41,919
1988	38,309	42,812	38,753	34,625	40,576
1987	38,007	41,074	37,604	34,954	40,645
1986	37,546	39,955	37,477	34,049	40,719
1985	36,246	39,111	36,143	32,837	39,567
1984	35,568	37,369	35,839	32,724	38,808
1983	34,462	36,002	34,764	31,989	36,660
1982	34,667	35,588	35,783	31,952	36,422
1981	34,696	36,062	35,819	31,544	37,188
1980	35,238	36,197	36,438	32,429	37,823
1979	36,399	37,290	38,270	33,098	38,577
1978	36,440	37,516	37,913	33,031	37,521
1977	34,242	35,907	36,003	31,303	35,272
1976	34,050	35,091	36,726	30,762	34,995
1975	33,489.	35,018	35,685	29,910	34,593
Percent change					
1990 to 2000	9.6%	7.5%	16.3%	11.0%	9.8%
1975 to 2000	25.9	28.8	25.1	28.4	29.4

Source: Bureau of the Census, Current Population Surveys, Internet site http://www.census.gov/hhes/income/histinc/h06.html; calculations by New Strategist

Dual-Income Couples Boost Affluence

As women have gone to work over the past few decades, the share of two-earner households has grown, boosting affluence. Between 1987 and 2000, two-earner households saw their incomes climb 17 percent, after adjusting for inflation, to $62,112. The median income of one-earner households grew only 6 percent during those years.

For couples in which both husband and wife work full-time, median household income reached a lofty $78,604 in 2000, 10 percent more than in 1987, after adjusting for inflation. For couples in which the wife did not work, median household income rose 3 percent during those years, to $53,577.

A growing number of wives earn more than their husbands. Their number increased from 4 million in 1981 to 7.5 million in 2000, while the proportion climbed from 16 to 22 percent. It's likely this trend will continue as career-oriented younger women replace older, just-a-job women in the labor force.

Many wives earn more than their husbands

(percent of wives who earn more than their husbands, 1981 and 2000)

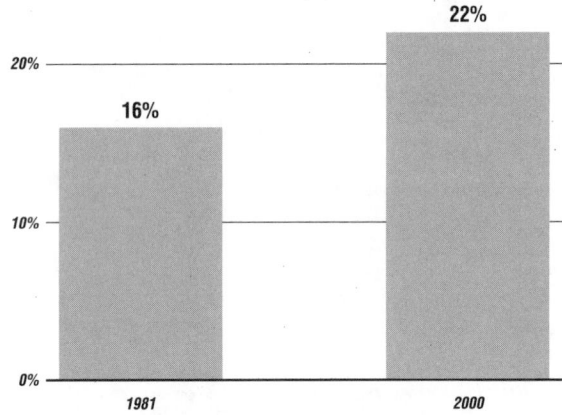

Table 5.9 Median Income of Households by Number of Earners, 1987 to 2000

(median household income by number of earners, and percent change, 1987 to 2000; in 2000 dollars)

	total households	no earners	one earner	two earners	three earners	four or more earners
2000	$42,151	$15,171	$33,399	$62,112	$76,263	$91,218
1999	42,187	15,922	33,021	61,704	76,562	92,424
1998	41,032	15,239	32,882	60,556	73,877	91,461
1997	39,594	15,132	31,864	57,984	71,883	90,751
1996	38,798	14,561	30,494	57,299	68,243	85,817
1995	38,262	14,711	30,953	56,142	70,953	83,362
1994	37,136	14,013	30,168	54,942	69,545	85,492
1993	36,746	13,888	30,064	54,649	67,365	84,973
1992	36,965	13,829	30,471	53,805	67,678	83,502
1991	37,314	14,256	30,759	53,301	68,629	85,669
1990	38,446	14,328	31,554	53,485	68,383	86,026
1989	38,979	14,437	32,106	54,224	69,483	87,923
1988	38,309	13,973	31,714	53,779	69,009	90,146
1987	38,007	13,881	31,478	53,203	69,089	88,007

Percent change

| 1987 to 2000 | 10.9% | 9.3% | 6.1% | 16.7% | 10.4% | 3.6% |

Source: Bureau of the Census, Current Population Surveys, Internet site http://www.census.gov/hhes/income/histinc/h12.html; calculations by New Strategist

Table 5.10 Median Income of Married Couples by Work Experience of Husband and Wife, 1987 to 2000

(median household income of married couples with husband working full-time, year-round by work experience of wife, and percent change, 1987 to 2000; in 2000 dollars)

	total couples	wife worked total	wife worked full-time, year-round	wife did not work
2000	$70,349	$74,362	$78,604	$53,577
1999	69,233	73,660	78,744	52,259
1998	67,269	71,833	76,956	51,192
1997	65,798	69,443	74,371	51,904
1996	64,615	68,031	72,287	49,172
1995	63,166	67,233	72,179	48,425
1994	62,772	66,620	71,779	48,422
1993	62,186	65,889	71,410	49,138
1992	62,077	65,734	71,296	49,673
1991	62,043	65,282	70,713	50,185
1990	61,086	64,571	70,706	50,181
1989	62,190	65,552	71,460	51,916
1988	61,620	65,371	71,609	50,861
1987	61,517	64,946	71,299	51,854
Percent change				
1987 to 2000	14.4%	14.5%	10.2%	3.3%

Source: Bureau of the Census, Current Population Surveys, Internet site http://www.census.gov/hhes/income/histinc/f13.html; calculations by New Strategist

Table 5.11   Wives Who Earn More than Their Husbands, 1981 to 2000

(number of married couples in which both husband and wife have earnings, and number and percent in which wives earn more than husbands, 1981 to 2000; couples in thousands as of the following year)

	husbands and wives with earnings	wives earning more than husbands	
		number	percent
2000	33,355	7,489	22.5%
1999	33,344	7,420	22.3
1998	32,783	7,435	22.7
1997	32,745	7,446	22.7
1996	32,390	7,327	22.6
1995	32,030	7,028	21.9
1994	32,093	7,218	22.5
1993	31,267	6,960	22.3
1992	31,224	6,979	22.4
1991	31,003	6,499	21.0
1987	29,079	5,266	18.1
1983	26,120	4,800	18.4
1981	25,744	4,088	15.9

Source: Bureau of the Census, Current Population Surveys, Internet site http://www.census.gov/hhes/income/histinc/f22.html

Women's Incomes Are Rising Faster Than Men's

The median income of women nearly tripled between 1950 and 2000, rising from just $5,808 to $16,188, after adjusting for inflation. Men's median income grew only 80 percent during those years. Consequently, women narrowed the income gap with men. In 1950, women's median income was just 37 percent as high as men's. By 2000, it was 57 percent of men's. Women's incomes are much lower than men's in part because these figures include both full- and part-time workers, and many more women than men work part-time.

Among both men and women, people aged 65 or older have seen their incomes grow the most since 1950. During the 1990s, however, the oldest age group made below-average income gains as interest rates fell. The income gains of black men and women have surpassed those of any other racial or ethnic group during the past half-century. Men and women in the South saw their incomes grow the fastest between 1950 and 2000, while women in the Northeast and men in the West experienced the slowest income growth.

Rising incomes for men and women

(median income of people aged 15 or older with income, by sex, 1950 and 2000; in 2000 dollars)

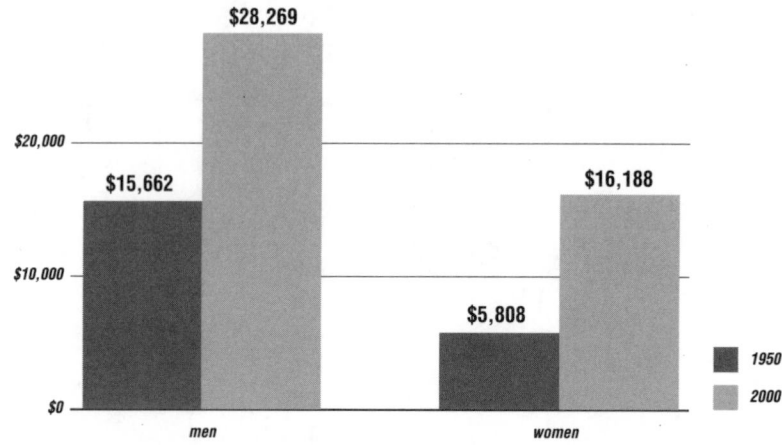

Table 5.12   Median Income of People by Sex, 1950 to 2000

(median income of people aged 15 or older with income by sex, and women's income as a percent of men's, 1950 to 2000; percent change for selected years; in 2000 dollars)

	men	women	women's income as a percent of men's
2000	$28,269	$16,188	57.3%
1999	28,191	15,825	56.1
1998	27,955	15,227	54.5
1997	26,976	14,662	54.4
1996	26,054	14,009	53.8
1995	25,333	13,620	53.8
1994	25,000	13,197	52.8
1993	24,821	12,993	52.3
1992	24,681	12,928	52.4
1991	25,353	12,975	51.2
1990	26,056	12,930	49.6
1989	26,825	12,978	48.4
1988	26,606	12,501	47.0
1987	25,939	12,097	46.6
1986	25,809	11,476	44.5
1985	25,032	11,076	44.2
1984	24,754	10,898	44.0
1983	24,143	10,427	43.2
1982	23,975	10,118	42.2
1981	24,508	9,928	40.5
1980	24,932	9,790	39.3
1979	26,046	9,623	36.9
1978	26,452	9,840	37.2
1977	25,540	9,943	38.9
1976	25,300	9,598	37.9
1975	25,125	9,607	38.2
1974	25,974	9,471	36.5
1973	27,209	9,444	34.7
1972	26,737	9,328	34.9
1971	25,537	8,908	34.9
1970	25,771	8,643	33.5
1969	26,036	8,634	33.2
1968	25,272	8,533	33.8
1967	24,408	7,916	32.4
1966	24,034	7,420	30.9
1965	23,425	7,093	30.3
1964	21,997	6,859	31.2
1963	21,637	6,581	30.4
1962	21,253	6,524	30.7
1961	20,562	6,278	30.5
1960	20,224	6,250	30.9
1959	20,169	6,171	30.6
1958	19,001	5,970	31.4
1957	19,207	6,268	32.6
1956	19,455	6,208	31.9
1955	18,378	6,130	33.4
1954	17,437	6,335	36.3
1953	17,705	6,409	36.2
1952	17,217	6,360	36.9
1951	16,662	5,898	35.4
1950	15,662	5,808	37.1

	percent change		percentage point change
1990 to 2000	8.5%	25.2%	7.6
1950 to 2000	80.5	178.7	20.2

Source: Bureau of the Census, Internet site http://www.census.gov/hhes/income/histinc/p08.html>; calculations by New Strategist

Table 5.13 Median Income of Men by Age, 1950 to 2000

(median income of men with income by age, 1950 to 2000; percent change for selected years; in 2000 dollars)

	total men	< 25	25 to 34	35 to 44	45 to 54	55 to 64	65+
2000	$28,269	$9,548	$30,633	$37,088	$41,072	$34,414	$19,167
1999	28,191	8,581	30,867	37,434	42,314	34,778	19,720
1998	27,955	8,642	29,669	37,119	41,071	34,585	19,169
1997	26,976	7,991	27,815	35,150	40,257	33,337	19,011
1996	26,054	7,608	27,525	35,163	39,607	32,276	18,238
1995	25,333	7,762	26,509	35,279	39,957	32,540	18,509
1994	25,000	8,112	26,020	35,344	40,208	31,163	17,553
1993	24,821	7,562	25,791	35,689	38,997	29,569	17,623
1992	24,681	7,598	25,938	35,584	38,830	30,907	17,613
1991	25,353	7,780	26,747	36,292	39,361	31,534	17,782
1990	26,056	8,113	27,468	38,228	39,812	31,848	18,211
1989	26,825	8,513	28,813	39,695	41,752	32,939	17,674
1988	26,606	8,222	29,243	40,167	41,620	31,867	17,548
1987	25,939	7,958	29,061	39,438	41,545	31,914	17,394
1986	25,809	7,967	28,898	39,469	41,858	31,721	17,409
1985	25,032	7,666	28,640	38,916	39,664	31,088	16,728
1984	24,754	7,472	28,710	38,981	39,018	30,985	16,582
1983	24,143	7,069	27,730	37,028	38,142	30,847	16,075
1982	23,975	7,609	28,214	37,207	37,025	30,640	15,791
1981	24,508	5,588	29,272	38,413	38,240	31,588	14,803
1980	24,932	9,147	31,000	39,869	39,743	31,665	14,603
1979	26,046	9,411	32,443	40,563	40,277	33,230	14,225
1978	26,452	8,834	32,439	40,087	40,092	32,956	14,432
1977	25,540	8,167	31,187	39,369	38,680	30,889	13,942
1976	25,300	7,974	31,449	38,452	37,829	30,928	14,207
1975	25,125	8,077	31,323	37,834	37,482	30,197	14,074
1974	25,974	8,337	32,215	38,724	37,747	30,648	14,253
1973	27,209	–	34,072	40,631	39,419	32,262	13,868
1972	26,737	–	33,083	39,604	38,656	31,948	13,444
1971	25,537	–	31,674	36,872	35,710	29,351	12,759
1970	25,771	–	31,899	36,570	35,442	29,666	11,885
1969	26,036	–	32,293	36,630	34,905	29,478	11,453
1968	25,272	–	30,982	34,992	32,976	28,387	11,208
1967	24,408	–	29,885	33,564	32,430	26,909	10,127
1966	24,034	–	29,474	33,089	31,336	26,045	9,793
1965	23,425	–	28,014	31,311	29,674	24,484	9,868
1964	21,997	–	27,138	30,768	28,757	23,389	9,642
1963	21,637	–	26,237	29,897	27,954	23,508	9,560
1962	21,253	–	25,347	29,104	27,330	23,334	9,285
1961	20,562	–	24,764	28,106	26,118	22,565	8,629
1960	20,224	–	24,308	27,406	25,676	21,260	8,417
1959	20,169	–	23,953	26,845	24,483	21,143	7,952
1958	19,001	–	22,636	24,996	22,849	20,143	7,554
1957	19,207	–	22,838	24,786	23,475	19,228	7,423
1956	19,455	–	22,750	24,717	23,290	19,271	7,677
1955	18,378	–	21,268	23,287	22,647	18,827	7,317
1954	17,437	–	20,009	22,123	20,812	17,448	6,925
1953	17,705	–	20,387	21,866	20,976	17,980	6,321
1952	17,217	–	19,369	20,567	19,330	16,685	6,915
1951	16,662	–	18,558	20,415	18,513	16,030	5,689
1950	15,662	–	18,045	19,831	18,837	15,199	6,009

Percent change

1990 to 2000	8.5%	17.7%	11.5%	–3.0%	3.2%	8.1%	5.2%
1950 to 2000	80.5	–	69.8	87.0	118.0	126.4	219.0

Note: (–) means data not available.
Source: Bureau of the Census, Current Populations Surveys, Internet site http://www.census.gov/hhes/income/histinc/p08.html; calculations by New Strategist

Table 5.14 Median Income of Women by Age, 1950 to 2000

(median income of women with income by age, 1950 to 2000; percent change for selected years; in 2000 dollars)

	total women	< 25	25 to 34	35 to 44	45 to 54	55 to 64	65+
2000	$16,188	$7,742	$20,940	$21,861	$24,193	$16,468	$10,898
1999	15,825	6,914	20,048	21,378	23,347	16,452	11,311
1998	15,227	6,895	19,265	21,405	22,780	15,485	11,084
1997	14,662	6,786	18,882	20,015	21,971	15,382	10,766
1996	14,009	6,429	17,910	20,165	20,820	14,556	10,523
1995	13,620	5,962	17,468	19,534	19,900	13,902	10,504
1994	13,197	6,340	17,132	18,634	19,626	12,508	10,301
1993	12,993	6,294	16,453	18,636	19,201	12,737	9,997
1992	12,928	6,238	16,447	18,602	19,127	12,226	9,874
1991	12,975	6,437	16,057	18,734	18,237	12,264	10,143
1990	12,930	6,294	16,164	18,623	18,271	12,069	10,328
1989	12,978	6,390	16,493	18,616	17,723	12,356	10,323
1988	12,501	6,311	16,274	17,654	16,914	11,788	9,995
1987	12,097	6,429	16,012	17,493	16,426	10,998	10,057
1986	11,476	6,099	15,548	16,685	15,654	11,125	9,689
1985	11,076	5,818	15,161	15,769	14,762	11,008	9,688
1984	10,898	5,727	14,903	15,171	14,127	10,849	9,552
1983	10,427	5,704	14,031	14,620	13,539	10,113	9,239
1982	10,118	5,761	13,701	13,493	12,893	10,152	9,221
1981	9,928	3,631	13,821	13,399	12,788	9,777	8,560
1980	9,790	6,216	13,875	12,864	12,740	9,801	8,409
1979	9,623	6,242	14,041	13,017	12,374	9,698	8,316
1978	9,840	6,246	14,124	14,040	13,720	10,820	8,176
1977	9,943	5,775	14,891	13,972	14,305	11,437	7,814
1976	9,598	5,390	14,419	13,844	14,309	10,881	7,558
1975	9,607	5,347	14,338	13,353	14,377	11,068	7,660
1974	9,471	5,446	13,872	13,678	14,502	11,134	7,495
1973	9,444	–	13,990	13,882	14,533	11,588	7,157
1972	9,328	–	13,656	13,860	14,596	11,517	6,815
1971	8,908	–	13,114	13,436	14,498	11,398	6,311
1970	8,643	–	12,460	13,330	14,284	11,382	5,881
1969	8,634	–	12,149	13,109	14,409	11,303	5,658
1968	8,533	–	12,175	12,864	13,790	10,887	5,540
1967	7,916	–	11,499	12,466	13,542	10,338	4,936
1966	7,420	–	10,645	11,732	12,493	10,029	4,915
1965	7,093	–	10,526	11,584	11,939	9,416	4,589
1964	6,859	–	9,638	10,693	11,408	9,041	4,506
1963	6,581	–	8,902	10,289	11,085	8,509	4,413
1962	6,524	–	8,624	10,116	10,991	8,113	4,472
1961	6,278	–	9,135	10,421	10,279	7,265	4,192
1960	6,250	–	8,699	10,082	10,419	7,014	4,070
1959	6,171	–	8,714	9,325	10,259	7,221	4,022
1958	5,970	–	8,483	9,224	9,564	6,731	3,939
1957	6,268	–	8,969	9,319	9,497	7,010	3,871
1956	6,208	–	8,504	9,379	9,454	7,369	3,987
1955	6,130	–	8,762	8,658	9,441	6,879	3,831
1954	6,335	–	8,645	8,639	8,912	6,526	3,790
1953	6,409	–	9,031	8,800	9,322	6,431	3,622
1952	6,360	–	8,750	8,800	8,739	6,515	3,626
1951	5,898	–	9,161	8,681	7,490	5,464	3,025
1950	5,808	–	8,258	7,971	7,569	5,594	3,236

Percent change

1990 to 2000	25.2%	23.0%	29.5%	17.4%	32.4%	36.4%	5.5%
1950 to 2000	178.7	–	153.6	174.3	219.6	194.4	236.8

Note: (–) means data not available.
Source: Bureau of the Census, Current Population Surveys, Internet site http://www.census.gov/hhes/income/histinc/p08.html; calculations by New Strategist

Table 5.15   Median Income of Men by Race and Hispanic Origin, 1950 to 2000

(median income of men aged 15 or older with income by race and Hispanic origin, 1950 to 2000; percent change for selected years; in 2000 dollars)

	total men	Asian	black	Hispanic	white total	white non-Hispanic
2000	$28,269	$30,445	$21,659	$19,829	$29,696	$31,213
1999	28,191	28,663	21,270	18,847	29,524	31,622
1998	27,955	26,511	20,388	18,210	29,172	31,511
1997	26,976	26,799	19,362	17,351	27,942	29,487
1996	26,054	25,551	18,027	16,875	27,273	28,739
1995	25,333	24,884	17,972	16,663	26,830	28,611
1994	25,000	26,346	17,244	16,690	26,092	27,765
1993	24,821	25,455	17,179	16,101	25,855	27,254
1992	24,681	23,999	15,763	16,178	25,828	27,027
1991	25,353	24,311	16,055	17,115	26,500	27,464
1990	26,056	24,901	16,522	17,295	27,182	28,193
1989	26,825	27,792	17,003	18,070	28,133	29,208
1988	26,606	25,922	16,948	18,335	28,085	29,132
1987	25,939	–	16,356	17,836	27,571	28,721
1986	25,809	–	16,320	17,391	27,236	28,460
1985	25,032	–	16,525	17,547	26,260	27,151
1984	24,754	–	14,992	17,615	26,130	26,907
1983	24,143	–	14,796	18,610	25,413	–
1982	23,975	–	15,190	17,996	25,347	25,995
1981	24,508	–	15,464	18,560	26,005	26,689
1980	24,932	–	15,936	19,219	26,519	27,222
1979	26,046	–	16,843	19,616	27,209	27,782
1978	26,452	–	16,597	20,271	27,705	28,000
1977	25,540	–	15,875	19,672	26,751	27,294
1976	25,300	–	16,059	18,923	26,671	27,160
1975	25,125	–	15,779	19,233	26,394	27,001
1974	25,974	–	16,859	19,800	27,209	27,784
1973	27,209	–	17,269	20,941	28,550	28,959
1972	26,737	–	16,986	20,765	28,044	28,363
1971	25,537	–	15,967	–	26,773	–
1970	25,771	–	16,061	–	27,088	–
1969	26,036	–	15,944	–	27,397	–
1968	25,272	–	15,713	–	26,485	–
1967	24,408	–	14,707	–	25,696	–
1966	24,034	–	14,028	–	25,330	–
1965	23,425	–	13,277	–	24,670	–
1964	21,997	–	13,245	–	23,365	–
1963	21,637	–	11,982	–	23,052	–
1962	21,253	–	11,147	–	22,639	–
1961	20,562	–	11,236	–	21,740	–
1960	20,224	–	11,202	–	21,294	–
1959	20,169	–	9,996	–	21,239	–
1958	19,001	–	10,056	–	20,184	–
1957	19,207	–	10,808	–	20,414	–
1956	19,455	–	10,821	–	20,622	–
1955	18,378	–	10,207	–	19,396	–
1954	17,437	–	9,142	–	18,371	–
1953	17,705	–	10,295	–	18,634	–
1952	17,217	–	9,892	–	18,049	–
1951	16,662	–	9,640	–	17,503	–
1950	15,662	–	8,965	–	16,509	–

Percent change

	total men	Asian	black	Hispanic	white total	white non-Hispanic
1990 to 2000	8.5%	22.3%	31.1%	14.7%	9.2%	10.7%
1950 to 2000	80.5	–	141.6	–	79.9	–

Note: (–) means data not available.
Source: Bureau of the Census, Current Population Surveys, Internet site http://www.census.gov/hhes/income/histinc/p02.html; calculations by New Strategist

Table 5.16 Median Income of Women by Race and Hispanic Origin, 1950 to 2000

(median income of women aged 15 or older with income by race and Hispanic origin, 1950 to 2000; percent change for selected years; in 2000 dollars)

	total women	Asian	black	Hispanic	white total	white non-Hispanic
2000	$16,188	$17,313	$16,084	$12,249	$16,216	$16,804
1999	15,825	17,406	15,267	11,694	15,878	16,457
1998	15,227	16,069	13,862	11,462	15,424	16,057
1997	14,662	15,313	13,961	10,978	14,757	15,396
1996	14,009	15,997	12,869	10,367	14,168	14,773
1995	13,620	14,442	12,307	10,025	13,829	14,380
1994	13,197	14,229	12,136	9,914	13,386	13,749
1993	12,993	14,544	11,184	9,527	13,251	13,643
1992	12,928	14,324	10,723	10,024	13,228	13,577
1991	12,975	13,657	10,919	9,925	13,279	13,624
1990	12,930	14,234	10,693	9,671	13,247	13,586
1989	12,978	15,115	10,619	10,312	13,231	13,502
1988	12,501	13,008	10,341	9,836	12,809	13,109
1987	12,097	–	10,134	9,669	12,406	12,685
1986	11,476	–	9,902	9,558	11,703	11,900
1985	11,076	–	9,633	9,239	11,291	11,415
1984	10,898	–	9,781	9,251	11,027	11,203
1983	10,427	–	9,146	8,914	10,595	–
1982	10,118	–	9,045	8,834	10,255	10,561
1981	9,928	–	8,919	9,204	10,039	10,219
1980	9,790	–	9,113	8,765	9,843	9,909
1979	9,623	–	8,840	9,177	9,714	9,966
1978	9,840	–	8,967	9,163	9,959	10,399
1977	9,943	–	8,717	9,257	10,095	10,556
1976	9,598	–	9,120	9,016	9,679	10,342
1975	9,607	–	8,818	9,087	9,706	10,262
1974	9,471	–	8,648	9,244	9,579	10,058
1973	9,444	–	8,606	8,957	9,535	9,737
1972	9,328	–	8,771	9,500	9,389	9,475
1971	8,908	–	7,935	–	9,056	–
1970	8,643	–	7,971	–	8,755	–
1969	8,634	–	7,452	–	8,837	–
1968	8,533	–	6,969	–	8,786	–
1967	7,916	–	6,417	–	8,154	–
1966	7,420	–	5,911	–	7,768	–
1965	7,093	–	5,475	–	7,522	–
1964	6,859	–	5,041	–	7,186	–
1963	6,581	–	4,619	–	6,897	–
1962	6,524	–	4,613	–	6,869	–
1961	6,278	–	4,462	–	6,656	–
1960	6,250	–	4,149	–	6,702	–
1959	6,171	–	4,077	–	6,620	–
1958	5,970	–	3,807	–	6,493	–
1957	6,268	–	3,970	–	6,859	–
1956	6,208	–	3,928	–	6,834	–
1955	6,130	–	3,574	–	6,852	–
1954	6,335	–	3,817	–	7,039	–
1953	6,409	–	4,161	–	7,107	–
1952	6,360	–	2,867	–	7,425	–
1951	5,898	–	2,924	–	6,892	–
1950	5,808	–	2,889	–	6,460	–
Percent change						
1990 to 2000	25.2%	21.6%	50.4%	26.7%	22.4%	23.7%
1950 to 2000	178.7	–	456.7	–	151.0	–

Note: (–) means data not available.
Source: Bureau of the Census, Current Population Surveys, Internet site http://www.census.gov/hhes/income/histinc/p02.html; calculations by New Strategist

Table 5.17 Median Income of Men by Educational Attainment, 1991 to 2000

(median income of men aged 25 or older by educational attainment, and percent change, 1991 to 2000; in 2000 dollars)

	total men	less than 9th grade	9th to 12th grade (no diploma)	high school graduate	some college, no degree	associate's degree	total	bachelor's degree	master's degree	professional degree	doctoral degree
								bachelor's degree or more			
2000	$32,092	$14,149	$18,952	$27,669	$33,035	$37,956	$53,457	$49,180	$59,376	$81,606	$71,732
1999	32,675	13,889	18,302	28,155	33,823	37,863	53,995	48,915	60,913	84,686	72,819
1998	32,346	13,265	18,426	28,007	33,373	37,947	53,047	48,275	58,864	80,578	68,925
1997	30,943	13,008	17,995	27,234	32,673	35,234	50,424	44,884	56,206	77,331	73,446
1996	29,786	13,308	17,554	27,126	31,876	36,145	48,275	43,315	54,661	78,564	68,054
1995	29,582	13,163	17,731	26,235	31,444	34,838	48,643	43,835	55,104	74,395	64,401
1994	29,310	13,034	16,786	25,768	30,810	35,270	48,373	44,545	53,677	71,062	66,157
1993	28,941	12,815	17,114	25,621	30,962	34,976	48,989	44,078	53,632	81,957	65,576
1992	28,830	12,517	17,155	26,117	31,755	34,739	48,936	44,337	53,444	82,566	62,358
1991	29,337	12,781	18,252	26,687	32,935	36,362	49,299	44,672	53,414	78,949	64,214
Percent change											
1991 to 2000	9.4%	10.7%	3.8%	3.7%	0.3%	4.4%	8.4%	10.1%	11.2%	3.4%	11.7%

Note: Because educational attainment categories changed in 1991, earlier data are not strictly comparable.
Source: Bureau of the Census, Current Population Surveys, Internet site http://www.census.gov/hhes/earnings/histinc/p16.html; calculations by New Strategist

Table 5.18 Median Income of Men by Educational Attainment, 1963 to 1990

(median income of men aged 25 or older by educational attainment, and percent change, 1967 to 1990; in 2000 dollars)

| | total men | less than 9 years | high school | | college | college, 4 years or more | | |
			1–3 years	4 years	1–3 years	total	4 years	5+ years
1990	$29,969	$13,225	$19,428	$27,879	$34,906	$48,611	$45,171	$54,673
1989	30,826	13,489	19,471	29,195	35,602	50,639	46,765	56,403
1988	31,011	13,962	19,794	29,812	35,737	50,231	45,490	56,352
1987	30,948	14,208	20,623	29,550	36,003	49,801	45,802	55,210
1986	30,973	13,935	20,210	29,818	35,799	50,225	47,658	54,654
1985	30,208	13,806	19,751	29,154	34,654	49,027	45,577	54,096
1984	29,994	13,653	19,881	29,871	33,922	48,077	44,757	52,191
1983	29,004	13,861	19,994	28,989	33,542	46,379	43,153	50,392
1982	29,092	13,873	20,760	29,312	34,339	45,443	42,331	49,437
1981	30,114	14,543	21,712	30,904	35,478	46,360	43,002	49,731
1980	30,998	14,812	22,954	32,256	35,835	46,126	43,452	50,209
1979	32,193	15,030	24,206	34,199	37,182	47,417	44,501	51,260
1978	32,359	15,772	25,203	34,691	37,395	48,745	45,414	51,834
1977	31,222	15,476	25,288	33,321	35,945	46,751	43,877	50,732
1976	31,033	15,618	25,595	33,263	35,824	46,496	44,195	49,537
1975	30,872	15,532	25,046	33,585	37,065	47,344	44,441	50,840
1974	31,972	16,333	27,409	34,843	38,143	49,172	44,255	49,667
1973	33,100	17,759	29,121	36,585	39,416	49,663	47,079	54,131
1972	32,261	17,561	28,625	35,548	39,374	50,693	48,522	53,676
1971	30,491	16,977	28,005	33,620	38,115	48,559	46,513	51,200
1970	30,489	17,078	28,340	33,892	38,170	48,996	46,921	51,874
1969	30,689	17,353	28,668	34,156	38,043	49,630	48,164	51,525
1968	29,520	17,260	27,761	32,672	36,421	47,574	45,921	49,602
1967	28,421	16,338	27,063	31,841	35,845	46,394	44,350	49,172
1966	27,758	15,799	27,096	31,363	34,919	44,571	44,064	45,482
1965	26,107	15,026	25,808	30,117	33,680	42,196	40,797	44,831
1964	25,609	14,821	25,334	29,661	33,287	41,679	39,904	44,330
1963	25,043	14,630	24,717	28,775	32,626	38,310	37,432	40,454

Percent change

	total men	less than 9 years	high school 1–3 years	high school 4 years	college 1–3 years	college total	college 4 years	college 5+ years
1963 to 1990	19.7%	–9.6%	–21.4%	–3.1%	7.0%	26.9%	20.7%	35.1%

Note: Because educational attainment categories changed in 1991, earlier data are not strictly comparable.
Source: Bureau of the Census, Current Population Surveys, Internet site http://www.census.gov/hhes/income/histinc/p17.html; calculations by New Strategist

Table 5.19 Median Income of Women by Educational Attainment, 1991 to 2000

(median income of women aged 25 or older by educational attainment, and percent change, 1991 to 2000; in 2000 dollars)

	total women	less than 9th grade	9th to 12th grade (no diploma)	high school graduate	some college, no degree	associate's degree	bachelor's degree or more				
							total	bachelor's degree	master's degree	professional degree	doctoral degree
2000	$18,025	$8,404	$9,995	$15,120	$20,181	$23,270	$33,366	$30,489	$40,246	$45,999	$48,885
1999	17,656	8,515	9,948	15,189	20,326	22,697	32,705	29,555	41,079	47,039	48,061
1998	17,156	8,351	10,111	14,547	19,463	22,465	32,386	28,929	38,924	45,891	48,830
1997	16,663	8,030	9,481	14,345	18,353	22,548	31,865	28,248	38,393	48,362	49,802
1996	16,050	7,954	9,340	13,885	17,769	22,366	30,123	27,539	36,404	45,977	46,384
1995	15,519	7,968	9,047	13,526	17,462	21,839	30,140	27,021	37,625	43,328	44,712
1994	14,694	7,902	8,768	13,110	16,787	20,665	30,199	26,939	36,912	41,213	46,953
1993	14,390	7,622	8,454	13,043	17,042	21,579	29,695	26,409	36,920	38,512	50,268
1992	14,385	7,646	8,800	13,153	17,376	20,912	30,277	27,007	36,402	44,210	47,446
1991	14,343	7,763	8,738	13,399	17,294	21,507	29,264	25,969	36,844	42,191	46,127
Percent change											
1991 to 2000	25.7%	8.3%	14.4%	12.8%	16.7%	8.2%	14.0%	17.4%	9.2%	9.0%	6.0%

Note: Because educational attainment categories changed in 1991, earlier data are not strictly comparable.
Source: Bureau of the Census, Current Population Surveys, Internet site http://www.census.gov/hhes/earnings/histinc/p16.html; calculations by New Strategist

Table 5.20 Median Income of Women by Educational Attainment, 1963 to 1990

(median income of women aged 25 or older by educational attainment, and percent change, 1963 to 1990; in 2000 dollars)

	total women	less than 9 years	high school 1–3 years	high school 4 years	college 1–3 years	college, 4 years or more total	college, 4 years or more 4 years	college, 4 years or more 5+ years
1990	$14,473	$7,599	$9,042	$13,678	$18,936	$28,901	$26,145	$34,677
1989	14,582	7,588	9,105	14,077	19,208	29,207	26,233	35,163
1988	14,187	7,324	8,858	13,717	18,809	28,797	25,912	33,035
1987	13,760	7,374	9,176	13,334	18,211	27,523	24,636	32,641
1986	12,942	7,368	8,794	12,617	17,454	27,243	24,319	32,573
1985	12,514	7,506	8,731	12,488	16,909	26,450	23,413	31,734
1984	12,307	7,494	8,821	12,439	16,618	25,184	21,650	31,234
1983	11,780	7,227	8,515	12,153	15,716	24,222	20,613	29,890
1982	11,396	7,208	8,473	11,971	14,751	23,174	20,138	28,796
1981	11,062	7,034	8,468	11,815	15,020	21,983	19,094	27,988
1980	10,928	7,018	8,460	11,745	14,981	21,909	19,116	27,737
1979	10,731	6,815	8,708	11,761	14,371	21,909	18,375	26,857
1978	11,214	6,972	8,953	12,630	15,007	22,431	19,570	27,492
1977	11,495	6,986	9,282	13,311	15,741	22,947	20,378	27,957
1976	11,120	6,965	9,187	13,219	14,768	22,922	20,514	28,180
1975	11,105	6,800	9,388	12,910	15,334	23,632	21,169	29,575
1974	10,814	6,884	9,616	12,916	15,270	23,703	19,904	28,217
1973	11,038	6,812	9,579	13,409	15,415	23,784	20,988	30,181
1972	10,878	6,521	9,661	13,484	14,793	24,753	21,559	30,793
1971	10,521	6,208	9,548	13,296	13,806	24,490	21,220	30,857
1970	10,026	6,047	9,223	13,137	14,381	23,858	20,717	30,481
1969	9,914	5,698	9,468	13,121	14,211	23,557	21,091	28,980
1968	9,729	5,828	9,200	12,987	13,722	22,420	18,751	28,548
1967	9,257	5,354	8,967	12,786	13,551	22,738	19,454	29,480
1966	8,724	5,390	8,665	12,108	12,805	21,597	18,866	27,694
1965	8,525	4,999	8,511	11,864	12,480	21,751	20,021	26,443
1964	8,170	4,696	7,744	11,214	11,815	20,629	18,608	26,120
1963	7,727	4,571	7,588	10,975	11,162	19,349	16,275	25,700

Percent change

1963 to 1990	87.3%	66.2%	19.2%	24.6%	69.6%	49.4%	60.6%	34.9%

Note: Because educational attainment categories changed in 1991, earlier data are not strictly comparable.
Source: Bureau of the Census, Current Population Surveys, Internet site http://www.census.gov/hhes/income/histinc/p17.html;
calculations by New Strategist

Table 5.21 Median Income of Men by Region, 1953 to 2000

(median income of men aged 15 or older with income by region, 1953 to 2000; percent change in income for selected years; in 2000 dollars)

	total men	Northeast	Midwest	South	West
2000	$28,269	$30,464	$29,935	$26,699	$28,009
1999	28,191	29,756	30,251	26,797	28,098
1998	27,955	29,040	29,195	26,694	27,813
1997	26,976	28,224	28,124	25,568	26,570
1996	26,054	27,637	27,773	24,305	25,574
1995	25,333	27,633	27,283	23,761	25,055
1994	25,000	27,289	25,639	23,415	25,355
1993	24,821	26,210	25,519	23,188	25,331
1992	24,681	26,654	25,304	22,431	25,337
1991	25,353	27,681	25,479	22,882	26,719
1990	26,056	28,128	26,544	23,662	26,949
1989	26,825	29,900	26,921	24,073	27,566
1988	26,606	30,315	26,955	23,602	27,342
1987	25,939	28,901	26,127	23,836	26,912
1986	25,809	28,546	26,298	23,324	27,601
1985	25,032	26,981	25,133	22,920	26,688
1984	24,754	26,445	24,895	22,547	26,841
1983	24,143	25,534	24,537	22,075	25,682
1982	23,975	24,996	25,075	22,033	25,125
1981	24,508	25,399	25,816	22,203	26,558
1980	24,932	26,189	26,543	22,723	27,293
1979	26,046	26,884	27,963	23,631	27,313
1978	26,452	27,001	28,445	23,858	28,292
1977	25,540	26,673	27,294	22,576	26,592
1976	25,300	26,626	27,444	22,406	26,373
1975	25,125	26,992	26,973	22,029	26,453
1974	25,974	28,235	28,100	22,504	26,865
1973	27,209	29,016	29,600	22,940	29,016
1972	26,737	28,690	28,718	22,804	28,629
1971	25,537	27,524	27,191	21,531	27,187
1970	25,771	27,803	27,533	21,641	27,525
1969	26,036	27,915	28,482	21,051	28,632
1968	25,272	26,692	27,402	20,353	28,264
1967	24,408	26,395	26,320	19,248	27,577
1966	24,034	26,154	25,900	18,232	27,087
1965	23,425	24,652	24,675	16,626	25,990
1964	21,997	24,321	23,999	16,615	24,984
1963	21,637	24,232	23,882	16,016	24,352
1962	21,253	23,961	23,164	15,313	24,822
1961	20,562	22,378	21,632	14,726	25,549
1960	20,224	22,177	21,468	14,399	24,437
1959	20,169	22,016	21,531	14,618	23,010
1958	19,001	21,189	19,961	13,950	21,981
1957	19,207	21,730	20,638	13,790	21,636
1956	19,455	21,632	21,194	14,057	22,377
1955	18,378	19,686	20,255	13,518	20,315
1954	17,437	18,781	18,649	13,199	18,912
1953	17,705	19,074	19,359	12,736	19,156
Percent change					
1990 to 2000	8.5%	8.3%	12.8%	12.8%	3.9%
1953 to 2000	59.7	59.7	54.6	109.6	46.2

Note: Men aged 14 or older in years prior to 1980.
Source: Bureau of the Census, Current Population Surveys, Internet site http://www.census.gov/hhes/income/histinc/p05.html; calculations by New Strategist

Table 5.22 Median Income of Women by Region, 1953 to 2000

(median income of women aged 15 or older with income by region, 1953 to 2000; percent change in income for selected years; in 2000 dollars)

	total women	Northeast	Midwest	South	West
2000	$16,188	$16,396	$16,417	$15,717	$16,653
1999	15,825	16,310	16,029	15,229	16,069
1998	15,227	15,629	15,325	14,749	15,482
1997	14,662	15,336	14,872	13,948	14,982
1996	14,009	14,704	14,267	13,508	14,026
1995	13,620	14,015	13,901	13,012	13,987
1994	13,197	13,769	13,319	12,591	13,578
1993	12,993	13,380	12,975	12,417	13,607
1992	12,928	13,635	12,714	12,242	13,689
1991	12,975	13,683	12,632	12,452	13,595
1990	12,930	13,780	12,992	12,091	13,439
1989	12,978	14,217	12,329	12,202	13,899
1988	12,501	13,524	11,678	11,854	13,648
1987	12,097	12,751	11,413	11,642	13,038
1986	11,476	12,095	10,956	10,988	12,336
1985	11,076	11,576	10,517	10,428	12,454
1984	10,898	11,112	10,357	10,622	12,010
1983	10,427	10,544	9,841	10,176	11,475
1982	10,118	10,269	9,645	9,759	11,352
1981	9,928	10,007	9,572	9,490	10,867
1980	9,790	9,829	9,527	9,457	10,725
1979	9,623	9,995	9,384	8,885	10,430
1978	9,840	10,648	9,683	9,006	10,406
1977	9,943	10,619	9,847	9,103	10,536
1976	9,598	10,210	9,652	8,959	9,904
1975	9,607	10,364	9,610	8,849	9,925
1974	9,471	10,332	9,394	8,602	9,868
1973	9,444	10,268	9,406	8,515	9,954
1972	9,328	10,307	9,389	8,477	9,507
1971	8,908	10,488	8,849	7,813	9,038
1970	8,643	10,138	8,369	7,658	8,805
1969	8,634	10,007	8,067	7,751	8,986
1968	8,533	9,665	8,127	7,565	9,264
1967	7,916	9,310	7,547	6,844	8,773
1966	7,420	9,050	7,170	6,283	7,959
1965	7,093	9,052	7,061	5,955	8,497
1964	6,859	8,658	6,812	5,586	7,261
1963	6,581	8,327	6,634	5,094	7,195
1962	6,524	8,172	6,650	4,958	7,059
1961	6,278	7,736	6,126	4,747	7,422
1960	6,250	8,089	6,082	4,763	7,148
1959	6,171	7,993	5,959	4,688	6,782
1958	5,970	7,823	6,041	4,483	6,559
1957	6,268	7,788	6,582	4,717	6,879
1956	6,208	7,834	6,753	4,711	6,834
1955	6,130	7,733	6,130	4,597	7,580
1954	6,335	8,366	6,482	4,849	5,991
1953	6,409	8,405	6,508	4,947	5,931

Percent change

1990 to 2000	25.2%	19.0%	26.4%	30.0%	23.9%
1953 to 2000	152.6	95.1	152.3	217.7	180.8

Note: Women aged 14 or older in years prior to 1980.
Source: Bureau of the Census, Current Population Surveys, Internet site http://www.census.gov/hhes/income/histinc/p05.html; calculations by New Strategist

Women Earn 73 Percent as Much as Men

Women who worked full-time earned a median of $27,352 in 2000, up from just $16,144 in 1960, after adjusting for inflation. Men earned $37,339 in 2000, up from $26,608 in 1960. Women's earnings have been growing faster than men's for the past four decades. Consequently, women are closing the earnings gap with men. Among full-time workers in 1960, women earned only 61 percent as much as men. By 2000, the figure had grown to 73 percent.

Among men working full-time, earnings have grown the fastest for blacks. The median earnings of black men rose from $20,997 in 1967 to $30,403 in 2000. During the 1990s, men with a college degree have gained ground while those who did not graduate from high school saw their earnings decline. The trends are similar for women. Black women enjoyed the fastest earnings growth between 1967 and 2000, and women with a bachelor's, master's, or doctoral degree experienced the biggest income gains during the 1990s.

Women's earnings are catching up to men's

(earnings of women working full-time, year-round as a percent of the earnings of men working full-time, year-round, 1960 to 2000)

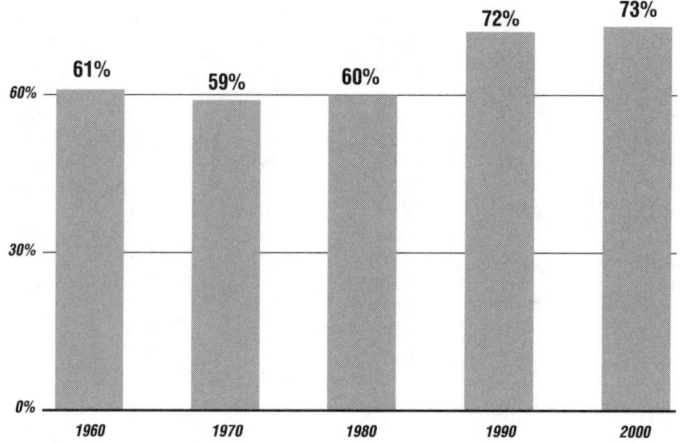

Table 5.23 Median Earnings of Full-Time Workers by Sex, 1960 to 2000

(median earnings of people aged 15 or older who work full-time, year-round by sex; women's earnings as a percent of men's, 1960 to 2000; percent change for selected years; in 2000 dollars)

	median earnings		women's earnings as a percent of men's
	men	women	
2000	$37,339	$27,352	73.3%
1999	37,701	27,208	72.2
1998	37,296	27,290	73.2
1997	36,030	26,720	74.2
1996	35,138	25,919	73.8
1995	35,365	25,260	71.4
1994	35,513	25,558	72.0
1993	35,765	25,579	71.5
1992	36,436	25,791	70.8
1991	36,440	25,457	69.9
1990	35,538	25,451	71.6
1989	36,855	25,310	68.7
1988	37,509	24,774	66.0
1987	37,839	24,663	65.2
1986	38,088	24,479	64.3
1985	37,131	23,978	64.6
1984	36,842	23,453	63.7
1983	36,106	22,961	63.6
1982	36,224	22,367	61.7
1981	36,854	21,830	59.2
1980	37,033	22,279	60.2
1979	37,622	22,446	59.7
1978	38,051	22,617	59.4
1977	36,901	21,743	58.9
1976	36,114	21,738	60.2
1975	36,207	21,297	58.8
1974	36,456	21,419	58.8
1973	37,781	21,397	56.6
1972	36,614	21,185	57.9
1971	34,771	20,691	59.5
1970	34,642	20,567	59.4
1969	34,241	20,156	58.9
1968	32,389	18,836	58.2
1967	31,568	18,241	57.8
1966	31,055	17,874	57.6
1965	29,791	17,852	59.9
1964	29,362	17,368	59.2
1963	28,684	16,908	58.9
1962	27,972	16,587	59.3
1961	27,463	16,272	59.3
1960	26,608	16,144	60.7
Percent change			
1990 to 2000	5.1%	7.5%	2.3%
1960 to 2000	40.3	69.4	20.7

Source: Bureau of the Census, Current Population Surveys, Internet site http://www.census.gov/hhes/income/histinc/p38.html; calculations by New Strategist

Table 5.24 Median Earnings of Men Who Work Full-Time by Race and Hispanic Origin, 1967 to 2000

(median earnings of men who work full-time, year-round by race and Hispanic origin, 1967 to 2000; percent change for selected years; in 2000 dollars)

	total men	Asian	black	Hispanic	white total	white non-Hispanic
2000	$37,339	$40,950	$30,403	$24,639	$38,870	$41,157
1999	37,701	38,055	31,035	23,728	38,499	41,679
1998	37,296	36,751	28,543	23,515	38,169	39,818
1997	36,030	37,109	28,282	23,128	37,656	39,158
1996	35,138	37,661	28,864	23,017	36,037	38,744
1995	35,365	35,452	27,429	22,882	36,124	38,628
1994	35,513	36,902	27,327	23,381	36,369	37,568
1993	35,765	36,349	27,075	23,700	36,568	37,605
1992	36,436	36,828	27,024	23,578	37,231	38,275
1991	36,440	37,355	27,342	24,488	37,487	38,454
1990	35,538	34,365	27,110	24,570	37,082	38,690
1989	36,855	37,961	27,544	24,755	38,487	40,411
1988	37,509	38,163	28,665	25,119	38,314	39,762
1987	37,839	–	27,889	25,425	38,689	39,630
1986	38,088	–	27,656	25,358	39,100	–
1985	37,131	–	26,825	26,168	38,462	–
1984	36,842	–	26,398	26,880	38,023	–
1983	36,106	–	26,654	26,680	36,990	–
1982	36,224	–	26,644	26,437	37,127	–
1981	36,854	–	26,789	26,776	37,665	–
1980	37,033	–	26,955	26,977	38,118	–
1979	37,622	–	27,945	27,375	38,484	–
1978	38,051	–	29,860	28,387	38,692	–
1977	36,901	–	26,353	27,221	37,996	–
1976	36,114	–	27,141	27,557	37,075	–
1975	36,207	–	27,549	26,714	37,048	–
1974	36,456	–	26,791	–	37,240	–
1973	37,781	–	26,615	–	38,895	–
1972	36,614	–	26,203	–	38,017	–
1971	34,771	–	24,671	–	35,733	–
1970	34,642	–	24,604	–	35,635	–
1969	34,241	–	23,813	–	35,379	–
1968	32,389	–	22,458	–	33,260	–
1967	31,568	–	20,997	–	32,509	–
Percent change						
1990 to 2000	5.1%	19.2%	12.1%	0.3%	4.8%	6.4%
1967 to 2000	18.3	–	44.8	–	19.6	–

Note: (–) means data not available.
Source: Bureau of the Census, Current Population Surveys, Internet sites http://www.census.gov/hhes/income/histinc/p38.html, http://www.census.gov/hhes/income/histinc/p38a.html, http:// www.census.gov/hhes/income/histinc/p38b.html, http:// www.census.gov/hhes/income/histinc/p38c.html, http://www.census.gov/hhes/income/histinc/p38d.html, and http:// www.census.gov/hhes/income/histinc/p38e.html; calculations by New Strategist

Table 5.25 Median Earnings of Women Who Work Full-Time by Race and Hispanic Origin, 1967 to 2000

(median earnings of women who work full-time, year-round by race and Hispanic origin, 1967 to 2000; percent change for selected years; in 2000 dollars)

	total women	Asian	black	Hispanic	white total	white non-Hispanic
2000	$27,352	$31,161	$25,107	$20,525	$28,080	$29,604
1999	27,208	29,633	25,043	20,063	27,559	28,340
1998	27,290	28,563	23,898	20,282	27,692	28,363
1997	26,720	29,725	23,577	20,301	27,104	27,728
1996	25,919	27,936	23,473	20,404	26,411	27,209
1995	25,260	27,933	23,203	19,288	25,725	26,568
1994	25,558	28,144	22,916	20,222	26,039	26,699
1993	25,579	28,635	23,308	19,711	25,904	26,327
1992	25,791	27,512	23,847	20,616	26,055	26,417
1991	25,457	26,226	23,186	20,120	25,755	26,127
1990	25,451	27,379	23,163	20,122	25,741	26,138
1989	25,310	28,806	23,449	21,120	25,516	25,946
1988	24,774	27,225	23,271	20,889	25,074	25,489
1987	24,663	–	22,971	21,183	24,902	25,172
1986	24,479	–	22,220	20,866	24,766	–
1985	23,978	–	21,958	20,052	24,242	–
1984	23,453	–	21,771	19,906	23,650	–
1983	22,961	–	20,940	19,247	23,210	–
1982	22,367	–	20,851	19,098	22,618	–
1981	21,830	–	20,371	19,516	22,025	–
1980	22,279	–	21,235	19,259	22,438	–
1979	22,446	–	20,839	18,669	22,621	–
1978	22,617	–	21,338	19,533	22,799	–
1977	21,743	–	20,429	18,963	21,879	–
1976	21,738	–	20,533	18,729	21,886	–
1975	21,297	–	20,539	18,251	21,322	–
1974	21,419	–	20,169	–	21,573	–
1973	21,397	–	18,532	–	21,731	–
1972	21,185	–	18,472	–	21,526	–
1971	20,691	–	18,549	–	20,905	–
1970	20,567	–	17,182	–	20,910	–
1969	20,156	–	16,235	–	20,565	–
1968	18,836	–	14,737	–	19,356	–
1967	18,241	–	14,039	–	18,808	–
Percent change						
1990 to 2000	7.5%	13.8%	8.4%	2.0%	9.1%	13.3%
1967 to 2000	49.9	–	78.8	–	49.3	–

Note: (–) means data not available.
Source: Bureau of the Census, Current Population Surveys, Internet sites http://www.census.gov/hhes/income/histinc/ p38.html>, http://www.census.gov/hhes/income/histinc/p38a.html, http:// www.census.gov/hhes/income/histinc/p38b.html, http://www.census.gov/hhes/income/histinc/p38c.html, http://www.census.gov/hhes/income/histinc/p38d.html, and http:// www.census.gov/hhes/income/histinc/p38e.html; calculations by New Strategist

Table 5.26 Median Earnings of Men Who Work Full-Time by Educational Attainment, 1987 to 2000

(median earnings of men aged 25 or older who work full-time, year-round by educational attainment, 1987 to 2000; percent change 1991 to 2000; in 2000 dollars)

	total men	less than 9th grade	9th to 12th grade (no diploma)	high school graduate	some college, no degree	associate's degree	bachelor's degree or more total	bachelor's degree	master's degree	professional degree	doctoral degree
2000	$40,181	$20,447	$24,439	$32,494	$38,650	$41,072	$60,449	$53,508	$65,058	$91,318	$75,630
1999	39,718	20,421	25,095	33,176	38,496	41,834	58,293	52,718	63,851	99,509	79,440
1998	38,704	19,577	24,732	32,572	37,934	40,608	55,201	52,741	63,490	95,658	73,008
1997	38,214	19,849	25,937	32,800	37,542	39,243	54,781	49,492	61,580	83,768	75,654
1996	37,673	18,853	24,275	32,893	36,394	39,432	54,804	47,858	61,300	85,423	72,322
1995	36,894	19,641	24,575	32,048	36,338	37,579	53,967	47,835	58,178	84,530	69,279
1994	36,983	19,741	25,032	31,350	36,077	40,424	54,070	48,399	59,109	82,976	69,371
1993	37,169	19,267	25,174	31,546	36,790	38,364	54,091	48,711	58,607	90,787	72,158
1992	37,789	20,335	25,407	32,215	37,816	39,021	52,788	48,679	56,984	88,808	67,987
1991	38,240	20,907	26,003	32,473	38,438	39,908	52,475	49,412	58,216	87,053	67,659
Percent change											
1991 to 2000	5.1%	-2.2%	-6.0%	0.1%	0.6%	2.9%	15.2%	8.3%	11.8%	4.9%	11.8%

	total	fewer than 9 years	high school 1-3 years	high school 4 years	college 1-3 years	college, 4 years or more total	4 years	5+ years
1990	$38,502	$21,622	$26,260	$33,219	$39,630	$52,811	$47,870	$60,515
1989	39,856	23,199	27,810	34,870	41,002	54,754	49,685	60,866
1988	39,653	23,560	28,607	35,702	41,167	53,888	50,076	58,707
1987	39,668	23,699	29,834	36,045	41,672	53,689	49,425	59,403

Note: Because educational attainment categories changed in 1991, earlier data are not strictly comparable.
Source: Bureau of the Census, Current Population Surveys, Internet sites http://www.census.gov/hhes/income/histinc/p24.html and http://www.census.gov/hhes/income/histinc/p25.html; calculations by New Strategist

Table 5.27 Median Earnings of Women Who Work Full-Time by Educational Attainment, 1987 to 2000

(median earnings of women aged 25 or older who work full-time, year-round by educational attainment, 1987 to 2000; percent change 1991 to 2000; in 2000 dollars)

	total women	less than 9th grade	9th to 12th grade (no diploma)	high school graduate	some college, no degree	associate's degree	bachelor's degree or more				
							total	bachelor's degree	master's degree	professional degree	doctoral degree
2000	$28,977	$15,399	$17,210	$23,721	$27,190	$30,180	$41,131	$38,213	$47,052	$56,089	$55,631
1999	28,049	14,858	16,879	22,708	27,345	31,141	41,466	37,561	46,868	58,632	58,238
1998	28,186	14,912	16,722	23,176	27,461	29,944	39,483	37,363	44,321	58,522	55,047
1997	27,630	14,388	17,020	22,781	26,787	29,110	38,889	35,771	44,785	58,344	54,310
1996	27,114	14,836	17,635	22,411	26,052	29,267	38,401	34,883	44,180	61,688	56,832
1995	26,520	14,345	16,958	22,062	25,277	29,509	37,501	34,581	43,333	54,020	47,069
1994	26,663	13,845	16,660	22,478	25,519	29,021	38,335	35,382	43,216	55,575	53,497
1993	26,373	13,969	17,290	22,546	25,873	29,484	37,981	35,691	43,431	56,936	54,600
1992	26,715	14,664	16,536	22,461	26,486	29,944	37,811	35,240	42,232	53,468	52,823
1991	26,347	14,413	16,768	22,347	26,417	29,555	37,644	34,252	41,024	52,769	49,756
Percent change											
1991 to 2000	10.0%	6.8%	2.6%	6.1%	2.9%	2.1%	9.3%	11.6%	14.7%	6.3%	11.8%

	total	fewer than 9 years	high school		college	college, 4 years or more		
			1–3 years	4 years	1–3 years	total	4 years	5+ years
1990	$26,393	$15,191	$17,793	$22,356	$27,379	$37,225	$34,446	$41,047
1989	26,635	15,793	17,830	22,742	28,000	36,986	34,936	41,672
1988	26,045	15,383	17,629	22,666	28,124	36,486	34,063	40,534
1987	25,724	15,253	18,065	23,210	27,617	35,961	32,386	40,986

Note: Because educational attainment categories changed in 1991, earlier data are not strictly comparable.
Source: Bureau of the Census, Current Population Surveys, Internet sites http://www.census.gov/hhes/income/histinc/p24.html and http://www.census.gov/hhes/income/histinc/p25.html; calculations by New Strategist

Less Poverty for Most Americans

The number of Americans living in poverty has fallen since 1959, despite the expanding population. Behind the decline in the number of poor is the plummeting poverty rate, which fell from 22 to 11 percent between 1959 and 2000.

There has been a 3- to 4-percentage point decline in the poverty rate by sex over the past three decades. Much bigger changes have occurred in poverty rates by age. Americans aged 65 or older are far less likely to be poor today than in 1959, the poverty rate falling from 35 to just 10 percent. Children are also less likely to be poor, as the poverty rate for people under age 18 fell from 27 to 16 percent between 1959 and 2000. Blacks continue to have a higher poverty rate than whites, but the black rate declined sharply. In 1959, the 55 percent majority of blacks were poor. By 2000, a considerably smaller 22 percent lived in poverty.

Families are less likely to be poor today than in 1959. The poverty rate for all families fell from 18 to 9 percent between 1959 and 2000. For families with children under age 18, the rate dropped from 20 to 13 percent. Among black female-headed families, the 52 percent majority were poor in 1974, a figure that fell to 35 percent by 2000.

Poverty rate is down

(percent of people living below the poverty level, 1959 to 2000)

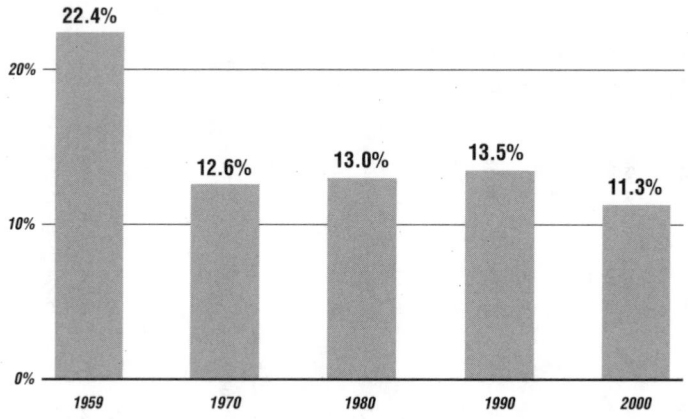

Table 5.28 People in Poverty, 1959 to 2000

(number and percent of people below poverty level, 1959 to 2000; percent and percentage point change for selected years; people in thousands as of the following year)

	number	percent
2000	31,054	11.3%
1999	32,258	11.8
1998	34,476	12.7
1997	35,574	13.3
1996	36,529	13.7
1995	36,425	13.8
1994	38,059	14.5
1993	39,265	15.1
1992	38,014	14.8
1991	35,708	14.2
1990	33,585	13.5
1989	31,528	12.8
1988	31,745	13.0
1987	32,221	13.4
1986	32,370	13.6
1985	33,064	14.0
1984	33,700	14.4
1983	35,303	15.2
1982	34,398	15.0
1981	31,822	14.0
1980	29,272	13.0
1979	26,072	11.7
1978	24,497	11.4
1977	24,720	11.6
1976	24,975	11.8
1975	25,877	12.3
1974	23,370	11.2
1973	22,973	11.1
1972	24,460	11.9
1971	25,559	12.5
1970	25,420	12.6
1969	24,147	12.1
1968	25,389	12.8
1967	27,769	14.2
1966	28,510	14.7
1965	33,185	17.3
1964	36,055	19.0
1963	36,436	19.5
1962	38,625	21.0
1961	39,628	21.9
1960	39,851	22.2
1959	39,490	22.4

	percent change	percentage point change
1990 to 2000	−7.5%	−2.2
1959 to 2000	−21.4	−11.1

Source: Bureau of the Census, Current Population Surveys, Internet site http://www.census.gov/hhes/poverty/histpov/hstpov2.html; calculations by New Strategist

Table 5.29 People in Poverty by Sex, 1966 to 2000

(number and percent of people below poverty level by sex, 1966 to 2000; percent and percentage point change for selected years; people in thousands as of the following year)

	number of poor		percent in poverty	
	female	*male*	*female*	*male*
2000	17,637	13,417	12.5%	9.9%
1999	18,445	13,813	13.2	10.3
1998	19,764	14,712	14.3	11.1
1997	20,387	15,187	14.9	11.6
1996	20,918	15,611	15.4	12.0
1995	20,742	15,683	15.4	12.2
1994	21,744	16,316	16.3	12.8
1993	22,365	16,900	16.9	13.3
1992	21,792	16,222	16.6	12.9
1991	20,626	15,082	16.0	12.3
1990	19,373	14,211	15.2	11.7
1989	18,162	13,366	14.4	11.2
1988	18,146	13,599	14.5	11.5
1987	18,518	14,029	15.0	12.0
1986	18,649	13,721	15.2	11.8
1985	18,923	14,140	15.6	12.3
1984	19,163	14,537	15.9	12.8
1983	20,084	15,182	16.8	13.5
1982	19,556	14,842	16.5	13.4
1981	18,462	13,360	15.8	12.1
1980	17,065	12,207	14.7	11.2
1979	14,810	10,535	13.2	10.0
1978	14,480	10,017	13.0	9.6
1977	14,381	10,340	13.0	10.0
1976	14,603	10,373	13.4	10.1
1975	14,970	10,908	13.8	10.7
1974	13,881	10,313	12.9	10.2
1973	13,316	9,642	12.5	9.6
1972	14,258	10,190	13.4	10.2
1971	14,841	10,708	14.1	10.8
1970	14,632	10,879	14.0	11.1
1969	13,978	10,292	13.6	10.6
1968	14,578	10,793	14.3	11.3
1967	15,951	11,813	15.8	12.5
1966	16,265	12,225	16.3	13.0
	percent change		percentage point change	
1990 to 2000	−9.0%	−5.6%	−2.7	−1.8
1966 to 2000	8.4	9.8	−3.8	−3.1

Source: Bureau of the Census, Current Population Surveys, Internet site http://www.census.gov/hhes/poverty/histpov/hstpov7.html; calculations by New Strategist

Table 5.30   People in Poverty by Age, 1959 to 2000

(number and percent of people below poverty level by age, 1959 to 2000; percent and percentage point change for selected years; people in thousands as of the following year)

	number of poor			percent in poverty		
	< 18	18 to 64	65+	< 18	18 to 64	65+
2000	11,553	16,143	3,359	16.1%	9.4%	10.2%
1999	12,109	16,982	3,167	16.9	10.0	9.7
1998	13,467	17,623	3,386	18.9	10.5	10.5
1997	14,113	18,084	3,376	19.9	10.9	10.5
1996	14,463	18,638	3,428	20.5	11.4	10.8
1995	14,665	18,442	3,318	20.8	11.4	10.5
1994	15,289	19,107	3,663	21.8	11.9	11.7
1993	15,727	19,781	3,755	22.7	12.4	12.2
1992	15,294	18,793	3,928	22.3	11.9	12.9
1991	14,341	17,586	3,781	21.8	11.4	12.4
1990	13,431	16,496	3,658	20.6	10.7	12.2
1989	12,590	15,575	3,363	19.6	10.2	11.4
1988	12,455	15,809	3,481	19.5	10.5	12.0
1987	12,843	15,815	3,563	20.3	10.6	12.5
1986	12,876	16,017	3,477	20.5	10.8	12.4
1985	13,010	16,598	3,456	20.7	11.3	12.6
1984	13,420	16,952	3,330	21.5	11.7	12.4
1983	13,911	17,767	3,625	22.3	12.4	13.8
1982	13,647	17,000	3,751	21.9	12.0	14.6
1981	12,505	15,464	3,853	20.0	11.1	15.3
1980	11,543	13,858	3,871	18.3	10.1	15.7
1979	10,377	12,014	3,682	16.4	8.9	15.2
1978	9,931	11,332	3,233	15.9	8.7	14.0
1977	10,288	11,316	3,177	16.2	8.8	14.1
1976	10,273	11,389	3,313	16.0	9.0	15.0
1975	11,104	11,456	3,317	17.1	9.2	15.3
1974	10,156	10,132	3,085	15.4	8.3	14.6
1973	9,642	9,977	3,354	14.4	8.3	16.3
1972	10,284	10,438	3,738	15.1	8.8	18.6
1971	10,551	10,735	4,273	15.3	9.3	21.6
1970	10,440	10,187	4,793	15.1	9.0	24.6
1969	9,691	9,669	4,787	14.0	8.7	25.3
1968	10,954	9,803	4,632	15.6	9.0	25.0
1967	11,656	10,725	5,388	16.6	10.0	29.5
1966	12,389	11,007	5,114	17.6	10.5	28.5
1965	14,676	–	–	21.0	–	–
1964	16,051	–	–	23.0	–	–
1963	16,005	–	–	23.1	–	–
1962	16,963	–	–	25.0	–	–
1961	16,909	–	–	25.6	–	–
1960	17,634	–	–	26.9	–	–
1959	17,552	16,457	5,481	27.3	17.0	35.2
	percent change			percentage point change		
1990 to 2000	−14.0%	−2.1%	−8.2%	−4.5	−1.3	−2.0
1959 to 2000	−34.2	−1.9	−38.7	−11.2	−7.6	−25.0

Note: (–) means data not available.
Source: Bureau of the Census, Current Population Surveys, Internet site http://www.census.gov/hhes/poverty/histpov/ hstpov3.html; calculations by New Strategist

Table 5.31 People in Poverty by Race and Hispanic Origin, 1959 to 2000

(number and percent of people below poverty level by race and Hispanic origin, 1959 to 2000; percent and percentage point change for selected years; people in thousands as of the following year)

| | number of poor | | | white | | percent in poverty | | | white | |
| | | | | | non- | | | | | non- |
	Asian	*black*	*Hispanic*	*total*	*Hispanic*	*Asian*	*black*	*Hispanic*	*total*	*Hispanic*
2000	1,214	7,862	7,153	21,242	14,532	10.7%	22.0%	21.2%	9.4%	7.5%
1999	1,163	8,360	7,439	21,922	14,875	10.7	23.6	22.8	9.8	7.7
1998	1,360	9,091	8,070	23,454	15,799	12.5	26.1	25.6	10.5	8.2
1997	1,468	9,116	8,308	24,396	16,491	14.0	26.5	27.1	11.0	8.6
1996	1,454	9,694	8,697	24,650	16,462	14.5	28.4	29.4	11.2	8.6
1995	1,411	9,872	8,574	24,423	16,267	14.6	29.3	30.3	11.2	8.5
1994	974	10,196	8,416	25,379	18,110	14.6	30.6	30.7	11.7	9.4
1993	1,134	10,877	8,126	26,226	18,882	15.3	33.1	30.6	12.2	9.9
1992	985	10,827	7,592	25,259	18,202	12.7	33.4	29.6	11.9	9.6
1991	996	10,242	6,339	23,747	17,741	13.8	32.7	28.7	11.3	9.4
1990	858	9,837	6,006	22,326	16,622	12.2	31.9	28.1	10.7	8.8
1989	939	9,302	5,430	20,785	15,599	14.1	30.7	26.2	10.0	8.3
1988	1,117	9,356	5,357	20,715	15,565	17.3	31.3	26.7	10.1	8.4
1987	1,021	9,520	5,422	21,195	16,029	16.1	32.4	28.0	10.4	8.7
1986	–	8,983	5,117	22,183	17,244	–	31.1	27.3	11.0	9.4
1985	–	8,926	5,236	22,860	17,839	–	31.3	29.0	11.4	9.7
1984	–	9,490	4,806	22,955	18,300	–	33.8	28.4	11.5	10.0
1983	–	9,882	4,633	23,984	19,538	–	35.7	28.0	12.1	10.8
1982	–	9,697	4,301	23,517	19,362	–	35.6	29.9	12.0	10.6
1981	–	9,173	3,713	21,553	17,987	–	34.2	26.5	11.1	9.9
1980	–	8,579	3,491	19,699	16,365	–	32.5	25.7	10.2	9.1
1979	–	8,050	2,921	17,214	14,419	–	31.0	21.8	9.0	8.1
1978	–	7,625	2,607	16,259	13,755	–	30.6	21.6	8.7	7.9
1977	–	7,726	2,700	16,416	13,802	–	31.3	22.4	8.9	8.0
1976	–	7,595	2,783	16,713	14,025	–	31.1	24.7	9.1	8.1
1975	–	7,545	2,991	17,770	14,883	–	31.3	26.9	9.7	8.6
1974	–	7,182	2,575	15,736	13,217	–	30.3	23.0	8.6	7.7
1973	–	7,388	2,366	15,142	12,864	–	31.4	21.9	8.4	7.5
1972	–	7,710	–	16,203	–	–	33.3	–	9.0	–
1971	–	7,396	–	17,780	–	–	32.5	–	9.9	–
1970	–	7,548	–	17,484	–	–	33.5	–	9.9	–
1969	–	7,095	–	16,659	–	–	32.2	–	9.5	–
1968	–	7,616	–	17,395	–	–	34.7	–	10.0	–
1967	–	8,486	–	18,983	–	–	39.3	–	11.0	–
1966	–	8,867	–	19,290	–	–	41.8	–	11.3	–
1965	–	–	–	22,496	–	–	–	–	13.3	–
1964	–	–	–	24,957	–	–	–	–	14.9	–
1963	–	–	–	25,238	–	–	–	–	15.3	–
1962	–	–	–	26,672	–	–	–	–	16.4	–
1961	–	–	–	27,890	–	–	–	–	17.4	–
1960	–	–	–	28,309	–	–	–	–	17.8	–
1959	–	9,927	–	28,484	–	–	55.1	–	18.1	–
	percent change					*percentage point change*				
1990 to 2000	41.5%	–20.1%	19.1%	–4.9%	–12.6%	–1.5	–9.9	–6.9	–1.3	–1.3
1959 to 2000	–	–20.8	–	–25.4	–	–	–33.1	–	–8.7	–

Note: (–) means data not available.
Source: Bureau of the Census, Current Population Surveys, Internet site http://www.census.gov/hhes/poverty/histpov/hstpov2.html; calculations by New Strategist

Table 5.32   Families in Poverty, 1959 to 2000

(total number of families, and number and percent below poverty level by presence of children under age 18 at home, 1959–00; percent and percentage point change for selected years; families in thousands as of the following year)

| | total families | | | families with children < 18 | | |
| | | in poverty | | | in poverty | |
	total	number	percent	total	number	percent
2000	72,388	6,222	8.6%	37,327	4,730	12.7%
1999	72,031	6,676	9.3	37,277	5,129	13.8
1998	71,551	7,186	10.0	37,268	5,628	15.1
1997	70,884	7,324	10.3	37,427	5,884	15.7
1996	70,241	7,708	11.0	37,204	6,131	16.5
1995	69,597	7,532	10.8	36,719	5,976	16.3
1994	69,313	8,053	11.6	36,782	6,408	17.4
1993	68,506	8,393	12.3	36,456	6,751	18.5
1992	68,216	8,144	11.9	35,851	6,457	18.0
1991	67,175	7,712	11.5	34,862	6,170	17.7
1990	66,322	7,098	10.7	34,503	5,676	16.4
1989	66,090	6,784	10.3	34,279	5,308	15.5
1988	65,837	6,874	10.4	34,251	5,373	15.7
1987	65,204	7,005	10.7	33,996	5,465	16.1
1986	64,491	7,023	10.9	33,801	5,516	16.3
1985	63,558	7,223	11.4	33,536	5,586	16.7
1984	62,706	7,277	11.6	32,942	5,662	17.2
1983	62,015	7,647	12.3	32,787	5,871	17.9
1982	61,393	7,512	12.2	32,565	5,712	17.5
1981	61,019	6,851	11.2	32,587	5,191	15.9
1980	60,309	6,217	10.3	32,773	4,822	14.7
1979	59,550	5,461	9.2	32,397	4,081	12.6
1978	57,804	5,280	9.1	31,735	4,060	12.8
1977	57,215	5,311	9.3	31,637	4,081	12.9
1976	56,710	5,311	9.4	31,434	4,060	12.9
1975	56,245	5,450	9.7	31,377	4,172	13.3
1974	55,698	4,922	8.8	31,319	3,789	12.1
1973	55,053	4,828	8.8	30,977	3,520	11.4
1972	54,373	5,075	9.3	30,807	3,621	11.8
1971	53,296	5,303	10.0	30,725	3,683	12.0
1970	52,227	5,260	10.1	30,070	3,491	11.6
1969	51,586	5,008	9.7	29,827	3,226	10.8
1968	50,511	5,047	10.0	29,325	3,347	11.4
1967	49,835	5,667	11.4	29,032	3,586	12.4
1966	48,921	5,784	11.8	28,592	3,734	13.4
1965	48,278	6,721	13.9	28,100	4,379	15.6
1964	47,836	7,160	15.0	28,277	4,771	16.9
1963	47,436	7,554	15.9	28,317	4,991	17.6
1962	46,998	8,077	17.2	28,174	5,460	19.4
1961	46,341	8,391	18.1	27,600	5,500	19.9
1960	45,435	8,243	18.1	27,102	5,328	19.7
1959	45,054	8,320	18.5	26,992	5,443	20.3

	percent change		percentage point change		percent change		percentage point change
1990 to 2000	9.1%	−12.3%	−2.1	8.2%	−16.7%	−3.7
1959 to 2000	60.7	−25.2	−9.9	38.3	−13.1	−7.6

Source: Bureau of the Census, Current Population Survey, Internet site http://www.census.gov/hhes/poverty/histpov/ hstpov4.html; calculations by New Strategist

Table 5.33 Married Couples in Poverty by Race and Hispanic Origin, 1974 to 2000

(number and percent of married couples below poverty level by race and Hispanic origin of householder, 1974 to 2000; percent and percentage point change for selected years; families in thousands as of the following year)

| | number of poor | | | | | percent in poverty | | | | |
| | | | | white | | | | | white | |
	total	black	Hispanic	total	non-Hispanic	total	black	Hispanic	total	non-Hispanic
2000	2,638	260	741	2,162	1,447	4.7%	6.1%	14.1%	4.4%	3.3%
1999	2,673	294	728	2,161	1,457	4.8	7.1	14.2	4.4	3.3
1998	2,879	290	775	2,400	1,639	5.3	7.3	15.7	5.0	3.8
1997	2,821	312	836	2,312	1,501	5.2	8.0	17.4	4.8	3.5
1996	3,010	352	815	2,416	1,628	5.6	9.1	18.0	5.1	3.8
1995	2,982	314	803	2,443	1,664	5.6	8.5	18.9	5.1	3.8
1994	3,272	336	827	2,629	1,915	6.1	8.7	19.5	5.5	4.3
1993	3,481	458	770	2,757	2,042	6.5	12.3	19.1	5.8	4.7
1992	3,385	490	743	2,677	1,978	6.4	13.0	18.8	5.7	4.5
1991	3,158	399	674	2,573	1,918	6.0	11.0	19.1	5.5	4.4
1990	2,981	448	605	2,386	1,799	5.7	12.6	17.5	5.1	4.1
1989	2,931	443	549	2,329	1,798	5.6	11.8	16.2	5.0	4.1
1988	2,897	421	547	2,294	1,763	5.6	11.3	16.1	4.9	4.0
1987	3,011	439	556	2,382	1,847	5.8	11.9	17.4	5.1	4.3
1986	3,123	403	518	2,591	2,081	6.1	10.8	16.6	5.6	4.8
1985	3,438	447	505	2,815	2,316	6.7	12.2	17.0	6.1	5.4
1984	3,488	479	469	2,858	2,400	6.9	13.8	16.6	6.3	5.6
1983	3,815	535	437	3,125	2,649	7.6	15.5	17.7	6.9	6.2
1982	3,789	543	465	3,104	2,648	7.6	15.6	19.0	6.9	6.2
1981	3,394	543	366	2,712	2,353	6.8	15.4	15.1	6.0	5.5
1980	3,032	474	363	2,437	2,083	6.2	14.0	15.3	5.4	4.9
1979	2,640	453	298	2,099	1,810	5.4	13.2	13.1	4.7	4.3
1978	2,474	366	248	2,033	1,790	5.2	11.3	11.9	4.7	4.3
1977	2,524	429	280	2,028	1,750	5.3	13.1	13.3	4.7	4.2
1976	2,606	450	312	2,071	1,759	5.5	13.2	15.8	4.8	4.2
1975	2,904	479	335	2,363	2,036	6.1	14.3	17.7	5.5	4.9
1974	2,474	435	278	1,977	1,700	5.3	13.0	14.4	4.6	4.1
	percent change					percentage point change				
1990 to 2000	−11.5%	−42.0%	22.5%	−9.4%	−19.6%	−1.0	−6.5	−3.4	−0.7	−0.8
1974 to 2000	6.6	−40.2	166.5	9.4	−14.9	−0.6	−6.9	−0.3	−0.2	−0.8

Source: Bureau of the Census, Current Population Surveys, Internet site http://www.census.gov/hhes/poverty/histpov/hstpov4.html; calculations by New Strategist

Table 5.34 Female-Headed Families in Poverty by Race and Hispanic Origin, 1974 to 2000

(number and percent of female-headed families below poverty level by race and Hispanic origin of householder, 1974 to 2000; percent and percentage point change for selected years; families in thousands as of the following year)

| | number of poor | | | | | percent in poverty | | | | |
| | | | | white | | | | | white | |
	total	black	Hispanic	total	non-Hispanic	total	black	Hispanic	total	non-Hispanic
2000	3,096	1,301	597	1,655	1,126	24.7%	34.6%	34.2%	20.0%	16.9%
1999	3,531	1,499	686	1,883	1,255	27.8	39.3	38.8	22.5	18.6
1998	3,831	1,557	756	2,123	1,428	29.9	40.8	43.7	24.9	20.7
1997	3,995	1,563	767	2,305	1,598	31.6	39.8	47.6	27.7	23.4
1996	4,167	1,724	823	2,276	1,538	32.6	43.7	50.9	27.3	22.4
1995	4,057	1,701	792	2,200	1,463	32.4	45.1	49.4	26.6	21.5
1994	4,232	1,715	773	2,329	1,678	34.6	46.2	52.1	29.0	24.8
1993	4,424	1,908	772	2,376	1,699	35.6	49.9	51.6	29.2	25.0
1992	4,275	1,878	664	2,245	1,637	35.4	50.2	49.3	28.5	24.7
1991	4,161	1,834	627	2,192	1,610	35.6	51.2	49.7	28.4	24.6
1990	3,768	1,648	573	2,010	1,480	33.4	48.1	48.3	26.8	23.1
1989	3,504	1,524	530	1,858	1,355	32.2	46.5	47.5	25.4	21.7
1988	3,642	1,579	546	1,945	1,426	33.4	49.0	49.1	26.5	22.7
1987	3,654	1,577	565	1,961	1,443	34.2	51.1	52.2	26.9	23.0
1986	3,613	1,488	528	2,041	1,542	34.6	50.1	51.2	28.2	24.7
1985	3,474	1,452	521	1,950	1,460	34.0	50.5	53.1	27.4	23.6
1984	3,498	1,533	483	1,878	1,422	34.5	51.7	53.4	27.1	23.4
1983	3,564	1,541	454	1,926	1,501	36.0	53.7	52.8	28.3	25.1
1982	3,434	1,535	425	1,813	1,413	36.3	56.2	55.4	27.9	24.5
1981	3,252	1,377	399	1,814	1,436	34.6	52.9	53.2	27.4	24.3
1980	2,972	1,301	362	1,609	1,264	32.7	49.4	51.3	25.7	22.6
1979	2,645	1,234	300	1,350	1,062	30.4	49.4	49.2	22.3	19.4
1978	2,654	1,208	288	1,391	1,047	31.4	50.6	53.1	23.5	20.0
1977	2,610	1,162	301	1,400	1,039	31.7	51.0	53.6	24.0	20.2
1976	2,543	1,122	275	1,379	1,059	33.0	52.2	53.1	25.2	21.8
1975	2,430	1,004	279	1,394	1,079	32.5	50.1	53.6	25.9	22.5
1974	2,324	1,010	229	1,289	1,005	32.1	52.2	49.6	24.8	21.5
	percent change					percentage point change				
1990 to 2000	−17.8%	−21.1%	4.2%	−17.7%	−23.9%	−8.7	−13.5	−14.1	−6.8	−6.2
1974 to 2000	33.2	28.8	160.7	28.4	12.0	−7.4	−17.6	−15.4	−4.8	−4.6

Source: Bureau of the Census, Current Population Surveys, Internet site http://www.census.gov/hhes/poverty/histpov/ hstpov4.html; calculations by New Strategist

6

Labor Force

■ A record proportion of Americans were in the labor force in 2000, as 67.2 percent of people aged 16 or older either worked or looked for work.

■ During the past half-century, the American labor force has changed dramatically. Women now account for nearly half of workers, while one in four workers is black, Hispanic or another minority.

■ Many of the occupations projected to grow the fastest between 2000 and 2010 are high-tech jobs such as computer software engineers, network systems and data communications analysts, and network administrators. While the total number of jobs is projected to increase 15 percent between 2000 and 2010, positions requiring a bachelor's degree or more education will grow 22 percent.

■ As women have entered the workforce, the dual-earner couple has become the norm. The majority of married women with children under age 18 are in the labor force. Among wives with children under age 3, the 59 percent majority were in the labor force in 2000, up from just 33 percent in 1975.

■ Long-term job tenure is on the decline among men. In 1983, the 51 percent majority of working men aged 40 to 44 had been with their current employer for 10 or more years. By 2000, the figure had fallen to 40 percent.

Face of Labor Force Has Changed

During the past half-century, the American labor force has changed dramatically. In 1950, women accounted for only 30 percent of the nation's workers. Today, they account for nearly half of workers, a figure that is not expected to change much during the next half century.

The age distribution of the labor force has also changed. The share of workers aged 16 to 24 fell between 1950 and 2000 as colleges lured many young adults away from jobs. The proportion of workers aged 55 or older also declined as early retirement became more popular. The older worker share of the labor force will grow during the next decade as the large baby-boom generation enters the age group. The number of workers aged 55 to 64 should grow 52 percent between 2000 and 2010. The number of working Americans aged 65 or older will expand by fully 142 percent between 2000 and 2050.

The minority share of the labor force increased substantially between 1980 and 2000. Eighty-two percent of workers were non-Hispanic white in 1980, a figure that fell to 73 percent by 2000. The non-Hispanic white share of the labor force will continue to decline, falling to just 53 percent by 2050. The number of non-Hispanic white workers will begin to decline after 2010.

More women in the labor force

(number of people aged 16 or older in the labor force, by sex, 1950 to 2050; numbers in millions)

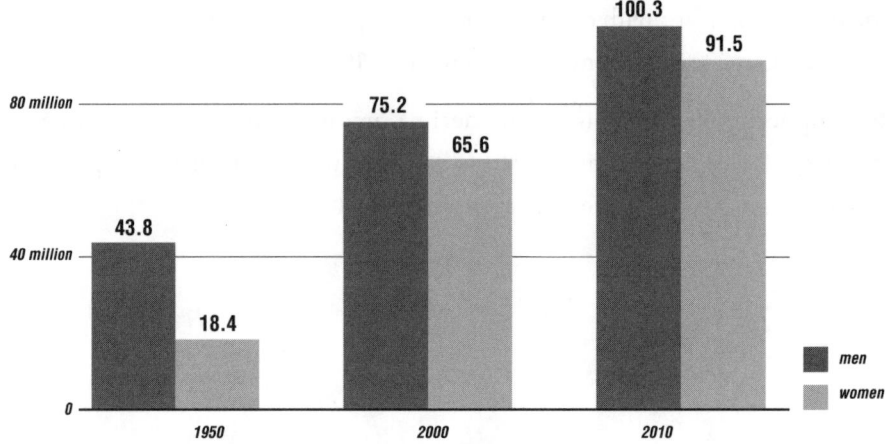

Table 6.1 Labor Force by Sex and Age, 1950 to 2000

(number and percent distribution of people aged 16 or older in the civilian labor force by sex and age, 1950 to 2000; percent change in number and percentage point change in share for selected years; numbers in thousands)

	1950	1960	1970	1980	1990	2000	percent change 1950–00	percent change 1990–00
Total	**62,208**	**69,628**	**82,771**	**106,940**	**125,840**	**140,863**	**126.4%**	**11.9%**
Men	43,819	46,388	51,228	61,453	69,011	75,247	71.7	9.0
Women	18,389	23,240	31,543	45,487	56,829	65,616	256.8	15.5
Aged 16 to 24	11,522	11,545	17,846	25,300	22,492	22,715	97.1	1.0
Aged 25 to 34	14,619	14,382	17,036	29,227	35,929	31,669	116.6	−11.9
Aged 35 to 44	13,954	16,269	16,437	20,463	32,145	37,838	171.2	17.7
Aged 45 to 54	11,444	14,852	16,949	16,910	20,248	30,467	166.2	50.5
Aged 55 to 64	7,633	9,385	11,283	11,985	11,575	13,974	83.1	20.7
Aged 65 or older	3,036	3,195	3,222	3,054	3,451	4,200	38.3	21.7

	1950	1960	1970	1980	1990	2000	percentage point change 1950–00	percentage point change 1990–00
Total	**100.0%**	**100.0%**	**100.0%**	**100.0%**	**100.0%**	**100.0%**	**–**	**–**
Men	70.4	66.6	61.9	57.5	54.8	53.4	−17.0	−1.4
Women	29.6	33.4	38.1	42.5	45.2	46.6	17.0	1.4
Aged 16 to 24	18.5	16.6	21.6	23.7	17.9	16.1	−2.4	−1.7
Aged 25 to 34	23.5	20.7	20.6	27.3	28.6	22.5	−1.0	−6.1
Aged 35 to 44	22.4	23.4	19.9	19.1	25.5	26.9	4.4	1.3
Aged 45 to 54	18.4	21.3	20.5	15.8	16.1	21.6	3.2	5.5
Aged 55 to 64	12.3	13.5	13.6	11.2	9.2	9.9	−2.3	0.7
Aged 65 or older	4.9	4.6	3.9	2.9	2.7	3.0	−1.9	0.2

Note: (–) means not applicable.
Source: Bureau of Labor Statistics, Monthly Labor Review, *May 2002; calculations by New Strategist*

Table 6.2 Labor Force by Sex and Age, 2000 to 2050

(number and percent distribution of people aged 16 or older in the civilian labor force by sex and age, 2000 to 2050; percent change in number and percentage point change in share for selected years; numbers in thousands)

	2000	2010	2020	2030	2040	2050	percent change 2000–10	2000–50
Total	**140,863**	**157,721**	**164,681**	**170,090**	**180,517**	**191,825**	**12.0%**	**36.2%**
Men	75,247	82,221	85,430	88,503	94,041	100,280	9.3	33.3
Women	65,616	75,500	79,250	81,588	86,476	91,545	15.1	39.5
Aged 16 to 24	22,715	26,081	25,653	27,518	29,792	31,317	14.8	37.9
Aged 25 to 34	31,669	34,222	37,905	37,828	41,099	44,156	8.1	39.4
Aged 35 to 44	37,838	33,990	35,277	38,968	39,336	42,647	–10.2	12.7
Aged 45 to 54	30,467	36,783	32,406	33,644	37,330	37,640	20.7	23.5
Aged 55 to 64	13,974	21,204	25,195	22,047	23,359	25,901	51.7	85.4
Aged 65 or older	4,200	5,442	8,243	10,086	9,601	10,164	29.6	142.0

	2000	2010	2020	2030	2040	2050	percentage point change 2000–10	2000–50
Total	**100.0%**	**100.0%**	**100.0%**	**100.0%**	**100.0%**	**100.0%**	**–**	**–**
Men	53.4	52.1	51.9	52.0	52.1	52.3	–1.3	–1.1
Women	46.6	47.9	48.1	48.0	47.9	47.7	1.3	1.1
Aged 16 to 24	16.1	16.5	15.6	16.2	16.5	16.3	0.4	0.2
Aged 25 to 34	22.5	21.7	23.0	22.2	22.8	23.0	–0.8	0.5
Aged 35 to 44	26.9	21.6	21.4	22.9	21.8	22.2	–5.3	–4.6
Aged 45 to 54	21.6	23.3	19.7	19.8	20.7	19.6	1.7	–0.2
Aged 55 to 64	9.9	13.4	15.3	13.0	12.9	13.5	3.5	3.6
Aged 65 or older	3.0	3.5	0.5	5.9	5.3	5.3	0.5	2.3

Note: (–) means not applicable.
Source: Bureau of Labor Statistics, Monthly Labor Review, *May 2002; calculations by New Strategist*

Table 6.3 Labor Force by Race and Hispanic Origin, 1980 to 2000

(number and percent distribution of people aged 16 or older in the civilian labor force by race and Hispanic origin, 1980 to 2000; percent change in number and percentage point change in share for selected years; numbers in thousands)

				percent change	
	1980	*1990*	*2000*	*1980–00*	*1990–00*
Total	**106,940**	**125,840**	**140,863**	**31.7%**	**11.9%**
Race					
Asian and other	2,476	4,653	6,687	170.1	43.7
Black	10,865	13,740	16,603	52.8	20.8
White	93,600	107,447	117,574	25.6	9.4
Hispanic origin					
Hispanic	6,146	10,720	15,368	150.1	43.4
Non-Hispanic	100,794	115,120	125,495	24.5	9.0
Non-Hispanic white	87,633	97,818	102,963	17.5	5.3

				percentage point change	
	1980	*1990*	*2000*	*1980–00*	*1990–00*
Total	**100.0%**	**100.0%**	**100.0%**	–	–
Race					
Asian and other	2.3	3.7	4.7	2.4	1.1
Black	10.2	10.9	11.8	1.6	0.9
White	87.5	85.4	83.5	–4.1	–1.9
Hispanic origin					
Hispanic	5.7	8.5	10.9	5.2	2.4
Non-Hispanic	94.3	91.5	89.1	–5.2	–2.4
Non-Hispanic white	81.9	77.7	73.1	–8.9	–4.6

Note: Hispanics may be of any race; (–) means not applicable.
Source: Bureau of Labor Statistics, Monthly Labor Review, *May 2002; calculations by New Strategist*

Table 6.4 Labor Force by Race and Hispanic Origin, 2000 to 2050

(number and percent distribution of people aged 16 or older in the civilian labor force by race and Hispanic origin, 2000 to 2050; percent change in number and percentage point change in share for selected years; numbers in thousands)

	2000	2010	2020	2030	2040	2050	percent change 2000–10	2000–50
Total	140,863	157,721	164,681	170,090	180,517	191,825	12.0%	36.2%
Race								
Asian and other	6,687	9,636	11,944	14,575	17,707	20,960	44.1	213.4
Black	16,603	20,041	21,856	23,399	25,316	27,094	20.7	63.2
White	117,574	128,043	130,881	132,116	137,494	143,770	8.9	22.3
Hispanic origin								
Hispanic	15,368	20,947	26,321	31,951	38,403	45,426	36.3	195.6
Non-Hispanic	125,495	136,774	138,359	138,140	142,114	146,399	9.0	16.7
Non-Hispanic white	102,963	109,118	107,043	103,138	102,637	102,506	6.0	–0.4

	2000	2010	2020	2030	2040	2050	percentage point change 2000–10	2000–50
Total	100.0%	100.0%	100.0%	100.0%	100.0%	100.0%	–	–
Race								
Asian and other	4.7	6.1	7.3	8.6	9.8	10.9	1.4	6.2
Black	11.8	13.9	14.2	14.9	1.5	0.0	2.1	–11.8
White	83.5	81.2	79.5	77.7	76.2	74.9	–2.3	–8.5
Hispanic origin								
Hispanic	10.9	13.3	16.0	18.8	21.3	23.7	2.4	12.8
Non-Hispanic	89.1	86.7	84.0	81.2	78.7	76.3	–2.4	–12.8
Non-Hispanic white	73.1	69.2	65.0	60.6	56.9	53.4	–3.9	–19.7

Note: Hispanics may be of any race; (–) means not applicable.
Source: Bureau of Labor Statistics, Monthly Labor Review, *May 2002; calculations by New Strategist*

Labor Force Participation Is at Record High

A record proportion of Americans were in the labor force in 2000, as 67.2 percent of people aged 16 or older either worked or looked for work. The labor force has more than doubled in size over the past half-century, from 62 million to 141 million. At the same time, the number of people employed in agriculture fell from 7 million to 3 million as farming became more efficient and required fewer laborers.

Three out of four men are in the labor force. The number grew 72 percent between 1950 and 2000, from 44 million to 75 million. The proportion of men aged 16 or older who are not in the labor force grew from 14 to 25 percent during those years as early retirement became increasingly popular.

Sixty percent of women are in the labor force. Their number grew 256 percent between 1950 and 2000, from 18 million to 66 million. The proportion of women aged 16 or older who are not in the labor force fell from 66 to 40 percent during those years as more women opted to go to work rather than devote themselves only to home and family.

Labor force more than doubles

(number of people aged 16 or older in the labor force, 1950 to 2000; numbers in millions)

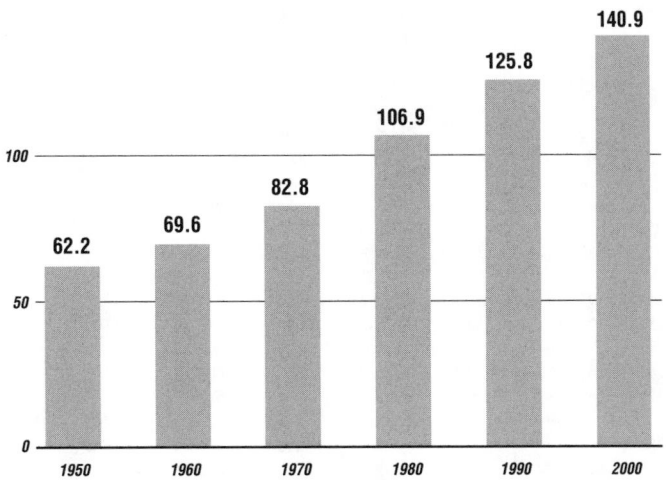

Table 6.5 Employment Status of the Population, 1950 to 2000

(employment status of the civilian noninstitutional population aged 16 or older, 1950 to 2000; numbers in thousands)

	civilian noninsitutional population	total	percent of population	employed total	agricultural	non-agric.	unemployed number	percent	not in labor force
				civilian labor force					
2000	209,699	140,863	67.2%	135,208	3,305	131,903	5,655	4.0%	68,836
1999	207,753	139,368	67.1	133,488	3,281	130,207	5,880	4.2	68,385
1998	205,220	137,673	67.1	131,463	3,378	128,085	6,210	4.5	67,547
1997	203,133	136,297	67.1	129,558	3,399	126,159	6,739	4.9	66,837
1996	200,591	133,943	66.8	126,708	3,443	123,264	7,236	5.4	66,647
1995	198,584	132,304	66.6	124,900	3,440	121,460	7,404	5.6	66,280
1994	196,814	131,056	66.6	123,060	3,409	119,651	7,996	6.1	65,758
1993	194,838	129,200	66.3	120,259	3,115	117,144	8,940	6.9	65,638
1992	192,805	128,105	66.4	118,492	3,247	115,245	9,613	7.5	64,700
1991	190,925	126,346	66.2	117,718	3,269	114,449	8,628	6.8	64,578
1990	189,164	125,840	66.5	118,793	3,223	115,570	7,047	5.6	63,324
1989	186,393	123,869	66.5	117,342	3,199	114,142	6,528	5.3	62,523
1988	184,613	121,669	65.9	114,968	3,169	111,800	6,701	5.5	62,944
1987	182,753	119,865	65.6	112,440	3,208	109,232	7,425	6.2	62,888
1986	180,587	117,834	65.3	109,597	3,163	106,434	8,237	7.0	62,752
1985	178,206	115,461	64.8	107,150	3,179	103,971	8,312	7.2	62,744
1984	176,383	113,544	64.4	105,005	3,321	101,685	8,539	7.5	62,839
1983	174,215	111,550	64.0	100,834	3,383	97,450	10,717	9.6	62,665
1982	172,271	110,204	64.0	99,526	3,401	96,125	10,678	9.7	62,067
1981	170,130	108,670	63.9	100,397	3,368	97,030	8,273	7.6	61,460
1980	167,745	106,940	63.8	99,303	3,364	95,938	7,637	7.1	60,806
1979	164,863	104,962	63.7	98,824	3,347	95,477	6,137	5.8	59,900
1978	161,910	102,251	63.2	96,048	3,387	92,661	6,202	6.1	59,659
1977	159,033	99,009	62.3	92,017	3,283	88,734	6,991	7.1	60,025
1976	156,150	96,158	61.6	88,752	3,331	85,421	7,406	7.7	59,991
1975	153,153	93,775	61.2	85,846	3,408	82,438	7,929	8.5	59,377
1974	150,120	91,949	61.3	86,794	3,515	83,279	5,156	5.6	58,171
1973	147,096	89,429	60.8	85,064	3,470	81,594	4,365	4.9	57,667
1972	144,126	87,034	60.4	82,153	3,484	78,669	4,882	5.6	57,091
1971	140,216	84,382	60.2	79,367	3,394	75,972	5,016	5.9	55,834
1970	137,085	82,771	60.4	78,678	3,463	75,215	4,093	4.9	54,315
1969	134,335	80,734	60.1	77,902	3,606	74,296	2,832	3.5	53,602
1968	132,028	78,737	59.6	75,920	3,817	72,103	2,817	3.6	53,291
1967	129,874	77,347	59.6	74,372	3,844	70,527	2,975	3.8	52,527
1966	128,058	75,770	59.2	72,895	3,979	68,915	2,875	3.8	52,288
1965	126,513	74,455	58.9	71,088	4,361	66,726	3,366	4.5	52,058
1964	124,485	73,091	58.7	69,305	4,523	64,782	3,786	5.2	51,394
1963	122,416	71,833	58.7	67,762	4,687	63,076	4,070	5.7	50,583
1962	120,153	70,614	58.8	66,702	4,944	61,759	3,911	5.5	49,539
1961	118,771	70,459	59.3	65,746	5,200	60,546	4,714	6.7	48,312
1960	117,245	69,628	59.4	65,778	5,458	60,318	3,852	5.5	47,617
1959	115,329	68,369	59.3	64,630	5,565	59,065	3,740	5.5	46,960
1958	113,727	67,639	59.5	63,036	5,586	57,450	4,602	6.8	46,088
1957	112,265	66,929	59.6	64,071	5,947	58,123	2,859	4.3	45,336
1956	110,954	66,552	60.0	63,799	6,283	57,514	2,750	4.1	44,402
1955	109,683	65,023	59.3	62,170	6,450	55,722	2,852	4.4	44,660
1954	108,321	63,643	58.8	60,109	6,205	53,904	3,532	5.5	44,678
1953	107,056	63,015	58.9	61,179	6,260	54,919	1,834	2.9	44,041
1952	105,231	62,138	59.0	60,250	6,500	53,749	1,883	3.0	43,093
1951	104,621	62,017	59.2	59,961	6,726	53,235	2,055	3.3	42,604
1950	104,995	62,208	59.2	58,918	7,160	51,758	3,288	5.3	42,787

Note: The civilian labor force includes both the employed and the unemployed. The civilian population includes both those in the labor force and those not in the labor force.
Source: Bureau of Labor Statistics, Employment and Earnings, *January 2001*

Table 6.6 Employment Status of Men, 1950 to 2000

(employment status of men aged 16 or older, 1950 to 2000; numbers in thousands)

	civilian noninstitutional population	civilian labor force total	percent of population	employed	unemployed number	unemployed percent	not in labor force number	not in labor force percent
2000	100,731	75,247	74.7%	72,293	2,954	3.9%	25,484	25.3%
1999	99,722	74,512	74.7	71,446	3,066	4.1	25,210	25.3
1998	98,758	73,959	74.9	70,693	3,266	4.4	24,799	25.1
1997	97,715	73,261	75.0	69,685	3,577	4.9	24,454	25.0
1996	96,206	72,087	74.9	68,207	3,880	5.4	24,119	25.1
1995	95,178	71,360	75.0	67,377	3,983	5.6	23,818	25.0
1994	94,355	70,817	75.1	66,450	4,367	6.2	23,538	24.9
1993	93,332	70,404	75.4	65,349	5,055	7.2	22,927	24.6
1992	92,270	69,964	75.8	64,440	5,523	7.9	22,306	24.2
1991	91,278	69,168	75.8	64,223	4,946	7.2	22,110	24.2
1990	90,377	69,011	76.4	65,104	3,906	5.7	21,367	23.6
1989	88,762	67,840	76.4	64,315	3,525	5.2	20,923	23.6
1988	87,857	66,927	76.2	63,273	3,655	5.5	20,930	23.8
1987	86,899	66,207	76.2	62,107	4,101	6.2	20,692	23.8
1986	85,798	65,422	76.3	60,892	4,530	6.9	20,376	23.7
1985	84,469	64,411	76.3	59,891	4,521	7.0	20,058	23.7
1984	83,605	63,835	76.4	59,091	4,744	7.4	19,771	23.6
1983	82,531	63,047	76.4	56,787	6,260	9.9	19,484	23.6
1982	81,523	62,450	76.6	56,271	6,179	9.9	19,073	23.4
1981	80,511	61,974	77.0	57,397	4,577	7.4	18,537	23.0
1980	79,398	61,453	77.4	57,186	4,267	6.9	17,945	22.6
1979	78,020	60,726	77.8	57,607	3,120	5.1	17,293	22.2
1978	76,576	59,620	77.9	56,479	3,142	5.3	16,956	22.1
1977	75,193	58,396	77.7	54,728	3,667	6.3	16,797	22.3
1976	73,759	57,174	77.5	53,138	4,036	7.1	16,585	22.5
1975	72,291	56,299	77.9	51,857	4,442	7.9	15,993	22.1
1974	70,808	55,739	78.7	53,024	2,714	4.9	15,069	21.3
1973	69,292	54,624	78.8	52,349	2,275	4.2	14,667	21.2
1972	67,835	53,555	78.9	50,896	2,659	5.0	14,280	21.1
1971	65,942	52,180	79.1	49,390	2,789	5.3	13,762	20.9
1970	64,304	51,228	79.7	48,990	2,238	4.4	13,076	20.3
1969	62,898	50,221	79.8	48,818	1,403	2.8	12,677	20.2
1968	61,847	49,533	80.1	48,114	1,419	2.9	12,315	19.9
1967	60,905	48,987	80.4	47,479	1,508	3.1	11,919	19.6
1966	60,262	48,471	80.4	46,919	1,551	3.2	11,792	19.6
1965	59,782	48,255	80.4	46,340	1,914	4.0	11,527	19.3
1964	58,847	47,679	80.7	45,474	2,205	4.6	11,169	19.0
1963	57,921	47,129	81.0	44,657	2,472	5.2	10,792	18.6
1962	56,831	46,600	81.4	44,177	2,423	5.2	10,231	18.0
1961	56,286	46,653	82.0	43,656	2,997	6.4	9,633	17.1
1960	55,662	46,388	82.9	43,904	2,486	5.4	9,274	16.7
1959	54,793	45,886	83.7	43,466	2,420	5.3	8,907	16.3
1958	54,033	45,521	84.2	42,423	3,098	6.8	8,514	15.8
1957	53,315	45,197	84.8	43,357	1,841	4.1	8,118	15.2
1956	52,723	45,091	85.5	43,379	1,711	3.8	7,633	14.5
1955	52,109	44,475	85.4	42,621	1,854	4.2	7,634	14.7
1954	51,395	43,965	85.5	41,619	2,344	5.3	7,431	14.5
1953	50,750	43,633	86.0	42,430	1,202	2.8	7,117	14.0
1952	49,700	42,869	86.3	41,682	1,185	2.8	6,832	13.7
1951	49,727	43,001	86.3	41,780	1,221	2.8	6,725	13.5
1950	50,725	43,819	86.4	41,578	2,239	5.1	6,906	13.6

Note: The civilian labor force includes both the employed and the unemployed. The civilian population includes both those in the labor force and those not in the labor force.
Source: Bureau of Labor Statistics, Handbook of Labor Statistics, Bulletin 2340, *1989; and Bureau of Labor Statistics,* Employment and Earnings, *January 2001; calculations by New Strategist*

Table 6.7 Employment Status of Women, 1950 to 2000

(employment status of women aged 16 or older, 1950 to 2000; numbers in thousands)

| | civilian noninstitutional population | civilian labor force | | | | | | |
		total	percent of population	employed	unemployed number	unemployed percent	not in labor force number	not in labor force percent
2000	108,968	65,616	60.2%	62,915	2,701	4.1%	43,352	39.8%
1999	108,031	64,855	60.0	62,042	2,814	4.3	43,175	40.0
1998	106,462	63,714	59.8	60,771	2,944	4.6	42,748	40.2
1997	105,418	63,036	59.8	59,873	3,162	5.0	42,382	40.2
1996	104,385	61,857	59.3	58,501	3,356	5.4	42,528	40.7
1995	103,406	60,944	58.9	57,523	3,421	5.6	42,462	41.1
1994	102,460	60,239	58.8	56,610	3,629	6.0	42,221	41.2
1993	101,506	58,795	57.9	54,910	3,885	6.6	42,711	42.1
1992	100,535	58,141	57.8	54,052	4,090	7.0	42,394	42.2
1991	99,646	57,178	57.4	53,496	3,683	6.4	42,468	42.6
1990	98,787	56,829	57.5	53,689	3,140	5.5	41,957	42.5
1989	97,630	56,030	57.4	53,027	3,003	5.4	41,601	42.6
1988	96,756	54,742	56.6	51,696	3,046	5.6	42,014	43.4
1987	95,853	53,658	56.0	50,334	3,324	6.2	42,195	44.0
1986	94,789	52,413	55.3	48,706	3,707	7.1	42,376	44.7
1985	93,736	51,050	54.5	47,259	3,791	7.4	42,686	45.5
1984	92,778	49,709	53.6	45,915	3,794	7.6	43,068	46.4
1983	91,684	48,503	52.9	44,047	4,457	9.2	43,181	47.1
1982	90,748	47,755	52.6	43,256	4,499	9.4	42,993	47.4
1981	89,618	46,696	52.1	43,000	3,696	7.9	42,922	47.9
1980	88,348	45,487	51.5	42,117	3,370	7.4	42,861	48.5
1979	86,843	44,235	50.9	41,217	3,018	6.8	42,608	49.1
1978	85,334	42,631	50.0	39,569	3,061	7.2	42,703	50.0
1977	83,840	40,613	48.4	37,289	3,324	8.2	43,227	51.6
1976	82,390	38,983	47.3	35,615	3,369	8.6	43,406	52.7
1975	80,860	37,475	46.3	33,989	3,486	9.3	43,386	53.7
1974	79,312	36,211	45.7	33,769	2,441	6.7	43,101	54.3
1973	77,804	34,804	44.7	32,715	2,089	6.0	43,000	55.3
1972	76,290	33,479	43.9	31,257	2,222	6.6	42,811	56.1
1971	74,274	32,202	43.4	29,976	2,227	6.9	42,072	56.6
1970	72,782	31,543	43.3	29,688	1,855	5.9	41,239	56.7
1969	71,436	30,513	42.7	29,084	1,429	4.7	40,924	57.3
1968	70,179	29,204	41.6	27,807	1,397	4.8	40,976	58.4
1967	68,968	28,360	41.1	26,893	1,468	5.2	40,608	58.9
1966	67,795	27,299	40.3	25,976	1,324	4.8	40,496	59.7
1965	66,731	26,200	39.3	24,748	1,452	5.5	40,531	60.7
1964	65,637	25,412	38.7	23,831	1,581	6.2	40,225	61.3
1963	64,494	24,704	38.3	23,105	1,598	6.5	39,791	61.7
1962	63,321	24,014	37.9	22,525	1,488	6.2	39,308	62.1
1961	62,484	23,806	38.1	22,090	1,717	7.2	38,679	61.9
1960	61,582	23,240	37.7	21,874	1,366	5.9	38,343	62.3
1959	60,534	22,483	37.1	21,164	1,320	5.9	38,053	62.9
1958	59,690	22,118	37.1	20,613	1,504	6.8	37,574	62.9
1957	58,951	21,732	36.9	20,714	1,018	4.7	37,218	63.1
1956	58,228	21,461	36.9	20,419	1,039	4.8	36,769	63.1
1955	57,574	20,548	35.7	19,551	998	4.9	37,026	64.3
1954	56,925	19,678	34.6	18,490	1,188	6.0	37,247	65.4
1953	56,305	19,382	34.4	18,749	632	3.3	36,924	65.6
1952	55,529	19,269	34.7	18,566	698	3.6	36,261	65.3
1951	54,895	19,016	34.6	18,181	834	4.4	35,879	65.4
1950	54,270	18,408	33.9	17,359	1,049	5.7	35,881	66.1

Note: The civilian labor force includes both the employed and the unemployed. The civilian population includes both those in the labor force and those not in the labor force.
Source: Bureau of Labor Statistics, Handbook of Labor Statistics, Bulletin 2340, 1989; Bureau of Labor Statistics, Employment and Earnings, January 2001; calculations by New Strategist

Labor Force Rate Higher for Women, Lower for Men

The labor force participation rate of women aged 16 or older has climbed from 34 percent in 1950 to 60 percent in 2000. At the same time, the labor force participation rate for men fell from 86 to 75 percent. Consequently, the gap between labor force participation rates of men and women dropped from 53 to just 15 percentage points during the past half-century. The gap is projected to shrink to just 10 percentage points by 2050.

The labor force participation rate of men fell in every age group between 1950 and 2000, particularly among men aged 55 or older because of early retirement. In contrast, the rate grew for all but the oldest women during those years, particularly among women aged 25 to 54.

During the next fifty years, the percentage of the population aged 16 or older in the labor force will decline as the large baby-boom generation retires. By 2050, boomers will be very old, ranging in age from 86 to 104, but still numerous enough to depress the overall labor force participation rate for both men and women. Interestingly, although women's labor force participation will rise in every age group between 2000 and 2050, their overall rate will fall because so many women will be very old and no longer working.

The gap between the sexes narrows

(percent of people aged 16 or older in the labor force, by sex, 1950 to 2050)

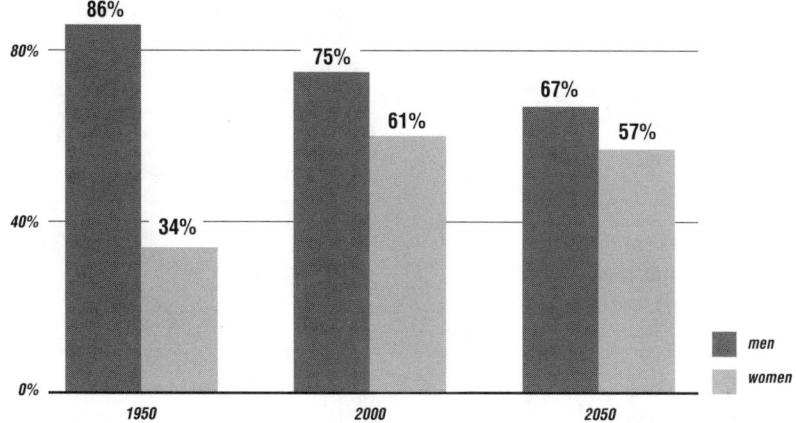

Table 6.8 Labor Force Participation Rate by Sex, 1950 to 2050

(percent of people aged 16 or older in the civilian labor force by sex, and percentage point difference between men and women, 1950 to 2050; percentage point change for selected years)

	total people	men	women	percentage point difference between men and women
2050	61.5%	66.8%	56.6%	10.2
2040	61.6	67.0	56.7	10.3
2030	62.3	67.6	57.4	10.2
2020	65.1	70.3	60.3	10.0
2010	67.5	73.2	62.2	11.0
2000	67.2	74.7	60.2	14.5
1999	67.1	74.7	60.0	14.7
1998	67.1	74.9	59.8	15.1
1997	67.1	75.0	59.8	15.2
1996	66.8	74.9	59.3	15.6
1995	66.6	75.0	58.9	16.1
1994	66.6	75.1	58.8	16.3
1993	66.3	75.4	57.9	17.5
1992	66.4	75.8	57.8	18.0
1991	66.2	75.8	57.4	18.4
1990	66.5	76.4	57.5	18.9
1989	66.5	76.4	57.4	19.0
1988	65.9	76.2	56.6	19.6
1987	65.6	76.2	56.0	20.2
1986	65.3	76.3	55.3	21.0
1985	64.8	76.3	54.5	21.8
1984	64.4	76.4	53.6	22.8
1983	64.0	76.4	52.9	23.5
1982	64.0	76.6	52.6	24.0
1981	63.9	77.0	52.1	24.9
1980	63.8	77.4	51.5	25.9
1979	63.7	77.8	50.9	26.9
1978	63.2	77.9	50.0	27.9
1977	62.3	77.7	48.4	29.3
1976	61.6	77.5	47.3	30.2
1975	61.2	77.9	46.3	31.6
1974	61.3	78.7	45.7	33.0
1973	60.8	78.8	44.7	34.1
1972	60.4	78.9	43.9	35.0
1971	60.2	79.1	43.4	35.7
1970	60.4	79.7	43.3	36.4
1969	60.1	79.8	42.7	37.1
1968	59.6	80.1	41.6	38.5
1967	59.6	80.4	41.1	39.3
1966	59.2	80.4	40.3	40.1
1965	58.9	80.4	39.3	41.1

(continued)

(continued from previous page)

	total people	men	women	percentage point difference between men and women
1964	58.7%	80.7%	38.7%	42.0
1963	58.7	81.0	38.3	42.7
1962	58.8	81.4	37.9	43.5
1961	59.3	82.0	38.1	43.9
1960	59.4	82.9	37.7	45.2
1959	59.3	83.7	37.1	46.6
1958	59.5	84.2	37.1	47.1
1957	59.6	84.8	36.9	47.9
1956	60.0	85.5	36.9	48.6
1955	59.3	85.4	35.7	49.7
1954	58.8	85.5	34.6	50.9
1953	58.9	86.0	34.4	51.6
1952	59.0	86.3	34.7	51.6
1951	59.2	86.3	34.6	51.7
1950	59.2	86.4	33.9	52.5
Percentage point change				
2000 to 2050	−5.7	−7.9	−3.6	−4.3
1950 to 2000	8.0	−11.7	26.3	−38.0

Source: Bureau of Labor Statistics, Handbook of Labor Statistics, *Bulletin 2340, 1989;* Employment and Earnings, *January 2001; and* Monthly Labor Review, *May 2002; calculations by New Strategist*

Table 6.9 Labor Force Participation Rate of Men by Age, 1950 to 2010

(percent of men aged 16 or older in the civilian labor force by age, 1950 to 2010; percentage point change for selected years)

	total men	16–19	20–24	25–34	35–44	45–54	55–64	65+
2010	73.2%	52.3%	81.2%	93.1%	92.3%	87.8%	67.0%	19.5%
2000	74.7	53.0	82.6	93.4	92.6	88.6	67.3	17.5
1999	74.7	52.9	81.9	93.3	92.8	88.8	67.9	16.9
1998	74.9	53.3	82.0	93.2	92.6	89.2	68.1	16.5
1997	75.0	52.3	82.5	93.0	92.6	89.5	67.6	17.1
1996	74.9	53.2	82.5	93.2	92.4	89.1	67.0	16.9
1995	75.0	54.8	83.1	93.0	92.3	88.8	66.0	16.8
1994	75.1	54.1	83.1	92.6	92.8	89.1	65.5	16.8
1993	75.4	53.2	83.2	93.4	93.4	90.1	66.5	15.6
1992	75.8	53.4	83.3	93.8	93.7	90.7	67.0	16.1
1991	75.8	53.2	83.5	93.6	94.1	90.5	67.0	15.7
1990	76.4	55.7	84.4	94.1	94.3	90.7	67.8	16.3
1989	76.4	57.9	85.3	94.4	94.5	91.1	67.2	16.6
1988	76.2	56.9	85.0	94.3	94.5	90.9	67.0	16.5
1987	76.2	56.1	85.2	94.6	94.6	90.7	67.6	16.3
1986	76.3	56.4	85.8	94.6	94.8	91.0	67.3	16.0
1985	76.3	56.8	85.0	94.7	95.0	91.0	67.9	15.8
1984	76.4	56.0	85.0	94.4	95.4	91.2	68.5	16.3
1983	76.4	56.2	84.8	94.2	95.2	91.2	69.4	17.4
1982	76.6	56.7	84.9	94.7	95.3	91.2	70.2	17.8
1981	77.0	59.0	85.5	94.9	95.4	91.4	70.6	18.4
1980	77.4	60.5	85.9	95.2	95.5	91.2	72.1	19.0
1979	77.8	61.5	86.4	95.3	95.7	91.4	72.8	19.9
1978	77.9	62.0	85.9	95.3	95.7	91.3	73.3	20.4
1977	77.7	60.9	85.6	95.3	95.7	91.1	73.8	20.0
1976	77.5	59.3	85.2	95.2	95.4	91.6	74.3	20.2
1975	77.9	59.1	84.5	95.2	95.6	92.1	75.6	21.6
1974	78.7	60.7	85.9	95.8	96.0	92.2	77.3	22.4
1973	78.8	59.7	85.2	95.7	96.2	93.0	78.2	22.7
1972	78.9	58.1	83.9	95.7	96.4	93.2	80.4	24.3
1971	79.1	56.1	83.0	95.9	96.5	93.9	82.1	25.5
1970	79.7	56.1	83.3	96.4	96.9	94.3	83.0	26.8
1969	79.8	55.9	82.8	96.7	96.9	94.6	83.4	27.2
1968	80.1	55.1	82.8	96.9	97.1	94.9	84.3	27.3
1967	80.4	55.6	84.4	97.2	97.3	95.2	84.4	27.1
1966	80.4	55.3	85.1	97.3	97.2	95.3	84.5	27.1
1965	80.4	53.8	85.8	97.2	97.3	95.6	84.6	27.9
1964	80.7	52.4	86.1	97.3	97.3	95.7	85.6	28.0
1963	81.0	52.9	86.1	97.1	97.5	95.7	86.2	28.4
1962	81.4	53.8	86.9	97.2	97.6	95.6	86.2	30.3
1961	82.0	54.6	87.8	97.5	97.6	95.6	87.3	31.7
1960	82.9	56.1	88.1	97.5	97.7	95.7	86.8	33.1
1959	83.7	55.8	87.8	97.4	97.8	96.0	87.4	34.2
1958	84.2	56.6	86.9	97.1	97.9	96.3	87.8	35.6
1957	84.8	59.1	87.1	97.1	97.9	96.3	87.5	37.5
1956	85.5	60.5	87.8	97.3	97.9	96.6	88.5	40.0
1955	85.4	58.9	86.9	97.6	98.1	96.4	87.9	39.6
1954	85.5	58.0	86.9	97.3	98.1	96.5	88.7	40.5
1953	86.0	60.7	87.7	97.4	98.2	96.5	87.9	41.6
1952	86.3	61.3	88.1	97.5	97.8	96.2	87.5	42.6
1951	86.3	63.0	88.4	96.9	97.5	95.9	87.2	44.9
1950	86.4	63.2	87.9	96.0	97.6	95.8	86.9	45.8
Percentage point change								
2000 to 2010	−1.5	−0.7	−1.4	−0.3	−0.3	−0.8	−0.3	2.0
1990 to 2000	−1.7	−2.7	−1.8	−0.7	−1.7	−2.1	−0.5	1.2
1950 to 2000	−11.7	−10.2	−5.3	−2.6	−5.0	−7.2	−19.6	−28.3

Source: Bureau of Labor Statistics, Internet site http://data.bls.gov/cgi-bin/srgate; and Monthly Labor Review, *November 2001; calculations by New Strategist*

Table 6.10   Labor Force Participation Rate of Men by Age, 2000 to 2050

(percent of men aged 16 or older in the civilian labor force by age, 2000 to 2050; percentage point change for selected years)

	total men	16–24	25–34	35–44	45–54	55–64	65+
2050	66.8%	67.0%	93.0%	92.1%	87.1%	66.2%	17.3%
2040	67.0	67.3	92.9	92.1	87.1	66.5	17.3
2030	67.6	67.2	93.0	92.1	87.3	65.7	19.6
2020	70.3	67.6	93.0	92.2	87.3	66.1	21.0
2010	73.2	67.9	93.1	92.3	87.8	67.0	19.5
2000	74.7	68.6	93.4	92.6	88.6	67.3	17.5
Percentage point change							
2000 to 2050	–7.9	–1.6	–0.4	–0.5	–1.5	–1.1	–0.2

Source: Bureau of Labor Statistics, Monthly Labor Review, *May 2002; calculations by New Strategist*

Table 6.11 Labor Force Participation Rate of Women by Age, 1950 to 2010

(percent of women aged 16 or older in the civilian labor force by age, 1950 to 2010; percentage point change for selected years)

	total women	16–19	20–24	25–34	35–44	45–54	55–64	65+
2010	62.2%	52.2%	75.7%	81.4%	80.0%	80.0%	55.2%	11.1%
2000	60.2	51.3	73.3	76.3	77.3	76.8	51.8	9.4
1999	60.0	51.0	73.2	76.4	77.2	76.7	51.5	8.9
1998	59.8	52.3	73.0	76.3	77.1	76.2	51.2	8.6
1997	59.8	51.0	72.7	76.0	77.7	76.0	50.9	8.6
1996	59.3	51.3	71.3	75.2	77.5	75.4	49.6	8.6
1995	58.9	52.2	70.3	74.9	77.2	74.4	49.2	8.8
1994	58.8	51.3	71.0	74.0	77.1	74.6	48.9	9.2
1993	57.9	49.7	70.9	73.4	76.6	73.5	47.2	8.1
1992	57.8	49.1	70.9	73.9	76.7	72.6	46.5	8.3
1991	57.4	50.0	70.1	73.1	76.5	72.0	45.2	8.5
1990	57.5	51.6	71.3	73.5	76.4	71.2	45.2	8.6
1989	57.4	53.9	72.4	73.5	76.0	70.5	45.0	8.4
1988	56.6	53.6	72.7	72.7	75.2	69.0	43.5	7.9
1987	56.0	53.3	73.0	72.4	74.5	67.1	42.7	7.4
1986	55.3	53.0	72.4	71.6	73.1	65.9	42.3	7.4
1985	54.5	52.1	71.8	70.9	71.8	64.4	42.0	7.3
1984	53.6	51.8	70.4	69.8	70.1	62.9	41.7	7.5
1983	52.9	50.8	69.9	69.0	68.7	61.9	41.5	7.8
1982	52.6	51.4	69.8	68.0	68.0	61.6	41.8	7.9
1981	52.1	51.8	69.6	66.7	66.8	61.1	41.4	8.0
1980	51.5	52.9	68.9	65.5	65.5	59.9	41.3	8.1
1979	50.9	54.2	69.0	63.9	63.6	58.3	41.7	8.3
1978	50.0	53.7	68.3	62.2	61.6	57.1	41.3	8.3
1977	48.4	51.2	66.5	59.7	59.6	55.8	40.9	8.1
1976	47.3	49.8	65.0	57.3	57.8	55.0	41.0	8.2
1975	46.3	49.1	64.1	54.9	55.8	54.6	40.9	8.2
1974	45.7	49.1	63.1	52.6	54.7	54.6	40.7	8.1
1973	44.7	47.8	61.1	50.4	53.3	53.7	41.1	8.9
1972	43.9	45.8	59.1	47.8	52.0	53.9	42.1	9.3
1971	43.4	43.4	57.7	45.6	51.6	54.3	42.9	9.5
1970	43.3	44.0	57.7	45.0	51.1	54.4	43.0	9.7
1969	42.7	43.2	56.7	43.7	49.9	53.8	43.1	9.9
1968	41.6	41.9	54.5	42.6	48.9	52.3	42.4	9.6
1967	41.1	41.6	53.3	41.9	48.1	51.8	42.4	9.6
1966	40.3	41.4	51.5	39.8	46.8	51.7	41.8	9.6
1965	39.3	38.0	49.9	38.5	46.1	50.9	41.1	10.0
1964	38.7	37.0	49.4	37.2	45.0	51.4	40.2	10.1
1963	38.3	38.0	47.5	37.2	44.9	50.6	39.7	9.6
1962	37.9	39.0	47.3	36.3	44.1	50.0	38.7	10.0
1961	38.1	39.7	47.0	36.4	43.8	50.1	37.9	10.7
1960	37.7	39.3	46.1	36.0	43.4	49.9	37.2	10.8
1959	37.1	38.2	45.1	35.3	43.4	49.0	36.6	10.2
1958	37.1	39.0	46.3	35.6	43.4	47.8	35.2	10.3
1957	36.9	41.1	45.9	35.6	43.3	46.5	34.5	10.5
1956	36.9	42.2	46.3	35.4	43.1	45.5	34.9	10.8
1955	35.7	39.7	45.9	34.9	41.6	43.8	32.5	10.6
1954	34.6	39.4	45.1	34.4	41.2	41.2	30.0	9.3
1953	34.4	40.7	44.3	34.0	41.3	40.4	29.1	10.0
1952	34.7	42.2	44.7	35.4	40.4	40.1	28.7	9.1
1951	34.6	42.4	46.5	35.4	39.8	39.7	27.6	8.9
1950	33.9	41.0	46.0	34.0	39.1	37.9	27.0	9.7
Percentage point change								
2000 to 2010	2.0	0.9	2.4	5.1	2.7	3.2	3.4	1.7
1990 to 2000	2.7	-0.3	2.0	2.8	0.9	5.6	6.6	0.8
1950 to 2000	26.3	10.3	27.3	42.3	38.2	38.9	24.8	–0.3

Source: Bureau of Labor Statistics, Internet site http://data.bls.gov/cgi-bin/srgate; and Monthly Labor Review, *November 2001; calculations by New Strategist*

Table 6.12 Labor Force Participation Rate of Women by Age, 2000 to 2050

(percent of women aged 16 or older in the civilian labor force by age, 2000 to 2050; percentage point change for selected years)

	total women	16–24	25–34	35–44	45–54	55–64	65+
2050	56.6%	64.0%	81.9%	80.5%	79.9%	54.7%	10.1%
2040	56.7	64.6	82.1	80.7	80.4	55.3	10.1
2030	57.4	64.8	82.4	81.0	80.7	54.9	11.7
2020	60.3	65.4	83.0	81.1	80.8	55.8	12.6
2010	62.2	65.1	81.4	80.0	80.0	55.2	11.1
2000	60.2	63.2	76.3	77.3	76.8	51.8	9.4

Percentage point change

2000 to 2050	–3.6	0.8	5.6	3.2	3.1	2.9	0.7

Source: Bureau of Labor Statistics, Monthly Labor Review, *May 2002; calculations by New Strategist*

Table 6.13 Labor Force Participation Rate of Men by Race and Hispanic Origin, 1972 to 2010

(percent of men aged 16 or older in the civilian labor force by race and Hispanic origin, 1972 to 2010; percentage point change for selected years)

	Asian, other	black	Hispanic	white total	white non-Hispanic
2010	74.8%	68.2%	79.0%	73.8%	72.9%
2000	74.9	69.0	80.6	75.4	74.7
1999	74.1	68.7	79.8	75.6	75.0
1998	75.5	69.0	79.8	75.6	75.0
1997	74.7	68.3	80.1	75.9	75.2
1996	73.4	68.7	79.6	75.8	75.3
1995	75.2	69.0	79.1	75.7	75.4
1994	74.3	69.1	79.2	75.9	75.5
1993	74.9	69.6	80.2	76.2	75.7
1992	75.2	70.7	80.7	76.5	76.0
1991	74.4	70.4	80.3	76.5	76.6
1990	75.0	71.1	81.4	77.1	76.5
1989	75.5	71.0	82.0	77.1	76.7
1988	74.4	71.0	81.9	76.9	76.4
1987	75.7	71.1	81.0	76.8	76.5
1986	75.0	71.2	81.0	76.9	76.5
1985	75.1	70.8	80.4	77.0	76.7
1984	74.0	70.8	80.6	77.1	76.8
1983	75.1	70.6	80.3	77.1	76.9
1982	76.0	70.1	79.5	77.4	77.2
1981	74.0	70.0	80.6	77.9	77.7
1980	74.5	70.6	81.4	78.2	78.0
1979	–	71.3	–	78.6	–
1978	–	71.5	–	78.6	–
1977	–	70.6	–	78.5	–
1976	–	70.0	–	78.4	–
1975	–	70.9	–	78.7	–
1974	–	72.9	–	79.4	–
1973	–	73.4	–	79.4	–
1972	–	73.6	–	79.6	–
Percentage point change					
2000 to 2010	–0.1	–0.8	–1.6	–1.6	–1.8
1990 to 2000	–0.1	–2.1	–0.8	–1.7	–1.8
1972 to 2000	–	–4.6	–	–4.2	–

Note: (–) means data not available.
Source: Bureau of Labor Statistics, Handbook of Labor Statistics, Bulletin 2340, 1989; and Internet site http://www.bls.gov/emp/emplab1.htm; and Monthly Labor Review, November 2001; calculations by New Strategist

Table 6.14 Labor Force Participation Rate of Women by Race and Hispanic Origin, 1972 to 2010

(percent of women aged 16 or older in the civilian labor force by race and Hispanic origin, 1972 to 2010; percentage point change for selected years)

	Asian, other	black	Hispanic	white total	white non-Hispanic
2010	60.9%	66.2%	59.4%	61.6%	62.0%
2000	58.9	63.2	56.9	59.8	60.3
1999	59.0	63.5	55.9	59.6	60.1
1998	59.2	62.8	55.6	59.4	59.9
1997	59.0	61.7	55.1	59.5	60.1
1996	58.8	60.4	53.4	59.1	59.8
1995	57.2	59.5	52.6	59.0	59.7
1994	56.9	58.7	52.9	59.0	59.5
1993	57.1	57.9	52.1	58.0	58.6
1992	58.2	58.5	52.8	57.7	58.1
1991	56.6	57.5	52.3	57.4	58.3
1990	57.4	58.3	53.1	57.4	57.8
1989	58.8	58.7	53.5	57.2	57.5
1988	56.5	58.0	53.2	56.4	56.7
1987	57.4	58.0	52.0	55.7	56.0
1986	57.0	56.9	50.1	55.0	55.4
1985	56.8	56.5	49.3	54.1	54.5
1984	55.6	55.2	49.7	53.3	53.5
1983	55.2	54.2	47.7	52.7	53.0
1982	54.8	53.7	48.2	52.4	52.7
1981	54.4	53.5	48.3	51.9	52.1
1980	55.4	53.2	47.4	51.2	51.3
1979	–	53.1	–	50.5	–
1978	–	53.1	–	49.4	–
1977	–	50.8	–	48.0	–
1976	–	49.8	–	46.9	–
1975	–	48.8	–	45.9	–
1974	–	49.0	–	45.2	–
1973	–	49.3	–	44.1	–
1972	–	48.7	–	43.2	–
Percentage point change					
2000 to 2010	2.0	3.0	2.5	1.8	1.7
1990 to 2000	1.5	4.9	3.8	2.4	2.5
1972 to 2000	–	14.5	–	16.6	–

Note: (–) means data not available.
Source: Bureau of Labor Statistics, Handbook of Labor Statistics, *Bulletin 2340, 1989; and Internet site http://www.bls.gov/emp/emplab1.htm; and* Monthly Labor Review, *November 2001; calculations by New Strategist*

Table 6.15   Median Age of the Labor Force by Sex, Race, and Hispanic Origin, 1962 to 2050

(median age of the civilian labor force by sex, race, and Hispanic origin, 1962 to 2050; percentage point change for selected years)

	total	men	women	Asian and other	black	Hispanic	white total	white non-Hispanic
2050	39.7	39.9	40.7	39.3	39.0	37.6	39.9	–
2040	39.9	40.0	40.6	39.1	38.9	37.1	40.3	–
2030	40.0	40.1	40.8	38.8	38.8	36.8	40.4	–
2020	40.2	40.2	40.7	38.8	38.2	36.7	40.7	–
2010	40.6	40.6	40.6	38.7	37.7	36.4	41.3	42.2
2000	39.3	39.3	39.3	37.8	37.3	34.9	39.7	40.4
1990	36.6	36.7	36.8	36.5	34.9	33.2	36.8	37.0
1980	34.6	35.1	33.9	34.1	33.3	32.0	34.8	35.0
1970	39.0	39.4	38.3	–	–	–	39.3	–
1962	40.5	40.5	40.4	–	–	–	40.9	–

Percentage point change

	total	men	women	Asian and other	black	Hispanic	white total	white non-Hispanic
2000 to 2050	0.4	0.6	1.4	1.5	1.7	2.7	0.2	–
1962 to 2000	−1.2	−1.2	−1.1	–	–	–	-1.2	–

Note: (−) means data not available.
Source: Bureau of Labor Statistics, Monthly Labor Review, *November 2001 and May 2002; calculations by New Strategist*

Women, Minorities, Gain in Occupations

As more women and minorities went to work during the past few decades, they entered occupations once dominated by white men. Women accounted for 50 percent of financial managers in 2000, up from 39 percent in 1983. They represented 28 percent of physicians and 30 percent of lawyers in 2000, up from 15 and 16 percent, respectively, in 1983. In some occupations, women have lost ground. They are a shrinking share of farm workers, for example, and they account for fewer operators, fabricators, and laborers.

Blacks accounted for 11 percent of workers in 2000, up from 9 percent in 1983. The Hispanic share of workers rose from 5 to 11 percent during those years. Blacks and Hispanics have made gains in professional jobs. Blacks accounted for 13 percent of administrators in public administration in 2000, up from 8 percent in 1983. They represent 18 percent of dieticians, 23 percent of social workers, and 20 percent of licensed practical nurses. Hispanics are over-represented in blue collar and farm work, but the proportion of Hispanics in managerial or professional specialty occupations nearly doubled between 1983 and 2000, rising from 3 to 5 percent.

More managers and professionals are women, minorities

(percent of workers in managerial and professional specialty occupations who are women, blacks, or Hispanics, 1983 and 2000)

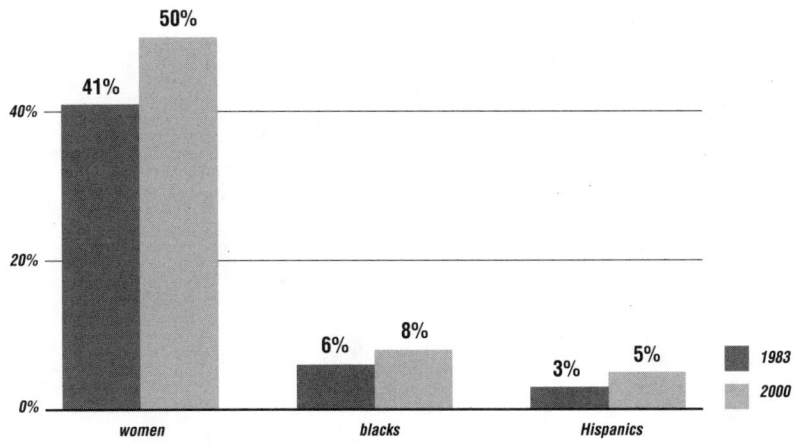

Table 6.16 Women's Share of Workers by Detailed Occupation, 1983 to 2000

(percent of employed civilians aged 16 or older who are women, by detailed occupation, 1983 to 2000; percentage point change, 1990–00 and 1983–00)

	2000	1990	1983	percentage point change 1990–00	percentage point change 1983–00
TOTAL EMPLOYED	**46.5%**	**45.4%**	**43.7%**	**1.1**	**2.8**
MANAGERIAL AND PROFESSIONAL SPECIALTY	**49.8**	**45.8**	**40.9**	**4.0**	**8.9**
Executive, administrative, and managerial	**45.3**	**40.0**	**32.4**	**5.3**	**12.9**
Officials and administrators, public administration	52.7	42.4	38.5	10.3	14.2
Financial managers	50.1	44.3	38.6	5.8	11.5
Personnel and labor relations managers	61.8	55.1	43.9	6.7	17.9
Purchasing managers	41.3	31.9	23.6	9.4	17.7
Managers, marketing, advertising, and public relations	37.6	31.1	21.8	6.5	15.8
Administrators, education and related fields	67.0	54.4	41.4	12.6	25.6
Managers, medicine and health	77.9	66.5	57.0	11.4	20.9
Managers, properties and real estate	50.9	45.2	42.8	5.7	8.1
Management-related occupations	56.5	49.9	40.3	6.6	16.2
Accountants and auditors	56.7	50.8	38.7	5.9	18.0
Professional specialty	**53.9**	**51.2**	**48.1**	**2.7**	**5.8**
Architects	23.5	18.4	12.7	5.1	10.8
Engineers	9.9	8.0	5.8	1.9	4.1
Aerospace engineers	9.7	7.3	6.9	2.4	2.8
Chemical engineers	10.4	10.9	6.1	–0.5	4.3
Civil engineers	9.7	5.0	4.0	4.7	5.7
Electrical and electronic engineers	9.8	8.7	6.1	1.1	3.7
Industrial engineers	15.3	11.9	11.0	3.4	4.3
Mechanical engineers	6.3	5.4	2.8	0.9	3.5
Mathematical and computer scientists	31.4	36.5	29.6	–5.1	1.8
Computer systems analysts and scientists	29.2	34.5	27.8	–5.3	1.4
Operations and systems researchers and analysts	45.5	41.5	31.3	4.0	14.2
Natural scientists	33.5	26.0	20.5	7.5	13.0
Chemists, except biochemists	30.3	27.0	23.3	3.3	7.0
Biological and life scientists	45.4	40.9	40.8	4.5	4.6
Health diagnosing occupations	27.1	17.8	13.3	9.3	13.8
Physicians	27.9	19.3	15.8	8.6	12.1
Dentists	18.7	9.5	6.7	9.2	12.0
Health assessment and treating occupations	85.7	86.2	85.8	–0.5	–0.1
Registered nurses	92.8	94.5	95.8	–1.7	–3.0
Pharmacists	46.5	37.2	26.7	9.3	19.8
Dieticians	89.9	95.0	90.8	–5.1	–0.9
Therapists	74.7	76.6	76.3	–1.9	–1.6
Respiratory therapists	62.4	60.1	69.4	2.3	–7.0
Physical therapists	61.1	75.0	77.0	–13.9	–15.9
Speech therapists	93.5	88.1	90.5	5.4	3.0
Physicians' assistants	57.6	39.6	36.3	18.0	21.3
Teachers, college and university	43.7	37.7	36.3	6.0	7.4
Teachers, except college and university	75.4	73.7	70.9	1.7	4.5
Prekindergarten and kindergarten	98.5	98.4	98.2	0.1	0.3
Elementary school	83.3	85.2	83.3	–1.9	0.0
Secondary school	57.9	53.1	51.8	4.8	6.1
Special education	82.6	84.8	82.2	–2.2	0.4
Counselors, educational and vocational	70.2	61.9	53.1	8.3	17.1
Librarians, archivists, and curators	84.4	81.1	84.4	3.3	0.0
Librarians	85.2	83.3	87.3	1.9	–2.1

(continued)

(continued from previous page)

	2000	1990	1983	percentage point change 1990–00	1983–00
Social scientists and urban planners	58.9%	51.5%	46.8%	7.4	12.1
Economists	53.3	43.8	37.9	9.5	15.4
Psychologists	64.6	58.4	57.1	6.2	7.5
Social, recreation, and religious workers	56.4	50.4	43.1	6.0	13.3
Social workers	72.4	68.2	64.3	4.2	8.1
Recreation workers	71.0	70.9	71.9	0.1	–0.9
Clergy	13.8	9.6	5.6	4.2	8.2
Lawyers and judges	29.7	20.8	15.8	8.9	13.9
Lawyers	29.6	20.6	15.3	9.0	14.3
Writers, artists, entertainers, and athletes	50.0	47.4	42.7	2.6	7.3
Authors	54.1	59.9	46.7	–5.8	7.4
Designers	57.2	53.3	52.7	3.9	4.5
Musicians and composers	34.1	31.9	28.0	2.2	6.1
Actors and directors	41.5	36.5	30.8	5.0	10.7
Painters, sculptors, craft artists, and artist printmakers	46.5	51.2	47.4	–4.7	–0.9
Photographers	32.6	27.8	20.7	4.8	11.9
Editors and reporters	55.8	52.0	48.4	3.8	7.4
Public relations specialists	61.1	58.7	50.1	2.4	11.0
Athletes	19.8	26.4	17.6	–6.6	2.2
TECHNICAL, SALES, ADMINISTRATIVE SUPPORT	**63.8**	**64.7**	**64.6**	**–0.9**	**–0.8**
Technicians and related support	**51.7**	**49.2**	**48.2**	**2.5**	**3.5**
Health technologists and technicians	80.5	83.5	84.3	–3.0	–3.8
Clinical laboratory technologists and technicians	75.0	76.3	76.2	–1.3	–1.2
Dental hygienists	98.5	99.1	98.6	–0.6	–0.1
Radiologic technicians	69.2	76.4	71.7	–7.2	–2.5
Licensed practical nurses	93.6	96.3	97.0	–2.7	–3.4
Engineering and related technologists and technicians	20.4	19.8	18.4	0.6	2.0
Electrical and electronic technicians	16.9	15.4	12.5	1.5	4.4
Drafting occupations	23.4	18.9	17.5	4.5	5.9
Science technicians	41.4	31.9	29.1	9.5	12.3
Biological technicians	59.5	40.7	37.7	18.8	21.8
Chemical technicians	21.2	28.1	26.9	–6.9	–5.7
Technicians, except health, engineering, and science	40.5	40.2	35.3	0.3	5.2
Airplane pilots and navigators	3.7	5.1	2.1	–1.4	1.6
Computer programmers	26.5	36.0	32.5	–9.5	–6.0
Legal assistants	84.4	78.8	74.0	5.6	10.4
Sales occupations	**49.6**	**49.2**	**47.5**	**0.4**	**2.1**
Supervisors and proprietors	40.3	34.8	28.4	5.5	11.9
Sales representatives, finance and business services	44.5	42.9	37.2	1.6	7.3
Insurance sales	42.5	32.7	25.1	9.8	17.4
Real estate sales	54.3	51.1	48.9	3.2	5.4
Securities and financial services sales	31.3	23.4	23.6	7.9	7.7
Advertising and related sales	61.9	50.9	47.9	11.0	14.0
Sales representatives, commodities, except retail	27.5	22.0	15.1	5.5	12.4
Sales workers, retail and personal services	63.5	67.4	69.7	–3.9	–6.2
Cashiers	77.5	81.4	84.4	–3.9	–6.9
Sales-related occupations	69.1	63.7	58.7	5.4	10.4
Administrative support occupations, including clerical	**79.0**	**79.8**	**79.9**	**–0.8**	**–0.9**
Supervisors, administrative support	60.3	31.5	53.4	28.8	6.9
Computer equipment operators	48.6	65.7	63.9	–17.1	–15.3
Computer operators	48.7	65.7	63.7	–17.0	–15.0

(continued)

(continued from previous page)

	2000	1990	1983	percentage point change 1990–00	1983–00
Secretaries, stenographers, and typists	98.0%	98.3%	98.2%	–0.3	–0.2
Secretaries	98.9	99.0	99.0	–0.1	–0.1
Typists	94.6	95.5	95.6	–0.9	–1.0
Information clerks	88.0	88.3	88.9	–0.3	–0.9
Receptionists	96.7	97.0	96.8	–0.3	–0.1
Records processing, except financial	81.5	81.3	82.4	0.2	–0.9
Order clerks	77.1	77.9	78.1	–0.8	–1.0
Personnel clerks, except payroll and timekeeping	82.5	88.6	91.1	–6.1	–8.6
Library clerks	87.0	76.2	81.9	10.8	5.1
File clerks	80.2	83.8	83.5	–3.6	–3.3
Records clerks	85.9	81.4	82.8	4.5	3.1
Financial records processing	91.8	91.6	89.4	0.2	2.4
Bookkeepers, accounting, and auditing clerks	92.2	92.2	91.0	0.0	1.2
Payroll and timekeeping clerks	91.3	91.0	82.2	0.3	9.1
Billing clerks	92.2	92.1	88.4	0.1	3.8
Cost and rate clerks	77.9	80.6	75.6	–2.7	2.3
Duplicating, mail and other office machine operators	54.2	62.4	62.6	–8.2	–8.4
Communications equipment operators	84.3	87.2	89.1	–2.9	–4.8
Telephone operators	83.9	89.0	90.4	–5.1	–6.5
Mail and message distributing	41.2	35.9	31.6	5.3	9.6
Postal clerks, except mail carriers	54.4	45.2	36.7	9.2	17.7
Mail carriers, postal service	30.6	24.9	17.1	5.7	13.5
Mail clerks, except postal service	54.0	47.0	50.0	7.0	4.0
Messengers	23.9	28.2	26.2	–4.3	–2.3
Material recording, scheduling, and distributing clerks	46.7	41.9	37.5	4.8	9.2
Dispatchers	51.7	54.8	45.7	–3.1	6.0
Production coordinators	58.5	49.3	44.0	9.2	14.5
Traffic, shipping, and receiving clerks	33.8	26.8	22.6	7.0	11.2
Stock and inventory clerks	44.9	43.2	38.7	1.7	6.2
Expediters	66.5	66.7	57.5	–0.2	9.0
Adjusters and investigators	75.5	75.1	69.9	0.4	5.6
Insurance adjusters, examiners, and investigators	73.9	72.2	65.0	1.7	8.9
Investigators and adjusters, except insurance	76.0	76.6	70.1	–0.6	5.9
Eligibility clerks, social welfare	89.2	90.1	88.7	–0.9	0.5
Bill and account collectors	69.4	67.5	66.4	1.9	3.0
Miscellaneous administrative support	83.9	84.6	85.2	–0.7	–1.3
General office clerks	83.6	81.8	80.6	1.8	3.0
Bank tellers	90.0	90.4	91.0	–0.4	–1.0
Data-entry keyers	83.5	87.2	93.6	–3.7	–10.1
Statistical clerks	88.5	72.3	75.7	16.2	12.8
Teachers' aides	91.0	94.5	93.7	–3.5	–2.7
SERVICE OCCUPATIONS	**60.4**	**60.1**	**60.1**	**0.3**	**0.3**
Private household	**95.5**	**96.3**	**96.1**	**–0.8**	**–0.6**
Child care workers	97.5	97.9	96.9	–0.4	0.6
Cleaners and servants	94.8	95.5	95.8	–0.7	–1.0
Protective service	**19.0**	**14.6**	**12.8**	**4.4**	**6.2**
Supervisors	15.1	8.0	4.7	7.1	10.4
Police and detectives	14.3	8.6	4.2	5.7	10.1
Firefighting and fire prevention	3.8	2.4	1.0	1.4	2.8
Firefighting	3.0	1.2	1.0	1.8	2.0
Police and detectives	16.5	13.8	9.4	2.7	7.1
Police and detectives, public service	12.1	12.1	5.7	0.0	6.4

(continued)

(continued from previous page)

	2000	1990	1983	percentage point change 1990–00	percentage point change 1983–00
Sheriffs, bailiffs, and other law enforcement officers	19.2%	12.8%	13.2%	6.4	6.0
Correctional institution officers	22.5	17.7	17.8	4.8	4.7
Guards	27.0	20.5	20.6	6.5	6.4
Guards and police, except public services	20.1	14.8	13.0	5.3	7.1
Service occupations, exc. private household, protective service	**65.1**	**64.9**	**64.0**	**0.2**	**1.1**
Food preparation and service occupations	57.7	59.5	63.3	–1.8	–5.6
Bartenders	51.8	55.6	48.4	–3.8	3.4
Waiters and waitresses	76.7	80.8	87.8	–4.1	–11.1
Cooks	43.3	47.7	50.0	–4.4	–6.7
Food counter, fountain and related occupations	67.9	72.7	76.0	–4.8	–8.1
Kitchen workers, food preparation	71.1	70.7	77.0	0.4	–5.9
Waiters' and waitresses' assistants	51.4	39.1	38.8	12.3	12.6
Health service occupations	89.5	90.2	89.2	–0.7	0.3
Dental assistants	96.4	98.7	98.1	–2.3	–1.7
Health aides, except nursing	82.6	84.8	86.8	–2.2	–4.2
Nursing aides, orderlies, and attendants	89.9	90.8	88.7	–0.9	1.2
Cleaning and building service occupations	45.0	44.0	38.8	1.0	6.2
Maids and housemen	81.3	82.0	81.2	–0.7	0.1
Janitors and cleaners	36.3	32.8	28.6	3.5	7.7
Personal service occupations	80.5	81.6	79.2	–1.1	1.3
Barbers	25.3	18.7	12.9	6.6	12.4
Hairdressers and cosmetologists	91.2	89.8	88.7	1.4	2.5
Attendants, amusement and recreation facilities	39.4	40.2	40.2	–0.8	–0.8
Public transportation attendants	80.9	83.2	74.3	–2.3	6.6
Welfare service aides	87.2	92.1	92.5	–4.9	–5.3
PRECISION PRODUCTION, CRAFT, AND REPAIR	**9.1**	**8.5**	**8.1**	**0.6**	**1.0**
Mechanics and repairers	**5.1**	**3.6**	**3.0**	**1.5**	**2.1**
Mechanics and repairers, except supervisors	5.0	3.3	2.8	1.7	2.2
Vehicle and mobile equipment mechanics and repairers	1.6	0.9	0.8	0.7	0.8
Automobile mechanics	1.2	0.8	0.5	0.4	0.7
Aircraft engine mechanics	6.1	2.8	2.5	3.3	3.6
Electrical and electronic equipment repairers	11.5	8.6	7.4	2.9	4.1
Data processing equipment repairers	15.4	11.4	9.3	4.0	6.1
Telephone installers and repairers	13.1	11.3	9.9	1.8	3.2
Construction trades	**2.6**	**1.9**	**1.8**	**0.7**	**0.8**
Construction trades, except supervisors	2.7	1.9	1.9	0.8	0.8
Carpenters	1.7	1.3	1.4	0.4	0.3
Extractive occupations	**1.9**	**1.9**	**2.3**	**0.0**	**–0.4**
Precision production occupations	**25.0**	**23.1**	**21.5**	**1.9**	**3.5**
OPERATORS, FABRICATORS, AND LABORERS	**23.6**	**25.5**	**26.6**	**–1.9**	**–3.0**
Machine operators, assemblers, and inspectors	**36.9**	**40.0**	**42.1**	**–3.1**	**–5.2**
Textile, apparel, and furnishings machine operators	69.2	78.3	82.1	–9.1	–12.9
Textile sewing machine operators	78.4	89.1	94.0	–10.7	–15.6
Pressing machine operators	66.6	69.0	66.4	–2.4	0.2
Fabricators, assemblers, and hand working occupations	33.5	32.5	33.7	1.0	–0.2
Production inspectors, testers, samplers, and weighers	48.5	51.4	53.8	–2.9	–5.3
Transportation and material moving occupations	**10.0**	**9.0**	**7.8**	**1.0**	**2.2**
Motor vehicle operators	11.5	10.8	9.2	0.7	2.3
Truck drivers	4.7	–	3.1	–	1.6
Transportation occupations, except motor vehicles	3.5	3.0	2.4	0.5	1.1
Material moving equipment operators	5.4	3.9	4.8	1.5	0.6
Industrial truck and tractor equipment operators	7.0	5.7	5.6	1.3	1.4

(continued)

(continued from previous page)

	2000	1990	1983	percentage point change	
				1990–00	1983–00
Handlers, equipment cleaners, helpers, and laborers	**19.8%**	**17.7%**	**16.8%**	**2.1**	**3.0**
Freight, stock, and material handlers	22.4	19.1	15.4	3.3	7.0
Laborers, except construction	20.8	18.8	19.4	2.0	1.4
FARMING, FORESTRY, FISHING	**20.6**	**18.8**	**16.0**	**1.8**	**4.6**
Farm operators and managers	**25.4**	**15.7**	**12.1**	**9.7**	**13.3**
Other agricultural and related occupations	**18.9**	**17.1**	**19.9**	**1.8**	**−1.0**
Farm workers	18.7	21.0	24.8	−2.3	−6.1
Forestry and logging occupations	**8.4**	**5.7**	**1.4**	**2.7**	**7.0**
Fishers, hunters, trappers	**11.9**	**4.7**	**4.5**	**7.2**	**7.4**

Note: (−) means data not available.
Source: Bureau of the Census, Statistical Abstract of the United States, 2001; *and Bureau of Labor Statistics,* Employment and Earnings, *January 1991; calculations by New Strategist*

Table 6.17 Black Share of Workers by Detailed Occupation, 1983 to 2000

(percent of employed civilians aged 16 or older who are black, by detailed occupation, 1983 to 2000; percentage point change, 1990–00 and 1983–00)

	2000	1990	1983	percentage point change 1990–00	percentage point change 1983–00
TOTAL EMPLOYED	**11.3%**	**10.1%**	**9.3%**	**1.2**	**2.0**
MANAGERIAL AND PROFESSIONAL SPECIALTY	**8.2**	**6.2**	**5.6**	**2.0**	**2.6**
Executive, administrative, and managerial	**7.6**	**5.7**	**4.7**	**1.9**	**2.9**
Officials and administrators, public administration	13.1	9.2	8.3	3.9	4.8
Financial managers	6.1	4.1	3.5	2.0	2.6
Personnel and labor relations managers	7.9	6.7	4.9	1.2	3.0
Purchasing managers	7.0	4.8	5.1	2.2	1.9
Managers, marketing, advertising, and public relations	4.2	2.9	2.7	1.3	1.5
Administrators, education and related fields	13.5	9.5	11.3	4.0	2.2
Managers, medicine and health	9.7	7.5	5.0	2.2	4.7
Managers, properties and real estate	8.2	6.5	5.5	1.7	2.7
Management-related occupations	9.5	7.6	5.8	1.9	3.7
Accountants and auditors	8.9	7.4	5.5	1.5	3.4
Professional specialty	**8.7**	**6.7**	**6.4**	**2.0**	**2.3**
Architects	1.6	0.9	1.6	0.7	0.0
Engineers	5.7	3.6	2.7	2.1	3.0
Aerospace engineers	5.4	4.8	1.5	0.6	3.9
Chemical engineers	5.1	1.7	3.0	3.4	2.1
Civil engineers	6.1	4.0	1.9	2.1	4.2
Electrical and electronic engineers	6.3	3.8	3.4	2.5	2.9
Industrial engineers	6.4	4.4	3.3	2.0	3.1
Mechanical engineers	4.7	3.5	3.2	1.2	1.5
Mathematical and computer scientists	8.1	6.5	5.4	1.6	2.7
Computer systems analysts and scientists	8.0	7.0	6.2	1.0	1.8
Operations and systems researchers and analysts	10.9	5.2	4.9	5.7	6.0
Natural scientists	5.4	2.7	2.6	2.7	2.8
Chemists, except biochemists	11.0	4.6	4.3	6.4	6.7
Biological and life scientists	4.0	2.7	2.4	1.3	1.6
Health diagnosing occupations	5.2	3.0	2.7	2.2	2.5
Physicians	6.3	3.0	3.2	3.3	3.1
Dentists	3.4	4.9	2.4	–1.5	1.0
Health assessment and treating occupations	9.0	7.4	7.1	1.6	1.9
Registered nurses	9.5	7.4	6.7	2.1	2.8
Pharmacists	3.3	4.1	3.8	–0.8	–0.5
Dieticians	18.4	20.1	21.0	–1.7	–2.6
Therapists	8.1	6.0	7.6	2.1	0.5
Respiratory therapists	10.8	11.7	6.5	–0.9	4.3
Physical therapists	6.5	4.1	9.7	2.4	–3.2
Speech therapists	4.5	2.8	1.5	1.7	3.0
Physicians' assistants	5.6	6.4	7.7	–0.8	–2.1
Teachers, college and university	6.4	4.5	4.4	1.9	2.0
Teachers, except college and university	10.4	8.7	9.1	1.7	1.3
Prekindergarten and kindergarten	13.3	10.7	11.8	2.6	1.5
Elementary school	11.3	9.7	11.1	1.6	0.2
Secondary school	8.9	7.1	7.2	1.8	1.7
Special education	9.2	11.8	10.2	–2.6	–1.0
Counselors, educational and vocational	17.1	16.3	13.9	0.8	3.2
Librarians, archivists, and curators	6.0	5.3	7.8	0.7	–1.8
Librarians	6.7	5.5	7.9	1.2	–1.2

(continued)

(continued from previous page)

	2000	1990	1983	percentage point change 1990–00	1983–00
Social scientists and urban planners	7.8%	5.4%	7.1%	2.4	0.7
Economists	6.3	4.0	6.3	2.3	0.0
Psychologists	8.1	6.6	8.6	1.5	–0.5
Social, recreation, and religious workers	17.4	15.2	12.1	2.2	5.3
Social workers	22.7	21.8	18.2	0.9	4.5
Recreation workers	9.5	14.7	15.7	–5.2	–6.2
Clergy	14.1	6.9	4.9	7.2	9.2
Lawyers and judges	5.7	3.4	2.7	2.3	3.0
Lawyers	5.4	3.2	2.6	2.2	2.8
Writers, artists, entertainers, and athletes	6.9	4.5	4.8	2.4	2.1
Authors	7.7	2.3	2.1	5.4	5.6
Designers	4.0	2.6	3.1	1.4	0.9
Musicians and composers	13.5	9.6	7.9	3.9	5.6
Actors and directors	12.8	5.9	6.6	6.9	6.2
Painters, sculptors, craft artists, and artist printmakers	6.8	2.8	2.1	4.0	4.7
Photographers	5.7	2.9	4.0	2.8	1.7
Editors and reporters	5.0	3.8	2.9	1.2	2.1
Public relations specialists	10.8	7.7	6.2	3.1	4.6
Athletes	10.9	9.7	9.4	1.2	1.5
TECHNICAL, SALES, ADMINISTRATIVE SUPPORT	**11.4**	**9.2**	**7.6**	**2.2**	**3.8**
Technicians and related support	**11.2**	**9.1**	**8.2**	**2.1**	**3.0**
Health technologists and technicians	15.0	14.1	12.7	0.9	2.3
Clinical laboratory technologists and technicians	18.0	15.1	10.5	2.9	7.5
Dental hygienists	2.4	2.5	1.6	–0.1	0.8
Radiologic technicians	10.8	12.8	8.6	–2.0	2.2
Licensed practical nurses	20.0	17.6	17.7	2.4	2.3
Engineering and related technologists and technicians	10.0	7.2	6.1	2.8	3.9
Electrical and electronic technicians	11.0	8.2	8.2	2.8	2.8
Drafting occupations	6.2	6.4	5.5	–0.2	0.7
Science technicians	8.7	7.5	6.6	1.2	2.1
Biological technicians	7.1	4.6	2.9	2.5	4.2
Chemical technicians	7.2	10.8	9.5	–3.6	–2.3
Technicians, except health, engineering, and science	7.9	5.7	5.0	2.2	2.9
Airplane pilots and navigators	1.9	0.6	–	1.3	–
Computer programmers	8.1	5.8	4.4	2.3	3.7
Legal assistants	8.4	6.1	4.3	2.3	4.1
Sales occupations	**8.8**	**6.4**	**4.7**	**2.4**	**4.1**
Supervisors and proprietors	6.6	4.5	3.6	2.1	3.0
Sales representatives, finance and business services	7.6	4.4	2.7	3.2	4.9
Insurance sales	6.5	5.2	3.8	1.3	2.7
Real estate sales	5.3	3.0	1.3	2.3	4.0
Securities and financial services sales	8.2	3.6	3.1	4.6	5.1
Advertising and related sales	9.2	4.4	4.5	4.8	4.7
Sales representatives, commodities, except retail	2.8	2.6	2.1	0.2	0.7
Sales workers, retail and personal services	12.3	9.5	6.7	2.8	5.6
Cashiers	16.5	13.5	10.1	3.0	6.4
Sales-related occupations	9.3	2.5	2.8	6.8	6.5
Administrative support occupations, including clerical	**13.7**	**11.4**	**9.6**	**2.3**	**4.1**
Supervisors, administrative support	17.0	14.2	9.3	2.8	7.7
Computer equipment operators	16.6	13.1	12.5	3.5	4.1
Computer operators	16.6	12.9	12.1	3.7	4.5

(continued)

(continued from previous page)

	2000	1990	1983	percentage point change 1990–00	1983–00
Secretaries, stenographers, and typists	9.9%	8.6%	7.3%	1.3	2.6
Secretaries	8.5	7.6	5.8	0.9	2.7
Typists	17.8	15.1	13.8	2.7	4.0
Information clerks	11.3	9.5	8.5	1.8	2.8
Receptionists	9.7	8.1	7.5	1.6	2.2
Records processing, except financial	16.9	14.1	13.9	2.8	3.0
Order clerks	24.4	15.1	10.6	9.3	13.8
Personnel clerks, except payroll and timekeeping	18.7	21.7	14.9	–3.0	3.8
Library clerks	10.8	9.1	15.4	1.7	–4.6
File clerks	15.3	14.0	16.7	1.3	–1.4
Records clerks	13.4	14.7	11.6	–1.3	1.8
Financial records processing	9.2	6.2	4.6	3.0	4.6
Bookkeepers, accounting, and auditing clerks	7.8	5.2	4.3	2.6	3.5
Payroll and timekeeping clerks	8.7	11.5	5.9	–2.8	2.8
Billing clerks	16.3	8.7	6.2	7.6	10.1
Cost and rate clerks	9.4	8.4	5.9	1.0	3.5
Duplicating, mail and other office machine operators	16.8	19.3	16.0	–2.5	0.8
Communications equipment operators	21.8	19.9	17.0	1.9	4.8
Telephone operators	22.9	19.7	17.0	3.2	5.9
Mail and message distributing	21.9	20.0	18.1	1.9	3.8
Postal clerks, except mail carriers	32.4	25.1	26.2	7.3	6.2
Mail carriers, postal service	14.7	14.4	12.5	0.3	2.2
Mail clerks, except postal service	22.6	23.8	15.8	–1.2	6.8
Messengers	16.7	17.9	16.7	–1.2	0.0
Material recording, scheduling, and distributing clerks	15.3	12.6	10.9	2.7	4.4
Dispatchers	15.1	9.2	11.4	5.9	3.7
Production coordinators	12.0	7.4	6.1	4.6	5.9
Traffic, shipping, and receiving clerks	16.1	15.3	9.1	0.8	7.0
Stock and inventory clerks	15.1	13.3	13.3	1.8	1.8
Expediters	13.4	11.1	8.4	2.3	5.0
Adjusters and investigators	17.5	12.9	11.1	4.6	6.4
Insurance adjusters, examiners, and investigators	14.6	12.1	11.5	2.5	3.1
Investigators and adjusters, except insurance	17.0	13.1	11.3	3.9	5.7
Eligibility clerks, social welfare	16.1	14.7	12.9	1.4	3.2
Bill and account collectors	28.2	13.1	8.5	15.1	19.7
Miscellaneous administrative support	14.3	14.0	12.5	0.3	1.8
General office clerks	12.9	13.1	12.7	–0.2	0.2
Bank tellers	13.7	9.9	7.5	3.8	6.2
Data-entry keyers	18.8	19.5	18.6	–0.7	0.2
Statistical clerks	15.8	12.9	7.5	2.9	8.3
Teachers' aides	12.8	14.1	17.8	–1.3	–5.0
SERVICE OCCUPATIONS	**18.1**	**17.3**	**16.6**	**0.8**	**1.5**
Private household	**14.9**	**24.7**	**27.8**	**–9.8**	**–12.9**
Child care workers	11.6	9.8	7.9	1.8	3.7
Cleaners and servants	16.9	35.6	42.4	–18.7	–25.5
Protective service	**19.6**	**16.6**	**13.6**	**3.0**	**6.0**
Supervisors	13.9	13.6	7.7	0.3	6.2
Police and detectives	10.5	12.9	9.3	–2.4	1.2
Firefighting and fire prevention	8.7	11.0	6.7	–2.3	2.0
Firefighting	9.0	11.5	7.3	–2.5	1.7
Police and detectives	18.3	16.0	13.1	2.3	5.2
Police and detectives, public service	13.0	13.5	9.5	–0.5	3.5

(continued)

(continued from previous page)

	2000	1990	1983	percentage point change 1990–00	percentage point change 1983–00
Sheriffs, bailiffs, and other law enforcement officers	20.2%	11.8%	11.5%	8.4	8.7
Correctional institution officers	25.9	22.8	24.0	3.1	1.9
Guards	25.7	19.4	17.0	6.3	8.7
Guards and police, except public services	27.5	21.2	18.9	6.3	8.6
Service occupations, exc. private household, protective service	**18.0**	**17.0**	**16.0**	**1.0**	**2.0**
Food preparation and service occupations	11.9	12.4	10.5	–0.5	1.4
Bartenders	2.0	3.6	2.7	–1.6	–0.7
Waiters and waitresses	4.4	4.7	4.1	–0.3	0.3
Cooks	17.6	18.3	15.8	–0.7	1.8
Food counter, fountain and related occupations	12.6	11.5	9.1	1.1	3.5
Kitchen workers, food preparation	13.0	12.8	13.7	0.2	–0.7
Waiters' and waitresses' assistants	10.5	16.0	12.6	–5.5	–2.1
Health service occupations	31.4	26.3	23.5	5.1	7.9
Dental assistants	5.1	5.6	6.1	–0.5	–1.0
Health aides, except nursing	26.4	21.0	16.5	5.4	9.9
Nursing aides, orderlies, and attendants	35.2	30.7	27.3	4.5	7.9
Cleaning and building service occupations	22.2	22.4	24.4	–0.2	–2.2
Maids and housemen	27.7	24.8	32.3	2.9	–4.6
Janitors and cleaners	20.9	21.8	22.6	–0.9	–1.7
Personal service occupations	14.8	12.0	11.1	2.8	3.7
Barbers	27.8	17.4	8.4	10.4	19.4
Hairdressers and cosmetologists	10.9	9.2	7.0	1.7	3.9
Attendants, amusement and recreation facilities	9.9	9.1	7.1	0.8	2.8
Public transportation attendants	12.3	11.2	11.3	1.1	1.0
Welfare service aides	30.3	24.1	24.2	6.2	6.1
PRECISION PRODUCTION, CRAFT, AND REPAIR	**8.0**	**7.8**	**6.8**	**0.2**	**1.2**
Mechanics and repairers	**8.2**	**8.1**	**6.8**	**0.1**	**1.4**
Mechanics and repairers, except supervisors	8.3	8.3	7.0	0.0	1.3
Vehicle and mobile equipment mechanics and repairers	7.1	7.5	6.9	–0.4	0.2
Automobile mechanics	7.3	8.7	7.8	–1.4	–0.5
Aircraft engine mechanics	8.3	9.8	4.0	–1.5	4.3
Electrical and electronic equipment repairers	10.7	10.6	7.3	0.1	3.4
Data processing equipment repairers	9.8	10.6	6.1	–0.8	3.7
Telephone installers and repairers	11.6	9.7	7.8	1.9	3.8
Construction trades	**7.0**	**6.9**	**6.6**	**0.1**	**0.4**
Construction trades, except supervisors	7.2	7.3	7.1	–0.1	0.1
Carpenters	6.0	4.8	5.0	1.2	1.0
Extractive occupations	**3.6**	**6.9**	**3.3**	**–3.3**	**0.3**
Precision production occupations	**9.5**	**8.6**	**7.3**	**0.9**	**2.2**
OPERATORS, FABRICATORS, AND LABORERS	**15.4**	**15.0**	**14.0**	**0.4**	**1.4**
Machine operators, assemblers, and inspectors	**14.7**	**14.4**	**14.0**	**0.3**	**0.7**
Textile, apparel, and furnishings machine operators	18.3	20.1	18.7	–1.8	–0.4
Textile sewing machine operators	16.3	16.4	15.5	–0.1	0.8
Pressing machine operators	13.9	26.8	27.1	–12.9	–13.2
Fabricators, assemblers, and hand working occupations	13.9	11.8	11.3	2.1	2.6
Production inspectors, testers, samplers, and weighers	16.3	13.5	13.0	2.8	3.3
Transportation and material moving occupations	**16.5**	**15.4**	**13.0**	**1.1**	**3.5**
Motor vehicle operators	16.7	15.4	13.5	1.3	3.2
Truck drivers	14.4	–	12.3	–	2.1
Transportation occupations, except motor vehicles	13.7	10.8	6.7	2.9	7.0
Material moving equipment operators	16.0	16.4	12.9	–0.4	3.1
Industrial truck and tractor equipment operators	22.1	23.5	19.6	–1.4	2.5

(continued)

(continued from previous page)

	2000	1990	1983	percentage point change 1990–00	1983–00
Handlers, equipment cleaners, helpers, and laborers	**15.3%**	**15.7%**	**15.1%**	**–0.4**	**0.2**
Freight, stock, and material handlers	17.7	16.4	15.3	1.3	2.4
Laborers, except construction	15.5	16.0	16.0	–0.5	–0.5
FARMING, FORESTRY, FISHING	**4.9**	**6.1**	**7.5**	**–1.2**	**–2.6**
Farm operators and managers	**0.9**	**0.9**	**1.3**	**0.0**	**–0.4**
Other agricultural and related occupations	**7.1**	**9.1**	**11.7**	**–2.0**	**–4.6**
Farm workers	4.7	8.2	11.6	–3.5	–6.9
Forestry and logging occupations	**4.4**	**10.1**	**12.8**	**–5.7**	**–8.4**
Fishers, hunters, trappers	**3.6**	**7.0**	**1.8**	**–3.4**	**1.8**

Note: (–) means data not available or sample is too small to make a reliable estimate.
Source: Bureau of the Census, Statistical Abstract of the United States, 2001; *and Bureau of Labor Statistics,* Employment and Earnings, *January 1991; calculations by New Strategist*

Table 6.18 Hispanic Share of Workers by Detailed Occupation, 1983 to 2000

(percent of employed civilians aged 16 or older who are Hispanic, by detailed occupation, 1983 to 2000; percentage point change, 1990–00 and 1983–00)

	2000	1990	1983	percentage point change 1990–00	percentage point change 1983–00
TOTAL EMPLOYED	10.7%	7.5%	5.3%	3.2	5.4
MANAGERIAL AND PROFESSIONAL SPECIALTY	5.0	3.6	2.6	1.4	2.4
Executive, administrative, and managerial	5.4	3.9	2.8	1.5	2.6
Officials and administrators, public administration	7.0	3.2	3.8	3.8	3.2
Financial managers	4.3	2.9	3.1	1.4	1.2
Personnel and labor relations managers	4.0	3.2	2.6	0.8	1.4
Purchasing managers	3.2	3.5	1.4	–0.3	1.8
Managers, marketing, advertising, and public relations	4.2	3.1	1.7	1.1	2.5
Administrators, education and related fields	5.7	3.8	2.4	1.9	3.3
Managers, medicine and health	5.4	2.9	2.0	2.5	3.4
Managers, properties and real estate	7.2	5.1	5.2	2.1	2.0
Management-related occupations	5.4	4.1	3.5	1.3	1.9
Accountants and auditors	5.1	3.8	3.3	1.3	1.8
Professional specialty	4.6	3.4	2.5	1.2	2.1
Architects	5.5	3.5	1.5	2.0	4.0
Engineers	3.7	2.8	2.2	0.9	1.5
Aerospace engineers	3.6	2.4	2.1	1.2	1.5
Chemical engineers	1.0	2.2	1.4	–1.2	–0.4
Civil engineers	2.7	3.2	3.2	–0.5	–0.5
Electrical and electronic engineers	3.6	3.3	3.1	0.3	0.5
Industrial engineers	4.0	3.2	2.4	0.8	1.6
Mechanical engineers	3.7	1.9	1.1	1.8	2.6
Mathematical and computer scientists	3.7	3.4	2.6	0.3	1.1
Computer systems analysts and scientists	3.6	3.3	2.7	0.3	0.9
Operations and systems researchers and analysts	4.4	4.2	2.2	0.2	2.2
Natural scientists	3.2	3.8	2.1	–0.6	1.1
Chemists, except biochemists	2.2	5.9	1.2	–3.7	1.0
Biological and life scientists	6.0	3.1	1.8	2.9	4.2
Health-diagnosing occupations	3.4	3.7	3.3	–0.3	0.1
Physicians	3.7	4.5	4.5	–0.8	–0.8
Dentists	2.2	3.5	1.0	–1.3	1.2
Health assessment and treating occupations	3.4	2.8	2.2	0.6	1.2
Registered nurses	2.8	2.5	1.8	0.3	1.0
Pharmacists	3.8	4.1	2.6	–0.3	1.2
Dieticians	4.8	3.5	3.7	1.3	1.1
Therapists	5.0	2.9	2.7	2.1	2.3
Respiratory therapists	5.3	2.8	3.7	2.5	1.6
Physical therapists	6.8	2.7	1.5	4.1	5.3
Speech therapists	2.0	3.3	–	–1.3	–
Physicians' assistants	7.8	5.2	4.4	2.6	3.4
Teachers, college and university	4.6	2.5	1.8	2.1	2.8
Teachers, except college and university	5.2	3.5	2.7	1.7	2.5
Prekindergarten and kindergarten	8.0	5.7	3.4	2.3	4.6
Elementary school	5.6	3.2	3.1	2.4	2.5
Secondary school	4.2	3.3	2.3	0.9	1.9
Special education	3.2	2.2	2.3	1.0	0.9
Counselors, educational and vocational	5.3	4.1	3.2	1.2	2.1
Librarians, archivists, and curators	5.8	3.3	1.6	2.5	4.2
Librarians	6.6	3.3	1.8	3.3	4.8

(continued)

(continued from previous page)

	2000	1990	1983	percentage point change 1990–00	percentage point change 1983–00
Social scientists and urban planners	4.1%	3.3%	2.1%	0.8	2.0
Economists	4.4	3.3	2.7	1.1	1.7
Psychologists	4.0	3.6	1.1	0.4	2.9
Social, recreation, and religious workers	6.4	4.6	3.8	1.8	2.6
Social workers	8.5	6.1	6.3	2.4	2.2
Recreation workers	4.9	6.1	2.0	–1.2	2.9
Clergy	4.5	2.1	1.4	2.4	3.1
Lawyers and judges	4.1	2.7	1.0	1.4	3.1
Lawyers	3.9	2.8	0.9	1.1	3.0
Writers, artists, entertainers, and athletes	5.6	4.0	2.9	1.6	2.7
Authors	2.2	0.7	0.9	1.5	1.3
Designers	6.3	4.4	2.7	1.9	3.6
Musicians and composers	6.0	4.5	4.4	1.5	1.6
Actors and directors	6.1	1.9	3.4	4.2	2.7
Painters, sculptors, craft artists, and artist printmakers	4.2	4.5	2.3	–0.3	1.9
Photographers	5.9	5.5	3.4	0.4	2.5
Editors and reporters	3.0	2.9	2.1	0.1	0.9
Public relations specialists	5.5	2.8	1.9	2.7	3.6
Athletes	5.5	4.3	1.7	1.2	3.8
TECHNICAL, SALES, ADMINISTRATIVE SUPPORT	**8.9**	**5.8**	**4.3**	**3.1**	**4.6**
Technicians and related support	**6.9**	**4.3**	**3.1**	**2.6**	**3.8**
Health technologists and technicians	8.2	4.5	3.1	3.7	5.1
Clinical laboratory technologists and technicians	7.5	4.1	2.9	3.4	4.6
Dental hygienists	1.7	3.0	–	–1.3	–
Radiologic technicians	7.7	4.8	4.5	2.9	3.2
Licensed practical nurses	5.0	3.8	3.1	1.2	1.9
Engineering and related technologists and technicians	6.1	4.8	3.5	1.3	2.6
Electrical and electronic technicians	7.1	5.8	4.6	1.3	2.5
Drafting occupations	4.7	5.1	2.3	–0.4	2.4
Science technicians	8.4	7.2	2.8	1.2	5.6
Biological technicians	8.2	9.0	2.0	–0.8	6.2
Chemical technicians	7.6	7.1	3.5	0.5	4.1
Technicians, except health, engineering, and science	5.7	3.1	2.7	2.6	3.0
Airplane pilots and navigators	4.3	3.3	1.6	1.0	2.7
Computer programmers	3.5	2.5	2.1	1.0	1.4
Legal assistants	9.8	3.7	3.6	6.1	6.2
Sales occupations	**8.5**	**5.3**	**3.7**	**3.2**	**4.8**
Supervisors and proprietors	7.3	4.4	3.4	2.9	3.9
Sales representatives, finance and business services	4.9	3.6	2.2	1.3	2.7
Insurance sales	4.4	3.5	2.5	0.9	1.9
Real estate sales	5.0	3.6	1.5	1.4	3.5
Securities and financial services sales	3.4	3.2	1.1	0.2	2.3
Advertising and related sales	5.7	2.8	3.3	2.9	2.4
Sales representatives, commodities, except retail	6.4	3.3	2.2	3.1	4.2
Sales workers, retail and personal services	11.4	7.0	4.8	4.4	6.6
Cashiers	13.5	8.4	5.4	5.1	8.1
Sales-related occupations	2.2	3.4	1.3	–1.2	0.9
Administrative support occupations, including clerical	**9.7**	**6.5**	**5.0**	**3.2**	**4.7**
Supervisors, administrative support	9.4	7.0	5.0	2.4	4.4
Computer equipment operators	7.4	6.9	6.0	0.5	1.4
Computer operators	7.4	6.9	6.0	0.5	1.4

(continued)

	2000	1990	1983	percentage point change 1990–00	1983–00
Secretaries, stenographers, and typists	8.6%	5.4%	4.5%	3.2	4.1
Secretaries	8.7	5.2	4.0	3.5	4.7
Typists	9.3	7.3	6.4	2.0	2.9
Information clerks	10.4	7.3	5.5	3.1	4.9
Receptionists	11.6	6.7	6.6	4.9	5.0
Records processing, except financial	10.6	7.2	4.8	3.4	5.8
Order clerks	12.4	6.5	4.4	5.9	8.0
Personnel clerks, except payroll and timekeeping	4.8	7.3	4.6	–2.5	0.2
Library clerks	6.5	5.0	2.5	1.5	4.0
File clerks	12.0	9.0	6.1	3.0	5.9
Records clerks	10.7	7.5	5.6	3.2	5.1
Financial records processing	7.3	5.1	3.7	2.2	3.6
Bookkeepers, accounting, and auditing clerks	6.1	5.0	3.3	1.1	2.8
Payroll and timekeeping clerks	8.4	3.6	5.0	4.8	3.4
Billing clerks	12.4	6.3	3.9	6.1	8.5
Cost and rate clerks	10.9	5.6	5.3	5.3	5.6
Duplicating, mail and other office machine operators	9.6	6.1	6.1	3.5	3.5
Communications equipment operators	10.7	7.1	4.4	3.6	6.3
Telephone operators	10.4	7.2	4.3	3.2	6.1
Mail and message distributing	7.7	6.3	4.5	1.4	3.2
Postal clerks, except mail carriers	6.2	4.7	5.2	1.5	1.0
Mail carriers, postal service	5.9	6.1	2.7	–0.2	3.2
Mail clerks, except postal service	11.2	7.7	5.9	3.5	5.3
Messengers	10.4	7.9	5.2	2.5	5.2
Material recording, scheduling, and distributing clerks	12.8	8.0	6.6	4.8	6.2
Dispatchers	9.0	4.4	4.3	4.6	4.7
Production coordinators	6.6	4.5	2.2	2.1	4.4
Traffic, shipping, and receiving clerks	17.5	11.7	11.1	5.8	6.4
Stock and inventory clerks	13.1	8.0	5.5	5.1	7.6
Expediters	10.5	4.9	4.3	5.6	6.2
Adjusters and investigators	10.1	5.6	5.1	4.5	5.0
Insurance adjusters, examiners, and investigators	7.0	3.9	3.3	3.1	3.7
Investigators and adjusters, except insurance	11.5	6.7	4.8	4.8	6.7
Eligibility clerks, social welfare	9.5	4.0	9.4	5.5	0.1
Bill and account collectors	9.5	6.7	6.5	2.8	3.0
Miscellaneous administrative support	10.4	7.7	5.9	2.7	4.5
General office clerks	10.5	7.0	5.2	3.5	5.3
Bank tellers	8.2	7.0	4.3	1.2	3.9
Data-entry keyers	11.2	8.0	5.6	3.2	5.6
Statistical clerks	8.4	6.7	3.4	1.7	5.0
Teachers' aides	14.4	11.8	12.6	2.6	1.8
SERVICE OCCUPATIONS	**15.7**	**11.2**	**6.8**	**4.5**	**8.9**
Private household	**31.7**	**19.7**	**8.5**	**12.0**	**23.2**
Child care workers	19.9	13.3	3.6	6.6	16.3
Cleaners and servants	37.7	23.8	11.8	13.9	25.9
Protective service	**8.7**	**5.9**	**4.6**	**2.8**	**4.1**
Supervisors	7.8	4.1	3.1	3.7	4.7
Police and detectives	3.0	2.4	1.2	0.6	1.8
Firefighting and fire prevention	5.4	4.4	4.1	1.0	1.3
Firefighting	5.0	4.5	3.8	0.5	1.2
Police and detectives	8.4	5.3	4.0	3.1	4.4
Police and detectives, public service	10.1	5.5	4.4	4.6	5.7

(continued)

(continued from previous page)

	2000	1990	1983	percentage point change 1990–00	1983–00
Sheriffs, bailiffs, and other law enforcement officers	5.8%	5.7%	4.0%	0.1	1.8
Correctional institution officers	6.9	4.7	2.8	2.2	4.1
Guards	10.0	7.4	5.6	2.6	4.4
Guards and police, except public services	10.6	7.8	6.2	2.8	4.4
Service occupations, exc. private household, protective service	**16.0**	**11.5**	**6.9**	**4.5**	**9.1**
Food preparation and service occupations	17.2	12.5	6.8	4.7	10.4
Bartenders	13.2	6.7	4.4	6.5	8.8
Waiters and waitresses	11.0	7.6	3.6	3.4	7.4
Cooks	21.6	14.6	6.5	7.0	15.1
Food counter, fountain and related occupations	11.8	7.3	6.7	4.5	5.1
Kitchen workers, food preparation	12.3	12.5	8.1	-0.2	4.2
Waiters' and waitresses' assistants	18.8	21.4	14.2	-2.6	4.6
Health service occupations	10.1	6.4	4.8	3.7	5.3
Dental assistants	10.6	7.4	5.7	3.2	4.9
Health aides, except nursing	8.7	5.6	4.8	3.1	3.9
Nursing aides, orderlies, and attendants	10.4	6.5	4.7	3.9	5.7
Cleaning and building service occupations	23.4	16.7	9.2	6.7	14.2
Maids and housemen	28.3	21.7	10.1	6.6	18.2
Janitors and cleaners	22.5	15.7	8.9	6.8	13.6
Personal service occupations	10.8	7.3	6.0	3.5	4.8
Barbers	12.7	9.9	12.1	2.8	0.6
Hairdressers and cosmetologists	10.7	7.1	5.7	3.6	5.0
Attendants, amusement and recreation facilities	6.0	5.7	4.3	0.3	1.7
Public transportation attendants	7.9	6.0	5.9	1.9	2.0
Welfare service aides	12.7	13.7	10.5	-1.0	2.2
PRECISION PRODUCTION, CRAFT, AND REPAIR	**13.9**	**8.5**	**6.2**	**5.4**	**7.7**
Mechanics and repairers	**10.7**	**7.0**	**5.3**	**3.7**	**5.4**
Mechanics and repairers, except supervisors	10.8	7.2	5.5	3.6	5.3
Vehicle and mobile equipment mechanics and repairers	13.1	8.4	6.0	4.7	7.1
Automobile mechanics	15.6	9.4	6.0	6.2	9.6
Aircraft engine mechanics	9.0	8.4	7.6	0.6	1.4
Electrical and electronic equipment repairers	7.8	6.0	4.5	1.8	3.3
Data processing equipment repairers	4.8	5.6	4.5	-0.8	0.3
Telephone installers and repairers	9.5	3.8	3.7	5.7	5.8
Construction trades	**16.4**	**8.9**	**6.0**	**7.5**	**10.4**
Construction trades, except supervisors	18.1	9.5	6.1	8.6	12.0
Carpenters	16.3	8.7	5.0	7.6	11.3
Extractive occupations	**7.8**	**6.9**	**6.0**	**0.9**	**1.8**
Precision production occupations	**14.4**	**9.8**	**7.4**	**4.6**	**7.0**
OPERATORS, FABRICATORS, AND LABORERS	**17.5**	**12.2**	**8.3**	**5.3**	**9.2**
Machine operators, assemblers, and inspectors	**19.3**	**13.9**	**9.4**	**5.4**	**9.9**
Textile, apparel, and furnishings machine operators	33.0	19.9	12.5	13.1	20.5
Textile sewing machine operators	40.6	23.1	14.5	17.5	26.1
Pressing machine operators	49.9	27.9	14.2	22.0	35.7
Fabricators, assemblers, and hand working occupations	17.1	12.7	8.7	4.4	8.4
Production inspectors, testers, samplers, and weighers	17.3	10.4	7.7	6.9	9.6
Transportation and material moving occupations	**11.9**	**8.5**	**5.9**	**3.4**	**6.0**
Motor vehicle operators	11.8	8.6	6.0	3.2	5.8
Truck drivers	12.5	–	5.7	–	6.8
Transportation occupations, except motor vehicles	3.6	5.1	3.0	-1.5	0.6
Material moving equipment operators	13.7	8.9	6.3	4.8	7.4
Industrial truck and tractor equipment operators	18.4	10.5	8.2	7.9	10.2

(continued)

(continued from previous page)

	2000	1990	1983	percentage point change	
				1990–00	1983–00
Handlers, equipment cleaners, helpers, and laborers	**20.7%**	**12.9%**	**8.6%**	**7.8**	**12.1**
Freight, stock, and material handlers	14.6	10.1	7.1	4.5	7.5
Laborers, except construction	18.4	12.0	8.6	6.4	9.8
FARMING, FORESTRY, FISHING	**23.7**	**14.2**	**8.2**	**9.5**	**15.5**
Farm operators and managers	**3.0**	**1.7**	**0.7**	**1.3**	**2.3**
Other agricultural and related occupations	**36.1**	**22.8**	**14.0**	**13.3**	**22.1**
Farm workers	47.4	26.9	15.9	20.5	31.5
Forestry and logging occupations	**7.8**	**5.4**	**2.1**	**2.4**	**5.7**
Fishers, hunters, trappers	**2.0**	**6.0**	**2.5**	**–4.0**	**–0.5**

Note: (–) means data are not available or sample is too small to make a reliable estimate.
Source: 1983 and 2000 data from Bureau of the Census, Statistical Abstract of the United States, 2001; *1990 data from Bureau of Labor Statistics,* Employment and Earnings, *January 1991; calculations by New Strategist*

Diverse, High-Tech Future for Labor Force

Between 2000 and 2010, the Bureau of Labor Statistics projects a changing labor force, in which women will outnumber men among labor force entrants and non-Hispanic whites account for only 61 percent of entering workers.

Many of the occupations projected to grow the fastest between 2000 and 2010 are high-tech jobs such as computer software engineers, network systems and data communications analysts, and network administrators. The occupations projected to gain the largest number of positions include computer jobs as well as blue-collar and service occupations such as cashiers, truck drivers, waiters and waitresses, nursing aides, and janitors.

While the total number of jobs is projected to increase 15 percent between 2000 and 2010, the number of positions requiring a bachelor's degree should climb 23 percent. The biggest increase is projected for jobs requiring an associate's degree—up 32 percent. Despite growing demand for educated workers, nearly 43 percent of net job openings projected for the next decade will require no more than short-term, on-the-job training.

Professional employment to grow the fastest

(percent change in employment by major occupational group, 2000–10)

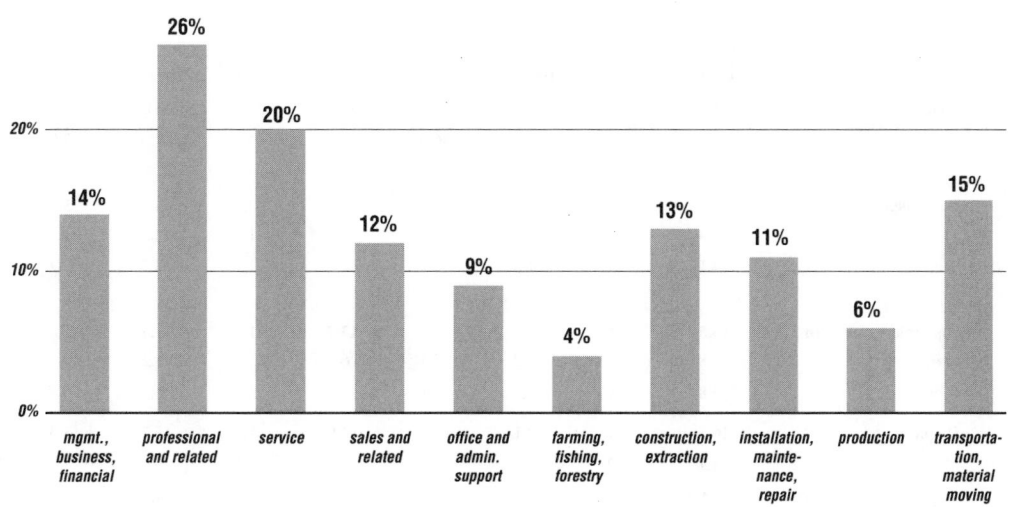

Table 6.19 Labor Force Entrants and Leavers, 1990 to 2010

(number and percent distribution of people aged 16 or older in the civilian labor force in 1990, 2000, and 2010, and number and percent distribution of entrants, leavers, and stayers, 1990–00 and 2000–10, by race, Hispanic origin, and sex; numbers in thousands)

	1990 labor force	1990–00 entrants	1990–00 leavers	1990–00 stayers	2000 labor force	2000–10 entrants	2000–10 leavers	2000–10 stayers	2010 labor force
Total	**125,840**	**34,669**	**19,646**	**106,194**	**140,864**	**41,048**	**24,191**	**116,673**	**157,721**
Men	69,011	17,783	11,547	57,464	75,247	20,379	13,406	61,842	82,221
Women	56,829	16,886	8,098	48,730	65,617	20,669	10,785	54,831	75,500
Asian, other, non-Hispanic	**3,735**	**2,946**	**277**	**3,459**	**6,404**	**3,218**	**879**	**5,526**	**8,743**
Men	2,007	1,539	145	1,862	3,401	1,513	461	2,940	4,453
Women	1,728	1,406	132	1,597	3,003	1,705	417	2,586	4,290
Black, non-Hispanic	**13,566**	**4,694**	**2,131**	**11,435**	**16,129**	**5,627**	**2,843**	**13,286**	**18,913**
Men	6,727	2,004	1,163	5,564	7,566	2,463	1,525	6,043	8,507
Women	6,839	2,689	967	5,872	8,561	3,164	1,318	7,243	10,407
Hispanic	**10,720**	**5,667**	**1,020**	**9,700**	**15,368**	**7,331**	**1,752**	**13,617**	**20,947**
Men	6,546	3,026	653	5,893	8,919	3,820	1,016	7,903	11,723
Women	4,174	2,641	367	3,807	6,449	3,511	736	5,713	9,224
White, non-Hispanic	**97,818**	**21,363**	**16,219**	**81,599**	**102,962**	**24,873**	**18,717**	**84,245**	**109,118**
Men	53,731	11,214	9,587	44,145	55,359	12,583	10,404	44,955	57,538
Women	44,087	10,149	6,632	37,455	47,604	12,290	8,314	39,290	51,580
Percent distribution									
Total	**100.0%**	**100.0%**	**100.0%**	**100.0%**	**100.0%**	**100.0%**	**100.0%**	**100.0%**	**100.0%**
Men	54.8	51.3	58.8	54.1	53.4	49.6	55.4	53.0	52.1
Women	45.2	48.7	41.2	45.9	46.6	50.4	44.6	47.0	47.9
Asian, other, non-Hispanic	**3.0**	**8.5**	**1.4**	**3.3**	**4.5**	**7.8**	**3.6**	**4.7**	**5.5**
Men	1.6	4.4	0.7	1.8	2.4	3.7	1.9	2.5	2.8
Women	1.4	4.1	0.7	1.5	2.1	4.2	1.7	3.7	2.7
Black, non-Hispanic	**10.8**	**13.5**	**10.8**	**10.8**	**11.5**	**13.7**	**11.8**	**11.4**	**12.0**
Men	5.3	5.8	5.9	5.2	5.4	6.0	6.3	5.2	5.4
Women	5.4	7.8	4.9	5.5	6.1	7.7	5.4	6.2	6.6
Hispanic	**8.5**	**16.3**	**5.2**	**9.1**	**10.9**	**17.9**	**7.2**	**11.7**	**13.3**
Men	5.2	8.7	3.3	5.5	6.3	9.3	4.2	6.8	7.4
Women	3.3	7.6	1.9	3.6	4.6	8.6	3.0	4.9	5.8
White, non-Hispanic	**77.7**	**8.5**	**82.6**	**76.8**	**73.1**	**60.6**	**77.4**	**72.2**	**69.2**
Men	42.7	4.4	48.8	41.6	39.3	30.7	43.0	38.5	36.5
Women	35.0	4.1	33.8	35.3	33.8	29.9	34.4	33.7	32.7

Source: Bureau of Labor Statistics, Monthly Labor Review, *November 2001*

Table 6.20   Employment by Major Occupational Group, 2000 and 2010

(number and percent distribution of people aged 16 or older employed by major occupational group, 2000 and 2010; percent and percentage point change, 2000–10; numbers in thousands)

	2000	2010	percent change 2000–10
Total employed	**145,594**	**167,754**	**15.2%**
Management, business, and financial occupations	15,519	17,635	13.6
Professional and related occupations	26,758	33,709	26.0
Service occupations	26,075	31,163	19.5
Sales and related occupations	15,513	17,365	11.9
Office and administrative support occupations	23,882	26,053	9.1
Farming, fishing, and forestry occupations	1,429	1,480	3.6
Construction and extraction occupations	7,451	8,439	13.3
Installation, maintenance, and repair occupations	5,820	6,482	11.4
Production occupations	13,060	13,811	5.7
Transportation and material moving occupations	10,088	11,618	15.2

			percentage point change 2000–10
Total employed	**100.0%**	**100.0%**	–
Management, business, and financial occupations	10.7	10.5	–0.2
Professional and related occupations	18.4	20.1	1.7
Service occupations	17.9	18.6	0.7
Sales and related occupations	10.7	10.4	–0.3
Office and administrative support occupations	16.4	15.5	–0.9
Farming, fishing, and forestry occupations	1.0	0.9	–0.1
Construction and extraction occupations	5.1	5.0	–0.1
Installation, maintenance, and repair occupations	4.0	3.9	–0.1
Production occupations	9.0	8.2	–0.8
Transportation and material moving occupations	6.9	6.9	0.0

Note: (–) means not applicable.
Source: Bureau of Labor Statistics, Internet site http://www.bls.gov/news.release/ecopro.t02.htm

Table 6.21 Employment by Major Industry, 1990 to 2010

(number and percent distribution of people aged 16 or older employed by major industry, 1990 to 2010; percent and percentage point change, 1990–00 and 2000–10; numbers in thousands)

	1990	2000	2010	percent change 1990–00	percent change 2000–10
Total employed	**124,324**	**145,594**	**167,754**	**17.1%**	**15.2%**
Nonfarm wage and salary	108,760	130,639	152,447	20.1	16.7
Goods producing	24,906	25,709	27,057	3.2	5.2
Mining	709	543	488	–23.4	–10.1
Construction	5,120	6,698	7,522	30.8	12.3
Manufacturing	19,077	18,469	19,047	–3.2	3.1
Durable	11,109	11,138	11,780	0.3	5.8
Nondurable	7,968	7,331	7,267	–8.0	–0.9
Service producing	83,854	104,930	125,390	25.1	19.5
Transportation, communications, and utilities	5,776	7,019	8,274	21.5	17.9
Wholesale trade	6,173	7,024	7,800	13.8	11.0
Retail trade	19,601	23,307	26,400	18.9	13.3
Finance, insurance, and real estate	6,709	7,560	8,247	12.7	9.1
Services	27,291	39,340	52,233	44.2	32.8
Government	18,304	20,680	22,436	13.0	8.5
Federal government	3,085	2,777	2,622	–10.0	–5.6
State and local government	15,219	17,903	19,814	17.6	10.7
Agriculture	3,340	3,526	3,849	5.6	9.2
Private household wage and salary	1,014	890	664	–12.2	–25.4
Nonagriculture self-employed and unpaid family workers	8,921	8,731	9,062	–2.1	3.8
Secondary wage and salary jobs in agriculture, forestry, fishing, trapping, and private households	205	155	150	–24.4	–3.2
Secondary jobs as self-employed or unpaid family workers	2,084	1,652	1,582	–20.7	–4.2

	1990	2000	2010	percentage point change 1990–00	percentage point change 2000–10
Total employed	**100.0%**	**100.0%**	**100.0%**	–	–
Nonfarm wage and salary	87.5	89.7	90.9	2.2	1.1
Goods producing	20.0	17.7	16.1	–2.4	–1.5
Mining	0.6	0.4	0.3	–0.2	–0.1
Construction	4.1	4.6	4.5	0.5	–0.1
Manufacturing	15.3	12.7	11.4	–2.7	–1.3
Durable	8.9	7.7	7.0	–1.3	–0.6
Nondurable	6.4	5.0	4.3	–1.4	–0.7
Service producing	67.4	72.1	74.7	4.6	2.7
Transportation, communications, and utilities	4.6	4.8	4.9	0.2	0.1
Wholesale trade	5.0	4.8	4.6	–0.1	–0.2
Retail trade	15.8	16.0	15.7	0.2	–0.3
Finance, insurance, and real estate	5.4	5.2	4.9	–0.2	–0.3
Services	22.0	27.0	31.1	5.1	4.1
Government	14.7	14.2	13.4	–0.5	–0.8
Federal government	2.5	1.9	1.6	–0.6	–0.3
State and local government	12.2	12.3	11.8	0.1	–0.5
Agriculture	2.7	2.4	2.3	–0.3	–0.1
Private household wage and salary	0.8	0.6	0.4	–0.2	–0.2
Nonagriculture self-employed and unpaid family workers	7.2	6.0	5.4	–1.2	–0.6
Secondary wage and salary jobs in agriculture, forestry, fishing, trapping, and private households	0.2	0.1	0.1	–0.1	0.0
Secondary jobs as self-employed or unpaid family workers	1.7	1.1	0.9	–0.5	–0.2

Source: Bureau of Labor Statistics, Internet site http://www.bls.gov/news.release/ecopro.t01.htm; calculations by New Strategist

Table 6.22 Fastest Growing Occupations, 2000 to 2010

(number of people aged 16 or older employed in the 30 fastest-growing occupations, 2000 and 2010; numerical and percent change, 2000–10; numbers in thousands)

	2000	2010	change, 2000–10	
			number	percent
Computer software engineers, applications	380	760	380	100.0%
Computer support specialists	506	996	490	97.0
Computer software engineers, systems software	317	601	284	90.0
Network and computer systems administrators	229	416	187	82.0
Network systems and data communications analysts	119	211	92	77.0
Desktop publishers	38	63	25	67.0
Database administrators	106	176	70	66.0
Personal and home care aides	414	672	258	62.0
Computer systems analysts	431	689	258	60.0
Medical assistants	329	516	187	57.0
Social and human service assistants	271	418	147	54.0
Physician assistants	58	89	31	53.0
Medical records and health information technicians	136	202	66	49.0
Computer and information systems managers	313	463	150	48.0
Home health aides	615	907	291	47.0
Physical therapist aides	36	53	17	46.0
Occupational therapist aides	9	12	4	45.0
Physical therapist assistants	44	64	20	45.0
Audiologists	13	19	6	45.0
Fitness trainers and aerobics instructors	158	222	64	40.0
Computer and information scientists, research	28	39	11	40.0
Veterinary assistants and laboratory animal caretakers	55	77	22	40.0
Occupational therapist assistants	17	23	7	40.0
Veterinary technologists and technicians	49	69	19	39.0
Speech-language pathologists and audiologists	88	122	34	39.0
Mental health and substance abuse social workers	83	116	33	39.0
Dental assistants	247	339	92	37.0
Dental hygienists	147	201	54	37.0
Special education teachers, preschool, kindergarten, and elementary school	234	320	86	37.0
Pharmacy technicians	190	259	69	36.0

Source: Bureau of Labor Statistics, Internet site http://www.bls.gov/emp/emptab3.htm

Table 6.23 Occupations with the Largest Job Growth, 2000 to 2010

(number of people aged 16 or older employed in the 30 occupations with the largest job growth, 2000 to 2010; numerical and percent change, 2000–10; numbers in thousands)

	2000	2010	change, 2000–10 number	change, 2000–10 percent
Combined food preparation and serving workers, including fast food	2,206	2,879	673	30.0%
Customer service representatives	1,946	2,577	631	32.0
Registered nurses	2,194	2,755	561	26.0
Retail salespersons	4,109	4,619	510	12.0
Computer support specialists	506	996	490	97.0
Cashiers, except gaming	3,325	3,799	474	14.0
Office clerks, general	2,705	3,135	430	16.0
Security guards	1,106	1,497	391	35.0
Computer software engineers, applications	380	760	380	100.0
Waiters and waitresses	1,983	2,347	364	18.0
General and operations managers	2,398	2,761	363	15.0
Truck drivers, heavy and tractor-trailer	1,749	2,095	346	20.0
Nursing aides, orderlies, and attendants	1,373	1,697	323	24.0
Janitors and cleaners, except maids and housekeeping cleaners	2,348	2,665	317	13.0
Postsecondary teachers	1,344	1,659	315	23.0
Teacher assistants	1,262	1,562	301	24.0
Home health aides	615	907	291	47.0
Laborers and freight, stock, and material movers, hand	2,084	2,373	289	14.0
Computer software engineers, systems software	317	601	284	90.0
Landscaping and groundskeeping workers	894	1,154	260	29.0
Personal and home care aides	414	672	258	62.0
Computer systems analysts	431	689	258	60.0
Receptionists and information clerks	1,078	1,334	256	24.0
Truck drivers, light or delivery services	1,117	1,331	215	19.0
Packers and packagers, hand	1,091	1,300	210	19.0
Elementary school teachers, except special education	1,532	1,734	202	13.0
Medical assistants	329	516	187	57.0
Network and computer systems administrators	229	416	187	82.0
Secondary school teachers, except special and vocational education	1,004	1,190	187	19.0
Accountants and auditors	976	1,157	181	19.0

Source: Bureau of Labor Statistics, Internet site http://www.bls.gov/emp/emptab4.htm

Table 6.24   Occupations with the Largest Job Decline, 2000 to 2010

(number of people aged 16 or older employed in the 30 occupations with the largest job decline, 2000 to 2010; numerical and percent change, 2000–10; numbers in thousands)

| | | | change, 2000–10 | |
	2000	2010	number	percent
Farmers and ranchers	1,294	965	–328	–25.0%
Order clerks	348	277	–71	–20.0
Tellers	499	440	–59	–12.0
Insurance claims and policy processing clerks	289	231	–58	–20.0
Word processors and typists	297	240	–57	–19.0
Sewing machine operators	399	348	–51	13.0
Dishwashers	525	483	–42	–8.0
Switchboard operators, including answering service	259	218	–41	–16.0
Loan interviewers and clerks	139	101	–38	–28.0
Computer operators	194	161	–33	–17.0
Dining room, cafeteria attendants and bartender helpers	431	402	–29	–7.0
Electrical and electronic equipment assemblers	379	355	–24	–6.0
Machine feeders and offbearers	182	159	–22	–12.0
Telephone operators	54	35	–19	–35.0
Secretaries, except legal, medical, and executive	1,864	1,846	–18	–1.0
Prepress technicians and workers	107	90	–17	–16.0
Office machine operators, except computer	84	68	–16	–19.0
Cutting, punching, press machine setters, operators, and tenders, metal and plastic	372	357	–15	–4.0
Postal service mail sorters, processors, and processing machine operators	289	275	–14	–5.0
Railroad brake, signal, and switch operators	22	9	–13	–61.0
Wholesale and retail buyers, except farm products	148	135	–13	–9.0
Meter readers, utilities	49	36	–13	–26.0
Butchers and meat cutters	141	128	–13	–9.0
Parts salespersons	260	248	–12	–4.0
Inspectors, testers, sorters, samplers, and weighers	602	591	–11	–2.0
Eligibility interviewers, government programs	117	106	–11	–9.0
Door-to-door sales workers, news and street vendors, and related workers	166	156	–10	–6.0
Procurement clerks	76	67	–9	–12.0
Railroad conductors and yardmasters	45	36	–8	–19.0
Barbers	73	64	–8	–12.0

Source: Bureau of Labor Statistics, Internet site http://www.bls.gov/emp/emptab5.htm

Table 6.25 Employment by Education and Training Requirements, 2000 and 2010

(number and percent distribution of employed people aged 16 or older by educational and training category, 2000 and 2010; numerical and percent change, 2000–10; number and percent distribution of net job openings by educational and training category; numbers in thousands)

	number		percent distribution		change, 2000–10		net job openings, 2000–10	
	2000	2010	2000	2010	number	percent	number	percent distribution
Total employed	145,594	167,754	100.0%	100.0%	22,160	15.2%	57,932	100.0%
Bachelor's or higher degree	30,072	36,556	20.7	21.8	6,484	21.6	12,130	20.9
First professional degree	2,034	2,404	1.4	1.4	370	18.2	691	1.2
Doctoral degree	1,492	1,845	1.0	1.1	353	23.7	760	1.3
Master's degree	1,426	1,759	1.0	1.0	333	23.4	634	1.1
Bachelor's or higher degree plus work experience	7,319	8,741	5.0	5.2	1,422	19.4	2,741	4.7
Bachelor's degree	17,801	21,807	12.2	13.0	4,006	22.5	7,304	12.6
Associate's degree or postsecondary vocational award	11,761	14,600	8.1	8.7	2,839	24.1	5,383	9.3
Associate's degree	5,083	6,710	3.5	4.0	1,626	32.0	2,608	4.5
Postsecondary vocational award	6,678	7,891	4.6	4.7	1,213	18.2	2,775	4.8
Work-related training	103,760	116,597	71.3	69.5	12,837	12.4	40,419	69.8
Work experience in related occupation	10,456	11,559	7.2	6.9	1,102	10.5	3,180	5.5
Long-term on-the-job training	12,435	13,373	8.5	8.0	938	7.5	3,737	6.5
Moderate-term on-the-job training	27,671	30,794	19.0	18.4	3,123	11.3	8,767	15.1
Short-term on-the-job training	53,198	60,871	36.5	36.3	7,673	14.4	24,735	42.7

Note: Net job openings include new positions as well as replacements due to retirement, etc.
Source: Bureau of Labor Statistics, Internet site http://www.bls.gov/news.release/ecopro.t04.htm

Table 6.26 Employment by Detailed Occupation, 2000 and 2010

(number of employed people aged 16 or older by occupation, 2000 and 2010; numerical and percent change, 2000–10; total job openings due to growth and net replacements, 2000–10; numbers in thousands)

	2000	2010	change, 2000–10 number	change, 2000–10 percent	net job openings 2000–10
TOTAL EMPLOYED	**145,594**	**167,754**	**22,160**	**15.2%**	**57,932**
MANAGEMENT, BUSINESS, AND FINANCIAL OCCUPATIONS	**15,519**	**17,635**	**2,115**	**13.6**	**5,109**
Management occupations	**10,564**	**11,834**	**1,270**	**12.0**	**3,330**
Administrative services managers	362	436	74	20.4	133
Advertising, marketing, promotions, public relations, and sales managers	707	936	229	32.4	331
Advertising and promotions managers	100	135	34	34.3	49
Marketing and sales managers	533	701	168	31.5	244
Marketing managers	190	246	55	29.1	83
Sales managers	343	455	112	32.8	162
Public relations managers	74	101	27	36.3	38
Agricultural managers	1,462	1,144	−318	−21.7	103
Farm, ranch, and other agricultural managers	169	179	10	6.0	30
Farmers and ranchers	1,294	965	−328	−25.4	74
Chief executives	547	641	94	17.2	266
Computer and information systems managers	313	463	150	47.9	203
Construction managers	308	358	50	16.3	100
Education administrators	453	513	61	13.4	178
Engineering managers	282	305	23	8.0	69
Financial managers	658	780	122	18.5	223
Food service managers	465	535	70	15.0	125
Funeral directors	32	32	1	3.0	6
Gaming managers	4	5	1	30.0	2
General and operations managers	2,398	2,761	363	15.2	767
Human resources managers	219	246	28	12.7	66
Industrial production managers	255	271	16	6.2	57
Legislators	54	61	7	12.7	24
Lodging managers	68	75	6	9.3	14
Medical and health services managers	250	330	81	32.3	123
Natural sciences managers	42	45	3	7.6	11
Postmasters and mail superintendents	25	26	1	2.5	5
Property, real estate, and community association managers	270	331	61	22.7	105
Purchasing managers	132	125	−7	−5.5	41
Social and community service managers	128	160	32	24.8	56
Transportation, storage, and distribution managers	149	179	30	20.2	55
All other managers	981	1,074	93	9.5	267
Business and financial operations specialists	**4,956**	**5,801**	**845**	**17.1**	**1,779**
Business operations specialists	2,841	3,320	479	16.8	1,053
Agents and business managers of artists, performers, athletes	17	22	5	27.9	8
Buyers and purchasing agents	404	424	20	4.8	128
Purchasing agents and buyers, farm products	20	23	3	16.8	7
Purchasing agents, except wholesale, retail, farm products	237	266	29	12.3	76
Wholesale and retail buyers, except farm products	148	135	−13	−8.7	45
Claims adjusters, appraisers, examiners, and investigators	207	238	31	15.0	54
Claims adjusters, examiners, and investigators	194	223	29	15.1	51
Insurance appraisers, auto damage	13	15	2	14.3	3
Compliance officers, except agriculture, construction, health and safety, and transportation	140	152	12	8.9	48
Cost estimators	211	246	35	16.5	81
Emergency management specialists	10	12	2	18.1	5
Human resources, training, and labor relations specialists	490	578	88	18.0	183

(continued)

(continued from previous page)

	2000	2010	change, 2000–10 number	change, 2000–10 percent	net job openings 2000–10
Compensation, benefits, and job analysis specialists	87	100	14	15.7%	30
Employment, recruitment, and placement specialists	199	234	35	17.6	73
Training and development specialists	204	244	40	19.4	79
Management analysts	501	646	145	28.9	189
Meeting and convention planners	34	42	8	23.3	14
All other business operations specialists	827	960	133	16.1	343
Financial specialists	2,115	2,481	367	17.3	726
Accountants and auditors	976	1,157	181	18.5	326
Appraisers and assessors of real estate	57	67	10	18.0	26
Budget analysts	70	80	10	14.6	24
Credit analysts	60	70	10	16.0	22
Financial analysts	145	182	37	25.5	57
Financial examiners	25	27	3	10.2	7
Insurance underwriters	107	109	2	2.0	18
Loan counselors and officers	265	281	16	6.1	69
Loan counselors	29	33	5	16.0	10
Loan officers	236	248	12	4.9	59
Personal financial advisors	94	126	32	34.0	43
Tax examiners, collectors, and revenue agents	79	86	7	8.3	28
Tax preparers	69	81	12	17.4	26
All other financial specialists	169	216	47	28.0	81
PROFESSIONAL AND RELATED OCCUPATIONS	**26,758**	**33,709**	**6,952**	**26.0**	**12,160**
Computer and mathematical occupations	**2,993**	**4,988**	**1,996**	**66.7**	**2,285**
Computer specialists	2,903	4,894	1,991	68.6	2,259
Computer programmers	585	680	95	16.2	217
Computer scientists and systems analysts	459	729	269	58.6	309
Computer and information scientists, research	28	39	11	40.3	14
Computer systems analysts	431	689	258	59.7	296
Computer software engineers	697	1,361	664	95.4	711
Computer software engineers, applications	380	760	380	100.0	406
Computer software engineers, systems software	317	601	284	89.7	306
Computer support specialists	506	996	490	97.0	512
Database administrators	106	176	70	65.9	74
Network and computer systems administrators	229	416	187	81.9	197
Network systems and data communications analysts	119	211	92	77.5	97
All other computer specialists	203	326	123	60.7	141
Mathematical science occupations	89	95	5	5.7	26
Mathematical scientists and technicians	85	90	5	5.9	25
Actuaries	14	15	1	5.4	3
Mathematicians	4	4	0	−1.9	0
Operations research analysts	47	51	4	8.0	19
Statisticians	19	20	0	2.3	3
Miscellaneous mathematical science occupations	5	5	0	2.7	1
Architecture and engineering occupations	**2,605**	**2,930**	**325**	**12.5**	**868**
Architects, surveyors, and cartographers	196	229	33	17.1	61
Architects, except naval	124	150	26	20.7	33
Architects, except landscape and naval	102	121	19	18.5	25
Landscape architects	22	29	7	31.1	8
Surveyors, cartographers, and photogrammetrists	65	71	6	9.2	26
Cartographers and photogrammetrists	7	8	1	18.5	3
Surveyors	58	63	5	8.1	22
All other architects, surveyors, and cartographers	6	8	2	28.5	2
Engineers	1,465	1,603	138	9.4	432
Aerospace engineers	50	57	7	13.9	22
Agricultural engineers	2	3	0	14.8	1

(continued)

(continued from previous page)

	2000	2010	change, 2000–10 number	change, 2000–10 percent	net job openings 2000–10
Biomedical engineers	7	9	2	31.4%	4
Chemical engineers	33	34	1	4.1	7
Civil engineers	232	256	24	10.2	60
Computer hardware engineers	60	75	15	24.9	23
Electrical and electronics engineers	288	319	31	10.9	84
Electrical engineers	157	175	18	11.3	47
Electronics engineers, except computer	130	144	14	10.4	37
Environmental engineers	52	66	14	26.0	24
Industrial engineers, including health and safety	198	210	12	5.9	45
Health and safety engineers, except mining safety engineers and inspectors	44	49	5	10.9	12
Industrial engineers	154	161	7	4.5	33
Marine engineers and naval architects	5	5	0	2.1	1
Materials engineers	33	35	2	5.3	9
Mechanical engineers	221	251	29	13.1	94
Mining and geological engineers, incl. mining safety engineers	6	6	0	−1.3	1
Nuclear engineers	14	14	0	1.8	3
Petroleum engineers	9	8	−1	−7.2	2
All other engineers	253	254	1	0.4	51
Drafters, engineering, and mapping technicians	944	1,098	154	16.3	375
Drafters	213	255	42	19.5	106
Architectural and civil drafters	102	123	21	20.8	52
Electrical and electronics drafters	41	51	10	23.3	22
Mechanical drafters	70	81	11	15.4	32
Engineering technicians, except drafters	519	582	62	12.0	167
Aerospace engineering and operations technicians	21	22	1	5.6	5
Civil engineering technicians	94	105	11	11.9	30
Electrical and electronic engineering technicians	233	258	25	10.8	72
Electro-mechanical technicians	43	50	6	14.5	15
Environmental engineering technicians	18	24	5	29.1	9
Industrial engineering technicians	52	57	5	10.1	16
Mechanical engineering technicans	58	66	8	13.9	20
Surveying and mapping technicians	55	70	14	25.3	32
All other drafters, engineering, and mapping technicians	156	192	36	23.2	70
Life, physical, and social science occupations	**1,164**	**1,386**	**223**	**19.1**	**559**
Life scientists	184	218	33	18.1	93
Agricultural and food scientists	17	19	2	8.8	7
Biological scientists	73	88	15	21.0	42
Conservation scientists and foresters	29	31	2	7.7	12
Conservation scientists	16	18	1	8.3	7
Foresters	12	13	1	7.0	5
Medical scientists	37	47	10	26.5	18
All other life scientists	28	33	4	15.9	15
Physical scientists	239	283	44	18.3	124
Astronomers and physicists	10	11	1	10.5	4
Atmospheric and space scientists	7	8	1	17.1	3
Chemists and materials scientists	92	110	18	19.2	47
Chemists	84	100	16	19.1	43
Materials scientists	8	9	2	19.8	4
Environmental scientists and geoscientists	97	118	21	21.5	52
Environmental scientists and specialists, including health	64	78	14	22.3	35
Geoscientists, except hydrologists and geographers	25	30	5	18.1	13
Hydrologists	8	10	2	25.7	5
All other physical scientists	33	36	3	9.4	17
Social scientists and related occupations	410	492	82	20.1	178

(continued)

(continued from previous page)

	2000	2010	change, 2000–10 number	change, 2000–10 percent	net job openings 2000–10
Economists	22	26	4	18.5%	9
Market and survey researchers	113	142	30	26.4	55
Market research analysts	90	112	22	24.4	42
Survey researchers	23	30	8	34.5	13
Psychologists	182	214	33	18.1	75
Social scientists, other	15	17	3	17.2	6
Urban and regional planners	30	35	5	16.4	12
All other social scientists and related workers	49	58	8	17.1	20
Life, physical, and social science technicians	330	393	63	19.0	164
Agricultural and food science technicians	18	20	3	15.2	7
Biological technicians	41	52	11	26.4	21
Chemical technicians	73	84	11	15.0	28
Geological and petroleum technicians	10	11	1	6.5	3
Nuclear technicians	3	4	1	20.7	2
Other life, physical, and social science technicians	184	221	37	20.0	104
Environmental science, protection technicians, incl. health	27	34	7	24.5	17
Forensic science technicians	6	7	1	13.0	3
Forest and conservation technicians	18	19	1	3.2	7
All other life, physical, and social science technicians	133	161	29	21.7	77
Community and social services occupations	**1,869**	**2,398**	**529**	**28.3**	**846**
Counselors	465	585	120	25.8	215
Educational, vocational, and school counselors	205	257	52	25.3	94
Marriage and family therapists	21	27	6	29.9	11
Mental health counselors	67	82	15	21.7	28
Rehabilitation counselors	110	136	26	23.6	49
Substance abuse and behavioral disorder counselors	61	82	21	35.0	34
Miscellaneous community and social service specialists	398	575	177	44.5	236
Health educators	43	53	10	23.5	17
Probation officers and correctional treatment specialists	84	105	20	23.8	33
Social and human service assistants	271	418	147	54.2	187
Religious workers	293	338	45	15.4	112
Clergy	171	197	26	15.0	73
Directors, religious activities and education	121	141	19	15.9	40
Social workers	468	609	141	30.1	193
Child, family, and school social workers	281	357	76	26.9	107
Medical and public health social workers	104	136	33	31.6	44
Mental health and substance abuse social workers	83	116	33	39.1	42
All other counselors, social, and religious workers	244	290	46	18.8	89
Legal occupations	**1,119**	**1,335**	**216**	**19.3**	**304**
Judges, magistrates, and other judicial workers	43	44	2	3.8	14
Administrative law judges, adjudicators, and hearing officers	14	14	0	1.1	4
Arbitrators, mediators, and conciliators	4	6	1	27.2	2
Judges, magistrate judges, and magistrates	24	24	0	1.1	7
Lawyers	681	803	123	18.0	168
Paralegals and legal assistants	188	251	62	33.2	74
Miscellaneous legal support workers	98	106	8	7.7	17
Court reporters	18	21	3	16.2	5
Law clerks	31	35	4	13.2	7
Title examiners, abstractors, and searchers	48	49	0	1.0	5
All other legal and related workers	109	131	22	20.2	32
Education, training, and library occupations	**8,260**	**9,831**	**1,571**	**19.0**	**3,356**
Postsecondary teachers	1,344	1,659	315	23.5	682
Primary, secondary, and special education teachers	4,284	4,995	711	16.6	1,663
Preschool and kindergarten teachers	597	707	110	18.4	184
Preschool teachers, except special education	423	507	85	20.0	137
Kindergarten teachers, except special education	175	200	25	14.5	47

(continued)

(continued from previous page)

	2000	2010	change, 2000–10 number	change, 2000–10 percent	net job openings 2000–10
Elementary and middle school teachers	2,122	2,381	260	12.2%	742
Elementary school teachers, except special education	1,532	1,734	202	13.2	551
Middle school teachers, except special ed. and vocational ed.	570	625	55	9.6	184
Vocational education teachers, middle school	20	22	3	13.1	7
Secondary school teachers	1,113	1,314	201	18.1	540
Secondary school teachers, except special and vocational ed.	1,004	1,190	187	18.6	492
Vocational education teachers, secondary school	109	123	15	13.4	48
Special education teachers	453	592	140	30.9	197
Special ed. teachers, preschool, kindergarten, elementary school	234	320	86	36.8	116
Special education teachers, middle school	96	119	23	24.4	35
Special education teachers, secondary school	123	153	30	24.6	46
Other teachers and instructors	901	1,076	175	19.4	266
Adult literacy, remedial education, GED teachers and instructors	67	80	13	19.4	20
Self-enrichment education teachers	186	220	34	18.5	53
All other teachers, primary, secondary, and adult	648	776	128	19.7	193
Library, museum, training, and other education occupations	1,731	2,101	370	21.4	745
Archivists, curators, and museum technicians	21	24	3	11.9	7
Librarians	149	160	10	7.0	41
Library technicians	109	130	21	19.5	70
Teacher assistants	1,262	1,562	301	23.9	565
Other education, training, library, and museum workers	190	225	35	18.2	62
Audiovisual collections specialists	11	13	2	13.6	3
Farm and home management advisors	11	11	1	6.1	2
Instructional coordinators	81	101	20	25.0	32
All other library, museum, training, other education workers	87	99	12	14.0	25
Arts, design, entertainment, sports, and media occupations	**2,371**	**2,864**	**493**	**20.8**	**947**
Art and design occupations	750	903	153	20.3	251
Artists and related workers	147	176	29	20.0	60
Art directors	47	56	10	21.1	19
Fine artists, including painters, sculptors, and illustrators	31	35	4	13.4	10
Multimedia artists and animators	69	85	15	22.2	30
Designers	492	596	104	21.2	154
Commercial and industrial designers	50	62	12	23.8	17
Fashion designers	16	19	3	20.3	5
Floral designers	102	118	15	14.9	26
Graphic designers	190	241	51	26.7	70
Interior designers	46	54	8	17.4	13
Merchandise displayers and window trimmers	76	88	12	15.9	20
Set and exhibit designers	12	15	3	27.0	4
All other art and design workers	112	130	19	16.8	37
Entertainers and performers, sports and related occupations	626	763	136	21.8	257
Actors, producers, and directors	158	200	42	26.9	73
Actors	99	126	26	26.7	46
Producers and directors	58	74	16	27.1	27
Athletes, coaches, umpires, and related workers	129	153	24	18.7	50
Athletes and sports competitors	18	22	4	22.5	7
Coaches and scouts	99	117	17	17.6	37
Umpires, referees, and other sports officials	11	14	3	22.7	5
Dancers and choreographers	26	30	4	16.3	9
Dancers	15	18	3	17.3	6
Choreographers	11	12	2	14.9	4
Musicians, singers, and related workers	240	285	45	18.7	90
Music directors and composers	50	56	6	13.1	16
Musicians and singers	191	229	38	20.1	74
All other entertainers and performers, sports, related workers	74	95	21	28.3	35

(continued)

(continued from previous page)

	2000	2010	change, 2000–10 number	change, 2000–10 percent	net job openings 2000–10
Media and communication occupations	703	856	153	21.8%	315
Announcers	71	68	–4	–5.5	11
News analysts, reporters, and correspondents	78	80	2	2.8	27
Public relations specialists	137	186	49	36.1	73
Writers and editors	305	385	80	26.3	158
Editors	122	149	27	22.6	67
Technical writers	57	74	17	29.6	34
Writers and authors	126	162	36	28.4	57
Miscellaneous media and communications workers	112	137	25	22.4	47
Interpreters and translators	22	27	5	23.8	9
All other media and communication workers	90	110	20	22.1	37
Media and communication equipment occupations	291	342	51	17.5	124
Broadcast, sound engineering technicians and radio operators	87	99	12	14.0	38
Audio and video equipment technicians	37	43	6	16.8	17
Broadcast technicians	36	40	4	10.2	14
Radio operators	3	3	0	6.2	1
Sound engineering technicians	11	13	2	19.0	5
Photographers	131	153	22	17.0	48
Television, video, motion picture camera operators and editors	43	53	11	25.8	19
Camera operators, television, video, and motion picture	27	33	7	25.8	12
Film and video editors	16	20	4	25.8	7
All other media and communication equipment workers	31	36	6	18.1	19
Healthcare practitioners and technical occupations	**6,379**	**7,978**	**1,599**	**25.1**	**2,995**
Health diagnosing and treating practitioners	3,921	4,888	966	24.6	1,773
Chiropractors	50	62	12	23.4	21
Dentists	152	161	9	5.7	43
Dieticians and nutritionists	49	56	7	15.2	21
Optometrists	31	37	6	18.7	12
Pharmacists	217	270	53	24.3	118
Physicians and surgeons	598	705	107	17.9	196
Physician assistants	58	89	31	53.5	43
Podiatrists	18	20	3	14.2	6
Registered nurses	2,194	2,755	561	25.6	1,004
Therapists	439	584	145	33.2	255
Audiologists	13	19	6	44.7	9
Occupational therapists	78	105	27	33.9	46
Physical therapists	132	176	44	33.3	77
Radiation therapists	16	19	4	22.8	7
Recreational therapists	29	32	2	8.6	10
Respiratory therapists	83	112	29	34.8	50
Speech-language pathologists	88	122	34	39.2	57
Veterinarians	59	77	19	31.8	29
All other health-diagnosing and treating practitioners	57	71	14	24.8	26
Other health professionals and technicians	2,457	3,090	633	25.7	1,222
Clinical laboratory technologists and technicians	295	348	53	18.0	122
Medical and clinical laboratory technologists	148	174	25	17.0	60
Medical and clinical laboratory technicians	147	175	28	19.0	62
Dental hygienists	147	201	54	37.1	76
Diagnostic-related technologists and technicians	257	322	65	25.2	121
Cardiovascular technologists and technicians	39	52	14	34.9	22
Diagnostic medical sonographers	33	41	9	26.1	16
Nuclear medicine technologists	18	22	4	22.4	8
Radiologic technologists and technicians	167	206	39	23.1	75
Emergency medical technicians and paramedics	172	226	54	31.3	97
Health-diagnosing and treating practitioner support technicians	417	551	134	32.2	242

(continued)

(continued from previous page)

	2000	2010	change, 2000–10 number	change, 2000–10 percent	net job openings 2000–10
Dietetic technicians	26	33	7	27.6%	14
Pharmacy technicians	190	259	69	36.4	118
Psychiatric technicians	54	59	5	8.5	19
Respiratory therapy technicians	27	36	9	34.6	16
Surgical technologists	71	96	25	34.7	43
Veterinary technologists and technicians	49	69	19	39.3	32
Licensed practical and licensed vocational nurses	700	842	142	20.3	322
Medical records and health information technicians	136	202	66	49.0	97
Opticians, dispensing	68	81	13	19.0	25
Other health practitioners and technical workers	266	317	50	19.0	119
Athletic trainers	15	17	3	18.5	6
Occupational health and safety specialists and technicians	35	40	5	15.0	14
Orthotists and prosthetists	5	6	1	17.3	2
All other health practitioners and technical workers	212	253	42	19.7	96
SERVICE OCCUPATIONS	**26,075**	**31,163**	**5,088**	**19.5**	**13,505**
Health care support occupations	**3,196**	**4,264**	**1,067**	**33.4**	**1,612**
Dental assistants	247	339	92	37.2	136
Massage therapists	34	45	10	30.4	18
Nursing, psychiatric, and home health aides	2,053	2,676	623	30.4	885
Home health aides	615	907	291	47.3	370
Nursing aides, orderlies, and attendants	1,373	1,697	323	23.5	498
Psychiatric aides	65	73	9	13.2	17
Occupational therapist assistants and aides	25	35	10	41.5	18
Occupational therapist assistants	17	23	7	39.7	11
Occupational therapist aides	9	12	4	45.2	6
Physical therapist assistants and aides	80	116	36	45.5	60
Physical therapist assistants	44	64	20	44.8	33
Physical therapist aides	36	53	17	46.3	27
Medical assistants and other health care support occupations	757	1,052	295	39.0	496
Medical assistants	329	516	187	57.0	274
Medical equipment preparers	33	39	6	18.2	15
Medical transcriptionists	102	132	30	29.8	57
Pharmacy aides	57	68	11	19.5	26
Veterinary assistants and laboratory animal caretakers	55	77	22	39.8	37
All other health care support workers	181	219	38	21.1	86
Protective service occupations	**3,087**	**3,896**	**809**	**26.2**	**1,677**
First-line supervisors/managers, protective service workers	273	319	46	16.7	122
First-line supervisors/managers of correctional officers	30	38	9	29.6	14
First-line supervisors/managers of firefighting, prevention workers	62	66	4	7.2	24
First-line supervisors/managers of police and detectives	121	136	16	13.1	48
First-line supervisors/managers of protective service workers, except police, fire, and corrections	61	78	17	27.1	35
Firefighters	258	280	23	8.9	90
Fire inspectors	13	15	2	15.1	5
Law enforcement workers	1,150	1,445	295	25.6	551
Bailiffs, correctional officers, and jailers	427	563	136	31.8	240
Bailiffs	14	15	2	12.5	5
Correctional officers and jailers	414	548	134	32.4	235
Detectives and criminal investigators	93	108	15	16.4	36
Fish and game wardens	8	9	1	11.4	2
Parking enforcement workers	9	10	1	13.2	2
Police and sheriff's patrol officers	607	748	141	23.2	269
Transit and railroad police	6	7	1	16.5	2
Other protective service workers	1,394	1,837	443	31.8	910
Animal control workers	9	10	1	12.8	8

(continued)

(continued from previous page)

	2000	2010	change, 2000–10 number	change, 2000–10 percent	net job openings 2000–10
Crossing guards	74	81	6	8.7%	32
Private detectives and investigators	39	48	9	23.5	20
Security guards and gaming surveillance officers	1,117	1,509	393	35.2	698
Gaming surveillance officers and gaming investigators	11	13	2	16.8	5
Security guards	1,106	1,497	391	35.4	693
All other protective service workers	156	190	34	21.7	153
Food preparation and serving related occupations	**10,140**	**11,717**	**1,577**	**15.6**	**6,256**
Supervisors, food preparation and serving workers	788	882	95	12.1	301
Chefs and head cooks	139	151	12	9.0	55
First-line supervisors/mgrs. of food preparation, serving workers	649	731	83	12.7	246
Cooks and food preparation workers	2,709	3,041	333	12.3	1,193
Cooks	1,864	2,054	190	10.2	725
Cooks, fast food	522	518	–4	–0.7	148
Cooks, institution and cafeteria	465	500	35	7.6	167
Cooks, private household	5	4	–1	–18.0	1
Cooks, restaurant	668	813	145	21.7	335
Cooks, short order	205	219	14	6.8	72
Food preparation workers	844	988	143	16.9	469
Food and beverage serving workers	5,201	6,384	1,182	22.7	4,218
Bartenders	387	439	52	13.4	204
Combined food preparation, serving workers, incl. fast food	2,206	2,879	673	30.5	2,023
Counter attendants, cafeteria, food concession, coffee shop	421	482	61	14.4	387
Food servers, nonrestaurant	205	238	34	16.4	124
Waiters and waitresses	1,983	2,347	364	18.3	1,479
Other food preparation and serving related workers	1,442	1,410	–33	–2.3	543
Dining room and cafeteria attendants and bartender helpers	431	402	–29	–6.7	145
Dishwashers	525	483	–42	–8.0	197
Hosts and hostesses, restaurant, lounge, and coffee shop	343	388	45	13.0	147
All other food preparation and serving related workers	143	137	–7	–4.6	54
Building, grounds cleaning, maintenance occupations	**5,549**	**6,328**	**779**	**14.0**	**1,912**
Supervisors, building, grounds cleaning, maintenance workers	378	441	63	16.7	131
First-line supervisors/managers of housekeeping and janitorial workers	219	250	31	14.2	91
First-line supervisors/managers of landscaping, lawn service, and groundskeeping workers	159	191	32	20.1	41
Building cleaning workers	3,981	4,381	400	10.1	1,179
Janitors and cleaners, except maids, housekeeping cleaners	2,348	2,665	317	13.5	741
Maids and housekeeping cleaners	1,633	1,716	83	5.1	438
Grounds maintenance workers	973	1,245	272	27.9	516
Landscaping and groundskeeping	894	1,154	260	29.0	484
Pesticide handlers, sprayers, and applicators, vegetation	27	30	4	13.6	10
Tree trimmers and pruners	52	61	8	16.3	22
Pest control workers	58	71	13	22.1	24
All other building, grounds cleaning, maintenance workers	159	190	31	19.6	63
Personal care and service occupations	**4,103**	**4,959**	**856**	**20.9**	**2,047**
First-line supervisors/managers of personal service workers	125	144	19	15.1	53
Animal care and service workers	145	176	31	21.2	61
Animal trainers	15	17	3	18.4	5
Nonfarm animal caretakers	131	159	28	21.6	56
Child care workers	1,193	1,319	127	10.6	531
Entertainment attendants and related workers	344	421	77	22.5	247
Motion picture projectionists	11	8	–3	–27.0	3
Ushers, lobby attendants, and ticket takers	112	124	12	11.0	102
Miscellaneous entertainment attendants and related workers	221	289	68	30.9	142
Amusement and recreation	197	260	64	32.4	130
Costume, locker room, and other attendants	24	28	5	19.1	13

(continued)

(continued from previous page)

	2000	2010	change, 2000–10 number	change, 2000–10 percent	net job openings 2000–10
Funeral service workers	33	38	5	13.8%	12
Embalmers	7	7	0	–0.6	2
Funeral attendants	26	31	5	17.8	11
Gaming occupations	167	211	44	26.5	98
First-line supervisors/managers, gaming workers	46	55	9	20.0	22
Gaming supervisors	31	37	6	18.4	15
Slot key persons	14	18	3	23.3	7
Gaming services workers	100	131	31	31.1	65
Gaming and sports book writers and runners	12	15	3	21.6	7
Gaming dealers	88	116	28	32.4	59
All other gaming service workers	21	25	4	18.7	11
Personal appearance workers	790	880	90	11.4	294
Barbers	73	64	–8	–11.5	21
Hairdressers, hairstylists, and cosmetologists	636	718	82	13.0	238
Miscellaneous personal appearance workers	81	97	16	19.8	36
Manicurists and pedicurists	40	51	11	26.5	21
Shampooers	20	22	3	13.2	7
Skin care specialists	21	24	3	13.3	8
Personal and home care aides	414	672	258	62.5	322
Recreation and fitness workers	427	545	118	27.6	206
Fitness trainers and aerobics instructors	158	222	64	40.3	97
Recreation workers	269	323	54	20.1	110
Residential advisors	44	55	11	24.0	21
Transportation, tourism, and lodging attendants	259	300	41	15.7	128
Baggage porters, bellhops, and concierges	68	78	9	13.4	33
Baggage porters and bellhops	51	57	6	12.6	24
Concierges	18	20	3	15.7	9
Tour and travel guides	44	48	4	9.5	18
Transportation attendants	147	174	27	18.6	78
Flight attendants	124	147	23	18.4	65
Transportation attendants, except flight attendants and baggage porters	23	27	5	20.0	12
All other personal care and service workers	163	198	35	21.7	72
SALES AND RELATED OCCUPATIONS	**15,513**	**17,365**	**1,852**	**11.9**	**6,712**
Advertising sales agents	**155**	**196**	**41**	**26.3**	**72**
Cashiers	**3,363**	**3,851**	**488**	**14.5**	**2,013**
Cashiers, except gaming	3,325	3,799	474	14.2	1,982
Gaming change persons and booth cashiers	38	52	14	36.1	31
Counter and rental clerks	**423**	**506**	**82**	**19.4**	**274**
Door-to-door sales workers, news and street vendors, and related workers	**166**	**156**	**–10**	**–6.2**	**42**
Insurance sales agents	**378**	**390**	**13**	**3.3**	**109**
Models, demonstrators, and product promoters	**121**	**152**	**30**	**24.9**	**70**
Demonstrators and product promoters	118	147	29	24.9	68
Models	4	5	1	26.0	2
Parts salespersons	**260**	**248**	**–12**	**–4.4**	**77**
Real estate brokers and sales agents	**432**	**473**	**41**	**9.5**	**116**
Real estate brokers	93	102	9	9.6	25
Real estate sales agents	339	371	32	9.5	91
Retail salespersons	**4,109**	**4,619**	**510**	**12.4**	**2,073**
Sales engineers	**85**	**100**	**15**	**17.7**	**37**
Sales representatives, wholesale and manufacturing	**1,821**	**1,932**	**111**	**6.1**	**606**
Sales representatives, wholesale and manufacturing, technical and scientific products	396	426	30	7.5	137

(continued)

(continued from previous page)

	2000	2010	change, 2000–10 number	change, 2000–10 percent	net job openings 2000–10
Sales representatives, wholesale and manufacturing, except technical and scientific products	1,425	1,507	82	5.7%	469
Securities, commodities, and financial services sales agents	**367**	**449**	**82**	**22.3**	**112**
Supervisors, sales workers	**2,504**	**2,697**	**193**	**7.7**	**556**
First-line supervisors/managers of retail sales workers	2,072	2,240	168	8.1	467
First-line supervisors/managers of non-retail sales workers	432	457	25	5.8	89
Telemarketers	**572**	**699**	**127**	**22.2**	**244**
Travel agents	**135**	**139**	**4**	**3.2**	**37**
All other sales and related workers	**621**	**758**	**137**	**22.0**	**273**
OFFICE, ADMIN. SUPPORT OCCUPATIONS	**23,882**	**26,053**	**2,171**	**9.1**	**7,667**
First-line supervisors/managers of office and administrative support workers	**1,392**	**1,522**	**130**	**9.4**	**399**
Communications equipment operators	**339**	**273**	**−65**	**−19.3**	**101**
Switchboard operators, including answering service	259	218	−41	−15.7	77
Telephone operators	54	35	−19	−35.3	16
All other communications equipment operators	26	20	−6	−21.8	9
Financial, information, and record clerks	**9,006**	**10,178**	**1,172**	**13.0**	**3,237**
Financial clerks	3,696	3,821	126	3.4	1,121
Bill and account collectors	400	502	101	25.3	201
Billing and posting clerks and machine operators	506	549	43	8.5	167
Bookkeeping, accounting, and auditing clerks	1,991	2,030	39	2.0	417
Gaming cage workers	22	27	6	25.2	15
Payroll and timekeeping clerks	201	206	5	2.3	63
Procurement clerks	76	67	−9	−12.2	17
Tellers	499	440	−59	−11.8	240
Information and record clerks	5,099	6,105	1,006	19.7	2,047
Brokerage clerks	70	69	−1	−1.4	9
Correspondence clerks	38	42	3	9.1	15
Court, municipal, and license clerks	105	117	13	12.0	29
Credit authorizers, checkers, and clerks	86	90	4	4.1	11
Customer service representatives	1,946	2,577	631	32.4	796
Eligibility interviewers, government programs	117	106	−11	−9.3	34
File clerks	288	314	26	9.1	118
Hotel, motel, and resort desk clerks	177	236	59	33.4	136
Human resources assistants, except payroll and timekeeping	177	211	34	19.3	74
Interviewers, except eligibility and loan	154	205	51	33.4	84
Library assistants, clerical	98	118	19	19.7	63
Loan interviewers and clerks	139	101	−38	−27.6	9
New accounts clerks	87	89	2	2.7	21
Order clerks	348	277	−71	−20.4	74
Receptionists and information clerks	1,078	1,334	256	23.7	493
Reservation and transportation ticket agents and travel clerks	191	219	28	14.5	79
All other financial, information, and record clerks	211	252	41	19.3	69
Material recording, scheduling, dispatching, and distributing occupations	**4,238**	**4,579**	**341**	**8.1**	**1,530**
Cargo and freight agents	60	65	5	8.3	17
Couriers and messengers	141	135	−5	−3.9	38
Dispatchers	254	304	50	19.6	92
Dispatchers, except police, fire, and ambulance	168	206	37	22.2	65
Police, fire, and ambulance dispatchers	86	98	12	14.5	27
Meter readers, utilities	49	36	−13	−26.0	12
Postal service workers	688	683	−5	−0.7	187
Postal service clerks	74	76	2	2.4	18
Postal service mail carriers	324	332	8	2.4	106
Postal service mail sorters, processors, and processing machine operators	289	275	−14	−4.9	63

(continued)

(continued from previous page)

	2000	2010	change, 2000–10 number	change, 2000–10 percent	net job openings 2000–10
Production, planning, and expediting clerks	332	391	60	17.9%	115
Shipping, receiving, and traffic clerks	890	973	83	9.3	262
Stock clerks and order fillers	1,679	1,821	142	8.5	740
Weighers, measurers, checkers, and samplers, recordkeeping	83	98	15	17.9	35
All other material recording, scheduling, dispatching, and distributing workers	63	73	10	15.5	32
Secretaries, administrative assistants, and other office support occupations	**8,908**	**9,500**	**592**	**6.6**	**2,400**
Computer operators	194	161	–33	–17.1	35
Data entry and information processing workers	806	774	–32	–3.9	165
Data entry keyers	509	534	25	4.9	106
Word processors and typists	297	240	–57	–19.1	60
Desktop publishers	38	63	25	66.7	32
Insurance claims and policy processing clerks	289	231	–58	–20.2	50
Mail clerks and mail machine operators, except postal service	188	207	19	9.9	74
Office clerks, general	2,705	3,135	430	15.9	949
Office machine operators, except computer	84	68	–16	–18.8	29
Proofreaders and copy markers	35	33	–2	–5.5	13
Secretaries and administrative assistants	3,902	4,167	265	6.8	946
Executive secretaries and administrative assistants	1,445	1,612	167	11.5	412
Legal secretaries	279	336	57	20.3	104
Medical secretaries	314	373	60	19.0	113
Secretaries, except legal, medical, and executive	1,864	1,846	–18	–1.0	317
Statistical assistants	21	22	0	2.1	2
All other secretaries, administrative assistants, and other office support workers	**645**	**639**	**–6**	**–0.9**	**104**
FARMING, FISHING, FORESTRY OCCUPATIONS	**1,429**	**1,480**	**51**	**3.6**	**485**
First-line supervisors/managers/contractors of farming, fishing, and forestry	**100**	**113**	**13**	**13.0**	**21**
Agricultural workers	**987**	**1,024**	**37**	**3.7**	**359**
Agricultural inspectors	15	16	1	6.6	5
Farmworkers	909	939	30	3.3	334
Graders and sorters, agricultural products	63	69	6	9.1	20
Fishers and fishing vessel operators	**53**	**46**	**–6**	**–12.2**	**17**
Forest, conservation, and logging workers	**90**	**88**	**–2**	**–1.8**	**19**
Forest and conservation workers	21	22	1	3.9	6
Logging workers	69	66	–2	–3.5	13
Fallers	13	12	–1	–8.7	3
Logging equipment operators	47	46	–1	–2.0	9
Log graders and scalers	8	8	0	–4.0	2
All other farming, fishing, and forestry workers	**199**	**209**	**10**	**4.9**	**70**
CONSTRUCTION AND EXTRACTION OCCUPATIONS	**7,451**	**8,439**	**989**	**13.3**	**2,469**
First-line supervisors/managers of construction trades and extraction workers	**792**	**923**	**131**	**16.5**	**311**
Construction trades and related workers	**6,466**	**7,328**	**862**	**13.3**	**2,086**
Boilermakers	27	28	1	2.1	8
Brickmasons, blockmasons, and stonemasons	158	179	21	13.2	50
Brickmasons and blockmasons	144	162	18	12.5	45
Stonemasons	14	17	3	20.8	5
Carpenters	1,204	1,302	98	8.2	302
Carpet, floor, and tile installers and finishers	167	189	22	13.2	50
Carpet installers	76	84	8	10.5	21
Floor layers, except carpet, wood, and hard tiles	23	27	4	15.8	8
Floor sanders and finishers	14	16	2	14.7	4
Tile and marble setters	54	62	8	15.6	17

(continued)

	2000	2010	change, 2000–10 number	change, 2000–10 percent	net job openings 2000–10
Cement masons, concrete finishers, and terrazzo workers	166	171	5	3.0%	19
Cement masons and concrete finishers	162	167	5	3.0	19
Terrazzo workers and finishers	3	4	0	2.0	–
Construction laborers	791	926	135	17.0	207
Construction equipment operators	416	450	34	8.1	123
Operating engineers, other construction equipment operators	357	382	25	6.9	103
Paving, surfacing, and tamping equipment operators	55	63	8	15.5	19
Pile-driver operators	4	5	1	14.0	1
Drywall installers, ceiling tile installers, and tapers	188	205	17	9.1	35
Drywall and ceiling tile installers	143	157	13	9.4	27
Tapers	44	48	4	8.3	8
Electricians	698	819	120	17.3	251
Glaziers	49	56	7	14.8	16
Insulation workers	53	60	7	13.6	23
Painters, construction and maintenance	491	585	94	19.1	180
Paperhangers	27	32	5	20.2	10
Pipelayers, plumbers, pipefitters, and steamfitters	568	627	59	10.4	153
Pipelayers	65	73	8	11.9	19
Plumbers, pipefitters, and steamfitters	503	554	51	10.2	134
Plasterers and stucco masons	54	61	6	11.9	16
Reinforcing iron and rebar workers	27	32	5	17.5	8
Roofers	158	188	31	19.4	67
Sheet metal workers	224	275	51	23.0	98
Structural iron and steel workers	84	99	15	18.4	24
Helpers, construction trades	450	510	60	13.3	283
Helpers for brickmasons, blockmasons, stonemasons, and tile and marble setters	58	66	8	14.1	37
Helpers for carpenters	101	108	7	6.6	57
Helpers for electricians	114	129	15	13.3	72
Helpers for painters, paperhangers, plasterers, stucco masons	27	30	3	12.9	17
Helpers for pipelayers, plumbers, pipefitters, and steamfitters	86	96	10	11.5	53
Helpers for roofers	23	28	5	19.3	16
All other helpers, construction trades	41	53	12	29.1	32
Other construction and related workers	465	534	69	14.8	162
Construction and building inspectors	75	86	11	15.0	28
Elevator installers and repairers	23	27	4	17.2	11
Fence erectors	29	30	1	4.6	6
Hazardous materials removal workers	37	49	12	32.8	23
Highway maintenance workers	151	159	8	5.2	31
Rail-track laying and maintenance equipment operators	12	9	–3	–26.1	3
Septic tank servicers and sewer pipe cleaners	15	18	3	16.5	6
All other construction and related workers	123	156	33	26.7	54
Extraction workers	**193**	**189**	**–4**	**–2.1**	**72**
Derrick, rotary drill, and service unit operators, oil, gas, mining	45	44	–2	–3.5	16
Derrick operators, oil and gas	16	16	0	0.1	6
Rotary drill operators, oil and gas	18	17	–1	–8.0	6
Service unit operators, oil, gas, and mining	11	11	0	–1.2	4
Earth drillers, except oil and gas	24	27	3	12.6	8
Explosives workers, ordnance handling experts, and blasters	5	5	0	1.9	2
Helpers for extraction workers	37	38	1	2.4	18
Mining machine operators	22	19	–3	–12.9	8
Continuous mining machine operators	10	8	–1	–13.4	3
Miscellaneous mining machine operators	12	11	–2	–12.5	4
Roustabouts, oil and gas	41	40	–2	–4.2	14
All other extraction workers	19	17	–2	–10.7	7

(continued)

(continued from previous page)

	2000	2010	change, 2000–10 number	change, 2000–10 percent	net job openings 2000–10
INSTALLATION, MAINTENANCE, AND REPAIR OCCUPATIONS	**5,820**	**6,482**	**662**	**11.4%**	**1,944**
First-line supervisors/managers of mechanics, installers, and repairers	**442**	**513**	**71**	**16.0**	**186**
Electrical and electronic equipment mechanics, installers, and repairers	**683**	**726**	**43**	**6.3**	**178**
Avionics technicians	16	17	2	9.8	5
Computer, automated teller, and office machine repairers	172	197	24	14.2	43
Electric motor, power tool, and related repairers	37	40	3	7.9	11
Electrical, electronics installers and repairers, transportation equip.	14	15	2	13.6	4
Electrical, electronics repairers, industrial and utility	108	116	8	7.3	30
Electrical, electronics repairers, commercial, industrial equipment	90	98	8	9.2	26
Electrical, electronics repairers, powerhouse, substation, relay	18	18	0	–2.3	4
Electronic equipment installers and repairers, motor vehicles	13	15	2	15.6	5
Electronic home entertainment equipment installers and repairers	37	30	–7	–17.9	7
Radio and telecommunications equipment installers and repairers	196	188	–7	–3.8	37
Radio mechanics	7	5	–2	–24.2	1
Telecommunications equipment installers and repairers, except line installers	189	183	–6	–3.1	36
Security and fire alarm systems installers	44	54	10	23.4	18
All other electrical, electronic equip. mechanics, installers, repairers	48	54	6	13.4	17
Vehicle and mobile equipment mechanics, installers, and repairers	**1,931**	**2,218**	**286**	**14.8**	**778**
Aircraft mechanics and service technicians	158	184	26	16.7	60
Automotive body and related repairers	199	219	20	10.2	69
Automotive glass installers and repairers	22	24	2	10.5	8
Automotive service technicians and mechanics	840	991	151	18.0	349
Bus and truck mechanics and diesel engine specialists	285	326	40	14.2	114
Heavy vehicle, mobile equip. service technicians, mechanics	185	203	17	9.4	66
Farm equipment mechanics	41	42	0	0.9	11
Mobile heavy equipment mechanics, except engines	130	148	18	14.0	52
Rail car repairers	14	13	–1	–7.6	4
Small engine mechanics	73	79	6	8.6	24
Motorboat mechanics	25	27	2	9.0	9
Motorcycle mechanics	14	16	1	8.6	5
Outdoor power equipment, other small engine mechanics	33	36	3	8.2	11
Miscellaneous vehicle and mobile equipment mechanics, installers, and repairers	170	192	22	13.2	87
Bicycle repairers	9	10	2	17.7	5
Recreational vehicle service technicians	12	15	3	25.4	8
Tire repairers and changers	89	95	6	6.8	40
All other vehicle and mobile equipment mechanics, installers, and repairers	60	72	12	19.6	35
Other installation, maintenance, and repair occupations	**2,764**	**3,026**	**262**	**9.5**	**802**
Coin, vending, and amusement machine servicers and repairers	37	44	7	18.5	15
Control and valve installers and repairers	46	48	2	5.2	17
Control and valve installers, repairers, except mechanical door	34	35	1	2.7	12
Mechanical door repairers	11	13	1	12.7	5
Heating, air conditioning, refrigeration mechanics and installers	243	297	54	22.3	79
Helpers for installation, maintenance, and repair workers	145	172	27	18.5	101
Home appliance repairers	43	46	3	6.2	11
Industrial machinery mechanics	198	205	7	3.4	60
Line installers and repairers	263	317	54	20.7	118
Electrical powerline installers and repairers	99	108	9	9.3	41
Telecommunications line installers and repairers	164	209	45	27.6	76

(continued)

(continued from previous page)

	2000	2010	change, 2000–10 number	change, 2000–10 percent	net job openings 2000–10
Locksmiths and safe repairers	23	25	2	8.7%	10
Maintenance and repair workers, general	1,251	1,310	59	4.7	221
Maintenance workers, machinery	114	120	7	5.8	37
Manufactured building and mobile home installers	17	20	3	19.1	7
Millwrights	72	75	3	3.9	25
Precision instrument and equipment repairers	63	69	6	9.7	22
Camera and photographic equipment repairers	7	7	0	−2.1	2
Medical equipment repairers	28	33	4	14.9	11
Musical instrument repairers and tuners	7	8	1	9.4	2
Watch repairers	5	6	0	6.2	2
All other precision instrument and equipment repairers	15	16	1	6.8	5
Riggers	20	22	2	10.1	6
All other installation, maintenance, and repair workers	228	254	26	11.5	73
PRODUCTION OCCUPATIONS	**13,060**	**13,811**	**750**	**5.7**	**3,932**
First-line supervisors/managers of production and operating workers	**819**	**827**	**9**	**1.0**	**224**
Assemblers and fabricators	**2,653**	**2,824**	**171**	**6.5**	**702**
Aircraft structure, surfaces, rigging, and systems assemblers	20	23	3	14.2	8
Electrical, electronics, and electromechanical assemblers	508	492	−16	−3.1	138
Coil winders, tapers, and finishers	56	61	5	8.2	19
Electrical and electronic equipment assemblers	379	355	−24	−6.3	97
Electromechanical equipment assemblers	73	76	3	4.5	22
Engine and other machine assemblers	67	72	5	7.1	18
Structural metal fabricators and fitters	101	120	20	19.5	35
Miscellaneous assemblers and fabricators	1,957	2,117	160	8.2	503
Fiberglass laminators and fabricators	48	53	5	11.4	14
Team assemblers	1,458	1,545	87	5.9	342
Timing device assemblers, adjusters, and calibrators	12	12	0	2.5	2
All other assemblers and fabricators	439	507	68	15.4	144
Food processing occupations	**760**	**783**	**23**	**3.0**	**214**
Bakers	160	187	27	16.8	52
Butchers and other meat, poultry, and fish processing workers	411	415	5	1.2	117
Butchers and meat cutters	141	128	−13	−8.9	34
Meat, poultry, and fish cutters and trimmers	148	162	14	9.5	50
Slaughterers and meat packers	122	125	3	2.6	33
Food, tobacco roasting, baking, drying machine operators, tenders	18	17	−2	−9.0	4
Food batchmakers	66	67	1	1.4	17
Food cooking machine operators and tenders	37	37	0	0.6	7
All other food processing workers	69	61	−8	−11.6	17
Metal workers and plastic workers	**2,907**	**3,156**	**249**	**8.6**	**994**
Computer control programmers and operators	186	222	36	19.3	102
Computer-controlled machine tool operators, metal, plastic	162	194	32	19.7	89
Numerical tool and process control programmers	24	28	4	16.6	12
Cutting, punching, and press machine setters, operators, and tenders, metal and plastic	372	357	−15	−4.0	73
Drilling and boring machine tool setters, operators, and tenders, metal and plastic	71	68	−3	−4.5	23
Extruding and drawing machine setters, operators, and tenders, metal and plastic	126	143	17	13.5	45
Forging machine setters, operators, and tenders, metal, plastic	54	59	5	9.1	22
Grinding, lapping, polishing, and buffing machine tool setters, operators, and tenders, metal and plastic	145	156	11	7.3	46
Heat treating equipment setters, operators, and tenders, metal and plastic	43	49	6	13.4	14

(continued)

(continued from previous page)

	2000	2010	change, 2000–10		net job openings 2000–10
			number	percent	
Lathe and turning machine tool setters, operators, and tenders, metal and plastic	84	78	–6	–7.4%	33
Layout workers, metal and plastic	18	17	–1	–6.0	5
Machinists	430	469	39	9.1	127
Metal furnace and kiln operators and tenders	40	43	3	7.2	14
Metal-refining furnace operators and tenders	24	26	2	7.4	8
Pourers and casters, metal	16	18	1	6.9	6
Milling and planing machine setters, operators, and tenders, metal and plastic	34	32	–2	–6.7	11
Model makers and patternmakers, metal and plastic	19	18	–1	–5.6	5
Model makers, metal and plastic	11	10	0	–3.2	3
Patternmakers, metal and plastic	9	8	–1	–8.4	2
Molders and molding machine setters, operators, and tenders, metal and plastic	235	252	17	7.0	65
Foundry mold and coremakers	59	59	–1	–1.2	12
Molding, coremaking, and casting machine setters, operators, and tenders, metal and plastic	176	193	17	9.8	53
Multiple machine tool setters, operators, tenders, metal, plastic	105	121	15	14.7	32
Plating and coating machine setters, operators, and tenders, metal and plastic	65	72	7	10.2	20
Rolling machine setters, operators, tenders, metal and plastic	49	50	1	1.4	17
Tool and die makers	130	132	3	2.2	35
Tool grinders, filers, and sharpeners	29	27	–2	–7.7	8
Welding, soldering, and brazing workers	521	618	97	18.7	244
Welders, cutters, solderers, and brazers	446	532	86	19.3	211
Welding, soldering, brazing machine setters, operators, tenders	74	86	11	15.1	32
All other metal workers and plastic workers	150	174	25	16.4	54
Plant and system operators	**368**	**384**	**16**	**4.4**	**133**
Power plant operators, distributors, and dispatchers	55	55	0	–0.4	17
Nuclear power reactor operators	4	4	0	–3.4	1
Power distributors and dispatchers	15	14	–1	–5.1	4
Power plant operators	36	37	1	1.8	11
Stationary engineers and boiler operators	57	56	–1	–1.3	16
Water and liquid waste treatment plant and system operators	88	104	16	18.1	44
Miscellaneous plant and system operators	167	168	1	0.6	56
Chemical plant and system operators	71	69	–2	–3.3	22
Gas plant operators	12	11	–1	–6.3	4
Petroleum pump system operators, refinery operators, gaugers	35	34	–1	–4.1	11
All other plant and system operators	49	54	6	11.4	20
Printing occupations	**534**	**543**	**8**	**1.6**	**160**
Bookbinders and bindery workers	115	124	9	7.4	39
Bindery workers	105	113	8	7.3	36
Bookbinders	10	10	1	8.2	3
Job printers	56	59	4	6.4	18
Prepress technicians and workers	107	90	–17	–15.6	26
Printing machine operators	222	234	12	5.5	68
All other printing workers	34	35	1	2.0	9
Textile, apparel, and furnishings occupations	**1,317**	**1,285**	**–32**	**–2.4**	**301**
Extruding and forming machine setters, operators, and tenders, synthetic and glass fibers	41	44	2	5.7	13
Fabric and apparel patternmakers	15	14	–1	–5.4	5
Laundry and dry-cleaning workers	236	263	27	11.4	89
Pressers, textile, garment, and related materials	110	112	2	1.7	17
Sewing machine operators	399	348	–51	–12.9	42
Shoe and leather workers and repairers	19	15	–4	–21.4	7

(continued)

	2000	2010	change, 2000–10 number	change, 2000–10 percent	net job openings 2000–10
Shoe machine operators and tenders	9	4	–5	–53.6%	1
Tailors, dressmakers, and sewers	101	91	–9	–9.3	22
Sewers, hand	43	40	–3	–6.6	9
Tailors, dressmakers, and custom sewers	58	51	–7	–11.4	13
Textile bleaching, dyeing machine operators and tenders	37	41	4	10.8	11
Textile cutting machine setters, operators, and tenders	38	35	–2	–6.5	6
Textile knitting, weaving machine setters, operators, tenders	70	68	–2	–2.4	11
Textile winding, twisting, and drawing-out machine setters, operators, and tenders	90	86	–4	–4.4	19
Upholsterers	58	53	–6	–9.5	19
All other textile, apparel, and furnishings workers	95	112	17	18.0	36
Woodworkers	**409**	**446**	**37**	**9.0**	**187**
Cabinetmakers and bench carpenters	159	175	16	9.8	66
Furniture finishers	45	49	4	8.4	22
Model makers and patternmakers, wood	10	12	2	16.0	6
Sawing machine setters, operators, and tenders, wood	57	64	7	11.7	29
Woodworking machine setters, operators, tenders, except sawing	103	108	5	5.3	47
All other woodworkers	35	38	4	10.6	18
Other production occupations	**3,293**	**3,563**	**269**	**8.2**	**1,017**
Cementing and gluing machine operators and tenders	36	38	2	6.7	11
Chemical processing machine setters, operators, and tenders	100	110	10	9.9	33
Chemical equipment operators and tenders	61	70	9	14.9	23
Separating, filtering, clarifying, precipitating, and still machine setters, operators, and tenders	39	40	1	2.2	10
Cleaning, washing, metal pickling equipment operators and tenders	20	17	–3	–14.2	5
Cooling and freezing equipment operators and tenders	7	7	0	–1.3	1
Crushing, grinding, polishing, mixing, and blending workers	202	222	21	10.3	65
Crushing, grinding, polishing machine setters, operators, tenders	44	49	4	9.8	14
Grinding and polishing workers, hand	49	55	7	13.7	17
Mixing and blending machine setters, operators, and tenders	109	118	10	9.0	33
Cutting workers	115	117	2	1.8	23
Cutters and trimmers, hand	32	33	1	2.2	6
Cutting and slicing machine setters, operators, and tenders	83	84	1	1.7	16
Etchers and engravers	15	16	2	11.1	5
Extruding, forming, pressing, and compacting machine setters, operators, and tenders	73	80	7	9.0	24
Furnace, kiln, oven, drier, and kettle operators and tenders	33	34	1	3.2	10
Helpers for production workers	525	587	62	11.9	194
Inspectors, testers, sorters, samplers, and weighers	602	591	–11	–1.9	133
Jewelers and precious stone and metal workers	43	44	1	1.3	12
Medical, dental, and ophthalmic laboratory workers	88	95	7	7.9	31
Dental laboratory technicians	43	46	3	6.3	14
Medical appliance technicians	13	15	2	19.0	6
Ophthalmic laboratory technicians	32	34	2	5.7	11
Molders, shapers, and casters, except metal and plastic	42	45	3	7.4	14
Packaging and filling machine operators and tenders	379	433	54	14.4	138
Painting workers	195	223	28	14.5	72
Coating, painting, spraying machine setters, operators, tenders	108	121	13	11.9	37
Painters, transportation equipment	49	57	9	17.5	19
Painting, coating, and decorating workers	38	45	7	17.9	15
Paper goods machine setters, operators, and tenders	123	116	–7	–5.4	24
Photographic process workers and processing machine operators	76	77	2	2.2	23
Photographic process workers	26	24	–2	–8.2	7
Photographic processing machine operators	50	53	4	7.6	17
Semiconductor processors	52	69	17	32.4	26

(continued)

(continued from previous page)

	2000	2010	change, 2000–10 number	change, 2000–10 percent	net job openings 2000–10
Tire builders	18	20	2	8.6%	5
All other production workers	549	619	70	12.7	168
TRANSPORTATION AND MATERIAL MOVING OCCUPATIONS	**10,088**	**11,618**	**1,530**	**15.2**	**3,949**
Supervisors, transportation and material moving workers	**357**	**427**	**70**	**19.7**	**147**
Aircraft cargo handling supervisors	10	13	3	27.7	5
First-line supervisors/managers of helpers, laborers, and material movers, hand	153	182	29	18.9	62
First-line supervisors/managers of transportation and material-moving machine and vehicle operators	194	233	39	19.9	80
Air transportation occupations	**166**	**186**	**20**	**12.2**	**68**
Aircraft pilots and flight engineers	117	129	11	9.8	38
Airline pilots, copilots, and flight engineers	98	104	6	6.4	29
Commercial pilots	19	24	5	26.9	10
Air traffic controllers and airfield operations specialists	31	35	3	10.2	17
Air traffic controllers	27	29	2	7.2	13
Airfield operations specialists	5	6	1	27.1	3
All other air transportation workers	17	22	5	32.2	13
Motor vehicle operators	**4,237**	**4,982**	**745**	**17.6**	**1,398**
Ambulance drivers and attendants, except emergency medical technicians	15	20	5	33.7	6
Bus drivers	666	754	88	13.2	257
Bus drivers, school	481	537	56	11.6	178
Bus drivers, transit and intercity	185	217	32	17.4	79
Driver/sales workers and truck drivers	3,268	3,857	589	18.0	1,038
Driver/sales workers	402	430	29	7.1	84
Truck drivers, heavy and tractor-trailer	1,749	2,095	346	19.8	586
Truck drivers, light or delivery services	1,117	1,331	215	19.2	368
Taxi drivers and chauffeurs	176	219	43	24.4	57
All other motor vehicle operators	112	132	20	18.2	39
Rail transportation occupations	**115**	**94**	**–21**	**–18.5**	**52**
Locomotive engineers and firers	37	38	1	2.3	18
Railroad brake, signal, and switch operators	22	9	–13	–60.8	10
Railroad conductors and yardmasters	45	36	–8	–18.9	20
Rail yard engineers, dinkey operators, and hostlers	4	4	0	–4.5	2
All other rail transportation workers	7	7	0	–4.1	3
Water transportation occupations	**70**	**74**	**3**	**4.4**	**27**
Sailors and marine oilers	32	33	2	4.9	12
Ship and boat captains and operators	25	26	1	3.4	9
Ship engineers	9	9	0	5.8	3
All other water transportation workers	5	5	0	4.2	2
Related transportation occupations	**309**	**341**	**32**	**10.4**	**139**
Bridge and lock tenders	4	4	–1	–19.1	2
Parking lot attendants	117	140	23	19.8	43
Service station attendants	112	110	–2	–1.7	57
Traffic technicians	4	5	1	14.1	2
Transportation inspectors	25	28	3	11.3	9
All other related transportation workers	46	54	8	17.9	26
Material-moving occupations	**4,833**	**5,514**	**681**	**14.1**	**2,118**
Cleaners of vehicles and equipment	322	382	60	18.8	183
Conveyor operators and tenders	63	71	8	13.3	26
Crane and tower operators	55	59	5	8.6	21
Excavating and loading machine and dragline operators	76	88	11	14.8	34
Hoist and winch operators	9	10	1	8.3	3
Industrial truck and tractor operators	635	707	72	11.3	160

(continued)

(continued from previous page)

	2000	2010	change, 2000–10 number	change, 2000–10 percent	net job openings 2000–10
Laborers and freight, stock, and material movers, hand	2,084	2,373	289	13.9%	985
Machine feeders and offbearers	182	159	–22	–12.3	63
Packers and packagers, hand	1,091	1,300	210	19.3	488
Pumping station operators	32	32	0	0.0	10
Gas compressor and gas pumping station operators	7	7	0	4.8	2
Pump operators, except wellhead pumpers	14	15	1	4.8	5
Wellhead pumpers	12	11	–1	–8.5	3
Refuse and recyclable material collectors	124	145	21	16.6	75
Tank car, truck, and ship loaders	19	21	3	13.5	8
All other material moving workers	142	165	23	16.4	62

Note: Net job openings include new positions as well as replacements due to retirement, etc. Employment estimates for 2000 and projections for 2010 are rounded to the nearest thousand. Numerical and percent change calculations are based on unrounded figures.

Source: Bureau of Labor Statistcs, Internet site http://www.bls.gov/emp/emptab21.htm

Most Married Couples Are Dual Earners

As women have entered the workforce over the past few decades, the dual-earner couple has become the norm. The 56 percent majority of married couples were dual earners in 2000, up from just under 50 percent in 1986. The 21 percent minority of couples are traditional, meaning only the husband is in the labor force. In 1986, a larger 29 percent were traditional.

Among couples with children under age 18, an even larger share are dual earners—68 percent in 2000. The proportion stands at 61 percent among couples with children under age 6. Since 1986, the proportion of couples with preschoolers in which only the husband is employed fell from 44 to 36 percent.

The majority of married women with children under age 18 are in the labor force—no matter how young their child. Among wives with children under age 3, the 59 percent majority were in the labor force in 2000, up from just 33 percent in 1975.

Most wives with young children work

(percent of married women with children under age 3 who are in the labor force, 1975 and 2000)

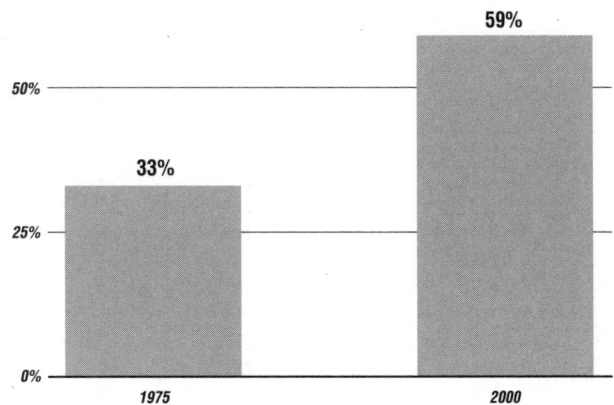

Table 6.27 Married Couples by Labor Force Status of Husband and Wife, 1986 to 2000: Total Couples

(number and percent distribution of married couples by labor force status of husband and wife, 1986 to 2000; percent and percentage point change for selected years; numbers in thousands)

	total couples	in labor force husband and wife	in labor force husband only	wife only	husband and wife not in labor force
2000	55,311	31,095	11,815	3,301	9,098
1999	54,770	30,635	11,704	3,185	9,245
1998	54,317	30,591	11,582	3,087	9,057
1997	53,604	30,466	11,369	2,891	8,878
1996	53,567	29,952	11,684	2,835	9,096
1995	53,858	29,999	11,777	3,043	9,039
1994	53,171	29,279	11,665	3,069	9,158
1993	53,171	28,898	12,268	2,804	9,200
1992	52,457	28,592	12,283	2,620	8,963
1991	52,147	28,167	12,680	2,454	8,845
1990	52,317	28,056	13,013	2,453	8,794
1989	52,100	27,731	13,292	2,348	8,729
1988	51,809	27,016	13,737	2,358	8,698
1987	51,537	26,466	14,144	2,317	8,611
1986	50,933	25,428	14,675	2,362	8,468
Percent change					
1990 to 2000	5.7%	10.8%	−9.2%	34.6%	3.5%
1986 to 2000	8.6	22.3	−19.5	39.8	7.4
Percent distribution					
2000	100.0%	56.2%	21.4%	6.0%	16.4%
1999	100.0	55.9	21.4	5.8	16.9
1998	100.0	56.3	21.3	5.7	16.7
1997	100.0	56.8	21.2	5.4	16.6
1996	100.0	55.9	21.8	5.3	17.0
1995	100.0	55.7	21.9	5.7	16.8
1994	100.0	55.1	21.9	5.8	17.2
1993	100.0	54.3	23.1	5.3	17.3
1992	100.0	54.5	23.4	5.0	17.1
1991	100.0	54.0	24.3	4.7	17.0
1990	100.0	53.6	24.9	4.7	16.8
1989	100.0	53.2	25.5	4.5	16.8
1988	100.0	52.1	26.5	4.6	16.8
1987	100.0	51.4	27.4	4.5	16.7
1986	100.0	49.9	28.8	4.6	16.6
Percentage point change					
1990 to 2000	–	2.6	−3.5	1.3	−0.4
1986 to 2000	–	6.3	−7.5	1.3	−0.2

Note: (–) means not applicable.
Source: Bureau of the Census, Current Population Surveys, Internet site http://www.census.gov/population/socdemo/hh-fam/ tabMC-1.txt; calculations by New Strategist

Table 6.28   Married Couples by Labor Force Status of Husband and Wife, 1986 to 2000: Couples with Children under Age 18

(number and percent distribution of married couples with children under age 18 at home by labor force status of husband and wife, 1986 to 2000; percent and percentage point change for selected years; numbers in thousands)

	total couples	in labor force			husband and wife not in labor force
		husband and wife	husband only	wife only	
2000	25,248	17,116	6,950	795	387
1999	25,066	16,887	6,998	765	418
1998	25,269	17,168	6,856	753	491
1997	25,083	17,160	6,713	732	478
1996	24,920	16,769	6,883	739	528
1995	25,241	17,024	6,863	756	598
1994	25,058	16,635	7,029	754	641
1993	24,707	16,064	7,431	680	532
1992	24,420	16,054	7,228	580	557
1991	24,397	15,778	7,542	581	495
1990	24,537	15,768	7,667	558	544
1989	24,735	15,757	7,929	488	560
1988	24,600	15,489	8,031	541	539
1987	24,645	15,238	8,345	528	534
1986	24,630	14,606	8,916	518	590
Percent change					
1990 to 2000	2.9%	8.5%	–9.4%	42.5%	–28.9%
1986 to 2000	2.5	17.2	–22.1	53.5	–34.4
Percent distribution					
2000	100.0%	67.8%	27.5%	3.1%	1.5%
1999	100.0	67.4	27.9	3.1	1.7
1998	100.0	67.9	27.1	3.0	1.9
1997	100.0	68.4	26.8	2.9	1.9
1996	100.0	67.3	27.6	3.0	2.1
1995	100.0	67.4	27.2	3.0	2.4
1994	100.0	66.4	28.1	3.0	2.6
1993	100.0	65.0	30.1	2.8	2.2
1992	100.0	65.7	29.6	2.4	2.3
1991	100.0	64.7	30.9	2.4	2.0
1990	100.0	64.3	31.2	2.3	2.2
1989	100.0	63.7	32.1	2.0	2.3
1988	100.0	63.0	32.6	2.2	2.2
1987	100.0	61.8	33.9	2.1	2.2
1986	100.0	59.3	36.2	2.1	2.4
Percentage point change					
1990 to 2000	–	3.5	–3.7	0.9	–0.7
1986 to 2000	–	8.5	–8.7	1.0	–0.9

Note: (–) means not applicable.
Source: Bureau of the Census, Current Population Surveys, Internet site http://www.census.gov/population/socdemo/hh-fam/ tabMC-1.txt; calculations by New Strategist

Table 6.29 Married Couples by Labor Force Status of Husband and Wife, 1986 to 2000: Couples with Children under Age 6

(number and percent distribution of married couples with children under age 6 at home by labor force status of husband and wife, 1986 to 2000; percent and percentage point change for selected years; numbers in thousands)

| | total couples | in labor force | | | husband and wife not in labor force |
		husband and wife	husband only	wife only	
2000	11,393	6,984	4,077	211	121
1999	11,461	6,878	4,182	257	144
1998	11,773	7,310	4,079	223	161
1997	11,584	7,142	4,022	260	162
1996	11,782	7,189	4,159	229	205
1995	11,951	7,406	4,059	233	253
1994	12,118	7,283	4,328	250	255
1993	11,942	6,934	4,535	231	241
1992	11,925	6,972	4,482	217	254
1991	12,100	7,061	4,593	223	222
1990	12,051	6,932	4,692	192	235
1989	12,011	6,772	4,867	148	224
1988	11,915	6,651	4,875	182	206
1987	11,966	6,618	4,947	199	202
1986	11,924	6,271	5,284	155	215
Percent change					
1990 to 2000	−5.5%	0.8%	−13.1%	9.9%	−48.5%
1986 to 2000	−4.5	11.4	−22.8	36.1	−43.7
Percent distribution					
2000	100.0%	61.3%	35.8%	1.9%	1.1%
1999	100.0	60.0	36.5	2.2	1.3
1998	100.0	62.1	34.6	1.9	1.4
1997	100.0	61.7	34.7	2.2	1.4
1996	100.0	61.0	35.3	1.9	1.7
1995	100.0	62.0	34.0	1.9	2.1
1994	100.0	60.1	35.7	2.1	2.1
1993	100.0	58.1	38.0	1.9	2.0
1992	100.0	58.5	37.6	1.8	2.1
1991	100.0	58.4	38.0	1.8	1.8
1990	100.0	57.5	38.9	1.6	2.0
1989	100.0	56.4	40.5	1.2	1.9
1988	100.0	55.8	40.9	1.5	1.7
1987	100.0	55.3	41.3	1.7	1.7
1986	100.0	52.6	44.3	1.3	1.8
Percentage point change					
1990 to 2000	–	3.8	−3.1	0.3	−0.9
1986 to 2000	–	8.7	−8.5	0.6	−0.7

Note: (−) means not applicable.
Source: Bureau of the Census, Current Population Surveys, Internet site http://www.census.gov/population/socdemo/hh-fam/ tabMC-1.txt; calculations by New Strategist

Table 6.30 Labor Force Participation of Wives by Age of Children at Home, 1960 to 2000

(labor force participation rate of wives aged 16 or older by presence and age of own children under age 18 at home, 1960 to 2000; percentage point change, 1960–00; numbers in thousands)

	total	no children < age 18	with children under age 18			
			total	6 to 17	under age 6	under age 3
2000	62.0%	54.7%	70.6%	77.2%	62.8%	59.0%
1999	61.6	54.4	70.1	77.1	61.8	59.2
1998	61.8	54.1	70.6	76.8	63.7	61.4
1997	62.1	54.2	71.1	77.6	63.6	61.3
1996	61.1	53.4	70.0	76.7	62.7	60.5
1995	61.1	53.2	70.2	76.2	63.5	60.9
1994	60.6	53.2	69.0	76.0	61.7	59.7
1993	59.4	52.4	67.5	74.9	59.6	57.3
1992	59.3	51.9	67.8	75.4	59.9	57.5
1991	58.5	51.2	66.8	73.6	59.9	56.8
1990	58.2	51.1	66.3	73.6	58.9	55.5
1989	57.6	50.5	65.6	73.4	57.4	55.2
1988	56.5	48.9	65.0	72.5	57.1	54.5
1987	55.8	48.4	63.8	70.6	56.8	54.2
1986	54.6	48.2	61.3	68.4	53.8	50.9
1985	54.2	48.2	60.8	67.8	53.4	50.5
1984	52.8	47.2	58.8	65.4	51.8	48.2
1983	51.8	46.6	57.2	63.8	49.9	46.0
1982	51.2	46.2	56.3	63.2	48.7	45.3
1981	51.0	46.3	55.7	62.5	47.8	43.7
1980	50.1	46.0	54.1	61.7	45.1	41.3
1979	49.3	46.6	51.9	59.0	43.3	39.6
1978	47.5	44.6	50.2	57.1	41.7	37.9
1977	46.6	44.8	48.2	55.5	39.4	34.7
1976	45.1	43.7	46.1	53.6	37.5	32.7
1975	44.4	43.8	44.9	52.2	36.7	32.7
1974	43.1	43.0	43.1	51.2	34.4	–
1973	42.2	42.8	41.7	50.1	32.7	–
1972	41.5	42.7	40.5	50.2	30.1	–
1971	40.8	42.1	39.7	49.4	29.6	–
1970	40.8	42.2	39.7	49.2	30.3	–
1969	39.6	41.0	38.6	48.6	28.5	–
1968	38.3	40.1	36.9	46.9	27.6	–
1967	36.8	38.9	35.3	45.0	26.5	–
1966	35.4	38.4	33.2	43.7	24.2	–
1965	34.7	38.3	32.2	42.7	23.3	–
1964	34.4	37.8	32.0	43.0	22.7	–
1963	33.7	37.4	31.2	41.5	22.5	–
1962	32.7	36.1	30.3	41.8	21.3	–
1961	32.7	37.3	29.6	41.7	20.0	–
1960	30.5	34.7	27.6	39.0	18.6	–
Percentage point change						
1990 to 2000	3.8	3.6	4.3	3.6	3.9	3.5
1960 to 2000	31.5	20.0	43.0	38.2	44.2	–

Note: (–) means data not available.
Source: Bureau of Labor Statistics, Handbook of Labor Statistics, *Bulletin 2340, 1989; and Bureau of the Census,* Statistical Abstracts of the United States, 1993 through 2001; *calculations by New Strategist*

Table 6.31 Child Care Arrangements of Working Mothers, 1977 to 1995

(percent distribution of children under age 5 with working mothers by child care arrangement, 1977 to 1995; percentage point change, 1977–95)

	1995	1993	1991	1990	1988	1985	1977	percentage point change 1977–95
Parents	**22.0%**	**22.1%**	**28.7%**	**22.9%**	**22.7%**	**23.8%**	**25.8%**	**–3.8**
Mother while working	5.4	6.2	8.7	6.4	7.6	8.1	11.4	–6.0
Father	16.6	15.9	20.0	16.5	15.1	15.7	14.4	2.2
Relatives	**21.4**	**26.0**	**23.5**	**23.1**	**21.1**	**24.1**	**30.9**	**–9.5**
Grandparent	15.9	17.0	15.8	14.3	13.9	15.9	–	–
Sibling, other relative	5.5	9.0	7.7	8.8	7.2	8.2	–	–
Organized facility	**25.1**	**29.9**	**23.1**	**27.5**	**25.8**	**23.1**	**13.0**	**12.1**
Day care center	17.7	18.3	15.8	20.6	16.6	14.0	–	–
Nursery/preschool	5.9	11.6	7.3	6.9	9.2	9.1	–	–
Federal Head Start program	1.5	–	–	–	–	–	–	–
Other nonrelative care	**28.4**	**21.6**	**23.3**	**25.1**	**28.9**	**28.2**	**29.4**	**–1.0**
In child's home	4.9	5.0	5.4	5.0	5.3	5.9	7.0	–2.1
In provider's home	23.5	16.6	17.9	20.1	23.6	22.3	22.4	1.1
Family day care	15.7	–	–	–	–	–	–	–
Other nonrelative	7.8	–	–	–	–	–	–	–
Other	**2.9**	**1.1**	**1.6**	**1.3**	**1.6**	**0.8**	**1.0**	**1.9**

Note: (–) means data not available.
Source: Bureau of the Census, Survey of Income and Program Participation, Internet site http://www.census.gov/pouplation/ socdemo/child/p70-62/tableA.txt; and Who's Minding the Kids? Child Care Arrangements: Fall 1995, *Current Population Report P70-70, 2000; calculations by New Strategist*

Self-Employment Is Becoming Less Common

Despite the popular perception that self-employment is on the rise, only 7.3 percent of workers aged 16 or older were self-employed in 2000, down from 17.6 percent in 1950. The long-term decline in self-employment occurred in part because of the dwindling number of farmers. In 1950, 7.4 percent of workers were self-employed farmers. The figure fell to just under 1 percent by 2000.

Nonagricultural self-employment also declined during the past half-century. In 1950, one in ten workers was self-employed in a nonagricultural industry. The figure fell to 6.4 percent in 2000. Although nonagricultural self-employment rose slightly in the early 1990s, it plummeted toward the end of the decade as the economy boomed and employers went begging for workers.

The Bureau of Labor Statistics counts as self-employed only those whose primary job is self-employment, not those who have a business on the side. If workers who are secondarily self-employed were counted, trends in self-employment might look different.

Nonagricultural self-employment fell in the 1990s

(percent of employed people aged 16 or older who are self-employed in nonagricultural occupations, 1950 to 2000)

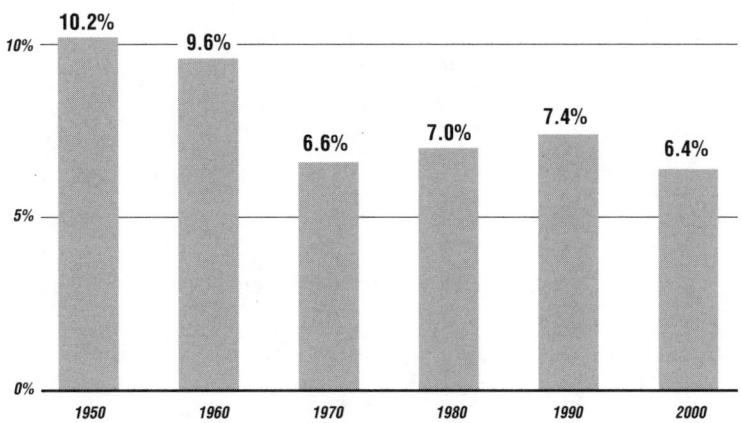

Table 6.32 Self-Employment, 1950 to 2000

(number and percent distribution of employed people aged 16 or older by self-employment status, 1950 to 2000; percent and percentage point change for selected years; numbers in thousands)

	total employed	self-employed total	self-employed nonagric.	self-employed agricultural	total employed	self-employed total	self-employed nonagric.	self-employed agricultural
2000	135,208	9,907	8,674	1,233	100.0%	7.3%	6.4%	0.9%
1999	133,488	10,087	8,790	1,297	100.0	7.6	6.6	1.0
1998	131,463	10,303	8,962	1,341	100.0	7.8	6.8	1.0
1997	129,558	10,513	9,056	1,457	100.0	8.1	7.0	1.1
1996	126,708	10,490	8,971	1,518	100.0	8.3	7.1	1.2
1995	124,900	10,482	8,902	1,580	100.0	8.4	7.1	1.3
1994	123,060	10,648	9,003	1,645	100.0	8.7	7.3	1.3
1993	119,306	10,335	9,003	1,332	100.0	8.7	7.5	1.1
1992	117,598	10,017	8,619	1,398	100.0	8.5	7.3	1.2
1991	116,877	10,341	8,899	1,442	100.0	8.8	7.6	1.2
1990	117,914	10,160	8,760	1,400	100.0	8.6	7.4	1.2
1989	117,342	10,008	8,605	1,403	100.0	8.5	7.3	1.2
1988	114,968	9,917	8,519	1,398	100.0	8.6	7.4	1.2
1987	112,440	9,624	8,201	1,423	100.0	8.6	7.3	1.3
1986	109,597	9,328	7,881	1,447	100.0	8.5	7.2	1.3
1985	107,150	9,269	7,811	1,458	100.0	8.7	7.3	1.4
1984	105,005	9,338	7,785	1,553	100.0	8.9	7.4	1.5
1983	100,834	9,140	7,575	1,565	100.0	9.1	7.5	1.6
1982	99,526	8,898	7,262	1,636	100.0	8.9	7.3	1.6
1981	100,397	8,735	7,097	1,638	100.0	8.7	7.1	1.6
1980	99,303	8,642	7,000	1,642	100.0	8.7	7.0	1.7
1979	98,824	8,384	6,791	1,593	100.0	8.5	6.9	1.6
1978	96,048	8,047	6,429	1,618	100.0	8.4	6.7	1.7
1977	92,017	7,694	6,114	1,580	100.0	8.4	6.6	1.7
1976	88,752	7,429	5,783	1,646	100.0	8.4	6.5	1.9
1975	85,846	7,427	5,705	1,722	100.0	8.7	6.6	2.0
1974	86,794	7,455	5,697	1,758	100.0	8.6	6.6	2.0
1973	85,064	7,254	5,474	1,780	100.0	8.5	6.4	2.1
1972	82,153	7,157	5,365	1,792	100.0	8.7	6.5	2.2
1971	79,367	7,077	5,327	1,750	100.0	8.9	6.7	2.2
1970	78,678	7,031	5,221	1,810	100.0	8.9	6.6	2.3
1969	77,902	7,148	5,252	1,896	100.0	9.2	6.7	2.4
1968	75,920	7,087	5,102	1,985	100.0	9.3	6.7	2.6
1967	74,372	7,170	5,174	1,996	100.0	9.6	7.0	2.7
1966	72,895	8,127	5,991	2,136	100.0	11.1	8.2	2.9
1965	71,088	8,394	6,097	2,297	100.0	11.8	8.6	3.2
1964	69,305	8,536	6,179	2,357	100.0	12.3	8.9	3.4
1963	67,762	8,541	6,114	2,427	100.0	12.6	9.0	3.6
1962	66,702	8,802	6,193	2,609	100.0	13.2	9.3	3.9
1961	65,746	9,045	6,308	2,737	100.0	13.8	9.6	4.2
1960	65,778	9,098	6,303	2,795	100.0	13.8	9.6	4.2
1959	64,630	9,242	6,222	3,020	100.0	14.3	9.6	4.7
1958	63,036	9,184	6,102	3,082	100.0	14.6	9.7	4.9
1957	64,071	9,312	6,011	3,301	100.0	14.5	9.4	5.2
1956	63,799	9,459	5,896	3,563	100.0	14.8	9.2	5.6
1955	62,170	9,577	5,851	3,726	100.0	15.4	9.4	6.0
1954	60,109	9,656	5,839	3,817	100.0	16.1	9.7	6.4
1953	61,179	9,556	5,740	3,816	100.0	15.6	9.4	6.2
1952	60,250	9,547	5,614	3,933	100.0	15.8	9.3	6.5
1951	59,961	9,821	5,804	4,017	100.0	16.4	9.7	6.7
1950	58,918	10,359	6,019	4,340	100.0	17.6	10.2	7.4
	percent change					*percentage point change*		
1990 to 2000	14.7%	−2.5%	−1.0%	−11.9%	–	−1.3	−1.0	−0.3
1950 to 2000	129.5	−4.4	44.1	−71.6	–	−10.3	−3.8	−6.5

Source: Bureau of Labor Statistics, Handbook of Labor Statistics, *Bulletin 2340, 1989;* Employment and Earnings, *1990–2001 January issues; calculations by New Strategist*

Job Tenure Drops for Men

While popular perceptions are often wrong, the sense that workers are not staying on the job as long as they once did is true, particularly for older men. The median number of years men aged 45 to 54 have been with their current employer fell fully 3.4 years between 1983 and 2000. Among those aged 55 to 64, the drop was an even larger 5.1 years. Among women, job tenure has not changed much since 1983.

The percentage of wage and salary workers aged 25 or older who have been with their current employer for 10 or more years has fallen 5.0 percentage points among men since 1983, while it has grown 3.5 percentage points among women. The biggest declines have been among men aged 40 to 49. In 1983, the 51 percent majority of men aged 40 to 44 had been with their current employer for 10 or more years. By 2000, only 40 percent had that kind of tenure. Among men aged 45 to 49, 58 percent had 10 or more years of tenure in 1983, a figure that fell to 49 percent in 2000.

While some of the decline in job tenure may result from voluntary job hopping, much of it is involuntary—especially among older men.

Long-term jobs decline for men, rise for women

(percent of wage and salary workers aged 25 or older who have been with their current employer for 10 or more years, by sex, 1983 and 2000)

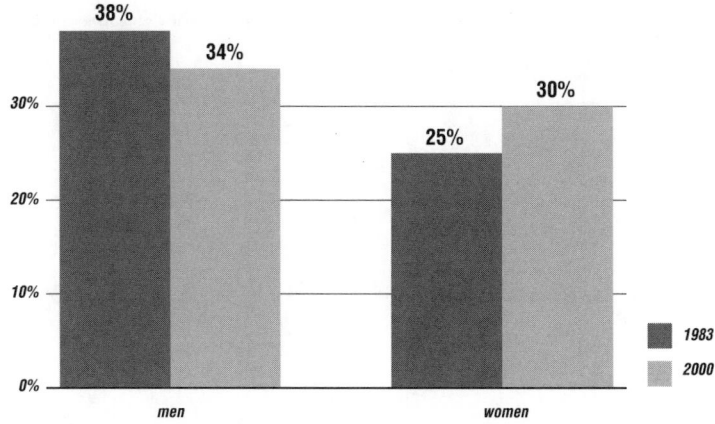

Table 6.33 Job Tenure by Sex and Age, 1983 to 2000

(median number of years workers aged 16 or older have been with their current employer by sex and age, 1983 to 2000; change in years, 1983–00)

	2000	1998	1996	1991	1987	1983	change in years 1983–00
Total employed men	**3.8**	**3.8**	**4.0**	**4.1**	**4.0**	**4.1**	**–0.3**
Aged 16 to 17	0.6	0.6	0.6	0.7	0.6	0.7	–0.1
Aged 18 to 19	0.7	0.7	0.7	0.8	0.7	0.8	–0.1
Aged 20 to 24	1.2	1.2	1.2	1.4	1.3	1.5	–0.3
Aged 25 to 34	2.7	2.8	3.0	3.1	3.1	3.2	–0.5
Aged 35 to 44	5.4	5.5	6.1	6.5	7.0	7.3	–1.9
Aged 45 to 54	9.4	9.4	10.1	11.2	11.8	12.8	–3.4
Aged 55 to 64	10.2	11.2	10.5	13.4	14.5	15.3	–5.1
Aged 65 or older	9.1	7.1	8.3	7.0	8.3	8.3	0.8
Total employed women	**3.3**	**3.4**	**3.5**	**3.2**	**3.0**	**3.1**	**0.2**
Aged 16 to 17	0.6	0.7	0.7	0.7	0.6	0.7	–0.1
Aged 18 to 19	0.7	0.7	0.7	0.8	0.7	0.8	–0.1
Aged 20 to 24	1.0	1.1	1.2	1.3	1.3	1.5	–0.5
Aged 25 to 34	2.5	2.5	2.7	2.7	2.6	2.8	–0.3
Aged 35 to 44	4.3	4.5	4.8	4.5	4.4	4.1	0.2
Aged 45 to 54	7.3	7.2	7.0	6.7	6.8	6.3	1.0
Aged 55 to 64	9.9	9.6	10.0	9.9	9.7	9.8	0.1
Aged 65 or older	9.7	8.7	8.4	9.5	9.9	10.1	–0.4

Source: Bureau of Labor Statistics, Current Population Surveys, Internet site http://www.bls.gov/news.release/tenure.t01.htm; calculations by New Strategist

Table 6.34 Long-Term Jobs by Sex and Age, 1983 to 2000

(percent of employed wage and salary workers aged 25 or older who have been with their current employer for 10 years or more, by sex and age, 1983 to 2000; percentage point change, 1983–00)

	2000	1998	1996	1991	1987	1983	percentage point change, 1983–00
Total employed men	**33.6%**	**32.7%**	**33.1%**	**35.9%**	**35.0%**	**37.7%**	**–5.0**
Aged 25 to 29	3.0	3.1	3.3	5.7	4.5	4.0	–0.9
Aged 30 to 34	15.3	15.3	15.6	21.1	18.7	18.7	–3.4
Aged 35 to 39	29.5	29.7	30.5	35.6	34.8	36.9	–7.2
Aged 40 to 44	40.4	39.1	41.7	46.3	48.5	51.1	–12.0
Aged 45 to 49	49.0	47.4	50.8	53.5	53.0	57.8	–10.4
Aged 50 to 54	51.6	52.8	54.9	58.5	59.4	62.3	–9.5
Aged 55 to 59	53.7	56.5	55.7	61.0	63.2	66.2	–9.7
Aged 60 to 64	52.5	55.7	50.4	57.5	58.7	65.6	–9.9
Aged 65 or older	48.9	42.3	47.6	42.6	47.4	47.6	–5.3
Total employed women	**29.5**	**28.4**	**27.6**	**28.2**	**25.7**	**24.9**	**3.5**
Aged 25 to 29	1.9	2.2	2.2	4.4	3.6	2.5	–0.3
Aged 30 to 34	12.6	14.0	13.6	17.3	14.7	14.8	–0.8
Aged 35 to 39	22.4	24.0	22.9	26.1	23.8	21.6	2.4
Aged 40 to 44	31.4	31.8	30.4	32.0	27.9	23.4	8.4
Aged 45 to 49	41.5	38.4	38.1	39.3	36.4	33.0	5.4
Aged 50 to 54	45.6	44.6	45.8	43.4	43.0	42.5	2.1
Aged 55 to 59	52.5	49.2	52.1	51.4	50.8	51.0	–1.8
Aged 60 to 64	54.0	53.0	52.7	53.1	52.4	52.6	0.4
Aged 65 or older	51.2	47.7	47.2	49.9	53.1	54.5	–6.8

Source: Bureau of Labor Statistics, Current Population Surveys, Internet site http://www.bls.gov/news.release/tenure.t02.htm; calculations by New Strategist

More Cars, Less Carpooling

Despite the efforts of many to encourage carpooling and the use of public transportation for the commute to work, Americans are increasingly likely to drive alone to their jobs. In 2000, 76 percent of workers drove to work alone as compared with 64 percent who did so in 1980. The percentage of workers who carpool fell from 20 percent in 1980 to 11 percent in 2000.

Most other means of transportation to work also experienced declines. The percentage of people using public transportation stood at 5 percent in 2000, down from 6 percent in 1980 and 12 percent in 1960. The percentage who walk to work fell from 10 to 3 percent between 1960 and 2000. The only means of transportation to work besides driving alone that experienced an increase between 1980 and 2000 was the proportion of workers who needed no transportation at all. The share of workers who work at home rose from 2 to 3 percent during those years.

More people drive to work alone

(percent of people who drive to work alone, 1980 and 2000)

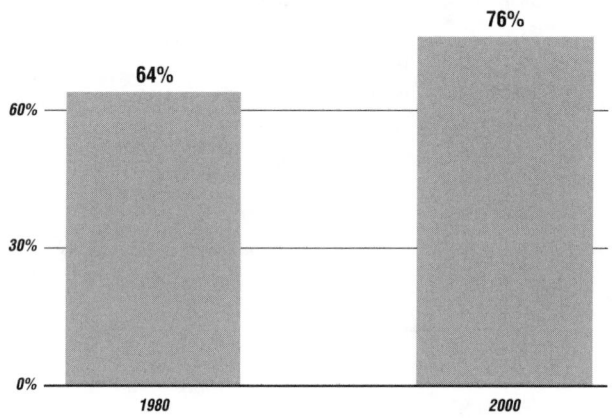

Table 6.35 Transportation to Work, 1960 to 2000

(number and percent distribution of workers aged 16 or older by primary means of transportation to work, 1960 to 2000; percent change in number and percentage point change in distribution, 1960–00; numbers in thousands)

	2000	1990	1980	1970	1960	percent change 1960–00
Total workers	**127,449**	**115,070**	**96,617**	**76,852**	**64,656**	**97.1**
Car, truck, or van	111,542	99,593	81,258	59,723	41,368	169.6
Drove alone	97,243	84,215	62,193	–	–	–
Carpooled	14,299	15,378	19,065	–	–	–
Public transportation	6,593	6,070	6,175	6,810	7,807	–15.5
Bus or trolley bus	–	3,445	3,925	4,245	5,323	–
Streetcar or trolley car	–	78	–	–	–	–
Subway or elevated	–	1,755	1,529	1,768	2,484	–
Railroad	–	574	554	502	–	–
Ferryboat	–	37	–	–	–	–
Taxicab	–	179	167	296	–	–
Motorcycle	–	237	419	–	–	–
Bicycle	–	467	468	–	–	–
Walked only	3,418	4,489	5,413	5,690	6,416	–46.7
Other means	–	809	703	1,944	1,620	–
Worked at home	4,075	3,406	2,180	2,685	4,663	–12.6

	2000	1990	1980	1970	1960	percentage point change, 1960–00
Total workers	**100.0%**	**100.0%**	**100.0%**	**100.0%**	**100.0%**	**–**
Car, truck, or van	87.5	86.5	84.1	77.7	64.0	23.5
Drove alone	76.3	73.2	64.4	–	–	–
Carpooled	11.2	13.4	19.7	–	–	–
Public transportation	5.2	5.3	6.4	8.9	12.1	–6.9
Bus or trolley bus	–	3.0	4.1	5.5	8.2	–
Streetcar or trolley car	–	0.1	–	–	–	–
Subway or elevated	–	1.5	1.6	2.3	3.8	–
Railroad	–	0.5	0.6	0.7	–	–
Ferryboat	–	0.0	–	–	–	–
Taxicab	–	0.2	0.2	0.4	–	–
Motorcycle	–	0.2	0.4	–	–	–
Bicycle	–	0.4	0.5	–	–	–
Walked only	2.7	3.9	5.6	7.4	9.9	–7.2
Other means	–	0.7	0.7	2.5	2.5	–
Worked at home	3.2	3.0	2.3	3.5	7.2	–4.0

Note: Workers aged 14 or older in 1960 and 1970; (–) means data not available.
Source: Bureau of the Census, Censuses of Population and Housing, Internet site http://www.census.gov/population/socdemo/ journey/mode6790.txt; and Census 2000 Supplementary Survey, Internet site http://www.census.gov/c2ss/www/Products/ Profiles/2000/index.htm; calculations by New Strategist

Employers Get Stingy with Employee Benefits

Forty-eight percent of the nation's employees participated in a retirement plan at work in 2000. The largest share were in a defined contribution, rather than a defined benefit, plan. Comparable data are not available for years earlier than 1999 because the Bureau of Labor Statistics replaced the Employee Benefit Survey, which collected data from small and large employers separately, with the National Compensation Survey, which examines employers of all sizes. Just over half of employees had medical coverage in 2000, and the majority was required to contribute to the cost.

Data from the Employee Benefit Survey through 1997 indicate employers are getting stingy with benefits. The percentage of employers with 100 or more workers who offered a defined benefit retirement plan fell from 84 to 50 percent between 1980 and 1997. The percentage who offered medical benefits fell from 97 to 76 percent. Among those who offer medical benefits, the percentage who require employees to contribute to the cost of coverage rose from 26 to 69 percent.

One reason for increasingly stingy benefits may be that fewer workers belong to unions. Between 1983 and 2000, the percentage of workers represented by unions fell from 23 to 15 percent.

Largest share of retirement plans are defined contribution

(percent of workers in private industry by type of retirement plan coverage, 2000)

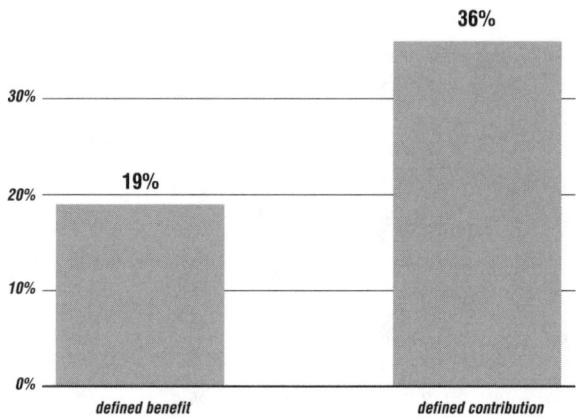

Table 6.36 Employee Benefits, 1999 and 2000

(percent of workers in private industry offered selected employee benefits, 1999 and 2000)

	2000	1999
Retirement benefits	48%	48%
Defined benefit	19	21
Defined contribution	36	36
Health care benefits		
Medical care	52	53
Single coverage		
Employee contributions not required	32	33
Employee contributions required	68	67
Average flat monthly contribution	$54.40	$48.30
Family coverage		
Employee contributions not required	19	19
Employee contributions required	81	81
Average flat monthly contribution	$179.75	$169.84
Dental care	29	32
Vision care	17	18
Survivor benefits		
Life insurance	54	56
Accidental death and dismemberment insurance	41	43
Survivor income benefits	2	3
Disability benefits		
Paid sick leave	–	53
Short-term disability	34	36
Long-term disability	26	25
Paid vacations	80	79
Paid holidays	77	75
Employer assistance for child care	4	6
Adoption assistance	5	6
Long-term care insurance	7	6
Flexible work place	5	3
Nonwage cash payments		
Nonproduction bonus	48	42
Supplemental unemployment benefits	1	2
Severance pay	20	22
Subsidized commuting	3	4
Section 125 cafeteria benefits	–	28
Flexible benefit plans	–	7
Reimbursement plans	–	15
Premium conversion plans	–	6
Education assistance		
Work-related	38	41
Nonwork-related	9	10
Travel accident insurance	15	20
Health promotion benefits		
Wellness programs	18	17
Employee assistance programs	–	33
Fitness centers	9	9

Note: (–) means data not available.
Source: Bureau of Labor Statistics, Employee Benefits in Private Industry: 1999 and 2000, *National Compensation Surveys, Internet site http://www.bls.gov/ncs/ebs/home.htm*

Table 6.37 Employee Benefits in Medium and Large Private Establishments, 1980 to 1987

(percent of employees in private establishments employing 100 or more workers with selected employee benefits, 1980 to 1997; percentage point change, 1980–97)

	defined benefit pension plan	defined contribution pension plan	medical benefits	percent of employees required to contribute to single medical coverage
1997	50%	57%	76%	69%
1995	52	55	77	67
1993	56	49	82	61
1991	59	48	83	51
1989	63	48	92	47
1988	63	45	90	44
1986	76	60	95	43
1985	80	53	96	36
1984	82	–	97	36
1983	82	–	96	33
1982	84	–	97	27
1981	84	–	97	27
1980	84	–	97	26
Percentage point change				
1980 to 1997	–34	–	–21	43

Note: (–) means data not available.
Source: Bureau of Labor Statistics, Employee Benefits Survey, Internet site http://data.bls.gov/servlet/SurveyOutputServlet; calculations by New Strategist

Table 6.38   Workers Represented by Unions, 1983 to 2000

(number and percent of employed wage and salary workers aged 16 or older who are represented by unions, 1983 to 2000; percent and percentage point change for selected years; numbers in thousands)

	number	percent
2000	17,944	14.9%
1999	18,182	15.3
1998	17,918	15.4
1997	17,923	15.6
1996	18,158	16.2
1995	18,346	16.7
1994	18,843	17.5
1993	18,646	17.7
1992	18,540	17.9
1991	18,734	18.2
1990	19,058	18.3
1989	19,198	18.6
1988	19,241	19.0
1985	19,358	20.5
1983	20,532	23.3
	percent change	*percentage point change*
1990 to 2000	−5.8%	−3.4
1983 to 2000	−12.6	−8.4

Source: Bureau of the Census, Employment and Earnings, *January issues*

7

Living Arrangements

■ In 1950, married couples headed fully 78 percent of the nation's households. By 2000, the share was just 53 percent as lifestyles grew more diverse.

■ One of the biggest lifestyle changes of the past half-century is the disappearance of children from the nation's households. In 1950, 47 percent of households included children under age 18. By 2000 the figure had fallen to just 33 percent.

■ Single-parent households have become much more numerous as divorce and out-of-wedlock births have become common. In 2000, only 69 percent of children lived with both parents, down from 88 percent in 1960.

■ Among Americans of all ages, a larger share lived alone in 2000 than in 1970, the biggest increase occurring among older women. In 2000, 49 percent of women aged 75 or older lived alone, up from 37 percent in 1970.

■ As people postponed marriage over the past few decades, the married share of the adult population declined. In 1950, two-thirds of men and women aged 15 or older were currently married. By 2000, only 58 percent of men and 55 percent of women were married.

Lifestyles Have Changed Dramatically

Americans live differently than they once did. In 1950, married couples headed fully 78 percent of the nation's households. By 2000, the share was just 53 percent as lifestyles grew more diverse. Baby boomers postponed marriage, then were quick to divorce after tying the knot. In 1950, people who lived alone or with nonrelatives headed only 11 percent of households. By 2000, fully 31 percent of households consisted of people who lived alone or with nonrelatives.

The age distribution of householders has also shifted over the years. As of 2000, however, the distribution was similar to what it had been in 1950—with one exception. The percentage of households headed by people aged 75 or older has nearly doubled in the past half-century, rising from 6 to 10 percent as more older people chose to live by themselves rather than move in with their children.

The white share of householders has fallen slightly over the past 50 years, from 89 to 84 percent. This figure includes most Hispanics, however, since most Hispanics are white.

Married couples are less common

(percent of households headed by married couples, 1950 to 2000)

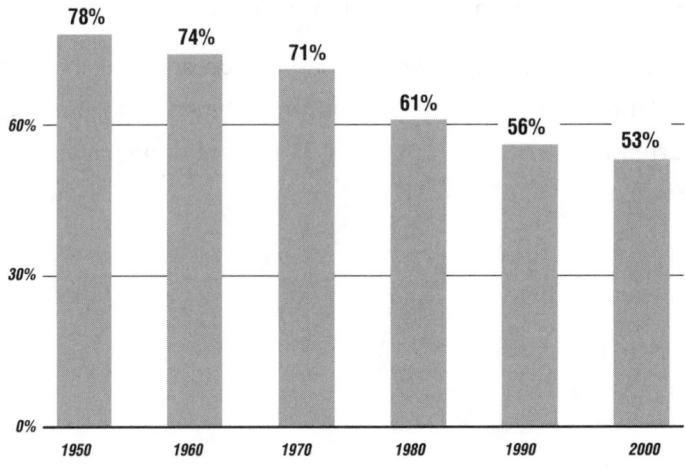

Table 7.1 Households by Type, 1950 to 2000

(number of households by type, 1950 to 2000; percent change for selected years; numbers in thousands)

| | total households | family households | | | | nonfamily households | | |
		total	married couples	female hh, no spouse present	male hh, no spouse present	total	female householder	male householder
2000	104,705	72,025	55,311	12,687	4,028	32,680	18,039	14,641
1999	103,874	71,535	54,770	12,789	3,976	32,339	17,971	14,368
1998	102,528	70,880	54,317	12,652	3,911	31,648	17,516	14,133
1997	101,018	70,241	53,604	12,790	3,847	30,777	17,070	13,707
1996	99,627	69,594	53,567	12,514	3,513	30,033	16,685	13,348
1995	98,990	69,305	53,858	12,220	3,226	29,686	16,496	13,190
1994	97,107	68,490	53,171	12,406	2,913	28,617	16,155	12,462
1993	96,426	68,216	53,090	12,061	3,065	28,210	15,914	12,297
1992	95,669	67,173	52,457	11,692	3,025	28,496	16,068	12,428
1991	94,312	66,322	52,147	11,268	2,907	27,990	15,840	12,150
1990	93,347	66,090	52,317	10,890	2,884	27,257	15,651	11,606
1989	92,830	65,837	52,100	10,890	2,847	26,994	15,120	11,874
1988	91,124	65,204	51,675	10,696	2,834	25,919	14,637	11,282
1987	89,479	64,491	51,537	10,445	2,510	24,988	14,336	10,652
1986	88,458	63,558	50,933	10,211	2,414	24,900	14,252	10,648
1985	86,789	62,706	50,350	10,129	2,228	24,082	13,968	10,114
1984	85,290	62,015	50,081	9,896	2,038	23,276	13,587	9,689
1983	83,918	61,393	49,908	9,469	2,016	22,525	13,011	9,514
1982	83,527	61,019	49,630	9,403	1,986	22,508	13,051	9,457
1981	82,368	60,309	49,294	9,082	1,933	22,059	12,780	9,279
1980	80,776	59,550	49,112	8,705	1,733	21,226	12,419	8,807
1979	77,330	57,498	47,662	8,220	1,616	19,831	11,767	8,064
1978	76,030	56,958	47,357	8,037	1,564	19,071	11,261	7,811
1977	74,142	56,472	47,471	7,540	1,461	17,669	10,698	6,971
1976	72,867	56,056	47,297	7,335	1,424	16,811	10,263	6,548
1975	71,120	55,563	46,951	7,127	1,485	15,557	9,645	5,912
1974	69,859	54,917	46,787	6,709	1,421	14,942	9,288	5,654
1973	68,251	54,264	46,297	6,535	1,432	13,986	8,858	5,129
1972	66,676	53,163	45,724	6,108	1,331	13,513	8,674	4,839
1971	64,778	52,102	44,928	5,920	1,254	12,676	8,273	4,403
1970	63,401	51,456	44,728	5,500	1,228	11,945	7,882	4,063
1969	62,214	50,729	44,086	5,422	1,221	11,485	7,595	3,890
1968	60,813	50,012	43,507	5,310	1,195	10,801	7,143	3,658
1967	59,236	49,086	42,743	5,153	1,190	10,150	6,731	3,419
1966	58,406	48,399	42,263	4,973	1,163	10,007	6,708	3,299
1965	57,436	47,838	41,689	4,982	1,167	9,598	6,321	3,277
1964	56,149	47,381	41,341	4,836	1,204	8,768	5,803	2,965
1963	55,270	46,872	40,888	4,689	1,295	8,398	5,560	2,838
1962	54,764	46,262	40,404	4,590	1,268	8,502	5,570	2,932
1961	53,557	45,383	39,620	4,564	1,199	8,174	5,395	2,779
1960	52,799	44,905	39,254	4,422	1,228	7,895	5,179	2,716
1959	51,435	43,971	38,410	4,276	1,285	7,464	5,015	2,449
1958	50,474	43,426	37,911	4,237	1,278	7,047	4,718	2,329
1957	49,673	43,262	37,718	4,304	1,241	6,411	4,374	2,038
1956	48,902	42,593	37,047	4,138	1,408	6,309	4,250	2,058
1955	47,874	41,732	36,251	4,153	1,328	6,142	4,083	2,059
1954	46,962	40,998	35,926	3,757	1,315	5,964	4,039	1,925
1953	46,385	40,540	35,577	3,757	1,206	5,845	3,943	1,902
1952	45,538	40,235	35,164	3,952	1,119	5,303	3,546	1,757
1951	44,673	39,502	34,391	3,957	1,154	5,171	3,439	1,732
1950	43,554	38,838	34,075	3,594	1,169	4,716	3,048	1,668
Percent change								
1990 to 2000	12.2%	9.0%	5.7%	16.5%	39.7%	19.9%	15.3%	26.2%
1950 to 2000	140.4	85.4	62.3	253.0	244.6	593.0	491.8	777.8

Source: Bureau of the Census, Current Population Surveys, Internet site http://www.census.gov/population/socdemo/hh-fam/ tabHH-1.txt; calculations by New Strategist

Table 7.2 Distribution of Households by Type, 1950 to 2000

(percent distribution of households by type, 1950 to 2000; percentage point change for selected years)

	total households	family households				nonfamily households		
		total	married couples	female hh, no spouse present	male hh, no spouse present	total	female householder	male householder
2000	100.0%	68.8%	52.8%	12.1%	3.8%	31.2%	17.2%	14.0%
1999	100.0	68.9	52.7	12.3	3.8	31.1	17.3	13.8
1998	100.0	69.1	53.0	12.3	3.8	30.9	17.1	13.8
1997	100.0	69.5	53.1	12.7	3.8	30.5	16.9	13.6
1996	100.0	69.9	53.8	12.6	3.5	30.1	16.7	13.4
1995	100.0	70.0	54.4	12.3	3.3	30.0	16.7	13.3
1994	100.0	70.5	54.8	12.8	3.0	29.5	16.6	12.8
1993	100.0	70.7	55.1	12.5	3.2	29.3	16.5	12.8
1992	100.0	70.2	54.8	12.2	3.2	29.8	16.8	13.0
1991	100.0	70.3	55.3	11.9	3.1	29.7	16.8	12.9
1990	100.0	70.8	56.0	11.7	3.1	29.2	16.8	12.4
1989	100.0	70.9	56.1	11.7	3.1	29.1	16.3	12.8
1988	100.0	71.6	56.7	11.7	3.1	28.4	16.1	12.4
1987	100.0	72.1	57.6	11.7	2.8	27.9	16.0	11.9
1986	100.0	71.9	57.6	11.5	2.7	28.1	16.1	12.0
1985	100.0	72.3	58.0	11.7	2.6	27.7	16.1	11.7
1984	100.0	72.7	58.7	11.6	2.4	27.3	15.9	11.4
1983	100.0	73.2	59.5	11.3	2.4	26.8	15.5	11.3
1982	100.0	73.1	59.4	11.3	2.4	26.9	15.6	11.3
1981	100.0	73.2	59.8	11.0	2.3	26.8	15.5	11.3
1980	100.0	73.7	60.8	10.8	2.1	26.3	15.4	10.9
1979	100.0	74.4	61.6	10.6	2.1	25.6	15.2	10.4
1978	100.0	74.9	62.3	10.6	2.1	25.1	14.8	10.3
1977	100.0	76.2	64.0	10.2	2.0	23.8	14.4	9.4
1976	100.0	76.9	64.9	10.1	2.0	23.1	14.1	9.0
1975	100.0	78.1	66.0	10.0	2.1	21.9	13.6	8.3
1974	100.0	78.6	67.0	9.6	2.0	21.4	13.3	8.1
1973	100.0	79.5	67.8	9.6	2.1	20.5	13.0	7.5
1972	100.0	79.7	68.6	9.2	2.0	20.3	13.0	7.3
1971	100.0	80.4	69.4	9.1	1.9	19.6	12.8	6.8
1970	100.0	81.2	70.5	8.7	1.9	18.8	12.4	6.4
1969	100.0	81.5	70.9	8.7	2.0	18.5	12.2	6.3
1968	100.0	82.2	71.5	8.7	2.0	17.8	11.7	6.0
1967	100.0	82.9	72.2	8.7	2.0	17.1	11.4	5.8
1966	100.0	82.9	72.4	8.5	2.0	17.1	11.5	5.6
1965	100.0	83.3	72.6	8.7	2.0	16.7	11.0	5.7
1964	100.0	84.4	73.6	8.6	2.1	15.6	10.3	5.3
1963	100.0	84.8	74.0	8.5	2.3	15.2	10.1	5.1
1962	100.0	84.5	73.8	8.4	2.3	15.5	10.2	5.4
1961	100.0	84.7	74.0	8.5	2.2	15.3	10.1	5.2
1960	100.0	85.0	74.3	8.4	2.3	15.0	9.8	5.1
1959	100.0	85.5	74.7	8.3	2.5	14.5	9.8	4.8
1958	100.0	86.0	75.1	8.4	2.5	14.0	9.3	4.6
1957	100.0	87.1	75.9	8.7	2.5	12.9	8.8	4.1
1956	100.0	87.1	75.8	8.5	2.9	12.9	8.7	4.2
1955	100.0	87.2	75.7	8.7	2.8	12.8	8.5	4.3
1954	100.0	87.3	76.5	8.0	2.8	12.7	8.6	4.1
1953	100.0	87.4	76.7	8.1	2.6	12.6	8.5	4.1
1952	100.0	88.4	77.2	8.7	2.5	11.6	7.8	3.9
1951	100.0	88.4	77.0	8.9	2.6	11.6	7.7	3.9
1950	100.0	89.2	78.2	8.3	2.7	10.8	7.0	3.8
Percentage point change								
1990 to 2000	–	–2.0	–3.2	0.5	0.8	2.0	0.5	1.5
1950 to 2000	–	–20.4	–25.4	3.9	1.2	20.4	10.2	10.2

Note: (–) means not applicable.
Source: Bureau of the Census, Current Population Surveys, Internet site http://www.census.gov/population/socdemo/hh-fam/ tabHH-1.txt; calculations by New Strategist

Table 7.3 Households by Age of Householder, 1960 to 2000

(number of households by age of householder, 1960 to 2000; percent change for selected years; numbers in thousands)

	total households	< 25	25–29	30–34	35–44	45–54	55–64	65–74	75+
2000	104,705	5,860	8,520	10,107	23,955	20,927	13,592	11,325	10,419
1999	103,874	5,770	8,519	10,300	23,969	20,158	13,571	11,373	10,216
1998	102,528	5,435	8,463	10,570	23,943	19,547	13,072	11,272	10,225
1997	101,018	5,160	8,647	10,667	23,823	18,843	12,469	11,679	9,729
1996	99,627	5,282	8,354	10,871	23,227	18,007	12,401	11,908	9,578
1995	98,990	5,444	8,400	11,052	22,914	17,590	12,224	11,803	9,562
1994	97,107	5,265	8,472	11,245	22,293	16,837	12,188	11,639	9,168
1993	96,426	5,257	8,859	11,198	21,862	16,413	12,154	11,668	9,014
1992	95,669	4,859	8,810	11,197	21,774	15,547	12,559	12,043	8,878
1991	94,312	4,882	9,246	11,077	21,304	14,751	12,524	12,001	8,526
1990	93,347	5,121	9,423	11,049	20,555	14,514	12,529	11,733	8,423
1989	92,830	5,415	9,624	11,300	19,952	14,018	12,805	11,590	8,127
1988	91,124	5,228	9,614	10,969	19,323	13,630	12,846	11,410	8,045
1987	89,479	5,197	9,652	10,850	18,703	13,211	12,868	11,250	7,748
1986	88,458	5,503	9,781	10,629	17,997	13,099	12,852	11,157	7,439
1985	86,789	5,438	9,637	10,377	17,481	12,628	13,073	10,851	7,305
1984	85,290	5,510	9,848	9,960	16,596	12,471	13,121	10,700	7,201
1983	83,918	5,695	9,465	9,639	16,020	12,354	13,074	10,603	7,067
1982	83,527	6,109	9,525	9,802	15,326	12,505	12,947	10,379	6,933
1981	82,368	6,443	9,514	9,639	14,463	12,694	12,704	10,226	6,685
1980	80,776	6,569	9,252	9,252	13,980	12,654	12,525	10,112	6,432
1979	77,330	6,342	8,679	8,317	13,328	12,585	12,284	9,753	6,042
1978	76,030	6,220	8,598	8,233	12,969	12,602	12,183	9,383	5,842
1977	74,142	5,991	8,385	7,782	12,482	12,905	11,780	9,210	5,606
1976	72,867	5,877	8,298	7,212	12,227	12,820	11,631	9,258	5,544
1975	71,120	5,834	7,810	7,137	11,861	12,916	11,301	8,910	5,350
1974	69,859	5,857	7,527	6,804	11,703	12,939	11,149	8,716	5,162
1973	68,251	5,476	7,116	6,447	11,721	12,805	11,212	8,369	5,104
1972	66,676	5,194	6,794	6,009	11,529	12,758	11,138	8,165	5,090
1971	64,778	4,737	6,239	5,682	11,813	12,588	11,021	7,793	4,909
1970	63,401	4,359	6,101	5,593	11,810	12,216	10,824	7,744	4,756
1969	62,214	4,094	5,910	5,447	11,817	12,230	10,622	7,540	4,554
1968	60,813	3,852	5,336	5,325	12,003	12,038	10,394	7,536	4,327
1967	59,236	3,587	5,288	5,099	11,998	11,892	9,909	7,321	4,143
1966	58,406	3,571	4,991	5,086	11,944	11,806	9,745	7,224	4,038
1965	57,436	3,413	4,808	5,119	12,009	11,523	9,600	7,173	3,790
1964	56,149	3,110	4,546	5,167	12,176	11,192	9,327	6,998	3,630
1963	55,270	2,889	4,386	5,314	12,005	11,072	9,103	6,909	3,592
1962	54,764	2,909	4,349	5,435	11,802	10,906	9,057	6,960	3,346
1961	53,557	2,628	4,341	5,387	11,596	11,047	9,026	6,355	3,179
1960	52,799	2,559	4,317	5,407	11,614	10,878	8,599	6,380	3,045
Percent change									
1990 to 2000	12.2%	14.4%	–9.6%	–8.5%	16.5%	44.2%	8.5%	–3.5%	23.7%
1960 to 2000	98.3	129.0	97.4	86.9	106.3	92.4	58.1	77.5	242.2

Source: Bureau of the Census, Current Population Surveys, Internet site http://www.census.gov/population/socdemo/hh-fam/tabHH-3.txt; calculations by New Strategist

Table 7.4 Distribution of Households by Age of Householder, 1960 to 2000

(percent distribution of households by age of householder, 1960 to 2000; percentage point change for selected years)

	total households	< 25	25–29	30–34	35–44	45–54	55–64	65–74	75+
2000	100.0%	5.6%	8.1%	9.7%	22.9%	20.0%	13.0%	10.8%	10.0%
1999	100.0	5.6	8.2	9.9	23.1	19.4	13.1	10.9	9.8
1998	100.0	5.3	8.3	10.3	23.4	19.1	12.7	11.0	10.0
1997	100.0	5.1	8.6	10.6	23.6	18.7	12.3	11.6	9.6
1996	100.0	5.3	8.4	10.9	23.3	18.1	12.4	12.0	9.6
1995	100.0	5.5	8.5	11.2	23.1	17.8	12.3	11.9	9.7
1994	100.0	5.4	8.7	11.6	23.0	17.3	12.6	12.0	9.4
1993	100.0	5.5	9.2	11.6	22.7	17.0	12.6	12.1	9.3
1992	100.0	5.1	9.2	11.7	22.8	16.3	13.1	12.6	9.3
1991	100.0	5.2	9.8	11.7	22.6	15.6	13.3	12.7	9.0
1990	100.0	5.5	10.1	11.8	22.0	15.5	13.4	12.6	9.0
1989	100.0	5.8	10.4	12.2	21.5	15.1	13.8	12.5	8.8
1988	100.0	5.7	10.6	12.0	21.2	15.0	14.1	12.5	8.8
1987	100.0	5.8	10.8	12.1	20.9	14.8	14.4	12.6	8.7
1986	100.0	6.2	11.1	12.0	20.3	14.8	14.5	12.6	8.4
1985	100.0	6.3	11.1	12.0	20.1	14.6	15.1	12.5	8.4
1984	100.0	6.5	11.5	11.7	19.5	14.6	15.4	12.5	8.4
1983	100.0	6.8	11.3	11.5	19.1	14.7	15.6	12.6	8.4
1982	100.0	7.3	11.4	11.7	18.3	15.0	15.5	12.4	8.3
1981	100.0	7.8	11.6	11.7	17.6	15.4	15.4	12.4	8.1
1980	100.0	8.1	11.5	11.5	17.3	15.7	15.5	12.5	8.0
1979	100.0	8.2	11.2	10.8	17.2	16.3	15.9	12.6	7.8
1978	100.0	8.2	11.3	10.8	17.1	16.6	16.0	12.3	7.7
1977	100.0	8.1	11.3	10.5	16.8	17.4	15.9	12.4	7.6
1976	100.0	8.1	11.4	9.9	16.8	17.6	16.0	12.7	7.6
1975	100.0	8.2	11.0	10.0	16.7	18.2	15.9	12.5	7.5
1974	100.0	8.4	10.8	9.7	16.8	18.5	16.0	12.5	7.4
1973	100.0	8.0	10.4	9.4	17.2	18.8	16.4	12.3	7.5
1972	100.0	7.8	10.2	9.0	17.3	19.1	16.7	12.2	7.6
1971	100.0	7.3	9.6	8.8	18.2	19.4	17.0	12.0	7.6
1970	100.0	6.9	9.6	8.8	18.6	19.3	17.1	12.2	7.5
1969	100.0	6.6	9.5	8.8	19.0	19.7	17.1	12.1	7.3
1968	100.0	6.3	8.8	8.8	19.7	19.8	17.1	12.4	7.1
1967	100.0	6.1	8.9	8.6	20.3	20.1	16.7	12.4	7.0
1966	100.0	6.1	8.5	8.7	20.4	20.2	16.7	12.4	6.9
1965	100.0	5.9	8.4	8.9	20.9	20.1	16.7	12.5	6.6
1964	100.0	5.5	8.1	9.2	21.7	19.9	16.6	12.5	6.5
1963	100.0	5.2	7.9	9.6	21.7	20.0	16.5	12.5	6.5
1962	100.0	5.3	7.9	9.9	21.6	19.9	16.5	12.7	6.1
1961	100.0	4.9	8.1	10.1	21.7	20.6	16.9	11.9	5.9
1960	100.0	4.8	8.2	10.2	22.0	20.6	16.3	12.1	5.8
Percentage point change									
1990 to 2000	–	0.1	–2.0	–2.1	0.9	4.5	–0.4	–1.8	1.0
1960 to 2000	–	0.8	–0.1	–0.5	0.9	–0.6	–3.3	–1.3	4.2

Note: (–) means not applicable.
Source: Bureau of the Census, Current Population Surveys, Internet site http://www.census.gov/population/socdemo/hh-fam/ tabHH-3.txt; calculations by New Strategist

Table 7.5 Households by Race and Hispanic Origin of Householder, 1970 to 2000

(number and percent distribution of households by race and Hispanic origin of householder, 1970 to 2000; percent and percentage point change for selected years; numbers in thousands)

	total households	black	Hispanic	white	total households	black	Hispanic	white
2000	104,705	12,849	9,319	87,671	100.0%	12.3%	8.9%	83.7%
1999	103,874	12,579	9,060	87,212	100.0	12.1	8.7	84.0
1998	102,528	12,474	8,590	86,106	100.0	12.2	8.4	84.0
1997	101,018	12,109	8,225	85,059	100.0	12.0	8.1	84.2
1996	99,627	11,577	7,939	84,511	100.0	11.6	8.0	84.8
1995	98,990	11,655	7,735	83,737	100.0	11.8	7.8	84.6
1994	97,107	11,281	7,362	82,387	100.0	11.6	7.6	84.8
1993	96,391	11,190	6,626	82,083	100.0	11.6	6.9	85.2
1992	95,669	11,083	6,379	81,675	100.0	11.6	6.7	85.4
1991	94,312	10,671	6,220	80,968	100.0	11.3	6.6	85.9
1990	93,347	10,486	5,933	80,163	100.0	11.2	6.4	85.9
1989	92,830	10,561	5,910	79,734	100.0	11.4	6.4	85.9
1988	91,124	10,186	5,698	78,469	100.0	11.2	6.3	86.2
1987	89,479	9,922	5,418	77,284	100.0	11.1	6.1	86.4
1986	88,458	9,797	5,213	76,576	100.0	11.1	5.9	86.6
1985	86,789	9,480	4,883	75,328	100.0	10.9	5.6	86.8
1984	85,290	9,236	4,326	74,376	100.0	10.8	5.1	87.1
1983	83,918	8,916	4,085	73,182	100.0	10.6	4.9	87.2
1982	83,527	8,961	3,980	72,845	100.0	10.7	4.8	87.2
1981	82,368	8,847	3,906	71,872	100.0	10.7	4.7	87.3
1980	80,776	8,586	3,684	70,766	100.0	10.6	4.6	87.6
1979	77,330	8,066	3,291	68,028	100.0	10.4	4.3	88.0
1978	76,030	7,977	3,304	66,934	100.0	10.5	4.3	88.0
1977	74,142	7,776	3,081	65,353	100.0	10.5	4.2	88.1
1976	72,867	7,486	2,948	64,392	100.0	10.3	4.0	88.4
1975	71,120	7,262	–	62,945	100.0	10.2	–	88.5
1974	69,859	7,040	–	61,965	100.0	10.1	–	88.7
1973	68,251	6,809	–	60,618	100.0	10.0	–	88.8
1972	66,676	6,578	–	59,463	100.0	9.9	–	89.2
1971	64,374	6,180	–	57,575	100.0	9.6	–	89.4
1970	63,401	6,223	–	56,602	100.0	9.8	–	89.3

	percent change					percentage point change		
1990 to 2000	12.2%	22.5%	57.1%	9.4%	–	1.0	2.5	–2.1
1970 to 2000	65.1	106.5	–	54.9	–	2.5	–	–5.5

Note: Numbers will not add to total because Hispanics may be of any race and not all races are shown. (–) means data not available or not applicable.
Source: Bureau of the Census, Current Population Surveys, Internet site http://www.census.gov/population/socdemo/hh-fam/ tabHH-2.txt; calculations by New Strategist

Fewer Households include Children

One of the biggest lifestyle changes of the past half-century is the disappearance of children from the nation's households. In 1950, 47 percent of households included children under age 18. By 2000 the figure had fallen to just 33 percent. The share of nuclear families (married couples with children under age 18 at home) fell from 43 percent of households in 1950 to just 24 percent in 2000. Only 7 percent of households had three or more children under age 18 at home in 2000, down from 17 percent in 1960.

As fewer households include children, and fewer children per household, household size has fallen. In 1950, the average household contained 3.4 people. By 2000, average household size was just 2.6 people. The share of households containing only one or two people rose from 40 percent in 1950 to the 59 percent majority by 2000.

Only one in three households includes children

(percent of households with children under age 18, 1950 to 2000)

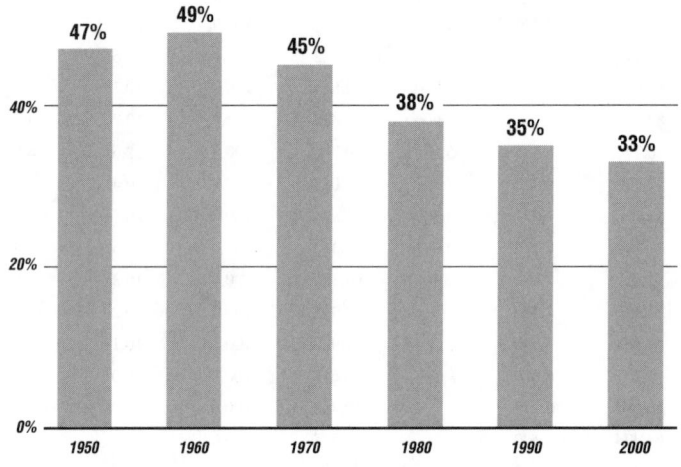

Table 7.6 Households with Children under Age 18 by Household Type, 1950 to 2000

(number of households by presence of own children under age 18 at home, 1950 to 2000; percent change for selected years; numbers in thousands)

	total households	families with children under age 18				
		total	married couples	single parent total	mother only	father only
2000	104,705	34,605	25,248	9,357	7,571	1,786
1999	103,874	34,613	25,066	9,547	7,841	1,706
1998	102,528	34,760	25,269	9,491	7,693	1,798
1997	101,018	34,665	25,083	9,583	7,874	1,709
1996	99,627	34,203	24,920	9,284	7,656	1,628
1995	98,990	34,296	25,241	9,055	7,615	1,440
1994	97,107	34,018	25,058	8,961	7,647	1,314
1993	96,426	33,257	24,707	8,550	7,226	1,324
1992	95,669	32,746	24,420	8,326	7,043	1,283
1991	94,312	32,401	24,397	8,004	6,823	1,181
1990	93,347	32,289	24,537	7,752	6,599	1,153
1989	92,830	32,322	24,735	7,587	6,519	1,068
1988	91,124	31,920	24,600	7,320	6,273	1,047
1987	89,479	31,898	24,646	7,252	6,297	955
1986	88,458	31,670	24,630	7,040	6,105	935
1985	86,789	31,112	24,210	6,902	6,006	896
1984	85,290	31,046	24,340	6,706	5,907	799
1983	83,918	30,818	24,363	6,455	5,718	737
1982	83,527	31,012	24,465	6,547	5,868	679
1981	82,368	31,227	24,927	6,300	5,634	666
1980	80,776	31,022	24,961	6,061	5,445	616
1979	77,330	30,371	24,514	5,857	5,288	569
1978	76,030	30,369	24,625	5,744	5,206	539
1977	74,142	30,145	24,875	5,270	4,784	486
1976	72,867	30,177	25,110	5,067	4,621	446
1975	71,120	30,057	25,169	4,888	4,404	484
1974	69,859	29,750	25,278	4,472	4,081	391
1973	68,251	29,571	25,387	4,184	3,798	386
1972	66,676	29,445	25,482	3,963	3,598	365
1971	64,778	28,786	25,091	3,695	3,365	331
1970	63,401	28,812	25,541	3,271	2,971	345
1969	62,214	28,347	25,136	3,211	2,888	323
1968	60,813	27,964	24,895	3,069	2,772	297
1967	59,236	27,561	24,646	2,915	2,584	331
1966	58,406	27,004	24,276	2,728	2,450	278
1965	57,436	27,140	24,406	2,734	2,485	249
1964	56,149	27,068	24,439	2,629	2,361	268
1963	55,270	26,911	24,321	2,590	2,229	361
1962	54,764	26,271	23,788	2,483	2,229	254
1961	53,557	25,889	23,514	2,375	2,185	190
1960	52,799	25,690	23,358	2,332	2,099	232
1959	51,435	25,069	22,894	2,175	1,943	232
1958	50,474	24,541	22,426	2,115	1,822	293
1957	49,673	24,260	22,139	2,121	1,855	265
1956	48,902	23,743	21,631	2,112	1,814	298
1955	47,874	23,190	21,064	2,126	1,870	256
1954	46,962	22,544	20,645	1,899	1,615	283
1953	46,385	21,718	19,920	1,798	1,521	277
1952	45,538	21,353	19,606	1,747	1,514	233
1951	44,673	21,279	19,389	1,890	1,659	231
1950	43,554	20,324	18,824	1,500	1,272	229
Percent change						
1990 to 2000	12.2%	7.2%	2.9%	20.7%	14.7%	54.9%
1950 to 2000	140.4	70.3	34.1	523.8	495.2	679.9

Source: Bureau of the Census, Current Population Surveys, Internet site http://www.census.gov/population/socdemo/hh-fam/ tabFM-1.txt; calculations by New Strategist

Table 7.7 Distribution of Households with Children under Age 18 by Household Type, 1950 to 2000

(percent distribution of households by presence of own children under age 18 at home, 1950 to 2000; percentage point change for selected years)

	total households	families with children under age 18				
				single parent		
		total	married couples	total	mother only	father only
2000	100.0%	33.0%	24.1%	8.9%	7.2%	1.7%
1999	100.0	33.3	24.1	9.2	7.5	1.6
1998	100.0	33.9	24.6	9.3	7.5	1.8
1997	100.0	34.3	24.8	9.5	7.8	1.7
1996	100.0	34.3	25.0	9.3	7.7	1.6
1995	100.0	34.6	25.5	9.1	7.7	1.5
1994	100.0	35.0	25.8	9.2	7.9	1.4
1993	100.0	34.5	25.6	8.9	7.5	1.4
1992	100.0	34.2	25.5	8.7	7.4	1.3
1991	100.0	34.4	25.9	8.5	7.2	1.3
1990	100.0	34.6	26.3	8.3	7.1	1.2
1989	100.0	34.8	26.6	8.2	7.0	1.2
1988	100.0	35.0	27.0	8.0	6.9	1.1
1987	100.0	35.6	27.5	8.1	7.0	1.1
1986	100.0	35.8	27.8	8.0	6.9	1.1
1985	100.0	35.8	27.9	8.0	6.9	1.0
1984	100.0	36.4	28.5	7.9	6.9	0.9
1983	100.0	36.7	29.0	7.7	6.8	0.9
1982	100.0	37.1	29.3	7.8	7.0	0.8
1981	100.0	37.9	30.3	7.6	6.8	0.8
1980	100.0	38.4	30.9	7.5	6.7	0.8
1979	100.0	39.3	31.7	7.6	6.8	0.7
1978	100.0	39.9	32.4	7.6	6.8	0.7
1977	100.0	40.7	33.6	7.1	6.5	0.7
1976	100.0	41.4	34.5	7.0	6.3	0.6
1975	100.0	42.3	35.4	6.9	6.2	0.7
1974	100.0	42.6	36.2	6.4	5.8	0.6
1973	100.0	43.3	37.2	6.1	5.6	0.6
1972	100.0	44.2	38.2	5.9	5.4	0.5
1971	100.0	44.4	38.7	5.7	5.2	0.5
1970	100.0	45.4	40.3	5.2	4.7	0.5
1969	100.0	45.6	40.4	5.2	4.6	0.5
1968	100.0	46.0	40.9	5.0	4.6	0.5
1967	100.0	46.5	41.6	4.9	4.4	0.6
1966	100.0	46.2	41.6	4.7	4.2	0.5
1965	100.0	47.3	42.5	4.8	4.3	0.4
1964	100.0	48.2	43.5	4.7	4.2	0.5
1963	100.0	48.7	44.0	4.7	4.0	0.7
1962	100.0	48.0	43.4	4.5	4.1	0.5
1961	100.0	48.3	43.9	4.4	4.1	0.4
1960	100.0	48.7	44.2	4.4	4.0	0.4
1959	100.0	48.7	44.5	4.2	3.8	0.5
1958	100.0	48.6	44.4	4.2	3.6	0.6
1957	100.0	48.8	44.6	4.3	3.7	0.5
1956	100.0	48.6	44.2	4.3	3.7	0.6
1955	100.0	48.4	44.0	4.4	3.9	0.5
1954	100.0	48.0	44.0	4.0	3.4	0.6
1953	100.0	46.8	42.9	3.9	3.3	0.6
1952	100.0	46.9	43.1	3.8	3.3	0.5
1951	100.0	47.6	43.4	4.2	3.7	0.5
1950	100.0	46.7	43.2	3.4	2.9	0.5
Percentage point change						
1990 to 2000	–	−1.5	−2.2	0.6	0.2	0.5
1950 to 2000	–	−13.6	−19.1	5.5	4.3	1.2

Note: (–) means not applicable.
Source: Bureau of the Census, Current Population Surveys, Internet site http://www.census.gov/population/socdemo/hh-fam/ tabFM-1.txt; calculations by New Strategist

Table 7.8 Households by Presence and Number of Children under Age 18, 1950 to 2000

(number and percent distribution of households by presence and number of own children under age 18 at home 1950 to 2000; percent and percentage point change for selected years; numbers in thousands)

| | total households | no children | households with children | | | | |
			total	one child	two children	three children	four or more children
2000	104,705	70,100	34,605	14,311	13,215	5,063	2,017
1990	93,347	61,058	32,289	13,530	12,263	4,650	1,846
1980	80,776	49,754	31,022	12,443	11,470	4,674	2,435
1970	63,401	34,589	28,812	9,364	8,961	5,445	5,042
1960	52,799	27,109	25,690	8,349	8,118	5,010	4,213
1950	43,554	23,230	20,324	8,292	6,483	3,069	2,480
Percent change							
1990 to 2000	12.2%	14.8%	7.2%	5.8%	7.8%	8.9%	9.3%
1950 to 2000	140.4	201.8	70.3	72.6	103.8	65.0	−18.7
Percent distribution							
2000	100.0	67.0	33.0	13.7	12.6	4.8	1.9
1990	100.0	65.4	34.6	14.5	13.1	5.0	2.0
1980	100.0	61.6	38.4	15.4	14.2	5.8	3.0
1970	100.0	54.6	45.4	14.8	14.1	8.6	8.0
1960	100.0	51.3	48.7	15.8	15.4	9.5	8.0
1950	100.0	53.3	46.7	19.0	14.9	7.0	5.7
Percentage point change							
1990 to 2000	–	1.5	−1.5	−0.8	−0.5	−0.1	−0.1
1950 to 2000	–	13.6	−13.6	−5.4	−2.3	−2.2	−3.8

Source: Bureau of the Census, Historical Statistics of the United States: Colonial Times to 1970, Part 1, *1975; and Internet site http://www.census.gov/population/socdemo/hh-fam/p20-537/2000/tabF1.txt; calculations by New Strategist*

Table 7.9 Households by Size, 1950 to 2000

(number of households by size, and average number of persons per household, 1950 to 2000; percent change for selected years; numbers in thousands)

	total households	one person	two people	three people	four people	five people	six people	seven+ people	aver. per household
2000	104,705	26,724	34,666	17,172	15,309	6,981	2,445	1,428	2.62
1999	103,874	26,606	34,262	17,386	15,030	6,962	2,367	1,261	2.61
1998	102,528	26,327	32,965	17,331	15,358	7,048	2,232	1,267	2.62
1997	101,018	25,402	32,736	17,065	15,396	6,774	2,311	1,334	2.64
1996	99,627	24,900	32,526	16,724	15,118	6,631	2,357	1,372	2.65
1995	98,990	24,732	31,834	16,827	15,321	6,616	2,279	1,382	2.65
1994	97,107	23,611	31,211	16,898	15,073	6,749	2,186	1,379	2.67
1993	96,426	23,558	31,041	16,964	14,997	6,404	2,217	1,244	2.66
1992	95,669	23,974	30,734	16,398	14,710	6,389	2,126	1,338	2.62
1991	94,312	23,590	30,181	16,082	14,556	6,206	2,237	1,459	2.63
1990	93,347	22,999	30,114	16,128	14,456	6,213	2,143	1,295	2.63
1989	92,830	22,708	29,976	16,276	14,550	6,232	2,003	1,084	2.62
1988	91,124	21,889	29,295	16,163	14,143	6,081	2,176	1,320	2.64
1987	89,479	21,128	28,602	16,159	13,984	6,162	2,176	1,268	2.66
1986	88,458	21,178	27,732	16,088	13,774	6,276	2,138	1,272	2.67
1985	86,789	20,602	27,389	15,465	13,631	6,108	2,299	1,296	2.69
1984	85,290	19,954	26,890	15,134	13,593	6,070	2,372	1,394	2.71
1983	83,918	19,250	26,439	14,793	13,303	6,105	2,460	1,568	2.73
1982	83,527	19,354	26,486	14,617	12,868	6,103	2,480	1,619	2.72
1981	82,368	18,936	25,787	14,569	12,768	6,117	2,549	1,643	2.73
1980	80,776	18,296	25,327	14,130	12,666	6,059	2,519	1,778	2.76
1979	77,330	17,201	23,928	13,392	12,274	6,187	2,573	1,774	2.78
1978	76,030	16,715	23,334	13,040	11,955	6,356	2,723	1,906	2.81
1977	74,142	15,532	22,775	12,794	11,630	6,285	2,864	2,263	2.86
1976	72,867	14,983	22,321	12,520	11,407	6,268	3,001	2,367	2.89
1975	71,120	13,939	21,753	12,384	11,103	6,399	3,059	2,484	2.94
1974	69,859	13,368	21,495	11,913	10,900	6,469	3,063	2,651	2.97
1973	68,251	12,635	20,632	11,804	10,739	6,426	3,245	2,769	3.01
1972	66,676	12,189	19,482	11,542	10,679	6,431	3,374	2,979	3.06
1971	64,778	11,446	18,892	11,071	10,059	6,640	3,435	3,234	3.11
1970	63,401	10,851	18,333	10,949	9,991	6,548	3,534	3,195	3.14
1969	62,214	10,401	18,034	10,769	9,778	6,387	3,557	3,288	3.16
1968	60,813	9,802	17,377	10,577	9,623	6,319	3,627	3,488	3.20
1967	59,236	9,200	16,770	10,403	9,559	6,276	3,491	3,550	3.26
1966	58,406	9,093	16,679	9,993	9,465	6,257	3,465	3,465	3.27
1965	57,436	8,631	16,119	10,263	9,269	6,313	3,327	3,514	3.29
1964	56,149	7,821	15,622	10,034	9,565	6,328	3,373	3,405	3.33
1963	55,270	7,501	15,279	9,989	9,445	6,240	3,473	3,342	3.33
1962	54,764	7,473	15,461	10,077	9,347	6,016	3,368	3,022	3.31
1961	53,557	7,112	15,185	9,780	9,390	6,052	3,085	2,953	3.34
1960	52,799	6,917	14,678	9,979	9,293	6,072	3,010	2,851	3.33
1950	43,468	4,737	12,529	9,808	7,729	4,357	2,196	2,113	3.37

Percent change

1990 to 2000	12.2%	16.2%	15.1%	6.5%	5.9%	12.4%	14.1%	10.3%	–0.4%
1950 to 2000	140.9	464.2	176.7	75.1	98.1	60.2	11.3	–32.4	–22.3

Source: Bureau of the Census, Historical Statistics of the United States: Colonial Times to 1970, Part 1, *1975; and Internet site http://www.census.gov/population/socdemo/hh-fam/tabHH-4.txt; calculations by New Strategist by New Strategist*

Table 7.10 Distribution of Households by Size, 1950 to 2000

(percent distribution of households by size, 1950 to 2000; percentage point change for selected years)

	total households	one person	two people	three people	four people	five people	six people	seven+ people
2000	100.0%	25.5%	33.1%	16.4%	14.6%	6.7%	2.3%	1.4%
1999	100.0	25.6	33.0	16.7	14.5	6.7	2.3	1.2
1998	100.0	25.7	32.2	16.9	15.0	6.9	2.2	1.2
1997	100.0	25.1	32.4	16.9	15.2	6.7	2.3	1.3
1996	100.0	25.0	32.6	16.8	15.2	6.7	2.4	1.4
1995	100.0	25.0	32.2	17.0	15.5	6.7	2.3	1.4
1994	100.0	24.3	32.1	17.4	15.5	7.0	2.3	1.4
1993	100.0	24.4	32.2	17.6	15.6	6.6	2.3	1.3
1992	100.0	25.1	32.1	17.1	15.4	6.7	2.2	1.4
1991	100.0	25.0	32.0	17.1	15.4	6.6	2.4	1.5
1990	100.0	24.6	32.3	17.3	15.5	6.7	2.3	1.4
1989	100.0	24.5	32.3	17.5	15.7	6.7	2.2	1.2
1988	100.0	24.0	32.1	17.7	15.5	6.7	2.4	1.4
1987	100.0	23.6	32.0	18.1	15.6	6.9	2.4	1.4
1986	100.0	23.9	31.4	18.2	15.6	7.1	2.4	1.4
1985	100.0	23.7	31.6	17.8	15.7	7.0	2.6	1.5
1984	100.0	23.4	31.5	17.7	15.9	7.1	2.8	1.6
1983	100.0	22.9	31.5	17.6	15.9	7.3	2.9	1.9
1982	100.0	23.2	31.7	17.5	15.4	7.3	3.0	1.9
1981	100.0	23.0	31.3	17.7	15.5	7.4	3.1	2.0
1980	100.0	22.7	31.4	17.5	15.7	7.5	3.1	2.2
1979	100.0	22.2	30.9	17.3	15.9	8.0	3.3	2.3
1978	100.0	22.0	30.7	17.2	15.7	8.4	3.6	2.5
1977	100.0	20.9	30.7	17.3	15.7	8.5	3.9	3.1
1976	100.0	20.6	30.6	17.2	15.7	8.6	4.1	3.2
1975	100.0	19.6	30.6	17.4	15.6	9.0	4.3	3.5
1974	100.0	19.1	30.8	17.1	15.6	9.3	4.4	3.8
1973	100.0	18.5	30.2	17.3	15.7	9.4	4.8	4.1
1972	100.0	18.3	29.2	17.3	16.0	9.6	5.1	4.5
1971	100.0	17.7	29.2	17.1	15.5	10.3	5.3	5.0
1970	100.0	17.1	28.9	17.3	15.8	10.3	5.6	5.0
1969	100.0	16.7	29.0	17.3	15.7	10.3	5.7	5.3
1968	100.0	16.1	28.6	17.4	15.8	10.4	6.0	5.7
1967	100.0	15.5	28.3	17.6	16.1	10.6	5.9	6.0
1966	100.0	15.6	28.6	17.1	16.2	10.7	5.9	5.9
1965	100.0	15.0	28.1	17.9	16.1	11.0	5.8	6.1
1964	100.0	13.9	27.8	17.9	17.0	11.3	6.0	6.1
1963	100.0	13.6	27.6	18.1	17.1	11.3	6.3	6.0
1962	100.0	13.6	28.2	18.4	17.1	11.0	6.2	5.5
1961	100.0	13.3	28.4	18.3	17.5	11.3	5.8	5.5
1960	100.0	13.1	27.8	18.9	17.6	11.5	5.7	5.4
1950	100.0	10.9	28.8	22.6	17.8	10.0	5.1	4.9
Percentage point change								
1990 to 2000	–	0.9	0.8	–0.9	–0.9	0.0	0.0	0.0
1950 to 2000	–	14.6	4.3	–6.2	–3.2	–3.4	–2.7	–3.5

Note: (–) means not applicable.
Source: Bureau of the Census, Historical Statistics of the United States: Colonial Times to 1970, Part 1, 1975; and Internet site http://www.census.gov/population/socdemo/hh-fam/tabHH-4.txt; calculations by New Strategist by New Strategist

More Children Live with Mother Only

Single-parent households have become much more numerous as divorce and out-of-wedlock births have become common. In 2000, only 69 percent of children lived with both parents, down from 88 percent in 1960. The percentage of children who live with their mother only has climbed from 8 percent in 1960 to 22 percent in 2000.

In 2000, 49 percent of black children lived with their mother only. Just 38 percent lived with both parents, down from 67 percent in 1960. Among Hispanic children, 65 percent live with both parents, down from 78 percent in 1970. Among white children 75 percent lived with both parents in 2000, down from 91 percent in 1960. Few children live with their fathers.

As out-of-wedlock births have soared, many more children live with mothers who have never married. Among children who lived with only their mother in 2000, 41 percent lived with a never-married mother. The share was only 4 percent in 1960. Five percent of children live with grandparents, up from 3 percent in 1970.

Fewer children live with both parents

(percent of children under age 18 who live with both parents, 1960 to 2000)

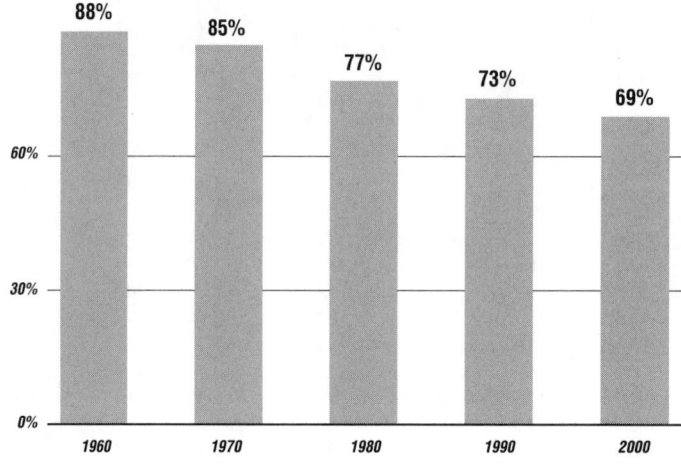

Table 7.11 Living Arrangements of Children under Age 18, 1960 to 2000: Total Children

(number and percent of children under age 18 by living arrangement, 1960 to 2000; numbers in thousands)

	total children	living with both parents		living with mother only		living with father only	
		number	percent	number	percent	number	percent
2000	72,012	49,795	69.1%	16,162	22.4%	3,058	4.2%
1999	71,703	48,775	68.0	16,805	23.4	3,094	4.3
1998	71,377	48,642	68.1	16,634	23.3	3,143	4.4
1997	70,983	48,386	68.2	16,740	23.6	3,059	4.3
1996	70,908	48,224	68.0	16,993	24.0	2,759	3.9
1995	70,254	48,276	68.7	16,477	23.5	2,461	3.5
1994	69,508	48,084	69.2	16,334	23.5	2,257	3.2
1993	66,893	47,181	70.5	15,586	23.3	2,286	3.4
1992	65,965	46,638	70.7	15,396	23.3	2,182	3.3
1991	65,093	46,658	71.7	14,608	22.4	2,016	3.1
1990	64,137	46,503	72.5	13,874	21.6	1,993	3.1
1989	63,637	46,549	73.1	13,700	21.5	1,793	2.8
1988	63,179	45,942	72.7	13,521	21.4	1,808	2.9
1987	62,932	46,009	73.1	13,420	21.3	1,651	2.6
1986	62,763	46,384	73.9	13,180	21.0	1,579	2.5
1985	62,475	46,149	73.9	13,081	20.9	1,554	2.5
1984	62,139	46,555	74.9	12,646	20.4	1,378	2.2
1983	62,281	46,632	74.9	12,739	20.5	1,267	2.0
1982	62,407	46,797	75.0	12,512	20.0	1,189	1.9
1981	62,918	48,040	76.4	11,416	18.1	1,203	1.9
1980	63,427	48,624	76.7	11,406	18.0	1,060	1.7
1979	62,389	48,295	77.4	10,531	16.9	997	1.6
1978	63,206	49,132	77.7	10,725	17.0	985	1.6
1977	64,062	50,735	79.2	10,419	16.3	892	1.4
1976	65,129	52,101	80.0	10,310	15.8	811	1.2
1975	66,087	53,072	80.3	10,231	15.5	1,014	1.5
1974	67,047	54,561	81.4	9,647	14.4	842	1.3
1973	67,950	55,807	82.1	9,272	13.6	821	1.2
1972	68,811	57,201	83.1	8,838	12.8	796	1.2
1971	70,255	58,606	83.4	8,714	12.4	764	1.1
1970	69,162	58,939	85.2	7,452	10.8	748	1.1
1969	70,317	59,857	85.1	7,744	11.0	765	1.1
1968	70,326	60,030	85.4	7,556	10.7	776	1.1
1960	63,727	55,877	87.7	5,105	8.0	724	1.1

Source: Bureau of the Census, 1960 Census and Current Population Surveys, Internet site http://www.census.gov/population/ socdemo/hh-fam/tabCH-1.txt; calculations by New Strategist

Table 7.12 Living Arrangements of Children under Age 18, 1960 to 2000: Black Children

(number and percent of black children under age 18 by living arrangement, 1960 to 2000; numbers in thousands)

	total children	living with both parents		living with mother only		living with father only	
		number	*percent*	*number*	*percent*	*number*	*percent*
2000	11,412	4,286	37.6%	5,596	49.0%	484	4.2%
1999	11,425	3,967	34.7	5,891	51.6	461	4.0
1998	11,414	4,137	36.2	5,830	51.1	424	3.7
1997	11,369	3,940	34.7	5,888	51.8	581	5.1
1996	11,434	3,816	33.4	6,056	53.0	504	4.4
1995	11,301	3,746	33.1	5,881	52.0	458	4.1
1994	11,177	3,722	33.3	5,967	53.4	417	3.7
1993	10,660	3,796	35.6	5,757	54.0	322	3.0
1992	10,427	3,714	35.6	5,607	53.8	327	3.1
1991	10,209	3,669	35.9	5,516	54.0	358	3.5
1990	10,018	3,781	37.7	5,132	51.2	353	3.5
1989	9,835	3,738	38.0	5,023	51.1	339	3.4
1988	9,699	3,739	38.6	4,959	51.1	288	3.0
1987	9,612	3,852	40.1	4,844	50.4	243	2.5
1986	9,532	3,869	40.6	4,827	50.6	231	2.4
1985	9,479	3,741	39.5	4,837	51.0	276	2.9
1984	9,375	3,845	41.0	4,705	50.2	273	2.9
1983	9,377	3,818	40.7	4,789	51.1	234	2.5
1982	9,377	3,978	42.4	4,422	47.2	192	2.0
1981	9,400	4,016	42.7	4,074	43.3	236	2.5
1980	9,375	3,956	42.2	4,117	43.9	180	1.9
1979	9,285	4,030	43.4	3,891	41.9	198	2.1
1978	9,394	4,094	43.6	3,978	42.3	195	2.1
1977	9,374	4,384	46.8	3,911	41.7	135	1.4
1976	9,461	4,688	49.6	3,791	40.1	145	1.5
1975	9,472	4,682	49.4	3,870	40.9	172	1.8
1974	9,526	4,831	50.7	3,602	37.8	171	1.8
1973	9,523	4,904	51.5	3,583	37.6	199	2.1
1972	9,583	5,201	54.3	3,207	33.5	178	1.9
1971	10,004	5,446	54.4	3,264	32.6	173	1.7
1970	9,422	5,508	58.5	2,783	29.5	213	2.3
1969	9,832	5,784	58.8	2,907	29.6	179	1.8
1968	9,714	5,702	58.7	2,842	29.3	210	2.2
1960	8,650	5,795	67.0	1,723	19.9	173	2.0

Source: Bureau of the Census, 1960 Census and Current Population Surveys, Internet site http://www.census.gov/population/socdemo/hh-fam/tabCH-3.txt; calculations by New Strategist

Table 7.13 Living Arrangements of Children under Age 18, 1970 to 2000: Hispanic Children

(number and percent of Hispanic children under age 18 by living arrangement, 1970 to 2000; numbers in thousands)

	total children	living with both parents		living with mother only		living with father only	
		number	percent	number	percent	number	percent
2000	11,613	7,561	65.1%	2,919	25.1%	506	4.4%
1999	11,236	7,127	63.4	3,023	26.9	506	4.5
1998	10,863	6,909	63.6	2,915	26.8	482	4.4
1997	10,526	6,748	64.1	2,819	26.8	441	4.2
1996	10,251	6,381	62.2	2,937	28.7	384	3.7
1995	9,843	6,191	62.9	2,798	28.4	417	4.2
1994	9,496	6,022	63.4	2,646	27.9	373	3.9
1993	7,776	5,017	64.5	2,176	28.0	296	3.8
1992	7,619	4,935	64.8	2,168	28.5	279	3.7
1991	7,462	4,944	66.3	1,983	26.6	239	3.2
1990	7,174	4,789	66.8	1,943	27.1	211	2.9
1989	6,973	4,673	67.0	1,940	27.8	189	2.7
1988	6,786	4,497	66.3	1,845	27.2	202	3.0
1987	6,647	4,355	65.5	1,843	27.7	184	2.8
1986	6,430	4,275	66.5	1,784	27.7	171	2.7
1985	6,057	4,110	67.9	1,612	26.6	134	2.2
1984	5,625	3,946	70.2	1,399	24.9	110	2.0
1983	5,513	3,774	68.5	1,475	26.8	99	1.8
1982	5,358	3,700	69.1	1,353	25.3	83	1.5
1981	5,267	3,703	70.3	1,212	23.0	129	2.4
1980	5,438	4,138	76.1	1,035	19.0	80	1.5
1970	4,006	3,111	77.7	–	–	–	–

Note: (–) means data not available.
Source: Bureau of the Census, Current Population Surveys, Internet site http://www.census.gov/population/socdemo/hh-fam/ tabCH-4.txt; calculations by New Strategist

Table 7.14 Living Arrangements of Children under Age 18, 1960 to 2000: White Children

(number and percent of white children under age 18 by living arrangement, 1960 to 2000; numbers in thousands)

	total children	living with both parents		living with mother only		living with father only	
		number	percent	number	percent	number	percent
2000	56,455	42,497	75.3%	9,765	17.3%	2,427	4.3%
1999	56,265	41,845	74.4	10,200	18.1	2,454	4.4
1998	56,124	41,547	74.0	10,210	18.2	2,562	4.6
1997	55,869	41,654	74.6	10,204	18.3	2,339	4.2
1996	55,714	41,609	74.7	10,239	18.4	2,096	3.8
1995	55,327	41,946	75.8	9,827	17.8	1,892	3.4
1994	54,795	41,766	76.2	9,724	17.7	1,710	3.1
1993	53,075	40,996	77.2	9,256	17.4	1,854	3.5
1992	52,493	40,635	77.4	9,250	17.6	1,721	3.3
1991	51,918	40,733	78.5	8,585	16.5	1,557	3.0
1990	51,390	40,593	79.0	8,321	16.2	1,549	3.0
1989	51,134	40,706	79.6	8,220	16.1	1,406	2.7
1988	51,030	40,287	78.9	8,160	16.0	1,464	2.9
1987	51,112	40,407	79.1	8,231	16.1	1,338	2.6
1986	50,931	40,681	79.9	8,021	15.7	1,282	2.5
1985	50,836	40,690	80.0	7,929	15.6	1,210	2.4
1984	50,620	41,009	81.0	7,641	15.1	1,061	2.1
1983	50,873	41,231	81.0	7,616	15.0	998	2.0
1982	51,086	41,285	80.8	7,831	15.3	949	1.9
1981	51,620	42,493	82.3	7,097	13.7	927	1.8
1980	52,242	43,200	82.7	7,059	13.5	842	1.6
1979	51,688	43,145	83.5	6,445	12.5	767	1.5
1978	52,523	44,001	83.8	6,592	12.6	770	1.5
1977	53,394	45,289	84.8	6,359	11.9	747	1.4
1976	54,411	46,342	85.2	6,421	11.8	634	1.2
1975	55,500	47,415	85.4	6,266	11.3	830	1.5
1974	56,437	48,910	86.7	5,889	10.4	661	1.2
1973	57,398	50,150	87.4	5,514	9.6	614	1.1
1972	58,221	51,159	87.9	5,510	9.5	610	1.0
1971	59,264	52,328	88.3	5,336	9.0	587	1.0
1970	58,791	52,624	89.5	4,581	7.8	528	0.9
1969	59,589	53,360	89.5	4,721	7.9	552	0.9
1968	59,724	53,599	89.7	4,613	7.7	563	0.9
1960	55,077	50,082	90.9	3,381	6.1	551	1.0

Source: Bureau of the Census, 1960 Census and Current Population Surveys, Internet site http://www.census.gov/population/socdemo/hh-fam/tabCH-2.txt; calculations by New Strategist

Table 7.15 Children under Age 18 Living with Mother Only, 1960 to 2000

(total number of children under age 18 living with only their mother and percent distribution by marital status of mother, 1960 to 2000; numbers in thousands)

	living with mother only		never married	married, spouse absent	divorced	widowed
	number	percent				
2000	16,162	100.0%	40.8%	19.9%	35.0%	4.3%
1999	16,805	100.0	40.1	21.2	34.7	4.0
1998	16,634	100.0	40.3	21.4	34.3	4.0
1997	16,740	100.0	39.4	22.4	34.8	3.4
1996	16,993	100.0	37.5	23.1	35.5	3.9
1995	16,477	100.0	35.6	23.7	36.5	4.2
1994	16,334	100.0	36.7	23.5	35.5	4.3
1993	15,586	100.0	35.4	24.0	36.5	4.2
1992	15,396	100.0	35.1	24.6	35.8	4.5
1991	14,608	100.0	34.5	24.5	35.6	5.3
1990	13,874	100.0	31.5	24.6	36.9	7.0
1989	13,700	100.0	31.3	24.7	38.2	5.9
1988	13,521	100.0	31.8	24.9	37.1	6.2
1987	13,420	100.0	29.7	24.5	39.7	6.1
1986	13,180	100.0	27.4	25.2	40.6	6.8
1985	13,081	100.0	26.7	25.7	40.4	7.2
1984	12,646	100.0	24.8	27.1	40.9	7.3
1983	12,739	100.0	25.2	26.2	40.7	7.9
1982	12,512	100.0	22.1	28.1	40.8	9.0
1981	11,416	100.0	15.8	31.0	43.0	10.1
1980	11,406	100.0	15.3	31.7	41.8	11.3
1979	10,531	100.0	14.7	33.1	40.4	11.8
1978	10,725	100.0	15.2	32.7	40.4	11.7
1977	10,419	100.0	12.8	34.7	40.4	12.0
1976	10,310	100.0	11.0	36.8	39.0	13.2
1975	10,231	100.0	11.4	37.7	35.6	15.3
1974	9,647	100.0	10.0	39.3	34.0	16.7
1973	9,272	100.0	9.6	40.4	33.5	16.5
1972	8,838	100.0	7.2	44.1	31.7	17.0
1971	8,714	100.0	8.9	44.4	30.1	16.6
1970	7,452	100.0	7.1	43.4	30.8	18.7
1969	7,744	100.0	5.7	47.8	26.5	19.9
1968	7,556	100.0	6.2	45.3	27.2	21.4
1960	5,105	100.0	4.3	46.3	23.7	25.7

Source: Bureau of the Census, Current Population Surveys, Internet site http://www.census.gov/population/socdemo/hh-fam/ tabCH-5.txt; calculations by New Strategist

Table 7.16　Grandchildren Living in the Home of Their Grandparents, 1970 to 2000

(number and percent distribution of children under age 18 living with their grandparents by presence of parent in the home, 1970 to 2000; numbers in thousands)

		living with grandparents				
	total children	total	with parents present			neither parent present
			both	mother only	father only	
2000	72,012	3,842	531	1,732	220	1,359
1999	71,703	3,919	535	1,803	250	1,331
1998	71,377	3,989	503	1,827	241	1,417
1997	70,983	3,894	554	1,785	247	1,309
1996	70,908	4,060	467	1,943	220	1,431
1995	70,254	3,965	427	1,876	195	1,466
1994	69,508	3,735	436	1,764	175	1,359
1993	66,893	3,368	475	1,647	229	1,017
1992	65,965	3,253	502	1,740	144	867
1991	65,093	3,320	559	1,674	151	937
1990	64,137	3,155	467	1,563	191	935
1980	63,369	2,306	310	922	86	988
1970	69,276	2,214	363	817	78	957
2000	100.0%	5.3%	0.7%	2.4%	0.3%	1.9%
1999	100.0	5.5	0.7	2.5	0.3	1.9
1998	100.0	5.6	0.7	2.6	0.3	2.0
1997	100.0	5.5	0.8	2.5	0.3	1.8
1996	100.0	5.7	0.7	2.7	0.3	2.0
1995	100.0	5.6	0.6	2.7	0.3	2.1
1994	100.0	5.4	0.6	2.5	0.3	2.0
1993	100.0	5.0	0.7	2.5	0.3	1.5
1992	100.0	4.9	0.8	2.6	0.2	1.3
1991	100.0	5.1	0.9	2.6	0.2	1.4
1990	100.0	4.9	0.7	2.4	0.3	1.5
1980	100.0	3.6	0.5	1.5	0.1	1.6
1970	100.0	3.2	0.5	1.2	0.1	1.4

Source: Bureau of the Census, 1970 and 1980 Censuses and Current Population Surveys, Internet site http://www.census.gov/population/socdemo/hh-fam/tabCH-7.txt; calculations by New Strategist

Changing Lifestyles of Young and Old

The living arrangements of both the young and the old have changed over the past few decades. Young adults are more likely to live with mom and dad and less likely to head their own households. Older Americans are more likely to live alone and less likely to live with adult children. The share of unmarried couples has increased as men and women opt for living together before marriage.

Among men aged 18 to 24, the 57 percent majority lived with their parents in 2000, up from 52 percent in 1960. Among women in the age group, the proportion living with their parents climbed from 35 to 47 percent. Men and women aged 25 to 34 are slightly more likely to live with their parents than they once were. The rate rose from 11 to 13 percent among men between 1960 and 2000, while it rose from 7 to 8 percent among women. (The shares include college students residing in dormitories.)

Among Americans of all ages, a larger share lived alone in 2000 than in 1970. The increase in lone living has been especially pronounced for women aged 75 or older. In 1970, 37 percent of women in the age group lived alone. By 2000, 49 percent lived by themselves, although this was down from 54 percent in 1990.

More older women live alone

(percent of people aged 75 or older who live alone, by sex, 1970 and 2000)

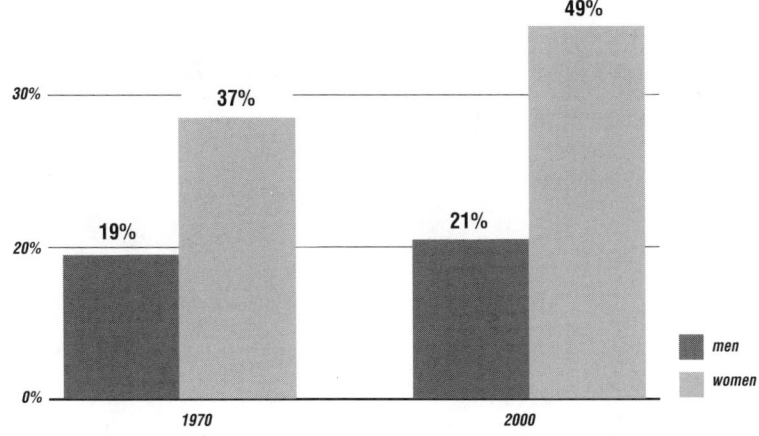

Table 7.17 Living Arrangements of Young Men, 1960 to 2000

(total number of men aged 18 to 34, and number and percent living with their parents, by age, 1960 to 2000; numbers in thousands)

| | men aged 18 to 24 | | | men aged 25 to 34 | | |
| | | living with parents | | | living with parents | |
	total	number	share of total	total	number	share of total
2000	13,291	7,593	57.1%	18,563	2,387	12.9%
1999	12,936	7,440	57.5	18,924	2,636	13.9
1998	12,633	7,399	58.6	19,526	2,845	14.6
1997	12,534	7,501	59.8	20,039	2,909	14.5
1996	12,402	7,327	59.1	20,390	3,213	15.8
1995	12,545	7,328	58.4	20,589	3,166	15.4
1994	12,683	7,547	59.5	20,873	3,261	15.6
1993	12,049	7,145	59.3	20,856	3,300	15.8
1992	12,083	7,296	60.4	21,125	3,225	15.3
1991	12,275	7,385	60.2	21,319	3,172	14.9
1990	12,450	7,232	58.1	21,462	3,213	15.0
1989	12,574	7,308	58.1	21,461	3,130	14.6
1988	12,835	7,792	60.7	21,320	3,207	15.0
1987	13,029	7,981	61.3	21,142	3,071	14.5
1986	13,324	7,831	58.8	20,956	2,981	14.2
1985	13,695	8,172	59.7	20,184	2,685	13.3
1984	14,196	8,764	61.7	19,876	2,626	13.2
1983	14,344	8,803	61.4	19,438	2,664	13.7
1980	14,278	7,755	54.3	18,107	1,894	10.5
1970	10,398	5,641	54.3	11,929	1,129	9.5
1960	6,842	3,583	52.4	10,896	1,185	10.9

Note: Unmarried college students living in dormitories are counted as living in their parents' home.
Source: Bureau of the Census, 1960, 1970, and 1980 Census and Current Population Surveys, Internet site http://www
.census.gov/population/socdemo/hh-fam/tabAD-1.txt; calculations by New Strategist

Table 7.18 Living Arrangements of Young Women, 1960 to 2000

(total number of women aged 18 to 34, and number and percent living with their parents, by age, 1960 to 2000; numbers in thousands)

| | women aged 18 to 24 | | | women aged 25 to 34 | | |
| | | living with parents | | | living with parents | |
	total	number	share of total	total	number	share of total
2000	13,242	6,232	47.1%	19,222	1,602	8.3%
1999	13,031	6,389	49.0	19,551	1,690	8.6
1998	12,568	5,974	47.5	19,828	1,680	8.5
1997	12,452	6,006	48.2	20,217	1,745	8.6
1996	12,441	5,955	48.0	20,528	1,810	9.0
1995	12,613	5,896	46.7	20,800	1,759	8.5
1994	12,792	5,924	46.3	21,073	1,859	8.8
1993	12,260	5,746	46.9	21,007	1,844	8.8
1992	12,351	5,929	48.0	21,368	1,874	8.8
1991	12,627	6,163	48.8	21,586	1,887	8.7
1990	12,860	6,135	47.7	21,779	1,774	8.1
1989	13,055	6,141	47.0	21,777	1,728	7.9
1988	13,226	6,398	48.4	21,649	1,791	8.3
1987	13,433	6,375	47.5	21,494	1,655	7.7
1986	13,787	6,433	46.7	21,097	1,686	8.0
1985	14,149	6,758	47.8	20,673	1,661	8.0
1984	14,482	6,779	46.8	20,297	1,548	7.6
1983	14,702	7,001	47.6	19,903	1,520	7.6
1980	14,844	6,336	42.7	18,689	1,300	7.0
1970	11,959	4,941	41.3	12,637	829	6.6
1960	7,876	2,750	34.9	11,587	853	7.4

Note: Unmarried college students living in dormitories are counted as living in their parents' home.
Source: Bureau of the Census, 1960, 1970, and 1980 Census and Current Population Surveys, Internet site http://www
.census.gov/population/socdemo/hh-fam/tabAD-1.txt; calculations by New Strategist

Table 7.19 People Who Live Alone by Sex and Age, 1970 to 2000

(total number of people and number and percent who live alone by sex and age, 1970 to 2000; numbers in thousands)

	2000			1990			1980			1970		
		living alone			living alone			living alone			living alone	
	total	number	percent	total	number	percent	total	number	percent	total	number	percent
Total men	103,114	11,181	10.8%	91,955	9,049	9.8%	81,947	6,966	8.5%	70,559	3,532	5.0%
15 to 24	19,502	556	2.9	17,533	674	3.8	20,558	947	4.6	18,695	274	1.5
25 to 34	18,562	2,279	12.3	21,462	2,395	11.2	18,051	1,975	10.9	12,191	535	4.4
35 to 44	22,135	2,569	11.6	18,331	1,836	10.0	12,435	945	7.6	11,277	398	3.5
45 to 54	17,890	2,146	12.0	12,292	1,167	9.5	10,938	804	7.4	11,224	513	4.6
55 to 64	11,137	1,276	11.5	10,002	1,036	10.4	10,014	809	8.1	8,835	639	7.2
65 to 74	8,048	1,108	13.8	8,013	1,042	13.0	6,657	775	11.6	5,393	611	11.3
75 or older	5,836	1,247	21.4	4,320	901	20.9	3,296	711	21.6	2,943	563	19.1
Total women	110,660	15,543	14.0	99,838	13,950	14.0	89,914	11,330	12.6	77,766	7,319	9.4
15 to 24	19,040	588	3.1	17,721	536	3.0	20,895	779	3.7	19,841	282	1.4
25 to 34	19,223	1,568	8.2	21,779	1,578	7.2	18,565	1,284	6.9	12,670	358	2.8
35 to 44	22,671	1,540	6.8	18,864	1,303	6.9	12,991	525	4.0	11,879	313	2.6
45 to 54	18,741	2,158	11.5	13,012	1,256	9.7	11,760	901	7.7	12,029	790	6.6
55 to 64	12,250	2,262	18.5	11,230	2,044	18.2	11,462	2,000	17.4	9,807	1,680	17.1
65 to 74	9,748	2,983	30.6	9,966	3,309	33.2	8,637	3,076	35.6	6,964	2,204	31.6
75 or older	8,988	4,444	49.4	7,267	3,924	54.0	5,605	2,766	49.3	4,575	1,693	37.0

Source: Bureau of the Census, Marital Status and Living Arrangements: March 1994, Current Population Reports, P20-484, 1996; and Internet site http://www.census.gov/population/socdemo/hh-fam/p20-537/2000/tabA2.txt; calculations by New Strategist

Table 7.20 Unmarried-Couple Households, 1960 to 2000

(total number of households, number and percent of households headed by people of the opposite sex sharing living quarters, and number and percent headed by unmarried partners, 1960 to 2000; numbers in thousands)

	total households	persons of opposite sex sharing living quarters		unmarried partners	
		number	percent	number	percent
2000	104,705	4,736	4.5%	3,822	3.7%
1999	103,874	4,486	4.3	3,380	3.3
1998	102,528	4,236	4.1	3,139	3.1
1997	101,018	4,130	4.1	3,087	3.1
1996	99,627	3,958	4.0	2,858	2.9
1995	98,990	3,668	3.7	–	–
1994	97,107	3,661	3.8	–	–
1993	96,426	3,510	3.6	–	–
1992	95,669	3,308	3.5	–	–
1991	94,312	3,039	3.2	–	–
1990	93,347	2,856	3.1	–	–
1989	92,830	2,764	3.0	–	–
1988	91,124	2,588	2.8	–	–
1987	89,479	2,334	2.6	–	–
1986	88,458	2,220	2.5	–	–
1985	86,789	1,983	2.3	–	–
1984	85,290	1,988	2.3	–	–
1983	83,918	1,891	2.3	–	–
1982	83,527	1,863	2.2	–	–
1981	82,368	1,808	2.2	–	–
1980	80,776	1,589	2.0	–	–
1970	63,401	523	0.8	–	–
1960	52,799	439	0.8	–	–

Note: People of the opposite sex sharing living quarters may or may not be unmarried partners; (–) means data not available.
Source: Bureau of the Census, 1960 and 1970 Censuses and Current Population Surveys, Internet site http://www.census.gov/ population/socdemo/hh-fam/tabUC-1.txt; calculations by New Strategist

Most People Marry, but Later

The median age at first marriage (meaning the age at which half of people have married) is at a record high of 25.1 years for women. For men, at 26.8 years in 2000, median age at first marriage closely matched its 1999 record high of 26.9 years. Fifty years ago, half of women married by age 20, that is, while in their teens.

The percentage of twentysomethings who have never married has grown enormously since 1950. Nearly 73 percent of women aged 20 to 24 had not yet married in 2000, up from 32 percent in 1950. Among men aged 20 to 24, the proportion of those who had not yet married rose from 59 to 84 percent between 1950 and 2000.

As people postponed marriage, the married share of the adult population declined. In 1950, two-thirds of men and women aged 15 or older were currently married. By 2000, only 58 percent of men and 55 percent of women were married.

The married are still the majority

(percent of people aged 15 or older who are married, by sex, 1950 to 2000)

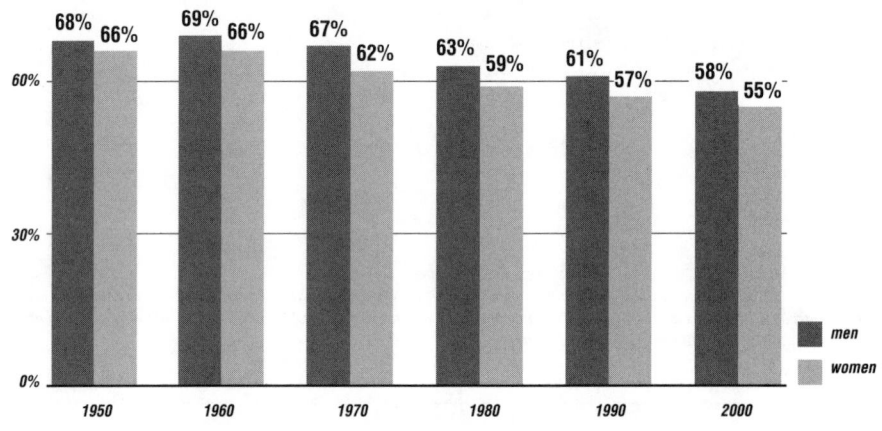

Table 7.21 Never-Married by Sex and Age, 1950 to 2000

(percent of people aged 18 or older who have never married, by sex and age, 1950 to 2000; percentage point change for selected years)

							percentage point change	
	2000	*1990*	*1980*	*1970*	*1960*	*1950*	*1990–00*	*1950–00*
Total men	**27.0%**	**25.8%**	**23.8%**	**18.9%**	**17.3%**	**20.2%**	**1.2**	**6.8**
Aged 18 to 19	98.3	96.8	94.3	92.8	91.1	93.4	1.5	4.9
Aged 20 to 24	83.7	79.3	68.8	54.7	53.1	59.0	4.4	24.7
Aged 25 to 29	51.7	45.2	33.1	19.1	20.8	23.8	6.5	27.9
Aged 30 to 34	30.0	27.0	15.9	9.4	11.9	13.2	3.0	16.8
Aged 35 to 39	20.3	14.7	7.8	7.2	8.8	–	5.6	–
Aged 40 to 44	15.7	10.5	7.1	6.3	7.3	–	5.2	–
Aged 45 to 54	9.5	6.3	6.1	7.5	7.4	8.5	3.2	1.0
Aged 55 to 64	5.5	5.8	5.3	7.8	8.0	8.4	–0.3	–2.9
Aged 65 or older	4.2	4.2	4.9	7.5	7.7	8.4	0.0	–4.2
Total women	**21.1**	**18.9**	**17.1**	**13.7**	**11.9**	**14.1**	**2.2**	**7.0**
Aged 18 to 19	93.0	90.3	82.8	75.6	67.9	68.9	2.7	24.1
Aged 20 to 24	72.8	62.8	50.2	35.8	28.4	32.3	10.0	40.5
Aged 25 to 29	38.9	31.1	20.9	10.5	10.5	13.3	7.8	25.6
Aged 30 to 34	21.9	16.4	9.5	6.2	6.9	9.3	5.5	12.6
Aged 35 to 39	14.3	10.4	6.2	5.4	6.1	–	3.9	–
Aged 40 to 44	11.8	8.0	4.8	4.9	6.1	–	3.8	–
Aged 45 to 54	8.6	5.0	4.7	4.9	7.0	7.8	3.6	0.8
Aged 55 to 64	4.9	3.9	4.5	6.8	8.0	7.9	1.0	–3.0
Aged 65 or older	3.6	4.9	5.9	7.7	8.5	8.9	–1.3	–5.3

Note: (–) means data are not available for five-year age groups. Among 35-to-44-year-olds in 1950, 9.6 percent of men and 8.3 percent of women had not married.
Source: Bureau of the Census, Historical Statistics of the United States: Colonial Times to 1970, Part 1, *1975; and* Statistical Abstract of the United States for 1980, 1993, *and* 2001; *calculations by New Strategist*

Table 7.22 Median Age at First Marriage by Sex, 1950 to 2000

(median age at first marriage by sex, 1950 to 2000)

	men	women
2000	26.8	25.1
1999	26.9	25.1
1998	26.7	25.0
1997	26.8	25.0
1996	27.1	24.8
1995	26.9	24.5
1994	26.7	24.5
1993	26.5	24.5
1992	26.5	24.4
1991	26.3	24.1
1990	26.1	23.9
1989	26.2	23.8
1988	25.9	23.6
1987	25.8	23.6
1986	25.7	23.1
1985	25.5	23.3
1984	25.4	23.0
1983	25.4	22.8
1982	25.2	22.5
1981	24.8	22.3
1980	24.7	22.0
1979	24.4	22.1
1978	24.2	21.8
1977	24.0	21.6
1976	23.8	21.3
1975	23.5	21.1
1974	23.1	21.1
1973	23.2	21.0
1972	23.3	20.9
1971	23.1	20.9
1970	23.2	20.8
1969	23.2	20.8
1968	23.1	20.8
1967	23.1	20.6
1966	22.8	20.5
1965	22.8	20.6
1964	23.1	20.5
1963	22.8	20.5
1962	22.7	20.3
1961	22.8	20.3
1960	22.8	20.3
1959	22.5	20.2
1958	22.6	20.2
1957	22.6	20.3
1956	22.5	20.1
1955	22.6	20.2
1954	23.0	20.3
1953	22.8	20.2
1952	23.0	20.2
1951	22.9	20.4
1950	22.8	20.3

Source: Bureau of the Census, Current Population Surveys, Internet site http://www.census.gov/population/socdemo/hh-fam/ tabMS-2.txt

Table 7.23 Marital Status of Men, 1950 to 2000

(total number of men aged 15 or older and percent distribution by marital status, 1950 to 2000; numbers in thousands)

	total men		never married	married	divorced	widowed
	number	*percent*				
2000	103,114	100.0%	31.3%	57.9%	8.3%	2.5%
1999	102,048	100.0	31.3	57.9	8.4	2.5
1998	101,123	100.0	31.2	58.0	8.2	2.5
1997	100,159	100.0	31.3	57.8	8.2	2.7
1996	98,593	100.0	31.1	58.5	7.9	2.5
1995	97,704	100.0	31.0	58.9	7.6	2.3
1994	96,768	100.0	31.2	59.0	7.5	2.3
1993	94,854	100.0	30.3	59.9	7.1	2.6
1992	93,760	100.0	30.2	59.9	7.2	2.7
1991	92,840	100.0	30.1	60.2	7.1	2.6
1990	91,955	100.0	29.9	60.7	6.8	2.5
1980	81,947	100.0	29.6	63.2	4.8	2.4
1970	70,559	100.0	28.1	66.8	2.2	2.9
1960	60,273	100.0	25.3	69.3	1.8	3.5
1950	54,601	100.0	26.4	67.5	2.0	4.1

Note: Figures for 1950 and 1960 are for men aged 14 or older.
Source: Bureau of the Census, Current Population Surveys, Internet site http://www.census.gov/population/socdemo/hh-fam/ tabMS-1.txt; and Statistical Abstract of the United States for 1992 and 1993; calculations by New Strategist

Table 7.24 Marital Status of Women, 1950 to 2000

(total number of women aged 15 or older and percent distribution by marital status, 1950 to 2000; numbers in thousands)

	total women		never married	married	divorced	widowed
	number	percent				
2000	110,660	100.0%	25.1%	54.7%	10.2%	10.0%
1999	109,628	100.0	25.1	54.7	10.2	10.0
1998	108,168	100.0	24.7	54.9	10.3	10.2
1997	107,076	100.0	24.3	54.9	10.4	10.3
1996	106,031	100.0	24.1	55.6	9.9	10.4
1995	105,028	100.0	23.5	56.2	9.8	10.6
1994	104,032	100.0	23.7	55.9	9.7	10.6
1993	102,400	100.0	23.0	56.4	9.7	11.0
1992	101,483	100.0	23.0	56.4	9.4	11.2
1991	100,680	100.0	23.2	56.5	9.1	11.2
1990	99,838	100.0	22.8	56.9	8.9	11.5
1980	89,914	100.0	22.5	58.9	6.6	12.0
1970	77,766	100.0	22.1	61.9	3.5	12.5
1960	64,607	100.0	19.0	65.9	2.6	12.5
1950	57,102	100.0	20.0	65.8	2.4	11.8

Note: Figures for 1950 and 1960 are for women aged 14 or older.
Source: Bureau of the Census, Current Population Surveys, Internet site http://www.census.gov/population/socdemo/hh-fam/tabMS-1.txt; and Statistical Abstract of the United States for 1991 and 1993; calculations by New Strategist

Table 7.25   Interracial Married Couples, 1960 to 2000

(total number of married couples, number of interracial couples, and interracial share of total, 1960 to 2000; numbers in thousands)

| | total couples | interracial couples | |
		number	share of total
2000	56,497	1,464	2.6%
1999	55,849	1,481	2.7
1998	55,305	1,348	2.4
1997	54,666	1,264	2.3
1996	54,664	1,260	2.3
1995	54,937	1,392	2.5
1994	54,251	1,283	2.4
1993	54,199	1,195	2.2
1992	53,512	1,161	2.2
1991	53,227	994	1.9
1990	53,256	964	1.8
1989	52,924	953	1.8
1988	52,613	956	1.8
1987	52,286	799	1.5
1986	51,704	827	1.6
1985	51,114	792	1.5
1984	50,864	762	1.5
1983	50,665	719	1.4
1982	50,294	697	1.4
1981	49,896	639	1.3
1980	49,714	651	1.3
1970	44,598	310	0.7
1960	40,491	149	0.4

Source: Bureau of the Census, 1960 and 1970 Censuses and Current Population Surveys, Internet site http://www.census.gov/ population/socdemo/hh-fam/tabMS-3.txt; calculations by New Strategist

Table 7.26 Interracial Married Couples by Race, 1960 to 2000

(total number of interracial married couples and percent distribution by race of husband and wife, 1960 to 2000; numbers in thousands)

| | interracial couples | | black/white | | | white/ | black/ |
	number	percent	total	black husband, white wife	white husband, black wife	other race	other race
2000	1,464	100.0%	24.8%	18.3%	6.5%	71.8%	3.4%
1999	1,481	100.0	24.6	16.2	8.4	73.3	2.1
1998	1,348	100.0	24.5	15.6	8.9	72.3	3.2
1997	1,264	100.0	24.6	15.9	8.7	70.9	4.5
1996	1,260	100.0	26.7	17.5	9.3	70.2	3.1
1995	1,392	100.0	23.6	14.8	8.8	71.0	5.5
1994	1,283	100.0	23.1	15.3	7.8	70.8	6.1
1993	1,195	100.0	20.3	15.2	5.0	77.0	2.8
1992	1,161	100.0	21.2	14.0	7.1	76.1	2.8
1991	994	100.0	23.2	15.7	7.5	72.4	4.3
1990	964	100.0	21.9	15.6	6.3	74.7	3.4
1989	953	100.0	23.0	16.3	6.7	73.8	3.3
1988	956	100.0	22.8	15.6	7.2	73.5	3.7
1987	799	100.0	22.2	15.1	7.0	72.7	5.1
1986	827	100.0	21.9	16.4	5.4	74.1	4.0
1985	792	100.0	20.7	14.8	5.9	75.6	3.7
1984	762	100.0	23.0	14.6	8.4	74.0	3.0
1983	719	100.0	22.8	16.4	6.4	72.6	4.6
1982	697	100.0	22.2	15.5	6.7	73.9	3.9
1981	639	100.0	20.7	16.3	4.4	75.7	3.6
1980	651	100.0	25.7	18.7	6.9	69.1	5.2
1970	310	100.0	21.0	13.2	7.7	75.2	3.9
1960	149	100.0	34.2	16.8	17.4	60.4	4.7

Source: Bureau of the Census, 1960 and 1970 Censuses and Current Population Surveys, Internet site http://www.census.gov/population/socdemo/hh-fam/tabMS-3.txt; calculations by New Strategist

8

Population

■ The population of the United States is projected to grow faster between 2000 and 2010 than in any decade since the 1950s. Behind the rapid growth is massive immigration.

■ The biggest ongoing change in the U.S. population is growing diversity. In 1950, 90 percent of Americans were white. By 2010, non-Hispanic whites will account for only 64 percent of the population.

■ The proportion of Americans who were born in another country is growing rapidly as immigrants flood to the United States. In 2000, nearly 1 in 9 Americans was foreign-born, up from 1 in 20 in 1970.

■ Americans move less than they once did. Between 1999 and 2000, only 16 percent of people aged 1 or older moved from one house to another, down from the 21 percent who moved between 1950 and 1951.

■ The West is by far the most diverse region, as non-Hispanic whites accounted for only 58 percent of its population in 2000. The Midwest is the least diverse region; 81 percent of its population is non-Hispanic white.

■ The growth of the elderly population varies dramatically by state. In 1950, the number of people aged 65 or older was greater in Iowa than in Florida. Today, Florida ranks second only to California in the number of people aged 65 or older.

Population Becoming Older, More Diverse

The population of the United States is projected to top 324 million by 2010. Rather than slowing, as demographers have long predicted, population growth in the United States will accelerate during the coming decade. The population will grow 15 percent between 2000 and 2010, the fastest growth since the 1950s. Behind the rapid growth is massive immigration to the U.S., as a record number of immigrants arrived here during the 1990s.

Americans are growing older as the enormous baby-boom generation ages. In 1960, 31 percent of the population was under age 15, a figure that fell to 21 percent in 2000 and will drop to 19 percent by 2010. While 21 percent of the population was aged 55 or older in 2000, by 2010 the proportion will climb to 26 percent as boomers age into their sixties.

Perhaps the biggest ongoing change is growing diversity. In 1950, 90 percent of Americans were white. By 2010, non-Hispanic whites will account for only 64 percent of the population. Among children under age 15, only 56 percent will be non-Hispanic white in 2010.

Children are much more diverse than older Americans

(non-Hispanic white share of population, by age, 2000)

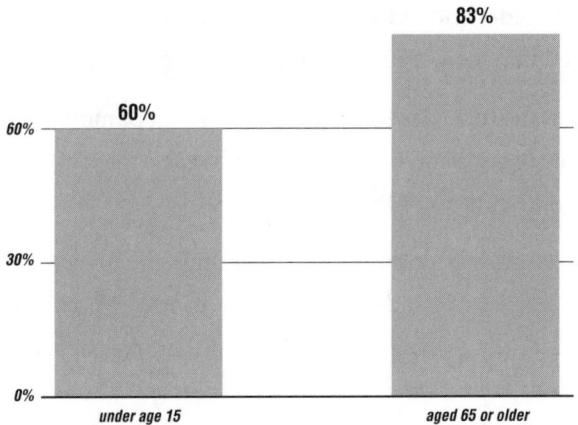

Table 8.1 Population of the United States, 1950 to 2010

(population of the United States, 1950 to 2010; numerical and percent change from preceding year and decade; numbers in thousands)

	population	increase from preceding year/decade	
		numerical	*percent*
2010	324,411	42,286	15.0%
2000	282,125	32,661	13.1
1981–90	**–**	**22,240**	**9.8**
1990	249,464	2,645	1.1
1989	246,819	2,320	0.9
1988	244,499	2,210	0.9
1987	242,289	2,156	0.9
1986	240,133	2,209	0.9
1985	237,924	2,099	0.9
1984	235,825	2,033	0.9
1983	233,792	2,128	0.9
1982	231,664	2,199	1.0
1981	229,466	2,241	1.0
1971–80	**–**	**22,173**	**10.8**
1980	227,225	2,169	1.0
1979	225,055	2,471	1.1
1978	222,585	2,345	1.1
1977	220,239	2,204	1.0
1976	218,035	2,062	1.0
1975	215,973	2,119	1.0
1974	213,854	1,945	0.9
1973	211,909	2,013	1.0
1972	209,896	2,235	1.1
1971	207,661	2,609	1.3
1961–70	**–**	**24,381**	**13.5**
1970	205,052	2,375	1.2
1969	202,677	1,971	1.0
1968	200,706	1,994	1.0
1967	198,712	2,152	1.1
1966	196,560	2,257	1.2
1965	194,303	2,414	1.3
1964	191,889	2,647	1.4
1963	189,242	2,704	1.4
1962	186,538	2,846	1.5
1961	183,691	3,020	1.7
1950–60	**–**	**28,400**	**18.7**
1960	180,671	2,842	1.6
1959	177,830	2,948	1.7
1958	174,882	2,898	1.7
1957	171,984	3,081	1.8
1956	168,903	2,972	1.8
1955	165,931	2,905	1.8
1954	163,026	2,842	1.8
1953	160,184	2,631	1.7
1952	157,553	2,675	1.7
1951	154,878	2,606	1.7
1950	152,271	–	–

Note: Figures are for July 1 of the year shown. Population estimates for single years during the 1990s adjusted to reflect 2000 census results were not available at time of publication.
Source: Bureau of the Census, Internet sites http://www.census.gov/population/estimates/nation/popclockest.txt and http:// eire.census.gov/popest/data/national/tables/NA-EST2001-01.php; and New Strategist projections, 2002 series; calculations by New Strategist

Table 8.2 Population by Sex, 1950 to 2010 Censuses

(number of people by sex and female share of total, 1950 to 2010; numbers in thousands)

	total	males	females number	females share of total
2010	324,411	161,175	163,236	50.3%
2000	281,422	138,054	143,368	50.9
1990	248,710	121,239	127,470	51.3
1980	226,546	110,053	116,493	51.4
1970	203,235	98,926	104,309	51.3
1960	179,323	88,331	90,992	50.7
1950	151,326	75,187	76,139	50.3

Source: Bureau of the Census, Gender: 2000, *2000 Census Brief, C2KBR/01-9, 2001; and* Statistical Abstract of the United States: 2001; *and New Strategist projections, 2002 series; calculations by New Strategist*

Table 8.3   Population by Age, 1950 to 2010 Censuses

(number and percent distribution of people by age, 1950 to 2010; numbers in thousands)

	total	*< age 15*	*15 to 24*	*25 to 34*	*35 to 44*	*45 to 54*	*55 to 64*	*65 or older*
2010	324,411	61,983	44,347	44,016	44,206	46,299	37,429	46,130
2000	281,422	60,253	39,184	39,892	45,149	37,678	24,275	34,992
1990	248,791	53,874	37,036	43,174	37,444	25,062	21,116	31,084
1980	226,546	51,290	42,487	37,082	25,634	22,800	21,703	25,550
1970	203,212	57,900	35,441	24,907	23,088	23,220	18,590	20,066
1960	179,323	55,786	24,020	22,818	24,081	20,485	15,572	16,560
1950	150,697	40,483	22,098	23,759	21,450	17,343	13,295	12,270
2010	100.0%	19.1%	13.7%	13.6%	13.6%	14.3%	11.5%	14.2%
2000	100.0	21.4	13.9	14.2	16.0	13.4	8.6	12.4
1990	100.0	21.7	14.9	17.4	15.1	10.1	8.5	12.5
1980	100.0	22.6	18.8	16.4	11.3	10.1	9.6	11.3
1970	100.0	28.5	17.4	12.3	11.4	11.4	9.1	9.9
1960	100.0	31.1	13.4	12.7	13.4	11.4	8.7	9.2
1950	100.0	26.9	14.7	15.8	14.2	11.5	8.8	8.1

Source: Bureau of the Census, Historical Statistics of the United States: Colonial Times to 1970, Part 1, *1975; and* Statistical Abstract of the United States: 2001*; and* Age: 2000*, 2000 Census Brief, C2KBR/01-12, 2001; and New Strategist projections, 2002 series; calculations by New Strategist*

Table 8.4 Population by Race and Hispanic Origin, 1950 to 2010 Censuses

(number and percent distribution of people by race and Hispanic origin, 1950 to 2010; numbers in thousands)

	total population	race alone				two or more races or other race	Hispanic origin		
		American Indian	Asian	black	white			non-Hispanic	
							Hispanic	total	white
2010	324,411	2,993	16,295	40,572	233,494	31,057	49,205	275,206	207,747
2000	281,422	2,476	10,642	34,658	211,461	22,185	35,306	246,116	194,553

Percent distribution

2010	100.0%	0.9%	5.0%	12.5%	72.0%	9.6%	15.2%	84.8%	64.0%
2000	100.0	0.9	3.8	12.3	75.1	7.9	12.5	87.5	69.1

	total population	American Indian	race				Hispanic origin		
			Asian	black	white			non-Hispanic	
							Hispanic	total	white
1990	248,791	2,067	7,467	30,517	208,741	–	22,379	226,412	188,315
1980	226,546	1,420	3,729	26,683	194,713	–	14,609	211,937	180,906

Percent distribution

1990	100.0%	0.8%	3.0%	12.3%	83.9%	–	9.0%	91.0%	75.7%
1980	100.0	0.6	1.6	11.8	85.9	–	6.4	93.6	79.9

	total population			black	white	other
1970	203,212	–	–	22,581	178,098	2,557
1960	179,323	–	–	18,872	158,832	1,620
1950	150,697	–	–	15,045	135,150	1,131

Percent distribution

				black	white	other
1970	100.0%	–	–	11.1%	87.6%	1.3%
1960	100.0	–	–	10.5	88.6	0.9
1950	100.0	–	–	10.0	89.7	0.8

Note: Hispanics may be of any race.
Source: Bureau of the Census, Statistical Abstract of the United States, 1990 *and* 2001; *and Census 2000 Redistricting Data, P.L. 94-171; New Strategist projections, 2002 series; calculations by New Strategist*

Table 8.5 Population under Age 15 by Race and Hispanic Origin, 1970 to 2010 Censuses

(number and percent distribution of people under age 15 by race and Hispanic origin, 1970 to 2010; numbers in thousands)

	population under age 15	American Indian	race alone			two or more races or other race	Hispanic origin		
			Asian	black	white		Hispanic	non-Hispanic total	non-Hispanic white
2010	61,983	709	3,347	8,841	41,965	7,120	13,053	48,930	34,863
2000	60,253	698	2,141	9,132	41,127	7,155	10,505	49,748	36,381
Percent distribution									
2010	100.0%	1.1%	5.4%	14.3%	67.7%	11.5%	21.1%	78.9%	56.2%
2000	100.0	1.2	3.6	15.2	68.3	11.9	17.4	82.6	60.4

	population under age 15	American Indian	race				Hispanic origin		
			Asian	black	white		Hispanic	non-Hispanic total	non-Hispanic white
1990	53,852	626	1,814	8,279	43,132	–	6,634	47,218	37,091
1980	51,290	452	954	7,659	42,226	–	4,675	46,615	37,807
Percent distribution									
1990	100.0%	1.2%	3.4%	15.4%	80.1%	–	12.3%	87.7%	68.9%
1980	100.0	0.9	1.9	14.9	82.3	–	9.1	90.9	73.7

	population under age 15			black	white	other
1970	57,936	–	–	7,995	49,129	812
Percent distribution						
1970	100.0%	–	–	13.8%	84.8%	1.4%

Note: Numbers will not add to total because Hispanics may be of any race.
Source: Bureau of the Census, Statistical Abstract of the United States, 1990 *and* 1995; *and* Age: 2000, 2000 Census Brief, *C2KBR/01-12, 2001; and New Strategist projections, 2002 series; calculations by New Strategist*

Table 8.6 Population Aged 65 or Older by Race and Hispanic Origin, 1970 to 2010 Censuses

(number and percent distribution of people aged 65 or older by race and Hispanic origin, 1970 to 2010; numbers in thousands)

	population aged 65 or older	American Indian	race alone			two or more races or other race	Hispanic origin		
			Asian	black	white		Hispanic	non-Hispanic total	white
2010	46,130	256	1,406	4,147	38,852	1,469	2,859	43,271	36,971
2000	34,992	138	822	2,823	30,406	803	1,734	33,258	29,245

Percent distribution

	population aged 65 or older	American Indian	Asian	black	white	two or more races or other race	Hispanic	non-Hispanic total	white
2010	100.0%	0.6%	3.0%	9.0%	84.2%	3.2%	6.2%	93.8%	80.1%
2000	100.0	0.4	2.3	8.1	86.9	2.3	5.0	95.0	83.6

	population aged 65 or older	American Indian	race			Hispanic origin		
			Asian	black	white	Hispanic	non-Hispanic total	white
1990	31,080	116	451	2,493	28,021	–	1,146	29,934	26,953
1980	25,550	75	221	2,091	23,162	–	709	24,841	22,491

Percent distribution

	population aged 65 or older	American Indian	Asian	black	white		Hispanic	non-Hispanic total	white
1990	100.0%	0.4%	1.5%	8.0%	90.2%	–	3.7%	96.3%	86.7%
1980	100.0	0.3	0.9	8.2	90.7	–	2.8	97.2	88.0

	population aged 65 or older			black	white	other
1970	19,972	–	–	1,544	18,272	156

Percent distribution

	population aged 65 or older			black	white	other
1970	100.0%	–	–	7.7%	91.5%	0.8%

Note: Numbers will not add to total because Hispanics may be of any race.
Source: Bureau of the Census, Statistical Abstract of the United States, 1990 *and* 1995; *and* Age: 2000, *2000 Census Brief, C2KBR/01-12, 2001; and New Strategist projections, 2002 series; calculations by New Strategist*

Table 8.7   Population Aged 65 or Older by Sex, 1950 to 2010 Censuses

(number of people aged 65 or older by sex and percent female, 1950 to 2010; numbers in thousands)

	total	men	women number	women percent
2010	46,130	20,857	25,273	54.8%
2000	34,992	14,410	20,582	58.8
1990	31,080	12,493	18,586	59.8
1980	25,550	10,306	15,245	59.7
1970	19,973	8,366	11,605	58.1
1960	16,560	7,503	9,056	54.7
1950	12,270	5,797	6,473	52.8

Source: Bureau of the Census, Historical Statistics of the United States, Colonial Times to 1970, Part 1, *1975; and* Statistical Abstract of the United States, 1995; *and* Age: 2000, *2000 Census Brief, C2KBR/01-12, 2001; and 2000 Census,* Table DP-1. Profiles of General Demographic Characteristics: 2000, *2001; and New Strategist projections, 2002 series; calculations by New Strategist*

Mobility Rate Has Fallen Since 1950

Americans move less than they once did. Between 1999 and 2000, only 16 percent of people aged 1 or older moved from one house to another. This is a decline from the 21 percent who moved between 1950 and 1951.

No one knows why the mobility rate has fallen so much, but there are a number of likely reasons. One reason may be that more Americans own a home today than half a century ago, and homeowners are less likely to move than renters. Another reason may be the rise in two-income couples, because it is more difficult to relocate when both husband and wife must find a job. The aging of the population is also important, since older people move less frequently than young adults.

Most moves are local, 56 percent of movers remaining in the same county. Many local moves are housing rather than job related. Only 19 percent of movers settle in a different state, slightly more than in 1950–51.

Mobility rate is down, but movers are up

(number and percent of people aged 1 or older moving in 1950–51 and 1999–00)

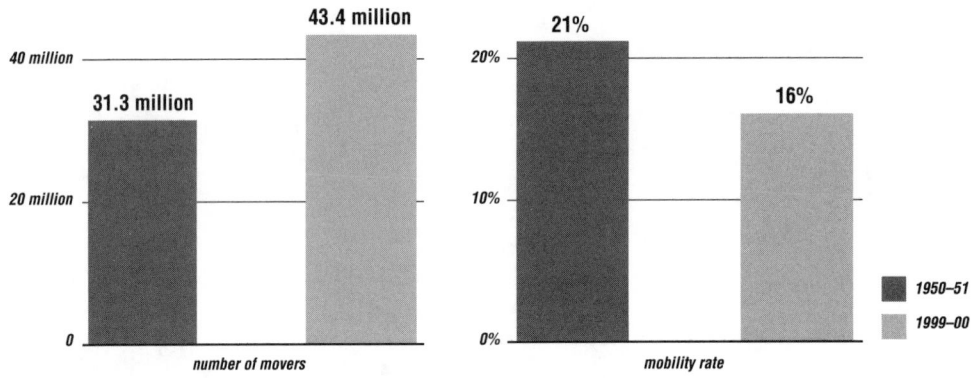

Table 8.8 Geographical Mobility, 1950 to 2000

(total number of people aged 1 or older, and number and percent moving by type of move, 1950–51 to 1999–00; numbers in thousands)

	total people aged 1+	same house (nonmovers)	total movers	total	different house in U.S. same county	different county	same state	different state	movers from abroad
1999–00	270,219	226,831	43,388	41,642	24,399	17,242	8,814	8,428	1,746
1998–99	267,933	225,297	42,636	41,207	25,268	15,939	8,423	7,516	1,429
1997–98	265,209	222,702	42,507	41,304	27,082	14,222	7,867	6,355	1,203
1996–97	262,976	219,585	43,391	42,088	27,740	14,348	7,960	6,389	1,303
1995–96	260,406	217,868	42,537	41,176	26,696	14,480	8,009	6,471	1,361
1994–95	258,248	215,931	42,317	41,539	27,908	13,631	7,888	5,743	778
1993–94	255,774	212,939	42,835	41,590	26,638	14,952	8,226	6,726	1,245
1992–93	252,799	209,700	43,099	41,704	26,932	14,772	7,855	6,916	1,395
1991–92	247,380	204,580	42,800	41,545	26,587	14,957	7,853	7,105	1,255
1990–91	244,884	203,345	41,539	40,154	25,151	15,003	7,881	7,122	1,385
1980–81	221,641	183,442	38,200	36,887	23,097	13,789	7,614	6,175	1,313
1970–71	201,506	163,800	37,705	36,161	23,018	13,143	6,197	6,946	1,544
1960–61	177,354	140,821	36,533	35,535	24,289	11,246	5,493	5,753	998
1950–51	148,400	116,936	31,464	31,158	20,694	10,464	5,276	5,188	306

Percent distribution of population by mobility status

1999–00	100.0%	83.9%	16.1%	15.4%	9.0%	6.4%	3.3%	3.1%	0.6%
1998–99	100.0	84.1	15.9	15.4	9.4	5.9	3.1	2.8	0.5
1997–98	100.0	84.0	16.0	15.6	10.2	5.4	3.0	2.4	0.5
1996–97	100.0	83.5	16.5	16.0	10.5	5.5	3.0	2.4	0.5
1995–96	100.0	83.7	16.3	15.8	10.3	5.6	3.1	2.5	0.5
1994–95	100.0	83.6	16.4	16.1	10.8	5.3	3.1	2.2	0.3
1993–94	100.0	83.3	16.7	16.3	10.4	5.8	3.2	2.6	0.5
1992–93	100.0	83.0	17.0	16.5	10.7	5.8	3.1	2.7	0.6
1991–92	100.0	82.7	17.3	16.8	10.7	6.0	3.2	2.9	0.5
1990–91	100.0	83.0	17.0	16.4	10.3	6.1	3.2	2.9	0.6
1980–81	100.0	82.8	17.2	16.6	10.4	6.2	3.4	2.8	0.6
1970–71	100.0	81.3	18.7	17.9	11.4	6.5	3.1	3.4	0.8
1960–61	100.0	79.4	20.6	20.0	13.7	6.3	3.1	3.2	0.6
1950–51	100.0	78.8	21.2	21.0	13.9	7.1	3.6	3.5	0.2

Percent distribution of movers by type of move

1999–00	–	–	100.0%	96.0%	56.2%	39.7%	20.3%	19.4%	4.0%
1998–99	–	–	100.0	96.6	59.3	37.4	19.8	17.6	3.4
1997–98	–	–	100.0	97.2	63.7	33.5	18.5	15.0	2.8
1996–97	–	–	100.0	97.0	63.9	33.1	18.3	14.7	3.0
1995–96	–	–	100.0	96.8	62.8	34.0	18.8	15.2	3.2
1994–95	–	–	100.0	98.2	65.9	32.2	18.6	13.6	1.8
1993–94	–	–	100.0	97.1	62.2	34.9	19.2	15.7	2.9
1992–93	–	–	100.0	96.8	62.5	34.3	18.2	16.0	3.2
1991–92	–	–	100.0	97.1	62.1	34.9	18.3	16.6	2.9
1990–91	–	–	100.0	96.7	60.5	36.1	19.0	17.1	3.3
1980–81	–	–	100.0	96.6	60.5	36.1	19.9	16.2	3.4
1970–71	–	–	100.0	95.9	61.0	34.9	16.4	18.4	4.1
1960–61	–	–	100.0	97.3	66.5	30.8	15.0	15.7	2.7
1950–51	–	–	100.0	99.0	65.8	33.3	16.8	16.5	1.0

Note: (–) means not applicable.
Source: Bureau of the Census, Internet site http://www.census.gov/population/socdemo/migration/tab-a-1.txt; calculations by New Strategist

Foreign-Born Population Is Growing

The proportion of Americans who were born in another country is growing rapidly as immigrants flood to the United States. In 2000, nearly 1 in 9 Americans was foreign born, up from 1 in 20 in 1970.

The 51 percent majority of foreign-born residents counted by the 2000 census hailed from Latin America. Another 26 percent came from Asia, and 16 percent stemmed from Europe. In 1960, Italy was the leading country of birth among the nation's foreign-born, followed by Germany, Canada, the United Kingdom, and Poland.

Behind the growth of the foreign-born population is immigration. More than 9 million immigrants came to the United States between 1991 and 2000, the largest number of immigrants to enter the United States in any decade in our history. Most immigrants in the 1990s came from Mexico, followed by the Philippines, the Soviet Union, China, and India. Mexico has been the top country of immigration to the U.S. since the 1960s.

One in nine Americans is foreign-born

(percent of Americans who were born in another country, 1950 to 2000)

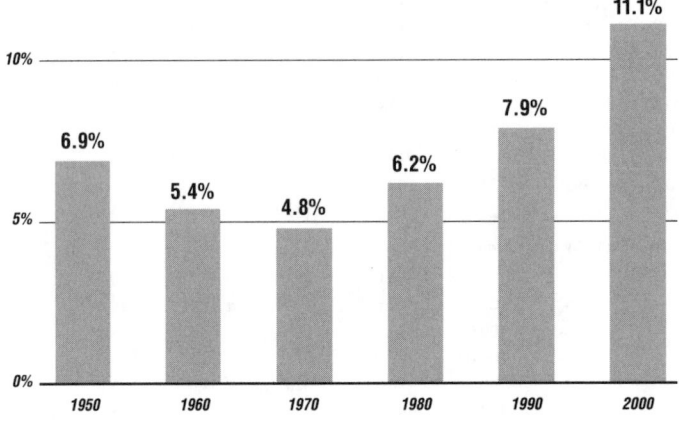

Table 8.9 Foreign-Born Population, 1950 to 2000 Censuses

(number and percent of people by foreign-born status, 1950 to 2000; numbers in thousands)

| | | native-born | | | foreign-born | |
| | | | born in state of residence | | | |
	total population	*total*	*number*	*percent of total population*	*number*	*percent of total population*
2000	281,422	250,314	168,729	60.0%	31,108	11.1%
1990	248,710	228,943	153,685	61.8	19,767	7.9
1980	226,546	212,466	144,871	63.9	14,080	6.2
1970	203,194	193,454	131,296	64.6	9,740	4.8
1960	178,467	168,806	118,802	66.6	9,661	5.4
1950	150,216	139,869	102,788	68.4	10,347	6.9

Source: Bureau of the Census, Census 2000, Table DP-2: Profile of Selected Social Characteristics: 2000*; and* Statistical Abstract of the United States: 2001

Table 8.10 Foreign-Born Population by Country of Birth, 1960 to 2000 Censuses

(number and percent distribution of foreign-born by country of birth for the ten largest foreign-born populations, 1960 to 1990; and number and percent distribution of foreign-born by world region of birth, 2000; numbers in thousands)

	number	percent distribution
2000		
Total foreign-born	**31,108**	**100.0%**
Latin America	16,087	51.7
Asia	8,226	26.4
Europe	4,916	15.8
Africa	881	2.8
North America	829	2.7
Oceania	168	0.5
1990		
Total foreign-born	**19,767**	**100.0**
Total from top ten	**10,267**	**51.9**
Mexico	4,298	21.7
Philippines	913	4.6
Canada	745	3.8
Cuba	737	3.7
Germany	712	3.6
United Kingdom	640	3.2
Italy	581	2.9
Korea	568	2.9
Vietnam	543	2.7
China	530	2.7
1980		
Total foreign-born	**14,080**	**100.0**
Total from top ten	**7,615**	**54.1**
Mexico	2,199	15.6
Germany	849	6.0
Canada	843	6.0
Italy	832	5.9
United Kingdom	669	4.8
Cuba	608	4.3
Philippines	501	3.6
Poland	418	3.0
Soviet Union	406	2.9
Korea	290	2.1
1970		
Total foreign-born	**9,740**	**100.0**
Total from top ten	**6,015**	**61.8**
Italy	1,009	10.4
Germany	833	8.6
Canada	812	8.3
Mexico	760	7.8
United Kingdom	686	7.0
Poland	548	5.6
Soviet Union	463	4.8
Cuba	439	4.5
Ireland	251	2.6
Austria	214	2.2
1960		
Total foreign-born	**9,661**	**100.0%**
Total from top ten	**6,937**	**71.8**
Italy	1,257	13.0
Germany	990	10.2
Canada	953	9.9
United Kingdom	833	8.6
Poland	748	7.7
Soviet Union	691	7.2
Mexico	576	6.0
Ireland	339	3.5
Austria	305	3.2
Hungary	245	2.5

Source: Bureau of the Census, Profile of the Foreign-Born Population in the United States: 1997, *Current Population Reports, Special Studies, P23-195, 1999; and Census 2000,* Table DP-2: Profile of Selected Social Characteristics: 2000; *calculations by New Strategist*

Table 8.11 Immigration to the U.S., 1950 to 2000

(number of immigrants granted permanent residence in the U.S. by decade and by single year, 1951 to 2000; percent change from previous decade and year; numbers in thousands)

	number	percent change
1991–00	**9,095**	**23.9%**
2000	850	31.4
1999	647	−1.1
1998	654	−18.1
1997	798	−12.8
1996	916	27.1
1995	720	−10.4
1994	804	−11.0
1993	904	−7.2
1992	974	−46.7
1991	1,827	18.9
1981–90	**7,338**	**63.3**
1990	1,536	40.8
1989	1,091	69.7
1988	643	6.9
1987	602	0.0
1986	602	5.6
1985	570	4.8
1984	544	−2.8
1983	560	−5.8
1982	594	−0.4
1981	597	12.4
1971–80	**4,493**	**35.3**
1980	531	15.3
1979	460	−23.5
1978	601	30.1
1977	462	−8.0
1976	502	30.1
1975	386	−2.2
1974	395	−1.3
1973	400	4.0
1972	385	3.8
1971	370	−0.8
1961–70	**3,322**	**32.0**
1970	373	4.1
1969	359	−21.1
1968	454	25.5
1967	362	12.1
1966	323	8.9
1965	297	1.5
1964	292	−4.6
1963	306	7.9
1962	284	4.6
1961	271	2.2
1951–60	**2,515**	**–**
1960	265	1.8I
1959	261	2.9
1958	253	−22.5
1957	327	1.6
1956	322	35.3
1955	238	14.2
1954	208	22.1
1953	170	−35.8
1952	266	29.1
1951	206	–

Note: Immigrants are people granted legal permanent residence in the United States. They either arrive in the U.S. with immigrant visas issued abroad or adjust their status in the United States from temporary to permanent residence. (–) means not applicable.
Source: Immigration and Naturalization Service, 2000 Statistical Yearbook of the Immigration and Naturalization Service, Internet site http://www.ins.usdoj.gov/graphics/aboutins/statistics/IMM00yrbk/IMM2000list.htm; calculations by New Strategist

Table 8.12 Immigrants by Country of Last Residence, 1950 to 2000

(country of last residence for immigrants from the ten countries sending the largest number of immigrants to the U.S., 1950 to 2000; numbers in thousands)

1991–00		1961–70	
Total immigrants	**9,095**	**Total immigrants**	**3,322**
Total from top ten	**5,207**	**Total from top ten**	**2,048**
Percent from top ten	**57.3%**	**Percent from top ten**	**61.7%**
Mexico	2,249	Mexico	454
Philippines	504	Canada	413
Soviet Union	463	Italy	214
China	419	United Kingdom	214
India	363	Cuba	209
Dominican Republic	335	Germany	191
Vietnam	286	Philippines	98
El Salvador	216	Dominican Republic	93
Canada	192	Greece	86
Haiti	180	Portugal	76
1981–90		**1951–60**	
Total immigrants	**7,338**	**Total immigrants**	**2,515**
Total from top ten	**4,250**	**Total from top ten**	**1,842**
Percent from top ten	**57.9%**	**Percent from top ten**	**73.2%**
Mexico	1,656	Germany	478
Philippines	549	Canada	378
China	347	Mexico	300
Korea	334	United Kingdom	203
Vietnam	281	Italy	185
Dominican Republic	252	Cuba	79
India	251	Austria	67
El Salvador	214	Netherlands	52
Jamaica	208	France	51
United Kingdom	159	Ireland	48
1971–80			
Total immigrants	**4,493**		
Total from top ten	**2,458**		
Percent from top ten	**54.7%**		
Mexico	640		
Philippines	355		
Korea	268		
Cuba	265		
Vietnam	173		
Canada	170		
India	164		
Dominican Republic	148		
Jamaica	138		
United Kingdom	137		

Note: Immigrants are persons granted legal permanent residence in the United States. They either arrive in the U.S. with immigrant visas issued abroad or adjust their status in the United States from temporary to permanent residence.
Source: Immigration and Naturalization Service, 2000 Statistical Yearbook of the Immigration and Naturalization Service, Internet site http://www.ins.usdoj.gov/graphics/aboutins/statistics/IMM00yrbk/IMM2000list.htm; calculations by New Strategist

Diversity Is Growing Faster in Some Regions

The South and West have grown much faster than the Northeast or Midwest during the past half-century. This trend continued during the 1990s, when the West grew 20 percent, the South 17 percent, the Midwest 8 percent, and the Northeast just 5 percent.

The West is by far the most diverse region, with non-Hispanic whites accounting for only 58 percent of its population in 2000. In the Pacific states, which include California, fully 26 percent of the population is Hispanic and 11 percent is Asian. The Midwest is the least diverse region, with non-Hispanic whites accounting for 81 percent of its population. The South is home to the 55 percent majority of the black population, up from 52 percent in 1990.

The West is most diverse

(minority share of population by region, 2000)

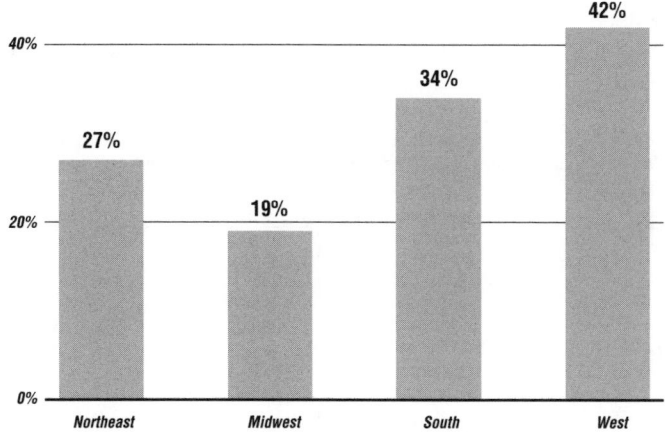

Table 8.13 Regional Populations, 1950 to 2000 Censuses

(population by region and division, 1950 to 2000; percent change 1950–00; numbers in thousands)

	2000	1990	1980	1970	1960	1950	percent change 1990–2000	percent change 1950–2000
UNITED STATES	**281,422**	**248,791**	**226,546**	**203,302**	**179,323**	**151,326**	**13.1%**	**46.2%**
Northeast	**53,594**	**50,828**	**49,135**	**49,061**	**44,678**	**39,478**	**5.4**	**26.3**
New England	13,923	13,207	12,348	11,847	10,509	9,315	5.4	33.1
Middle Atlantic	39,672	37,621	36,787	37,213	34,168	30,163	5.5	24.0
Midwest	**64,393**	**59,669**	**58,866**	**56,590**	**51,619**	**44,461**	**7.9**	**31.0**
E. North Central	45,155	42,009	41,682	40,263	36,224	30,400	7.5	32.7
W. North Central	19,238	17,660	17,183	16,328	15,395	14,062	8.9	26.9
South	**100,237**	**85,456**	**75,372**	**62,813**	**54,973**	**47,197**	**17.3**	**52.9**
South Atlantic	51,769	43,571	36,959	30,679	25,972	21,183	18.8	59.1
E. South Central	17,023	15,180	14,666	12,808	12,050	11,478	12.1	32.6
W. South Central	31,445	26,704	23,747	19,326	16,951	14,538	17.8	53.8
West	**63,198**	**52,837**	**43,172**	**34,838**	**28,053**	**20,190**	**19.6**	**68.1**
Mountain	18,172	13,659	11,373	8,290	6,855	5,076	33.0	72.1
Pacific	45,026	39,179	31,800	26,548	21,198	15,115	14.9	66.4

Source: Bureau of the Census, Internet site http://www.census.gov/population/www/censusdata/hiscendata.html; and 2000 Census, Table DP-1. Profiles of General Demographic Characteristics, 2001; calculations by New Strategist

Table 8.14 Regional Populations by Race and Hispanic Origin, 1990 Census

(number and percent distribution of people by region and division, race, and Hispanic origin, 1990; numbers in thousands)

	total people	race American Indian	Asian	black	white	Hispanic origin Hispanic	non-Hispanic total	white
UNITED STATES	**248,765**	**2,065**	**7,462**	**30,511**	**208,727**	**22,372**	**226,394**	**188,307**
Northeast	**50,828**	**132**	**1,362**	**5,915**	**43,420**	**3,762**	**47,066**	**40,422**
New England	13,207	34	236	667	12,269	568	12,639	11,792
Middle Atlantic	37,621	98	1,126	5,247	31,150	3,194	34,427	28,630
Midwest	**59,669**	**348**	**781**	**5,750**	**52,790**	**1,727**	**57,943**	**51,202**
E. North Central	42,009	156	583	4,847	36,423	1,438	40,571	35,094
W. North Central	17,660	192	198	904	16,367	289	17,371	16,108
South	**85,456**	**578**	**1,145**	**15,907**	**67,825**	**6,767**	**78,689**	**61,403**
South Atlantic	43,571	175	640	8,964	33,793	2,133	41,439	31,840
E. South Central	15,180	41	85	2,982	12,071	95	15,085	11,994
W. South Central	26,704	362	420	3,962	21,961	4,539	22,165	17,569
West	**52,837**	**1,007**	**4,174**	**2,939**	**44,692**	**10,116**	**42,721**	**35,281**
Mountain	13,659	502	225	384	12,547	1,992	11,667	10,655
Pacific	39,153	505	3,949	2,554	32,145	8,124	31,029	24,626

Percent distribution by race and Hispanic origin

	total people	American Indian	Asian	black	white	Hispanic	non-Hispanic total	white
UNITED STATES	**100.0%**	**0.8%**	**3.0%**	**12.3%**	**83.9%**	**9.0%**	**91.0%**	**75.7%**
Northeast	**100.0**	**0.3**	**2.7**	**11.6**	**85.4**	**7.4**	**92.6**	**79.5**
New England	100.0	0.3	1.8	5.1	92.9	4.3	95.7	89.3
Middle Atlantic	100.0	0.3	3.0	13.9	82.8	8.5	91.5	76.1
Midwest	**100.0**	**0.6**	**1.3**	**9.6**	**88.5**	**2.9**	**97.1**	**85.8**
E. North Central	100.0	0.4	1.4	11.5	86.7	3.4	96.6	83.5
W. North Central	100.0	1.1	1.1	5.1	92.7	1.6	98.4	91.2
South	**100.0**	**0.7**	**1.3**	**18.6**	**79.4**	**7.9**	**92.1**	**71.9**
South Atlantic	100.0	0.4	1.5	20.6	77.6	4.9	95.1	73.1
E. South Central	100.0	0.3	0.6	19.6	79.5	0.6	99.4	79.0
W. South Central	100.0	1.4	1.6	14.8	82.2	17.0	83.0	65.8
West	**100.0**	**1.9**	**7.9**	**5.6**	**84.6**	**19.1**	**80.9**	**66.8**
Mountain	100.0	3.7	1.7	2.8	91.9	14.6	85.4	78.0
Pacific	100.0	1.3	10.1	6.5	82.1	20.7	79.3	62.9

Percent distribution by region/division

	total people	American Indian	Asian	black	white	Hispanic	non-Hispanic total	white
UNITED STATES	**100.0%**	**100.0%**	**100.0%**	**100.0%**	**100.0%**	**100.0%**	**100.0%**	**100.0%**
Northeast	**20.4**	**6.4**	**18.3**	**19.4**	**20.8**	**16.8**	**20.8**	**21.5**
New England	5.3	1.6	3.2	2.2	5.9	2.5	5.6	6.3
Middle Atlantic	15.1	4.7	15.1	17.2	14.9	14.3	15.2	15.2
Midwest	**24.0**	**16.9**	**10.5**	**18.8**	**25.3**	**7.7**	**25.6**	**27.2**
E. North Central	16.9	7.6	7.8	15.9	17.5	6.4	17.9	18.6
W. North Central	7.1	9.3	2.7	3.0	7.8	1.3	7.7	8.6
South	**34.4**	**28.0**	**15.3**	**52.1**	**32.5**	**30.2**	**34.8**	**32.6**
South Atlantic	17.5	8.5	8.6	29.4	16.2	9.5	18.3	16.9
E. South Central	6.1	2.0	1.1	9.8	5.8	0.4	6.7	6.4
W. South Central	10.7	17.5	5.6	13.0	10.5	20.3	9.8	9.3
West	**21.2**	**48.8**	**55.9**	**9.6**	**21.4**	**45.2**	**18.9**	**18.7**
Mountain	5.5	24.3	3.0	1.3	6.0	8.9	5.2	5.7
Pacific	15.7	24.4	52.9	8.4	15.4	36.3	13.7	13.1

Note: Numbers will not add to total because Hispanics may be of any race.
Source: Bureau of the Census, Internet site http://eire.census.gov/popest/archives/state/srh/srhmars.txt; calculations by New Strategist

Table 8.15 Regional Populations by Race and Hispanic Origin, 2000 Census

(number and percent distribution of people by region and division, race, and Hispanic origin, 2000)

| | | race alone | | | | two or more races or other race | Hispanic origin | | |
| | | American | | | | | | non-Hispanic | |
	total	Indian	Asian	black	white		Hispanic	total	white
UNITED STATES	281,422	2,476	10,642	34,658	211,461	22,185	35,306	246,116	194,553
Northeast	53,594	163	2,140	6,100	41,534	3,658	5,254	48,340	39,327
New England	13,923	42	379	719	12,051	730	875	13,047	11,687
Middle Atlantic	39,672	120	1,761	5,381	29,483	2,927	4,379	35,293	27,641
Midwest	64,393	399	1,220	6,500	53,834	2,439	3,125	61,268	52,386
E. North Central	45,155	177	895	5,405	36,827	1,852	2,479	42,676	35,670
West North Central	19,238	222	326	1,094	17,007	589	646	18,592	16,716
South	100,237	726	1,973	18,982	72,819	5,736	11,587	88,650	65,928
South Atlantic	51,769	233	1,128	11,027	37,284	2,098	4,244	47,525	34,576
East South Central	17,023	58	142	3,419	13,113	291	299	16,724	12,968
West South Central	31,445	435	704	4,536	22,423	3,347	7,044	24,401	18,384
West	63,198	1,188	5,308	3,077	43,274	10,351	15,341	47,857	36,912
Mountain	18,172	615	392	523	14,592	2,051	3,544	14,629	12,884
Pacific	45,026	573	4,916	2,554	28,682	8,300	11,797	33,229	24,028

Percent distribution by race and Hispanic origin

	total	American Indian	Asian	black	white	two or more races or other race	Hispanic	non-Hispanic total	non-Hispanic white
UNITED STATES	100.0%	0.9%	3.8%	12.3%	75.1%	7.9%	12.5%	87.5%	69.1%
Northeast	100.0	0.3	4.0	11.4	77.5	6.8	9.8	90.2	73.4
New England	100.0	0.3	2.7	5.2	86.6	5.2	6.3	93.7	83.9
Middle Atlantic	100.0	0.3	4.4	13.6	74.3	7.4	11.0	89.0	69.7
Midwest	100.0	0.6	1.9	10.1	83.6	3.8	4.9	95.1	81.4
East North Central	100.0	0.4	2.0	12.0	81.6	4.1	5.5	94.5	79.0
West North Central	100.0	1.2	1.7	5.7	88.4	3.1	3.4	96.6	86.9
South	100.0	0.7	2.0	18.9	72.6	5.7	11.6	88.4	65.8
South Atlantic	100.0	0.5	2.2	21.3	72.0	4.1	8.2	91.8	66.8
East South Central	100.0	0.3	0.8	20.1	77.0	1.7	1.8	98.2	76.2
West South Central	100.0	1.4	2.2	14.4	71.3	10.6	22.4	77.6	58.5
West	100.0	1.9	8.4	4.9	68.5	16.4	24.3	75.7	58.4
Mountain	100.0	3.4	2.2	2.9	80.3	11.3	19.5	80.5	70.9
Pacific	100.0	1.3	10.9	5.7	63.7	18.4	26.2	73.8	53.4

Percent distribution by region/division

	total	American Indian	Asian	black	white	two or more races or other race	Hispanic	non-Hispanic total	non-Hispanic white
UNITED STATES	100.0%	100.0%	100.0%	100.0%	100.0%	100.0%	100.0%	100.0%	100.0%
Northeast	19.0	6.6	20.1	17.6	19.6	16.5	14.9	19.6	20.2
New England	4.9	1.7	3.6	2.1	5.7	3.3	2.5	5.3	6.0
Middle Atlantic	14.1	4.8	16.5	15.5	13.9	13.2	12.4	14.3	14.2
Midwest	22.9	16.1	11.5	18.8	25.5	11.0	8.8	24.9	26.9
East North Central	16.0	7.1	8.4	15.6	17.4	8.3	7.0	17.3	18.3
West North Central	6.8	9.0	3.1	3.2	8.0	2.7	1.8	7.6	8.6
South	35.6	29.3	18.5	54.8	34.4	25.9	32.8	36.0	33.9
South Atlantic	18.4	9.4	10.6	31.8	17.6	9.5	12.0	19.3	17.8
East South Central	6.0	2.3	1.3	9.9	6.2	1.3	0.8	6.8	6.7
West South Central	11.2	17.6	6.6	13.1	10.6	15.1	20.0	9.9	9.4
West	22.5	48.0	49.9	8.9	20.5	46.7	43.5	19.4	19.0
Mountain	6.5	24.8	3.7	1.5	6.9	9.2	10.0	5.9	6.6
Pacific	16.0	23.1	46.2	7.4	13.6	37.4	33.4	13.5	12.4

Note: Asians include Native Hawaiians and other Pacific Islanders; numbers will not add to total because Hispanics may be of any race.
Source: Bureau of the Census, 2000 Census, Table DP-1. Profiles of General Demographic Characteristics, 2001; calculations by New Strategist

Big Changes for States

During the past half-century, the population of some states has increased tenfold while other states have lost people. The population of Nevada grew from just 160,000 in 1950 to nearly 2 million in 2000. In contrast, West Virginia lost 10 percent of its population during the past half-century.

One dramatic change that has occurred among states is the growth of the elderly population. In 1950, the number of people aged 65 or older was greater in Iowa than in Florida. Today, Florida ranks second only to California in the number of people aged 65 or older.

The racial and ethnic diversity of some states is much greater than that of others, differences that are certain to grow during the next few decades. Minorities account for the majority of the population in the nation's most populous state, California; non-Hispanic whites accounted for only 52 percent of its population in 2000. Texas, the nation's second most populous state, will soon join California with a minority majority.

States with the biggest gains

(states gaining the largest number of people, 1950–2000)

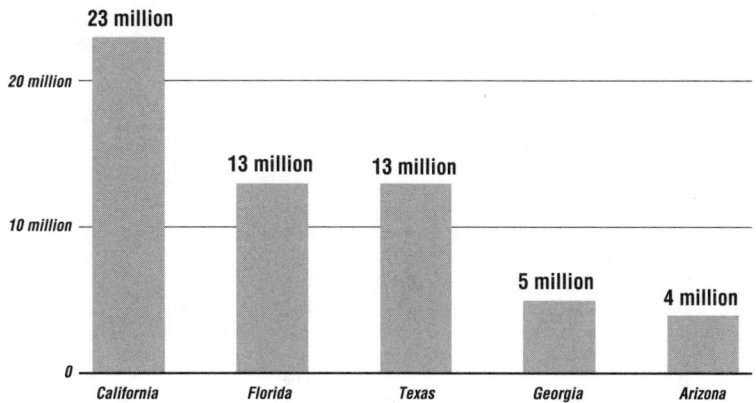

Table 8.16 State Populations, 1950 to 2000 Censuses

(population by state, 1950 to 2000; percent change 1950–2000; numbers in thousands)

	2000	1990	1980	1970	1960	1950	percent change 1990–2000	percent change 1950–2000
United States	**281,422**	**248,791**	**226,546**	**203,302**	**179,323**	**151,326**	**13.1%**	**86.0%**
Alabama	4,447	4,040	3,894	3,444	3,267	3,062	10.1	45.2
Alaska	627	550	402	303	226	129	14.0	386.0
Arizona	5,131	3,665	2,718	1,775	1,302	750	40.0	584.1
Arkansas	2,673	2,351	2,286	1,923	1,786	1,910	13.7	40.0
California	33,872	29,811	23,668	19,971	15,717	10,586	13.6	220.0
Colorado	4,301	3,294	2,890	2,210	1,754	1,325	30.6	224.6
Connecticut	3,406	3,287	3,108	3,032	2,535	2,007	3.6	69.7
Delaware	784	666	594	548	446	318	17.6	146.4
District of Columbia	572	607	638	757	764	802	–5.7	–28.7
Florida	15,982	12,938	9,746	6,791	4,952	2,771	23.5	476.8
Georgia	8,186	6,478	5,463	4,588	3,943	3,445	26.4	137.6
Hawaii	1,212	1,108	965	770	633	500	9.3	142.3
Idaho	1,294	1,007	944	713	667	589	28.5	119.7
Illinois	12,419	11,431	11,427	11,110	10,081	8,712	8.6	42.6
Indiana	6,080	5,544	5,490	5,195	4,662	3,934	9.7	54.6
Iowa	2,926	2,777	2,914	2,825	2,758	2,621	5.4	11.6
Kansas	2,688	2,478	2,364	2,249	2,179	1,905	8.5	41.1
Kentucky	4,042	3,687	3,661	3,221	3,038	2,945	9.6	37.2
Louisiana	4,469	4,222	4,206	3,645	3,257	2,684	5.9	66.5
Maine	1,275	1,228	1,125	994	969	914	3.8	39.5
Maryland	5,296	4,781	4,217	3,924	3,101	2,343	10.8	126.1
Massachusetts	6,349	6,016	5,737	5,689	5,149	4,691	5.5	35.3
Michigan	9,938	9,295	9,262	8,882	7,823	6,372	6.9	56.0
Minnesota	4,919	4,376	4,076	3,806	3,414	2,982	12.4	65.0
Mississippi	2,845	2,575	2,521	2,217	2,178	2,179	10.5	30.5
Missouri	5,595	5,117	4,917	4,678	4,320	3,955	9.3	41.5
Montana	902	799	787	694	675	591	12.9	52.7
Nebraska	1,711	1,578	1,570	1,485	1,411	1,326	8.4	29.1
Nevada	1,998	1,202	800	489	285	160	66.3	1,148.9
New Hampshire	1,236	1,109	921	738	607	533	11.4	131.9
New Jersey	8,414	7,748	7,365	7,171	6,067	4,835	8.6	74.0
New Mexico	1,819	1,515	1,303	1,017	951	681	20.1	167.1
New York	18,976	17,991	17,558	18,241	16,782	14,830	5.5	28.0
North Carolina	8,049	6,632	5,882	5,084	4,556	4,062	21.4	98.2
North Dakota	642	639	653	618	632	620	0.5	3.6
Ohio	11,353	10,847	10,798	10,657	9,706	7,947	4.7	42.9
Oklahoma	3,451	3,146	3,025	2,559	2,328	2,233	9.7	54.5
Oregon	3,421	2,842	2,633	2,092	1,769	1,521	20.4	124.9
Pennsylvania	12,281	11,883	11,864	11,801	11,319	10,498	3.4	17.0
Rhode Island	1,048	1,003	947	950	859	792	4.5	32.4
South Carolina	4,012	3,486	3,122	2,591	2,383	2,117	15.1	89.5
South Dakota	755	696	691	666	681	653	8.5	15.6
Tennessee	5,689	4,877	4,591	3,926	3,567	3,292	16.7	72.8
Texas	20,852	16,986	14,229	11,199	9,580	7,711	22.8	170.4
Utah	2,233	1,723	1,461	1,059	891	689	29.6	224.1
Vermont	609	563	511	445	390	378	8.2	61.1
Virginia	7,079	6,189	5,347	4,651	3,967	3,319	14.4	113.3
Washington	5,894	4,867	4,132	3,413	2,853	2,379	21.1	147.8
West Virginia	1,808	1,793	1,950	1,744	1,860	2,006	0.8	–9.9
Wisconsin	5,364	4,892	4,706	4,418	3,952	3,435	9.6	56.1
Wyoming	494	454	470	332	330	291	8.9	69.7

Source: Bureau of the Census, Internet sites http://www.census.gov/population/www/censusdata/hiscendata.html and http://www.census.gov/population/cen2000/phc-t2/tab01.xls; calculations by New Strategist

Table 8.17 States Ranked by Population, 1950 and 2000 Censuses

(states ranked by population in 1950 and 2000; numbers in thousands)

1950		2000	
New York	14,830	California	33,872
California	10,586	Texas	20,852
Pennsylvania	10,498	New York	18,976
Illinois	8,712	Florida	15,982
Ohio	7,947	Illinois	12,419
Texas	7,711	Pennsylvania	12,281
Michigan	6,372	Ohio	11,353
New Jersey	4,835	Michigan	9,938
Massachusetts	4,691	New Jersey	8,414
North Carolina	4,062	Georgia	8,186
Missouri	3,955	North Carolina	8,049
Indiana	3,934	Virginia	7,079
Georgia	3,445	Massachusetts	6,349
Wisconsin	3,435	Indiana	6,080
Virginia	3,319	Washington	5,894
Tennessee	3,292	Tennessee	5,689
Alabama	3,062	Missouri	5,595
Minnesota	2,982	Wisconsin	5,364
Kentucky	2,945	Maryland	5,296
Florida	2,771	Arizona	5,131
Louisiana	2,684	Minnesota	4,919
Iowa	2,621	Louisiana	4,469
Washington	2,379	Alabama	4,447
Maryland	2,343	Colorado	4,301
Oklahoma	2,233	Kentucky	4,042
Mississippi	2,179	South Carolina	4,012
South Carolina	2,117	Oklahoma	3,451
Connecticut	2,007	Oregon	3,421
West Virginia	2,006	Connecticut	3,406
Arkansas	1,910	Iowa	2,926
Kansas	1,905	Mississippi	2,845
Oregon	1,521	Kansas	2,688
Nebraska	1,326	Arkansas	2,673
Colorado	1,325	Utah	2,233
Maine	914	Nevada	1,998
District of Columbia	802	New Mexico	1,819
Rhode Island	792	West Virginia	1,808
Arizona	750	Nebraska	1,711
Utah	689	Idaho	1,294
New Mexico	681	Maine	1,275
South Dakota	653	New Hampshire	1,236
North Dakota	620	Hawaii	1,212
Montana	591	Rhode Island	1,048
Idaho	589	Montana	902
New Hampshire	533	Delaware	784
Hawaii	500	South Dakota	755
Vermont	378	North Dakota	642
Delaware	318	Alaska	627
Wyoming	291	Vermont	609
Nevada	160	District of Columbia	572
Alaska	129	Wyoming	494

Source: Bureau of the Census, Internet sites http://www.census.gov/population/www/censusdata/hiscendata.html and http://www.census.gov/population/cen2000/phc-t2/tab01.xls; calculations by New Strategist

Table 8.18 States Ranked by Population Change, 1950 to 2000 Censuses

(states ranked by numerical and percent change in population, 1950 to 2000; numbers in thousands)

numerical change		percent change	
California	23,286	Nevada	1,148.9%
Florida	13,211	Arizona	584.1
Texas	13,141	Florida	476.8
Georgia	4,741	Alaska	386.0
Arizona	4,381	Colorado	224.6
New York	4,146	Utah	224.1
North Carolina	3,987	California	220.0
Virginia	3,760	Texas	170.4
Illinois	3,707	New Mexico	167.1
New Jersey	3,579	Washington	147.8
Michigan	3,566	Delaware	146.4
Washington	3,515	Hawaii	142.3
Ohio	3,406	Georgia	137.6
Colorado	2,976	New Hampshire	131.9
Maryland	2,953	Maryland	126.1
Tennessee	2,397	Oregon	124.9
Indiana	2,146	Idaho	119.7
Minnesota	1,937	Virginia	113.3
Wisconsin	1,929	North Carolina	98.2
Oregon	1,900	South Carolina	89.5
South Carolina	1,895	New Jersey	74.0
Nevada	1,838	Tennessee	72.8
Louisiana	1,785	Wyoming	69.7
Pennsylvania	1,783	Connecticut	69.7
Massachusetts	1,658	Louisiana	66.5
Missouri	1,640	Minnesota	65.0
Utah	1,544	Vermont	61.1
Connecticut	1,399	Wisconsin	56.1
Alabama	1,385	Michigan	56.0
Oklahoma	1,218	Indiana	54.6
New Mexico	1,138	Oklahoma	54.5
Kentucky	1,097	Montana	52.7
Kansas	783	Alabama	45.2
Arkansas	763	Ohio	42.9
Hawaii	712	Illinois	42.6
Idaho	705	Missouri	41.5
New Hampshire	703	Kansas	41.1
Mississippi	666	Arkansas	40.0
Alaska	498	Maine	39.5
Delaware	466	Kentucky	37.2
Nebraska	385	Massachusetts	35.3
Maine	361	Rhode Island	32.4
Montana	311	Mississippi	30.5
Iowa	305	Nebraska	29.1
Rhode Island	256	New York	28.0
Vermont	231	Pennsylvania	17.0
Wyoming	203	South Dakota	15.6
South Dakota	102	Iowa	11.6
North Dakota	22	North Dakota	3.6
West Virginia	−198	West Virginia	−9.9
District of Columbia	−230	District of Columbia	−28.7

Source: Calculations by New Strategist based on Bureau of the Census, Internet sites http://www.census.gov/population/www/ censusdata/hiscendata.html and http://www.census.gov/population/cen2000/phc-t2/tab01.xls

Table 8.19   People Aged 65 or Older by State, 1950 and 2000 Censuses

(number of people aged 65 or older by state, 1950 to 2000; percent change 1950–00; numbers in thousands)

	2000	1950	percent change 1950–2000
United States	**34,992**	**12,270**	**185.2%**
Alabama	580	199	191.5
Alaska	36	5	620.0
Arizona	668	44	1,418.2
Arkansas	374	150	149.3
California	3,596	895	301.8
Colorado	416	116	258.6
Connecticut	470	177	165.5
Delaware	102	26	292.3
District of Columbia	70	57	22.8
Florida	2,808	237	1,084.8
Georgia	785	220	256.8
Hawaii	161	20	705.0
Idaho	146	44	231.8
Illinois	1,500	754	98.9
Indiana	753	361	108.6
Iowa	436	273	59.7
Kansas	356	194	83.5
Kentucky	505	235	114.9
Louisiana	517	177	192.1
Maine	183	94	94.7
Maryland	599	164	265.2
Massachusetts	860	468	83.8
Michigan	1,219	462	163.9
Minnesota	594	269	120.8
Mississippi	344	153	124.8
Missouri	755	407	85.5
Montana	121	51	137.3
Nebraska	232	130	78.5
Nevada	219	11	1,890.9
New Hampshire	148	58	155.2
New Jersey	1,113	394	182.5
New Mexico	212	33	542.4
New York	2,448	1,258	94.6
North Carolina	969	225	330.7
North Dakota	94	48	95.8
Ohio	1,508	709	112.7
Oklahoma	456	194	135.1
Oregon	438	133	229.3
Pennsylvania	1,919	887	116.3
Rhode Island	152	70	117.1
South Carolina	485	115	321.7
South Dakota	108	55	96.4
Tennessee	703	235	199.1
Texas	2,073	513	304.1
Utah	190	42	352.4
Vermont	78	40	95.0
Virginia	792	215	268.4
Washington	662	211	213.7
West Virginia	277	139	99.3
Wisconsin	703	310	126.8
Wyoming	58	18	222.2

Source: Bureau of the Census, Historical Statistics of the United States, Colonial Times to 1970, Part 1, *1975; and* The 65 Years and Over Population: 2000, *Census 2000 Brief, C2KBR/01-10, 2001; calculations by New Strategist*

Table 8.20 State Populations by Race and Hispanic Origin, 1990 Census

(number of people by state, race, and Hispanic origin, 1990; numbers in thousands)

	total population	race American Indian	race Asian	race black	race white	Hispanic origin Hispanic	Hispanic origin non-Hispanic total	Hispanic origin non-Hispanic white
United States	**248,765**	**2,065**	**7,462**	**30,511**	**208,727**	**22,372**	**226,394**	**188,307**
Alabama	4,040	17	22	1,021	2,980	25	4,016	2,960
Alaska	550	86	20	23	421	18	532	407
Arizona	3,665	214	58	115	3,278	688	2,977	2,630
Arkansas	2,351	13	13	374	1,951	20	2,331	1,933
California	29,786	285	2,947	2,304	24,249	7,697	22,088	17,064
Colorado	3,294	31	62	136	3,066	424	2,870	2,663
Connecticut	3,287	7	52	282	2,946	213	3,074	2,757
Delaware	666	2	9	113	541	16	650	528
District of Columbia	607	2	12	402	191	33	574	166
Florida	12,938	37	156	1,772	10,972	1,574	11,364	9,482
Georgia	6,478	14	77	1,751	4,636	109	6,369	4,545
Hawaii	1,108	5	696	28	379	81	1,027	349
Idaho	1,007	15	10	4	979	53	954	929
Illinois	11,431	24	292	1,707	9,407	904	10,526	8,556
Indiana	5,544	13	38	434	5,059	99	5,445	4,967
Iowa	2,777	8	26	48	2,695	33	2,744	2,665
Kansas	2,478	23	32	145	2,277	94	2,384	2,192
Kentucky	3,687	6	18	264	3,399	22	3,665	3,380
Louisiana	4,222	19	42	1,303	2,858	93	4,129	2,778
Maine	1,228	6	7	5	1,210	7	1,221	1,204
Maryland	4,781	13	141	1,196	3,430	125	4,656	3,328
Massachusetts	6,016	13	146	327	5,530	288	5,729	5,298
Michigan	9,295	58	106	1,298	7,833	202	9,094	7,654
Minnesota	4,376	51	79	96	4,150	54	4,322	4,104
Mississippi	2,575	9	13	917	1,636	16	2,559	1,625
Missouri	5,117	20	42	550	4,505	62	5,055	4,450
Montana	799	48	4	2	744	12	787	734
Nebraska	1,578	13	13	58	1,495	37	1,541	1,461
Nevada	1,202	21	39	80	1,061	124	1,077	947
New Hampshire	1,109	2	9	7	1,090	11	1,098	1,080
New Jersey	7,748	16	277	1,077	6,378	748	7,000	5,726
New Mexico	1,515	138	15	32	1,331	579	936	767
New York	17,991	66	709	3,065	14,150	2,214	15,777	12,475
North Carolina	6,632	81	53	1,462	5,037	77	6,556	4,975
North Dakota	639	26	4	4	606	5	634	602
Ohio	10,847	21	92	1,160	9,575	140	10,707	9,450
Oklahoma	3,146	258	35	236	2,617	86	3,059	2,549
Oregon	2,842	41	70	47	2,685	113	2,730	2,581
Pennsylvania	11,883	15	140	1,105	10,622	232	11,651	10,428
Rhode Island	1,003	4	19	43	937	46	958	901
South Carolina	3,486	8	23	1,042	2,414	31	3,456	2,390
South Dakota	696	51	3	3	639	5	691	635
Tennessee	4,877	10	32	779	4,056	33	4,844	4,029
Texas	16,986	72	331	2,048	14,534	4,340	12,646	10,308
Utah	1,723	25	34	12	1,651	85	1,638	1,572
Vermont	563	2	3	2	556	4	559	552
Virginia	6,189	16	161	1,168	4,844	160	6,029	4,706
Washington	4,867	87	215	153	4,411	215	4,652	4,225
West Virginia	1,793	2	7	56	1,727	8	1,785	1,719
Wisconsin	4,892	40	54	247	4,550	93	4,799	4,466
Wyoming	454	10	3	4	437	26	428	413

Note: Asians include Pacific Islanders; numbers will not add to total because Hispanics may be of any race.
Source: Bureau of the Census, Internet site http://eire.census.gov/popest/archives/state/srh/srhmars.txt

Table 8.21 Distribution of State Populations by Race and Hispanic Origin, 1990 Census

(percent distribution of people by race and Hispanic origin, by state, 1990)

| | total population | race | | | | Hispanic origin | | |
		American Indian	Asian	black	white	Hispanic	non-Hispanic total	non-Hispanic white
United States	**100.0%**	**0.8%**	**3.0%**	**12.3%**	**83.9%**	**9.0%**	**91.0%**	**75.7%**
Alabama	100.0	0.4	0.5	25.3	73.8	0.6	99.4	73.3
Alaska	100.0	15.7	3.7	4.2	76.5	3.2	96.8	74.0
Arizona	100.0	5.9	1.6	3.1	89.4	18.8	81.2	71.7
Arkansas	100.0	0.6	0.5	15.9	83.0	0.8	99.2	82.2
California	100.0	1.0	9.9	7.7	81.4	25.8	74.2	57.3
Colorado	100.0	0.9	1.9	4.1	93.1	12.9	87.1	80.8
Connecticut	100.0	0.2	1.6	8.6	89.6	6.5	93.5	83.9
Delaware	100.0	0.3	1.4	17.0	81.3	2.4	97.6	79.3
District of Columbia	100.0	0.3	1.9	66.3	31.5	5.4	94.6	27.4
Florida	100.0	0.3	1.2	13.7	84.8	12.2	87.8	73.3
Georgia	100.0	0.2	1.2	27.0	71.6	1.7	98.3	70.2
Hawaii	100.0	0.5	62.8	2.5	34.2	7.3	92.7	31.5
Idaho	100.0	1.5	1.0	0.3	97.2	5.3	94.7	92.3
Illinois	100.0	0.2	2.6	14.9	82.3	7.9	92.1	74.9
Indiana	100.0	0.2	0.7	7.8	91.2	1.8	98.2	89.6
Iowa	100.0	0.3	0.9	1.7	97.1	1.2	98.8	96.0
Kansas	100.0	0.9	1.3	5.8	91.9	3.8	96.2	88.5
Kentucky	100.0	0.2	0.5	7.2	92.2	0.6	99.4	91.7
Louisiana	100.0	0.4	1.0	30.9	67.7	2.2	97.8	65.8
Maine	100.0	0.5	0.5	0.4	98.5	0.6	99.4	98.0
Maryland	100.0	0.3	3.0	25.0	71.7	2.6	97.4	69.6
Massachusetts	100.0	0.2	2.4	5.4	91.9	4.8	95.2	88.1
Michigan	100.0	0.6	1.1	14.0	84.3	2.2	97.8	82.3
Minnesota	100.0	1.2	1.8	2.2	94.8	1.2	98.8	93.8
Mississippi	100.0	0.3	0.5	35.6	63.5	0.6	99.4	63.1
Missouri	100.0	0.4	0.8	10.7	88.0	1.2	98.8	87.0
Montana	100.0	6.0	0.5	0.3	93.1	1.5	98.5	91.9
Nebraska	100.0	0.8	0.8	3.7	94.7	2.3	97.7	92.6
Nevada	100.0	1.8	3.3	6.6	88.3	10.4	89.6	78.8
New Hampshire	100.0	0.2	0.8	0.7	98.3	1.0	99.0	97.4
New Jersey	100.0	0.2	3.6	13.9	82.3	9.7	90.3	73.9
New Mexico	100.0	9.1	1.0	2.1	87.8	38.2	61.8	50.6
New York	100.0	0.4	3.9	17.0	78.7	12.3	87.7	69.3
North Carolina	100.0	1.2	0.8	22.0	75.9	1.2	98.8	75.0
North Dakota	100.0	4.1	0.5	0.6	94.8	0.7	99.3	94.2
Ohio	100.0	0.2	0.8	10.7	88.3	1.3	98.7	87.1
Oklahoma	100.0	8.2	1.1	7.5	83.2	2.7	97.3	81.0
Oregon	100.0	1.4	2.5	1.7	94.4	4.0	96.0	90.8
Pennsylvania	100.0	0.1	1.2	9.3	89.4	2.0	98.0	87.8
Rhode Island	100.0	0.4	1.9	4.3	93.4	4.6	95.4	89.8
South Carolina	100.0	0.2	0.7	29.9	69.2	0.9	99.1	68.6
South Dakota	100.0	7.3	0.5	0.5	91.8	0.8	99.2	91.2
Tennessee	100.0	0.2	0.7	16.0	83.2	0.7	99.3	82.6
Texas	100.0	0.4	2.0	12.1	85.6	25.5	74.5	60.7
Utah	100.0	1.5	2.0	0.7	95.9	4.9	95.1	91.2
Vermont	100.0	0.3	0.6	0.4	98.8	0.7	99.3	98.2
Virginia	100.0	0.3	2.6	18.9	78.3	2.6	97.4	76.0
Washington	100.0	1.8	4.4	3.1	90.6	4.4	95.6	86.8
West Virginia	100.0	0.1	0.4	3.1	96.3	0.5	99.5	95.9
Wisconsin	100.0	0.8	1.1	5.0	93.0	1.9	98.1	91.3
Wyoming	100.0	2.2	0.6	0.8	96.4	5.7	94.3	91.0

Note: Asians include Pacific Islanders; numbers will not add to total because Hispanics may be of any race.
Source: Bureau of the Census, Internet site http://eire.census.gov/popest/archives/state/srh/srhmars.txt; calculations by New Strategist

Table 8.22 State Populations by Race and Hispanic Origin, 2000 Census

(number of people by state, race, and Hispanic origin, 2000; numbers in thousands)

	total	race alone				two or more races or other race	Hispanic origin		
		American Indian	Asian	black	white		Hispanic	non-Hispanic total	non-Hispanic white
United States	**281,422**	**2,476**	**10,642**	**34,658**	**211,461**	**22,185**	**35,306**	**246,116**	**194,553**
Alabama	4,447	22	33	1,156	3,163	73	76	4,371	3,126
Alaska	627	98	28	22	435	44	26	601	424
Arizona	5,131	256	99	159	3,874	743	1,296	3,835	3,274
Arkansas	2,673	18	22	419	2,139	76	87	2,587	2,100
California	33,872	333	3,814	2,264	20,170	7,290	10,967	22,905	15,817
Colorado	4,301	44	100	165	3,560	432	736	3,566	3,203
Connecticut	3,406	10	84	310	2,780	222	320	3,085	2,639
Delaware	784	3	17	151	585	29	37	746	568
Dist. Columbia	572	2	16	343	176	35	45	527	159
Florida	15,982	54	275	2,336	12,465	853	2,683	13,300	10,459
Georgia	8,186	22	177	2,350	5,327	310	435	7,751	5,129
Hawaii	1,212	4	617	22	294	274	88	1,124	277
Idaho	1,294	18	13	5	1,177	80	102	1,192	1,139
Illinois	12,419	31	428	1,877	9,125	958	1,530	10,889	8,424
Indiana	6,080	16	61	510	5,320	173	215	5,866	5,219
Iowa	2,926	9	38	62	2,749	69	82	2,844	2,710
Kansas	2,688	25	48	154	2,314	147	188	2,500	2,234
Kentucky	4,042	9	31	296	3,641	65	60	3,982	3,608
Louisiana	4,469	25	56	1,452	2,856	79	108	4,361	2,794
Maine	1,275	7	9	7	1,236	16	9	1,266	1,230
Maryland	5,296	15	213	1,477	3,391	199	228	5,069	3,287
Massachusetts	6,349	15	241	343	5,367	383	429	5,920	5,198
Michigan	9,938	58	179	1,413	7,966	322	324	9,615	7,807
Minnesota	4,919	55	144	172	4,400	149	143	4,776	4,337
Mississippi	2,845	12	19	1,034	1,746	34	40	2,805	1,728
Missouri	5,595	25	65	629	4,748	128	119	5,477	4,686
Montana	902	56	5	3	817	21	18	884	808
Nebraska	1,711	15	23	69	1,533	72	94	1,617	1,494
Nevada	1,998	26	99	135	1,502	236	394	1,604	1,303
New Hampshire	1,236	3	16	9	1,187	21	20	1,215	1,175
New Jersey	8,414	19	484	1,142	6,105	665	1,117	7,297	5,557
New Mexico	1,819	173	21	34	1,214	376	765	1,054	813
New York	18,976	82	1,054	3,014	12,894	1,932	2,868	16,109	11,761
North Carolina	8,049	100	118	1,738	5,805	290	379	7,670	5,647
North Dakota	642	31	4	4	593	10	8	634	589
Ohio	11,353	24	135	1,301	9,645	247	217	11,136	9,538
Oklahoma	3,451	273	49	261	2,628	239	179	3,271	2,556
Oregon	3,421	45	109	56	2,962	250	275	3,146	2,858
Pennsylvania	12,281	18	223	1,225	10,484	331	394	11,887	10,322
Rhode Island	1,048	5	24	47	891	81	91	957	858
South Carolina	4,012	14	38	1,185	2,696	80	95	3,917	2,652
South Dakota	755	62	5	5	669	14	11	744	665
Tennessee	5,689	15	59	933	4,563	119	124	5,565	4,506
Texas	20,852	118	577	2,405	14,800	2,953	6,670	14,182	10,933
Utah	2,233	30	52	18	1,993	141	202	2,032	1,904
Vermont	609	2	5	3	589	9	6	603	585
Virginia	7,079	21	265	1,390	5,120	282	330	6,749	4,966
Washington	5,894	93	346	190	4,822	442	442	5,453	4,652
West Virginia	1,808	4	10	57	1,719	19	12	1,796	1,710
Wisconsin	5,364	47	90	304	4,770	152	193	5,171	4,682
Wyoming	494	11	3	4	455	21	32	462	439

Note: Numbers will not add to total because Hispanics may be of any race; Asians include Native Hawaiians and other Pacific Islanders.

Source: Bureau of the Census, 2000 Census, Table DP-1. Profiles of General Demographic Characteristics, *2001*

Table 8.23 Distribution of State Populations by Race and Hispanic Origin, 2000 Census

(percent distribution of people by race and Hispanic origin, by state, 2000)

	total population	race alone				two or more races or other race	Hispanic origin		
		American Indian	Asian	black	white		Hispanic	non-Hispanic	
								total	white
United States	**100.0%**	**0.9%**	**3.8%**	**12.3%**	**75.1%**	**7.9%**	**12.5%**	**87.5%**	**69.1%**
Alabama	100.0	0.5	0.7	26.0	71.1	1.6	1.7	98.3	70.3
Alaska	100.0	15.6	4.5	3.5	69.3	7.0	4.1	95.9	67.6
Arizona	100.0	5.0	1.9	3.1	75.5	14.5	25.3	74.7	63.8
Arkansas	100.0	0.7	0.8	15.7	80.0	2.8	3.2	96.8	78.6
California	100.0	1.0	11.3	6.7	59.5	21.5	32.4	67.6	46.7
Colorado	100.0	1.0	2.3	3.8	82.8	10.0	17.1	82.9	74.5
Connecticut	100.0	0.3	2.5	9.1	81.6	6.5	9.4	90.6	77.5
Delaware	100.0	0.3	2.1	19.2	74.6	3.7	4.8	95.2	72.5
Dist. Columbia	100.0	0.3	2.7	60.0	30.8	6.2	7.9	92.1	27.8
Florida	100.0	0.3	1.7	14.6	78.0	5.3	16.8	83.2	65.4
Georgia	100.0	0.3	2.2	28.7	65.1	3.8	5.3	94.7	62.6
Hawaii	100.0	0.3	51.0	1.8	24.3	22.7	7.2	92.8	22.9
Idaho	100.0	1.4	1.0	0.4	91.0	6.2	7.9	92.1	88.0
Illinois	100.0	0.2	3.4	15.1	73.5	7.7	12.3	87.7	67.8
Indiana	100.0	0.3	1.0	8.4	87.5	2.9	3.5	96.5	85.8
Iowa	100.0	0.3	1.3	2.1	93.9	2.4	2.8	97.2	92.6
Kansas	100.0	0.9	1.8	5.7	86.1	5.5	7.0	93.0	83.1
Kentucky	100.0	0.2	0.8	7.3	90.1	1.6	1.5	98.5	89.3
Louisiana	100.0	0.6	1.3	32.5	63.9	1.8	2.4	97.6	62.5
Maine	100.0	0.6	0.7	0.5	96.9	1.2	0.7	99.3	96.5
Maryland	100.0	0.3	4.0	27.9	64.0	3.8	4.3	95.7	62.1
Massachusetts	100.0	0.2	3.8	5.4	84.5	6.0	6.8	93.2	81.9
Michigan	100.0	0.6	1.8	14.2	80.2	3.2	3.3	96.7	78.6
Minnesota	100.0	1.1	2.9	3.5	89.4	3.0	2.9	97.1	88.2
Mississippi	100.0	0.4	0.7	36.3	61.4	1.2	1.4	98.6	60.7
Missouri	100.0	0.4	1.2	11.2	84.9	2.3	2.1	97.9	83.8
Montana	100.0	6.2	0.6	0.3	90.6	2.3	2.0	98.0	89.5
Nebraska	100.0	0.9	1.3	4.0	89.6	4.2	5.5	94.5	87.3
Nevada	100.0	1.3	4.9	6.8	75.2	11.8	19.7	80.3	65.2
New Hampshire	100.0	0.2	1.3	0.7	96.0	1.7	1.7	98.3	95.1
New Jersey	100.0	0.2	5.7	13.6	72.6	7.9	13.3	86.7	66.0
New Mexico	100.0	9.5	1.1	1.9	66.8	20.7	42.1	57.9	44.7
New York	100.0	0.4	5.6	15.9	67.9	10.2	15.1	84.9	62.0
North Carolina	100.0	1.2	1.5	21.6	72.1	3.6	4.7	95.3	70.2
North Dakota	100.0	4.9	0.6	0.6	92.4	1.5	1.2	98.8	91.7
Ohio	100.0	0.2	1.2	11.5	85.0	2.2	1.9	98.1	84.0
Oklahoma	100.0	7.9	1.4	7.6	76.2	6.9	5.2	94.8	74.1
Oregon	100.0	1.3	3.2	1.6	86.6	7.3	8.0	92.0	83.5
Pennsylvania	100.0	0.1	1.8	10.0	85.4	2.7	3.2	96.8	84.1
Rhode Island	100.0	0.5	2.3	4.5	85.0	7.7	8.7	91.3	81.9
South Carolina	100.0	0.3	0.9	29.5	67.2	2.0	2.4	97.6	66.1
South Dakota	100.0	8.3	0.6	0.6	88.7	1.8	1.4	98.6	88.0
Tennessee	100.0	0.3	1.0	16.4	80.2	2.1	2.2	97.8	79.2
Texas	100.0	0.6	2.8	11.5	71.0	14.2	32.0	68.0	52.4
Utah	100.0	1.3	2.3	0.8	89.2	6.3	9.0	91.0	85.3
Vermont	100.0	0.4	0.9	0.5	96.8	1.4	0.9	99.1	96.2
Virginia	100.0	0.3	3.7	19.6	72.3	4.0	4.7	95.3	70.2
Washington	100.0	1.6	5.9	3.2	81.8	7.5	7.5	92.5	78.9
West Virginia	100.0	0.2	0.5	3.2	95.0	1.0	0.7	99.3	94.6
Wisconsin	100.0	0.9	1.7	5.7	88.9	2.8	3.6	96.4	87.3
Wyoming	100.0	2.3	0.6	0.8	92.1	4.3	6.4	93.6	88.9

Note: Numbers will not add to total because Hispanics may be of any race; Asians include Native Hawaiians and other Pacific Islanders.
Source: Bureau of the Census, 2000 Census, Table DP-1. Profiles of General Demographic Characteristics, 2001; calculations by New Strategist

The Suburbs Are Home to Half of Americans

The nation's suburbs (the portions of metropolitan areas that are outside the central cities) were home to 50 percent of Americans in 2000, up from just 23 percent in 1950. Overall, 80 percent of the U.S. population lives in metropolitan areas, up from 56 percent in 1950. Meanwhile, the proportion of the population living outside of metropolitan areas has fallen from 44 to just 20 percent during the past half-century.

New York is by far the most populous metropolitan area, with more than 21 million people in 2000. Los Angeles is second, followed by Chicago, Washington, D.C., and San Francisco. Las Vegas was the fastest growing metropolitan area during the 1990s, posting an 83 percent gain. Naples, Florida, and Yuma, Arizona, were second and third in growth rate, gaining 65 percent and 50 percent, respectively.

Suburbs are growing at the expense of nonmetro areas

(percent of people living in central cities, suburbs, and nonmetropolitan areas, 1950 and 2000)

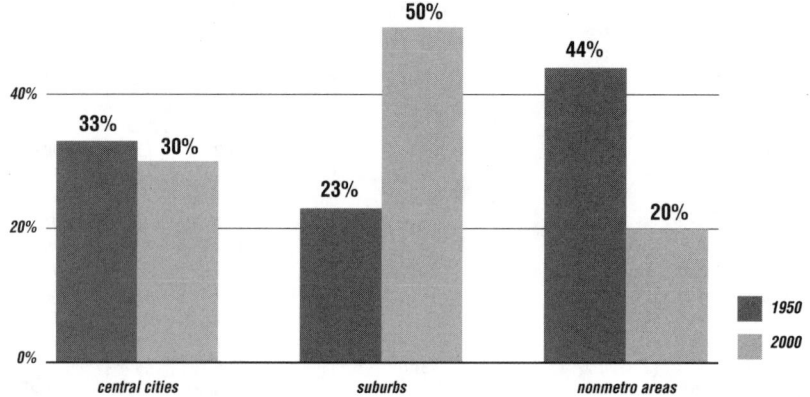

Table 8.24   Population by Metropolitan Status, 1950 to 2000 Censuses

(number and percent distribution of people by metropolitan status, 1950 to 2000; numbers in thousands; metropolitan areas as defined at each time period)

| | number | | | percent distribution by metropolitan status | | | | |
| | | | | | metropolitan | | | nonmetro |
	total	metropolitan	total	total	central cities	suburbs	areas
2000	281,422	225,968	100.0%	80.3%	30.3%	50.0%	19.7%
1990	249,464	198,249	100.0	77.5	31.3	46.2	22.5
1980	227,225	177,361	100.0	74.8	30.0	44.8	25.2
1970	203,212	139,480	100.0	69.0	31.4	37.6	31.0
1960	179,323	112,885	100.0	63.3	32.3	30.9	36.7
1950	150,697	84,501	100.0	56.1	32.8	23.3	43.9

Note: The suburbs are the portion of a metropolitan area outside the central city.
Source: Bureau of the Census, Metropolitan Areas and Cities, *1990 Census Profile, No. 3, 1991; and 2000 Census,* Table DP-1: Profile of General Demographic Characteristics: 2000; *and* Historical Statistics of the United States, Colonial Times to 1970, Part 1, *1975; calculations by New Strategist*

Table 8.25 Metropolitan Populations, 1990 and 2000 Censuses: Alphabetical Ranking

(number of people by metropolitan area, 1990 and 2000; change and percent change in number, 1990–2000; metropolitan areas as defined on June 30, 1999; metropolitan areas ranked alphabetically)

				change, 1990–2000	
		2000	*1990*	*number*	*percent*
1.	Abilene, TX MSA	126,555	119,655	6,900	5.8%
2.	Aguadilla, PR MSA	146,424	128,172	18,252	14.2
3.	Albany, GA MSA	120,822	112,561	8,261	7.3
4.	Albany–Schenectady–Troy, NY MSA	875,583	861,424	14,159	1.6
5.	Albuquerque, NM MSA	712,738	589,131	123,607	21.0
6.	Alexandria, LA MSA	126,337	131,556	–5,219	–4.0
7.	Allentown–Bethlehem–Easton, PA MSA	637,958	595,081	42,877	7.2
8.	Altoona, PA MSA	129,144	130,542	–1,398	–1.1
9.	Amarillo, TX MSA	217,858	187,547	30,311	16.2
10.	Anchorage, AK MSA	260,283	226,338	33,945	15.0
11.	Anniston, AL MSA	112,249	116,034	–3,785	–3.3
12.	Appleton–Oshkosh–Neenah, WI MSA	358,365	315,121	43,244	13.7
13.	Asheville, NC MSA	225,965	191,774	34,191	17.8
14.	Athens, GA MSA	153,444	126,262	27,182	21.5
15.	Atlanta, GA MSA	4,112,198	2,959,950	1,152,248	38.9
16.	Auburn–Opelika, AL MSA	115,092	87,146	27,946	32.1
17.	Augusta–Aiken, GA–SC MSA	477,441	415,184	62,257	15.0
18.	Austin–San Marcos, TX MSA	1,249,763	846,227	403,536	47.7
19.	Bakersfield, CA MSA	661,645	543,477	118,168	21.7
20.	Bangor, ME MSA	90,864	91,629	–765	–0.8
21.	Barnstable–Yarmouth, MA MSA	162,582	134,954	27,628	20.5
22.	Baton Rouge, LA MSA	602,894	528,264	74,630	14.1
23.	Beaumont–Port Arthur, TX MSA	385,090	361,226	23,864	6.6
24.	Bellingham, WA MSA	166,814	127,780	39,034	30.5
25.	Benton Harbor, MI MSA	162,453	161,378	1,075	0.7
26.	Billings, MT MSA	129,352	113,419	15,933	14.0
27.	Biloxi–Gulfport–Pascagoula, MS MSA	363,988	312,368	51,620	16.5
28.	Binghamton, NY MSA	252,320	264,497	–12,177	–4.6
29.	Birmingham, AL MSA	921,106	840,140	80,966	9.6
30.	Bismarck, ND MSA	94,719	83,831	10,888	13.0
31.	Bloomington, IN MSA	120,563	108,978	11,585	10.6
32.	Bloomington–Normal, IL MSA	150,433	129,180	21,253	16.5
33.	Boise City, ID MSA	432,345	295,851	136,494	46.1
34.	Boston–Worcester–Lawrence, MA–NH–ME–CT CMSA	5,819,100	5,455,403	363,697	6.7
35.	Brownsville–Harlingen–San Benito, TX MSA	335,227	260,120	75,107	28.9
36.	Bryan–College Station, TX MSA	152,415	121,862	30,553	25.1
37.	Buffalo–Niagara Falls, NY MSA	1,170,111	1,189,288	–19,177	–1.6
38.	Burlington, VT MSA	169,391	151,506	17,885	11.8
39.	Canton–Massillon, OH MSA	406,934	394,106	12,828	3.3
40.	Casper, WY MSA	66,533	61,226	5,307	8.7
41.	Cedar Rapids, IA MSA	191,701	168,767	22,934	13.6
42.	Champaign–Urbana, IL MSA	179,669	173,025	6,644	3.8
43.	Charleston, WV MSA	251,662	250,454	1,208	0.5
44.	Charleston–North Charleston, SC MSA	549,033	506,875	42,158	8.3
45.	Charlotte–Gastonia–Rock Hill, NC–SC MSA	1,499,293	1,162,093	337,200	29.0
46.	Charlottesville, VA MSA	159,576	131,107	28,469	21.7
47.	Chattanooga, TN–GA MSA	465,161	424,347	40,814	9.6
48.	Cheyenne, WY MSA	81,607	73,142	8,465	11.6

(continued)

(continued from previous page)

		2000	1990	change, 1990–2000 number	change, 1990–2000 percent
49.	Chicago–Gary–Kenosha, IL–IN–WI CMSA	9,157,540	8,239,820	917,720	11.1%
50.	Chico–Paradise, CA MSA	203,171	182,120	21,051	11.6
51.	Cincinnati–Hamilton, OH–KY–IN CMSA	1,979,202	1,817,571	161,631	8.9
52.	Clarksville–Hopkinsville, TN–KY MSA	207,033	169,439	37,594	22.2
53.	Cleveland–Akron, OH CMSA	2,945,831	2,859,644	86,187	3.0
54.	Colorado Springs, CO MSA	516,929	397,014	119,915	30.2
55.	Columbia, MO MSA	135,454	112,379	23,075	20.5
56.	Columbia, SC MSA	536,691	453,331	83,360	18.4
57.	Columbus, GA–AL MSA	274,624	260,860	13,764	5.3
58.	Columbus, OH MSA	1,540,157	1,345,450	194,707	14.5
59.	Corpus Christi, TX MSA	380,783	349,894	30,889	8.8
60.	Corvallis, OR MSA	78,153	70,811	7,342	10.4
61.	Cumberland, MD–WV MSA	102,008	101,643	365	0.4
62.	Dallas–Fort Worth, TX CMSA	5,221,801	4,037,282	1,184,519	29.3
63.	Danville, VA MSA	110,156	108,711	1,445	1.3
64.	Davenport–Moline–Rock Island, IA–IL MSA	359,062	350,861	8,201	2.3
65.	Daytona Beach, FL MSA	493,175	399,413	93,762	23.5
66.	Dayton–Springfield, OH MSA	950,558	951,270	–712	–0.1
67.	Decatur, AL MSA	145,867	131,556	14,311	10.9
68.	Decatur, IL MSA	114,706	117,206	–2,500	–2.1
69.	Denver–Boulder–Greeley, CO CMSA	2,581,506	1,980,140	601,366	30.4
70.	Des Moines, IA MSA	456,022	392,928	63,094	16.1
71.	Detroit–Ann Arbor–Flint, MI CMSA	5,456,428	5,187,171	269,257	5.2
72.	Dothan, AL MSA	137,916	130,964	6,952	5.3
73.	Dover, DE MSA	126,697	110,993	15,704	14.1
74.	Dubuque, IA MSA	89,143	86,403	2,740	3.2
75.	Duluth–Superior, MN–WI MSA	243,815	239,971	3,844	1.6
76.	Eau Claire, WI MSA	148,337	137,543	10,794	7.8
77.	El Paso, TX MSA	679,622	591,610	88,012	14.9
78.	Elkhart–Goshen, IN MSA	182,791	156,198	26,593	17.0
79.	Elmira, NY MSA	91,070	95,195	–4,125	–4.3
80.	Enid, OK MSA	57,813	56,735	1,078	1.9
81.	Erie, PA MSA	280,843	275,572	5,271	1.9
82.	Eugene–Springfield, OR MSA	322,959	282,912	40,047	14.2
83.	Evansville–Henderson, IN–KY MSA	296,195	278,990	17,205	6.2
84.	Fargo–Moorhead, ND–MN MSA	174,367	153,296	21,071	13.7
85.	Fayetteville, NC MSA	302,963	274,566	28,397	10.3
86.	Fayetteville–Springdale–Rogers, AR MSA	311,121	210,908	100,213	47.5
87.	Flagstaff, AZ–UT MSA	122,366	101,760	20,606	20.2
88.	Florence, AL MSA	142,950	131,327	11,623	8.9
89.	Florence, SC MSA	125,761	114,344	11,417	10.0
90.	Fort Collins–Loveland, CO MSA	251,494	186,136	65,358	35.1
91.	Fort Myers–Cape Coral, FL MSA	440,888	335,113	105,775	31.6
92.	Fort Pierce–Port St. Lucie, FL MSA	319,426	251,071	68,355	27.2
93.	Fort Smith, AR–OK MSA	207,290	175,911	31,379	17.8
94.	Fort Walton Beach, FL MSA	170,498	143,776	26,722	18.6
95.	Fort Wayne, IN MSA	502,141	456,281	45,860	10.1
96.	Fresno, CA MSA	922,516	755,580	166,936	22.1
97.	Gadsden, AL MSA	103,459	99,840	3,619	3.6
98.	Gainesville, FL MSA	217,955	181,596	36,359	20.0
99.	Glens Falls, NY MSA	124,345	118,539	5,806	4.9
100.	Goldsboro, NC MSA	113,329	104,666	8,663	8.3
101.	Grand Forks, ND–MN MSA	97,478	103,181	–5,703	–5.5
102.	Grand Junction, CO MSA	116,255	93,145	23,110	24.8

(continued)

(continued from previous page)

	2000	1990	change, 1990–2000 number	change, 1990–2000 percent
103. Grand Rapids–Muskegon–Holland, MI MSA	1,088,514	937,891	150,623	16.1%
104. Great Falls, MT MSA	80,357	77,691	2,666	3.4
105. Green Bay, WI MSA	226,778	194,594	32,184	16.5
106. Greensboro–Winston-Salem–High Point, NC MSA	1,251,509	1,050,304	201,205	19.2
107. Greenville, NC MSA	133,798	107,924	25,874	24.0
108. Greenville–Spartanburg–Anderson, SC MSA	962,441	830,563	131,878	15.9
109. Harrisburg–Lebanon–Carlisle, PA MSA	629,401	587,986	41,415	7.0
110. Hartford, CT MSA	1,183,110	1,157,585	25,525	2.2
111. Hattiesburg, MS MSA	111,674	98,738	12,936	13.1
112. Hickory–Morganton–Lenoir, NC MSA	341,851	292,409	49,442	16.9
113. Honolulu, HI MSA	876,156	836,231	39,925	4.8
114. Houma, LA MSA	194,477	182,842	11,635	6.4
115. Houston–Galveston–Brazoria, TX CMSA	4,669,571	3,731,131	938,440	25.2
116. Huntington–Ashland, WV–KY–OH MSA	315,538	312,529	3,009	1.0
117. Huntsville, AL MSA	342,376	293,047	49,329	16.8
118. Indianapolis, IN MSA	1,607,486	1,380,491	226,995	16.4
119. Iowa City, IA MSA	111,006	96,119	14,887	15.5
120. Jackson, MI MSA	158,422	149,756	8,666	5.8
121. Jackson, MS MSA	440,801	395,396	45,405	11.5
122. Jackson, TN MSA	107,377	90,801	16,576	18.3
123. Jacksonville, FL MSA	1,100,491	906,727	193,764	21.4
124. Jacksonville, NC MSA	150,355	149,838	517	0.3
125. Jamestown, NY MSA	139,750	141,895	−2,145	−1.5
126. Janesville–Beloit, WI MSA	152,307	139,510	12,797	9.2
127. Johnson City–Kingsport–Bristol, TN–VA MSA	480,091	436,047	44,044	10.1
128. Johnstown, PA MSA	232,621	241,247	−8,626	−3.6
129. Jonesboro, AR MSA	82,148	68,956	13,192	19.1
130. Joplin, MO MSA	157,322	134,910	22,412	16.6
131. Kalamazoo–Battle Creek, MI MSA	452,851	429,453	23,398	5.4
132. Kansas City, MO–KS MSA	1,776,062	1,582,875	193,187	12.2
133. Killeen–Temple, TX MSA	312,952	255,301	57,651	22.6
134. Knoxville, TN MSA	687,249	585,960	101,289	17.3
135. Kokomo, IN MSA	101,541	96,946	4,595	4.7
136. La Crosse, WI–MN MSA	126,838	116,401	10,437	9.0
137. Lafayette, IN MSA	182,821	161,572	21,249	13.2
138. Lafayette, LA MSA	385,647	344,953	40,694	11.8
139. Lake Charles, LA MSA	183,577	168,134	15,443	9.2
140. Lakeland–Winter Haven, FL MSA	483,924	405,382	78,542	19.4
141. Lancaster, PA MSA	470,658	422,822	47,836	11.3
142. Lansing–East Lansing, MI MSA	447,728	432,674	15,054	3.5
143. Laredo, TX MSA	193,117	133,239	59,878	44.9
144. Las Cruces, NM MSA	174,682	135,510	39,172	28.9
145. Las Vegas, NV–AZ MSA	1,563,282	852,737	710,545	83.3
146. Lawrence, KS MSA	99,962	81,798	18,164	22.2
147. Lawton, OK MSA	114,996	111,486	3,510	3.1
148. Lewiston–Auburn, ME MSA	90,830	93,679	−2,849	−3.0
149. Lexington, KY MSA	479,198	405,936	73,262	18.0
150. Lima, OH MSA	155,084	154,340	744	0.5
151. Lincoln, NE MSA	250,291	213,641	36,650	17.2
152. Little Rock–North Little Rock, AR MSA	583,845	513,117	70,728	13.8
153. Longview–Marshall, TX MSA	208,780	193,801	14,979	7.7
154. Los Angeles–Riverside–Orange County, CA CMSA	16,373,645	14,531,529	1,842,116	12.7
155. Louisville, KY–IN MSA	1,025,598	948,829	76,769	8.1
156. Lubbock, TX MSA	242,628	222,636	19,992	9.0

(continued)

(continued from previous page)

	2000	1990	change, 1990–2000 number	percent
157. Lynchburg, VA MSA	214,911	193,928	20,983	10.8%
158. Macon, GA MSA	322,549	290,909	31,640	10.9
159. Madison, WI MSA	426,526	367,085	59,441	16.2
160. Mansfield, OH MSA	175,818	174,007	1,811	1.0
161. Mayaguez, PR MSA	253,347	237,143	16,204	6.8
162. McAllen–Edinburg–Mission, TX MSA	569,463	383,545	185,918	48.5
163. Medford–Ashland, OR MSA	181,269	146,389	34,880	23.8
164. Melbourne–Titusville–Palm Bay, FL MSA	476,230	398,978	77,252	19.4
165. Memphis, TN–AR–MS MSA	1,135,614	1,007,306	128,308	12.7
166. Merced, CA MSA	210,554	178,403	32,151	18.0
167. Miami–Fort Lauderdale, FL CMSA	3,876,380	3,192,582	683,798	21.4
168. Milwaukee–Racine, WI CMSA	1,689,572	1,607,183	82,389	5.1
169. Minneapolis–St. Paul, MN–WI MSA	2,968,806	2,538,834	429,972	16.9
170. Missoula, MT MSA	95,802	78,687	17,115	21.8
171. Mobile, AL MSA	540,258	476,923	63,335	13.3
172. Modesto, CA MSA	446,997	370,522	76,475	20.6
173. Monroe, LA MSA	147,250	142,191	5,059	3.6
174. Montgomery, AL MSA	333,055	292,517	40,538	13.9
175. Muncie, IN MSA	118,769	119,659	−890	−0.7
176. Myrtle Beach, SC MSA	196,629	144,053	52,576	36.5
177. Naples, FL MSA	251,377	152,099	99,278	65.3
178. Nashville, TN MSA	1,231,311	985,026	246,285	25.0
179. New London–Norwich, CT–RI MSA	293,566	290,734	2,832	1.0
180. New Orleans, LA MSA	1,337,726	1,285,270	52,456	4.1
181. New York–Northern New Jersey–Long Island, NY–NJ–CT–PA CMSA	21,199,865	19,549,649	1,650,216	8.4
182. Norfolk–Virginia Beach–Newport News, VA–NC MSA	1,569,541	1,443,244	126,297	8.8
183. Ocala, FL MSA	258,916	194,833	64,083	32.9
184. Odessa–Midland, TX MSA	237,132	225,545	11,587	5.1
185. Oklahoma City, OK MSA	1,083,346	958,839	124,507	13.0
186. Omaha, NE–IA MSA	716,998	639,580	77,418	12.1
187. Orlando, FL MSA	1,644,561	1,224,852	419,709	34.3
188. Owensboro, KY MSA	91,545	87,189	4,356	5.0
189. Panama City, FL MSA	148,217	126,994	21,223	16.7
190. Parkersburg–Marietta, WV–OH MSA	151,237	149,169	2,068	1.4
191. Pensacola, FL MSA	412,153	344,406	67,747	19.7
192. Peoria–Pekin, IL MSA	347,387	339,172	8,215	2.4
193. Philadelphia–Wilmington–Atlantic City, PA–NJ–DE–MD CMSA	6,188,463	5,892,937	295,526	5.0
194. Phoenix–Mesa, AZ MSA	3,251,876	2,238,480	1,013,396	45.3
195. Pine Bluff, AR MSA	84,278	85,487	−1,209	−1.4
196. Pittsburgh, PA MSA	2,358,695	2,394,811	−36,116	−1.5
197. Pittsfield, MA MSA	84,699	88,695	−3,996	−4.5
198. Pocatello, ID MSA	75,565	66,026	9,539	14.4
199. Ponce, PR MSA	361,094	342,660	18,434	5.4
200. Portland, ME MSA	243,537	221,095	22,442	10.2
201. Portland–Salem, OR–WA CMSA	2,265,223	1,793,476	471,747	26.3
202. Providence–Fall River–Warwick, RI–MA MSA	1,188,613	1,134,350	54,263	4.8
203. Provo–Orem, UT MSA	368,536	263,590	104,946	39.8
204. Pueblo, CO MSA	141,472	123,051	18,421	15.0
205. Punta Gorda, FL MSA	141,627	110,975	30,652	27.6
206. Raleigh–Durham–Chapel Hill, NC MSA	1,187,941	855,545	332,396	38.9
207. Rapid City, SD MSA	88,565	81,343	7,222	8.9

(continued)

(continued from previous page)

	2000	1990	change, 1990–2000 number	percent
208. Reading, PA MSA	373,638	336,523	37,115	11.0%
209. Redding, CA MSA	163,256	147,036	16,220	11.0
210. Reno, NV MSA	339,486	254,667	84,819	33.3
211. Richland–Kennewick–Pasco, WA MSA	191,822	150,033	41,789	27.9
212. Richmond–Petersburg, VA MSA	996,512	865,640	130,872	15.1
213. Roanoke, VA MSA	235,932	224,477	11,455	5.1
214. Rochester, MN MSA	124,277	106,470	17,807	16.7
215. Rochester, NY MSA	1,098,201	1,062,470	35,731	3.4
216. Rockford, IL MSA	371,236	329,676	41,560	12.6
217. Rocky Mount, NC MSA	143,026	133,235	9,791	7.3
218. Sacramento–Yolo, CA CMSA	1,796,857	1,481,102	315,755	21.3
219. Saginaw–Bay City–Midland, MI MSA	403,070	399,320	3,750	0.9
220. Salinas, CA MSA	401,762	355,660	46,102	13.0
221. Salt Lake City–Ogden, UT MSA	1,333,914	1,072,227	261,687	24.4
222. San Angelo, TX MSA	104,010	98,458	5,552	5.6
223. San Antonio, TX MSA	1,592,383	1,324,749	267,634	20.2
224. San Diego, CA MSA	2,813,833	2,498,016	315,817	12.6
225. San Francisco–Oakland–San Jose, CA CMSA	7,039,362	6,253,311	786,051	12.6
226. San Juan–Caguas–Arecibo, PR CMSA	2,450,292	2,270,808	179,484	7.9
227. San Luis Obispo–Atascadero–Paso Robles, CA MSA	246,681	217,162	29,519	13.6
228. Santa Barbara–Santa Maria–Lompoc, CA MSA	399,347	369,608	29,739	8.0
229. Santa Fe, NM MSA	147,635	117,043	30,592	26.1
230. Sarasota–Bradenton, FL MSA	589,959	489,483	100,476	20.5
231. Savannah, GA MSA	293,000	258,060	34,940	13.5
232. Scranton–Wilkes-Barre–Hazleton, PA MSA	624,776	638,466	−13,690	−2.1
233. Seattle–Tacoma–Bremerton, WA CMSA	3,554,760	2,970,328	584,432	19.7
234. Sharon, PA MSA	120,293	121,003	−710	−0.6
235. Sheboygan, WI MSA	112,646	103,877	8,769	8.4
236. Sherman–Denison, TX MSA	110,595	95,021	15,574	16.4
237. Shreveport–Bossier City, LA MSA	392,302	376,330	15,972	4.2
238. Sioux City, IA–NE MSA	124,130	115,018	9,112	7.9
239. Sioux Falls, SD MSA	172,412	139,236	33,176	23.8
240. South Bend, IN MSA	265,559	247,052	18,507	7.5
241. Spokane, WA MSA	417,939	361,364	56,575	15.7
242. Springfield, IL MSA	201,437	189,550	11,887	6.3
243. Springfield, MA MSA	591,932	587,884	4,048	0.7
244. Springfield, MO MSA	325,721	264,346	61,375	23.2
245. St. Cloud, MN MSA	167,392	148,976	18,416	12.4
246. St. Joseph, MO MSA	102,490	97,715	4,775	4.9
247. St. Louis, MO–IL MSA	2,603,607	2,492,525	111,082	4.5
248. State College, PA MSA	135,758	123,786	11,972	9.7
249. Steubenville–Weirton, OH–WV MSA	132,008	142,523	−10,515	−7.4
250. Stockton–Lodi, CA MSA	563,598	480,628	82,970	17.3
251. Sumter, SC MSA	104,646	102,637	2,009	2.0
252. Syracuse, NY MSA	732,117	742,177	−10,060	−1.4
253. Tallahassee, FL MSA	284,539	233,598	50,941	21.8
254. Tampa–St. Petersburg–Clearwater, FL MSA	2,395,997	2,067,959	328,038	15.9
255. Terre Haute, IN MSA	149,192	147,585	1,607	1.1
256. Texarkana, TX–Texarkana, AR MSA	129,749	120,132	9,617	8.0
257. Toledo, OH MSA	618,203	614,128	4,075	0.7
258. Topeka, KS MSA	169,871	160,976	8,895	5.5
259. Tucson, AZ MSA	843,746	666,880	176,866	26.5
260. Tulsa, OK MSA	803,235	708,954	94,281	13.3
261. Tuscaloosa, AL MSA	164,875	150,522	14,353	9.5

(continued)

(continued from previous page)

		2000	1990	change, 1990–2000 number	change, 1990–2000 percent
262.	Tyler, TX MSA	174,706	151,309	23,397	15.5%
263.	Utica–Rome, NY MSA	299,896	316,633	–16,737	–5.3
264.	Victoria, TX MSA	84,088	74,361	9,727	13.1
265.	Visalia–Tulare–Porterville, CA MSA	368,021	311,921	56,100	18.0
266.	Waco, TX MSA	213,517	189,123	24,394	12.9
267.	Washington–Baltimore, DC–MD–VA–WV CMSA	7,608,070	6,727,050	881,020	13.1
268.	Waterloo–Cedar Falls, IA MSA	128,012	123,798	4,214	3.4
269.	Wausau, WI MSA	125,834	115,400	10,434	9.0
270.	West Palm Beach–Boca Raton, FL MSA	1,131,184	863,518	267,666	31.0
271.	Wheeling, WV–OH MSA	153,172	159,301	–6,129	–3.8
272.	Wichita Falls, TX MSA	140,518	130,351	10,167	7.8
273.	Wichita, KS MSA	545,220	485,270	59,950	12.4
274.	Williamsport, PA MSA	120,044	118,710	1,334	1.1
275.	Wilmington, NC MSA	233,450	171,269	62,181	36.3
276.	Yakima, WA MSA	222,581	188,823	33,758	17.9
277.	York, PA MSA	381,751	339,574	42,177	12.4
278.	Youngstown–Warren, OH MSA	594,746	600,895	–6,149	–1.0
279.	Yuba City, CA MSA	139,149	122,643	16,506	13.5
280.	Yuma, AZ MSA	160,026	106,895	53,131	49.7

Note: For the definition of MSA, PMSA, and CMSA, see the glossary.
Source: Bureau of the Census, Census 2000 PHC–T–3. Ranking Tables for Metropolitan Areas: 1990 and 2000, Table 3:
Metropolitan Areas Ranked by Population: 2000

Table 8.26 Metropolitan Populations, 1990 and 2000 Censuses: Population Ranking

(number of people by metropolitan area, 1990 and 2000; change and percent change in number, 1990–00; metropolitan areas as defined on June 30, 1999; metropolitan areas ranked by population in 2000)

				change, 1990–2000	
		2000	1990	number	percent
1.	New York–Northern New Jersey–Long Island, NY–NJ–CT–PA CMSA	21,199,865	19,549,649	1,650,216	8.4%
2.	Los Angeles–Riverside–Orange County, CA CMSA	16,373,645	14,531,529	1,842,116	12.7
3.	Chicago–Gary–Kenosha, IL–IN–WI CMSA	9,157,540	8,239,820	917,720	11.1
4.	Washington–Baltimore, DC–MD–VA–WV CMSA	7,608,070	6,727,050	881,020	13.1
5.	San Francisco–Oakland–San Jose, CA CMSA	7,039,362	6,253,311	786,051	12.6
6.	Philadelphia–Wilmington–Atlantic City, PA–NJ–DE–MD CMSA	6,188,463	5,892,937	295,526	5.0
7.	Boston–Worcester–Lawrence, MA–NH–ME–CT CMSA	5,819,100	5,455,403	363,697	6.7
8.	Detroit–Ann Arbor–Flint, MI CMSA	5,456,428	5,187,171	269,257	5.2
9.	Dallas–Fort Worth, TX CMSA	5,221,801	4,037,282	1,184,519	29.3
10.	Houston–Galveston–Brazoria, TX CMSA	4,669,571	3,731,131	938,440	25.2
11.	Atlanta, GA MSA	4,112,198	2,959,950	1,152,248	38.9
12.	Miami–Fort Lauderdale, FL CMSA	3,876,380	3,192,582	683,798	21.4
13.	Seattle–Tacoma–Bremerton, WA CMSA	3,554,760	2,970,328	584,432	19.7
14.	Phoenix–Mesa, AZ MSA	3,251,876	2,238,480	1,013,396	45.3
15.	Minneapolis–St. Paul, MN–WI MSA	2,968,806	2,538,834	429,972	16.9
16.	Cleveland–Akron, OH CMSA	2,945,831	2,859,644	86,187	3.0
17.	San Diego, CA MSA	2,813,833	2,498,016	315,817	12.6
18.	St. Louis, MO–IL MSA	2,603,607	2,492,525	111,082	4.5
19.	Denver–Boulder–Greeley, CO CMSA	2,581,506	1,980,140	601,366	30.4
20.	San Juan–Caguas–Arecibo, PR CMSA	2,450,292	2,270,808	179,484	7.9
21.	Tampa–St. Petersburg–Clearwater, FL MSA	2,395,997	2,067,959	328,038	15.9
22.	Pittsburgh, PA MSA	2,358,695	2,394,811	−36,116	−1.5
23.	Portland–Salem, OR–WA CMSA	2,265,223	1,793,476	471,747	26.3
24.	Cincinnati–Hamilton, OH–KY–IN CMSA	1,979,202	1,817,571	161,631	8.9
25.	Sacramento–Yolo, CA CMSA	1,796,857	1,481,102	315,755	21.3
26.	Kansas City, MO–KS MSA	1,776,062	1,582,875	193,187	12.2
27.	Milwaukee–Racine, WI CMSA	1,689,572	1,607,183	82,389	5.1
28.	Orlando, FL MSA	1,644,561	1,224,852	419,709	34.3
29.	Indianapolis, IN MSA	1,607,486	1,380,491	226,995	16.4
30.	San Antonio, TX MSA	1,592,383	1,324,749	267,634	20.2
31.	Norfolk–Virginia Beach–Newport News, VA–NC MSA	1,569,541	1,443,244	126,297	8.8
32.	Las Vegas, NV–AZ MSA	1,563,282	852,737	710,545	83.3
33.	Columbus, OH MSA	1,540,157	1,345,450	194,707	14.5
34.	Charlotte–Gastonia–Rock Hill, NC–SC MSA	1,499,293	1,162,093	337,200	29.0
35.	New Orleans, LA MSA	1,337,726	1,285,270	52,456	4.1
36.	Salt Lake City–Ogden, UT MSA	1,333,914	1,072,227	261,687	24.4
37.	Greensboro–Winston-Salem–High Point, NC MSA	1,251,509	1,050,304	201,205	19.2
38.	Austin–San Marcos, TX MSA	1,249,763	846,227	403,536	47.7
39.	Nashville, TN MSA	1,231,311	985,026	246,285	25.0
40.	Providence–Fall River–Warwick, RI–MA MSA	1,188,613	1,134,350	54,263	4.8
41.	Raleigh–Durham–Chapel Hill, NC MSA	1,187,941	855,545	332,396	38.9
42.	Hartford, CT MSA	1,183,110	1,157,585	25,525	2.2
43.	Buffalo–Niagara Falls, NY MSA	1,170,111	1,189,288	−19,177	−1.6
44.	Memphis, TN–AR–MS MSA	1,135,614	1,007,306	128,308	12.7
45.	West Palm Beach–Boca Raton, FL MSA	1,131,184	863,518	267,666	31.0

(continued)

(continued from previous page)

		2000	1990	change, 1990–2000 number	change, 1990–2000 percent
46.	Jacksonville, FL MSA	1,100,491	906,727	193,764	21.4%
47.	Rochester, NY MSA	1,098,201	1,062,470	35,731	3.4
48.	Grand Rapids–Muskegon–Holland, MI MSA	1,088,514	937,891	150,623	16.1
49.	Oklahoma City, OK MSA	1,083,346	958,839	124,507	13.0
50.	Louisville, KY–IN MSA	1,025,598	948,829	76,769	8.1
51.	Richmond–Petersburg, VA MSA	996,512	865,640	130,872	15.1
52.	Greenville–Spartanburg–Anderson, SC MSA	962,441	830,563	131,878	15.9
53.	Dayton–Springfield, OH MSA	950,558	951,270	–712	–0.1
54.	Fresno, CA MSA	922,516	755,580	166,936	22.1
55.	Birmingham, AL MSA	921,106	840,140	80,966	9.6
56.	Honolulu, HI MSA	876,156	836,231	39,925	4.8
57.	Albany–Schenectady–Troy, NY MSA	875,583	861,424	14,159	1.6
58.	Tucson, AZ MSA	843,746	666,880	176,866	26.5
59.	Tulsa, OK MSA	803,235	708,954	94,281	13.3
60.	Syracuse, NY MSA	732,117	742,177	–10,060	–1.4
61.	Omaha, NE–IA MSA	716,998	639,580	77,418	12.1
62.	Albuquerque, NM MSA	712,738	589,131	123,607	21.0
63.	Knoxville, TN MSA	687,249	585,960	101,289	17.3
64.	El Paso, TX MSA	679,622	591,610	88,012	14.9
65.	Bakersfield, CA MSA	661,645	543,477	118,168	21.7
66.	Allentown–Bethlehem–Easton, PA MSA	637,958	595,081	42,877	7.2
67.	Harrisburg–Lebanon–Carlisle, PA MSA	629,401	587,986	41,415	7.0
68.	Scranton–Wilkes-Barre–Hazleton, PA MSA	624,776	638,466	–13,690	–2.1
69.	Toledo, OH MSA	618,203	614,128	4,075	0.7
70.	Baton Rouge, LA MSA	602,894	528,264	74,630	14.1
71.	Youngstown–Warren, OH MSA	594,746	600,895	–6,149	–1.0
72.	Springfield, MA MSA	591,932	587,884	4,048	0.7
73.	Sarasota–Bradenton, FL MSA	589,959	489,483	100,476	20.5
74.	Little Rock–North Little Rock, AR MSA	583,845	513,117	70,728	13.8
75.	McAllen–Edinburg–Mission, TX MSA	569,463	383,545	185,918	48.5
76.	Stockton–Lodi, CA MSA	563,598	480,628	82,970	17.3
77.	Charleston–North Charleston, SC MSA	549,033	506,875	42,158	8.3
78.	Wichita, KS MSA	545,220	485,270	59,950	12.4
79.	Mobile, AL MSA	540,258	476,923	63,335	13.3
80.	Columbia, SC MSA	536,691	453,331	83,360	18.4
81.	Colorado Springs, CO MSA	516,929	397,014	119,915	30.2
82.	Fort Wayne, IN MSA	502,141	456,281	45,860	10.1
83.	Daytona Beach, FL MSA	493,175	399,413	93,762	23.5
84.	Lakeland–Winter Haven, FL MSA	483,924	405,382	78,542	19.4
85.	Johnson City–Kingsport–Bristol, TN–VA MSA	480,091	436,047	44,044	10.1
86.	Lexington, KY MSA	479,198	405,936	73,262	18.0
87.	Augusta–Aiken, GA–SC MSA	477,441	415,184	62,257	15.0
88.	Melbourne–Titusville–Palm Bay, FL MSA	476,230	398,978	77,252	19.4
89.	Lancaster, PA MSA	470,658	422,822	47,836	11.3
90.	Chattanooga, TN–GA MSA	465,161	424,347	40,814	9.6
91.	Des Moines, IA MSA	456,022	392,928	63,094	16.1
92.	Kalamazoo–Battle Creek, MI MSA	452,851	429,453	23,398	5.4
93.	Lansing–East Lansing, MI MSA	447,728	432,674	15,054	3.5
94.	Modesto, CA MSA	446,997	370,522	76,475	20.6
95.	Fort Myers–Cape Coral, FL MSA	440,888	335,113	105,775	31.6
96.	Jackson, MS MSA	440,801	395,396	45,405	11.5
97.	Boise City, ID MSA	432,345	295,851	136,494	46.1
98.	Madison, WI MSA	426,526	367,085	59,441	16.2
99.	Spokane, WA MSA	417,939	361,364	56,575	15.7

(continued)

(continued from previous page)

		2000	1990	change, 1990–2000 number	percent
100.	Pensacola, FL MSA	412,153	344,406	67,747	19.7%
101.	Canton–Massillon, OH MSA	406,934	394,106	12,828	3.3
102.	Saginaw–Bay City–Midland, MI MSA	403,070	399,320	3,750	0.9
103.	Salinas, CA MSA	401,762	355,660	46,102	13.0
104.	Santa Barbara–Santa Maria–Lompoc, CA MSA	399,347	369,608	29,739	8.0
105.	Shreveport–Bossier City, LA MSA	392,302	376,330	15,972	4.2
106.	Lafayette, LA MSA	385,647	344,953	40,694	11.8
107.	Beaumont–Port Arthur, TX MSA	385,090	361,226	23,864	6.6
108.	York, PA MSA	381,751	339,574	42,177	12.4
109.	Corpus Christi, TX MSA	380,783	349,894	30,889	8.8
110.	Reading, PA MSA	373,638	336,523	37,115	11.0
111.	Rockford, IL MSA	371,236	329,676	41,560	12.6
112.	Provo–Orem, UT MSA	368,536	263,590	104,946	39.8
113.	Visalia–Tulare–Porterville, CA MSA	368,021	311,921	56,100	18.0
114.	Biloxi–Gulfport–Pascagoula, MS MSA	363,988	312,368	51,620	16.5
115.	Ponce, PR MSA	361,094	342,660	18,434	5.4
116.	Davenport–Moline–Rock Island, IA–IL MSA	359,062	350,861	8,201	2.3
117.	Appleton–Oshkosh–Neenah, WI MSA	358,365	315,121	43,244	13.7
118.	Peoria–Pekin, IL MSA	347,387	339,172	8,215	2.4
119.	Huntsville, AL MSA	342,376	293,047	49,329	16.8
120.	Hickory–Morganton–Lenoir, NC MSA	341,851	292,409	49,442	16.9
121.	Reno, NV MSA	339,486	254,667	84,819	33.3
122.	Brownsville–Harlingen–San Benito, TX MSA	335,227	260,120	75,107	28.9
123.	Montgomery, AL MSA	333,055	292,517	40,538	13.9
124.	Springfield, MO MSA	325,721	264,346	61,375	23.2
125.	Eugene–Springfield, OR MSA	322,959	282,912	40,047	14.2
126.	Macon, GA MSA	322,549	290,909	31,640	10.9
127.	Fort Pierce–Port St. Lucie, FL MSA	319,426	251,071	68,355	27.2
128.	Huntington–Ashland, WV–KY–OH MSA	315,538	312,529	3,009	1.0
129.	Killeen–Temple, TX MSA	312,952	255,301	57,651	22.6
130.	Fayetteville–Springdale–Rogers, AR MSA	311,121	210,908	100,213	47.5
131.	Fayetteville, NC MSA	302,963	274,566	28,397	10.3
132.	Utica–Rome, NY MSA	299,896	316,633	−16,737	−5.3
133.	Evansville–Henderson, IN–KY MSA	296,195	278,990	17,205	6.2
134.	New London–Norwich, CT–RI MSA	293,566	290,734	2,832	1.0
135.	Savannah, GA MSA	293,000	258,060	34,940	13.5
136.	Tallahassee, FL MSA	284,539	233,598	50,941	21.8
137.	Erie, PA MSA	280,843	275,572	5,271	1.9
138.	Columbus, GA–AL MSA	274,624	260,860	13,764	5.3
139.	South Bend, IN MSA	265,559	247,052	18,507	7.5
140.	Anchorage, AK MSA	260,283	226,338	33,945	15.0
141.	Ocala, FL MSA	258,916	194,833	64,083	32.9
142.	Mayaguez, PR MSA	253,347	237,143	16,204	6.8
143.	Binghamton, NY MSA	252,320	264,497	−12,177	−4.6
144.	Charleston, WV MSA	251,662	250,454	1,208	0.5
145.	Fort Collins–Loveland, CO MSA	251,494	186,136	65,358	35.1
146.	Naples, FL MSA	251,377	152,099	99,278	65.3
147.	Lincoln, NE MSA	250,291	213,641	36,650	17.2
148.	San Luis Obispo–Atascadero–Paso Robles, CA MSA	246,681	217,162	29,519	13.6
149.	Duluth–Superior, MN–WI MSA	243,815	239,971	3,844	1.6
150.	Portland, ME MSA	243,537	221,095	22,442	10.2
151.	Lubbock, TX MSA	242,628	222,636	19,992	9.0
152.	Odessa–Midland, TX MSA	237,132	225,545	11,587	5.1
153.	Roanoke, VA MSA	235,932	224,477	11,455	5.1

(continued)

(continued from previous page)

	2000	1990	change, 1990–2000	
			number	percent
154. Wilmington, NC MSA	233,450	171,269	62,181	36.3%
155. Johnstown, PA MSA	232,621	241,247	−8,626	−3.6
156. Green Bay, WI MSA	226,778	194,594	32,184	16.5
157. Asheville, NC MSA	225,965	191,774	34,191	17.8
158. Yakima, WA MSA	222,581	188,823	33,758	17.9
159. Gainesville, FL MSA	217,955	181,596	36,359	20.0
160. Amarillo, TX MSA	217,858	187,547	30,311	16.2
161. Lynchburg, VA MSA	214,911	193,928	20,983	10.8
162. Waco, TX MSA	213,517	189,123	24,394	12.9
163. Merced, CA MSA	210,554	178,403	32,151	18.0
164. Longview–Marshall, TX MSA	208,780	193,801	14,979	7.7
165. Fort Smith, AR–OK MSA	207,290	175,911	31,379	17.8
166. Clarksville–Hopkinsville, TN–KY MSA	207,033	169,439	37,594	22.2
167. Chico–Paradise, CA MSA	203,171	182,120	21,051	11.6
168. Springfield, IL MSA	201,437	189,550	11,887	6.3
169. Myrtle Beach, SC MSA	196,629	144,053	52,576	36.5
170. Houma, LA MSA	194,477	182,842	11,635	6.4
171. Laredo, TX MSA	193,117	133,239	59,878	44.9
172. Richland–Kennewick–Pasco, WA MSA	191,822	150,033	41,789	27.9
173. Cedar Rapids, IA MSA	191,701	168,767	22,934	13.6
174. Lake Charles, LA MSA	183,577	168,134	15,443	9.2
175. Lafayette, IN MSA	182,821	161,572	21,249	13.2
176. Elkhart–Goshen, IN MSA	182,791	156,198	26,593	17.0
177. Medford–Ashland, OR MSA	181,269	146,389	34,880	23.8
178. Champaign–Urbana, IL MSA	179,669	173,025	6,644	3.8
179. Mansfield, OH MSA	175,818	174,007	1,811	1.0
180. Tyler, TX MSA	174,706	151,309	23,397	15.5
181. Las Cruces, NM MSA	174,682	135,510	39,172	28.9
182. Fargo–Moorhead, ND–MN MSA	174,367	153,296	21,071	13.7
183. Sioux Falls, SD MSA	172,412	139,236	33,176	23.8
184. Fort Walton Beach, FL MSA	170,498	143,776	26,722	18.6
185. Topeka, KS MSA	169,871	160,976	8,895	5.5
186. Burlington, VT MSA	169,391	151,506	17,885	11.8
187. St. Cloud, MN MSA	167,392	148,976	18,416	12.4
188. Bellingham, WA MSA	166,814	127,780	39,034	30.5
189. Tuscaloosa, AL MSA	164,875	150,522	14,353	9.5
190. Redding, CA MSA	163,256	147,036	16,220	11.0
191. Barnstable–Yarmouth, MA MSA	162,582	134,954	27,628	20.5
192. Benton Harbor, MI MSA	162,453	161,378	1,075	0.7
193. Yuma, AZ MSA	160,026	106,895	53,131	49.7
194. Charlottesville, VA MSA	159,576	131,107	28,469	21.7
195. Jackson, MI MSA	158,422	149,756	8,666	5.8
196. Joplin, MO MSA	157,322	134,910	22,412	16.6
197. Lima, OH MSA	155,084	154,340	744	0.5
198. Athens, GA MSA	153,444	126,262	27,182	21.5
199. Wheeling, WV–OH MSA	153,172	159,301	−6,129	−3.8
200. Bryan–College Station, TX MSA	152,415	121,862	30,553	25.1
201. Janesville–Beloit, WI MSA	152,307	139,510	12,797	9.2
202. Parkersburg–Marietta, WV–OH MSA	151,237	149,169	2,068	1.4
203. Bloomington–Normal, IL MSA	150,433	129,180	21,253	16.5
204. Jacksonville, NC MSA	150,355	149,838	517	0.3
205. Terre Haute, IN MSA	149,192	147,585	1,607	1.1
206. Eau Claire, WI MSA	148,337	137,543	10,794	7.8
207. Panama City, FL MSA	148,217	126,994	21,223	16.7

(continued)

(continued from previous page)

		2000	1990	change, 1990–2000	
				number	percent
208.	Santa Fe, NM MSA	147,635	117,043	30,592	26.1%
209.	Monroe, LA MSA	147,250	142,191	5,059	3.6
210.	Aguadilla, PR MSA	146,424	128,172	18,252	14.2
211.	Decatur, AL MSA	145,867	131,556	14,311	10.9
212.	Rocky Mount, NC MSA	143,026	133,235	9,791	7.3
213.	Florence, AL MSA	142,950	131,327	11,623	8.9
214.	Punta Gorda, FL MSA	141,627	110,975	30,652	27.6
215.	Pueblo, CO MSA	141,472	123,051	18,421	15.0
216.	Wichita Falls, TX MSA	140,518	130,351	10,167	7.8
217.	Jamestown, NY MSA	139,750	141,895	−2,145	−1.5
218.	Yuba City, CA MSA	139,149	122,643	16,506	13.5
219.	Dothan, AL MSA	137,916	130,964	6,952	5.3
220.	State College, PA MSA	135,758	123,786	11,972	9.7
221.	Columbia, MO MSA	135,454	112,379	23,075	20.5
222.	Greenville, NC MSA	133,798	107,924	25,874	24.0
223.	Steubenville–Weirton, OH–WV MSA	132,008	142,523	−10,515	−7.4
224.	Texarkana, TX–Texarkana, AR MSA	129,749	120,132	9,617	8.0
225.	Billings, MT MSA	129,352	113,419	15,933	14.0
226.	Altoona, PA MSA	129,144	130,542	−1,398	−1.1
227.	Waterloo–Cedar Falls, IA MSA	128,012	123,798	4,214	3.4
228.	La Crosse, WI–MN MSA	126,838	116,401	10,437	9.0
229.	Dover, DE MSA	126,697	110,993	15,704	14.1
230.	Abilene, TX MSA	126,555	119,655	6,900	5.8
231.	Alexandria, LA MSA	126,337	131,556	−5,219	−4.0
232.	Wausau, WI MSA	125,834	115,400	10,434	9.0
233.	Florence, SC MSA	125,761	114,344	11,417	10.0
234.	Glens Falls, NY MSA	124,345	118,539	5,806	4.9
235.	Rochester, MN MSA	124,277	106,470	17,807	16.7
236.	Sioux City, IA–NE MSA	124,130	115,018	9,112	7.9
237.	Flagstaff, AZ–UT MSA	122,366	101,760	20,606	20.2
238.	Albany, GA MSA	120,822	112,561	8,261	7.3
239.	Bloomington, IN MSA	120,563	108,978	11,585	10.6
240.	Sharon, PA MSA	120,293	121,003	−710	−0.6
241.	Williamsport, PA MSA	120,044	118,710	1,334	1.1
242.	Muncie, IN MSA	118,769	119,659	−890	−0.7
243.	Grand Junction, CO MSA	116,255	93,145	23,110	24.8
244.	Auburn–Opelika, AL MSA	115,092	87,146	27,946	32.1
245.	Lawton, OK MSA	114,996	111,486	3,510	3.1
246.	Decatur, IL MSA	114,706	117,206	−2,500	−2.1
247.	Goldsboro, NC MSA	113,329	104,666	8,663	8.3
248.	Sheboygan, WI MSA	112,646	103,877	8,769	8.4
249.	Anniston, AL MSA	112,249	116,034	−3,785	−3.3
250.	Hattiesburg, MS MSA	111,674	98,738	12,936	13.1
251.	Iowa City, IA MSA	111,006	96,119	14,887	15.5
252.	Sherman–Denison, TX MSA	110,595	95,021	15,574	16.4
253.	Danville, VA MSA	110,156	108,711	1,445	1.3
254.	Jackson, TN MSA	107,377	90,801	16,576	18.3
255.	Sumter, SC MSA	104,646	102,637	2,009	2.0
256.	San Angelo, TX MSA	104,010	98,458	5,552	5.6
257.	Gadsden, AL MSA	103,459	99,840	3,619	3.6
258.	St. Joseph, MO MSA	102,490	97,715	4,775	4.9
259.	Cumberland, MD–WV MSA	102,008	101,643	365	0.4
260.	Kokomo, IN MSA	101,541	96,946	4,595	4.7
261.	Lawrence, KS MSA	99,962	81,798	18,164	22.2

(continued)

(continued from previous page)

		2000	1990	change, 1990–2000	
				number	percent
262.	Grand Forks, ND–MN MSA	97,478	103,181	–5,703	–5.5%
263.	Missoula, MT MSA	95,802	78,687	17,115	21.8
264.	Bismarck, ND MSA	94,719	83,831	10,888	13.0
265.	Owensboro, KY MSA	91,545	87,189	4,356	5.0
266.	Elmira, NY MSA	91,070	95,195	–4,125	–4.3
267.	Bangor, ME MSA	90,864	91,629	–765	–0.8
268.	Lewiston–Auburn, ME MSA	90,830	93,679	–2,849	–3.0
269.	Dubuque, IA MSA	89,143	86,403	2,740	3.2
270.	Rapid City, SD MSA	88,565	81,343	7,222	8.9
271.	Pittsfield, MA MSA	84,699	88,695	–3,996	–4.5
272.	Pine Bluff, AR MSA	84,278	85,487	–1,209	–1.4
273.	Victoria, TX MSA	84,088	74,361	9,727	13.1
274.	Jonesboro, AR MSA	82,148	68,956	13,192	19.1
275.	Cheyenne, WY MSA	81,607	73,142	8,465	11.6
276.	Great Falls, MT MSA	80,357	77,691	2,666	3.4
277.	Corvallis, OR MSA	78,153	70,811	7,342	10.4
278.	Pocatello, ID MSA	75,565	66,026	9,539	14.4
279.	Casper, WY MSA	66,533	61,226	5,307	8.7
280.	Enid, OK MSA	57,813	56,735	1,078	1.9

Note: For the definition of MSA, PMSA, and CMSA, see the glossary.
Source: Bureau of the Census, Census 2000 PHC-T-3. Ranking Tables for Metropolitan Areas: 1990 and 2000, Table 3: Metropolitan Areas Ranked by Population: 2000

Table 8.27 Metropolitan Populations, 1990 and 2000 Censuses: Percent Change Ranking

(number of people by metropolitan area, 1990 and 2000; change and percent change in number, 1990–2000; metropolitan areas as defined on June 30, 1999; metropolitan areas ranked by percent change in population, 1990–2000)

				change, 1990–2000	
		2000	1990	number	percent
1.	Las Vegas, NV–AZ MSA	1,563,282	852,737	710,545	83.3%
2.	Naples, FL MSA	251,377	152,099	99,278	65.3
3.	Yuma, AZ MSA	160,026	106,895	53,131	49.7
4.	McAllen–Edinburg–Mission, TX MSA	569,463	383,545	185,918	48.5
5.	Austin–San Marcos, TX MSA	1,249,763	846,227	403,536	47.7
6.	Fayetteville–Springdale–Rogers, AR MSA	311,121	210,908	100,213	47.5
7.	Boise City, ID MSA	432,345	295,851	136,494	46.1
8.	Phoenix–Mesa, AZ MSA	3,251,876	2,238,480	1,013,396	45.3
9.	Laredo, TX MSA	193,117	133,239	59,878	44.9
10.	Provo–Orem, UT MSA	368,536	263,590	104,946	39.8
11.	Atlanta, GA MSA	4,112,198	2,959,950	1,152,248	38.9
12.	Raleigh–Durham–Chapel Hill, NC MSA	1,187,941	855,545	332,396	38.9
13.	Myrtle Beach, SC MSA	196,629	144,053	52,576	36.5
14.	Wilmington, NC MSA	233,450	171,269	62,181	36.3
15.	Fort Collins–Loveland, CO MSA	251,494	186,136	65,358	35.1
16.	Orlando, FL MSA	1,644,561	1,224,852	419,709	34.3
17.	Reno, NV MSA	339,486	254,667	84,819	33.3
18.	Ocala, FL MSA	258,916	194,833	64,083	32.9
19.	Auburn–Opelika, AL MSA	115,092	87,146	27,946	32.1
20.	Fort Myers–Cape Coral, FL MSA	440,888	335,113	105,775	31.6
21.	West Palm Beach–Boca Raton, FL MSA	1,131,184	863,518	267,666	31.0
22.	Bellingham, WA MSA	166,814	127,780	39,034	30.5
23.	Denver–Boulder–Greeley, CO CMSA	2,581,506	1,980,140	601,366	30.4
24.	Colorado Springs, CO MSA	516,929	397,014	119,915	30.2
25.	Dallas–Fort Worth, TX CMSA	5,221,801	4,037,282	1,184,519	29.3
26.	Charlotte–Gastonia–Rock Hill, NC–SC MSA	1,499,293	1,162,093	337,200	29.0
27.	Las Cruces, NM MSA	174,682	135,510	39,172	28.9
28.	Brownsville–Harlingen–San Benito, TX MSA	335,227	260,120	75,107	28.9
29.	Richland–Kennewick–Pasco, WA MSA	191,822	150,033	41,789	27.9
30.	Punta Gorda, FL MSA	141,627	110,975	30,652	27.6
31.	Fort Pierce–Port St. Lucie, FL MSA	319,426	251,071	68,355	27.2
32.	Tucson, AZ MSA	843,746	666,880	176,866	26.5
33.	Portland–Salem, OR–WA CMSA	2,265,223	1,793,476	471,747	26.3
34.	Santa Fe, NM MSA	147,635	117,043	30,592	26.1
35.	Houston–Galveston–Brazoria, TX CMSA	4,669,571	3,731,131	938,440	25.2
36.	Bryan–College Station, TX MSA	152,415	121,862	30,553	25.1
37.	Nashville, TN MSA	1,231,311	985,026	246,285	25.0
38.	Grand Junction, CO MSA	116,255	93,145	23,110	24.8
39.	Salt Lake City–Ogden, UT MSA	1,333,914	1,072,227	261,687	24.4
40.	Greenville, NC MSA	133,798	107,924	25,874	24.0
41.	Sioux Falls, SD MSA	172,412	139,236	33,176	23.8
42.	Medford–Ashland, OR MSA	181,269	146,389	34,880	23.8
43.	Daytona Beach, FL MSA	493,175	399,413	93,762	23.5
44.	Springfield, MO MSA	325,721	264,346	61,375	23.2
45.	Killeen–Temple, TX MSA	312,952	255,301	57,651	22.6
46.	Lawrence, KS MSA	99,962	81,798	18,164	22.2
47.	Clarksville–Hopkinsville, TN–KY MSA	207,033	169,439	37,594	22.2
48.	Fresno, CA MSA	922,516	755,580	166,936	22.1
49.	Tallahassee, FL MSA	284,539	233,598	50,941	21.8

(continued)

(continued from previous page)

		2000	1990	change, 1990–2000	
				number	percent
50.	Missoula, MT MSA	95,802	78,687	17,115	21.8%
51.	Bakersfield, CA MSA	661,645	543,477	118,168	21.7
52.	Charlottesville, VA MSA	159,576	131,107	28,469	21.7
53.	Athens, GA MSA	153,444	126,262	27,182	21.5
54.	Miami–Fort Lauderdale, FL CMSA	3,876,380	3,192,582	683,798	21.4
55.	Jacksonville, FL MSA	1,100,491	906,727	193,764	21.4
56.	Sacramento–Yolo, CA CMSA	1,796,857	1,481,102	315,755	21.3
57.	Albuquerque, NM MSA	712,738	589,131	123,607	21.0
58.	Modesto, CA MSA	446,997	370,522	76,475	20.6
59.	Columbia, MO MSA	135,454	112,379	23,075	20.5
60.	Sarasota–Bradenton, FL MSA	589,959	489,483	100,476	20.5
61.	Barnstable–Yarmouth, MA MSA	162,582	134,954	27,628	20.5
62.	Flagstaff, AZ–UT MSA	122,366	101,760	20,606	20.2
63.	San Antonio, TX MSA	1,592,383	1,324,749	267,634	20.2
64.	Gainesville, FL MSA	217,955	181,596	36,359	20.0
65.	Seattle–Tacoma–Bremerton, WA CMSA	3,554,760	2,970,328	584,432	19.7
66.	Pensacola, FL MSA	412,153	344,406	67,747	19.7
67.	Lakeland–Winter Haven, FL MSA	483,924	405,382	78,542	19.4
68.	Melbourne–Titusville–Palm Bay, FL MSA	476,230	398,978	77,252	19.4
69.	Greensboro–Winston-Salem–High Point, NC MSA	1,251,509	1,050,304	201,205	19.2
70.	Jonesboro, AR MSA	82,148	68,956	13,192	19.1
71.	Fort Walton Beach, FL MSA	170,498	143,776	26,722	18.6
72.	Columbia, SC MSA	536,691	453,331	83,360	18.4
73.	Jackson, TN MSA	107,377	90,801	16,576	18.3
74.	Lexington, KY MSA	479,198	405,936	73,262	18.0
75.	Merced, CA MSA	210,554	178,403	32,151	18.0
76.	Visalia–Tulare–Porterville, CA MSA	368,021	311,921	56,100	18.0
77.	Yakima, WA MSA	222,581	188,823	33,758	17.9
78.	Fort Smith, AR–OK MSA	207,290	175,911	31,379	17.8
79.	Asheville, NC MSA	225,965	191,774	34,191	17.8
80.	Knoxville, TN MSA	687,249	585,960	101,289	17.3
81.	Stockton–Lodi, CA MSA	563,598	480,628	82,970	17.3
82.	Lincoln, NE MSA	250,291	213,641	36,650	17.2
83.	Elkhart–Goshen, IN MSA	182,791	156,198	26,593	17.0
84.	Minneapolis–St. Paul, MN–WI MSA	2,968,806	2,538,834	429,972	16.9
85.	Hickory–Morganton–Lenoir, NC MSA	341,851	292,409	49,442	16.9
86.	Huntsville, AL MSA	342,376	293,047	49,329	16.8
87.	Rochester, MN MSA	124,277	106,470	17,807	16.7
88.	Panama City, FL MSA	148,217	126,994	21,223	16.7
89.	Joplin, MO MSA	157,322	134,910	22,412	16.6
90.	Green Bay, WI MSA	226,778	194,594	32,184	16.5
91.	Biloxi–Gulfport–Pascagoula, MS MSA	363,988	312,368	51,620	16.5
92.	Bloomington–Normal, IL MSA	150,433	129,180	21,253	16.5
93.	Indianapolis, IN MSA	1,607,486	1,380,491	226,995	16.4
94.	Sherman–Denison, TX MSA	110,595	95,021	15,574	16.4
95.	Madison, WI MSA	426,526	367,085	59,441	16.2
96.	Amarillo, TX MSA	217,858	187,547	30,311	16.2
97.	Grand Rapids–Muskegon–Holland, MI MSA	1,088,514	937,891	150,623	16.1
98.	Des Moines, IA MSA	456,022	392,928	63,094	16.1
99.	Greenville–Spartanburg–Anderson, SC MSA	962,441	830,563	131,878	15.9
100.	Tampa–St. Petersburg–Clearwater, FL MSA	2,395,997	2,067,959	328,038	15.9
101.	Spokane, WA MSA	417,939	361,364	56,575	15.7
102.	Iowa City, IA MSA	111,006	96,119	14,887	15.5
103.	Tyler, TX MSA	174,706	151,309	23,397	15.5

(continued)

(continued from previous page)

	2000	1990	change, 1990–2000 number	percent
104. Richmond–Petersburg, VA MSA	996,512	865,640	130,872	15.1%
105. Anchorage, AK MSA	260,283	226,338	33,945	15.0
106. Augusta–Aiken, GA–SC MSA	477,441	415,184	62,257	15.0
107. Pueblo, CO MSA	141,472	123,051	18,421	15.0
108. El Paso, TX MSA	679,622	591,610	88,012	14.9
109. Columbus, OH MSA	1,540,157	1,345,450	194,707	14.5
110. Pocatello, ID MSA	75,565	66,026	9,539	14.4
111. Aguadilla, PR MSA	146,424	128,172	18,252	14.2
112. Eugene–Springfield, OR MSA	322,959	282,912	40,047	14.2
113. Dover, DE MSA	126,697	110,993	15,704	14.1
114. Baton Rouge, LA MSA	602,894	528,264	74,630	14.1
115. Billings, MT MSA	129,352	113,419	15,933	14.0
116. Montgomery, AL MSA	333,055	292,517	40,538	13.9
117. Little Rock–North Little Rock, AR MSA	583,845	513,117	70,728	13.8
118. Fargo–Moorhead, ND–MN MSA	174,367	153,296	21,071	13.7
119. Appleton–Oshkosh–Neenah, WI MSA	358,365	315,121	43,244	13.7
120. San Luis Obispo–Atascadero–Paso Robles, CA MSA	246,681	217,162	29,519	13.6
121. Cedar Rapids, IA MSA	191,701	168,767	22,934	13.6
122. Savannah, GA MSA	293,000	258,060	34,940	13.5
123. Yuba City, CA MSA	139,149	122,643	16,506	13.5
124. Tulsa, OK MSA	803,235	708,954	94,281	13.3
125. Mobile, AL MSA	540,258	476,923	63,335	13.3
126. Lafayette, IN MSA	182,821	161,572	21,249	13.2
127. Hattiesburg, MS MSA	111,674	98,738	12,936	13.1
128. Washington–Baltimore, DC–MD–VA–WV CMSA	7,608,070	6,727,050	881,020	13.1
129. Victoria, TX MSA	84,088	74,361	9,727	13.1
130. Bismarck, ND MSA	94,719	83,831	10,888	13.0
131. Oklahoma City, OK MSA	1,083,346	958,839	124,507	13.0
132. Salinas, CA MSA	401,762	355,660	46,102	13.0
133. Waco, TX MSA	213,517	189,123	24,394	12.9
134. Memphis, TN–AR–MS MSA	1,135,614	1,007,306	128,308	12.7
135. Los Angeles–Riverside–Orange County, CA CMSA	16,373,645	14,531,529	1,842,116	12.7
136. San Diego, CA MSA	2,813,833	2,498,016	315,817	12.6
137. Rockford, IL MSA	371,236	329,676	41,560	12.6
138. San Francisco–Oakland–San Jose, CA CMSA	7,039,362	6,253,311	786,051	12.6
139. York, PA MSA	381,751	339,574	42,177	12.4
140. St. Cloud, MN MSA	167,392	148,976	18,416	12.4
141. Wichita, KS MSA	545,220	485,270	59,950	12.4
142. Kansas City, MO–KS MSA	1,776,062	1,582,875	193,187	12.2
143. Omaha, NE–IA MSA	716,998	639,580	77,418	12.1
144. Burlington, VT MSA	169,391	151,506	17,885	11.8
145. Lafayette, LA MSA	385,647	344,953	40,694	11.8
146. Cheyenne, WY MSA	81,607	73,142	8,465	11.6
147. Chico–Paradise, CA MSA	203,171	182,120	21,051	11.6
148. Jackson, MS MSA	440,801	395,396	45,405	11.5
149. Lancaster, PA MSA	470,658	422,822	47,836	11.3
150. Chicago–Gary–Kenosha, IL–IN–WI CMSA	9,157,540	8,239,820	917,720	11.1
151. Redding, CA MSA	163,256	147,036	16,220	11.0
152. Reading, PA MSA	373,638	336,523	37,115	11.0
153. Decatur, AL MSA	145,867	131,556	14,311	10.9
154. Macon, GA MSA	322,549	290,909	31,640	10.9
155. Lynchburg, VA MSA	214,911	193,928	20,983	10.8
156. Bloomington, IN MSA	120,563	108,978	11,585	10.6
157. Corvallis, OR MSA	78,153	70,811	7,342	10.4

(continued)

(continued from previous page)

		2000	1990	change, 1990–2000	
				number	percent
158.	Fayetteville, NC MSA	302,963	274,566	28,397	10.3%
159.	Portland, ME MSA	243,537	221,095	22,442	10.2
160.	Johnson City–Kingsport–Bristol, TN–VA MSA	480,091	436,047	44,044	10.1
161.	Fort Wayne, IN MSA	502,141	456,281	45,860	10.1
162.	Florence, SC MSA	125,761	114,344	11,417	10.0
163.	State College, PA MSA	135,758	123,786	11,972	9.7
164.	Birmingham, AL MSA	921,106	840,140	80,966	9.6
165.	Chattanooga, TN–GA MSA	465,161	424,347	40,814	9.6
166.	Tuscaloosa, AL MSA	164,875	150,522	14,353	9.5
167.	Lake Charles, LA MSA	183,577	168,134	15,443	9.2
168.	Janesville–Beloit, WI MSA	152,307	139,510	12,797	9.2
169.	Wausau, WI MSA	125,834	115,400	10,434	9.0
170.	Lubbock, TX MSA	242,628	222,636	19,992	9.0
171.	La Crosse, WI–MN MSA	126,838	116,401	10,437	9.0
172.	Cincinnati–Hamilton, OH–KY–IN CMSA	1,979,202	1,817,571	161,631	8.9
173.	Rapid City, SD MSA	88,565	81,343	7,222	8.9
174.	Florence, AL MSA	142,950	131,327	11,623	8.9
175.	Corpus Christi, TX MSA	380,783	349,894	30,889	8.8
176.	Norfolk–Virginia Beach–Newport News, VA–NC MSA	1,569,541	1,443,244	126,297	8.8
177.	Casper, WY MSA	66,533	61,226	5,307	8.7
178.	Sheboygan, WI MSA	112,646	103,877	8,769	8.4
179.	New York–Northern New Jersey–Long Island, NY–NJ–CT–PA CMSA	21,199,865	19,549,649	1,650,216	8.4
180.	Charleston–North Charleston, SC MSA	549,033	506,875	42,158	8.3
181.	Goldsboro, NC MSA	113,329	104,666	8,663	8.3
182.	Louisville, KY–IN MSA	1,025,598	948,829	76,769	8.1
183.	Santa Barbara–Santa Maria–Lompoc, CA MSA	399,347	369,608	29,739	8.0
184.	Texarkana, TX–Texarkana, AR MSA	129,749	120,132	9,617	8.0
185.	Sioux City, IA–NE MSA	124,130	115,018	9,112	7.9
186.	San Juan–Caguas–Arecibo, PR CMSA	2,450,292	2,270,808	179,484	7.9
187.	Eau Claire, WI MSA	148,337	137,543	10,794	7.8
188.	Wichita Falls, TX MSA	140,518	130,351	10,167	7.8
189.	Longview–Marshall, TX MSA	208,780	193,801	14,979	7.7
190.	South Bend, IN MSA	265,559	247,052	18,507	7.5
191.	Rocky Mount, NC MSA	143,026	133,235	9,791	7.3
192.	Albany, GA MSA	120,822	112,561	8,261	7.3
193.	Allentown–Bethlehem–Easton, PA MSA	637,958	595,081	42,877	7.2
194.	Harrisburg–Lebanon–Carlisle, PA MSA	629,401	587,986	41,415	7.0
195.	Mayaguez, PR MSA	253,347	237,143	16,204	6.8
196.	Boston–Worcester–Lawrence, MA–NH–ME–CT CMSA	5,819,100	5,455,403	363,697	6.7
197.	Beaumont–Port Arthur, TX MSA	385,090	361,226	23,864	6.6
198.	Houma, LA MSA	194,477	182,842	11,635	6.4
199.	Springfield, IL MSA	201,437	189,550	11,887	6.3
200.	Evansville–Henderson, IN–KY MSA	296,195	278,990	17,205	6.2
201.	Jackson, MI MSA	158,422	149,756	8,666	5.8
202.	Abilene, TX MSA	126,555	119,655	6,900	5.8
203.	San Angelo, TX MSA	104,010	98,458	5,552	5.6
204.	Topeka, KS MSA	169,871	160,976	8,895	5.5
205.	Kalamazoo–Battle Creek, MI MSA	452,851	429,453	23,398	5.4
206.	Ponce, PR MSA	361,094	342,660	18,434	5.4
207.	Dothan, AL MSA	137,916	130,964	6,952	5.3
208.	Columbus, GA–AL MSA	274,624	260,860	13,764	5.3
209.	Detroit–Ann Arbor–Flint, MI CMSA	5,456,428	5,187,171	269,257	5.2

(continued)

(continued from previous page)

| | | 2000 | 1990 | change, 1990–2000 | |
				number	percent
210.	Odessa–Midland, TX MSA	237,132	225,545	11,587	5.1%
211.	Milwaukee–Racine, WI CMSA	1,689,572	1,607,183	82,389	5.1
212.	Roanoke, VA MSA	235,932	224,477	11,455	5.1
213.	Philadelphia–Wilmington–Atlantic City, PA–NJ–DE–MD CMSA	6,188,463	5,892,937	295,526	5.0
214.	Owensboro, KY MSA	91,545	87,189	4,356	5.0
215.	Glens Falls, NY MSA	124,345	118,539	5,806	4.9
216.	St. Joseph, MO MSA	102,490	97,715	4,775	4.9
217.	Providence–Fall River–Warwick, RI–MA MSA	1,188,613	1,134,350	54,263	4.8
218.	Honolulu, HI MSA	876,156	836,231	39,925	4.8
219.	Kokomo, IN MSA	101,541	96,946	4,595	4.7
220.	St. Louis, MO–IL MSA	2,603,607	2,492,525	111,082	4.5
221.	Shreveport–Bossier City, LA MSA	392,302	376,330	15,972	4.2
222.	New Orleans, LA MSA	1,337,726	1,285,270	52,456	4.1
223.	Champaign–Urbana, IL MSA	179,669	173,025	6,644	3.8
224.	Gadsden, AL MSA	103,459	99,840	3,619	3.6
225.	Monroe, LA MSA	147,250	142,191	5,059	3.6
226.	Lansing–East Lansing, MI MSA	447,728	432,674	15,054	3.5
227.	Great Falls, MT MSA	80,357	77,691	2,666	3.4
228.	Waterloo–Cedar Falls, IA MSA	128,012	123,798	4,214	3.4
229.	Rochester, NY MSA	1,098,201	1,062,470	35,731	3.4
230.	Canton–Massillon, OH MSA	406,934	394,106	12,828	3.3
231.	Dubuque, IA MSA	89,143	86,403	2,740	3.2
232.	Lawton, OK MSA	114,996	111,486	3,510	3.1
233.	Cleveland–Akron, OH CMSA	2,945,831	2,859,644	86,187	3.0
234.	Peoria–Pekin, IL MSA	347,387	339,172	8,215	2.4
235.	Davenport–Moline–Rock Island, IA–IL MSA	359,062	350,861	8,201	2.3
236.	Hartford, CT MSA	1,183,110	1,157,585	25,525	2.2
237.	Sumter, SC MSA	104,646	102,637	2,009	2.0
238.	Erie, PA MSA	280,843	275,572	5,271	1.9
239.	Enid, OK MSA	57,813	56,735	1,078	1.9
240.	Albany–Schenectady–Troy, NY MSA	875,583	861,424	14,159	1.6
241.	Duluth–Superior, MN–WI MSA	243,815	239,971	3,844	1.6
242.	Parkersburg–Marietta, WV–OH MSA	151,237	149,169	2,068	1.4
243.	Danville, VA MSA	110,156	108,711	1,445	1.3
244.	Williamsport, PA MSA	120,044	118,710	1,334	1.1
245.	Terre Haute, IN MSA	149,192	147,585	1,607	1.1
246.	Mansfield, OH MSA	175,818	174,007	1,811	1.0
247.	New London–Norwich, CT–RI MSA	293,566	290,734	2,832	1.0
248.	Huntington–Ashland, WV–KY–OH MSA	315,538	312,529	3,009	1.0
249.	Saginaw–Bay City–Midland, MI MSA	403,070	399,320	3,750	0.9
250.	Springfield, MA MSA	591,932	587,884	4,048	0.7
251.	Benton Harbor, MI MSA	162,453	161,378	1,075	0.7
252.	Toledo, OH MSA	618,203	614,128	4,075	0.7
253.	Charleston, WV MSA	251,662	250,454	1,208	0.5
254.	Lima, OH MSA	155,084	154,340	744	0.5
255.	Cumberland, MD–WV MSA	102,008	101,643	365	0.4
256.	Jacksonville, NC MSA	150,355	149,838	517	0.3
257.	Dayton–Springfield, OH MSA	950,558	951,270	–712	–0.1
258.	Sharon, PA MSA	120,293	121,003	–710	–0.6
259.	Muncie, IN MSA	118,769	119,659	–890	–0.7
260.	Bangor, ME MSA	90,864	91,629	–765	–0.8
261.	Youngstown–Warren, OH MSA	594,746	600,895	–6,149	–1.0
262.	Altoona, PA MSA	129,144	130,542	–1,398	–1.1

(continued)

(continued from previous page)

		2000	1990	change, 1990–2000	
				number	percent
263.	Syracuse, NY MSA	732,117	742,177	–10,060	–1.4%
264.	Pine Bluff, AR MSA	84,278	85,487	–1,209	–1.4
265.	Pittsburgh, PA MSA	2,358,695	2,394,811	–36,116	–1.5
266.	Jamestown, NY MSA	139,750	141,895	–2,145	–1.5
267.	Buffalo–Niagara Falls, NY MSA	1,170,111	1,189,288	–19,177	–1.6
268.	Decatur, IL MSA	114,706	117,206	–2,500	–2.1
269.	Scranton–Wilkes-Barre–Hazleton, PA MSA	624,776	638,466	–13,690	–2.1
270.	Lewiston–Auburn, ME MSA	90,830	93,679	–2,849	–3.0
271.	Anniston, AL MSA	112,249	116,034	–3,785	–3.3
272.	Johnstown, PA MSA	232,621	241,247	–8,626	–3.6
273.	Wheeling, WV–OH MSA	153,172	159,301	–6,129	–3.8
274.	Alexandria, LA MSA	126,337	131,556	–5,219	–4.0
275.	Elmira, NY MSA	91,070	95,195	–4,125	–4.3
276.	Pittsfield, MA MSA	84,699	88,695	–3,996	–4.5
277.	Binghamton, NY MSA	252,320	264,497	–12,177	–4.6
278.	Utica–Rome, NY MSA	299,896	316,633	–16,737	–5.3
279.	Grand Forks, ND–MN MSA	97,478	103,181	–5,703	–5.5
280.	Steubenville–Weirton, OH–WV MSA	132,008	142,523	–10,515	–7.4

Note: For the definition of MSA, PMSA, and CMSA, see the glossary.
Source: Bureau of the Census, Census 2000 PHC–T–3. Ranking Tables for Metropolitan Areas: 1990 and 2000, Table 3:
Metropolitan Areas Ranked by Population: 2000

9

Spending

■ Between 1950 and 2000, spending by the average household rose 47 percent, after adjusting for inflation. Most of the increase occurred before the mid-1980s. Between 1984 and 2000, spending by the average household grew only 4 percent, after adjusting for inflation.

■ Households cut their spending so deeply during the recession of the early 1990s that many are still playing catch-up. Householders aged 35 to 54 spent less in 2000 than their counterparts did in 1984, contrary to the popular perception that boomers are big spenders.

■ Spending by blacks rose 16 percent between 1984 and 2000 as they made gains in education and income. Blacks still spend much less than whites, but the gap is narrowing.

■ Married couples without children at home (some of them young couples, but most of them older empty-nesters) spent 10 percent more in 2000 than in 1984, after adjusting for inflation. This household type enjoyed a bigger spending increase than any other during those years.

■ Spending trends varied greatly by region between 1984 and 2000. Households in the Midwest spent 12 percent more in 2000 than in 1984, after adjusting for inflation, a much larger spending increase than in any other region.

Spending Grows with Standard of Living

Between 1950 and 2000, spending by the average household rose 47 percent, after adjusting for inflation. Behind the increase was a substantial rise in our standard of living. Houses grew larger and housing quality improved. Most households now own more than one vehicle. Food and clothing prices dropped. And households devoted more of their dollars to having fun.

In 1950, 31 percent of the household budget was devoted to food. Today, the figure is just 14 percent. At the same time, the share of the budget allotted to shelter rose substantially, from 11 to 19 percent. Vehicle expenses also command more of the household budget, rising from a 12 percent share in 1950 to 18 percent in 2000. The average household spends more on entertainment and health care today than in 1950, but less on alcoholic beverages, apparel, household furnishings, and personal care products and services.

Most of the increase in spending during the past half-century occurred before the mid-1980s. Since 1984, spending by the average household has grown only 4 percent, after adjusting for inflation. Between 1984 and 2000, spending fell in many discretionary categories because households were paying more for nondiscretionary items such as housing, vehicles, and health insurance.

Rise in spending slows

(average annual spending by households, 1950 to 2000; in 2000 dollars)

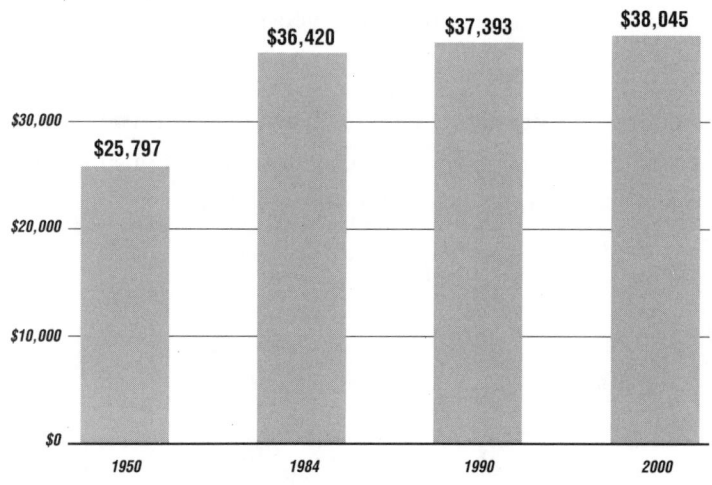

Table 9.1 Spending on Major Categories of Goods and Services, 1950 and 2000

(average annual spending of consumer units on major categories of goods and services, and percent distribution of spending, 1950 and 2000; percent change and percentage point change, 1950–00; in 2000 dollars)

	average spending			percent distribution		
	2000	**1950**	**percent change 1950–00**	**2000**	**1950**	**percentage point change 1950–00**
Total spending by the average consumer unit	**$38,045**	**$25,797**	**47.5%**	**100.0%**	**100.0%**	**–**
Food	5,158	7,920	–34.9	13.6	30.7	–17.1
Alcoholic beverages	372	460	–19.1	1.0	1.8	–0.8
Shelter	7,114	2,728	160.8	18.7	10.6	8.1
Utilities, fuels, and public services	2,489	1,071	132.3	6.5	4.2	2.4
Household operations	1,166	1,019	14.5	3.1	3.9	–0.9
Household furnishings and equipment	1,549	1,827	–15.2	4.1	7.1	–3.0
Apparel and services	1,856	2,977	–37.7	4.9	11.5	–6.7
Vehicle expenses	6,990	3,102	125.3	18.4	12.0	6.3
Public transportation	427	454	–5.8	1.1	1.8	–0.6
Health care	2,066	1,315	57.2	5.4	5.1	0.3
Entertainment and reading	2,009	1,387	44.9	5.3	5.4	–0.1
Personal care	564	598	–5.7	1.5	2.3	–0.8
Education	632	112	465.6	1.7	0.4	1.2
Tobacco	319	519	–38.6	0.8	2.0	–1.2
Miscellaneous	5,333	309	1,626.4	14.0	1.2	12.8

Note: Miscellaneous includes cash contributions, personal insurance, and pensions.
Source: Bureau of the Census, Historical Statistics of the United States, Colonial Times to 1970, Part 1, *1975; and Bureau of Labor Statistics, Internet site http://www.bls.gov/cex/; calculations by New Strategist*

Table 9.2 Spending on Detailed Categories of Goods and Services, 1984, 1990, and 2000

(number of consumer units (CU), and average annual spending on products and services, 1984, 1990, and 2000; percent change, 1990–00 and 1984–00; in 2000 dollars)

	2000	1990	1984	percent change 1990–00	percent change 1984–00
Number of consumer units (in 000s)	109,367	96,968	90,223	12.8%	21.2%
Average annual spending	$38,045	$37,393	$36,420	1.7	4.5
FOOD	**$5,158**	**$5,660**	**$5,453**	**–8.9%**	**–5.4%**
Food at home	**3,021**	**3,274**	**3,265**	**–7.7**	**–7.5**
Cereals and bakery products	453	485	434	–6.6	4.4
Cereals and cereal products	156	170	139	–8.2	12.2
Bakery products	297	316	295	–6.0	0.7
Meats, poultry, fish, and eggs	795	880	971	–9.7	–18.1
Beef	238	287	330	–17.1	–27.9
Pork	167	174	197	–4.0	–15.2
Other meats	101	130	134	–22.3	–24.6
Poultry	145	142	141	2.1	2.8
Fish and seafood	110	108	111	1.9	–0.9
Eggs	34	40	58	–15.0	–41.4
Dairy products	325	389	419	–16.5	–22.4
Fresh milk and cream	131	184	212	–28.8	–38.2
Other dairy products	193	204	207	–5.4	–6.8
Fruits and vegetables	521	538	519	–3.2	0.4
Fresh fruits	163	167	154	–2.4	5.8
Fresh vegetables	159	155	152	2.6	4.6
Processed fruits	115	123	119	–6.5	–3.4
Processed vegetables	84	92	93	–8.7	–9.7
Other food at home	927	983	872	–5.7	6.3
Sugar and other sweets	117	124	123	–5.6	–4.9
Fats and oils	83	90	93	–7.8	–10.8
Miscellaneous foods	437	443	361	–1.4	21.1
Nonalcoholic beverages	250	281	295	–11.0	–15.3
Food prepared by CU, out-of-town trips	40	46	50	–13.0	–20.0
Food away from home	**2,137**	**2,386**	**2,188**	**–10.4**	**–2.3**
ALCOHOLIC BEVERAGES	**372**	**386**	**456**	**–3.6**	**–18.4**
HOUSING	**12,319**	**11,466**	**11,061**	**7.4**	**11.4**
Shelter	**7,114**	**6,372**	**5,782**	**11.6**	**23.0**
Owned dwellings*	4,602	3,891	3,417	18.3	34.7
Mortgage interest and charges	2,639	2,394	2,073	10.2	27.3
Property taxes	1,139	787	698	44.7	63.2
Maintenance, repairs, insurance, other expenses	825	711	646	16.0	27.7
Rented dwellings	2,034	2,020	1,773	0.7	14.7
Other lodging	478	460	592	3.9	–19.3
Utilities, fuels, public services	**2,489**	**2,490**	**2,715**	**0.0**	**–8.3**
Natural gas	307	324	492	–5.2	–37.6
Electricity	911	999	1,042	–8.8	–12.6
Fuel oil and other fuels	97	132	232	–26.5	–58.2
Telephone	877	780	721	12.4	21.6
Water and other public services	296	254	229	16.5	29.3
Household services	**684**	**588**	**522**	**16.3**	**31.0**
Personal services	326	289	212	12.8	53.8
Other household services	358	299	310	19.7	15.5
Housekeeping supplies	**482**	**535**	**509**	**–9.9**	**–5.3**
Laundry and cleaning supplies	131	149	144	–12.1	–9.0
Other household products	226	225	222	0.4	1.8
Postage and stationery	126	161	143	–21.7	–11.9
Household furnishings and equipment	**1,549**	**1,482**	**1,535**	**4.5**	**0.9**
Household textiles	106	130	143	–18.5	–25.9

(continued)

(continued from previous page)

	2000	1990	1984	percent change 1990–00	percent change 1984–00
Furniture	$391	$408	$447	–4.2%	–12.5%
Floor coverings	44	121	129	–63.6	–65.9
Major appliances	189	194	237	–2.6	–20.3
Small appliances, misc. houseware	87	99	111	–12.1	–21.6
Miscellaneous household equipment	731	530	467	37.9	56.5
APPAREL AND SERVICES	**1,856**	**2,132**	**2,186**	**–12.9**	**–15.1**
Men and boys	**440**	**518**	**580**	**–15.1**	**–24.1**
Men, aged 16 or older	344	427	464	–19.4	–25.9
Boys, aged 2 to 15	96	92	116	4.3	–17.2
Women and girls	**725**	**887**	**868**	**–18.3**	**–16.5**
Women, aged 16 or older	607	772	736	–21.4	–17.5
Girls, aged 2 to 15	118	115	131	2.6	–9.9
Children under age 2	**82**	**92**	**83**	**–10.9**	**–1.2**
Footwear	**343**	**296**	**307**	**15.9**	**11.7**
Other apparel products and services	**266**	**340**	**350**	**–21.8**	**–24.0**
TRANSPORTATION	**7,417**	**6,746**	**7,133**	**9.9**	**4.0**
Vehicle purchases	**3,418**	**2,805**	**3,005**	**21.9**	**13.7**
Cars and trucks, new	1,605	1,527	1,707	5.1	–6.0
Cars and trucks, used	1,770	1,249	1,253	41.7	41.3
Other vehicles	43	29	45	48.3	–4.4
Gasoline and motor oil	**1,291**	**1,379**	**1,753**	**–6.4**	**–26.4**
Other vehicle expenses	**2,281**	**2,163**	**1,952**	**5.5**	**16.9**
Vehicle finance charges	328	395	353	–17.0	–7.1
Maintenance and repairs	624	776	797	–19.6	–21.7
Vehicle insurance	778	742	578	4.9	34.6
Vehicle rent, lease, license, other	551	250	222	120.4	148.2
Public transportation	**427**	**398**	**423**	**7.3**	**0.9**
HEALTH CARE	**2,066**	**1,950**	**1,739**	**5.9**	**18.8**
Health insurance	983	765	613	28.5	60.4
Medical services	568	740	752	–23.2	–24.5
Drugs	416	332	277	25.3	50.2
Medical supplies	99	112	96	–11.6	3.1
ENTERTAINMENT	**1,863**	**1,874**	**1,748**	**–0.6**	**6.6**
Fees and admissions	515	489	519	5.3	–0.8
Television, radios, sound equipment	622	598	534	4.0	16.5
Pets, toys, and playground equipment	334	364	315	–8.2	6.0
Other supplies, equipment, and services	393	423	381	–7.1	3.1
PERSONAL CARE PRODUCTS, SERVICES	**564**	**480**	**479**	**17.5**	**17.7**
READING	**146**	**202**	**219**	**–27.7**	**–33.3**
EDUCATION	**632**	**535**	**502**	**18.1**	**25.9**
TOBACCO PRODUCTS AND SMOKING SUPPLIES	**319**	**361**	**378**	**–11.6**	**–15.6**
MISCELLANEOUS	**776**	**1,109**	**747**	**–30.0**	**3.9**
CASH CONTRIBUTIONS	**1,192**	**1,075**	**1,170**	**10.9**	**1.9**
PERSONAL INSURANCE, PENSIONS	**3,365**	**3,415**	**3,144**	**–1.5**	**7.0**
Life and other personal insurance	399	455	497	–12.3	–19.7
Pensions and Social Security	2,966	2,962	2,648	0.1	12.0
PERSONAL TAXES	**3,117**	**3,889**	**3,691**	**–19.9**	**–15.6**
Federal income taxes	2,409	3,055	2,872	–21.1	–16.1
State and local income taxes	562	735	714	–23.5	–21.3
Other taxes	146	99	104	47.5	40.4
GIFTS**	**1,083**	**1,200**	**1,154**	**–9.8**	**–6.2**

* This figure does not include the amount paid for mortgage principle, which is considered an asset.
** Expenditures on gifts are also included in the preceding product and service categories.
Note: The Bureau of Labor Statistics uses consumer unit rather than household as the sampling unit in the Consumer Expenditure Survey. For the definition of consumer unit, see the glossary. Average annual spending total does not include the amount spent on personal taxes.
Source: Bureau of Labor Statistics, Consumer Expenditure Surveys, Internet site http://www.bls.gov/cex/; calculations by New Strategist

Householders Aged 35 to 54 Are Spending Less

While many people believe the booming economy of the 1990s resulted in a spending spree, in fact the average household spent only 2 percent more in 2000 than in 1990, after adjusting for inflation. Households cut their spending so deeply in the recession of the early 1990s that many still haven't caught up. In particular, householders aged 35 to 54, the age group now filled with the baby-boom generation, spent less in 2000 than people in that age group did in 1984.

Householders aged 65 or older boosted their spending the most between 1984 and 2000, posting a 15 percent increase in spending after adjusting for inflation. Retirees spent 12 percent more in 2000 than in 1984. Behind the increase in spending by older Americans was the entry of a more educated and affluent cohort into the 65-or-older age group.

Spending fell in many discretionary categories between 1984 and 2000, particularly among middle-aged adults. Householders aged 35 to 44, for example, spent 44 percent less on "other lodging" (which includes hotels and motels) in 2000 than in 1984. They spent 23 percent less on women's clothes, and 19 percent less on furniture. Behind the discretionary spending cuts was a rise in spending on nondiscretionary items such as property taxes, Social Security taxes, health and vehicle insurance, and shelter.

Older householders are spending more

(percent change in average annual spending of households by age of householder, 1984 to 2000; in 2000 dollars)

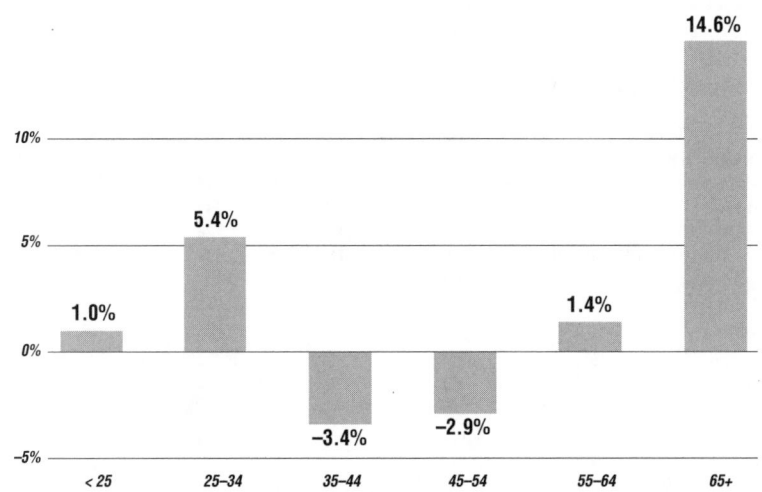

Table 9.3 Spending by Householders under Age 25, 1984, 1990, and 2000

(number of consumer units (CU) headed by people under age 25, and average annual spending on products and services, 1984, 1990 and 2000; percent change, 1990–00 and 1984–00; in 2000 dollars)

	2000	1990	1984	percent change 1990–00	percent change 1984–00
Number of consumer units (in 000s)	8,306	7,581	8,811	9.6%	–5.7%
Average annual spending	$22,543	$21,772	$22,309	3.5	1
FOOD	**$3,213**	**$3,638**	**$3,457**	**–11.7%**	**–7.1%**
Food at home	**1,643**	**1,693**	**1,747**	**–3.0**	**–6.0**
Cereals and bakery products	238	241	227	–1.2	4.8
Cereals and cereal products	90	95	81	–5.3	11.1
Bakery products	148	146	146	1.4	1.4
Meats, poultry, fish, and eggs	437	390	472	12.1	–7.4
Beef	135	128	166	5.5	–18.7
Pork	89	78	104	14.1	–14.4
Other meats	55	63	68	–12.7	–19.1
Poultry	86	51	70	68.6	22.9
Fish and seafood	52	46	36	13.0	44.4
Eggs	21	22	28	–4.5	–25.0
Dairy products	175	206	242	–15	–27.7
Fresh milk and cream	73	107	134	–31.8	–45.5
Other dairy products	101	99	108	2.0	–6.5
Fruits and vegetables	253	248	250	2.0	1.2
Fresh fruits	77	61	68	26.2	13.2
Fresh vegetables	74	75	73	–1.3	1.4
Processed fruits	62	63	53	–1.6	17.0
Processed vegetables	41	49	56	–16.3	–26.8
Other food at home	541	609	535	–11.2	1.1
Sugar and other sweets	60	63	58	–4.8	3.4
Fats and oils	42	41	51	2.4	–17.6
Miscellaneous foods	271	318	244	–14.8	11.1
Nonalcoholic beverages	147	167	184	–12.0	–20.1
Food prepared by CU, out-of-town trips	19	20	18	–5.0	5.6
Food away from home	**1,569**	**1,945**	**1,712**	**–19.3**	**–8.4**
ALCOHOLIC BEVERAGES	**392**	**419**	**436**	**–6.4**	**–10.1**
HOUSING	**7,109**	**6,383**	**6,218**	**11.4**	**14.3**
Shelter	**4,574**	**3,971**	**3,780**	**15.2**	**21.0**
Owned dwellings*	634	410	767	54.6	–17.3
Mortgage interest and charges	386	307	597	25.7	–35.3
Property taxes	176	36	65	388.9	170.8
Maintenance, repairs, insurance, other expenses	72	67	106	7.5	–32.1
Rented dwellings	3,618	3,299	2,693	9.7	34.3
Other lodging	322	264	320	22.0	0.6
Utilities, fuels, public services	**1,248**	**1,194**	**1,185**	**4.5**	**5.3**
Natural gas	102	124	136	–17.7	–25.0
Electricity	444	418	459	6.2	–3.3
Fuel oil and other fuels	21	22	51	–4.5	–58.8
Telephone	589	567	484	3.9	21.7
Water and other public services	91	63	55	44.4	65.5
Household services	**226**	**192**	**192**	**17.7**	**17.7**
Personal services	154	132	134	16.7	14.9
Other household services	72	61	58	18.0	24.1
Housekeeping supplies	**194**	**235**	**234**	**–17.4**	**–17.1**
Laundry and cleaning supplies	55	62	78	–11.3	–29.5
Other household products	89	78	71	14.1	25.4
Postage and stationery	50	95	86	–47.4	–41.9
Household furnishings, equipment	**867**	**792**	**827**	**9.5**	**4.8**
Household textiles	35	51	66	–31.4	–47.0

(continued)

(continued from previous page)

	2000	1990	1984	percent change 1990–00	percent change 1984–00
Furniture	$270	$335	$348	–19.4%	–22.4%
Floor coverings	6	12	22	–50.0	–72.7
Major appliances	77	86	108	–10.5	–28.7
Small appliances, misc. houseware	50	53	75	–5.7	–33.3
Miscellaneous household equipment	429	256	209	67.6	105.3
APPAREL AND SERVICES	**1,420**	**1,362**	**1,553**	**4.3**	**–8.6**
Men and boys	**320**	**415**	**409**	**–22.9**	**–21.8**
Men, aged 16 or older	294	399	381	–26.3	–22.8
Boys, aged 2 to 15	26	17	28	52.9	–7.1
Women and girls	**435**	**415**	**550**	**4.8**	**–20.9**
Women, aged 16 or older	405	382	529	6.0	–23.4
Girls, aged 2 to 15	31	34	22	–8.8	40.9
Children under age 2	**101**	**111**	**93**	**–9.0**	**8.6**
Footwear	**363**	**124**	**197**	**192.7**	**84.3**
Other apparel products, services	**201**	**298**	**303**	**–32.6**	**–33.7**
TRANSPORTATION	**5,189**	**4,603**	**5,499**	**12.7**	**–5.6**
Vehicle purchases	**2,628**	**2,096**	**2,711**	**25.4**	**–3.1**
Cars and trucks, new	1,061	967	880	9.7	20.6
Cars and trucks, used	1,547	1,100	1,712	40.6	–9.6
Other vehicles	–	30	118	–	–
Gasoline and motor oil	**947**	**951**	**1,281**	**–0.4**	**–26.1**
Other vehicle expenses	**1,397**	**1,320**	**1,304**	**5.8**	**7.1**
Vehicle finance charges	228	256	268	–10.9	–14.9
Maintenance and repairs	442	513	565	–13.8	–21.8
Vehicle insurance	449	426	341	5.4	31.7
Vehicle rent, lease, license, other	278	128	·129	117.2	115.5
Public transportation	**216**	**236**	**202**	**–8.5**	**6.9**
HEALTH CARE	**504**	**531**	**615**	**–5.1**	**–18.0**
Health insurance	211	140	179	50.7	17.9
Medical services	178	250	308	–28.8	–42.2
Drugs	81	86	93	–5.8	–12.9
Medical supplies	34	54	36	–37.0	–5.6
ENTERTAINMENT	**1,091**	**1,097**	**1,082**	**–0.5**	**0.8**
Fees and admissions	271	287	317	–5.6	–14.5
Television, radios, sound equipment	473	453	381	4.4	24.1
Pets, toys, and playground equipment	173	154	146	12.3	18.5
Other supplies, equipment, and services	175	204	239	–14.2	–26.8
PERSONAL CARE PRODUCTS, SERVICES	**345**	**279**	**265**	**23.7**	**30.2**
READING	**57**	**99**	**103**	**–42.4**	**–44.7**
EDUCATION	**1,257**	**1,076**	**945**	**16.8**	**33.0**
TOBACCO PRODUCTS AND SMOKING SUPPLIES	**237**	**285**	**264**	**–16.8**	**–10.2**
MISCELLANEOUS	**322**	**526**	**398**	**–38.8**	**–19.1**
CASH CONTRIBUTIONS	**189**	**192**	**171**	**–1.6**	**10.5**
PERSONAL INSURANCE, PENSIONS	**1,216**	**1,281**	**1,304**	**–5.1**	**–6.7**
Life and other personal insurance	54	65	106	–16.9	–49.1
Pensions and Social Security	1,162	1,215	1,198	–4.4	–3.0
PERSONAL TAXES	**931**	**1,111**	**1,730**	**–16.2**	**–46.2**
Federal income taxes	696	846	1,367	–17.7	–49.1
State and local income taxes	226	253	350	–10.7	–35.4
Other taxes	9	13	12	–30.8	–25.0
GIFTS**	**597**	**553**	**633**	**8.0**	**–5.7**

* This figure does not include the amount paid for mortgage principle, which is considered an asset.
** Expenditures on gifts are also included in the preceding product and service categories.
Note: The Bureau of Labor Statistics uses consumer unit rather than household as the sampling unit in the Consumer Expenditure Survey. For the definition of consumer unit, see the glossary. Average annual spending total does not include the amount spent on personal taxes; (–) means sample is too small to make a reliable estimate.
Source: Bureau of Labor Statistics, Consumer Expenditure Surveys, Internet site http://www.bls.gov/cex/; calculations by New Strategist

Table 9.4 Spending by Householders Aged 25 to 34, 1984, 1990, and 2000

(number of consumer units (CU) headed by people aged 25 to 34, and average annual spending on products and services, 1984, 1990, and 2000; percent change, 1990–00 and 1984–00; in 2000 dollars)

	2000	1990	1984	percent change 1990–00	percent change 1984–00
Number of consumer units (in 000s)	18,887	7,581	20,058	149.1%	–5.8%
Average annual spending	$38,945	$37,045	$36,949	5.1	5.4
FOOD	**$5,260**	**$5,402**	**$5,191**	**–2.6%**	**1.3%**
Food at home	2,951	3,083	3,033	–4.3	–2.7
Cereals and bakery products	429	437	409	–1.8	4.9
Cereals and cereal products	167	165	143	1.2	16.8
Bakery products	263	271	267	–3.0	–1.5
Meats, poultry, fish, and eggs	770	827	882	–6.9	–12.7
Beef	239	286	312	–16.4	–23.4
Pork	155	150	176	3.3	–11.9
Other meats	98	123	126	–20.3	–22.2
Poultry	145	136	134	6.6	8.2
Fish and seafood	102	96	80	6.3	27.5
Eggs	30	38	53	–21.1	–43.4
Dairy products	317	385	399	–17.7	–20.6
Fresh milk and cream	134	187	207	–28.3	–35.3
Other dairy products	183	198	192	–7.6	–4.7
Fruits and vegetables	488	482	441	1.2	10.7
Fresh fruits	146	149	119	–2.0	22.7
Fresh vegetables	148	136	124	8.8	19.4
Processed fruits	113	112	104	0.9	8.7
Processed vegetables	82	86	93	–4.7	–11.8
Other food at home	946	951	860	–0.5	10.0
Sugar and other sweets	105	107	109	–1.9	–3.7
Fats and oils	77	75	85	2.7	–9.4
Miscellaneous foods	485	451	398	7.5	21.9
Nonalcoholic beverages	247	273	268	–9.5	–7.8
Food prepared by CU, out-of-town trips	31	46	45	–32.6	–31.1
Food away from home	**2,309**	**2,319**	**2,158**	**–0.4**	**7.0**
ALCOHOLIC BEVERAGES	**431**	**481**	**555**	**–10.4**	**–22.3**
HOUSING	**13,050**	**12,133**	**11,878**	**7.6**	**9.9**
Shelter	**7,905**	**7,266**	**6,784**	**8.8**	**16.5**
Owned dwellings*	4,142	3,826	3,727	8.3	11.1
Mortgage interest and charges	2,888	2,979	2,879	–3.1	0.3
Property taxes	755	401	404	88.3	86.9
Maintenance, repairs, insurance, other expenses	499	447	443	11.6	12.6
Rented dwellings	3,514	3,216	2,677	9.3	31.3
Other lodging	248	224	380	10.7	–34.7
Utilities, fuels, public services	**2,341**	**2,219**	**2,450**	**5.5**	**–4.4**
Natural gas	273	262	404	4.2	–32.4
Electricity	826	880	955	–6.1	–13.5
Fuel oil and other fuels	58	83	154	–30.1	–62.3
Telephone	950	796	746	19.3	27.3
Water and other public services	234	198	191	18.2	22.5
Household services	**871**	**748**	**683**	**16.4**	**27.5**
Personal services	641	592	497	8.3	29.0
Other household services	230	157	186	46.5	23.7
Housekeeping supplies	**437**	**485**	**474**	**–9.9**	**–7.8**
Laundry and cleaning supplies	125	149	141	–16.1	–11.3
Other household products	201	198	212	1.5	–5.2
Postage and stationery	112	138	121	–18.8	–7.4
Household furnishings, equipment	**1,495**	**1,416**	**1,490**	**5.6**	**0.3**
Household textiles	120	104	126	15.4	–4.8

(continued)

(continued from previous page)

	2000	1990	1984	percent change 1990–00	percent change 1984–00
Furniture	$457	$440	$535	3.9%	−14.6%
Floor coverings	42	71	41	−40.8	2.4
Major appliances	181	198	259	−8.6	−30.1
Small appliances, misc. houseware	78	91	89	−14.3	−12.4
Miscellaneous household equipment	617	514	439	20.0	40.5
APPAREL AND SERVICES	**2,059**	**2,070**	**2,271**	**−0.5**	**−9.3**
Men and boys	**511**	**516**	**628**	**−1.0**	**−18.6**
Men, aged 16 or older	368	395	484	−6.8	−24
Boys, aged 2 to 15	143	121	143	18.2	0.0
Women and girls	**704**	**748**	**771**	**−5.9**	**−8.7**
Women, aged 16 or older	561	622	633	−9.8	−11.4
Girls, aged 2 to 15	144	126	138	14.3	4.3
Children under age 2	**165**	**177**	**162**	**−6.8**	**1.9**
Footwear	**394**	**275**	**312**	**43.3**	**26.3**
Other apparel products, services	**285**	**353**	**398**	**−19.3**	**−28.4**
TRANSPORTATION	**8,357**	**7,130**	**7,602**	**17.2**	**9.9**
Vehicle purchases	**4,139**	**3,190**	**3,543**	**29.7**	**16.8**
Cars and trucks, new	1,845	1,656	2,083	11.4	−11.4
Cars and trucks, used	2,217	1,480	1,419	49.8	56.2
Other vehicles	77	54	41	42.6	87.8
Gasoline and motor oil	**1,341**	**1,423**	**1,709**	**−5.8**	**−21.5**
Other vehicle expenses	**2,482**	**2,224**	**1,961**	**11.6**	**26.6**
Vehicle finance charges	436	489	438	−10.8	−0.5
Maintenance and repairs	570	763	766	−25.3	−25.6
Vehicle insurance	774	686	510	12.8	51.8
Vehicle rent, lease, license, other	701	286	247	145.1	183.8
Public transportation	**395**	**294**	**388**	**34.4**	**1.8**
HEALTH CARE	**1,256**	**1,292**	**1,236**	**−2.8**	**1.6**
Health insurance	640	515	411	24.3	55.7
Medical services	367	515	598	−28.7	−38.6
Drugs	181	178	162	1.7	11.7
Medical supplies	69	84	63	−17.9	9.5
ENTERTAINMENT	**1,876**	**1,939**	**1,997**	**−3.2**	**−6.1**
Fees and admissions	460	451	492	2.0	−6.5
Television, radios, sound equipment	680	663	678	2.6	0.3
Pets, toys, and playground equipment	351	404	408	−13.1	−14.0
Other supplies, equipment, and services	385	423	419	−9.0	−8.1
PERSONAL CARE PRODUCTS, SERVICES	**576**	**415**	**452**	**38.8**	**27.4**
READING	**118**	**177**	**220**	**−33.3**	**−46.4**
EDUCATION	**585**	**428**	**360**	**36.7**	**62.5**
TOBACCO PRODUCTS AND SMOKING SUPPLIES	**310**	**362**	**368**	**−14.4**	**−15.8**
MISCELLANEOUS	**804**	**1,036**	**878**	**−22.4**	**−8.4**
CASH CONTRIBUTIONS	**648**	**542**	**587**	**19.6**	**10.4**
PERSONAL INSURANCE, PENSIONS	**3,614**	**3,638**	**3,351**	**−0.7**	**7.8**
Life and other personal insurance	242	296	391	−18.2	−38.1
Pensions and Social Security	3,373	3,341	2,960	1.0	14.0
PERSONAL TAXES	**2,833**	**3,892**	**4,263**	**−27.2**	**−33.5**
Federal income taxes	2,205	3,024	3,323	−27.1	−33.6
State and local income taxes	570	825	885	−30.9	−35.6
Other taxes	58	43	55	34.9	5.5
GIFTS**	**716**	**793**	**805**	**−9.7**	**−11.1**

* This figure does not include the amount paid for mortgage principle, which is considered an asset.
** Expenditures on gifts are also included in the preceding product and service categories.
Note: The Bureau of Labor Statistics uses consumer unit rather than household as the sampling unit in the Consumer Expenditure Survey. For the definition of consumer unit, see the glossary. Average annual spending total does not include the amount spent on personal taxes.
Source: Bureau of Labor Statistics, Consumer Expenditure Surveys, Internet site http://www.bls.gov/cex/; calculations by New Strategist

Table 9.5 Spending of Householders Aged 35 to 44, 1984, 1990, and 2000

(number of consumer units (CU) headed by people aged 35 to 44, and average annual spending on products and services, 1984, 1990, and 2000; percent change, 1990–00 and 1984–00; in 2000 dollars)

	2000	1990	1984	percent change 1990–00	percent change 1984–00
Number of consumer units (in 000s)	23,983	21,003	17,118	14.2%	40.1%
Average annual spending	$45,149	$46,896	$46,760	–3.7	–3.4
FOOD	**$6,092**	**$7,088**	**$7,130**	**–14.1%**	**–14.6%**
Food at home	3,484	4,129	4,170	–15.6	–16.5
Cereals and bakery products	531	626	550	–15.2	–3.5
Cereals and cereal products	190	224	187	–15.2	1.6
Bakery products	341	402	363	–15.2	–6.1
Meats, poultry, fish, and eggs	918	1,055	1,215	–13.0	–24.4
Beef	270	345	423	–21.7	–36.2
Pork	186	206	242	–9.7	–23.1
Other meats	120	153	174	–21.6	–31.0
Poultry	178	166	186	7.2	–4.3
Fish and seafood	126	141	121	–10.6	4.1
Eggs	37	45	70	–17.8	–47.1
Dairy products	383	497	544	–22.9	–29.6
Fresh milk and cream	157	231	270	–32.0	–41.9
Other dairy products	226	266	272	–15.0	–16.9
Fruits and vegetables	552	646	643	–14.6	–14.2
Fresh fruits	169	186	182	–9.1	–7.1
Fresh vegetables	164	191	187	–14.1	–12.3
Processed fruits	125	150	159	–16.7	–21.4
Processed vegetables	92	117	114	–21.4	–19.3
Other food at home	1,101	1,306	1,162	–15.7	–5.2
Sugar and other sweets	147	163	161	–9.8	–8.7
Fats and oils	90	116	119	–22.4	–24.4
Miscellaneous foods	518	609	492	–14.9	5.3
Nonalcoholic beverages	300	361	389	–16.9	–22.9
Food prepared by CU, out-of-town trips	46	57	58	–19.3	–20.7
Food away from home	**2,607**	**2,959**	**2,958**	**–11.9**	**–11.9**
ALCOHOLIC BEVERAGES	**420**	**487**	**479**	**–13.8**	**–12.3**
HOUSING	**15,111**	**14,559**	**14,535**	**3.8**	**4.0**
Shelter	**8,930**	**8,178**	**7,978**	**9.2**	**11.9**
Owned dwellings*	6,433	5,697	5,257	12.9	22.4
Mortgage interest and charges	4,302	4,059	3,867	6.0	11.2
Property taxes	1,246	946	729	31.7	70.9
Maintenance, repairs, insurance, other expenses	884	692	660	27.7	33.9
Rented dwellings	2,067	2,017	1,951	2.5	5.9
Other lodging	430	464	771	–7.3	–44.2
Utilities, fuels, public services	**2,810**	**2,837**	**3,214**	**–1.0**	**–12.6**
Natural gas	350	361	549	–3.0	–36.2
Electricity	1,009	1,133	1,294	–10.9	–22.0
Fuel oil and other fuels	97	144	222	–32.6	–56.3
Telephone	1,018	899	852	13.2	19.5
Water and other public services	336	302	297	11.3	13.1
Household services	**896**	**804**	**646**	**11.4**	**38.7**
Personal services	542	466	307	16.3	76.5
Other household services	354	337	340	5.0	4.1
Housekeeping supplies	**570**	**651**	**640**	**–12.4**	**–10.9**
Laundry and cleaning supplies	157	187	179	–16.0	–12.3
Other household products	280	287	293	–2.4	–4.4
Postage and stationery	133	175	167	–24.0	–20.4
Household furnishings, equipment	**1,906**	**2,090**	**2,055**	**–8.8**	**–7.3**
Household textiles	124	163	184	–23.9	–32.6

(continued)

(continued from previous page)

	2000	1990	1984	percent change 1990–00	percent change 1984–00
Furniture	$499	$538	$615	–7.2%	–18.9%
Floor coverings	53	202	139	–73.8	–61.9
Major appliances	212	228	285	–7.0	–25.6
Small appliances, misc. houseware	93	116	151	–19.8	–38.4
Miscellaneous household equipment	926	843	680	9.8	36.2
APPAREL AND SERVICES	**2,323**	**3,046**	**3,131**	**–23.7**	**–25.8**
Men and boys	**551**	**740**	**903**	**–25.5**	**–39.0**
Men, aged 16 or older	367	553	603	–33.6	–39.1
Boys, aged 2 to 15	184	186	300	–1.1	–38.7
Women and girls	**935**	**1,292**	**1,246**	**–27.6**	**–25.0**
Women, aged 16 or older	692	1,024	897	–32.4	–22.9
Girls, aged 2 to 15	242	269	348	–10.0	–30.5
Children under age 2	**105**	**91**	**80**	**15.4**	**31.3**
Footwear	**401**	**457**	**464**	**–12.3**	**–13.6**
Other apparel products, services	**331**	**465**	**439**	**–28.8**	**–24.6**
TRANSPORTATION	**8,702**	**8,009**	**8,484**	**8.7**	**2.6**
Vehicle purchases	**3,996**	**3,324**	**3,326**	**20.2**	**20.1**
Cars and trucks, new	1,724	1,780	1,966	–3.1	–12.3
Cars and trucks, used	2,198	1,513	1,311	45.3	67.7
Other vehicles	74	33	50	124.2	48.0
Gasoline and motor oil	**1,577**	**1,640**	**2,160**	**–3.8**	**–27.0**
Other vehicle expenses	**2,677**	**2,615**	**2,527**	**2.4**	**5.9**
Vehicle finance charges	406	520	477	–21.9	–14.9
Maintenance and repairs	708	912	1,033	–22.4	–31.5
Vehicle insurance	884	858	703	3.0	25.7
Vehicle rent, lease, license, other	680	325	315	109.2	115.9
Public transportation	**451**	**430**	**472**	**4.9**	**–4.4**
HEALTH CARE	**1,774**	**1,864**	**1,618**	**–4.8**	**9.6**
Health insurance	850	639	502	33.0	69.3
Medical services	555	851	817	–34.8	–32.1
Drugs	284	241	222	17.8	27.9
Medical supplies	85	132	78	–35.6	9.0
ENTERTAINMENT	**2,464**	**2,420**	**2,476**	**1.8**	**–0.5**
Fees and admissions	715	694	754	3.0	–5.2
Television, radios, sound equipment	789	768	691	2.7	14.2
Pets, toys, and playground equipment	451	473	456	–4.7	–1.1
Other supplies, equipment, and services	509	484	575	5.2	–11.5
PERSONAL CARE PRODUCTS, SERVICES	**644**	**589**	**575**	**9.3**	**12.0**
READING	**151**	**248**	**270**	**–39.1**	**–44.1**
EDUCATION	**615**	**613**	**655**	**0.3**	**–6.1**
TOBACCO PRODUCTS AND SMOKING SUPPLIES	**427**	**416**	**454**	**2.6**	**–5.9**
MISCELLANEOUS	**852**	**1,526**	**1,024**	**–44.2**	**–16.8**
CASH CONTRIBUTIONS	**1,003**	**1,154**	**1,637**	**–13.1**	**–38.7**
PERSONAL INSURANCE, PENSIONS	**4,570**	**4,875**	**4,294**	**–6.3**	**6.4**
Life and other personal insurance	412	585	593	–29.6	–30.5
Pensions and Social Security	4,158	4,290	3,701	–3.1	12.3
PERSONAL TAXES	**3,874**	**5,891**	**5,017**	**–34.2**	**–22.8**
Federal income taxes	3,014	4,663	3,943	–35.4	–23.6
State and local income taxes	734	1,088	955	–32.5	–23.1
Other taxes	126	140	121	–10.0	4.1
GIFTS**	**1,001**	**1,182**	**1,321**	**–15.3**	**–24.2**

* This figure does not include the amount paid for mortgage principle, which is considered an asset.
** Expenditures on gifts are also included in the preceding product and service categories.
Note: The Bureau of Labor Statistics uses consumer unit rather than household as the sampling unit in the Consumer Expenditure Survey. For the definition of consumer unit, see the glossary. Average annual spending total does not include the amount spent on personal taxes.
Source: Bureau of Labor Statistics, Consumer Expenditure Surveys, Internet site http://www.bls.gov/cex/; calculations by New Strategist

Table 9.6   Spending of Householders Aged 45 to 54, 1984, 1990, and 2000

(number of consumer units (CU) headed by people aged 45 to 54, and average annual spending on products and services, 1984, 1990, and 2000; percent change, 1990–00 and 1984–00; in 2000 dollars)

	2000	1990	1984	percent change 1990–00	percent change 1984–00
Number of consumer units (in 000s)	21,874	14,855	13,027	47.3%	67.9%
Average annual spending	$46,160	$48,764	$47,559	–5.3	–2.9
FOOD	**$6,295**	**$7,233**	**$7,195**	**–13.0%**	**–12.5%**
Food at home	**3,657**	**3,963**	**4,278**	**–7.7**	**–14.5**
Cereals and bakery products	560	580	555	–3.4	0.9
Cereals and cereal products	180	188	172	–4.3	4.7
Bakery products	380	391	383	–2.8	–0.8
Meats, poultry, fish, and eggs	970	1,120	1,391	–13.4	–30.3
Beef	296	353	466	–16.1	–36.5
Pork	198	237	267	–16.5	–25.8
Other meats	121	171	182	–29.2	–33.5
Poultry	169	179	174	–5.6	–2.9
Fish and seafood	146	134	222	9.0	–34.2
Eggs	40	46	78	–13.0	–48.7
Dairy products	377	455	542	–17.1	–30.4
Fresh milk and cream	146	213	275	–31.5	–46.9
Other dairy products	232	242	265	–4.1	–12.5
Fruits and vegetables	626	617	665	1.5	–5.9
Fresh fruits	187	190	204	–1.6	–8.3
Fresh vegetables	201	184	201	9.2	0.0
Processed fruits	133	137	146	–2.9	–8.9
Processed vegetables	105	105	114	0.0	–7.9
Other food at home	1,124	1,191	1,057	–5.6	6.3
Sugar and other sweets	143	157	152	–8.9	–5.9
Fats and oils	102	109	111	–6.4	–8.1
Miscellaneous foods	528	519	409	1.7	29.1
Nonalcoholic beverages	300	352	385	–14.8	–22.1
Food prepared by CU, out-of-town trips	52	54	70	–3.7	–25.7
Food away from home	**2,638**	**3,270**	**2,915**	**–19.3**	**–9.5**
ALCOHOLIC BEVERAGES	**417**	**427**	**608**	**–2.3**	**–31.4**
HOUSING	**14,179**	**13,735**	**13,292**	**3.2**	**6.7**
Shelter	**8,297**	**7,664**	**6,575**	**8.3**	**26.2**
Owned dwellings*	5,964	5,209	4,463	14.5	33.6
Mortgage interest and charges	3,558	3,458	2,696	2.9	32.0
Property taxes	1,471	937	931	57.0	58.0
Maintenance, repairs, insurance, other expenses	935	814	835	14.9	12.0
Rented dwellings	1,614	1,609	1,235	0.3	30.7
Other lodging	719	846	877	–15.0	–18.0
Utilities, fuels, public services	**2,857**	**3,105**	**3,474**	**–8.0**	**–17.8**
Natural gas	344	403	645	–14.6	–46.7
Electricity	1,045	1,248	1,342	–16.3	–22.1
Fuel oil and other fuels	109	146	259	–25.3	–57.9
Telephone	1,007	988	925	1.9	8.9
Water and other public services	352	321	303	9.7	16.2
Household services	**583**	**415**	**496**	**40.5**	**17.5**
Personal services	147	71	70	107.0	110.0
Other household services	435	344	426	26.5	2.1
Housekeeping supplies	**532**	**636**	**656**	**–16.4**	**–18.9**
Laundry and cleaning supplies	137	181	197	–24.3	–30.5
Other household products	247	261	293	–5.4	–15.7
Postage and stationery	147	195	166	–24.6	–11.4
Household furnishings, equipment	**1,911**	**1,914**	**2,092**	**–0.2**	**–8.7**
Household textiles	125	191	177	–34.6	–29.4

(continued)

(continued from previous page)

	2000	1990	1984	percent change 1990–00	1984–00
Furniture	$471	$493	$524	–4.5%	–10.1%
Floor coverings	51	198	252	–74.2	–79.8
Major appliances	223	231	303	–3.5	–26.4
Small appliances, misc. houseware	126	130	157	–3.1	–19.7
Miscellaneous household equipment	915	669	678	36.8	35.0
APPAREL AND SERVICES	**2,371**	**2,854**	**2,687**	**–16.9**	**–11.8**
Men and boys	**577**	**752**	**724**	**–23.3**	**–20.3**
Men, aged 16 or older	482	663	622	–27.3	–22.5
Boys, aged 2 to 15	95	90	104	5.6	–8.7
Women and girls	**977**	**1,192**	**1,074**	**–18.0**	**–9.0**
Women, aged 16 or older	850	1,091	936	–22.1	–9.2
Girls, aged 2 to 15	126	101	139	24.8	–9.4
Children under age 2	**54**	**76**	**76**	**–28.9**	**–28.9**
Footwear	**438**	**379**	**356**	**15.6**	**23.0**
Other apparel products, services	**325**	**455**	**454**	**–28.6**	**–28.4**
TRANSPORTATION	**8,827**	**9,283**	**9,841**	**–4.9**	**–10.3**
Vehicle purchases	**3,863**	**3,909**	**4,201**	**–1.2**	**–8.0**
Cars and trucks, new	1,690	2,204	2,198	–23.3	–23.1
Cars and trucks, used	2,128	1,669	1,931	27.5	10.2
Other vehicles	45	36	73	25.0	–38.4
Gasoline and motor oil	**1,592**	**1,833**	**2,463**	**–13.1**	**–35.4**
Other vehicle expenses	**2,868**	**2,947**	**2,655**	**–2.7**	**8.0**
Vehicle finance charges	391	565	512	–30.8	–23.6
Maintenance and repairs	801	1,018	1,052	–21.3	–23.9
Vehicle insurance	1,002	1,033	799	–3.0	25.4
Vehicle rent, lease, license, other	674	331	292	103.6	130.8
Public transportation	**505**	**593**	**522**	**–14.8**	**–3.3**
HEALTH CARE	**2,200**	**2,104**	**2,063**	**4.6**	**6.6**
Health insurance	976	768	653	27.1	49.5
Medical services	699	875	1,011	–20.1	–30.9
Drugs	407	311	298	30.9	36.6
Medical supplies	118	149	101	–20.8	16.8
ENTERTAINMENT	**2,231**	**2,590**	**2,083**	**–13.9**	**7.1**
Fees and admissions	637	577	689	10.4	–7.5
Television, radios, sound equipment	696	780	600	–10.8	16.0
Pets, toys, and playground equipment	384	540	375	–28.9	2.4
Other supplies, equipment, and services	514	694	419	–25.9	22.7
PERSONAL CARE PRODUCTS, SERVICES	**682**	**630**	**643**	**8.3**	**6.1**
READING	**178**	**242**	**267**	**–26.4**	**–33.3**
EDUCATION	**1,146**	**964**	**822**	**18.9**	**39.4**
TOBACCO PRODUCTS AND SMOKING SUPPLIES	**376**	**476**	**540**	**–21.0**	**–30.4**
MISCELLANEOUS	**927**	**1,445**	**961**	**–35.8**	**–3.5**
CASH CONTRIBUTIONS	**1,537**	**1,711**	**1,790**	**–10.2**	**–14.1**
PERSONAL INSURANCE, PENSIONS	**4,795**	**5,068**	**4,767**	**–5.4**	**0.6**
Life and other personal insurance	549	731	804	–24.9	–31.7
Pensions and Social Security	4,246	4,337	3,963	–2.1	7.1
PERSONAL TAXES	**4,740**	**5,362**	**5,093**	**–11.6**	**–6.9**
Federal income taxes	3,707	4,217	3,988	–12.1	–7.0
State and local income taxes	848	1,020	971	–16.9	–12.7
Other taxes	185	125	136	48.0	36.0
GIFTS**	**1,724**	**2,337**	**1,797**	**–26.2**	**–4.1**

* This figure does not include the amount paid for mortgage principle, which is considered an asset.
** Expenditures on gifts are also included in the preceding product and service categories.
Note: The Bureau of Labor Statistics uses consumer unit rather than household as the sampling unit in the Consumer Expenditure Survey.
For the definition of consumer unit, see the glossary. Average annual spending total does not include the amount spent on personal taxes.
Source: Bureau of Labor Statistics, Consumer Expenditure Surveys, Internet site http://www.bls.gov/cex/; calculations by New Strategist

Table 9.7 Spending of Householders Aged 55 to 64, 1984, 1990, and 2000

(number of consumer units (CU) headed by people aged 55 to 64, and average annual spending on products and services, 1984, 1990, and 2000; percent change, 1990–00 and 1984–00; in 2000 dollars)

	2000	1990	1984	percent change 1990–00	percent change 1984–00
Number of consumer units (in 000s)	14,161	12,162	13,343	16.4%	6.1%
Average annual spending	$39,340	$38,555	$38,783	2.0	1.4
FOOD	**$5,168**	**$5,837**	**$5,743**	**–11.5%**	**–10.0%**
Food at home	3,071	3,427	3,509	–10.4	–12.5
Cereals and bakery products	441	498	462	–11.4	–4.5
Cereals and cereal products	140	170	126	–17.6	11.1
Bakery products	301	328	336	–8.2	–10.4
Meats, poultry, fish, and eggs	832	984	1,037	–15.4	–19.8
Beef	243	304	343	–20.1	–29.2
Pork	186	202	217	–7.9	–14.3
Other meats	99	152	151	–34.9	–34.4
Poultry	146	165	156	–11.5	–6.4
Fish and seafood	115	119	99	–3.4	16.2
Eggs	43	43	70	0.0	–38.6
Dairy products	321	383	436	–16.2	–26.4
Fresh milk and cream	126	169	209	–25.4	–39.7
Other dairy products	195	215	227	–9.3	–14.1
Fruits and vegetables	558	589	600	–5.3	–7.0
Fresh fruits	185	204	189	–9.3	–2.1
Fresh vegetables	173	173	182	0.0	–4.9
Processed fruits	115	116	126	–0.9	–8.7
Processed vegetables	87	95	103	–8.4	–15.5
Other food at home	918	971	902	–5.5	1.8
Sugar and other sweets	115	125	136	–8.0	–15.4
Fats and oils	90	95	104	–5.3	–13.5
Miscellaneous foods	398	399	356	–0.3	11.8
Nonalcoholic beverages	263	285	305	–7.7	–13.8
Food prepared by CU, out-of-town trips	52	67	70	–22.4	–25.7
Food away from home	**2,097**	**2,411**	**2,234**	**–13.0**	**–6.1**
ALCOHOLIC BEVERAGES	**371**	**335**	**492**	**10.7**	**–24.6**
HOUSING	**12,362**	**11,145**	**11,147**	**10.9**	**10.9**
Shelter	**6,587**	**5,560**	**5,171**	**18.5**	**27.4**
Owned dwellings*	4,780	3,784	3,389	26.3	41.0
Mortgage interest and charges	2,278	1,646	1,270	38.4	79.4
Property taxes	1,462	1,120	1,188	30.5	23.1
Maintenance, repairs, insurance, other expenses	1,040	1,017	931	2.3	11.7
Rented dwellings	1,123	1,150	1,047	–2.3	7.3
Other lodging	685	627	734	9.3	–6.7
Utilities, fuels, public services	**2,756**	**2,846**	**3,112**	**–3.2**	**–11.4**
Natural gas	341	383	646	–11.0	–47.2
Electricity	1,048	1,209	1,180	–13.3	–11.2
Fuel oil and other fuels	113	170	278	–33.5	–59.4
Telephone	909	777	747	17.0	21.7
Water and other public services	345	306	259	12.7	33.2
Household services	**542**	**509**	**438**	**6.5**	**23.7**
Personal services	93	75	65	24.0	43.1
Other household services	449	432	373	3.9	20.4
Housekeeping supplies	**585**	**643**	**568**	**–9.0**	**3.0**
Laundry and cleaning supplies	184	165	157	11.5	17.2
Other household products	262	296	252	–11.5	4.0
Postage and stationery	139	182	157	–23.6	–11.5
Household furnishings, equipment	**1,891**	**1,588**	**1,860**	**19.1**	**1.7**
Household textiles	125	161	146	–22.4	–14.4

(continued)

(continued from previous page)

	2000	1990	1984	percent change 1990–00	percent change 1984–00
Furniture	$361	$487	$469	−25.9%	−23.0%
Floor coverings	56	120	280	−53.3	−80.0
Major appliances	221	248	280	−10.9	−21.1
Small appliances, misc. houseware	106	119	131	−10.9	−19.1
Miscellaneous household equipment	1,022	455	554	124.6	84.5
APPAREL AND SERVICES	**1,694**	**2,055**	**2,216**	**−17.6**	**−23.6**
Men and boys	**395**	**472**	**527**	**−16.3**	**−25.0**
Men, aged 16 or older	352	428	469	−17.8	−24.9
Boys, aged 2 to 15	42	45	58	−6.7	−27.6
Women and girls	**687**	**909**	**943**	**−24.4**	**−27.1**
Women, aged 16 or older	630	870	887	−27.6	−29.0
Girls, aged 2 to 15	57	40	56	42.5	1.8
Children under age 2	**53**	**67**	**50**	**−20.9**	**6.0**
Footwear	**300**	**286**	**346**	**4.9**	**−13.3**
Other apparel products, services	**259**	**320**	**351**	**−19.1**	**−26.2**
TRANSPORTATION	**7,842**	**6,979**	**7,445**	**12.4**	**5.3**
Vehicle purchases	**3,623**	**2,653**	**3,006**	**36.6**	**20.5**
Cars and trucks, new	2,097	1,507	1,939	39.2	8.1
Cars and trucks, used	1,508	1,124	1,057	34.2	42.7
Other vehicles	–	21	8	–	–
Gasoline and motor oil	**1,349**	**1,494**	**1,881**	**−9.7**	**−28.3**
Other vehicle expenses	**2,375**	**2,287**	**2,047**	**3.8**	**16.0**
Vehicle finance charges	349	345	312	1.2	11.9
Maintenance and repairs	672	866	842	−22.4	−20.2
Vehicle insurance	796	851	675	−6.5	17.9
Vehicle rent, lease, license, other	559	224	217	149.6	157.6
Public transportation	**495**	**545**	**510**	**−9.2**	**−2.9**
HEALTH CARE	**2,508**	**2,360**	**2,080**	**6.3**	**20.6**
Health insurance	1,132	922	751	22.8	50.7
Medical services	721	862	870	−16.4	−17.1
Drugs	538	448	366	20.1	47.0
Medical supplies	117	126	93	−7.1	25.8
ENTERTAINMENT	**1,955**	**1,986**	**1,767**	**−1.6**	**10.6**
Fees and admissions	509	481	517	5.8	−1.5
Television, radios, sound equipment	581	514	461	13.0	26.0
Pets, toys, and playground equipment	358	336	285	6.5	25.6
Other supplies, equipment, and services	507	655	504	−22.6	0.6
PERSONAL CARE PRODUCTS, SERVICES	**569**	**543**	**540**	**4.8**	**5.4**
READING	**179**	**215**	**234**	**−16.7**	**−23.5**
EDUCATION	**380**	**495**	**411**	**−23.2**	**−7.5**
TOBACCO PRODUCTS AND SMOKING SUPPLIES	**349**	**430**	**438**	**−18.8**	**−20.3**
MISCELLANEOUS	**824**	**1,091**	**769**	**−24.5**	**7.2**
CASH CONTRIBUTIONS	**1,301**	**1,190**	**1,449**	**9.3**	**−10.2**
PERSONAL INSURANCE, PENSIONS	**3,838**	**3,897**	**4,054**	**−1.5**	**−5.3**
Life and other personal insurance	587	615	766	−4.6	−23.4
Pensions and Social Security	3,252	3,282	3,288	−0.9	−1.1
PERSONAL TAXES	**3,999**	**4,621**	**4,051**	**−13.5**	**−1.3**
Federal income taxes	3,062	3,665	3,078	−16.5	−0.5
State and local income taxes	702	830	799	−15.4	−12.1
Other taxes	235	125	174	88.0	35.1
GIFTS**	**1,345**	**1,505**	**1,606**	**−10.6**	**−16.3**

* This figure does not include the amount paid for mortgage principle, which is considered an asset.
** Expenditures on gifts are also included in the preceding product and service categories.
Note: The Bureau of Labor Statistics uses consumer unit rather than household as the sampling unit in the Consumer Expenditure Survey. For the definition of consumer unit, see the glossary. Average annual spending total does not include the amount spent on personal taxes; (–) means sample is too small to make a reliable estimate.
Source: Bureau of Labor Statistics, Consumer Expenditure Surveys, Internetsite http://www.bls.gov/cex/; calculations by New Strategist

Table 9.8 Spending of Householders Aged 65 or Older, 1984, 1990, and 2000

(number of consumer units (CU) headed by people aged 65 or older, and average annual spending on products and services, 1984, 1990, and 2000; percent change, 1990–00 and 1984–00; in 2000 dollars)

	2000	1990	1984	percent change 1990–00	percent change 1984–00
Number of consumer units (in 000s)	22,155	20,079	17,866	10.3%	24.0%
Average annual spending	$26,533	$24,441	$23,145	8.6	14.6
FOOD	**$3,652**	**$3,855**	**$3,721**	**–5.3%**	**–1.9%**
Food at home	2,448	2,526	2,522	–3.1	–2.9
Cereals and bakery products	376	395	351	–4.8	7.1
Cereals and cereal products	123	128	107	–3.9	15.0
Bakery products	253	267	244	–5.2	3.7
Meats, poultry, fish, and eggs	626	681	739	–8.1	–15.3
Beef	182	223	242	–18.4	–24.8
Pork	143	136	156	5.1	–8.3
Other meats	79	94	92	–16.0	–14.1
Poultry	108	115	105	–6.1	2.9
Fish and seafood	84	82	97	2.4	–13.4
Eggs	30	33	48	–9.1	–37.5
Dairy products	275	300	315	–8.3	–12.7
Fresh milk and cream	112	149	157	–24.8	–28.7
Other dairy products	163	152	159	7.2	2.5
Fruits and vegetables	495	491	460	0.8	7.6
Fresh fruits	169	165	149	2.4	13.4
Fresh vegetables	146	134	130	9.0	12.3
Processed fruits	109	119	108	–8.4	0.9
Processed vegetables	71	75	72	–5.3	–1.4
Other food at home	676	656	627	3.0	7.8
Sugar and other sweets	93	99	101	–6.1	–7.9
Fats and oils	74	75	73	–1.3	1.4
Miscellaneous foods	304	269	229	13.0	32.8
Nonalcoholic beverages	176	187	223	–5.9	–21.1
Food prepared by CU, out-of-town trips	29	26	30	11.5	–3.3
Food away from home	**1,205**	**1,329**	**1,198**	**–9.3**	**0.6**
ALCOHOLIC BEVERAGES	**211**	**166**	**201**	**27.1**	**5.0**
HOUSING	**8,759**	**7,938**	**7,533**	**10.3**	**16.3**
Shelter	**4,597**	**3,975**	**3,419**	**15.6**	**34.5**
Owned dwellings*	3,043	2,477	1,874	22.9	62.4
Mortgage interest and charges	793	484	321	63.8	147.0
Property taxes	1,175	1,001	774	17.4	51.8
Maintenance, repairs, insurance, other expenses	1,075	992	779	8.4	38.0
Rented dwellings	1,140	1,105	1,070	3.2	6.5
Other lodging	413	394	475	4.8	–13.1
Utilities, fuels, public services	**2,198**	**2,236**	**2,437**	**–1.7**	**–9.8**
Natural gas	310	336	482	–7.7	–35.7
Electricity	834	893	867	–6.6	–3.8
Fuel oil and other fuels	137	181	360	–24.3	–61.9
Telephone	620	569	516	9.0	20.2
Water and other public services	298	257	212	16.0	40.6
Household services	**661**	**519**	**471**	**27.4**	**40.3**
Personal services	215	130	60	65.4	258.3
Other household services	446	389	412	14.7	8.3
Housekeeping supplies	**421**	**428**	**409**	**–1.6**	**2.9**
Laundry and cleaning supplies	95	104	99	–8.7	–4.0
Other household products	196	170	164	15.3	19.5
Postage and stationery	130	154	145	–15.6	–10.3
Household furnishings, equipment	**882**	**780**	**796**	**13.1**	**10.8**
Household textiles	73	87	128	–16.1	–43.0

(continued)

(continued from previous page)

	2000	1990	1984	percent change 1990–00	percent change 1984–00
Furniture	$201	$161	$164	24.8%	22.6%
Floor coverings	38	72	70	–47.2	–45.7
Major appliances	160	137	152	16.8	5.3
Small appliances, misc. houseware	54	69	67	–21.7	–19.4
Miscellaneous household equipment	356	254	215	40.2	65.6
APPAREL AND SERVICES	**925**	**1,012**	**1,165**	**–8.6**	**–20.6**
Men and boys	**196**	**174**	**252**	**12.6**	**–22.2**
Men, aged 16 or older	177	155	239	14.2	–25.9
Boys, aged 2 to 15	19	18	14	5.6	35.7
Women and girls	**400**	**530**	**587**	**–24.5**	**–31.9**
Women, aged 16 or older	378	503	562	–24.9	–32.7
Girls, aged 2 to 15	22	28	25	–21.4	–12.0
Children under age 2	**20**	**21**	**21**	**–4.8**	**–4.8**
Footwear	**159**	**150**	**147**	**6.0**	**8.2**
Other apparel products, services	**150**	**136**	**156**	**10.3**	**–3.8**
TRANSPORTATION	**4,397**	**3,798**	**3,923**	**15.8**	**12.1**
Vehicle purchases	**1,904**	**1,394**	**1,364**	**36.6**	**39.6**
Cars and trucks, new	1,076	845	916	27.3	17.5
Cars and trucks, used	823	548	438	50.2	87.9
Other vehicles	–	0	11	–	–
Gasoline and motor oil	**735**	**816**	**1,035**	**–9.9**	**–29.0**
Other vehicle expenses	**1,374**	**1,283**	**1,137**	**7.1**	**20.8**
Vehicle finance charges	115	121	96	–5.0	19.8
Maintenance and repairs	441	507	514	–13.0	–14.2
Vehicle insurance	557	519	418	7.3	33.3
Vehicle rent, lease, license, other	260	134	108	94.0	140.7
Public transportation	**385**	**306**	**387**	**25.8**	**–0.5**
HEALTH CARE	**3,247**	**2,909**	**2,474**	**11.6**	**31.2**
Health insurance	1,619	1,304	1,029	24.2	57.3
Medical services	672	875	810	–23.2	–17.0
Drugs	822	626	462	31.3	77.9
Medical supplies	133	105	173	26.7	–23.1
ENTERTAINMENT	**1,069**	**922**	**839**	**15.9**	**27.4**
Fees and admissions	319	332	303	–3.9	5.3
Television, radios, sound equipment	399	320	290	24.7	37.6
Pets, toys, and playground equipment	187	169	139	10.7	34.5
Other supplies, equipment, and services	164	101	107	62.4	53.3
PERSONAL CARE PRODUCTS, SERVICES	**426**	**353**	**359**	**20.7**	**18.7**
READING	**148**	**181**	**178**	**–18.2**	**–16.9**
EDUCATION	**108**	**71**	**136**	**52.1**	**–20.6**
TOBACCO PRODUCTS AND SMOKING SUPPLIES	**163**	**207**	**211**	**–21.3**	**–22.7**
MISCELLANEOUS	**661**	**730**	**341**	**–9.5**	**93.8**
CASH CONTRIBUTIONS	**1,828**	**1,352**	**1,207**	**35.2**	**51.4**
PERSONAL INSURANCE, PENSIONS	**939**	**946**	**856**	**–0.7**	**9.7**
Life and other personal insurance	378	328	288	15.2	31.3
Pensions and Social Security	561	617	567	–9.1	–1.1
PERSONAL TAXES	**1,330**	**1,498**	**1,459**	**–11.2**	**–8.8**
Federal income taxes	979	1,161	1,117	–15.7	–12.4
State and local income taxes	145	221	217	–34.4	–33.2
Other taxes	205	117	126	75.2	62.7
GIFTS**	**866**	**860**	**840**	**0.7**	**3.1**

* This figure does not include the amount paid for mortgage principle, which is considered an asset.

** Expenditures on gifts are also included in the preceding product and service categories.

Note: The Bureau of Labor Statistics uses consumer unit rather than household as the sampling unit in the Consumer Expenditure Survey. For the definition of consumer unit, see the glossary. Average annual spending total does not include the amount spent on personal taxes; (–) means sample is too small to make a reliable estimate.

Source: Bureau of Labor Statistics, Consumer Expenditure Surveys, Internet site http://www.bls.gov/cex/; calculations by New Strategist

Table 9.9 Spending by Households Headed by Retirees, 1984, 1990, and 2000

(number of consumer units (CU) headed by retirees, and average annual spending on products and services, 1984, 1990, and 2000; percent change, 1990–00 and 1984–00; in 2000 dollars)

	2000	1990	1984	percent change 1990–00	1984–00
Number of consumer units (in 000s)	19,499	16,253	14,491	20.0%	34.6%
Average annual spending	$25,938	$23,909	$23,199	8.5	11.8
FOOD	**$3,686**	**$3,910**	**$3,877**	**–5.7%**	**–4.9%**
Food at home	2,453	2,644	2,645	–7.2	–7.3
Cereals and bakery products	374	408	371	–8.3	0.8
Cereals and cereal products	120	132	111	–9.1	8.1
Bakery products	254	277	260	–8.3	–2.3
Meats, poultry, fish, and eggs	636	719	757	–11.5	–16.0
Beef	185	232	267	–20.3	–30.7
Pork	145	152	152	–4.6	–4.6
Other meats	79	107	101	–26.2	–21.8
Poultry	108	115	106	–6.1	1.9
Fish and seafood	87	78	81	11.5	7.4
Eggs	31	37	51	–16.2	–39.2
Dairy products	277	325	328	–14.8	–15.5
Fresh milk and cream	113	161	171	–29.8	–33.9
Other dairy products	164	165	157	–0.6	4.5
Fruits and vegetables	487	485	486	0.4	0.2
Fresh fruits	163	157	154	3.8	5.8
Fresh vegetables	146	138	138	5.8	5.8
Processed fruits	107	113	113	–5.3	–5.3
Processed vegetables	69	76	81	–9.2	–14.8
Other food at home	680	708	665	–4.0	2.3
Sugar and other sweets	96	109	114	–11.9	–15.8
Fats and oils	73	82	76	–11.0	–3.9
Miscellaneous foods	303	285	245	6.3	23.7
Nonalcoholic beverages	177	199	227	–11.1	–22.0
Food prepared by CU, out-of-town trips	30	33	38	–9.1	–21.1
Food away from home	1,233	1,266	1,231	–2.6	0.2
ALCOHOLIC BEVERAGES	**226**	**181**	**207**	**24.9**	**9.2**
HOUSING	**8,663**	**7,736**	**7,637**	**12.0**	**13.4**
Shelter	4,413	3,810	3,500	15.8	26.1
Owned dwellings*	2,937	2,402	2,055	22.3	42.9
Mortgage interest and charges	754	431	371	74.9	103.2
Property taxes	1,136	979	812	16.0	39.9
Maintenance, repairs, insurance, other expenses	1,047	992	872	5.5	20.1
Rented dwellings	1,098	1,045	1,029	5.1	6.7
Other lodging	379	362	416	4.7	–8.9
Utilities, fuels, public services	2,179	2,219	2,426	–1.8	–10.2
Natural gas	309	323	479	–4.3	–35.5
Electricity	835	896	882	–6.8	–5.3
Fuel oil and other fuels	124	186	335	–33.3	–63.0
Telephone	613	560	517	9.5	18.6
Water and other public services	297	257	214	15.6	38.8
Household services	574	462	396	24.2	44.9
Personal services	194	129	56	50.4	246.4
Other household services	380	333	340	14.1	11.8
Housekeeping supplies	436	428	438	1.9	–0.5
Laundry and cleaning supplies	98	108	108	–9.3	–9.3
Other household products	199	175	176	13.7	13.1
Postage and stationery	139	144	154	–3.5	–9.7
Household furnishings, equipment	1,060	818	877	29.6	20.9
Household textiles	81	79	118	2.5	–31.4

(continued)

(continued from previous page)

	2000	1990	1984	percent change 1990–00	percent change 1984–00
Furniture	$204	$209	$214	–2.4%	–4.7%
Floor coverings	33	58	75	–43.1	–56.0
Major appliances	177	146	179	21.2	–1.1
Small appliances, misc. houseware	57	65	73	–12.3	–21.9
Miscellaneous household equipment	508	260	220	95.4	130.9
APPAREL AND SERVICES	**926**	**934**	**1,154**	**–0.9**	**–19.8**
Men and boys	**180**	**188**	**282**	**–4.3**	**–36.2**
Men, aged 16 or older	161	167	260	–3.6	–38.1
Boys, aged 2 to 15	19	21	22	–9.5	–13.6
Women and girls	**433**	**445**	**489**	**–2.7**	**–11.5**
Women, aged 16 or older	402	420	456	–4.3	–11.8
Girls, aged 2 to 15	30	26	33	15.4	–9.1
Children under age 2	**23**	**24**	**31**	**–4.2**	**–25.8**
Footwear	**158**	**158**	**179**	**0.0**	**–11.7**
Other apparel products, services	**132**	**119**	**172**	**10.9**	**–23.3**
TRANSPORTATION	**4,399**	**4,142**	**3,989**	**6.2**	**10.3**
Vehicle purchases	**1,866**	**1,722**	**1,351**	**8.4**	**38.1**
Cars and trucks, new	982	1,236	1,006	–20.6	–2.4
Cars and trucks, used	884	478	331	84.9	167.1
Other vehicles	–	8	13	–	–
Gasoline and motor oil	**761**	**843**	**1,086**	**–9.7**	**–29.9**
Other vehicle expenses	**1,404**	**1,274**	**1,200**	**10.2**	**17.0**
Vehicle finance charges	130	119	106	9.2	22.6
Maintenance and repairs	452	487	524	–7.2	–13.7
Vehicle insurance	573	539	457	6.3	25.4
Vehicle rent, lease, license, other	249	130	113	91.5	120.4
Public transportation	**368**	**303**	**353**	**21.5**	**4.2**
HEALTH CARE	**3,172**	**2,711**	**2,546**	**17.0**	**24.6**
Health insurance	1,580	1,264	1,006	25.0	57.1
Medical services	668	773	928	–13.6	–28.0
Drugs	793	570	451	39.1	75.8
Medical supplies	130	103	161	26.2	–19.3
ENTERTAINMENT	**1,105**	**946**	**810**	**16.8**	**36.4**
Fees and admissions	340	308	275	10.4	23.6
Television, radios, sound equipment	398	336	270	18.5	47.4
Pets, toys, and playground equipment	191	187	148	2.1	29.1
Other supplies, equipment, and services	176	115	116	53.0	51.7
PERSONAL CARE PRODUCTS, SERVICES	**427**	**323**	**378**	**32.2**	**13.0**
READING	**142**	**171**	**181**	**–17.0**	**–21.5**
EDUCATION	**123**	**84**	**139**	**46.4**	**–11.5**
TOBACCO PRODUCTS AND SMOKING SUPPLIES	**179**	**216**	**239**	**–17.1**	**–25.1**
MISCELLANEOUS	**609**	**698**	**360**	**–12.8**	**69.2**
CASH CONTRIBUTIONS	**1,681**	**1,279**	**1,059**	**31.4**	**58.7**
PERSONAL INSURANCE, PENSIONS	**600**	**574**	**625**	**4.5**	**–4.0**
Life and other personal insurance	338	260	272	30.0	24.3
Pensions and Social Security	262	315	353	–16.8	–25.8
PERSONAL TAXES	**885**	**1,353**	**1,110**	**–34.6**	**–20.3**
Federal income taxes	577	1,050	802	–45.0	–28.1
State and local income taxes	98	198	156	–50.5	–37.2
Other taxes	209	105	152	99.0	37.5
GIFTS**	**801**	**780**	**887**	**2.7**	**–9.7**

* This figure does not include the amount paid for mortgage principle, which is considered an asset.
** Expenditures on gifts are also included in the preceding product and service categories.
Note: The Bureau of Labor Statistics uses consumer unit rather than household as the sampling unit in the Consumer Expenditure Survey. For the definition of consumer unit, see the glossary. Average annual spending total does not include the amount spent on personal taxes.
Source: Bureau of Labor Statistics, Consumer Expenditure Surveys, Internet site http://www.bls.gov/cex/; calculations by New Strategist

Black Households Saw the Biggest Gain

Between 1984 and 2000, average annual spending by black households rose 16 percent, after adjusting for inflation. The rise was much greater than the 4 percent increase for other households during those years.

Black spending rose substantially because black householders have made significant gains in education and income over the past few decades. While blacks still spend much less than whites ($28,152 versus $39,406 in 2000), the gap is narrowing. In 1984, the average black household spent only 64 percent as much as the average white household. By 2000, blacks were spending 71 percent as much as whites. Blacks made these gains although a much smaller share of black households are headed by married couples, the most affluent household type.

The Bureau of Labor Statistics has collected comparable spending data for Hispanics only since 1994. Between 1994 and 2000, the spending of Hispanic households rose 7 percent, after adjusting for inflation. The average Hispanic household spent $32,735 in 2000, 83 percent as much as white households.

Blacks are narrowing the gap

(average annual spending of households by race of householder, 1984 and 2000; in 2000 dollars)

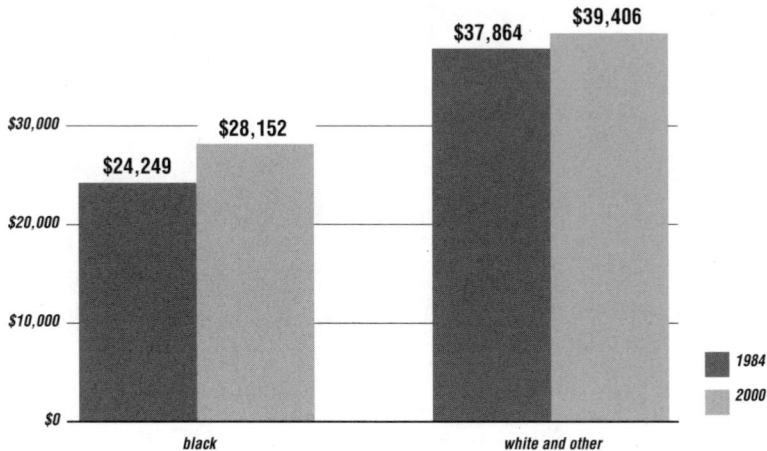

Table 9.10 Spending by Black Households, 1984, 1990 and 2000

(number of consumer units (CU) headed by blacks, and average annual spending on products and services, 1984, 1990, and 2000; percent change, 1990–00 and 1984–00; in 2000 dollars)

	2000	1990	1984	percent change 1990–00	percent change 1984–00
Number of consumer units (in 000s)	13,230	11,128	9,389	18.9%	40.9%
Average annual spending	$28,152	$25,211	$24,249	11.7	16.1
FOOD	**$4,095**	**$4,124**	**$3,807**	**–0.7%**	**7.6%**
Food at home	**2,691**	**2,802**	**2,612**	**–4.0**	**3.0**
Cereals and bakery products	393	381	341	3.1	15.2
Cereals and cereal products	159	155	133	2.6	19.5
Bakery products	234	225	210	4.0	11.4
Meats, poultry, fish, and eggs	909	960	1,004	–5.3	–9.5
Beef	236	277	287	–14.8	–17.8
Pork	199	231	227	–13.9	–12.3
Other meats	106	123	118	–13.8	–10.2
Poultry	185	175	177	5.7	4.5
Fish and seafood	139	111	133	25.2	4.5
Eggs	43	45	63	–4.4	–31.7
Dairy products	245	258	278	–5.0	–11.9
Fresh milk and cream	102	125	162	–18.4	–37.0
Other dairy products	143	133	116	7.5	23.3
Fruits and vegetables	454	480	424	–5.4	7.1
Fresh fruits	131	138	121	–5.1	8.3
Fresh vegetables	129	133	128	–3.0	0.8
Processed fruits	118	121	98	–2.5	20.4
Processed vegetables	76	86	78	–11.6	–2.6
Other food at home	691	723	555	–4.4	24.5
Sugar and other sweets	89	99	86	–10.1	3.5
Fats and oils	83	84	78	–1.2	6.4
Miscellaneous foods	316	325	201	–2.8	57.2
Nonalcoholic beverages	186	207	191	–10.1	–2.6
Food prepared by CU, out-of-town trips	17	8	10	112.5	70.0
Food away from home	**1,404**	**1,321**	**1,193**	**6.3**	**17.7**
ALCOHOLIC BEVERAGES	**211**	**213**	**290**	**–0.9**	**–27.2**
HOUSING	**9,906**	**8,283**	**7,902**	**19.6**	**25.4**
Shelter	**5,678**	**4,478**	**3,994**	**26.8**	**42.2**
Owned dwellings*	2,607	1,892	1,762	37.8	48.0
Mortgage interest and charges	1,574	1,299	1,190	21.2	32.3
Property taxes	640	225	275	184.4	132.7
Maintenance, repairs, insurance, other expenses	393	369	295	6.5	33.2
Rented dwellings	2,843	2,466	2,030	15.3	40.0
Other lodging	227	119	204	90.8	11.3
Utilities, fuels, public services	**2,571**	**2,333**	**2,572**	**10.2**	**0.0**
Natural gas	342	368	527	–7.1	–35.1
Electricity	938	876	935	7.1	0.3
Fuel oil and other fuels	43	63	149	–31.7	–71.1
Telephone	986	822	766	20.0	28.7
Water and other public services	261	204	197	27.9	32.5
Household services	**468**	**271**	**264**	**72.7**	**77.3**
Personal services	292	163	157	79.1	86.0
Other household services	176	107	104	64.5	69.2
Housekeeping supplies	**303**	**391**	**320**	**–22.5**	**–5.3**
Laundry and cleaning supplies	126	153	134	–17.6	–6.0
Other household products	126	144	113	–12.5	11.5
Postage and stationery	51	95	73	–46.3	–30.1
Household furnishings, equipment	**887**	**809**	**751**	**9.6**	**18.1**
Household textiles	57	62	70	–8.1	–18.6

(continued)

(continued from previous page)

	2000	1990	1984	percent change 1990–00	1984–00
Furniture	$283	$264	$252	7.2%	12.3%
Floor coverings	25	36	25	–30.6	0.0
Major appliances	108	145	161	–25.5	–32.9
Small appliances, misc. houseware	36	46	70	–21.7	–48.6
Miscellaneous household equipment	377	257	174	46.7	116.7
APPAREL AND SERVICES	**1,695**	**1,855**	**1,860**	**–8.6**	**–8.9**
Men and boys	**390**	**462**	**403**	**–15.6**	**–3.2**
Men, aged 16 or older	245	314	312	–22.0	–21.5
Boys, aged 2 to 15	145	149	89	–2.7	62.9
Women and girls	**604**	**692**	**739**	**–12.7**	**–18.3**
Women, aged 16 or older	473	578	625	–18.2	–24.3
Girls, aged 2 to 15	131	113	114	15.9	14.9
Children under age 2	**89**	**94**	**65**	**–5.3**	**36.9**
Footwear	**352**	**306**	**333**	**15.0**	**5.7**
Other apparel products, services	**260**	**300**	**322**	**–13.3**	**–19.3**
TRANSPORTATION	**5,214**	**4,228**	**4,488**	**23.3**	**16.2**
Vehicle purchases	**2,285**	**1,511**	**1,444**	**51.2**	**58.2**
Cars and trucks, new	869	653	655	33.1	32.7
Cars and trucks, used	1,414	858	774	64.8	82.7
Other vehicles	–	0	15	–	–
Gasoline and motor oil	**956**	**949**	**1,402**	**0.7**	**–31.8**
Other vehicle expenses	**1,705**	**1,464**	**1,331**	**16.5**	**28.1**
Vehicle finance charges	290	289	239	0.3	21.3
Maintenance and repairs	452	522	590	–13.4	–23.4
Vehicle insurance	634	487	376	30.2	68.6
Vehicle rent, lease, license, other	330	165	124	100.0	166.1
Public transportation	**268**	**304**	**313**	**–11.8**	**–14.4**
HEALTH CARE	**1,107**	**1,028**	**1,021**	**7.7**	**8.4**
Health insurance	639	452	426	41.4	50.0
Medical services	191	343	360	–44.3	–46.9
Drugs	235	179	192	31.3	22.4
Medical supplies	41	54	43	–24.1	–4.7
ENTERTAINMENT	**1,014**	**835**	**824**	**21.4**	**23.1**
Fees and admissions	181	182	179	–0.5	1.1
Television, radios, sound equipment	567	440	361	28.9	57.1
Pets, toys, and playground equipment	159	154	138	3.2	15.2
Other supplies, equipment, and services	107	61	148	75.4	–27.7
PERSONAL CARE PRODUCTS, SERVICES	**627**	**397**	**383**	**57.9**	**63.7**
READING	**72**	**95**	**111**	**–24.2**	**–35.1**
EDUCATION	**383**	**274**	**336**	**39.8**	**14.0**
TOBACCO PRODUCTS AND SMOKING SUPPLIES	**243**	**283**	**303**	**–14.1**	**–19.8**
MISCELLANEOUS	**572**	**621**	**520**	**–7.9**	**10.0**
CASH CONTRIBUTIONS	**700**	**709**	**519**	**–1.3**	**34.9**
PERSONAL INSURANCE, PENSIONS	**2,313**	**2,267**	**1,886**	**2.0**	**22.6**
Life and other personal insurance	358	385	419	–7.0	–14.6
Pensions and Social Security	1,955	1,883	1,467	3.8	33.3
PERSONAL TAXES	**1,626**	**2,452**	**2,150**	**–33.7**	**–24.4**
Federal income taxes	1,240	1,856	1,628	–33.2	–23.8
State and local income taxes	338	561	477	–39.8	–29.1
Other taxes	48	34	43	41.2	11.6
GIFTS**	**571**	**519**	**592**	**10.0**	**–3.5**

* This figure does not include the amount paid for mortgage principle, which is considered an asset.
** Expenditures on gifts are also included in the preceding product and service categories.
Note: The Bureau of Labor Statistics uses consumer unit rather than household as the sampling unit in the Consumer Expenditure Survey.
For the definition of consumer unit, see the glossary. Average annual spending total does not include the amount spent on personal taxes;
(–) means sample is too small to make a reliable estimate.
Source: Bureau of Labor Statistics, Consumer Expenditure Surveys, Internet site http://www.bls.gov/cex/; calculations by New Strategist

Table 9.11 Spending by White and Other Households, 1984, 1990 and 2000

(number of consumer units (CU) headed by whites and others, and average annual spending on products and services, 1984, 1990, and 2000; percent change, 1990–00 and 1984–00; in 2000 dollars)

	2000	1990	1984	percent change 1990–00	percent change 1984–00
Number of consumer units (in 000s)	96,137	85,840	80,834	12.0%	18.9%
Average annual spending	$39,406	$38,946	$37,864	1.2	4.1
FOOD	**$5,304**	**$5,846**	**$5,660**	**–9.3%**	**–6.3%**
Food at home	**3,066**	**3,331**	**3,348**	**–8.0**	**–8.4**
Cereals and bakery products	462	498	447	–7.2	3.4
Cereals and cereal products	156	171	141	–8.8	10.6
Bakery products	306	327	307	–6.4	–0.3
Meats, poultry, fish, and eggs	780	871	966	–10.4	–19.3
Beef	239	289	336	–17.3	–28.9
Pork	163	167	192	–2.4	–15.1
Other meats	100	132	136	–24.2	–26.5
Poultry	140	138	136	1.4	2.9
Fish and seafood	106	108	108	–1.9	–1.9
Eggs	33	38	58	–13.2	–43.1
Dairy products	336	404	438	–16.8	–23.3
Fresh milk and cream	135	191	217	–29.3	–37.8
Other dairy products	200	213	219	–6.1	–8.7
Fruits and vegetables	530	544	532	–2.6	–0.4
Fresh fruits	168	170	159	–1.2	5.7
Fresh vegetables	163	158	154	3.2	5.8
Processed fruits	115	123	123	–6.5	–6.5
Processed vegetables	85	92	96	–7.6	–11.5
Other food at home	959	1,013	912	–5.3	5.2
Sugar and other sweets	121	126	128	–4.0	–5.5
Fats and oils	83	90	94	–7.8	–11.7
Miscellaneous foods	454	456	381	–0.4	19.2
Nonalcoholic beverages	258	290	308	–11.0	–16.2
Food prepared by CU, out-of-town trips	43	51	53	–15.7	–18.9
Food away from home	**2,238**	**2,516**	**2,312**	**–11.0**	**–3.2**
ALCOHOLIC BEVERAGES	**394**	**407**	**477**	**–3.2**	**–17.4**
HOUSING	**12,651**	**11,875**	**11,434**	**6.5**	**10.6**
Shelter	**7,312**	**6,617**	**5,990**	**10.5**	**22.1**
Owned dwellings*	4,877	4,150	3,610	17.5	35.1
Mortgage interest and charges	2,785	2,535	2,174	9.9	28.1
Property taxes	1,207	860	747	40.3	61.6
Maintenance, repairs, insurance, other expenses	884	755	688	17.1	28.5
Rented dwellings	1,923	1,962	1,744	–2.0	10.3
Other lodging	512	505	636	1.4	–19.5
Utilities, fuels, public services	**2,478**	**2,511**	**2,731**	**–1.3**	**–9.3**
Natural gas	303	319	487	–5.0	–37.8
Electricity	908	1,014	1,056	–10.5	–14.0
Fuel oil and other fuels	104	141	240	–26.2	–56.7
Telephone	862	775	716	11.2	20.4
Water and other public services	301	261	232	15.3	29.7
Household services	**714**	**630**	**552**	**13.3**	**29.3**
Personal services	331	304	219	8.9	51.1
Other household services	383	324	333	18.2	15.0
Housekeeping supplies	**507**	**552**	**532**	**–8.2**	**–4.7**
Laundry and cleaning supplies	131	148	146	–11.5	–10.3
Other household products	240	235	235	2.1	2.1
Postage and stationery	136	169	151	–19.5	–9.9
Household furnishings, equipment	**1,640**	**1,567**	**1,629**	**4.7**	**0.7**
Household textiles	113	138	151	–18.1	–25.2

(continued)

(continued from previous page)

	2000	1990	1984	percent change 1990–00	percent change 1984–00
Furniture	$405	$428	$469	–5.4%	–13.6%
Floor coverings	47	132	141	–64.4	–66.7
Major appliances	200	200	247	0.0	–19.0
Small appliances, misc. houseware	94	105	116	–10.5	–19.0
Miscellaneous household equipment	779	563	504	38.4	54.6
APPAREL AND SERVICES	**1,878**	**2,166**	**2,227**	**–13.3**	**–15.7**
Men and boys	**447**	**526**	**602**	**–15.0**	**–25.7**
Men, aged 16 or older	358	440	482	–18.6	–25.7
Boys, aged 2 to 15	89	86	119	3.5	–25.2
Women and girls	**742**	**909**	**885**	**–18.4**	**–16.2**
Women, aged 16 or older	626	794	751	–21.2	–16.6
Girls, aged 2 to 15	116	115	133	0.9	–12.8
Children under age 2	**81**	**91**	**86**	**–11.0**	**–5.8**
Footwear	**342**	**295**	**303**	**15.9**	**12.9**
Other apparel products, services	**267**	**344**	**353**	**–22.4**	**–24.4**
TRANSPORTATION	**7,721**	**7,071**	**7,441**	**9.2**	**3.8**
Vehicle purchases	**3,574**	**2,972**	**3,187**	**20.3**	**12.1**
Cars and trucks, new	1,706	1,639	1,830	4.1	–6.8
Cars and trucks, used	1,819	1,299	1,309	40.0	39.0
Other vehicles	49	33	48	48.5	2.1
Gasoline and motor oil	**1,337**	**1,435**	**1,795**	**–6.8**	**–25.5**
Other vehicle expenses	**2,361**	**2,253**	**2,025**	**4.8**	**16.6**
Vehicle finance charges	334	408	366	–18.1	–8.7
Maintenance and repairs	647	808	822	–19.9	–21.3
Vehicle insurance	798	776	602	2.8	32.6
Vehicle rent, lease, license, other	582	261	234	123.0	148.7
Public transportation	**448**	**411**	**436**	**9.0**	**2.8**
HEALTH CARE	**2,198**	**2,069**	**1,821**	**6.2**	**20.7**
Health insurance	1,030	806	635	27.8	62.2
Medical services	620	792	799	–21.7	–22.4
Drugs	441	350	287	26.0	53.7
Medical supplies	107	119	101	–10.1	5.9
ENTERTAINMENT	**1,980**	**2,007**	**1,858**	**–1.3**	**6.6**
Fees and admissions	561	530	559	5.8	0.4
Television, radios, sound equipment	629	618	554	1.8	13.5
Pets, toys, and playground equipment	358	390	336	–8.2	6.5
Other supplies, equipment, and services	433	469	409	–7.7	5.9
PERSONAL CARE PRODUCTS, SERVICES	**555**	**490**	**491**	**13.3**	**13.0**
READING	**157**	**216**	**232**	**–27.3**	**–32.3**
EDUCATION	**666**	**569**	**522**	**17.0**	**27.6**
TOBACCO PRODUCTS AND SMOKING SUPPLIES	**329**	**372**	**388**	**–11.6**	**–15.2**
MISCELLANEOUS	**804**	**1,173**	**774**	**–31.5**	**3.9**
CASH CONTRIBUTIONS	**1,260**	**1,123**	**1,245**	**12.2**	**1.2**
PERSONAL INSURANCE, PENSIONS	**3,510**	**3,564**	**3,291**	**–1.5**	**6.7**
Life and other personal insurance	404	464	505	–12.9	–20.0
Pensions and Social Security	3,105	3,101	2,786	0.1	11.5
PERSONAL TAXES	**3,318**	**4,070**	**3,867**	**–18.5**	**–14.2**
Federal income taxes	2,566	3,206	3,015	–20.0	–14.9
State and local income taxes	592	758	741	–21.9	–20.1
Other taxes	159	107	113	48.6	40.7
GIFTS**	**1,154**	**1,286**	**1,221**	**–10.3**	**–5.5**

* This figure does not include the amount paid for mortgage principle, which is considered an asset.
** Expenditures on gifts are also included in the preceding product and service categories.
Note: The Bureau of Labor Statistics uses consumer unit rather than household as the sampling unit in the Consumer Expenditure Survey. For the definition of consumer unit, see the glossary. Average annual spending total does not include the amount spent on personal taxes. The white and other category includes a small number of Asians and Native Americans.
Source: Bureau of Labor Statistics, Consumer Expenditure Surveys, Internet site http://www.bls.gov/cex/; calculations by New Strategist

Table 9.12 Spending by Hispanic Households, 1994 and 2000

(number of consumer units (CU) headed by Hispanics, and average annual spending on products and services, 1994 and 2000; percent change, 1994–00; in 2000 dollars)

	2000	1994	percent change 1994–00
Number of consumer units (in 000s)	9,473	7,730	22.5%
Average annual spending	$32,735	$30,714	6.6
FOOD	**$5,362**	**$5,224**	**2.6%**
Food at home	**3,496**	**3,860**	**–9.4**
Cereals and bakery products	491	558	–12.0
Cereals and cereal products	201	265	–24.2
Bakery products	290	293	–1.0
Meats, poultry, fish, and eggs	1,036	1,194	–13.2
Beef	326	423	–22.9
Pork	213	232	–8.2
Other meats	116	132	–12.1
Poultry	190	209	–9.1
Fish and seafood	136	123	10.6
Eggs	55	74	–25.7
Dairy products	359	396	–9.3
Fresh milk and cream	170	213	–20.2
Other dairy products	189	184	2.7
Fruits and vegetables	670	660	1.5
Fresh fruits	228	214	6.5
Fresh vegetables	228	221	3.2
Processed fruits	125	129	–3.1
Processed vegetables	89	96	–7.3
Other food at home	940	1,052	–10.6
Sugar and other sweets	110	135	–18.5
Fats and oils	100	124	–19.4
Miscellaneous foods	405	452	–10.4
Nonalcoholic beverages	292	310	–5.8
Food prepared by CU, out-of-town trips	34	30	13.3
Food away from home	**1,865**	**1,364**	**36.7**
ALCOHOLIC BEVERAGES	**285**	**245**	**16.3**
HOUSING	**10,850**	**10,385**	**4.5**
Shelter	**6,437**	**6,175**	**4.2**
Owned dwellings*	2,949	2,686	9.8
Mortgage interest and charges	1,751	1,809	–3.2
Property taxes	665	523	27.2
Maintenance, repairs, insurance, other expenses	533	354	50.6
Rented dwellings	3,307	3,338	–0.9
Other lodging	181	150	20.7
Utilities, fuels, public services	**2,170**	**2,280**	**–4.8**
Natural gas	242	256	–5.5
Electricity	749	830	–9.8
Fuel oil and other fuels	30	22	36.4
Telephone	889	921	–3.5
Water and other public services	259	252	2.8
Household services	**465**	**411**	**13.1**
Personal services	255	236	8.1
Other household services	211	174	21.3
Housekeeping supplies	**474**	**416**	**13.9**
Laundry and cleaning supplies	172	163	5.5
Other household products	227	199	14.1
Postage and stationery	76	53	43.4
Household furnishings, equipment	**1,303**	**1,105**	**17.9**
Household textiles	89	109	–18.3

(continued)

(continued from previous page)

	2000	1994	percent change 1994–00
Furniture	$447	$333	34.2%
Floor coverings	27	20	35.0
Major appliances	166	148	12.2
Small appliances, misc. houseware	66	73	–9.6
Miscellaneous household equipment	508	422	20.4
APPAREL AND SERVICES	**2,076**	**2,194**	**–5.4**
Men and boys	**483**	**648**	**–25.5**
Men, aged 16 or older	359	437	–17.8
Boys, aged 2 to 15	124	211	–41.2
Women and girls	**691**	**616**	**12.2**
Women, aged 16 or older	540	467	15.6
Girls, aged 2 to 15	150	149	0.7
Children under age 2	**137**	**168**	**–18.5**
Footwear	**516**	**472**	**9.3**
Other apparel products, services	**249**	**289**	**–13.8**
TRANSPORTATION	**6,719**	**5,632**	**19.3**
Vehicle purchases	**3,146**	**2,512**	**25.2**
Cars and trucks, new	1,079	1,009	6.9
Cars and trucks, used	2,058	1,502	37.0
Other vehicles	–	–	–
Gasoline and motor oil	**1,244**	**1,053**	**18.1**
Other vehicle expenses	**1,945**	**1,721**	**13.0**
Vehicle finance charges	274	208	31.7
Maintenance and repairs	546	623	–12.4
Vehicle insurance	696	605	15.0
Vehicle rent, lease, license, other	428	284	50.7
Public transportation	**385**	**347**	**11.0**
HEALTH CARE	**1,243**	**1,233**	**0.8**
Health insurance	600	554	8.3
Medical services	364	461	–21.0
Drugs	211	172	22.7
Medical supplies	69	45	53.3
ENTERTAINMENT	**1,186**	**1,089**	**8.9**
Fees and admissions	262	225	16.4
Television, radios, sound equipment	545	536	1.7
Pets, toys, and playground equipment	218	199	9.5
Other supplies, equipment, and services	162	129	25.6
PERSONAL CARE PRODUCTS, SERVICES	**564**	**528**	**6.8**
READING	**59**	**88**	**–33.0**
EDUCATION	**363**	**389**	**–6.7**
TOBACCO PRODUCTS AND SMOKING SUPPLIES	**173**	**159**	**8.8**
MISCELLANEOUS	**602**	**673**	**–10.5**
CASH CONTRIBUTIONS	**645**	**526**	**22.6**
PERSONAL INSURANCE, PENSIONS	**2,608**	**2,349**	**11.0**
Life and other personal insurance	189	223	–15.2
Pensions and Social Security	2,420	2,126	13.8
PERSONAL TAXES	**1,518**	**2,038**	**–25.5**
Federal income taxes	1,258	1,562	–19.5
State and local income taxes	271	426	–36.4
Other taxes	52	50	4.0
GIFTS**	**825**	**691**	**19.4**

* This figure does not include the amount paid for mortgage principle, which is considered an asset.
** Expenditures on gifts are also included in the preceding product and service categories.
Note: 1994 is the earliest year for which Hispanic spending statistics are available. The Bureau of Labor Statistics uses consumer unit rather than household as the sampling unit in the Consumer Expenditure Survey. For the definition of consumer unit, see the glossary. Average annual spending total does not include the amount spent on personal taxes. (–) means sample is too small to make a reliable estimate.
Source: Bureau of Labor Statistics, Consumer Expenditure Surveys, Internet site http://www.bls.gov/cex/; calculations by New Strategist

The Rich Spend More

Between 1984 and 2000, households in the top quintile of the income distribution (the richest one-fifth of households) boosted their spending by 8 percent, after adjusting for inflation. Households in the bottom income quintile (the poorest one-fifth of households) spent about 1 percent less in 2000 than in 1984. Consequently, the spending gap between the richest and the poorest households grew during those years. In 1984, the average household in the bottom income quintile spent 26 percent as much as the average household in the top quintile. By 2000, the bottom quintile spent just 24 percent as much as the top quintile ($17,940 versus $75,102).

By product and service category, spending trends have been similar for the poorest and the richest households. Both rich and poor spent considerably less in 2000 than in 1984 on many items, including food and clothing. They spent more on many nondiscretionary items such as property taxes, drugs, health insurance, and telephone services. Both spent more on entertainment and less on transportation. Some of the reasons for the bigger spending increase among the well-off are the substantial rise in spending on mortgage interest and on pensions and Social Security payments.

The gap between rich and poor widens

(average annual spending of households by income quintile, 1984 and 2000; in 2000 dollars)

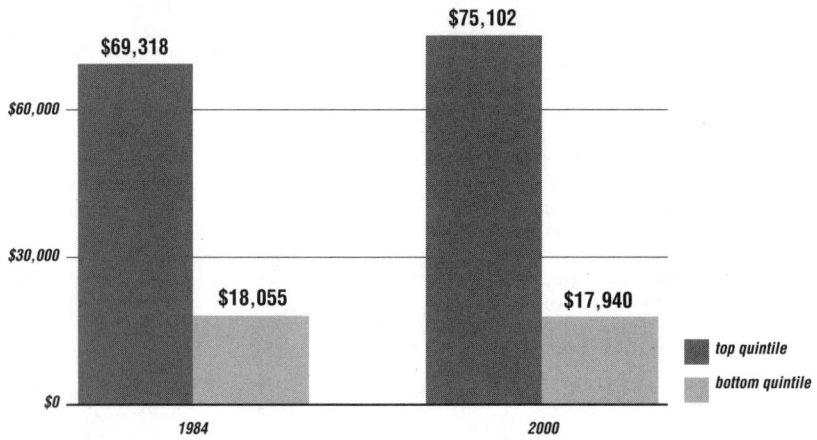

Table 9.13 Spending by Households in the Lowest Income Quintile, 1984, 1990, and 2000

(number of consumer units (CU) in the poorest 20 percent of households, and average annual spending on products and services, 1984, 1990, and 2000; percent change, 1990–00 and 1984–00; in 2000 dollars)

	2000	1990	1984	percent change 1990–00	percent change 1984–00
Number of consumer units (in 000s)	16,268	16,653	16,190	–2.3%	0.5%
Average annual spending	$17,940	$17,008	$18,055	5.5	–0.6
FOOD	$2,673	$3,163	$2,910	–15.5%	–8.1%
Food at home	1,826	2,120	1,966	–13.9	–7.1
Cereals and bakery products	270	306	272	–11.8	–0.7
Cereals and cereal products	96	115	89	–16.5	7.9
Bakery products	174	191	182	–8.9	–4.4
Meats, poultry, fish, and eggs	492	618	615	–20.4	–20.0
Beef	141	211	187	–33.2	–24.6
Pork	114	130	131	–12.3	–13.0
Other meats	65	84	78	–22.6	–16.7
Poultry	89	99	99	–10.1	–10.1
Fish and seafood	57	63	76	–9.5	–25.0
Eggs	26	30	43	–13.3	–39.5
Dairy products	197	254	255	–22.4	–22.7
Fresh milk and cream	92	136	151	–32.4	–39.1
Other dairy products	105	119	104	–11.8	1.0
Fruits and vegetables	326	358	305	–8.9	6.9
Fresh fruits	102	108	86	–5.6	18.6
Fresh vegetables	97	104	94	–6.7	3.2
Processed fruits	77	79	68	–2.5	13.2
Processed vegetables	50	69	56	–27.5	–10.7
Other food at home	541	582	496	–7.0	9.1
Sugar and other sweets	66	76	78	–13.2	–15.4
Fats and oils	53	63	61	–15.9	–13.1
Miscellaneous foods	241	253	181	–4.7	33.1
Nonalcoholic beverages	156	173	176	–9.8	–11.4
Food prepared by CU, out-of-town trips	25	17	23	47.1	8.7
Food away from home	848	1,043	945	–18.7	–10.3
ALCOHOLIC BEVERAGES	206	167	187	23.4	10.2
HOUSING	6,509	5,767	6,334	12.9	2.8
Shelter	3,735	3,092	3,419	20.8	9.2
Owned dwellings*	1,466	1,128	1,594	30.0	–8.0
Mortgage interest and charges	524	407	860	28.7	–39.1
Property taxes	510	364	353	40.1	44.5
Maintenance, repairs, insurance, other expenses	431	356	381	21.1	13.1
Rented dwellings	2,035	1,801	1,487	13.0	36.9
Other lodging	234	165	338	41.8	–30.8
Utilities, fuels, public services	1,632	1,599	1,792	2.1	–8.9
Natural gas	188	216	320	–13.0	–41.3
Electricity	618	628	661	–1.6	–6.5
Fuel oil and other fuels	84	84	187	0.0	–55.1
Telephone	575	530	489	8.5	17.6
Water and other public services	168	141	133	19.1	26.3
Household services	270	229	247	17.9	9.3
Personal services	100	95	70	5.3	42.9
Other household services	171	134	176	27.6	–2.8
Housekeeping supplies	249	311	255	–19.9	–2.4
Laundry and cleaning supplies	73	96	86	–24.0	–15.1
Other household products	102	113	99	–9.7	3.0
Postage and stationery	74	101	68	–26.7	8.8
Household furnishings, equipment	622	536	623	16.0	–0.2
Household textiles	43	72	46	–40.3	–6.5

(continued)

(continued from previous page)

	2000	1990	1984	percent change 1990–00	percent change 1984–00
Furniture	$150	$109	$214	37.6%	–29.9%
Floor coverings	15	28	60	–46.4	–75.0
Major appliances	117	94	118	24.5	–0.8
Small appliances, misc. houseware	37	40	51	–7.5	–27.5
Miscellaneous household equipment	261	194	134	34.5	94.8
APPAREL AND SERVICES	**844**	**879**	**976**	**–4.0**	**–13.5**
Men and boys	**171**	**198**	**207**	**–13.6**	**–17.4**
Men, aged 16 or older	134	144	167	–6.9	–19.8
Boys, aged 2 to 15	38	54	40	–29.6	–5.0
Women and girls	**299**	**382**	**383**	**–21.7**	**–21.9**
Women, aged 16 or older	252	345	322	–27.0	–21.7
Girls, aged 2 to 15	47	37	61	27.0	–23.0
Children under age 2	**50**	**40**	**36**	**25.0**	**38.9**
Footwear	**198**	**115**	**179**	**72.2**	**10.6**
Other apparel products, services	**127**	**145**	**171**	**–12.4**	**–25.7**
TRANSPORTATION	**3,212**	**2,688**	**3,268**	**19.5**	**–1.7**
Vehicle purchases	**1,443**	**1,051**	**1,218**	**37.3**	**18.5**
Cars and trucks, new	443	306	680	44.8	–34.9
Cars and trucks, used	996	721	519	38.1	91.9
Other vehicles	–	24	20	–	–
Gasoline and motor oil	**631**	**686**	**926**	**–8.0**	**–31.9**
Other vehicle expenses	**925**	**796**	**863**	**16.2**	**7.2**
Vehicle finance charges	82	90	96	–8.9	–14.6
Maintenance and repairs	325	350	447	–7.1	–27.3
Vehicle insurance	344	281	229	22.4	50.2
Vehicle rent, lease, license, other	175	76	91	130.3	92.3
Public transportation	**212**	**153**	**260**	**38.6**	**–18.5**
HEALTH CARE	**1,470**	**1,333**	**1,064**	**10.3**	**38.2**
Health insurance	690	536	394	28.7	75.1
Medical services	339	440	421	–23.0	–19.5
Drugs	381	287	197	32.8	93.4
Medical supplies	60	71	53	–15.5	13.2
ENTERTAINMENT	**837**	**730**	**772**	**14.7**	**8.4**
Fees and admissions	198	130	232	52.3	–14.7
Television, radios, sound equipment	363	275	249	32.0	45.8
Pets, toys, and playground equipment	122	181	179	–32.6	–31.8
Other supplies, equipment, and services	154	145	111	6.2	38.7
PERSONAL CARE PRODUCTS, SERVICES	**318**	**241**	**249**	**32.0**	**27.7**
READING	**73**	**82**	**111**	**–11.0**	**–34.2**
EDUCATION	**430**	**464**	**560**	**–7.3**	**–23.2**
TOBACCO PRODUCTS AND SMOKING SUPPLIES	**257**	**266**	**268**	**–3.4**	**–4.1**
MISCELLANEOUS	**365**	**490**	**303**	**–25.5**	**20.5**
CASH CONTRIBUTIONS	**332**	**307**	**414**	**8.1**	**–19.8**
PERSONAL INSURANCE, PENSIONS	**413**	**431**	**638**	**–4.2**	**–35.3**
Life and other personal insurance	144	155	313	–7.1	–54.0
Pensions and Social Security	269	274	325	–1.8	–17.2
PERSONAL TAXES	**226**	**109**	**53**	**107.3**	**326.4**
Federal income taxes	142	47	–	202.1	–
State and local income taxes	41	32	27	28.1	51.9
Other taxes	43	30	35	43.3	22.9
GIFTS**	**555**	**638**	**479**	**–13.0**	**15.9**

* This figure does not include the amount paid for mortgage principle, which is considered an asset.
** Expenditures on gifts are also included in the preceding product and service categories.
Note: The Bureau of Labor Statistics uses consumer unit rather than household as the sampling unit in the Consumer Expenditure Survey. For the definition of consumer unit, see the glossary. Average annual spending total does not include the amount spent on personal taxes; (–) means sample is too small to make a reliable estimate.
Source: Bureau of Labor Statistics, Consumer Expenditure Surveys, Internet site http://www.bls.gov/cex/; calculations by New Strategist

Table 9.14 Spending by Households in the Highest Income Quintile, 1984, 1990 and 2000

(number of consumer units (CU) in the richest 20 percent of households, and average annual spending on products and services, 1984, 1990, and 2000; percent change, 1990–00 and 1984–00; in 2000 dollars)

	2000	1990	1984	percent change 1990–00	percent change 1984–00
Number of consumer units (in 000s)	16,321	16,722	16,273	–2.4%	0.3%
Average annual spending	$75,102	$73,039	$69,318	2.8	8.3
FOOD	**$8,679**	**$9,390**	**$9,150**	**–7.6%**	**–5.1%**
Food at home	4,507	4,623	4,841	–2.5	–6.9
Cereals and bakery products	683	709	610	–3.7	12.0
Cereals and cereal products	215	236	172	–8.9	25.0
Bakery products	469	473	436	–0.8	7.6
Meats, poultry, fish, and eggs	1,101	1,162	1,334	–5.2	–17.5
Beef	330	373	481	–11.5	–31.4
Pork	204	206	255	–1.0	–20.0
Other meats	133	175	184	–24.0	–27.7
Poultry	208	192	197	8.3	5.6
Fish and seafood	186	173	146	7.5	27.4
Eggs	41	43	71	–4.7	–42.3
Dairy products	474	528	620	–10.2	–23.5
Fresh milk and cream	181	213	270	–15.0	–33.0
Other dairy products	293	315	350	–7.0	–16.3
Fruits and vegetables	790	771	797	2.5	–0.9
Fresh fruits	249	254	237	–2.0	5.1
Fresh vegetables	248	221	229	12.2	8.3
Processed fruits	176	171	191	2.9	–7.9
Processed vegetables	116	124	143	–6.5	–18.9
Other food at home	1,459	1,453	1,361	0.4	7.2
Sugar and other sweets	194	177	189	9.6	2.6
Fats and oils	110	113	121	–2.7	–9.1
Miscellaneous foods	714	677	602	5.5	18.6
Nonalcoholic beverages	356	391	447	–9.0	–20.4
Food prepared by CU, out-of-town trips	84	95	119	–11.6	–29.4
Food away from home	4,173	4,767	4,311	–12.5	–3.2
ALCOHOLIC BEVERAGES	**780**	**730**	**878**	**6.8**	**–11.2**
HOUSING	**22,611**	**21,275**	**19,872**	**6.3**	**13.8**
Shelter	13,004	12,039	10,390	8.0	25.2
Owned dwellings*	10,459	9,490	7,770	10.2	34.6
Mortgage interest and charges	6,729	6,602	5,363	1.9	25.5
Property taxes	2,226	1,611	1,248	38.2	78.4
Maintenance, repairs, insurance, other expenses	1,503	1,277	1,158	17.7	29.8
Rented dwellings	1,364	1,306	1,231	4.4	10.8
Other lodging	1,181	1,244	1,389	–5.1	–15.0
Utilities, fuels, public services	3,522	3,502	3,936	0.6	–10.5
Natural gas	451	448	689	0.7	–34.5
Electricity	1,178	1,398	1,538	–15.7	–23.4
Fuel oil and other fuels	121	175	283	–30.9	–57.2
Telephone	1,305	1,078	1,044	21.1	25.0
Water and other public services	467	401	381	16.5	22.6
Household services	**1,685**	**1,345**	**1,134**	**25.3**	**48.6**
Personal services	820	680	423	20.6	93.9
Other household services	865	665	711	30.1	21.7
Housekeeping supplies	**951**	**980**	**978**	**–3.0**	**–2.8**
Laundry and cleaning supplies	244	231	229	5.6	6.6
Other household products	445	433	496	2.8	–10.3
Postage and stationery	261	315	254	–17.1	2.8
Household furnishings, equipment	**3,450**	**3,408**	**3,432**	**1.2**	**0.5**
Household textiles	233	275	312	–15.3	–25.3

(continued)

(continued from previous page)

	2000	1990	1984	percent change 1990–00	percent change 1984–00
Furniture	$989	$804	$963	23.0%	2.7%
Floor coverings	112	362	255	–69.1	–56.1
Major appliances	365	340	423	7.4	–13.7
Small appliances, misc. houseware	178	215	244	–17.2	–27.0
Miscellaneous household equipment	1,573	1,414	1,236	11.2	27.3
APPAREL AND SERVICES	**3,989**	**4,472**	**4,390**	**–10.8**	**–9.1**
Men and boys	**1,021**	**1,190**	**1,183**	**–14.2**	**–13.7**
Men, aged 16 or older	825	1,054	981	–21.7	–15.9
Boys, aged 2 to 15	197	136	202	44.9	–2.5
Women and girls	**1,553**	**1,760**	**1,811**	**–11.8**	**–14.2**
Women, aged 16 or older	1,285	1,544	1,546	–16.8	–16.9
Girls, aged 2 to 15	268	217	265	23.5	1.1
Children under age 2	**149**	**152**	**131**	**–2.0**	**13.7**
Footwear	**605**	**611**	**537**	**–1.0**	**12.7**
Other apparel products, services	**660**	**759**	**726**	**–13.0**	**–9.1**
TRANSPORTATION	**13,315**	**12,673**	**13,347**	**5.1**	**–0.2**
Vehicle purchases	**6,018**	**5,440**	**5,995**	**10.6**	**0.4**
Cars and trucks, new	3,377	3,565	4,104	–5.3	–17.7
Cars and trucks, used	2,521	1,802	1,821	39.9	38.4
Other vehicles	119	72	71	65.3	67.6
Gasoline and motor oil	**2,053**	**2,125**	**2,733**	**–3.4**	**–24.9**
Other vehicle expenses	**4,286**	**4,126**	**3,734**	**3.9**	**14.8**
Vehicle finance charges	598	775	800	–22.8	–25.3
Maintenance and repairs	1,110	1,393	1,374	–20.3	–19.2
Vehicle insurance	1,275	1,377	1,049	–7.4	21.5
Vehicle rent, lease, license, other	1,302	582	512	123.7	154.3
Public transportation	**959**	**983**	**885**	**–2.4**	**8.4**
HEALTH CARE	**2,864**	**2,740**	**2,421**	**4.5**	**18.3**
Health insurance	1,254	935	733	34.1	71.1
Medical services	968	1,262	1,233	–23.3	–21.5
Drugs	470	375	326	25.3	44.2
Medical supplies	172	167	129	3.0	33.3
ENTERTAINMENT	**3,866**	**4,050**	**3,817**	**–4.5**	**1.3**
Fees and admissions	1,349	1,165	1,192	15.8	13.2
Television, radios, sound equipment	1,071	1,092	1,064	–1.9	0.7
Pets, toys, and playground equipment	656	653	582	0.5	12.7
Other supplies, equipment, and services	790	1,140	979	–30.7	–19.3
PERSONAL CARE PRODUCTS, SERVICES	**983**	**871**	**863**	**12.9**	**13.9**
READING	**291**	**385**	**399**	**–24.4**	**–27.1**
EDUCATION	**1,462**	**1,191**	**900**	**22.8**	**62.4**
TOBACCO PRODUCTS AND SMOKING SUPPLIES	**336**	**383**	**449**	**–12.3**	**–25.2**
MISCELLANEOUS	**1,318**	**2,250**	**1,376**	**–41.4**	**–4.2**
CASH CONTRIBUTIONS	**3,050**	**2,694**	**2,879**	**13.2**	**5.9**
PERSONAL INSURANCE, PENSIONS	**11,557**	**9,933**	**8,577**	**16.3**	**34.7**
Life and other personal insurance	880	1,072	1,016	–17.9	–13.4
Pensions and Social Security	10,677	8,862	7,562	20.5	41.2
PERSONAL TAXES	**9,749**	**11,627**	**10,864**	**–16.2**	**–10.3**
Federal income taxes	7,815	9,389	8,636	–16.8	–9.5
State and local income taxes	1,646	2,057	1,992	–20.0	–17.4
Other taxes	289	182	235	58.8	23.0
GIFTS**	**2,553**	**2,812**	**2,307**	**–9.2**	**10.7**

* This figure does not include the amount paid for mortgage principle, which is considered an asset.
** Expenditures on gifts are also included in the preceding product and service categories.
Note: The Bureau of Labor Statistics uses consumer unit rather than household as the sampling unit in the Consumer Expenditure Survey.
For the definition of consumer unit, see the glossary. Average annual spending total does not include the amount spent on personal taxes.
Source: Bureau of Labor Statistics, Consumer Expenditure Surveys, Internet site http://www.bls.gov/cex/; calculations by New Strategist

Empty-Nesters Boost Spending

Married couples without children at home (some of them young couples, but most of them older empty-nesters) spent 10 percent more in 2000 than in 1984, after adjusting for inflation. This household type enjoyed a bigger spending increase than any other during those years, which is consistent with the fact that the householders aged 65 or older were the ones to increase their spending the most between 1984 and 2000.

Married couples with children at home spent 9 percent more in 2000 than in 1984, after adjusting for inflation. Single-person households, many of which are headed by older Americans, spent 7 percent more, while single-parent households spent 4 percent more.

Between 1990 and 2000, these spending patterns changed. Single parents made the biggest spending gains as the booming economy and tight labor market boosted wages. The spending of married couples without children at home and of single-person households increased the least during the 1990s as interest rates fell, reducing income growth among older Americans.

Married, no kids enjoyed biggest spending increase

(percent change in average annual spending of households by household type, 1984 to 2000; in 2000 dollars)

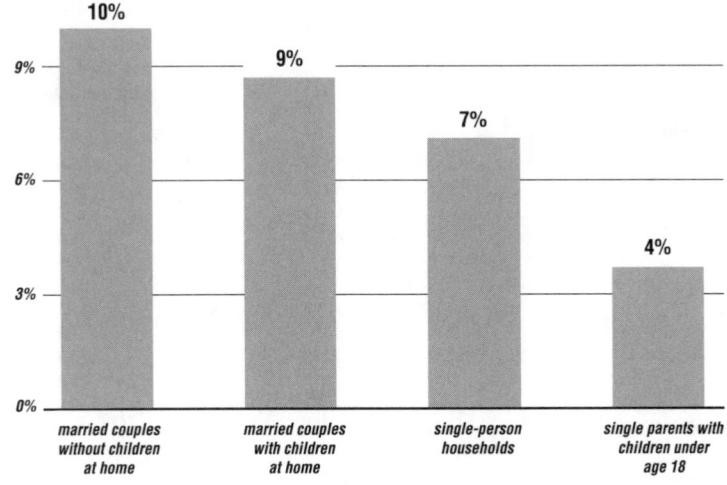

Table 9.15 Spending of Married Couples with Children at Home, 1984, 1990, and 2000

(number of consumer units (CU) headed by married couples with children at home, and average annual spending on products and services, 1984, 1990, and 2000; percent change, 1990–00 and 1984–00; in 2000 dollars)

	2000	1990	1984	percent change 1990–00	percent change 1984–00
Number of consumer units (in 000s)	28,777	27,991	28,064	2.8%	2.5%
Average annual spending	$53,586	$51,410	$49,296	4.2	8.7
FOOD	**$7,251**	**$7,913**	**$7,741**	**–8.4%**	**–6.3%**
Food at home	**4,357**	**4,729**	**4,808**	**–7.9**	**–9.4**
Cereals and bakery products	680	722	646	–5.8	5.3
Cereals and cereal products	240	258	215	–7.0	11.6
Bakery products	440	464	432	–5.2	1.9
Meats, poultry, fish, and eggs	1,113	1,240	1,445	–10.2	–23.0
Beef	335	407	495	–17.7	–32.3
Pork	226	244	293	–7.4	–22.9
Other meats	148	187	206	–20.9	–28.2
Poultry	207	198	195	4.5	6.2
Fish and seafood	153	150	173	2.0	–11.6
Eggs	44	54	82	–18.5	–46.3
Dairy products	481	585	635	–17.8	–24.3
Fresh milk and cream	201	283	326	–29.0	–38.3
Other dairy products	280	302	310	–7.3	–9.7
Fruits and vegetables	710	717	715	–1.0	–0.7
Fresh fruits	216	216	204	0.0	5.9
Fresh vegetables	211	206	204	2.4	3.4
Processed fruits	164	169	171	–3.0	–4.1
Processed vegetables	119	125	136	–4.8	–12.5
Other food at home	1,373	1,466	1,292	–6.3	6.3
Sugar and other sweets	172	184	182	–6.5	–5.5
Fats and oils	113	128	133	–11.7	–15.0
Miscellaneous foods	677	681	558	–0.6	21.3
Nonalcoholic beverages	356	410	419	–13.2	–15.0
Food prepared by CU, out-of-town trips	54	62	74	–12.9	–27.0
Food away from home	**2,894**	**3,184**	**2,933**	**–9.1**	**–1.3**
ALCOHOLIC BEVERAGES	**396**	**391**	**485**	**1.3**	**–18.4**
HOUSING	**17,132**	**15,216**	**14,488**	**12.6**	**18.2**
Shelter	**9,693**	**8,123**	**7,320**	**19.3**	**32.4**
Owned dwellings*	7,587	5,939	5,230	27.7	45.1
Mortgage interest and charges	4,940	4,130	3,616	19.6	36.6
Property taxes	1,618	1,041	866	55.4	86.8
Maintenance, repairs, insurance, other expenses	1,029	768	747	34.0	37.8
Rented dwellings	1,502	1,590	1,333	–5.5	12.7
Other lodging	604	593	758	1.9	–20.3
Utilities, fuels, public services	**3,180**	**3,170**	**3,479**	**0.3**	**–8.6**
Natural gas	396	419	603	–5.5	–34.3
Electricity	1,161	1,302	1,422	–10.8	–18.4
Fuel oil and other fuels	120	181	268	–33.7	–55.2
Telephone	1,097	916	865	19.8	26.8
Water and other public services	405	352	321	15.1	26.2
Household services	**1,221**	**1,009**	**803**	**21.0**	**52.1**
Personal services	750	686	471	9.3	59.2
Other household services	471	321	332	46.7	41.9
Housekeeping supplies	**703**	**752**	**713**	**–6.5**	**–1.4**
Laundry and cleaning supplies	203	223	215	–9.0	–5.6
Other household products	338	331	327	2.1	3.4
Postage and stationery	162	199	171	–18.6	–5.3
Household furnishings, equipment	**2,336**	**2,163**	**2,174**	**8.0**	**7.5**
Household textiles	162	208	178	–22.1	–9.0

(continued)

(continued from previous page)

	2000	1990	1984	percent change 1990–00	percent change 1984–00
Furniture	$608	$556	$574	9.4%	5.9%
Floor coverings	71	244	231	−70.9	−69.3
Major appliances	290	258	323	12.4	−10.2
Small appliances, misc. houseware	122	130	151	−6.2	−19.2
Miscellaneous household equipment	1,082	768	717	40.9	50.9
APPAREL AND SERVICES	**2,749**	**2,999**	**3,042**	**−8.3**	**−9.6**
Men and boys	**683**	**791**	**902**	**−13.7**	**−24.3**
Men, aged 16 or older	467	592	652	−21.1	−28.4
Boys, aged 2 to 15	216	199	250	8.5	−13.6
Women and girls	**1,052**	**1,198**	**1,151**	**−12.2**	**−8.6**
Women, aged 16 or older	778	935	872	−16.8	−10.8
Girls, aged 2 to 15	274	262	278	4.6	−1.4
Children under age 2	**173**	**190**	**169**	**−8.9**	**2.4**
Footwear	**480**	**386**	**412**	**24.4**	**16.5**
Other apparel products, services	**361**	**436**	**408**	**−17.2**	**−11.5**
TRANSPORTATION	**11,088**	**9,829**	**9,804**	**12.8**	**13.1**
Vehicle purchases	**5,365**	**4,485**	**4,260**	**19.6**	**25.9**
Cars and trucks, new	2,478	2,423	2,370	2.3	4.6
Cars and trucks, used	2,817	2,021	1,831	39.4	53.9
Other vehicles	70	41	59	70.7	18.6
Gasoline and motor oil	**1,879**	**1,963**	**2,472**	**−4.3**	**−24.0**
Other vehicle expenses	**3,352**	**2,982**	**2,661**	**12.4**	**26.0**
Vehicle finance charges	534	632	550	−15.5	−2.9
Maintenance and repairs	851	1,003	1,012	−15.2	−15.9
Vehicle insurance	1,097	1,004	792	9.3	38.5
Vehicle rent, lease, license, other	871	341	307	155.4	183.7
Public transportation	**491**	**401**	**411**	**22.4**	**19.5**
HEALTH CARE	**2,306**	**2,228**	**2,006**	**3.5**	**15.0**
Health insurance	1,131	843	650	34.2	74.0
Medical services	698	937	996	−25.5	−29.9
Drugs	361	324	268	11.4	34.7
Medical supplies	116	124	92	−6.5	26.1
ENTERTAINMENT	**2,864**	**2,656**	**2,587**	**7.8**	**10.7**
Fees and admissions	850	694	697	22.5	22.0
Television, radios, sound equipment	854	821	758	4.0	12.7
Pets, toys, and playground equipment	498	538	475	−7.4	4.8
Other supplies, equipment, and services	662	603	657	9.8	0.8
PERSONAL CARE PRODUCTS, SERVICES	**769**	**659**	**644**	**16.7**	**19.4**
READING	**176**	**254**	**266**	**−30.7**	**−33.8**
EDUCATION	**1,126**	**899**	**755**	**25.3**	**49.1**
TOBACCO PRODUCTS AND SMOKING SUPPLIES	**358**	**448**	**474**	**−20.1**	**−24.5**
MISCELLANEOUS	**893**	**1,389**	**874**	**−35.7**	**2.2**
CASH CONTRIBUTIONS	**1,220**	**1,232**	**1,417**	**−1.0**	**−13.9**
PERSONAL INSURANCE, PENSIONS	**5,257**	**5,299**	**4,714**	**−0.8**	**11.5**
Life and other personal insurance	601	718	734	−16.3	−18.1
Pensions and Social Security	4,656	4,581	3,980	1.6	17.0
PERSONAL TAXES	**4,457**	**5,307**	**4,935**	**−16.0**	**−9.7**
Federal income taxes	3,467	4,187	3,810	−17.2	−9.0
State and local income taxes	816	1,013	983	−19.4	−17.0
Other taxes	175	107	142	63.6	23.2
GIFTS**	**1,266**	**1,456**	**1,301**	**−13.0**	**−2.7**

* This figure does not include the amount paid for mortgage principle, which is considered an asset.
** Expenditures on gifts are also included in the preceding product and service categories.
Note: The Bureau of Labor Statistics uses consumer unit rather than household as the sampling unit in the Consumer Expenditure Survey.
For the definition of consumer unit, see the glossary. Average annual spending total does not include the amount spent on personal taxes.
Source: Bureau of Labor Statistics, Consumer Expenditure Surveys, Internet site http://www.bls.gov/cex/; calculations by New Strategist

Table 9.16 Spending of Married Couples without Children at Home, 1984, 1990, and 2000

(number of consumer units (CU) headed by married couples without children at home, and average annual spending on products and services, 1984, 1990, and 2000; percent change, 1990–00 and 1984–00; in 2000 dollars)

	2000	1990	1984	percent change 1990–00	percent change 1984–00
Number of consumer units (in 000s)	22,805	20,653	19,337	10.4%	17.9%
Average annual spending	$42,196	$41,536	$38,363	1.6	10.0
FOOD	**$5,575**	**$6,017**	**$5,204**	**–7.3%**	**7.1%**
Food at home	3,155	3,303	2,968	–4.5	6.3
Cereals and bakery products	456	469	381	–2.8	19.7
Cereals and cereal products	149	154	111	–3.2	34.2
Bakery products	307	315	270	–2.5	13.7
Meats, poultry, fish, and eggs	846	918	875	–7.8	–3.3
Beef	251	316	312	–20.6	–19.6
Pork	189	174	181	8.6	4.4
Other meats	100	132	114	–24.2	–12.3
Poultry	143	149	124	–4.0	15.3
Fish and seafood	126	112	91	12.5	38.5
Eggs	37	37	51	0.0	–27.5
Dairy products	335	364	363	–8.0	–7.7
Fresh milk and cream	121	157	162	–22.9	–25.3
Other dairy products	214	207	201	3.4	6.5
Fruits and vegetables	578	586	525	–1.4	10.1
Fresh fruits	180	196	172	–8.2	4.7
Fresh vegetables	183	170	154	7.6	18.8
Processed fruits	123	125	114	–1.6	7.9
Processed vegetables	91	95	85	–4.2	7.1
Other food at home	940	964	757	–2.5	24.2
Sugar and other sweets	123	128	108	–3.9	13.9
Fats and oils	94	94	85	0.0	10.6
Miscellaneous foods	413	410	292	0.7	41.4
Nonalcoholic beverages	252	271	273	–7.0	–7.7
Food prepared by CU, out-of-town trips	58	62	65	–6.5	–10.8
Food away from home	**2,420**	**2,715**	**2,236**	**–10.9**	**8.2**
ALCOHOLIC BEVERAGES	**461**	**444**	**484**	**3.8**	**–4.8**
HOUSING	**12,832**	**12,331**	**11,752**	**4.1**	**9.2**
Shelter	**7,153**	**6,498**	**5,942**	**10.1**	**20.4**
Owned dwellings*	5,234	4,422	3,921	18.4	33.5
Mortgage interest and charges	2,692	2,298	2,065	17.1	30.4
Property taxes	1,460	1,062	923	37.5	58.2
Maintenance, repairs, insurance, other expenses	1,082	1,063	935	1.8	15.7
Rented dwellings	1,121	1,353	1,208	–17.1	–7.2
Other lodging	798	723	812	10.4	–1.7
Utilities, fuels, public services	**2,689**	**2,688**	**2,836**	**0.0**	**–5.2**
Natural gas	318	328	502	–3.0	–36.7
Electricity	1,022	1,120	1,122	–8.8	–8.9
Fuel oil and other fuels	129	170	283	–24.1	–54.4
Telephone	871	775	688	12.4	26.6
Water and other public services	348	295	240	18.0	45.0
Household services	**533**	**505**	**512**	**5.5**	**4.1**
Personal services	54	62	58	–12.9	–6.9
Other household services	478	443	454	7.9	5.3
Housekeeping supplies	**573**	**644**	**557**	**–11.0**	**2.9**
Laundry and cleaning supplies	134	159	134	–15.7	0.0
Other household products	286	273	237	4.8	20.7
Postage and stationery	154	212	184	–27.4	–16.3
Household furnishings, equipment	**1,884**	**1,995**	**1,904**	**–5.6**	**–1.1**
Household textiles	129	170	167	–24.1	–22.8

(continued)

(continued from previous page)

	2000	1990	1984	percent change 1990–00	percent change 1984–00
Furniture	$437	$535	$618	–18.3%	–29.3%
Floor coverings	61	115	148	–47.0	–58.8
Major appliances	218	258	308	–15.5	–29.2
Small appliances, misc. houseware	110	138	141	–20.3	–22.0
Miscellaneous household equipment	929	779	522	19.3	78.0
APPAREL AND SERVICES	**1,725**	**2,184**	**2,082**	**–21.0**	**–17.1**
Men and boys	**424**	**523**	**512**	**–18.9**	**–17.2**
Men, aged 16 or older	400	495	487	–19.2	–17.9
Boys, aged 2 to 15	25	28	27	–10.7	–7.4
Women and girls	**691**	**987**	**915**	**–30.0**	**–24.5**
Women, aged 16 or older	657	955	892	–31.2	–26.3
Girls, aged 2 to 15	34	30	23	13.3	47.8
Children under age 2	**38**	**42**	**45**	**–9.5**	**–15.6**
Footwear	**298**	**310**	**272**	**–3.9**	**9.6**
Other apparel products, services	**274**	**324**	**336**	**–15.4**	**–18.5**
TRANSPORTATION	**8,309**	**7,569**	**7,627**	**9.8**	**8.9**
Vehicle purchases	**3,824**	**3,137**	**3,250**	**21.9**	**17.7**
Cars and trucks, new	2,113	2,067	2,103	2.2	0.5
Cars and trucks, used	1,685	1,047	1,127	60.9	49.5
Other vehicles	–	22	20	–	–
Gasoline and motor oil	**1,411**	**1,498**	**1,770**	**–5.8**	**–20.3**
Other vehicle expenses	**2,493**	**2,415**	**2,088**	**3.2**	**19.4**
Vehicle finance charges	350	391	345	–10.5	1.4
Maintenance and repairs	673	859	852	–21.7	–21.0
Vehicle insurance	837	854	638	–2.0	31.2
Vehicle rent, lease, license, other	633	312	254	102.9	149.2
Public transportation	**581**	**518**	**519**	**12.2**	**11.9**
HEALTH CARE	**3,044**	**2,755**	**2,411**	**10.5**	**26.3**
Health insurance	1,479	1,132	960	30.7	54.1
Medical services	738	941	888	–21.6	–16.9
Drugs	671	530	414	26.6	62.1
Medical supplies	157	153	149	2.6	5.4
ENTERTAINMENT	**1,968**	**2,198**	**1,740**	**–10.5**	**13.1**
Fees and admissions	595	582	560	2.2	6.3
Television, radios, sound equipment	570	584	484	–2.4	17.8
Pets, toys, and playground equipment	388	372	307	4.3	26.4
Other supplies, equipment, and services	414	660	389	–37.3	6.4
PERSONAL CARE PRODUCTS, SERVICES	**611**	**551**	**527**	**10.9**	**15.9**
READING	**197**	**245**	**249**	**–19.6**	**–20.9**
EDUCATION	**447**	**333**	**345**	**34.2**	**29.6**
TOBACCO PRODUCTS AND SMOKING SUPPLIES	**286**	**354**	**389**	**–19.2**	**–26.5**
MISCELLANEOUS	**878**	**1,190**	**622**	**–26.2**	**41.2**
CASH CONTRIBUTIONS	**1,915**	**1,577**	**1,463**	**21.4**	**30.9**
PERSONAL INSURANCE, PENSIONS	**3,949**	**3,788**	**3,469**	**4.3**	**13.8**
Life and other personal insurance	613	590	593	3.9	3.4
Pensions and Social Security	3,335	3,198	2,875	4.3	16.0
PERSONAL TAXES	**4,358**	**4,809**	**3,998**	**–9.4**	**9.0**
Federal income taxes	3,396	3,784	3,096	–10.3	9.7
State and local income taxes	726	863	757	–15.9	–4.1
Other taxes	236	162	146	45.7	61.6
GIFTS**	**1,477**	**1,547**	**1,409**	**–4.5**	**4.8**

* This figure does not include the amount paid for mortgage principle, which is considered an asset.
** Expenditures on gifts are also included in the preceding product and service categories.
Note: The Bureau of Labor Statistics uses consumer unit rather than household as the sampling unit in the Consumer Expenditure Survey. For the definition of consumer unit, see the glossary. Average annual spending total does not include the amount spent on personal taxes; (–) means sample is too small to make a reliable estimate
Source: Bureau of Labor Statistics, Consumer Expenditure Surveys, Internet site http://www.bls.gov/cex/; calculations by New Strategist

Table 9.17 Spending of Single Parents with Children under Age 18 at Home, 1984, 1990, and 2000

(number of consumer units (CU) headed by single parents with children under age 18 at home, and average annual spending on products and services, 1984, 1990, and 2000; percent change, 1990–00 and 1984–00; in 2000 dollars)

	2000	1990	1984	percent change 1990–00	percent change 1984–00
Number of consumer units (in 000s)	6,132	6,074	5,086	1.0%	20.6%
Average annual spending	$28,923	$25,348	$27,903	14.1	3.7
FOOD	**$4,255**	**$4,663**	**$4,365**	**–8.7%**	**–2.5%**
Food at home	2,647	3,158	2,856	–16.2	–7.3
Cereals and bakery products	388	473	401	–18.0	–3.2
Cereals and cereal products	153	186	161	–17.7	–5.0
Bakery products	234	289	240	–19.0	–2.5
Meats, poultry, fish, and eggs	754	913	912	–17.4	–17.3
Beef	223	324	317	–31.2	–29.7
Pork	159	182	186	–12.6	–14.5
Other meats	91	132	119	–31.1	–23.5
Poultry	153	140	151	9.3	1.3
Fish and seafood	93	92	78	1.1	19.2
Eggs	33	42	61	–21.4	–45.9
Dairy products	279	381	371	–26.8	–24.8
Fresh milk and cream	117	196	214	–40.3	–45.3
Other dairy products	162	184	157	–12.0	3.2
Fruits and vegetables	408	477	418	–14.5	–2.4
Fresh fruits	114	130	106	–12.3	7.5
Fresh vegetables	117	133	126	–12.0	–7.1
Processed fruits	105	121	101	–13.2	4.0
Processed vegetables	72	92	86	–21.7	–16.3
Other food at home	818	913	739	–10.4	10.7
Sugar and other sweets	107	119	99	–10.1	8.1
Fats and oils	78	84	76	–7.1	2.6
Miscellaneous foods	359	435	297	–17.5	20.9
Nonalcoholic beverages	241	254	267	–5.1	–9.7
Food prepared by CU, out-of-town trips	32	21	15	52.4	113.3
Food away from home	1,608	1,505	1,508	6.8	6.6
ALCOHOLIC BEVERAGES	**187**	**216**	**222**	**–13.4**	**–15.8**
HOUSING	**10,732**	**9,123**	**9,598**	**17.6**	**11.8**
Shelter	6,331	5,125	5,187	23.5	22.1
Owned dwellings*	2,797	2,049	2,261	36.5	23.7
Mortgage interest and charges	1,694	1,314	1,581	28.9	7.1
Property taxes	646	337	340	91.7	90.0
Maintenance, repairs, insurance, other expenses	457	397	338	15.1	35.2
Rented dwellings	3,315	2,929	2,546	13.2	30.2
Other lodging	219	149	381	47.0	–42.5
Utilities, fuels, public services	2,335	2,105	2,496	10.9	–6.5
Natural gas	306	289	509	5.9	–39.9
Electricity	863	833	933	3.6	–7.5
Fuel oil and other fuels	43	63	136	–31.7	–68.4
Telephone	893	725	713	23.2	25.2
Water and other public services	230	198	207	16.2	11.1
Household services	**786**	**763**	**665**	**3.0**	**18.2**
Personal services	586	569	494	3.0	18.6
Other household services	200	194	171	3.1	17.0
Housekeeping supplies	**368**	**357**	**322**	**3.1**	**14.3**
Laundry and cleaning supplies	151	129	113	17.1	33.6
Other household products	140	137	131	2.2	6.9
Postage and stationery	77	92	78	–16.3	–1.3
Household furnishings, equipment	**912**	**771**	**928**	**18.3**	**–1.7**
Household textiles	60	45	156	33.3	–61.5

(continued)

(continued from previous page)

	2000	1990	1984	percent change 1990–00	1984–00
Furniture	$272	$274	$325	−0.7%	−16.3%
Floor coverings	22	38	28	−42.1	−21.4
Major appliances	104	148	177	−29.7	−41.2
Small appliances, misc. houseware	36	42	70	−14.3	−48.6
Miscellaneous household equipment	417	224	171	86.2	143.9
APPAREL AND SERVICES	**1,921**	**1,980**	**2,188**	**−3.0**	**−12.2**
Men and boys	**406**	**383**	**499**	**6.0**	**−18.6**
Men, aged 16 or older	148	109	259	35.8	−42.9
Boys, aged 2 to 15	259	274	240	−5.5	7.9
Women and girls	**812**	**863**	**933**	**−5.9**	**−13.0**
Women, aged 16 or older	532	636	593	−16.4	−10.3
Girls, aged 2 to 15	279	227	340	22.9	−17.9
Children under age 2	**111**	**88**	**66**	**26.1**	**68.2**
Footwear	**411**	**349**	**409**	**17.8**	**0.5**
Other apparel products, services	**180**	**295**	**280**	**−39.0**	**−35.7**
TRANSPORTATION	**5,017**	**3,568**	**4,660**	**40.6**	**7.7**
Vehicle purchases	**2,338**	**1,354**	**1,845**	**72.7**	**26.7**
Cars and trucks, new	524	229	936	128.8	−44.0
Cars and trucks, used	1,810	1,084	888	67.0	103.8
Other vehicles	–	41	18	–	–
Gasoline and motor oil	**894**	**810**	**1,162**	**10.4**	**−23.1**
Other vehicle expenses	**1,518**	**1,216**	**1,323**	**24.8**	**14.7**
Vehicle finance charges	217	181	237	19.9	−8.4
Maintenance and repairs	470	458	550	2.6	−14.5
Vehicle insurance	554	404	381	37.1	45.4
Vehicle rent, lease, license, other	276	173	156	59.5	76.9
Public transportation	**267**	**187**	**331**	**42.8**	**−19.3**
HEALTH CARE	**1,014**	**829**	**973**	**22.3**	**4.2**
Health insurance	453	302	297	50.0	52.5
Medical services	363	358	507	1.4	−28.4
Drugs	145	111	123	30.6	17.9
Medical supplies	54	58	46	−6.9	17.4
ENTERTAINMENT	**1,433**	**1,159**	**1,158**	**23.6**	**23.7**
Fees and admissions	404	289	414	39.8	−2.4
Television, radios, sound equipment	591	523	348	13.0	69.8
Pets, toys, and playground equipment	255	219	264	16.4	−3.4
Other supplies, equipment, and services	182	128	133	42.2	36.8
PERSONAL CARE PRODUCTS, SERVICES	**569**	**356**	**378**	**59.8**	**50.5**
READING	**76**	**104**	**143**	**−26.9**	**−46.9**
EDUCATION	**395**	**344**	**489**	**14.8**	**−19.2**
TOBACCO PRODUCTS AND SMOKING SUPPLIES	**299**	**274**	**317**	**9.1**	**−5.7**
MISCELLANEOUS	**784**	**744**	**630**	**5.4**	**24.4**
CASH CONTRIBUTIONS	**407**	**462**	**1,149**	**−11.9**	**−64.6**
PERSONAL INSURANCE, PENSIONS	**1,834**	**1,524**	**1,637**	**20.3**	**12.0**
Life and other personal insurance	150	181	255	−17.1	−41.2
Pensions and Social Security	1,683	1,344	1,384	25.2	21.6
PERSONAL TAXES	**597**	**1,360**	**1,636**	**−56.1**	**−63.5**
Federal income taxes	353	988	1,314	−64.3	−73.1
State and local income taxes	203	320	298	−36.6	−31.9
Other taxes	41	51	23	−19.6	78.3
GIFTS**	**683**	**661**	**933**	**3.3**	**−26.8**

* This figure does not include the amount paid for mortgage principle, which is considered an asset.
** Expenditures on gifts are also included in the preceding product and service categories.
Note: The Bureau of Labor Statistics uses consumer unit rather than household as the sampling unit in the Consumer Expenditure Survey. For the definition of consumer unit, see the glossary. Average annual spending total does not include the amount spent on personal taxes. (–) means sample is too small to make a reliable estimate.
Source: Bureau of Labor Statistics, Consumer Expenditure Surveys, Internet site http://www.bls.gov/cex/; calculations by New Strategist

Table 9.18 Spending of Single-Person Households, 1984, 1990, and 2000

(number of consumer units (CU) headed by people living alone, and average annual spending on products and services, 1984, 1990, and 2000; percent change, 1990–00 and 1984–00; in 2000 dollars)

	2000	1990	1984	percent change 1990–00	percent change 1984–00
Number of consumer units (in 000s)	32,323	27,263	24,563	18.6%	31.6%
Average annual spending	$23,059	$22,566	$21,536	2.2	7.1
FOOD	**$2,825**	**$3,033**	**$2,940**	**–6.9%**	**–3.9%**
Food at home	**1,477**	**1,489**	**1,419**	**–0.8**	**4.1**
Cereals and bakery products	221	223	194	–0.9	13.9
Cereals and cereal products	69	72	55	–4.2	25.5
Bakery products	151	150	141	0.7	7.1
Meats, poultry, fish, and eggs	352	358	375	–1.7	–6.1
Beef	100	104	123	–3.8	–18.7
Pork	71	67	65	6.0	9.2
Other meats	47	57	50	–17.5	–6.0
Poultry	68	65	61	4.6	11.5
Fish and seafood	50	49	53	2.0	–5.7
Eggs	18	18	25	0.0	–28.0
Dairy products	162	177	186	–8.5	–12.9
Fresh milk and cream	65	84	91	–22.6	–28.6
Other dairy products	98	94	96	4.3	2.1
Fruits and vegetables	279	271	254	3.0	9.8
Fresh fruits	93	87	78	6.9	19.2
Fresh vegetables	86	79	75	8.9	14.7
Processed fruits	60	63	60	–4.8	0.0
Processed vegetables	40	42	41	–4.8	–2.4
Other food at home	462	458	389	0.9	18.8
Sugar and other sweets	56	57	56	–1.8	0.0
Fats and oils	39	41	38	–4.9	2.6
Miscellaneous foods	221	200	154	10.5	43.5
Nonalcoholic beverages	125	141	139	–11.3	–10.1
Food prepared by CU, out-of-town trips	22	20	22	10.0	0.0
Food away from home	**1,348**	**1,544**	**1,521**	**–12.7**	**–11.4**
ALCOHOLIC BEVERAGES	**325**	**344**	**398**	**–5.5**	**–18.3**
HOUSING	**8,189**	**7,746**	**7,001**	**5.7**	**17.0**
Shelter	**5,054**	**4,913**	**4,180**	**2.9**	**20.9**
Owned dwellings*	2,332	2,107	1,415	10.7	64.8
Mortgage interest and charges	1,005	1,104	636	–9.0	58.0
Property taxes	723	487	391	48.5	84.9
Maintenance, repairs, insurance, other expenses	604	515	388	17.3	55.7
Rented dwellings	2,435	2,532	2,395	–3.8	1.7
Other lodging	287	275	370	4.4	–22.4
Utilities, fuels, public services	**1,628**	**1,578**	**1,603**	**3.2**	**1.6**
Natural gas	208	206	297	1.0	–30.0
Electricity	569	588	535	–3.2	6.4
Fuel oil and other fuels	68	75	149	–9.3	–54.4
Telephone	607	580	515	4.7	17.9
Water and other public services	175	132	108	32.6	62.0
Household services	**387**	**292**	**227**	**32.5**	**70.5**
Personal services	124	58	10	113.8	1,140.0
Other household services	264	235	219	12.3	20.5
Housekeeping supplies	**224**	**264**	**242**	**–15.2**	**–7.4**
Laundry and cleaning supplies	53	61	58	–13.1	–8.6
Other household products	102	101	88	1.0	15.9
Postage and stationery	69	101	96	–31.7	–28.1
Household furnishings, equipment	**895**	**698**	**747**	**28.2**	**19.8**
Household textiles	63	53	89	18.9	–29.2

(continued)

(continued from previous page)

	2000	1990	1984	percent change 1990–00	1984–00
Furniture	$226	$231	$234	–2.2%	–3.4%
Floor coverings	20	47	28	–57.4	–28.6
Major appliances	104	90	109	15.6	–4.6
Small appliances, misc. houseware	49	51	56	–3.9	–12.5
Miscellaneous household equipment	433	227	230	90.7	88.3
APPAREL AND SERVICES	**1,028**	**1,169**	**1,212**	**–12.1**	**–15.2**
Men and boys	**223**	**283**	**290**	**–21.2**	**–23.1**
Men, aged 16 or older	211	273	273	–22.7	–22.7
Boys, aged 2 to 15	12	11	18	9.1	–33.3
Women and girls	**414**	**464**	**487**	**–10.8**	**–15.0**
Women, aged 16 or older	397	449	472	–11.6	–15.9
Girls, aged 2 to 15	16	16	15	0.0	6.7
Children under age 2	**17**	**14**	**12**	**21.4**	**41.7**
Footwear	**191**	**162**	**149**	**17.9**	**28.2**
Other apparel products, services	**183**	**244**	**273**	**–25.0**	**–33.0**
TRANSPORTATION	**3,732**	**3,503**	**3,815**	**6.5**	**–2.2**
Vehicle purchases	**1,456**	**1,170**	**1,452**	**24.4**	**0.3**
Cars and trucks, new	797	578	897	37.9	–11.1
Cars and trucks, used	628	580	522	8.3	20.3
Other vehicles	32	12	31	166.7	3.2
Gasoline and motor oil	**682**	**733**	**923**	**–7.0**	**–26.1**
Other vehicle expenses	**1,272**	**1,246**	**1,046**	**2.1**	**21.6**
Vehicle finance charges	129	182	138	–29.1	–6.5
Maintenance and repairs	396	513	466	–22.8	–15.0
Vehicle insurance	437	415	305	5.3	43.3
Vehicle rent, lease, license, other	310	138	136	124.6	127.9
Public transportation	**322**	**353**	**394**	**–8.8**	**–18.3**
HEALTH CARE	**1,488**	**1,287**	**1,034**	**15.6**	**43.9**
Health insurance	657	513	355	28.1	85.1
Medical services	418	469	411	–10.9	1.7
Drugs	351	228	191	53.9	83.8
Medical supplies	62	76	78	–18.4	–20.5
ENTERTAINMENT	**1,026**	**1,108**	**1,076**	**–7.4**	**–4.6**
Fees and admissions	281	310	376	–9.4	–25.3
Television, radios, sound equipment	429	382	373	12.3	15.0
Pets, toys, and playground equipment	177	221	152	–19.9	16.4
Other supplies, equipment, and services	139	195	171	–28.7	–18.7
PERSONAL CARE PRODUCTS, SERVICES	**338**	**275**	**283**	**22.9**	**19.4**
READING	**113**	**144**	**167**	**–21.5**	**–32.3**
EDUCATION	**407**	**411**	**429**	**–1.0**	**–5.1**
TOBACCO PRODUCTS AND SMOKING SUPPLIES	**203**	**206**	**206**	**–1.5**	**–1.5**
MISCELLANEOUS	**561**	**838**	**613**	**–33.1**	**–8.5**
CASH CONTRIBUTIONS	**1,047**	**802**	**786**	**30.5**	**33.2**
PERSONAL INSURANCE, PENSIONS	**1,778**	**1,704**	**1,574**	**4.3**	**13.0**
Life and other personal insurance	155	148	219	4.7	–29.2
Pensions and Social Security	1,623	1,555	1,354	4.4	19.9
PERSONAL TAXES	**2,090**	**2,596**	**2,662**	**–19.5**	**–21.5**
Federal income taxes	1,621	2,082	2,105	–22.1	–23.0
State and local income taxes	360	464	484	–22.4	–25.6
Other taxes	109	51	71	113.7	53.5
GIFTS**	**807**	**930**	**898**	**–13.2**	**–10.1**

* This figure does not include the amount paid for mortgage principle, which is considered an asset.
** Expenditures on gifts are also included in the preceding product and service categories.
Note: The Bureau of Labor Statistics uses consumer unit rather than household as the sampling unit in the Consumer Expenditure Survey. For the definition of consumer unit, see the glossary. Average annual spending total does not include the amount spent on personal taxes.
Source: Bureau of Labor Statistics, Consumer Expenditure Surveys, Internet site http://www.bls.gov/cex/; calculations by New Strategist

Spending in the Midwest Rose the Most

Spending trends varied greatly by region between 1984 and 2000. Households in the Midwest spent 12 percent more in 2000 than in 1984, after adjusting for inflation. This increase was much larger than in any other region. Households in the Northeast boosted their spending by 9 percent during those years, while households in the West spent 3 percent more. Spending by households in the South fell 3 percent between 1984 and 2000, after adjusting for inflation.

The spending gains in the Midwest between 1984 and 2000 occurred entirely during the 1990s, since spending in the Midwest was lower in 1990 than in 1984. The booming economy of the 1990s created jobs and lifted incomes in most of the nation, but growth was greatest in the Midwest. As in other regions, however, much of the increased spending in the Midwest was devoted to nondiscretionary items such as health insurance (up 67 percent between 1984 and 2000), property taxes (up 42 percent), and mortgage interest (up 40 percent).

In the South, spending fell on most items between 1984 and 2000. While entertainment spending rose 24 percent in the Midwest and 19 percent in the Northeast, it fell 1 percent in the South and was down fully 10 percent in the West. Households in the West spent 28 percent more on mortgage interest in 2000 than in 1984. In the South, spending fell even on this item during those years.

Spending fell in the South

(percent change in average annual spending of households by region, 1984 to 2000; in 2000 dollars)

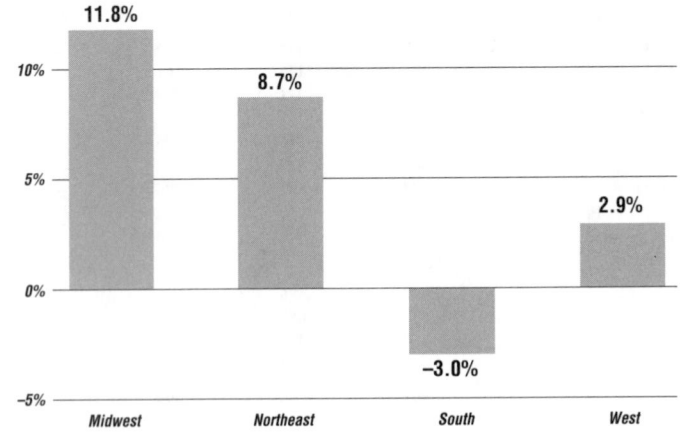

Table 9.19 Spending by Households in the Northeast, 1984, 1990, and 2000

(number of consumer units (CU) in the Northeast, and average annual spending on products and services, 1984, 1990, and 2000; percent change, 1990–00 and 1984–00; in 2000 dollars)

	2000	1990	1984	percent change 1990–00	percent change 1984–00
Number of consumer units (in 000s)	20,994	20,259	19,686	3.6%	6.6%
Average annual spending	$38,902	$38,862	$35,787	0.1	8.7
FOOD	**$5,377**	**$6,091**	**$5,779**	**–11.7%**	**–7.0%**
Food at home	3,202	3,424	3,462	–6.5	–7.5
Cereals and bakery products	491	536	472	–8.4	4.0
Cereals and cereal products	164	174	129	–5.7	27.1
Bakery products	326	362	343	–9.9	–5.0
Meats, poultry, fish, and eggs	883	989	1,084	–10.7	–18.5
Beef	248	298	353	–16.8	–29.7
Pork	162	171	196	–5.3	–17.3
Other meats	116	146	162	–20.5	–28.4
Poultry	174	183	167	–4.9	4.2
Fish and seafood	149	148	143	0.7	4.2
Eggs	35	43	63	–18.6	–44.4
Dairy products	354	412	459	–14.1	–22.9
Fresh milk and cream	132	200	217	–34.0	–39.2
Other dairy products	222	212	242	4.7	–8.3
Fruits and vegetables	579	585	598	–1.0	–3.2
Fresh fruits	181	179	182	1.1	–0.5
Fresh vegetables	184	169	174	8.9	5.7
Processed fruits	131	144	144	–9.0	–9.0
Processed vegetables	83	95	98	–12.6	–15.3
Other food at home	895	901	800	–0.7	11.9
Sugar and other sweets	126	117	113	7.7	11.5
Fats and oils	89	80	83	11.3	7.2
Miscellaneous foods	398	382	317	4.2	25.6
Nonalcoholic beverages	240	281	290	–14.6	–17.2
Food prepared by CU, out-of-town trips	41	42	48	–2.4	–14.6
Food away from home	**2,175**	**2,667**	**2,317**	**–18.4**	**–6.1**
ALCOHOLIC BEVERAGES	**390**	**437**	**461**	**–10.8**	**–15.4**
HOUSING	**13,505**	**12,652**	**10,831**	**6.7**	**24.7**
Shelter	**8,222**	**7,456**	**5,715**	**10.3**	**43.9**
Owned dwellings*	5,229	4,354	3,177	20.1	64.6
Mortgage interest and charges	2,574	2,440	1,535	5.5	67.7
Property taxes	1,780	1,165	963	52.8	84.8
Maintenance, repairs, insurance, other expenses	874	750	680	16.5	28.5
Rented dwellings	2,434	2,414	1,941	0.8	25.4
Other lodging	559	688	595	–18.8	–6.1
Utilities, fuels, public services	**2,570**	**2,610**	**2,912**	**–1.5**	**–11.7**
Natural gas	413	375	549	10.1	–24.8
Electricity	816	916	975	–10.9	–16.3
Fuel oil and other fuels	271	339	507	–20.1	–46.5
Telephone	856	776	718	10.3	19.2
Water and other public services	214	203	166	5.4	28.9
Household services	**643**	**498**	**452**	**29.1**	**42.3**
Personal services	312	242	169	28.9	84.6
Other household services	331	256	285	29.3	16.1
Housekeeping supplies	**530**	**561**	**492**	**–5.5**	**7.7**
Laundry and cleaning supplies	146	161	138	–9.3	5.8
Other household products	245	224	209	9.4	17.2
Postage and stationery	139	177	144	–21.5	–3.5
Household furnishings, equipment	**1,540**	**1,526**	**1,260**	**0.9**	**22.2**
Household textiles	134	116	104	15.5	28.8

(continued)

(continued from previous page)

	2000	1990	1984	percent change 1990–00	percent change 1984–00
Furniture	$388	$449	$325	–13.6%	19.4%
Floor coverings	47	208	63	–77.4	–25.4
Major appliances	179	191	230	–6.3	–22.2
Small appliances, misc. houseware	91	82	94	11.0	–3.2
Miscellaneous household equipment	702	478	443	46.9	58.5
APPAREL AND SERVICES	**2,115**	**2,383**	**2,393**	**–11.2**	**–11.6**
Men and boys	**484**	**548**	**636**	**–11.7**	**–23.9**
Men, aged 16 or older	374	445	484	–16.0	–22.7
Boys, aged 2 to 15	110	103	152	6.8	–27.6
Women and girls	**849**	**980**	**943**	**–13.4**	**–10.0**
Women, aged 16 or older	705	860	792	–18.0	–11.0
Girls, aged 2 to 15	144	120	151	20.0	–4.6
Children under age 2	**82**	**94**	**81**	**–12.8**	**1.2**
Footwear	**382**	**402**	**363**	**–5.0**	**5.2**
Other apparel products, services	**318**	**360**	**371**	**–11.7**	**–14.3**
TRANSPORTATION	**6,664**	**6,337**	**6,605**	**5.2**	**0.9**
Vehicle purchases	**2,719**	**2,530**	**2,728**	**7.5**	**–0.3**
Cars and trucks, new	1,456	1,541	1,840	–5.5	–20.9
Cars and trucks, used	1,246	974	878	27.9	41.9
Other vehicles	–	14	10	–	–
Gasoline and motor oil	**1,094**	**1,142**	**1,465**	**–4.2**	**–25.3**
Other vehicle expenses	**2,251**	**2,099**	**1,841**	**7.2**	**22.3**
Vehicle finance charges	228	314	270	–27.4	–15.6
Maintenance and repairs	570	701	731	–18.7	–22.0
Vehicle insurance	808	830	631	–2.7	28.1
Vehicle rent, lease, license, other	646	254	209	154.3	209.1
Public transportation	**600**	**567**	**568**	**5.8**	**5.6**
HEALTH CARE	**1,862**	**1,839**	**1,631**	**1.3**	**14.2**
Health insurance	908	729	504	24.6	80.2
Medical services	504	736	797	–31.5	–36.8
Drugs	349	270	252	29.3	38.5
Medical supplies	101	105	78	–3.8	29.5
ENTERTAINMENT	**1,915**	**1,754**	**1,616**	**9.2**	**18.5**
Fees and admissions	577	524	549	10.1	5.1
Television, radios, sound equipment	627	565	481	11.0	30.4
Pets, toys, and playground equipment	316	356	282	–11.2	12.1
Other supplies, equipment, and services	395	310	303	27.4	30.4
PERSONAL CARE PRODUCTS, SERVICES	**578**	**464**	**449**	**24.6**	**28.7**
READING	**172**	**225**	**254**	**–23.6**	**–32.3**
EDUCATION	**823**	**781**	**638**	**5.4**	**29.0**
TOBACCO PRODUCTS AND SMOKING SUPPLIES	**326**	**368**	**404**	**–11.4**	**–19.3**
MISCELLANEOUS	**738**	**1,054**	**598**	**–30.0**	**23.4**
CASH CONTRIBUTIONS	**1,064**	**933**	**1,155**	**14.0**	**–7.9**
PERSONAL INSURANCE, PENSIONS	**3,371**	**3,544**	**2,975**	**–4.9**	**13.3**
Life and other personal insurance	423	449	401	–5.8	5.5
Pensions and Social Security	2,948	3,095	2,574	–4.7	14.5
PERSONAL TAXES	**2,983**	**4,076**	**3,578**	**–26.8**	**–16.6**
Federal income taxes	2,196	3,174	2,642	–30.8	–16.9
State and local income taxes	633	817	812	–22.5	–22.0
Other taxes	154	87	124	77.0	24.2
GIFTS**	**1,096**	**1,453**	**1,306**	**–24.6**	**–16.1**

This figure does not include the amount paid for mortgage principle, which is considered an asset.
** Expenditures on gifts are also included in the preceding product and service categories.
Note: The Bureau of Labor Statistics uses consumer unit rather than household as the sampling unit in the Consumer Expenditure Survey. For the definition of consumer unit, see the glossary. Average annual spending total does not include the amount spent on personal taxes. (–) means sample is too small to make a reliable estimate.
Source: Bureau of Labor Statistics, Consumer Expenditure Surveys, Internet site http://www.bls.gov/cex/; calculations by New Strategist

Table 9.20 Spending by Households in the Midwest, 1984, 1990, and 2000

(number of consumer units (CU) in the Midwest, and average annual spending on products and services, 1984, 1990, and 2000; percent change, 1990–00 and 1984–00; in 2000 dollars)

	2000	1990	1984	percent change 1990–00	percent change 1984–00
Number of consumer units (in 000s)	25,717	24,205	23,737	6.2%	8.3%
Average annual spending	$39,213	$34,170	$35,081	14.8	11.8
FOOD	**$5,255**	**$5,299**	**$5,360**	**–0.8%**	**–2.0%**
Food at home	2,933	3,047	3,252	–3.7	–9.8
Cereals and bakery products	444	457	454	–2.8	–2.2
Cereals and cereal products	152	157	148	–3.2	2.7
Bakery products	292	300	305	–2.7	–4.3
Meats, poultry, fish, and eggs	721	779	938	–7.4	–23.1
Beef	226	260	326	–13.1	–30.7
Pork	160	171	214	–6.4	–25.2
Other meats	103	129	157	–20.2	–34.4
Poultry	125	108	114	15.7	9.6
Fish and seafood	78	80	73	–2.5	6.8
Eggs	28	32	53	–12.5	–47.2
Dairy products	330	369	404	–10.6	–18.3
Fresh milk and cream	132	174	204	–24.1	–35.3
Other dairy products	197	195	201	1.0	–2.0
Fruits and vegetables	482	490	491	–1.6	–1.8
Fresh fruits	151	159	151	–5.0	0.0
Fresh vegetables	137	133	139	3.0	–1.4
Processed fruits	113	116	109	–2.6	3.7
Processed vegetables	81	82	91	–1.2	–11.0
Other food at home	957	953	915	0.4	4.6
Sugar and other sweets	124	120	129	3.3	–3.9
Fats and oils	75	86	93	–12.8	–19.4
Miscellaneous foods	468	444	393	5.4	19.1
Nonalcoholic beverages	249	267	298	–6.7	–16.4
Food prepared by CU, out-of-town trips	41	37	48	10.8	–14.6
Food away from home	**2,322**	**2,252**	**2,110**	**3.1**	**10.0**
ALCOHOLIC BEVERAGES	**388**	**386**	**403**	**0.5**	**–3.7**
HOUSING	**11,961**	**10,133**	**10,415**	**18.0**	**14.8**
Shelter	**6,633**	**5,345**	**5,118**	**24.1**	**29.6**
Owned dwellings*	4,599	3,381	3,262	36.0	41.0
Mortgage interest and charges	2,471	1,901	1,765	30.0	40.0
Property taxes	1,224	842	865	45.4	41.5
Maintenance, repairs, insurance, other expenses	903	638	631	41.5	43.1
Rented dwellings	1,531	1,581	1,354	–3.2	13.1
Other lodging	503	383	502	31.3	0.2
Utilities, fuels, public services	**2,513**	**2,422**	**2,872**	**3.8**	**–12.5**
Natural gas	430	491	766	–12.4	–43.9
Electricity	834	880	1,021	–5.2	–18.3
Fuel oil and other fuels	73	109	192	–33.0	–62.0
Telephone	884	721	675	22.6	31.0
Water and other public services	291	220	217	32.3	34.1
Household services	**670**	**481**	**466**	**39.3**	**43.8**
Personal services	369	267	191	38.2	93.2
Other household services	301	213	275	41.3	9.5
Housekeeping supplies	**514**	**514**	**530**	**0.0**	**–3.0**
Laundry and cleaning supplies	133	145	151	–8.3	–11.9
Other household products	238	216	230	10.2	3.5
Postage and stationery	143	152	149	–5.9	–4.0
Household furnishings, equipment	**1,631**	**1,373**	**1,429**	**18.8**	**14.1**
Household textiles	117	133	133	–12.0	–12.0

(continued)

(continued from previous page)

	2000	1990	1984	percent change 1990–00	percent change 1984–00
Furniture	$378	$383	$404	–1.3%	–6.4%
Floor coverings	54	138	131	–60.9	–58.8
Major appliances	198	173	225	14.5	–12.0
Small appliances, misc. houseware	103	96	109	7.3	–5.5
Miscellaneous household equipment	782	449	426	74.2	83.6
APPAREL AND SERVICES	**1,917**	**1,791**	**2,100**	**7.0**	**–8.7**
Men and boys	**489**	**437**	**587**	**11.9**	**–16.7**
Men, aged 16 or older	386	353	467	9.3	–17.3
Boys, aged 2 to 15	103	84	119	22.6	–13.4
Women and girls	**771**	**762**	**854**	**1.2**	**–9.7**
Women, aged 16 or older	646	651	706	–0.8	–8.5
Girls, aged 2 to 15	125	111	146	12.6	–14.4
Children under age 2	**88**	**83**	**89**	**6.0**	**–1.1**
Footwear	**324**	**216**	**283**	**50.0**	**14.5**
Other apparel products, services	**245**	**292**	**288**	**–16.1**	**–14.9**
TRANSPORTATION	**7,841**	**6,314**	**6,923**	**24.2**	**13.3**
Vehicle purchases	**3,759**	**2,725**	**3,013**	**37.9**	**24.8**
Cars and trucks, new	1,540	1,174	1,558	31.2	–1.2
Cars and trucks, used	2,132	1,522	1,400	40.1	52.3
Other vehicles	86	29	55	196.6	56.4
Gasoline and motor oil	**1,352**	**1,318**	**1,760**	**2.6**	**–23.2**
Other vehicle expenses	**2,327**	**1,996**	**1,840**	**16.6**	**26.5**
Vehicle finance charges	353	395	328	–10.6	7.6
Maintenance and repairs	610	704	739	–13.4	–17.5
Vehicle insurance	750	639	517	17.4	45.1
Vehicle rent, lease, license, other	615	260	255	136.5	141.2
Public transportation	**403**	**275**	**312**	**46.5**	**29.2**
HEALTH CARE	**2,172**	**1,760**	**1,651**	**23.4**	**31.6**
Health insurance	1,047	725	626	44.4	67.3
Medical services	575	602	686	–4.5	–16.2
Drugs	439	327	264	34.3	66.3
Medical supplies	111	108	75	2.8	48.0
ENTERTAINMENT	**2,040**	**1,787**	**1,642**	**14.2**	**24.2**
Fees and admissions	566	457	509	23.9	11.2
Television, radios, sound equipment	665	570	477	16.7	39.4
Pets, toys, and playground equipment	360	356	298	1.1	20.8
Other supplies, equipment, and services	449	403	358	11.4	25.4
PERSONAL CARE PRODUCTS, SERVICES	**544**	**432**	**496**	**25.9**	**9.7**
READING	**164**	**211**	**229**	**–22.3**	**–28.4**
EDUCATION	**667**	**519**	**517**	**28.5**	**29.0**
TOBACCO PRODUCTS AND SMOKING SUPPLIES	**360**	**393**	**389**	**–8.4**	**–7.5**
MISCELLANEOUS	**798**	**992**	**626**	**–19.6**	**27.5**
CASH CONTRIBUTIONS	**1,615**	**982**	**1,205**	**64.5**	**34.0**
PERSONAL INSURANCE, PENSIONS	**3,490**	**3,173**	**3,127**	**10.0**	**11.6**
Life and other personal insurance	429	468	496	–8.3	–13.5
Pensions and Social Security	3,061	2,705	2,632	13.2	16.3
PERSONAL TAXES	**3,667**	**3,196**	**3,552**	**14.7**	**3.2**
Federal income taxes	2,699	2,314	2,564	16.6	5.3
State and local income taxes	815	748	812	9.0	0.4
Other taxes	153	136	176	12.5	–13.1
GIFTS **	**1,291**	**1,090**	**1,096**	**18.4**	**17.8**

* This figure does not include the amount paid for mortgage principle, which is considered an asset.
** Expenditures on gifts are also included in the preceding product and service categories.
Note: The Bureau of Labor Statistics uses consumer unit rather than household as the sampling unit in the Consumer Expenditure Survey.
For the definition of consumer unit, see the glossary. Average annual spending total does not include the amount spent on personal taxes.
Source: Bureau of Labor Statistics, Consumer Expenditure Surveys, Internet site http://www.bls.gov/cex/; calculations by New Strategist

Table 9.21 Spending by Households in the South, 1984, 1990, and 2000

(number of consumer units (CU) in the South, and average annual spending on products and services, 1984, 1990, and 2000; percent change, 1990–00 and 1984–00; in 2000 dollars)

	2000	1990	1984	percent change 1990–00	percent change 1984–00
Number of consumer units (in 000s)	38,245	32,651	29,852	17.1%	28.1%
Average annual spending	$34,707	$35,599	$35,777	–2.5	–3.0
FOOD	**$4,724**	**$5,372**	**$5,053**	**–12.1%**	**–6.5%**
Food at home	**2,823**	**3,137**	**3,035**	**–10.0**	**–7.0**
Cereals and bakery products	422	455	398	–7.3	6.0
Cereals and cereal products	148	167	136	–11.4	8.8
Bakery products	274	287	262	–4.5	4.6
Meats, poultry, fish, and eggs	779	863	953	–9.7	–18.3
Beef	230	281	325	–18.1	–29.2
Pork	176	187	191	–5.9	–7.9
Other meats	94	124	108	–24.2	–13.0
Poultry	142	138	144	2.9	–1.4
Fish and seafood	100	95	126	5.3	–20.6
Eggs	36	38	60	–5.3	–40.0
Dairy products	286	357	375	–19.9	–23.7
Fresh milk and cream	122	171	204	–28.7	–40.2
Other dairy products	164	186	171	–11.8	–4.1
Fruits and vegetables	470	501	451	–6.2	4.2
Fresh fruits	141	150	123	–6.0	14.6
Fresh vegetables	139	145	134	–4.1	3.7
Processed fruits	103	107	101	–3.7	2.0
Processed vegetables	86	99	94	–13.1	–8.5
Other food at home	867	962	819	–9.9	5.9
Sugar and other sweets	107	123	113	–13.0	–5.3
Fats and oils	82	95	91	–13.7	–9.9
Miscellaneous foods	410	432	335	–5.1	22.4
Nonalcoholic beverages	238	273	280	–12.8	–15.0
Food prepared by CU, out-of-town trips	29	38	38	–23.7	–23.7
Food away from home	**1,901**	**2,235**	**2,019**	**–14.9**	**–5.8**
ALCOHOLIC BEVERAGES	**304**	**328**	**423**	**–7.3**	**–28.1**
HOUSING	**10,855**	**10,282**	**10,985**	**5.6**	**–1.2**
Shelter	**5,839**	**5,228**	**5,453**	**11.7**	**7.1**
Owned dwellings*	3,803	3,199	3,356	18.9	13.3
Mortgage interest and charges	2,238	1,984	2,295	12.8	–2.5
Property taxes	825	515	419	60.2	96.9
Maintenance, repairs, insurance, other expenses	739	700	641	5.6	15.3
Rented dwellings	1,643	1,665	1,510	–1.3	8.8
Other lodging	393	364	587	8.0	–33.0
Utilities, fuels, public services	**2,596**	**2,635**	**2,738**	**–1.5**	**–5.2**
Natural gas	190	198	268	–4.0	–29.1
Electricity	1,148	1,252	1,296	–8.3	–11.4
Fuel oil and other fuels	57	74	169	–23.0	–66.3
Telephone	891	812	738	9.7	20.7
Water and other public services	311	299	267	4.0	16.5
Household services	**645**	**617**	**547**	**4.5**	**17.9**
Personal services	284	279	240	1.8	18.3
Other household services	361	337	307	7.1	17.6
Housekeeping supplies	**440**	**501**	**499**	**–12.2**	**–11.8**
Laundry and cleaning supplies	126	144	143	–12.5	–11.9
Other household products	213	219	240	–2.7	–11.3
Postage and stationery	101	138	114	–26.8	–11.4
Household furnishings, equipment	**1,334**	**1,302**	**1,747**	**2.5**	**–23.6**
Household textiles	85	125	151	–32.0	–43.7

(continued)

(continued from previous page)

	2000	1990	1984	percent change 1990–00	percent change 1984–00
Furniture	$338	$369	$549	–8.4%	–38.4%
Floor coverings	41	63	192	–34.9	–78.6
Major appliances	168	202	247	–16.8	–32.0
Small appliances, misc. houseware	72	91	121	–20.9	–40.5
Miscellaneous household equipment	630	451	491	39.7	28.3
APPAREL AND SERVICES	**1,617**	**2,041**	**2,136**	**–20.8**	**–24.3**
Men and boys	**382**	**501**	**534**	**–23.8**	**–28.5**
Men, aged 16 or older	295	412	438	–28.4	–32.6
Boys, aged 2 to 15	87	88	94	–1.1	–7.4
Women and girls	**612**	**870**	**857**	**–29.7**	**–28.6**
Women, aged 16 or older	499	763	744	–34.6	–32.9
Girls, aged 2 to 15	113	107	113	5.6	0.0
Children under age 2	**82**	**87**	**80**	**–5.7**	**2.5**
Footwear	**303**	**254**	**308**	**19.3**	**–1.6**
Other apparel products, services	**238**	**331**	**358**	**–28.1**	**–33.5**
TRANSPORTATION	**7,211**	**6,992**	**7,170**	**3.1**	**0.6**
Vehicle purchases	**3,566**	**2,997**	**3,041**	**19.0**	**17.3**
Cars and trucks, new	1,632	1,721	1,735	–5.2	–5.9
Cars and trucks, used	1,909	1,241	1,270	53.8	50.3
Other vehicles	–	36	38	–	–
Gasoline and motor oil	**1,290**	**1,518**	**1,891**	**–15.0**	**–31.8**
Other vehicle expenses	**2,073**	**2,149**	**1,926**	**–3.5**	**7.6**
Vehicle finance charges	366	456	428	–19.7	–14.5
Maintenance and repairs	584	791	786	–26.2	–25.7
Vehicle insurance	747	717	555	4.2	34.6
Vehicle rent, lease, license, other	376	186	157	102.2	139.5
Public transportation	**283**	**328**	**312**	**–13.7**	**–9.3**
HEALTH CARE	**2,147**	**2,108**	**1,921**	**1.9**	**11.8**
Health insurance	1,063	839	738	26.7	44.0
Medical services	533	755	759	–29.4	–29.8
Drugs	470	391	320	20.2	46.9
Medical supplies	82	123	104	–33.3	–21.2
ENTERTAINMENT	**1,617**	**1,668**	**1,641**	**–3.1**	**–1.5**
Fees and admissions	395	403	421	–2.0	–6.2
Television, radios, sound equipment	574	578	517	–0.7	11.0
Pets, toys, and playground equipment	313	357	315	–12.3	–0.6
Other supplies, equipment, and services	335	329	386	1.8	–13.2
PERSONAL CARE PRODUCTS, SERVICES	**550**	**473**	**466**	**16.3**	**18.0**
READING	**114**	**173**	**184**	**–34.1**	**–38.0**
EDUCATION	**477**	**420**	**396**	**13.6**	**20.5**
TOBACCO PRODUCTS AND SMOKING SUPPLIES	**334**	**377**	**396**	**–11.4**	**–15.7**
MISCELLANEOUS	**729**	**1,107**	**781**	**–34.1**	**–6.7**
CASH CONTRIBUTIONS	**953**	**1,105**	**1,124**	**–13.8**	**–15.2**
PERSONAL INSURANCE, PENSIONS	**3,077**	**3,155**	**3,104**	**–2.5**	**–0.9**
Life and other personal insurance	407	485	555	–16.1	–26.7
Pensions and Social Security	2,670	2,671	2,549	0.0	4.7
PERSONAL TAXES	**2,516**	**3,577**	**3,696**	**–29.7**	**–31.9**
Federal income taxes	2,053	2,997	3,084	–31.5	–33.4
State and local income taxes	321	481	532	–33.3	–39.7
Other taxes	142	99	80	43.4	77.5
GIFTS**	**908**	**1,112**	**1,057**	**–18.3**	**–14.1**

* This figure does not include the amount paid for mortgage principle, which is considered an asset.
** Expenditures on gifts are also included in the preceding product and service categories.
Note: The Bureau of Labor Statistics uses consumer unit rather than household as the sampling unit in the Consumer Expenditure Survey. For the definition of consumer unit, see the glossary. Average annual spending total does not include the amount spent on personal taxes. (–) means sample is too small to make a reliable estimate.
Source: Bureau of Labor Statistics, Consumer Expenditure Surveys, Internet site http://www.bls.gov/cex/; calculations by New Strategist

Table 9.22 Spending by Households in the West, 1984, 1990, and 2000

(number of consumer units (CU) in the West, and average annual spending on products and services, 1984, 1990, and 2000; percent change, 1990–00 and 1984–00; in 2000 dollars)

	2000	1990	1984	percent change 1990–00	percent change 1984–00
Number of consumer units (in 000s)	24,410	19,853	16,948	23.0%	44.0%
Average annual spending	$41,328	$42,768	$40,171	−3.4	2.9
FOOD	**$5,554**	**$6,137**	**$5,915**	**−9.5%**	**−6.1%**
Food at home	**3,269**	**3,622**	**3,464**	**−9.7**	**−5.6**
Cereals and bakery products	480	516	431	−7.0	11.4
Cereals and cereal products	167	183	146	−8.7	14.4
Bakery products	313	332	285	−5.7	9.8
Meats, poultry, fish, and eggs	821	922	915	−11.0	−10.3
Beef	255	318	320	−19.8	−20.3
Pork	164	161	181	1.9	−9.4
Other meats	94	126	116	−25.4	−19.0
Poultry	146	146	141	0.0	3.5
Fish and seafood	124	124	96	0.0	29.2
Eggs	38	46	61	−17.4	−37.7
Dairy products	356	444	476	−19.8	−25.2
Fresh milk and cream	145	204	230	−28.9	−37.0
Other dairy products	211	240	244	−12.1	−13.5
Fruits and vegetables	592	605	592	−2.1	0.0
Fresh fruits	196	191	186	2.6	5.4
Fresh vegetables	190	190	177	0.0	7.3
Processed fruits	123	133	138	−7.5	−10.9
Processed vegetables	84	91	89	−7.7	−5.6
Other food at home	1,021	1,134	984	−10.0	3.8
Sugar and other sweets	117	138	141	−15.2	−17.0
Fats and oils	87	96	101	−9.4	−13.9
Miscellaneous foods	484	516	418	−6.2	15.8
Nonalcoholic beverages	277	308	325	−10.1	−14.8
Food prepared by CU, out-of-town trips	55	75	70	−26.7	−21.4
Food away from home	**2,285**	**2,515**	**2,450**	**−9.1**	**−6.7**
ALCOHOLIC BEVERAGES	**449**	**432**	**585**	**3.9**	**−23.2**
HOUSING	**13,972**	**13,831**	**12,374**	**1.0**	**12.9**
Shelter	**8,667**	**8,397**	**7,372**	**3.2**	**17.6**
Owned dwellings*	5,320	5,180	4,026	2.7	32.1
Mortgage interest and charges	3,498	3,619	2,738	−3.3	27.8
Property taxes	987	783	648	26.1	52.3
Maintenance, repairs, insurance, other expenses	834	779	640	7.1	30.3
Rented dwellings	2,832	2,736	2,630	3.5	7.7
Other lodging	515	480	716	7.3	−28.1
Utilities, fuels, public services	**2,226**	**2,215**	**2,221**	**0.5**	**0.2**
Natural gas	272	279	434	−2.5	−37.3
Electricity	704	812	704	−13.3	0.0
Fuel oil and other fuels	35	43	75	−18.6	−53.3
Telephone	864	805	759	7.3	13.8
Water and other public services	351	275	249	27.6	41.0
Household services	**796**	**764**	**641**	**4.2**	**24.2**
Personal services	360	377	247	−4.5	45.7
Other household services	436	387	393	12.7	10.9
Housekeeping supplies	**472**	**589**	**514**	**−19.9**	**−8.2**
Laundry and cleaning supplies	122	150	143	−18.7	−14.7
Other household products	216	249	189	−13.3	14.3
Postage and stationery	135	191	182	−29.3	−25.8
Household furnishings, equipment	**1,811**	**1,866**	**1,626**	**−2.9**	**11.4**
Household textiles	106	149	186	−28.9	−43.0

(continued)

(continued from previous page)

	2000	1990	1984	percent change 1990–00	1984–00
Furniture	$489	$464	$471	5.4%	3.8%
Floor coverings	37	104	89	−64.4	−58.4
Major appliances	221	211	247	4.7	−10.5
Small appliances, misc. houseware	93	129	116	−27.9	−19.8
Miscellaneous household equipment	865	809	517	6.9	67.3
APPAREL AND SERVICES	**1,945**	**2,441**	**2,155**	**−20.3**	**−9.7**
Men and boys	**445**	**615**	**585**	**−27.6**	**−23.9**
Men, aged 16 or older	354	520	479	−31.9	−26.1
Boys, aged 2 to 15	91	95	106	−4.2	−14.2
Women and girls	**746**	**971**	**819**	**−23.2**	**−8.9**
Women, aged 16 or older	652	842	699	−22.6	−6.7
Girls, aged 2 to 15	95	129	119	−26.4	−20.2
Children under age 2	**75**	**109**	**85**	**−31.2**	**−11.8**
Footwear	**391**	**356**	**270**	**9.8**	**44.8**
Other apparel products, services	**288**	**390**	**396**	**−26.2**	**−27.3**
TRANSPORTATION	**7,943**	**7,282**	**7,982**	**9.1**	**−0.5**
Vehicle purchases	**3,430**	**2,864**	**3,250**	**19.8**	**5.5**
Cars and trucks, new	1,759	1,622	1,717	8.4	2.4
Cars and trucks, used	1,620	1,206	1,455	34.3	11.3
Other vehicles	51	37	80	37.8	−36.3
Gasoline and motor oil	**1,400**	**1,469**	**1,836**	**−4.7**	**−23.7**
Other vehicle expenses	**2,586**	**2,455**	**2,285**	**5.3**	**13.2**
Vehicle finance charges	329	378	353	−13.0	−6.8
Maintenance and repairs	749	916	979	−18.2	−23.5
Vehicle insurance	831	822	643	1.1	29.2
Vehicle rent, lease, license, other	677	339	312	99.7	117.0
Public transportation	**527**	**494**	**610**	**6.7**	**−13.6**
HEALTH CARE	**2,001**	**2,034**	**1,662**	**−1.6**	**20.4**
Health insurance	853	735	502	16.1	69.9
Medical services	669	891	786	−24.9	−14.9
Drugs	368	303	245	21.5	50.2
Medical supplies	111	105	131	5.7	−15.3
ENTERTAINMENT	**2,021**	**2,441**	**2,246**	**−17.2**	**−10.0**
Fees and admissions	595	635	675	−6.3	−11.9
Television, radios, sound equipment	648	696	699	−6.9	−7.3
Pets, toys, and playground equipment	355	394	376	−9.9	−5.6
Other supplies, equipment, and services	423	715	497	−40.8	−14.9
PERSONAL CARE PRODUCTS, SERVICES	**594**	**564**	**517**	**5.3**	**14.9**
READING	**158**	**216**	**227**	**−26.9**	**−30.4**
EDUCATION	**674**	**494**	**515**	**36.4**	**30.9**
TOBACCO PRODUCTS AND SMOKING SUPPLIES	**245**	**291**	**302**	**−15.8**	**−18.9**
MISCELLANEOUS	**859**	**1,311**	**1,034**	**−34.5**	**−16.9**
CASH CONTRIBUTIONS	**1,233**	**1,285**	**1,218**	**−4.0**	**1.2**
PERSONAL INSURANCE, PENSIONS	**3,679**	**4,008**	**3,439**	**−8.2**	**7.0**
Life and other personal insurance	333	393	505	−15.3	−34.1
Pensions and Social Security	3,346	3,615	2,932	−7.4	14.1
PERSONAL TAXES	**3,582**	**4,995**	**3,989**	**−28.3**	**−10.2**
Federal income taxes	2,827	3,881	3,156	−27.2	−10.4
State and local income taxes	614	1,042	797	−41.1	−23.0
Other taxes	140	70	36	100.0	288.9
GIFTS**	**1,131**	**1,223**	**1,228**	**−7.5**	**−7.9**

* This figure does not include the amount paid for mortgage principle, which is considered an asset.
** Expenditures on gifts are also included in the preceding product and service categories.
Note: The Bureau of Labor Statistics uses consumer unit rather than household as the sampling unit in the Consumer Expenditure Survey. For the definition of consumer unit, see the glossary. Average annual spending total does not include the amount spent on personal taxes.
Source: Bureau of Labor Statistics, Consumer Expenditure Surveys, Internet site http://www.bls.gov/cex/; calculations by New Strategist

10

Wealth

■ The median net worth, or assets minus debts, of the average American household stood at $71,600 in 1998. While modest, the figure is 20 percent higher than it was in 1989.

■ Householders aged 55 or older saw their net worth rise between 1989 and 1998, those aged 65 to 74 enjoying the biggest gains. Householders under age 55 saw their net worth shrink as homeownership among young and middle-aged adults declined.

■ The median value of financial assets owned by the average American household surged between 1989 and 1998, rising 64 percent because of the booming stock market. Despite this growth, nonfinancial assets continue to account for most of Americans' wealth. Housing equity is the largest component of net worth.

■ Three out of four American households are in debt, a ratio that did not change much between 1989 and 1998. The median amount owed by the average household with debt rose a substantial 67 percent during those years as more households took on mortgage debt.

Net Worth Rose during the 1990s

The median net worth, or assets minus debts, of the average American household stood at $71,600 in 1998 (the latest data available). While modest, the figure is 20 percent higher than it was in 1989, the earliest comparable figure available. Some demographic segments gained during those years while others lost ground. Householders aged 55 or older saw their net worth rise, those aged 65 to 74 enjoying the biggest gains. Householders under age 55 saw their net worth shrink as homeownership fell among young and middle-aged adults. Home equity accounts for the largest share of net worth.

The net worth of non-Hispanic whites is much greater than that of nonwhites and Hispanics, $94,900 versus $16,400 in 1998. But the net worth of nonwhites and Hispanics grew much faster than that of non-Hispanic whites between 1989 and 1998, thanks to the rise in minority homeownership.

Net worth rose 20 percent

(median net worth of households, 1989 and 1998; in 1998 dollars)

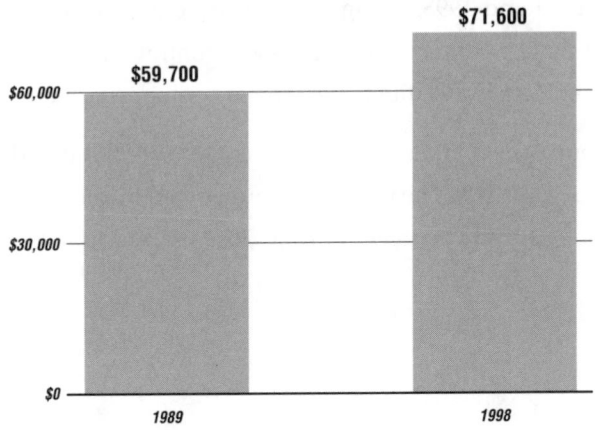

Table 10.1 Net Worth of Households by Age of Householder, 1989 and 1998

(median net worth of households by age of householder, 1989 and 1998; percent change, 1989–98; in 1998 dollars)

	1998	1989	percent change 1989–98
Total households	**$71,600**	**$59,700**	**19.9%**
Under age 35	9,000	9,900	–9.1
Aged 35 to 44	63,400	71,800	–11.7
Aged 45 to 54	105,500	125,700	–16.1
Aged 55 to 64	127,500	124,600	2.3
Aged 65 to 74	146,500	97,100	50.9
Aged 75 or older	125,600	92,200	36.2

Source: Federal Reserve Board, Recent Changes in U.S. Family Finances: Results from the 1998 Survey of Consumer Finances, *Federal Reserve Bulletin, January 2000; calculations by New Strategist*

Table 10.2 Net Worth of Households by Race and Hispanic Origin of Householder, 1989 and 1998

(median net worth of households by race and Hispanic origin of householder, 1989 and 1998; percent change, 1989–98; in 1998 dollars)

	1998	1989	percent change 1989–98
Total households	**$71,600**	**$59,700**	**19.9%**
White, non-Hispanic	94,900	90,500	4.9
Nonwhite or Hispanic	16,400	8,500	92.9

Source: Federal Reserve Board, Recent Changes in U.S. Family Finances: Results from the 1998 Survey of Consumer Finances, *Federal Reserve Bulletin, January 2000; calculations by New Strategist*

Financial Assets Soared in the 1990s

The median value of financial assets owned by the average American household surged between 1989 and 1998, rising from $13,671 to $22,400—a 64 percent gain.

Behind the rise in financial assets was the stock market boom of the 1990s. The proportion of households owning stock either directly or indirectly climbed from 32 percent in 1989 to 49 percent in 1998. The value of the stock owned by stockholders more than doubled. Consequently, stocks accounted for the 54 percent majority of Americans' financial assets in 1998, up from just 28 percent in 1989.

Despite the growth in financial assets, nonfinancial assets continue to account for most of Americans' wealth. Housing equity is the largest component of net worth. The median value of nonfinancial assets owned by the average household stood at $97,800 in 1998, up from $87,677 in 1989. Householders aged 65 or older saw the biggest gain in the value of their nonfinancial assets during those years as homeownership rates among older Americans rose.

Nonfinancial assets are most important

(median value of financial and nonfinancial assets of households, 1989 and 1998; in 1998 dollars)

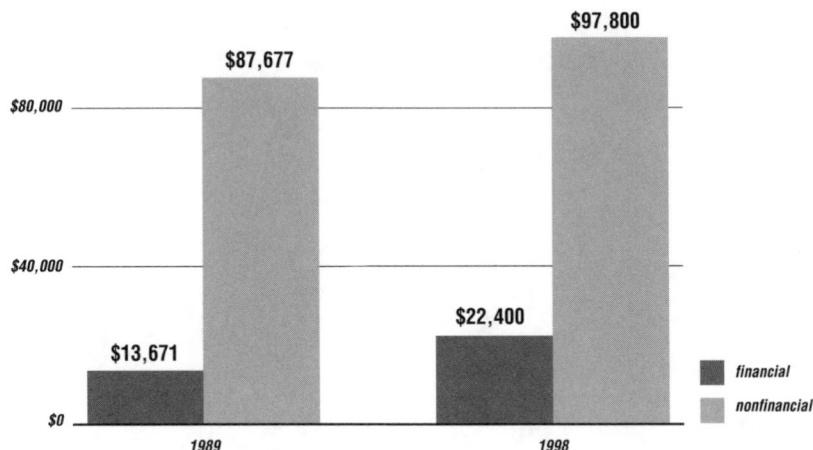

Table 10.3 Financial Assets of Households by Age of Householder, 1989 and 1998

(percentage of households owning financial assets and median value of assets for owners, by age of householder, 1989 and 1998; percentage point change in ownership and percent change in value of asset, 1989–98; in 1998 dollars)

	percent owning any financial asset			median value of financial assets		
	1998	1989	percentage point change 1989–98	1998	1989	percent change 1989–98
Total households	**92.9%**	**87.5%**	**5.4**	**$22,400**	**$13,671**	**63.9%**
Under age 35	88.6	82.2	6.4	4,500	3,286	36.9
Aged 35 to 44	93.3	88.4	4.9	22,900	14,722	55.5
Aged 45 to 54	94.9	90.4	4.5	37,800	19,060	98.3
Aged 55 to 64	95.6	87.5	8.1	45,600	26,290	73.4
Aged 65 to 74	95.6	91.5	4.1	45,800	23,924	91.4
Aged 75 or older	92.1	90.6	1.5	36,600	27,605	32.6

Source: Federal Reserve Board, Recent Changes in U.S. Family Finances: Results from the 1998 Survey of Consumer Finances, *Federal Reserve Bulletin, January 2000; and* Changes in Family Finances from 1983 to 1989: Evidence from the Survey of Consumer Finances, *Federal Reserve Bulletin, January 1992; calculations by New Strategist*

Table 10.4   Financial Assets of Households by Race and Hispanic Origin of Householder, 1989 and 1998

(percentage of households owning financial assets and median value of assets for owners, by race and Hispanic origin of householder, 1989 and 1998; percentage point change in ownership and percent change in value of asset, 1989–98; in 1998 dollars)

	percent owning any financial asset			median value of financial assets		
	1998	*1989*	*percentage point change 1989–98*	*1998*	*1989*	*percent change 1989–98*
Total households	**92.9%**	**87.5%**	**5.4**	**$22,400**	**$13,671**	**63.9%**
White, non-Hispanic	96.3	91.4	4.9	29,900	15,117	97.8
Nonwhite or Hispanic	81.2	60.9	20.3	6,400	2,629	143.4

Source: Federal Reserve Board, Recent Changes in U.S. Family Finances: Results from the 1998 Survey of Consumer Finances, *Federal Reserve Bulletin, January 2000; and* Changes in Family Finances from 1983 to 1989: Evidence from the Survey of Consumer Finances, *Federal Reserve Bulletin, January 1992; calculations by New Strategist*

Table 10.5 Stock Ownership of Households by Age of Householder, 1989 and 1998

(percent of households owning stock directly or indirectly, median value of stock holdings for owners, and stock holdings as a percent of financial assets, by age of householder, 1989 and 1998; percentage point change in ownership and share, and percent change in value of holdings, 1989–98)

	1998	1989	percentage point change 1989–98
Percent owning stock			
Total households	**48.8%**	**31.6%**	**17.2**
Under age 35	40.7	22.4	18.3
Aged 35 to 44	56.5	38.9	17.6
Aged 45 to 54	58.6	41.8	16.8
Aged 55 to 64	55.9	36.2	19.7
Aged 65 to 74	42.6	26.7	15.9
Aged 75 or older	29.4	25.9	3.5

			percent change 1989–98
Median value for owners			
Total households	**$25,000**	**$10,800**	**131.5%**
Under age 35	7,000	3,800	84.2
Aged 35 to 44	20,000	6,600	203.0
Aged 45 to 54	38,000	16,700	127.5
Aged 55 to 64	47,000	23,400	100.9
Aged 65 to 74	56,000	25,800	117.1
Aged 75 or older	60,000	31,800	88.7

			percentage point change 1989–98
Stock holdings as share of financial assets			
Total households	**53.9%**	**27.8%**	**26.1**
Under age 35	44.8	20.2	24.6
Aged 35 to 44	54.7	29.2	25.5
Aged 45 to 54	55.7	33.5	22.2
Aged 55 to 64	58.3	27.6	30.7
Aged 65 to 74	51.3	26.0	25.3
Aged 75 or older	48.7	25.0	23.7

Note: Indirect holdings are stocks in mutual funds, retirement accounts, and other managed assets.
Source: Federal Reserve Board, Recent Changes in U.S. Family Finances: Results from the 1998 Survey of Consumer Finances, *Federal Reserve Bulletin, January 2000; calculations by New Strategist*

Table 10.6 Nonfinancial Assets of Households by Age of Householder, 1989 and 1998

(percentage of households owning nonfinancial assets and median value of assets for owners, by age of householder, 1989 and 1998; percentage point change in ownership and percent change in value of asset, 1989–98; in 1998 dollars)

	percent owning any nonfinancial asset			median value of nonfinancial assets		
	1998	*1989*	*percentage point change 1989–98*	*1998*	*1989*	*percent change 1989–98*
Total households	**89.9%**	**90.2%**	**–0.3**	**$97,800**	**$87,677**	**11.5%**
Under age 35	83.3	84.4	–1.1	22,700	20,375	11.4
Aged 35 to 44	92.0	92.8	–0.8	103,500	106,869	–3.2
Aged 45 to 54	92.9	93.3	–0.4	126,800	138,417	–8.4
Aged 55 to 64	93.8	92.1	1.7	126,900	123,432	2.8
Aged 65 to 74	92.0	93.8	–1.8	109,900	82,945	32.5
Aged 75 or older	87.2	87.3	–0.1	96,100	68,354	40.6

Source: Federal Reserve Board, Recent Changes in U.S. Family Finances: Results from the 1998 Survey of Consumer Finances, *Federal Reserve Bulletin, January 2000; and* Changes in Family Finances from 1983 to 1989: Evidence from the Survey of Consumer Finances, *Federal Reserve Bulletin, January 1992; calculations by New Strategist*

Table 10.7 Nonfinancial Assets of Households by Race and Hispanic Origin of Householder, 1989 and 1998

(percentage of households owning nonfinancial assets and median value of assets for owners, by race and Hispanic origin of householder, 1989 and 1998; percentage point change in ownership and percent change in value of asset, 1989–98; in 1998 dollars)

	percent owning any nonfinancial asset			median value of nonfinancial assets		
	1998	*1989*	*percentage point change 1989–98*	*1998*	*1989*	*percent change 1989–98*
Total households	**89.9%**	**90.2%**	**0.3**	**$97,800**	**$87,677**	**11.5%**
White, non-Hispanic	93.8	93.2	–0.6	107,600	93,330	15.3
Nonwhite or Hispanic	76.4	70.0	6.4	52,000	39,566	31.4

Source: Federal Reserve Board, Recent Changes in U.S. Family Finances: Results from the 1998 Survey of Consumer Finances, *Federal Reserve Bulletin, January 2000; and* Changes in Family Finances from 1983 to 1989: Evidence from the Survey of Consumer Finances, *Federal Reserve Bulletin, January 1992; calculations by New Strategist*

More Debt for Most Households

Three out of four American households are in debt, a ratio that did not change much between 1989 and 1998. The median amount owed by the average household with debt soared during those years, rising from $19,980 to $33,300—a 67 percent gain.

Behind the rise in debt was the increase in homeownership during the 1990s. The median amount of debt rose the most for householders aged 55 or older, and it is older householders who enjoyed the biggest gains in homeownership. Similarly, debt rose the fastest among nonwhites and Hispanics as more minority households became homeowners.

Householders aged 35 to 54 are most likely to be in debt. At that age, many are recent homeowners and have little housing equity. As people age, they pay off their mortgages, lower their debts, and make gains in net worth.

Debt rose sharply during the 1990s

(median amount of debt for households with debts, 1989 and 1998; in 1998 dollars)

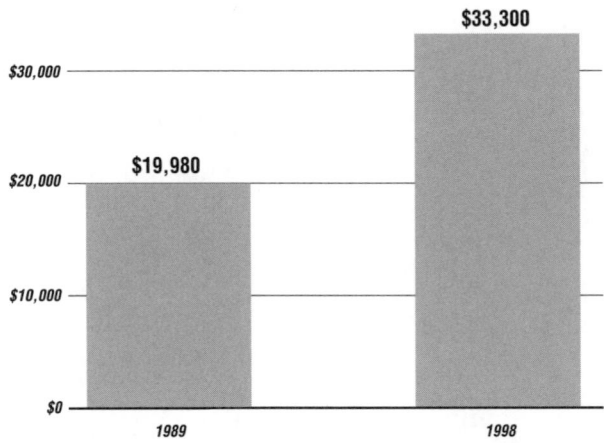

Table 10.8 Debt of Households by Age of Householder, 1989 and 1998

(percentage of households with debt and median amount of debt for debtors, by age of householder, 1989 and 1998; percentage point change in households with debt and percent change in amount of debt, 1989–98; in 1998 dollars)

	percent with debt			median amount of debt		
	1998	*1989*	*percentage point change 1989–98*	*1998*	*1989*	*percent change 1989–98*
Total households	**74.1%**	**72.7%**	**1.4**	**$33,300**	**$19,980**	**66.7%**
Under age 35	81.2	79.5	1.7	19,200	14,460	32.8
Aged 35 to 44	87.6	89.6	–2.0	55,700	40,881	36.2
Aged 45 to 54	87.0	85.9	1.1	48,400	31,154	55.4
Aged 55 to 64	76.4	74.0	2.4	34,600	14,197	143.7
Aged 65 to 74	51.4	47.9	3.5	11,900	6,573	81.1
Aged 75 or older	24.6	23.8	0.8	8,000	3,944	102.9

Source: Federal Reserve Board, Recent Changes in U.S. Family Finances: Results from the 1998 Survey of Consumer Finances, *Federal Reserve Bulletin, January 2000; and* Changes in Family Finances from 1983 to 1989: Evidence from the Survey of Consumer Finances, *Federal Reserve Bulletin, January 1992; calculations by New Strategist*

Table 10.9 Debt of Households by Race and Hispanic Origin of Householder, 1989 and 1998

(percentage of households with debt and median amount of debt for debtors, by race and Hispanic origin of householder, 1989 and 1998; percentage point change in households with debt and percent change in amount of debt, 1989–98; in 1998 dollars)

	percent with debt			median amount of debt		
	1998	1989	percentage point change 1989–98	1998	1989	percent change 1989–98
Total households	**74.1%**	**72.7%**	**1.4**	**$33,300**	**$19,980**	**66.7%**
White, non-Hispanic	74.9	73.9	1.0	40,000	22,741	75.9
Nonwhite or Hispanic	71.1	65.0	6.1	15,300	5,915	158.7

Source: Federal Reserve Board, Recent Changes in U.S. Family Finances: Results from the 1998 Survey of Consumer Finances, *Federal Reserve Bulletin, January 2000; and* Changes in Family Finances from 1983 to 1989: Evidence from the Survey of Consumer Finances, *Federal Reserve Bulletin, January 1992; calculations by New Strategist*

For More Information

The federal government is a rich source of data on almost every aspect of American life. Below are the Internet addresses of federal and other agencies collecting the demographic data analyzed in this book. Also shown are phone numbers of the agencies and of the subject specialists at the Census Bureau and the Bureau of Labor Statistics, organized alphabetically by name of agency or specialty topic. A list of State Data Centers and Small Business Development Centers is also below to help you track down demographic and economic information for your state or local area. E-mail addresses are shown when available. Note: Telephone numbers at the Census Bureau change regularly. If the numbers below do not allow you to reach the specialists you need, go to http://www.census.gov/contacts/www/contacts.html for the most up-to-date lists.

Internet addresses

- American Hospital Association, http://www.aha.org
- Bureau of the Census, http://www.census.gov
- Bureau of Justice Statistics, http://www.ojp.usdoj.gov/bjs
- Bureau of Labor Statistics, http://www.bls.gov
- Current Population Survey, http://www.bls.census.gov/cps
- Federal Reserve Board, Survey of Consumer Finances, http://www.federalreserve.gov/pubs/OSS/oss2/scfindex.html
- The Gallup Organization, http://www.gallup.com
- Immigration and Naturalization Service http://www.ins.usdoj.gov/graphics/aboutins/statistics/index.htm
- National Center for Education Statistics, http://nces.ed.gov
- National Center for Health Statistics, http://www.cdc.gov/nchs
- National Opinion Research Center, http://www.norc.uchicago.edu
- National Telecommunications and Information Administration, http://www.ntia.doc.gov
- University of Michigan, Monitoring the Future Study, http://monitoringthefuture.org
- USDA, Economic Research Service, http://www.ers.usda.gov/

Subject Specialists

Absences from work, Staff 202-691-6378
Aging population, Staff 301-763-2378
American Community Survey/C2SS Results, Larry McGinn 301-457-8050
Ancestry, Staff 301-763-2403
Apportionment, Edwin Byerly 301-763-2381
Apportionment and redistricting, Cathy McCully 301-457-4039
Business expenditures, Sheldon Ziman 301-763-3315
Business investment, Charles Funk 301-763-3324
Business owners, characteristics of, Valerie Strang 301-457-3316
Census 1990 and earlier, Staff 301-763-2422
Census 2000
- Aging population, Staff 301-763-2378
- American Community Survey, Larry McGinn 301-457-8050
- American Factfinder, Staff 301-763-INFO (4636)
- Annexations/boundary changes, Joe Marinucci 301-457-1099
- Apportionment, Edwin Byerly 301-763-2381
- Census 2000 Briefs, Staff 301-763-2437
- Census 2000 tabulations, Staff 301-763-2422
- Census 2010, Ed Gore 301-457-3998
- Census history, Dave Pemberton 301-457-1167
- Citizenship, Staff 301-763-2411
- Commuting and place of work, Clara Reschovsky/Celia Boertlein 301-763-2454
- Confidentiality and privacy, Jerry Gates 301-457-2515
- Count question resolution, Staff 866-546-0527
- Count review, Paul Campbell 301-763-2381
- Data dissemination, Staff 301-763-INFO (4636)
- Disability, Staff 301-763-3242
- Education, Staff 301-763-2464
- Employment/unemployment, Staff 301-763-3242
- Foreign born, Staff 301-763-2411
- Geographic entities, Staff 301-457-1099
- Grandparents as caregivers, Staff 301-763-2416
- Group quarters population, Denise Smith 301-763-2378
- Hispanic origin, ethnicity, ancestry, Staff 301-763-2403
- Homeless, Edison Gore 301-457-3998
- Housing, Staff 301-763-3237
- Immigration/emigration, Staff 301-763-2411
- Income, Staff 301-763-3242

- Island areas, Idabelle Hovland 301-457-8443
- Labor force status/work experience, Staff 301-763-3230
- Language spoken in home, Staff 301-763-2464
- Living arrangements, Staff 301-763-2416
- Maps, customer services 301-763-INFO (4636)
- Marital status, Staff 301-763-2416
- Metropolitan areas, concepts and standards, Michael Ratcliffe 301-763-2419
- Microdata files, Amanda Shields 301-457-1326
- Migration, Jason Schachter/Carol Faber 301-763-2454
- Occupation/industry, Staff 301-763-3239
- Place of birth/native born, Carol Faber/Bonny Berkner 301-763-2454
- Population (general information), Staff 301-763-2422
- Poverty, Alemayehu Bishaw 301-457-3213
- Race, Staff 301-763-2402
- Redistricting, Cathy McCully 301-457-4039
- Residence rules, Karen Mills 301-763-2381
- Small area income and poverty estimates, David Waddington 301-457-3195
- Special censuses, Mike Stump 301-457-3577
- Special populations, Staff 301-763-2378
- Special tabulations, Linda Showalter 301-763-2429
- Undercount, Rajendra Singh 301-457-4199
  - Demographic analysis, Greg Robinson 301-763-2110
- Unmarried partners, Staff 301-763-2416
- Urban/rural, Ryan Short 301-457-1099
- U.S. citizens abroad, Staff 301-763-2422
- Veteran status, Staff 301-763-3230
- Voting districts, John Byle 301-457-1099
- Women, Staff 301-763-2378
- ZIP codes, Staff 301-763-2422

Census Bureau customer service, Staff 301-763-INFO (4636)

Child care, Martin O'Connell/Kristin Smith 301-763-2416

Children, Staff 301-763-2416

Citizenship, Staff 301-763-2411

Communications and Utilities
- Current programs, Ruth Bramblett 301-763-2787
- Economic census, Jim Barron 301-763-2786

Commuting and place of work, Phil Salopek/Celia Boertlein 301-763-2454

Construction
- Building permits, Staff 301-457-1321
- Economic census, Staff 301-457-4680
- Housing starts and completions, Staff 301-457-1321
- Residential characteristics, price index, and sales, Staff 301-457-1321

- Residential improvements and repairs, Joe Huesman 301-457-1605
- Value of new construction, Mike Davis 301-457-1605

Consumer Expenditure Survey, Staff 202-691-6900, cexinfo@bls.gov

Contingent workers, Staff 202-691-6378

County Business Patterns, Paul Hanczaryk 301-763-2580

County populations, Staff 301-763-2422

Crime, Marilyn Monahan 301-457-3925

Current Population Survey, general information, Staff, 301-457-3806

Demographic surveys, demographic statistics, Staff 301-763-2422

Disability, Staff 301-763-3242

Discouraged workers, Staff 202-691-6378

Displaced workers, Staff 202-691-6378

Economic census 1997
- Accommodations and food services, Fay Dorsett 301-763-5180
- Construction, Staff 301-457-4680
- Finance and insurance, Faye Jacobs 301-763-2824
- General information, Robert Marske 301-763-2547
- Internet dissemination, Paul Zeisset 301-763-4151
- Manufacturing:
  - Consumer goods industries, Robert Reinard 301-457-4810
  - Investment goods industries, Kenneth Hansen 301-457-4755
  - Primary goods industries, Nat Shelton 301-457-6614
- Mining, Staff 301-457-4680
- Minority/women-owned businesses, Valerie Strang 301-763-3316
- North American Industry Class. System, Wanda Dougherty 301-763-2790
- Puerto Rico and the Insular Areas, Irma Harahush 301-763-3319
- Real estate and rental/leasing, Pam Palmer 301-763-2824
- Retail trade, Fay Dorsett 301-763-5180
- Services:
  - Administrative, waste management, remediation, Dan Wellwood 301-763-5181
  - Arts, entertainment, and recreation, Tara Dryden 301-763-5181
  - Educational services, Kim Casey 301-763-5181
  - Health care and social assistance, Laurie Davis 301-763-5181
  - Information, Joyce Kiessling/Joy Pierson/Steve Cornell 301-763-5181

- New York City Housing and Vacancy Survey, Alan Friedman/Robert Callis 301-457-3199
- Residential finance, Howard Savage 301-457-3199

Illegal immigration, Staff 301-763-2461

Immigration, general information, Staff 301-763-2422

Income statistics, Staff 301-763-3242

Industry and commodity classification, James Kristoff 301-763-4631

Industry employment projections, demographics, Howard Fullerton 202-691-5711

International Statistics:
- Africa, Asia, Latin Am., North Am., and Oceania, Staff 301-763-1358
- Aging population, Victoria Velkoff 301-763-1371
- China, People's Republic, Staff 301-763-1360
- Europe, former Soviet Union, Staff 301-763-1360
- Health, Staff 301-763-1433
- International data base, Pat Dickerson/Peter Johnson 301-763-1351
- Technical assistance and training, Diana Lopez-Meisel 301-763-1444
- Women in development, Victoria Velkoff 301-763-1371

Job tenure, Staff 202-691-6378

Journey to work, Phil Salopek/Celia Boertlein 301-763-2454

Labor force concepts, Staff 202-691-6378

Language, Staff 301-763-2464

Longitudinal data/gross flows, Staff 202-691-6345

Longitudinal surveys, Ron Dopkowski 301-457-3801

Manufacturing and mining:
- Concentration, Patrick Duck 301-457-4699
- Exports from manufacturing establishments, John Gates 301-457-4589
- Financial statistics (Quarterly Financial Report), Ronald Horton 301-763-3343
- Foreign direct investment, Julius Smith, Jr. 301-457-1313
- Fuels, electric energy consumed and prod. index, Staff 301-457-4680
- General information and data requests, Nishea Quash 301-457-4673
- Industries:
  - Electrical and trans. equip., instruments, misc., Milbren Thomas 301-457-4821
  - Food, textiles, and apparel, Robert Reinard 301-457-4810
  - Furniture, printing, Robert Reinard 301-457-4810
  - Metals and industrial machinery, Kenneth Hansen 301-457-4757

- Wood, paper, chem., pet. prod., rubber, plastics, Nat Shelton 301-457-6614
- Mining, Staff 301-457-4680
- Monthly shipments, inventories, and orders, Dan Sansbury 301-457-4832
- Technology, research and development, and capacity use, Ron Taylor 301-457-4683

Marital and family characteristics of workers, Staff 202-691-6378

Metropolitan areas, Staff 301-763-2422

Metropolitan standards, Michael Ratcliffe 301-763-2419

Migration, Jason Schachter/Carol Faber 301-763-2454

Mineral industries, Staff 301-457-4680

Minimum wage data, Steven Haugen 202-691-6378

Minority/women-owned businesses, Valerie Strang 301-457-3316

Minority workers, Staff 202-691-6378

Multiple jobholders, Staff 202-691-6373

National Center for Education Statistics, Staff 202-502-7300

National Center for Health Statistics, Staff 301-458-4636

National Compensation Survey, Staff 202-691-6199; ocltinfo@bls.gov

National Opinion Research Center, Staff 773-256-6000; norcinfo@norcmail.uchicago.edu

National Telecommunications and Information Administration, Staff 202-482-7002

Nonemployer statistics, Staff 301-763-2580

North Am. Industry Class. System (NAICS), Wanda Dougherty 301-763-2790

Occupational and industrial statistics, Staff 301-763-3239

Occupational data, Staff 202-691-6378

Occupational employment statistics, Staff 202-691-6569; oesinfo@bls.gov

Occupational Outlook Quarterly, Kathleen Green 202-691-5717

Occupational projections:
- College graduate outlook, Arlene Dohn 202-691-5727
- Education and training, Alan Eck/Chet Levine 202-691-5695/5715
- General information, Chet Levine/Jon Sargent 202-691-5715/5722
- Industry-occupation matrix, David Frank 202-691-5708
- Mobility and tenure, Alan Eck 202-691-5705
- Projections:
  - Computer, Carolyn Veneri/Roger Moncarz 202-691-5714/5694
  - Construction, Doug Braddock/Hall Dillon 202-691-5695/5704
  - Education, Arlene Dohm 202-691-5727

- Engineering, Doug Braddock/Azure Reaser
  202-691-5695/5682
- Food and lodging, Carolyn Veneri/Tiffany Stringer
  202-691-5714/5730
- Health, Theresa Cosca/Alan Lacey/Terry Schau
  202-601-5712/5731/5720
- Legal, Tamara Dillon 202-691-5733
- Mechanics and repairers, Theresa Cosca
  202-691-5712
- Sales, Doug Braddock/Andrew Nelson
  202-691-5695/5718
- Scientific, Henry Kasper 292-691-5696
- Replacement and separation rates, Alan Eck
  202-691-5705
Older workers, Staff 202-691-6378
Outlying areas, Michael Levin 301-763-1444
Part-time workers, Staff 202-691-6378
Place of birth, Bonnie Berkner/Carol Faber 301-763-2454
Population estimates and projections, Staff 301-763-2422
Population information, Staff 301-763-2422
Poverty statistics, Staff 301-457-3242
Prisoner surveys, Marilyn Monahan 301-457-3925
Puerto Rico, Idabelle Hovland 301-457-8443
Quarterly Financial Report, Ronald Horton 301-457-3343
Race, concepts and interpretation, Staff 301-763-2402
Race statistics, Staff 301-763-2422
Retail Trade:
- Advance monthly, Scott Scheleur 301-763-2713;
  svsd@census.gov
- Annual retail, Scott Scheleur 301-763-2713;
  svsd@census.gov
- Economic census, Fay Dorsett 301-763-5180;
  rcb@census.gov
- Monthly sales and inventory, Nancy Piesto
  301-763-2747; retail.trade@census.gov
- Quarterly Financial Report, Ronald Horton
  301-763-3343; cad@census.gov
School enrollment, Staff 301-763-2464
Seasonal adjustment methodology, Robert McIntire
  202-691-6345
Services
- Current Reports, Ruth Bramblett 301-763-2787;
  svsd@census.gov
- Economic census, Jack Moody 301-763-5181;
  scb@census.gov
- General information, Staff 1-800-541-8345;
  scb@census.gov
Small area income and poverty estimates, David
  Waddington 301-457-3195
Special censuses, Mike Stump 301-457-3577

Special surveys, Ron Dopkowski 301-457-3801
Special tabulations, Linda Showalter 301-763-2429
State population estimates, Staff 301-763-2422
Statistics of U.S. businesses, Melvin Cole 301-763-3321
Survey of Income and Program Participation (SIPP),
  Staff 301-457-3242
Transportation
- Commodity Flow Survey, John Fowler 301-763-2108;
  svsd@census.gov
- Economic census, James Barron 301-763-2786;
  ucb@census.gov
- Vehicle inventory and use, Dave Lassman
  301-763-2797; vius@census.gov
- Warehousing and trucking, Ruth Bramblett
  301-763-2787; svsd@census.gov
Undercount, demographic analysis, Gregg Robinson
  301-763-2110
Union membership, Staff 202-691-6378
Urban/rural population, Michael Ratcliff/Rodger Johnson
  301-763-2419
USDA, Economic Research Service, Staff 202-694-5050;
  service@ers.usda.gov
Veterans in labor force, Staff 202-691-6378
Veterans' status, Staff 301-763-3230
Voters, characteristics, Staff 301-763-2464
Voting age population, Staff 301-763-2464
Weekly earnings, Staff 202-691-6378
Wholesale Trade
- Annual wholesale, Scott Scheleur 301-763-2713;
  svsd@census.gov
- Current sales and inventories, Scott Scheleur
  301-763-2713; svsd@census.gov
- Economic census, Donna Hambric 301-763-2725;
  wcb@census.gov
- Quarterly Financial Report, Ronald Horton
  301-763-3343; csd@census.gov
Women, Staff 301-763-2378
Women in the labor force, Staff 202-691-6378
Work experience, Staff 202-691-6378
Working poor, Staff 202-691-6378
Youth, students, and dropouts in labor force, Staff
  202-691-6378

Census Regional Offices

Information specialists in the Census Bureau's 12 regional
offices answer thousands of questions each year. If you have
questions about the CensusBureau's products and services,
contact the regional office serving your state. The states
served by each regional office are listed in parentheses.
- Atlanta (AL, FL, GA) 404-730-3833
  www.census.gov/atlanta

- Boston, MA (CT, MA, ME, NH, NY, RI, VT) 617-424-0510; www.census.gov/boston
- Charlotte (KY, NC, SC, TN, VA) 704-344-6144 www.census.gov/charlotte
- Chicago (IL, IN, WI) 708-562-1350 www.census.gov/chicago
- Dallas (LA, MS, TX) 214-253-4481 www.census.gov/dallas
- Denver (AZ, CO, MT, NE, ND, NM, NV, SD, UT, WY) 303-969-7750; www.census.gov/denver
- Detroit (MI, OH, WV) 313-259-1875 www.census.gov/detroit
- Kansas City (AR, IA, KS, MN, MO, OK) 913-551-6711; www.census.gov/kansascity
- Los Angeles (southern CA, HI) 818-904-6339 www.census.gov/losangeles
- New York (NY, NJ-selected counties) 212-264-4730 www.census.gov/newyork
- Philadelphia (DE, DC, MD, NJ-selected counties, PA) 215-656-7578; www.census.gov/philadelphia
- Seattle (northern CA, AK, ID, OR, WA) 206-553-5835 www.census.gov/seattle
- Puerto Rico and the U.S. Virgin Islands are serviced by the Boston regional office. All other outlying areas are serviced by the Los Angeles regional office.

State Data Centers and Business and Industry Data Centers

For demographic and economic information about states and local areas, contact your State Data Center (SDC) or Business and Industry Data Center (BIDC). Every state has a State Data Center. Below are listed the leading centers for each state-usually a state government agency, university, or library that heads a network of affiliate centers. Asterisks (*) identify states that also have BIDCs. In some states, one agency serves as the lead for both the SDC and the BIDC. The BIDC is listed separately if a separate agency serves as the lead.

- Alabama, Annette Watters, University of Alabama 205-348-6191; awatters@cba.ua.edu
- Alaska, Kathryn Lizik, Department of Labor 907-465-2437; kathryn_lizik@labor.state.ak.us
- American Samoa, Vaitoelav Filiga, Department of Commerce 684-633-5155; vfiliga@doc.asg.as
- Arizona,* Betty Jeffries, Department of Economic Security 602-542-5984; betty.jeffries@de.state.az.us
- Arkansas, Sarah Breshears, University of Arkansas/ Little Rock 501-569-8530; sgbreshears@ualr.edu
- California, Julie Hoang, Department of Finance 916-323-4086; fijhoang@dof.ca.gov

- Colorado, Rebecca Picaso, Department of Local Affairs 303-866-2156; rebecca.picaso@state.co.us
- Connecticut, Bill Kraynak, Office of Policy and Management 860-418-6230; william.kraynak@po.state.ct.us
- Delaware,* O'Shell Howell, Economic Development Office 302-739-4271; oshowell@state.de.us
- District of Columbia, Herb Bixhorn, Mayor's Office of Planning 202-442-7603; herb.bixhorn@dc.gov
- Florida,* Pam Schenker, Dept. of Labor and Employment Security 850-488-1048; pamela.schenker@awi.state.fl.us
- Georgia, Robert Giacomini, Office of Planning and Budget 404-463-1115; robert.giacomini@sdrc.gadata.org
- Guam, Isabel Lujan, Department of Commerce 671-475-0321; idlujan@mail.gov.gu
- Hawaii, Jan Nakamoto, Dept. of Business, Ec. Dev., and Tourism 808-586-2493; jnakamot@dbedt.hawaii.gov
- Idaho, Alan Porter, Department of Commerce 208-334-2470; aporter@idoc.state.id.us
- Illinois,* Suzanne Ebetsch, Bureau of the Budget 217-782-1381; sebetsch@commerce.state.il.us
- Illinois BIDC, Ed Taft, Bureau of the Budget 217-785-7545; etaft@commerce.state.il.us
- Indiana,* Roberta Brooker, State Library 317-232-3733; rbrooker@statelib.lib.in.us
- Indiana BIDC, Carol Rogers, Business Research Center 317-274-2205; rogersc@indiana.edu
- Iowa, Beth Henning, State Library 515-281-4350; beth.henning@lib.state.ia.us
- Kansas, Marc Galbraith, State Library 785-296-3296; marcg@kslib.info
- Kentucky,* Ron Crouch, University of Louisville 502-852-7990; rtcrou01@gwise.louisville.edu
- Louisiana, Karen Paterson, Office of Planning and Budget 225-219-4025; webmaster@doa.state.la.us
- Maine,* Eric Vonmagnus, State Planning Office 207-287-3261; eric.vonmagnus@state.me.us
- Maryland,* Jane Traynham, Office of Planning 410-767-4450; jtraynham@mdp.state.md.us
- Massachusetts,* John Gaviglio, Institute for Social and Ec. Research 413-545-3460; miser@miser.umass.edu
- Michigan, Carolyn Lauer, Dept. of Management and Budget 517-373-7910; lauerc@state.mi.us
- Minnesota,* David Birkholz, State Demographer's Office 651-296-2557; david.birkholz@mnplan.state.mn.us

- Minnesota BIDC, Barbara Ronningen, State Demographer's Office 651-296-4886; barbara.ronningen@mnplan.state.mn.us
- Mississippi,* Rachel McNeely, University of Mississippi 662-915-7288; rmcneely@olemiss.edu
- Mississippi BIDC, Deloise Tate, Dept. of Ec. and Comm. Dev. 601-359-3593; dtate@mississippi.org
- Missouri,* Debra Pitts, State Library 573-526-7648; pittsd@sosmail.state.mo.us
- Missouri BIDC, Cathy Frank, Small Business Development Center 573-341-6484; cfrank@umr.edu
- Montana,* Pam Harris, Department of Commerce 406-841-2740; paharris@state.mt.us
- Nebraska, Jerome Deichert, University of Nebraska at Omaha 402-554-2134; jerome_deichert@unomaha.edu
- Nevada, Ramona Reno, State Library and Archives 775-684-332; rlreno@clan.lib.nv.us
- New Hampshire, Thomas Duffy, Office of State Planning 603-271-2155; t_duffy@osp.state.nh.us
- New Jersey,* David Joye, Department of Labor 609-984-2595; djoye@dol.state.nj.us
- New Mexico,* Kevin Kargacin, University of New Mexico 505-277-6626; kargacin@unm.edu
- New Mexico BIDC, Beth Davis, Economic Development Dept. 505-827-0264; edavis@edd.state.nm.us
- New York,* Staff, Department of Economic Development 518-292-5300; rscardamalia@empire.state.ny.us
- North Carolina,* Staff, State Library 919-733-3270; francine.stephenson@ncmail.net
- North Dakota, Richard Rathge, State University 701-231-8621; richard.rathge@ndsu.nodak.edu
- Northern Mariana Islands, Diego A. Sasamoto, Dept. of Commerce 670-664-3033; csd@itecnmi.com
- Ohio,* Erin Jones, Department of Development 614-466-2116; ejones@odod.state.oh.us
- Oklahoma,* Jeff Wallace, Department of Commerce 405-815-5184; jeff_wallace@odoc.state.ok.us
- Oregon, George Hough, Portland State University. 503-725-5159; houghg@mail.pdx.edu
- Pennsylvania,* Sue Copella, Pennsylvania State Univ./ Harrisburg 717-948-6336; sdc3@psu.edu
- Puerto Rico, Lillian Torres Aguirre, Planning Bd. 787-727-4444; torres_l@jp.gobierno.pr
- Rhode Island, Mark Brown, Department of Administration 401-222-6183; mbrown@planning.state.ri.us
- South Carolina, Mike MacFarlane, Budget and Control Board 803-734-3780; mmacfarl@drss.state.sc.us
- South Dakota, Nancy Nelson, University of South Dakota 605-677-5287; nnelson@usd.edu
- Tennessee, Betty Vickers, University of Tennessee 423-974-6080; bvickers@utk.edu
- Texas,* Steve Murdock, Texas A&M University 979-845-5115/5332; smurdock@rsocsun.tamu.edu
- Texas BIDC, Julie Leung, Dept. of Economic Dev. 512-936-0256; julie@txed.state.tx.us
- Utah,* Neena Verma, Office of Planning and Budget 801-537-9013; nverma@gov.state.ut.us
- Vermont, Sharon Whitaker, University of Vermont 802-656-3021; sharon.whitaker@uvm.edu
- Virgin Islands, Frank Mills, University of the Virgin Islands 340-693-1027; fmills@uvi.edu
- Virginia,* Don Lillywhite, Virginia Employment Commission 804-786-7496; dlillywhite@vec.state.va.us
- Washington,* Yi Zhao, Office of Financial Management 360-902-0599; yi.zhao@ofm.wa.gov
- West Virginia,* Delphine Coffey, Office of Comm. and Ind. Dev. 304-558-4010; dcoffey@wvdo.org
- West Virginia BIDC, Randy Childs, Center for Economic Research 304-293-6524; childs@mail.wvu.edu
- Wisconsin,* Robert Naylor, Department of Administration 608-266-1927; bob.naylor@doa.state.wi.us
- Wisconsin BIDC, Dan Veroff, University of Wisconsin 608-265-9545; dlveroff@facstaff.wisc.edu
- Wyoming, Wenlin Liu, Dept. of Administration and Information 307-766-2925; wliu@state.wy.us

Glossary

adjusted for inflation Income or a change in income that has been adjusted for the rise in the cost of living, or the consumer price index. The income tables are adjusted for inflation using the CPI-U-RS index. The spending tables are adjusted for inflation using the CPI-U index.

American Indian In this book, the term "American Indian" includes Alaska Natives.

Asian In this book, the term "Asian" includes Asians, Native Hawaiians, and other Pacific Islanders.

baby boom Americans born between 1946 and 1964. Baby boomers were aged 36 to 54 in 2000.

baby bust Americans born between 1965 and 1976, also known as Generation X. In 2000, baby busters were aged 24 to 35.

birth rate The number of births in a year per 1,000 mid-year population. The rate may be restricted to women of a specific age or race.

Census 2000 Supplementary Survey This was an operational test conducted as part of Census 2000. The survey collected demographic, social, economic, and housing data from a national sample, testing the feasibility of converting from the census long form to the new American Community Survey. The American Community Survey is planned to be a continuous demographic survey conducted by the Census Bureau to provide accurate and up-to-date annual profiles of America's communities. The survey will provide data for the nation, states, and most cities and counties with 250,000 or more population.

central cities The largest city in a metropolitan area is called the central city. The balance of the metropolitan area outside the central city is regarded as the "suburbs."

Consolidated metropolitan statistical area (CMSA) An area that meets the requirements for recognition as an MSA (metropolitan statistical area) and also has a population of 1 million or more may be recognized as a consolidated metropolitan statistical area (or CMSA) if it includes separate component areas that meet the statistical criteria specified in the standards for metropolitan areas, and if local opinion indicates there is support for the component areas. The components of CMSAs are called primary metropolitan statistical areas (or PMSAs).

Consumer Expenditure Survey The Consumer Expenditure Survey (CEX) is an ongoing study of the day-to-day spending of American households administered by the Bureau of Labor Statistics. The survey is used to update prices for the Consumer Price Index. The CEX includes an interview survey and a diary survey. The average spending figures shown in this book are the integrated data from both the diary and interview components of the survey. Two separate, nationally representative samples are used for the interview and diary surveys. For the interview survey, about 7,500 consumer units are interviewed on a rotating panel basis each quarter for five consecutive quarters. For the diary survey, 7,500 consumer units keep weekly diaries of spending for two consecutive weeks.

consumer unit For convenience, the terms consumer unit and household are used interchangeably in the spending tables of this book, although consumer units are somewhat different from the Census Bureau's households. Consumer units are all related members of a household, or financially independent members of a household. A household may include more than one consumer unit.

Current Population Survey A nationally representative survey of the civilian noninstitutional population aged 15 or older. It is taken monthly by the Census Bureau, collecting information from 51,000 households on employment and unemployment. In March of each year, the survey includes a demographic supplement which is the source of most national data on the characteristics of Americans, such as their educational attainment, living arrangements, and incomes.

crime The crime statistics in this book are based on the FBI's Uniform Crime Reports (UCR) program which collects information on the following crimes reported to law enforcement authorities: homicide, forcible rape, robbery, aggravated assault, burglary, larceny-theft, motor vehicle theft, and arson. In 2000, law enforcement agencies active in the UCR program represented approximately 96 percent of the total population.

death rate The number of deaths in a year per 1,000 mid-year population.

dual-earner couple A married couple in which both husband and wife are in the labor force.

earnings A type of income, earnings is the amount of money a person receives from his or her job. *See also* Income.

employed All civilians who did any work as a paid employee or farmer/self-employed worker, or who worked 15 hours or more as an unpaid farm worker or in a family-owned business, during the reference period. All those who have jobs but who are temporarily absent from their jobs due to illness, bad weather, vacation, labor management dispute, or personal reasons are considered employed.

expenditure The transaction cost including excise and sales taxes of goods and services acquired during the survey period. The full cost of each purchase is recorded even though full payment may not have been made at the date of purchase. Average expenditure figures may be artificially low for infrequently purchased items such as cars because figures are calculated using all consumer units within a demographic segment rather than just purchasers. Expenditure estimates include money spent on gifts for others.

family A group of two or more people (one of whom is the householder) related by birth, marriage, or adoption and living in the same household.

family household A household maintained by a householder who lives with one or more people related to him or her by blood, marriage, or adoption.

female/male householder A woman or man who maintains a household without a spouse present. May head family or nonfamily households.

foreign-born population People who are not U.S. citizens at birth.

full-time employment Full-time is 35 or more hours of work per week during a majority of the weeks worked during the preceding calendar year.

full-time, year-round Indicates 50 or more weeks of full-time employment during the previous calendar year.

General Social Survey The General Social Survey (GSS) is a biennial survey of the attitudes of Americans taken by the University of Chicago's National Opinion Research Center (NORC). NORC is the oldest nonprofit, university-affiliated national survey research facility in the nation. It conducts the GSS through face-to-face interviews with an independently drawn, representative sample of 1,500 to 3,000 noninstitutionalized English-speaking people aged 18 or older who live in the United States.

Generation X Americans born between 1965 and 1976, also known as the baby-bust generation. Generation Xers were aged 24 to 35 in 2000.

Hispanic People or householders who identify their origin as Mexican, Puerto Rican, Central or South American, or some other Hispanic origin. People of Hispanic origin may be of any race. In other words, there are American Indian Hispanics, Asian Hispanics, black Hispanics, and white Hispanics.

household All the people occupying a housing unit. A household includes the related family members and all the unrelated people, if any, such as lodgers, foster children, wards, or employees who share the housing unit. A person living alone is counted as a household. A group of unrelated people who share a housing unit as roommates or unmarried partners is also counted as a household. Households do not include group quarters such as college dormitories, prisons, or nursing homes.

household, race/ethnicity of Households are categorized according to the race or ethnicity of the householder only.

householder The householder is the person (or one of the persons) in whose name the housing unit is owned or rented or, if there is no such person, any adult member. With married couples, the householder may be either the husband or wife. The householder is the reference person for the household.

householder, age of The age of the householder is used to categorize households into age groups such as those used in this book. Married couples, for example, are classified according to the age of either the husband or wife, depending on which one identified him or herself as the householder.

householder, race of A household is assigned the race of the householder.

housing unit A housing unit is a house, an apartment, a group of rooms, or a single room occupied or intended for occupancy as separate living quarters. Separate living quarters are those in which the occupants do not live and eat with any other persons in the structure and that have direct access from the outside of the building or through a common hall that is used or intended for use by the occupants of another unit or by the general public. The occupants may be a single family, one person living alone, two or more families living together, or any other group of related or unrelated persons who share living arrangements.

Housing Vacancy Survey A supplement to the Current Population Survey, this survey provides quarterly and annual data on rental and homeowner vacancy rates, characteristics of units available for occupancy, and homeownership rates by age, household type, region, state, and metropolitan area. The Current Population Survey sample includes 51,000 occupied housing units and 9,000 vacant units.

immigration The relatively permanent movement (change of residence) of people into the country of reference.

in-migration The relatively permanent movement (change of residence) of people into a subnational geographic entity, such as a region, division, state, metropolitan area, or county.

income Money received in the preceding calendar year by each person aged 15 or older from each of the following sources: (1) earnings from longest job (or self-employment); (2) earnings from jobs other than longest job; (3) unemployment compensation; (4) workers' compensation; (5) Social Security; (6) Supplemental Security income; (7) public assistance; (8) veterans' payments; (9) survivor benefits; (10) disability benefits; (11) retirement pensions; (12) interest; (13) dividends; (14) rents and royalties or estates and trusts; (15) educational assistance; (16) alimony; (17) child support; (18) financial assistance from outside the household, and other periodic income. Income is reported in several ways in this book. Household income is the combined income of all household members. Income of persons is all income accruing to a person from all sources. Earnings is the amount of money a person receives from his or her job.

industry Refers to the industry in which a person worked longest in the preceding calendar year.

job tenure The length of time a person has been employed continuously by the same employer.

labor force The labor force tables in this book show the civilian labor force only. The labor force includes both the employed and the unemployed (people who are looking for work). People are counted as in the labor force if they were working or looking for work during the reference week in which the Census Bureau fields the Current Population Survey.

labor force participation rate The percent of a population that is in the labor force, which includes both the employed and unemployed. Labor force participation rates may be shown for sex-age groups or other special populations such as mothers of children of a given age.

married couples with or without children under age 18 Refers to married couples with or without children under age 18 living in the same household. Couples without children under age 18 may be parents of grown children who live elsewhere, or they could be childless couples.

median The median is the amount that divides the population or households into two equal portions: one below and one above the median. Medians can be calculated for income, age, and many other characteristics.

median income The amount that divides the income distribution into two equal groups, half having incomes above the median, half having incomes below the median. The medians for households or families are based on all households or families. The median for persons are based on all persons aged 15 or older with income.

metropolitan statistical area (MSA) To be defined as a metropolitan statistical area (or MSA), an area must include a city with 50,000 or more inhabitants, or a Census Bureau-defined urbanized area of at least 50,000 inhabitants and a total metropolitan population of at least 100,000 (75,000 in New England). The county (or counties) that contains the largest city becomes the "central county" (counties), along with any adjacent counties that have at least 50 percent of their population in the urbanized area surrounding the largest city. Additional "outlying counties" are included in the MSA if they meet specified requirements of commuting to the central counties and other selected requirements of metropolitan character (such as population density and percent urban). In New England, MSAs are defined in terms of cities and towns rather than counties. For this reason, the concept of NECMA is used to define metropolitan areas in the New England division.

millennial generation Americans born between 1977 and 1994. Millennials were aged 6 to 23 in 2000.

mobility status People are classified according to their mobility status on the basis of a comparison between their place of residence at the time of the March Current Population Survey and their place of residence in March of the previous year. Nonmovers are people living in the same house at the end of the period as at the beginning of the period. Movers are people living in a different house at the end of period than at the beginning of the period. Movers from abroad are either citizens or aliens whose place of residence is outside the United States at the beginning of the period, that is, in an outlying area under the jurisdiction of the United States or in a foreign country. The mobility status for children is fully allocated from the mother if she is in the household; otherwise it is allocated from the householder.

other race The 2000 census included "other race" as a racial category. The category was meant to capture the few Americans, such as Creoles, who may not consider themselves as belonging to the other five racial groups. In fact, more than 18 million Americans identified themselves as "other race," including 42 percent of the nation's Hispanics. Among the 18 million people who claim to be of "other" race, 90 percent also identified themselves as Hispanic. The government considers Hispanic to be an ethnic identification rather than a race since there are white, black, American Indian, and Asian Hispanics. But many Hispanics consider their ethnicity to be a separate race.

net migration Net migration is the result of subtracting out-migration from in-migration for an area. Another way to derive net migration is to subtract natural increase (births minus deaths) from total population change in an area.

nonfamily household A household maintained by a householder who lives alone or who lives with people to whom he or she is not related.

nonfamily householder A householder who lives alone or with nonrelatives.

nonmetropolitan area Counties that are not classified as metropolitan areas.

occupation Occupational classification is based on the kind of work a person did at his or her job during the previous calendar year. If a person changed jobs during the year, the data refer to the occupation of the job held the longest during that year.

occupied housing units A housing unit is classified as occupied if a person or group of people is living in it or if the occupants are only temporarily absent-on vacation, example. By definition, the count of occupied housing units is the same as the count of households.

out-migration The permanent movement (change of residence) of people out of a subnational geographic entity, such as a region, division, state, metropolitan area, or county.

outside central city The portion of a metropolitan county or counties that falls outside of the central city or cities; generally regarded as the suburbs.

own children Own children are sons and daughters, including stepchildren and adopted children, of the householder. The totals include never-married children living away from home in college dormitories.

owner occupied A housing unit is "owner occupied" if the owner lives in the unit, even if it is mortgaged or not fully paid for. A cooperative or condominium unit is "owner occupied" only if the owner lives in it. All other occupied units are classified as "renter occupied."

part-time employment Part-time employment is less than 35 hours of work per week in a majority of the weeks worked during the year.

percent change The change (either positive or negative) in a measure that is expressed as a proportion of the starting measure. When median income changes from $20,000 to $25,000, for example, this is a 25 percent increase.

percentage point change The change (either positive or negative) in a value which is already expressed as a percentage. When a labor force participation rate changes from 70 percent of 75 percent, for example, this is a 5 percentage point increase.

poverty level The official income threshold below which families and persons are classified as living in poverty. The threshold rises each year with inflation and varies depending on family size and age of householder. In 2000, the poverty threshold for a four-person family with two children under age 18 stood at $17,463.

Primary metropolitan statistical area (PMSA) PMSAs are metropolitan statistical areas that are components of consolidated metropolitan statistical areas (CMSAs).

proportion or share The value of a part expressed as a percentage of the whole. If there are 4 million people aged 25 and 3 million of them are white, then the white proportion is 75 percent.

race Race is self-reported and defined differently depending on the data source. On the 2000 census, respondents identified themselves as belonging to one or more of six racial groups: American Indian and Alaska Native, Asian, black, Native Hawaiian and other Pacific Islander, white, and other. In publishing the results, the Census Bureau created three new terms to distinguish one group from another. The "race alone" population is people who identified themselves as only one race. The "race in combination" population is people who identified themselves as more than one race, such as white and black. The "race, alone or in combination" population includes both those who identified themselves as one race and those who identified themselves as more than one race. Other government data collection efforts must offer the multiracial option by 2003. Race data from government surveys or from censuses prior to 2000 do not include the multiracial option.

regions The four major regions and nine census divisions of the United States are the state groupings as shown below:

Northeast
• New England: Connecticut, Maine, Massachusetts, New Hampshire, Rhode Island, and Vermont
• Middle Atlantic: New Jersey, New York, and Pennsylvania

Midwest
• East North Central: Illinois, Indiana, Michigan, Ohio, and Wisconsin
• West North Central: Iowa, Kansas, Minnesota, Missouri, Nebraska, North Dakota, and South Dakota

South
• South Atlantic: Delaware, District of Columbia, Florida, Georgia, Maryland, North Carolina, South Carolina, Virginia, and West Virginia
• East South Central: Alabama, Kentucky, Mississippi, and Tennessee
• West South Central: Arkansas, Louisiana, Oklahoma, and Texas

West
• Mountain: Arizona, Colorado, Idaho, Montana, Nevada, New Mexico, Utah, and Wyoming
• Pacific: Alaska, California, Hawaii, Oregon, and Washington

renter occupied *See* Owner Occupied.

rounding Percentages are rounded to the nearest tenth of a percent; therefore, the percentages in a distribution do not always add exactly to 100.0 percent. The totals, however, are always shown as 100.0. Moreover, individual figures are rounded to the nearest thousand without being adjusted to group totals, which are independently rounded; percentages are based on the unrounded numbers.

self-employment A person is categorized as self-employed if he or she was self-employed in the job held longest during the reference period. Persons who report self-employment from a second job are excluded, but those who report wage-and-salary income from a second job are included. Unpaid workers in family businesses are excluded. Self-employment statistics exclude people who work for themselves in an incorporated business.

sex ratio The number of men per 100 women.

suburbs The portion of a metropolitan area that is outside the central city.

Survey of Consumer Finances The Survey of Consumer Finances is a triennial survey taken by the Federal Reserve Board. It collects data on the assets, debts, and net worth of American households. For the 1998 survey, the Federal Reserve Board interviewed a random sample of 2,813 households and a supplemental sample of 1,496 wealthy households based on tax-return data.

two or more races People who identified themselves as belonging to two or more racial groups on the 2000 Census. See Race.

unemployed Unemployed people are those who, during the survey period, had no employment but were available and looking for work. Those who were laid off from their jobs and were waiting to be recalled are also classified as unemployed.

Bibliography

American Hospital Association
>Internet site http://www.aha.org
>—*Hospital Statistics Annual*

Bureau of the Census
>Internet site http://www.census.gov
>—1950 to 1990 Censuses
>—2000 and 2001 Current Population Surveys
>—*Access Denied: Changes in Computer Ownership and Use: 1984–1997*, Robert Kominski and Eric Newburger, 1999
>—*Age: 2000*, 2000 Census Brief, C2KBR/01-12, 2001
>—*America's Families and Living Arrangements: March 2000*, detailed tables for Current Population Reports, P20-537, 2001
>—*Census 2000*, Internet site http://www.census.gov/main/www/cen2000.html
>—*Census 2000* Supplementary Survey, Internet site http://www.census.gov/c2ss/www/Products/Profiles/2000/index.htm
>—*Educational Attainment in the United States: March 2000*, detailed tables from Current Population Reports, P20-536, 2000
>—*Gender: 2000*, 2000 Census Brief, C2KBR/01-9, 2001
>—*Geographic Mobility: March 1999 to March 2000*, detailed tables for Current Population Reports, P20-538, 2001
>—*Historical Statistics of the United States, Colonial Times to 1970, Part 1*, 1975
>—*Home Computers and Internet Use in the United States: 2000*, Current Population Reports, P23-207, 2001
>—*Housing Characteristics 2000*, 2000 Census Brief, C2KBR/01-13, 2001
>—Housing Vacancy Surveys, Internet site http://www.census.gov/hhes/www/housing/hvs/
>—*Metropolitan Areas and Cities*, 1990 Census Profile, No. 3, 1991
>—*Profile of the Foreign-Born Population in the United States: 1997*, Current Population Reports Special Studies, P23-195, 1999
>—*School Enrollment—Social and Economic Characteristics of Students: October 2000*, Current Population Reports, PPL-148, 2001
>—*The 65 Years and Over Population: 2000*, Census 2000 Brief, C2KBR/01-10, 2001
>—*Statistical Abstract of the United States: 1980 to 2001 editions*
>—*Voting and Registration in the Election of November 1998*, Current Population Reports, P20-523RV, 2000
>—*Voting and Registration in the Election of November 2000*, Current Population Reports, P20-542, 2002
>—*Who's Minding the Kids? Child Care Arrangements: Fall 1995*, Current Population Reports, P70-70, 2000

Bureau of Justice Statistics

Internet site http://www.ojp.usdoj.gov/bjs

—*Sourcebook of Criminal Justice Statistics, 2000*

Bureau of Labor Statistics

Internet site http://www.bls.gov

—1984 1990, and 2000 Consumer Expenditure Surveys, Internet site http://www.bls.gov/cex/

—*Employee Benefits in Private Industry*, 1999 and 2000

—Employee Benefits Survey, 1980 to 1997

—*Employment and Earnings*, January 1991, January 2001

—*Handbook of Labor Statistics*, Bulletin 2340, 1989

—*Monthly Labor Review*, June 1994, November 2001, May 2002

Federal Reserve Board

Internet site http://www.federalreserve.gov/pubs/oss/oss2/scfindex.html

—*Recent Changes in U.S. Family Finances: Results from the 1998 Survey of Consumer Finances*, Federal Reserve Bulletin, January 2000

Immigration and Naturalization Service

Internet site http://www.usdoj.gov/ins

—*2000 Statistical Yearbook of the Immigration and Naturalization Service*

The Gallup Organization

Internet site http://www.gallup.com

—public opinion data on crime

National Center for Education Statistics

Internet site http://nces.ed.gov

—*Digest of Education Statistics 2001*

—*Projections of Education Statistics to 2012*

National Center for Health Statistics

Internet site http://www.cdc.gov/nchs

—*Births: Final Data for 1999*, National Vital Statistics Report, Vol. 49, No. 2, 2001

—*Births: Final Data for 2000*, National Vital Statistics Report, Vol. 50, No. 5, 2002

—*Deaths: Preliminary Data for 2000*, National Vital Statistics Report, Vol. 49, No. 12, 2001

—Health E-Stats, Internet site http://www.cdc.gov/nchs/products/pubs/pubd/hestats/obese/obse99.htm

—*Health, United States, 2001* and *2002*

—*Nonmarital Childbearing in the United States, 1940–99*, National Vital Statistics Report, Vol. 48, No. 16, 2000

National Opinion Research Center

Internet site http://www.norc.uchicago.edu

—General Social Surveys, unpublished data

National Telecommunications and Information Administration
Internet site http://www.ntia.doc.gov
—*Falling Through the Net: Defining the Digital Divide*, 1999

University of Michigan
Internet site http://monitoringthefuture.org
—*Monitoring the Future Study*

U.S. Department of Agriculture
Internet site http://www.ers.usda.gov
—*Food Consumption, Prices, and Expenditures*, 1970–1997

Index

accidents as cause of death, 125, 128
administrative support occupations:
   black share of employment, 222–223;
   employment, 231, 233, 248–249;
   female share of employment, 217–218;
   Hispanic share of employment, 227–228
Africa, foreign-born from, 320
age:
   assets, financial, 412, 414;
   assets, nonfinancial, 411, 415;
   at first marriage, median, 300, 302;
   births, 98, 102–103,
   blacks pushing, attitudes toward, 22;
   business, confidence in, 33;
   cholesterol, high serum, by age, 109, 112;
   cigarette smoking, 113;
   college enrollment, 69, 72–73;
   college graduates, 55;
   computer use, 46–48;
   Congress, confidence in, 28;
   contraceptive use, 99;
   debts, 417–418;
   educational attainment, 52, 55;
   educational establishment, confidence in, 31;
   employment, long–term, 265, 267;
   executive branch of government, confidence in, 27;
   finances, personal, satisfaction with, 8;
   God, belief in, 11;
   gun control, attitudes toward, 25;
   happiness, personal, 3;
   health status, perceived, 96–97;
   helpfulness of others, perceived, 5;
   high school graduates, 52;
   homeowners, 134, 136;
   homeownership rates, 134, 137;
   homosexuality, attitudes toward, 20;
   householders, 276, 279–280;
   hypertension, 109, 111;
   income of households, 157–158;
   income of men and women, 168, 170–171;
   Internet access, 46, 48;
   job satisfaction, 9;
   job tenure, 265–266;
   labor force, 196–198;
   labor force, median age of 214;
   labor force participation rates, 205, 208–211;
   labor force projections, 196, 198, 205, 208–211;
   life, excitement of, 4;
   life expectancy at birth, 125, 129–131;
   living alone, 295, 298;
   marital happiness, 15;
   marital status, 300–301;
   marriage, interracial, attitudes toward, 23;
   medical establishment, confidence in, 32;
   net worth, 408–409;
   never married, 300–301;
   obesity, 109–110;
   political party identification, 35;
   population, 308, 311–315, 327, 331;
   poverty, 186, 189;
   press, confidence in, 30;
   religious preference, 12;
   religious services, attendance at, 13;
   sex, premarital, attitudes toward, 19;
   sex roles, attitudes toward, 16;
   sexual behaviors, attitudes toward, 19–20;
   spending, 362–374;
   sterilization, 99;
   suicide, physician–assisted, attitudes toward, 125–126;
   Supreme Court, confidence in, 29;
   voting rates, 34, 36;
   work, if rich, 7;
   working mothers, attitudes toward, 17;
   young adults, living arrangements, 295–297
agriculture. *See* Farming, fishing, and forestry occupations.
AIDS (acquired immune deficiency syndrome):
   cases by race and Hispanic origin, 122, 124;
   cases by sex, 122–123
Alabama:
   homeownership rate, 144;
   population, 328;
   population aged 65 or older, 331;
   population by race and Hispanic origin, 332–335;
   population ranking, 329–330
Alaska:
   homeownership rate, 142, 144;
   population, 328;
   population aged 65 or older, 331;
   population by race and Hispanic origin, 332–335;
   population ranking, 329–330

education, spending on:
  by age, 364, 366, 368, 370, 372, 374;
  by household income quintile, 386, 388;
  by household type, 391, 393, 395, 397;
  by race and Hispanic origin, 379, 381, 383;
  by region of the U.S., 400, 402, 404, 406;
  by retirees, 376;
  by total households, 359, 361
educational attainment, 50–56. *See also* Degrees
    conferred:
  blacks pushing, attitude toward, 21–22;
  business, confidence in, 33;
  computer ownership, 46–48;
  Congress, confidence in, 28;
  earnings of people by, 180, 184–185;
  educational establishment, confidence in, 31;
  employment, 231, 238;
  executive branch of government, confidence
    in, 27;
  finances, personal, satisfaction with, 6, 8;
  God, belief in, 11;
  gun control, attitudes toward, 24–25;
  happiness, personal, 2–3;
  health status, perceived, 96–97;
  helpfulness of others, perceived, 5;
  homosexuality, attitudes toward, 20;
  income of households by, 161–162;
  income of men and women by, 174–177;
  Internet access by, 46, 48;
  job opportunities, 231, 238;
  job satisfaction, 6, 9;
  life, excitement of, 2, 4;
  marital happiness, 15;
  marriage, interracial, attitudes toward, 23;
  medical establishment, confidence in, 32;
  political party identification, 35;
  press, confidence in, 30;
  racial tolerance, 21–23;
  religious preference, 12;
  religious services, attendance at, 13;
  sex, premarital, attitudes toward, 19;
  sex roles, attitudes toward, 16;
  sexual behaviors, attitudes toward, 19–20;
  Supreme Court, confidence in, 29;
  work, if rich, 6–7;
  working mothers, attitudes toward, 17
educational establishment, confidence in, 26, 31
El Salvador:
  foreign-born from, 320;
  immigrants from, 322
employment benefits, by benefit type, 270–272
employment, long-term, 265, 266

employment status, 201–204
entertainment and reading, spending on:
  by age, 364, 366, 368, 370, 372, 374;
  by household income quintile, 384, 386, 388;
  by household type, 391, 393, 395, 397;
  by race and Hispanic origin, 379, 381, 383;
  by region of the U.S., 400, 402, 404, 406;
  by retirees, 376;
  by total households, 358–359, 361
Europe, foreign-born from, 320
executive, administrative and managerial
    occupations:
  black share of employment, 221–222;
  employment, 231, 233, 239–240;
  female share of employment, 215–216;
  Hispanic share of employment, 226–227
executive branch of government, confidence in,
    26–27

farming, fishing, and forestry occupations:
  black share of employment, 225;
  employment, 231, 233, 249;
  female share of employment, 220;
  Hispanic share of employment, 230;
  self-employment, 263–264
finance, insurance, and real estate industry,
    employment in, 234
finances, personal, satisfaction with, 6, 8
Florida:
  homeownership rate, 144;
  population, 327–328;
  population aged 65 or older, 327, 331;
  population by race and Hispanic origin,
    332–335;
  population ranking, 329–330
food and beverage consumption, by type of
    food, 43–45
food, spending on:
  by age, 363, 365, 367, 369, 371, 373;
  by household income quintile, 384–385, 387;
  by household type, 390, 392, 394, 396;
  by race and Hispanic origin, 378, 380, 382;
  by region of the U.S., 399, 401, 403, 405;
  by retirees, 375;
  by total households, 358–360
foreign-born population. *See also* Immigration,
    318–320
France, immigrants from, 322

Georgia:
  homeownership rate, 144;
  population, 328;

housing, spending on:
  by age, 362–374;
  by household income quintile, 384–388;
  by household type, 390–397;
  by race and Hispanic origin, 378–383;
  by region of the U.S., 398–406;
  by retirees, 375–376;
  by total households, 358–361
Hungary, foreign-born from, 320
husbands. *See* Men and Households,
      married-couple
hypertension, 109, 111

Idaho:
  homeownership rate, 144;
  population, 328;
  population aged 65 or older, 331;
  population by race and Hispanic origin,
      332–335;
  population ranking, 329–330
Illinois:
  homeownership rate, 144;
  population, 328;
  population aged 65 or older, 331;
  population by race and Hispanic origin,
      332–335;
  population ranking, 329–330
immigration, 318, 321–322
income, of households:
  by age of householder, 157–158;
  by educational attainment, 161–162;
  by number of earners, 164–165;
  by race and Hispanic origin, 157, 160;
  by region, 157, 163;
  by type of household, 157, 159;
  distribution, 154–155;
  married couples by work experience of wife,
      164, 166;
  quintiles, 154, 156;
  quintiles, spending by, 384–388
income, of people:
  by age, 168, 170–171;
  by educational attainment, 174–177;
  by race and Hispanic origin, 172–173;
  by region, 178–179;
  by sex, 168–185
independent (no political party affiliation),
      34–35
India:
  foreign-born from, 320;
  immigrants from, 318, 322

Indiana:
  homeownership rate, 144;
  population, 328;
  population aged 65 or older, 331;
  population by race and Hispanic origin,
      332–335;
  population ranking, 329–330
installation, maintenance, and repair
      occupations, 231, 233, 251–252
insurance benefits for employed workers,
      270–272
Internet access:
  by age of householder, 46, 48;
  by educational attainment, 46, 48;
  by race and Hispanic origin, 46, 48;
  by type of household, 46, 48;
  of households with children, 46, 48
Iowa:
  homeownership rate, 144;
  population, 328;
  population aged 65 or older, 327, 331;
  population by race and Hispanic origin,
      332–335;
  population ranking, 329–330
Ireland:
  foreign-born from, 320;
  immigrants from, 322
Italy:
  foreign-born from, 318, 320;
  immigrants from, 322

Jamaica, immigrants from, 322
Jewish religion, preference toward, 10, 12
job satisfaction, 6, 9
job tenure, 265–266

Kansas:
  homeownership rate, 142, 144;
  population, 328;
  population aged 65 or older, 331;
  population by race and Hispanic origin,
      332–335;
  population ranking, 329–330
Kentucky:
  homeownership rate, 144;
  population, 328;
  population aged 65 or older, 331;
  population by race and Hispanic origin,
      332–335;
  population ranking, 329–330

Korea:
  foreign-born from, 320;
  immigrants from, 322

labor force. *See also* Occupations:
  employment benefits, 270–272;
  employment by education and training
      requirements, 231, 238;
  employment by major industry, 234;
  employment by occupation, 215–231, 233,
      235–256;
  entrants and leavers, 231–232;
  median age, 214;
  participation by age, 196–198, 205, 208–211;
  participation by race and Hispanic origin,
      196, 199–200, 205, 212–213;
  participation by sex, 196–198, 201–204,
      205–213;
  projections, 196, 198, 200, 205–214, 231–256;
  self-employment, 263–264;
  size of, 196–204;
  union representation, 270, 273,
larceny and theft. *See also* Motor vehicle theft:
  by rates of crime, 42;
  by type of crime, 41
Latin America, foreign-born from, 318, 320
life, excitement of, 2, 4
life expectancy:
  at age 65, 125, 129–131;
  at birth, 125, 129–131;
  by race, 130;
  by sex, 131
liver disease as cause of death, 128
living arrangements, 276–306
Louisiana:
  homeownership rate, 144;
  population, 328;
  population aged 65 or older, 331;
  population by race and Hispanic origin,
      332–335;
  population ranking, 329–330

Maine:
  homeownership rate, 144;
  population, 328;
  population aged 65 or older, 331;
  population by race and Hispanic origin,
      332–335;
  population ranking, 329–330
management, business, and financial
      occupations, 233, 239–240
manufacturing industry, employment in, 234

marital happiness, 14–15
marriage and marital status:
  age at first marriage, median, 300, 302;
  interracial marriage, 305–306;
  marital status, by sex, 300, 303–304;
  never-married, 300–301;
marriage, interracial, attitudes toward, 21, 23
marriage, interracial, number of, 305–306
married couples. *See* Households,
      married-couple.
Maryland:
  homeownership rate, 144;
  population, 328;
  population aged 65 or older, 331;
  population by race and Hispanic origin,
      332–335;
  population ranking, 329–330
Massachusetts:
  homeownership rate, 144;
  population, 328;
  population aged 65 or older, 331;
  population by race and Hispanic origin,
      332–335;
  population ranking, 329–330
Master's degrees conferred, 76–78, 85–87:
  by race and Hispanic origin, 76, 87;
  by sex, 76, 86–87
medical establishment, confidence in, 26, 32
men:
  age at first marriage, 300, 302;
  AIDS cases, 122–123;
  blacks pushing, attitudes toward, 22;
  business, confidence in, 33;
  cancer incidence rates, 119–120;
  cancer survival rates, 119, 121;
  children living with father only, 288–292;
  cholesterol, high serum, 112;
  cigarette smoking, 113;
  college enrollment, 69–71;
  college enrollment rate, 66–67;
  college graduates, 50, 54;
  Congress, confidence in, 28;
  degrees conferred, 76, 79–80, 82–83, 85–86,
      88–89, 91–92;
  earnings of full–time workers, 180–182, 184;
  educational attainment, 50–56;
  educational establishment, confidence in, 31;
  employment, long-term, 265, 267;
  employment status, 201, 203;
  executive branch of government, confidence
      in, 27;
  finances, personal, satisfaction with, 8;

God, belief in, 11;
gun control, attitudes toward, 25;
happiness, personal, 3;
health status, perceived, 97;
helpfulness of others, perceived, 5;
high school graduates, 50, 51;
homosexuality, attitudes toward, 20;
householders, 277–278;
hypertension, 111;
income, 168–170, 172, 174–175, 178;
interracial marriage, attitudes toward, 23;
interracial marriages, 306;
job satisfaction, 9;
job tenure, 265–266;
labor force, 196–198, 201, 203, 231–232;
labor force, median age, 214;
labor force participation rates, 201, 203,
    205–209, 212;
labor force projections, 197, 198, 205–209, 212;
life, excitement of, 4;
life expectancy, 125, 131;
living alone, 295, 298;
marital happiness, 15;
marital status, 300, 303;
medical establishment, confidence in, 32;
never married, 300–301;
obesity, 110;
political party identification, 35;
population, 310, 315;
poverty, 188;
press, confidence in, 30;
religious preference, 12;
religious services, attendance at, 13;
SAT scores, 63–64;
sex, premarital, attitudes toward, 19;
sex roles, attitudes toward, 16;
sexual behaviors, attitudes toward, 19–20;
single parents, 282–284, 288–292;
sterilization, 99;
suicide, physician-assisted, attitudes toward,
    126;
Supreme Court, confidence in, 29;
voting rates, 37;
work, if rich, 7;
working mothers, attitudes toward, 17;
young adults, living arrangements, 295–297
metropolitan areas, individual areas:
alphabetical ranking, 338–343;
homeownership rate, 142, 145–147;
population, 336, 338–355;
population growth ranking, 350–355;
population ranking, 344–349;

metropolitan status:
homeownership rate, 142, 145;
population, 336, 338–355
Mexican Americans, SAT scores, 63, 65
Mexico:
foreign-born from, 320;
immigrants from, 318, 322
Michigan:
homeownership rate, 144;
population, 328;
population aged 65 or older, 331;
population by race and Hispanic origin,
    332–335;
population ranking, 329–330
Middle Atlantic division of U.S.:
population, 324;
population by race and Hispanic origin,
    325–326
Midwest region of U.S.:
homeownership rate, 142–143;
income of households, 157, 163;
income of men and women, 178–179;
population, 323–324;
population by race and Hispanic origin, 323,
    325–326;
spending by households, 398, 401–402
mining industry, employment in, 234
Minnesota:
homeownership rate, 144;
population, 328;
population aged 65 or older, 331;
population by race and Hispanic origin,
    332–335;
population ranking, 329–330
Mississippi:
homeownership rate, 144;
population, 328;
population aged 65 or older, 331;
population by race and Hispanic origin,
    332–335;
population ranking, 329–330
Missouri:
homeownership rate, 144;
population, 328;
population aged 65 or older, 331;
population by race and Hispanic origin,
    332–335;
population ranking, 329–330
mobility, geographical, 316–317
Montana:
homeownership rate, 144;
population, 328;

labor force, 199–200;
labor force, median age, 214;
labor force participation, 212–213;
labor force projections, 200;
life, excitement of, 4;
life expectancy, 130;
marital happiness, 15;
medical establishment, confidence in, 32;
political party identification, 35;
population, 308, 312;
population by age, 313–314;
population by region 325–326;
population by state, 332–335;
poverty of families, 191–193;
poverty of people, 190;
press, confidence in, 30;
religious preference, 12;
religious services, attendance at, 13;
SAT scores, 65;
sex, premarital, attitudes toward, 19;
sex roles, attitudes toward, 16;
sexual behaviors, attitudes toward, 19–20;
spending, 377, 380–381;
suicide, physician-assisted, attitudes toward, 126;
Supreme Court, confidence in, 29;
voting rates, 38;
work, if rich, 7;
working mothers, attitudes toward, 17
white Americans, non-Hispanic:
AIDS, cases of, 122, 124;
assets, financial, 411, 413;
assets, nonfinancial, 411, 416;
births, 98, 104–106, 108;
births to unmarried women, 108;
college enrollment, 75;
computer ownership, 46–48;
debt, household, 417, 419;
degrees conferred, 81, 84, 87, 90, 93;
earnings of men and women, 182–183;
income, of households, 160;
income, of persons, 172–173;
Internet access, 46, 48;
labor force, 196, 199–200;
labor force entrants and leavers, 231–232;
labor force, median age, 214;
labor force participation, 212–213;
labor force projections, 196, 200;
net worth, 408, 410;
population, 308, 312;
population by age, 313–314;
population by region 323, 325–326;

population by state, 327, 332–335;
poverty of families, 191–193;
poverty of people, 190;
voting rates, 38;
wholesale trade industry, employment in, 234
Wisconsin:
homeownership rate, 144;
population, 328;
population aged 65 or older, 331;
population by race and Hispanic origin, 332–335;
population ranking, 329–330
wives. *See also* Women and Households, married-couple:
earning more than husbands, 164–167;
participation in labor force, 257–261
women. *See also* Working mothers, Households, married-couple and Households, female-headed:
age at first marriage, median, 300, 302;
AIDS cases, 122–123;
births, 98, 100–108;
births to unmarried women, 98, 108;
blacks pushing, attitudes toward, 22;
business, confidence in, 33;
cancer incidence rates, 119–120;
cancer survival rates, 121;
children living with mother only, 288–293;
cholesterol, high serum, 112;
cigarette smoking, 113;
college enrollment, 69–71;
college enrollment rate, 66–67;
college graduates, 50, 54;
Congress, confidence in, 28;
contraceptive use, 99;
degrees conferred, 76, 79–80, 82–83, 85–86, 88–89, 91–92;
earnings of full–time workers, 180–181, 183, 185;
earnings of full-time workers as a percent of men's, 180–181;
educational attainment, 50–51, 54;
educational establishment, confidence in, 31;
employment, long-term, 265, 267;
employment share by detailed occupation, 216–220;
employment status, 201, 204;
executive branch of government, confidence in, 27;
finances, personal, satisfaction with, 8;
God, belief in, 11;
gun control, attitudes toward, 25;

happiness, personal, 3;
health status, perceived, 97;
helpfulness of others, perceived, 5;
high school graduates, 50–51;
homosexuality, attitudes toward, 20;
householders, 277–278;
hypertension, 111;
income, 168–169, 171, 173, 176–177, 179;
income, as a percent of men's, 168–169;
interracial marriage, attitudes toward, 23;
interracial marriages, 306;
job satisfaction, 9;
job tenure, 265–266;
labor force, 196–198, 201, 204, 231–232;
labor force, median age, 214;
labor force participation rates, 201, 204,
    205–207, 210–211, 213;
labor force projections, 196, 198, 205–207,
    210–211, 213;
life, excitement of, 4;
life expectancy at birth, 125, 131;
living alone, 295, 298;
marital happiness, 15;
marital status, 300, 304;
medical establishment, confidence in, 32;
never married, 300–301;
obesity, 110;
political party identification, 35;
population, 310, 315;
poverty, 188;
press, confidence in, 30;
religious preference, 12;
religious services, attendance at, 13;
SAT scores, 63–64;
sex, premarital, attitudes toward, 19;
sex roles, attitudes toward, 16;
sexual behaviors, attitudes toward, 19–20;
single parents, 282–284;
sterilization, 99;
suicide, physician-assisted, attitudes toward,
    126;
Supreme Court, confidence in, 29;
voting rates, 37;
wives earning more than husbands, 164, 167;
wives, labor force participation by age of
    children, 257, 261;
work if rich, 7;
working mothers, attitudes toward, 17;
working mothers, child care arrangements,
    262;
young adults, living arrangements, 295, 297

work, attitudes toward, 6–7, 9
workers, full-time, earnings by sex, 180–185
working mothers, child care arrangements, 262
working mothers, attitudes toward, 14, 17
Wyoming:
    homeownership rate, 144;
    population, 328;
    population aged 65 or older, 331;
    population by race and Hispanic origin,
        332–335;
    population ranking, 329–330

young adults, living arrangements, 295–297